To Kathy,
Come join me o[illegible]
down Memory L[illegible]
Enjoy,
Marilyn Kilpatrick
2014

The World Is My Oyster

Travels With A Cheapskate

Marilyn Kilpatrick

Published in the United States by CreateSpace

ISBN-13: 978-1497500402
ISBN-10: 1497500400
Library of Congress Control Number: 2014906644
CreateSpace Independent Publishing Platform
North Charleston, South Carolina

For permission write to: Marilyn Kilpatrick
P.O. Box 1216
Fort Jones, CA 96032

Dedication

For my beloved husband, Marlow.
Without his enduring patience and tolerance, my travels would never have happened.

Contents

Acknowledgments

Thanks to the critique group of Siskiyou Writers Club for their consistent efforts to turn my travel journals into a readable book. Thanks also to my travel companions, hosts and hostesses, and all the wonderful people I met on my journeys. What a grand life I've had because of you.

Thank you to Shakespeare for the title inspiration from his play, *The Merry Wives of Windsor*:

"Why, then the world is my oyster, which I with sword will open."

Introduction

By Marilyn Kilpatrick

While working for Lockheed in Sunnyvale, California, in 1969, Marlow, my husband, was offered his first assignment with the title of *engineer.* He would be working for Raytheon in Sudbury, Massachusetts. Of course, he accepted the job. The trip to Massachusetts from San Jose with three kids, a cat, and a goldfish was when I started journaling. Hence, my story starts with that adventure.

From 1983 to 1993, Marlow and I made trips together whenever we had the opportunity and money. Marlow and I worked at Aerojet, Sacramento, California, and were finally making a wage to support international excursions. In 1993, I was working at Aerojet, and Marlow had been laid-off from that company and accepted a temporary job working for Boeing near Seattle, Washington. My night-school teacher offered a chance to go to Europe with a class of engineering students to see how factories were preparing for joining the common market. I went and loved the experience, and it had no detrimental effect on our marriage. We decided we could go on separate vacations when we wanted to do different things. I loved camping in the wilderness. Marlow considered cruises ideal vacations.

We took trips over the next several years – sometimes together, sometimes separately. I went to thirty-three countries. The journals from some those trips are the crux of my story.

My writing style has been compared to Erma Bombeck, whom I adored. I hope my readers will find humor while watching a naïve Catholic girl from Columbus, Ohio, grow and learn from exposure to other cultures and lifestyles. After spending a childhood going thirty-five miles from home to a cabin on a lake for vacations, it was a mind-expanding experience to see the wonders of Europe, Africa, Mexico, South America, and the South Pacific.

Marlow and I are happily sharing our retirement, after almost sixty years of marriage, living in Northern California. We still travel at every opportunity. And each trip is an adventure.

One

Go East, Young Man

1969

My husband, Marlow, and I lived with our sons, Craig, Scott, and Darryl, in San Jose, California, in 1968. Marlow, a draftsman for Lockheed at Sunnyvale, received a telephone call in the wee small hours one autumn morning. The caller introduced himself as one of Marlow's former coworkers, Paul, who had been laid off from Lockheed and went to work at Raytheon in Boston. Paul wanted to know if Marlow would be interested in an engineering position at Raytheon. When one is a draftsman, that's a "job." Engineering is a "position," a "career."

Marlow told Paul he'd have to talk it over with his wife. He hung up the phone, and we discussed it. I walked from side to side in the bedroom, saying, "Take it, take it, *take it*!" Marlow phoned Paul within five minutes, saying he'd take the offer. He excitedly claimed another dream had come true; he was going to be an engineer. Neither one said aloud that we had dollar signs floating in our brains. We were both thinking of this as a giant step toward financial security. It also meant we could live among the Puritans, with no more worries about drugs and gangs, and no more fear for our children's well-being.

January 26, 1969, moving day finally arrived. San Jose's welfare department leased our house on Annona Avenue for three years. They planned on using it as a rental to integrate welfare recipients who didn't speak English into American life by putting them in a middle-class neighborhood. The city employees felt the children would become immersed in middle-class ideals. The whole family would learn to speak American more quickly than in a neighborhood of non-English-speaking occupants. The city promised, in writing, to return our house to us in the same condition in which we left it. Because of that, every room had to be meticulously examined for peeled paint, cracks, or dents. Every window, appliance, and fixture was scrutinized and described at length on a form before the transfer of possession. The city employees arrived for the inspection at four in the afternoon and left at eight. We were not allowed to spend another night in the house after the inspection sign-off.

Cold rain pushed by swirling winds swished back and forth across the highway as the Kilpatrick family left San Jose at nine p.m. and drove as far as Sacramento before stopping for sleep. At midnight we pulled into an inviting-looking motel with gardens and a swimming pool, but the time didn't stop the children from begging for a swim before bed. It was forty degrees outside! I convinced them they'd turn into icicles as soon as they got out of the heated pool.

Once inside the room, Scott, the eight-year-old, headed directly to the bathroom to flush the toilet. "It works!" he announced loudly.

I hushed the boys, explaining we had neighbors trying to sleep.

Craig put his goldfish jar on the bedside table so he could see it first thing in the morning. Boots, the cat, went in the bathroom with his sandbox, a bowl of water, and a bowl of dry cat food. The boys were sound asleep within five minutes of being tucked into a queen-sized bed. Marlow and I were only minutes behind them.

The next morning we drank coffee and hot chocolate and ate bowls of cereal while sitting on the edge of the bed. That was to be our routine while we wended our way across the continent. I made sandwiches for lunch while Marlow packed the cars. Raytheon, Marlow's new employer, paid a moving van company to take our household goods. They removed our belongings from the house in San Jose the day before our departure and wouldn't arrive in Boston until May, so we had to take enough supplies to get by until then.

The last items to go into the three-month-old Chevy Nova were pets, sandbox, a water bowl, and cat food. The water and food went on the back window's shelf in the two-door car. The boys straddled the sandbox that sat on the floor. I drove the Nova, and Marlow drove our 1965 Chevy Biscayne.

We headed east on Route 80 and were an hour out of Sacramento when the rain turned to snow flurries. Our children were delighted, we parents apprehensive. The flurries thickened as snow accumulated on the road. Marlow and I drove on, following a long stream of cars heading into the Sierras.

Highway patrolmen directed us to shoulder parking with a directive to put on snow chains. Marlow went through the arduous task of putting chains on two cars, the Biscayne he was driving packed with our belongings, and then the Chevy Nova I drove with three boys, a cat, and a goldfish.

That finger-numbing chore accomplished, we progressed eastward. The cat yowled, and the boys were tired of riding already. My hands gripped the steering wheel tighter as we became embroiled in a blizzard approaching infamous Donner Summit. I could barely see the Biscayne's tail-lights several feet in front of my car. Traffic traveled on one wide lane following the snowplow.

Driving around a curve, I saw pedestrians beside two parked cars. Two people laid a third in the snow on the roadway next to the rear parked car. I released the gas and slowed to a crawl as I approached. There wasn't much room to safely proceed around the commotion.

I heard a loud crashing sound, and our vehicle lurched toward the parked car. *Wham*! Our front end hit the back fender of the second parked car.

Instantly hysterical, I screamed, "I just killed a man, I just killed a man!" I was froze to my seat with fear.

Scott, our middle son, climbed over the back of the seat and across my lap to get out of the Chevy coupe. "I'll check it out," he said.

"Good news, Mom, you missed the man's head by this much," Scott said, holding up his little hands to indicate about six inches. With a struggle I managed to stop screaming and regain my breath.

A frightened man knocked on my car door. "Are you okay in here? I'm so sorry. All of a sudden you weren't moving, and I hit my brakes and slid into you. Is anyone hurt?"

My semiparalyzed head turned and looked into the backseat. Craig, our ten-year-old, clutched his goldfish in a jar of vibrating water. His eyes were enlarged with fright, but he looked unhurt. Darryl, the six-year-old baby of the family, had the cat in a stranglehold in the passenger seat beside me. He looked scared but unhurt. The worst damage the kids sustained was watching their mother go berserk.

"Oh my gosh! Marlow! Marlow isn't here," I yelled at no one in particular.

He was probably a couple of miles away by now. I jumped out of the car and attempted to run through the snow. I found his car just around the curve a few feet in front of the wreck. He had stopped as soon as our headlights disappeared from his rearview mirror.

"I almost killed a man, I almost killed a man." The hysteria returned as I ran in slow motion toward him. He calmed me enough to tell him what happened.

We returned to our Chevy Nova. All three boys were out of the car. A crowd gathered, and explanations were passed from one person to another.

The three attached cars had traffic blocked. Marlow and I approached the original perpetrators. The driver of the first car said he came around the curve just as the driver of a parked car opened his door. The moving vehicle clipped the door. The driver of the parked car was so startled, he went into shock. The people from the offending car laid the victim on the ground to cover him with blankets.

As they told their story, a highway patrolman arrived. The policeman instructed the first people involved in the accident to take the victim to Truckee Hospital and then wait at Mom's Truck Stop to make an accident report.

The patrolman organized a group of men to disconnect the rear end of our car from the front end of the car that hit us. The same group tried in vain to disconnect the front end of our car from the rear end of the car of the original victim. The cars were welded together.

The policeman put our sons in the backseat of his patrol car and me in his front passenger seat while he called for a tow truck. Then traffic proceeded past the accident scene under the direction of the patrolman.

He got into his car to warm up and take a statement from me. As he settled in, a woman drove around the curve, saw the scene, hit her brakes, and slid into the rear end of our wrecked car. Our Chevy Nova now looked like an accordion-pleated camel. Traffic was blocked again, and we had an additional driver involved.

The tow truck arrived, and the driver disconnected all attached vehicles with the help of several people. He called for more tow trucks, because there were three wrecked cars. The patrolman arranged for all parties to meet at Mom's Truck Stop, where our cars were towed. Kind strangers gave stranded drivers and passengers a ride to the town of Truckee.

It was late evening by the time reports were made, and no mechanics were on duty to help accident victims become mobile. Marlow and I rented a motel room and considered our options. Marlow had to report for work at a new job three thousand miles away in one week. We had traveled a hundred and six miles on Saturday, only twenty-nine hundred miles to go. At this rate it would take us a month to get to Boston, Massachusetts!

Sunday morning the first thing Craig said was, "Where's my goldfish?"

Oh my heavens! We'd left it in the wrecked car overnight in freezing weather! The water was frozen; the goldfish stared glassily at us from the bottom of the jar. I took the jar to Mom's Truck Stop restroom and ran warm water over it while Marlow searched for a mechanic. Amazingly, the goldfish eventually swam to the top of the water to greet a greatly relieved owner. Craig had won the fish at a church bazaar the week before we left home.

Marlow returned to the restaurant with bad news—no mechanics were on duty on Sunday. Marlow didn't want to waste a day sitting in Truckee, so he and a Good Samaritan jury-rigged the Nova enough to get the wheels turning and to make the car capable of being steered down the mountain into Reno, seventy-five miles east. Marlow hoped he'd find mechanics on duty in the larger city.

He started from the garage on that cloudy, windy morning driving the wrecked car packed with household equipment we had transferred from the Chevy Biscayne. I followed in the four-year-old Biscayne with three kids, a cat, and a goldfish. The wind buffeted us from side to side on the snow-cleared lane. We traveled slowly, not knowing what might fall off the Nova.

We descended in elevation to the point where the snow lay shallow on the roadway and gravel shoulder. Guardrails and brush could be seen on the roadside. Suddenly, we were engulfed in fog! It was a cloud, really, but at any rate, I couldn't see Marlow's dark-blue car ahead of me anymore. I couldn't even see the road! If I stopped and someone came up from behind, they'd never see my white car in this blinding haze. If I kept going, I might go off the side of the mountain.

I proceeded slowly with all the windows of the car rolled down and everyone stone silent. I edged to the right until I heard the tires hit the gravel shoulder. Then I edged back to the left just a little until the sound stopped. Inch by inch, I progressed, listening intently for the sound of another car approaching, for the blessed sound of tires hitting the edge of the gravel, to the gurgling of the cat being held extremely tight, and I listened to my pounding heart.

I probably drove less than a mile in this condition, but it seemed like miles and miles. My eyelids were frozen open staring at the nothingness in front of me. Then I picked out a faint glimmer of red taillights and felt overwhelmed with relief. Soon vision returned; we were through the cloud. We rolled up the windows, and Darryl released the gasping cat. Boots promptly ducked under the front seat to escape the animal abuser.

Marlow stopped at the first gas station on the edge of Reno and asked if they had a mechanic on duty.

"No mechanics on duty in Reno on Sunday," was the answer. "Have to wait 'til Monday." It wasn't quite ten o'clock in the morning, and Marlow didn't want to waste a whole day sitting in Reno waiting for the mechanic to return to work, and another whole day waiting for him to make repairs to the car. We agreed to wend our way farther east. Marlow felt that even at our speed, we could make it to Salt Lake City by midnight and would be in position to get into a mechanic's shop first thing Monday morning.

We drove the major freeway, barely maintaining the minimum legal speed limit. The inclement weather and the day of the week meant there was little traffic. Road conditions improved as we descended in elevation. Marlow clunked, rattled, and rolled across the bleak, desolate winterscape of Nevada. Everyone was grouchy. We stopped every couple of hours for one excuse or another, mainly to relieve the tension. Marlow said the springs of the car were broken, and every little bump felt like the chassis bottomed out on the road. Bigger bumps could throw the car out of control. We slowed to thirty-five miles an hour.

Day became night, and we were still a long way from Salt Lake City. Marlow chose to continue. The wind died down after dark, and the kids and pets went to sleep, so the interior atmosphere improved. Driving was still tense as we watched for a new danger—black ice. Bridges froze in the cold night air, making the road extremely slippery with no visible evidence. Also, drainage from earthen banks froze at night on an otherwise clear roadway. We drove all night and approached Bonneville, Utah, as lavender rays of daylight appeared.

By the time we reached the gleaming salt flats, the sun blasted into our windshields, making visibility almost impossible. I squinted against the glare. My eyes seemed to relax in this almost-closed position after being open for twenty four hours. It was just too inviting to take turns closing first one eye, then the other. Somewhere along the flats, both eyes closed at the same time. I don't know how many seconds or possibly minutes went by. A loud blast from a passing truck horn brought me back to consciousness with a start. I pulled over and shook violently from the realization that I could have killed us all.

An hour later we were in the hubbub of Salt Lake City's morning rush-hour traffic. Marlow found an auto mechanic and scheduled car repairs. We found a motel. Because the boys had slept in the car, they no longer wanted to sleep, but they were too tired to be in good moods. They played games and grumbled and growled at one another while Marlow and I slept fitfully.

In the early afternoon, we got the car from the mechanic. He had done wheel repairs, checked the fluid containers, hoses, and belts, and repaired wiring, giving Marlow two headlights. The springs remained broken, but the car was steerable and reasonably safe to drive at very slow speeds. It still had multiple folds in the exterior, not a pretty sight.

We drove until ten p.m. Everyone was exhausted as we pulled into a motel. Marlow paid for a room, and five sleepy people started for the motel room door. When the boys climbed out of the car, the cat saw his chance to escape this madness. He darted out of the car and up the nearest tree. Marlow and I looked at Boots clinging to the limb in fear, his tail twitching in agitation, and decided that looked like a good place for him to spend the night. The boys thought otherwise, and their pleading convinced Marlow to borrow a ladder from the motel manager and get the cat. By midnight Boots was in the bathroom and we were snug in warm beds sound asleep.

"Mom, Mom, Mom, wake up," Craig said, jiggling my shoulder. I thought if I ignored him, he would go away, and I could sleep for a few more hours. "Mom, Mom, where's my goldfish? Mom, Mom…" It was no use; I finally woke up enough to tell him to look where he had left it before he went to bed. Of course, all the rustling around and the grumbling of waking brothers and a father made it impossible for me to sleep anymore. We all looked for the goldfish. We found it. The jar had been left in the car. The fish was encased in ice.

We sympathized with Craig on the loss of the goldfish. Craig was certain the fish was not dead, just frozen (again). He ran warm water over the jar while we dressed for the day's trip. Sure enough, Craig was right! The fish was not dead! When the water thawed, the fish wiggled and swam around and around. Jubilation! That got everyone started down the highway in a good mood.

Even the cat seemed more conducive to spending another day in the car. It only took fifteen minutes to sort out whose turn it was—whose turn it was to sit in the front seat, whose turn it was to hold the cat, and whose turn it was to choose the radio station.

We managed to get up to forty-five miles an hour on the clean, clear roads of Utah. We were whizzing right along and hoped to make up some lost time.

Once we were on that glorious high plateau known as Wyoming, we traveled at a crawl again. In January in Wyoming, the whole state is covered with four inches of ice. We crept along the icy road, clenching steering wheels. When we did slide into the occasional rest stop, it was hazardous inching our way from the car to the restroom. Of course, boys who were six, eight, and ten thought it was great fun to slide into one another. The old folks on the brink of thirty had more common sense and knew that falling down hurt.

Twelve hours after starting the day's drive, we dragged our tired bodies into another motel. We had been lucky enough to consistently find motel rooms with two big beds for ten dollars. Craig held the goldfish jar, and Darryl clutched the cat as we exited the car and headed for the room.

Scott rushed ahead to test the toilet. For some reason he felt it was necessary to be the first to try out the toilet when we stopped for the night. I carried groceries for making breakfast and for making our sandwiches for lunch on the road. Marlow carried suitcases. He stopped to chat with the motel manager, so I closed the door.

Craig and Darryl put the pets on the floor and experimented with the bounceability of the bed. As soon as Marlow opened the door, the cat ran out. How did that cat know to head for the tallest tree in the vicinity? Fortunately, the motel manager had not yet returned to his cozy abode; he and Marlow worked for an hour to coax the cat out of the tree. I suspected some of the coaxing was done with large rocks. Marlow appeared in the bedroom after the rest of the family was tucked in for the night. The boys were happy to see Boots; they thought their dad was a hero. I didn't ask what Marlow thought.

Marlow was concerned about our progress, so the following morning he set Davenport, Iowa, as our goal for the day's drive. That meant we had to drive across the tip of Wyoming, all the way across Nebraska, and all the way across Iowa. The weather favored us; the ice melted off the roads, the wind died down, and we even saw some sunshine. The highway in Nebraska ran straight and smooth between neat, well-kept farms. In Iowa the farms were still orderly, but the road picked up a definite hilliness. It was harder for the Nova with no springs to speed along at forty-five miles an hour. We slowed to thirty-five.

Once more we approached our destination near midnight. I took the cat into the chosen motel and locked him in the closet before I helped Marlow struggle with three sleeping boys, a cooler of food, and suitcases. The boys slept in their clothes minus their jackets and shoes. Marlow and I collapsed into bed, mumbling about showering in the morning. We all slept soundly until Craig woke us up at eight o'clock with his routine question. I knew as soon as he asked that the fish was still in the car.

Yes, it was frozen. Yes, we ran warm water over the jar. The usual miracle was anticipated. No such luck. The darn fish had tired of playing that silly game. He floated to the top and stayed immobile. Shaking the jar didn't help, and no one was willing to give mouth-to-mouth resuscitation. We had a quiet, dignified funeral before we put the fish into the ceramic casket and flushed. I saw Marlow trying to figure out if he could flush the cat.

That day we caravanned all the way to Cleveland. The price of gasoline went up considerably, which was a sign of things to come. We pulled into a clean-looking motel, but it had no vacancies—a convention was in town. We tried another and then a third one before we found a vacancy. The price had jumped to $20.00 for the night. Marlow tried to bargain with the desk clerk, who was adamant. After all, President Kennedy had once stayed at that motel. Oh well, in that case, we would be honored to stay there and pay twice the usual price. Yes, the motel was twice as nice as any we had stayed in before. It even had a television, not that we were in any condition to stay up and watch television. The next morning the boys did enjoy cartoons with their breakfast, and Marlow watched news and weather before we started out.

We didn't need a weather forecast to tell us it was cold. The wind blew off Lake Erie for most of the day's journey. At least we had not been caught in any snowstorms since we left the Sierras. We made reasonable time the whole day and spent that night in Syracuse, New York. When the desk clerk told Marlow the motel room cost $20.00, the obvious question was, "Did Kennedy sleep here too?" The man looked at Marlow like he had a screw loose.

The next day we made it all the way to suburban Boston, to a little town named Wayland. Marlow was scheduled to start work at Raytheon in Wayland at seven the next morning. We made it! Now Marlow could start his new career as an engineer. Nothing could stand in his way.

The motel owner forewarned him that snow was expected, so Marlow parked the most presentable car as close to the street as possible and still be in the motel parking lot. He put a borrowed snow shovel next to the front door. When he arose the next morning, he opened the door and found snow up to his waist. He looked across the parking lot and saw a two-foot-high bump in the snow representing the Biscayne. I knew he would love to lie on the floor and kick his feet and scream, but he didn't. He put on old clothes and shoveled a narrow path from the room to the car. Then he dug out the car and a path to the road.

Totally exhausted, he retreated to the motel room for hot coffee, a shower, and a change into his engineering costume. As he was on the path between the door and the car, the street-cleaning plow, with its funnel-shaped scraper, came along Route 20, cleaned the snow off the street, and dumped it onto Marlow's recently retrieved car. Marlow knew he didn't have the time or energy to dig the car out again, so he climbed over the newly created drift blocking the parking lot and walked into the street. He hitchhiked to his new employer's factory, arriving two hours late for work. That would be a black mark against him, but he felt lucky to have made it at all. He walked to the guard at the entrance of Raytheon's property and reported for his first day.

The guard looked at him in astonishment. "Didn't you hear our report on WBZ? The plant is closed due to the storm. It's the first snow we've had all winter. Really came down, didn't it?"

Two

Mexico or Bust

1983

In mid-1982 I said I'd like to go to Mexico. It seemed a perfect place for Californians to take a winter vacation. Mexico was closer to the equator and bound to be warmer than Sacramento, where we lived. It only took nine hours of freeway driving to reach the border.

Marlow, Craig, our eldest son, and I studied Spanish in high school and could communicate with the natives. It was cheap. Baja had lots of water as it was a peninsula, so we could take our raft and do some fishing as well as beachcombing.

Workmates at Aerojet had advice or warnings to offer. We were warned that if we had an accident, we'd end up in jail with no chance for parole. We'd be robbed, beaten, cheated, molested, or poisoned. We'd have to watch for people whistling through their teeth. That was a sure sign they were cheating us. We'd have to keep the doors locked at all times, so the prostitutes couldn't drag Marlow or Craig out of the car.

We'd have to avoid the children because, as everyone knew, they were the sneakiest of all. We were told Mexican kids carried dead cats, and when they saw a Yankee coming down the street, they threw the dead cat under the car and screamed at the top of their lungs. That was done in the vicinity of a policeman. If the Yankee didn't jump out of his car and give the kids some *pesos*, they would cause so much commotion, claiming the driver deliberately ran over their little pet, that the policeman would arrest the driver (unless, of course, the driver paid the policeman a sizable number of *pesos*).

We decided to take our chances. I promised friends I'd carefully check our car tires. I'd not pay for any cats where the tire tracks didn't match ours. I'd not pay for a cat where *rigor mortis* had set in, whether the tread marks matched or not.

We'd not drink the water. What the heck, we could live on beer for a week. Sacrifices, sacrifices. We'd carefully check restaurant food for beetles, horsemeat, dog meat, and roaches.

Marlow and I both worked for the same aerospace company; both of us were working on the huge MX missile, also known as the Peacekeeper. Congress was having a hot debate on whether the US needed the expensive giant missile. We ended up not going to Mexico for Christmas 1982 because of the threat of being out of jobs by January 1983. That gave us another year to listen to warnings about those devious devils living south of the border. We didn't get laid off work in the Peacekeeper cutback, so we had extra money accumulated to buy a nice new truck for 1983's trip.

We bought the truck the first of December, and it took California sixty days to type up one of those little registration slips that proved ownership. How could we insure a truck if it wasn't ours? That's what the Mexican authorities would ask. So okay, we'd take the camper shell off the new truck and put it on the old truck. With a bit of luck, the old truck should be good for one more trip.

Craig, our eldest son, wanted to go with us. He had two years of high school Spanish and two years of college Spanish in which he received As or Bs, so he volunteered to be our interpreter. Fine. One less worry. But wait, where was his birth certificate? He'd have to prove he was a US citizen to get a visa to visit Mexico south of Ensenada. He had lost any citizenship proof he had. Los Angeles County, where Craig was born, said it would take thirty days to send a new copy of his birth certificate.

Seasoned travelers told us if we passed the Mexican inspector a few *pesos*, he'd give Craig a visitor's pass with an outdated passport. We decided to give it a try. We had the passport from when the family migrated to Australia in 1972. Craig was fourteen at that time, almost half his current age.

December 24, 1983 Marlow wanted to get to the border early enough to get Craig's papers in order and get Mexican car insurance. We did not want to drive in Mexico after dark as we were warned that potholes resembled the Grand Canyon.

We arrived in Tijuana at four p.m., and I got the necessary papers while Marlow and Craig scarfed down "genuine Mexican tamales" from a street vendor. The Mexican insurance man laughed and told me the tamales were imported from San Diego. I didn't tell my menfolk.

We were only about a hundred feet inside Mexico at that time. We turned around and started across the border to stay in one of our membership Thousand Trails campgrounds near San Diego. US customs inspectors wanted to know what we had brought from Mexico. We told him, "Nothing but car insurance," and said we had only gone to the office across the street for paperwork.

He was skeptical. Did we have fruit, dairy products, meat, alcohol, cameras, and radios? Yes, sure, we had all that stuff. The camper was packed with a week's supply of food, water, beer, Marlow's new camera and heaps of film, and my little cassette/television combination for watching football games. Well, we'd have to prove we had bought them in the United States, or all food would have to be destroyed and duty paid on any electrical equipment. I didn't know if Marlow paid the US inspector or not, but after an hour, we were escorted through the gate into the United States with all our goods intact.

We went to the Thousand Trails campground, which was now full because of the late hour. They let us stay in the parking lot beside the swimming pool, so we had showers, toilets, electricity, and everything we needed.

December 25, 1983 Christmas morning we woke up early and decided to avoid the hubbub of the big city of Tijuana and cross the border at the sleepy little village of Tecáte, fifty miles east of Tijuana. We were welcomed with a cheery, "Feliz Navidad!" We crossed the border without questions and proceeded on perfectly good roads to our first night's destination of San Felipe.

Among the three of us, we were able to decipher the road signs, and the trip was not only beautiful, but also lacked any hazards. We passed an area of outstanding rock formations. If they'd been located a hundred miles north, they'd have been a US national park. The clouds couldn't make up their minds whether they wanted to stay or go, and that added muted colors and textures to the scenery.

We passed the suburbs of Mexicali about noon, and many people were eating their holiday feast. Neighbors and relatives got together for Christmas barbecues. The people mostly went about their business, totally ignoring us, while some smiled and waved. No one looked threatening. We didn't see a single dead cat among the cheerful youngsters.

The odor of the holiday feasts made us hungry, so we stopped at a little cafe. We felt confident they spoke English, as there was a sign on the door that said, "Open," with the *N* written backward. Inside we ordered our preferences—Marlow wanted a taco combination plate, I ordered an enchilada, and Craig wanted a burrito combination plate. The girl was confused and kept asking us how many we wanted.

Thank goodness we had an interpreter with us! I thought it seemed very simple, as we were ordering Mexican food in Mexico. Craig told the waitress what we wanted; he repeated what we had just enunciated. A young man at the counter told Craig (in Spanish) that he had lived in America and had gone to college there. At least that's what Craig said the man told us. The man offered to clarify the order for us. He smiled and said thirty seconds worth of gibberish to the girl; she smiled and returned to the kitchen.

Marlow and I sat at the table and waited for the food. Craig settled at the counter and talked to the young man for almost ten minutes. There was lots of laughing, knee slapping, and hand maneuvers; they certainly had a good time.

The waitress brought three identical plates with one teensy taquito on each plate and three bottles of beer.

"Forget it, boys," I said. "We'll eat this, go to the camper, and I'll fix us sandwiches."

After we got back in the truck, I told Craig I was glad he used his Spanish and had such a nice conversation with the young man. Craig said, "I never did figure out what the heck that guy said." So much for our interpreter.

South of Mexicali, we found marshland and a few water birds. Within a couple of miles, the number of birds dramatically increased, and suddenly we were in a reserve. There were many varieties of egrets, herons, pelicans, and gulls. Each of us said, "Wow! Look at that one!" at the same time, but pointed in different directions. The marshland was the northern tip of the Gulf of California; we followed it for several miles, enjoying outstanding scenery.

Then we were away from the bay and driving through sand dunes that looked like they had just blown in from Arabia. The dunes moderated into chaparral like we see in Eastern California and Nevada.

We arrived in San Felipe in mid-afternoon and walked around town awhile before going to a campground located on the beach. We did a bit of shell searching, and then had a Christmas dinner of ham, dressing, vegetables, and dessert. We shared a sedate gift exchange with smiles and hugs all around.

The clouds played hide-and-seek in the western sky, and we were treated to a beautiful sunset behind the mountains.

December 26, 1983 I arose at sunrise and walked along the beach collecting choice shells. I added those to the ones collected the previous evening. I had something to play with in the car, trying to decide which ones were really "keepers." Craig studied Spanish (he had a final coming up at school in January). Marlow gripped the steering wheel in anticipation of the horrendous roads expected. They turned out to be no worse than dirt roads anywhere else in the world—a little bumpy, a little dusty.

We arrived at Puertocitos about noon. The one lonely gas station looked closed. An American worked on his Volkswagen bus in the shadow of the building. I asked if it was possible to get gas. He said to ring the doorbell on the front of the station, and the owner would come from his house to serve us. We rang and waited. After a couple of minutes, I decided this would be a good spot for me to fix lunch. I fixed, we ate, I cleaned up the dishes, and we got back in the truck ready to drive away. *Then* the owner showed up to give us gas. He had to finish his siesta before coming to the station. Fancy running a business like that! He must have been independently wealthy.

We took pictures, played among the rocks, and talked to a few residents. The community turned out to be almost entirely *Norteamericanos* (Yankees). Very few Mexicans lived in town. That was confirmed by the satellite television antennas on top of most homes.

The man fixing his VW said he wouldn't suggest we take the dirt road as far as we originally intended, as it was for four-wheel-drive vehicles only. Some of the road had been washed out by a recent storm.

We headed back toward San Felipe. We viewed enormous cacti and a nice variety of eagles and hawks. The landscape changed color and texture often enough to prevent boredom.

Once we arrived in town, we went shopping for bargains, then tried our luck with another restaurant. What a great meal we had! Whatever we ordered showed up on our plate, and there were no extra dishes set before us. Horse or not, it was not only edible, but it was also delicious.

We stayed at the same free campground as the previous night. They had flush toilets and brick shower houses. They also had a series of brick cabanas with no roofs. Electrical wiring and plumbing had not been completed. That was something we noticed time after time while on our tour. The Mexicans had the materials for laying bricks, but not the money or knowledge to complete a building once they got the walls up. So often we'd see people living in hovels made of bits and pieces of old cars, cardboard, and scrap metal, even though they had a nice, partially completed, empty brick structure deteriorating on the same block of land.

December 27, 1983 We went northwesterly toward the Pacific Ocean. We crossed an extension of the California Coastal Range and saw snow on the peaks. We didn't run into any foul weather except a bit of wind at one stage. We descended out of the mountains and into the beachside city of Ensenada.

I was disappointed to see Mexicans dressed like Americans—in blue jeans and T-shirts. I had expected to see a wild combination of bright colors in both clothing and housing. They lived in white or brown houses, much the same as Americans.

We spent the night at a fishing village on the ocean and were delighted to find sand dollars and enormous clamshells, as well as small conch shells. Marlow went surf fishing, and Craig made friends with US students in Baja on a lark. They had a beat-up old bus dating back to the fifties that they managed to drive into deep sand. After much digging, pushing, and swearing, they were free to drive to higher ground.

While I cooked dinner, Craig asked if I would feed these boys also.

I asked, "Why?" He said they didn't have anything to cook with, and they didn't know how to use a can opener, and all they had with them were canned goods. We were being scammed by Americans, not Mexicans! They didn't sound too bright, but we fed them anyhow. I imagined they'd get a different tourist/mom to feed them each day of their trip. Why didn't we think of that plan?

December 28, 1983 The three of us toured further south, stopping at old missions, some dating back to the 1700s. We drove through many miles of farmland and enjoyed seeing the change from cacti to corn. We spent the next night on a peninsula jutting into the ocean. The sunset was breathtaking.

We stayed in a quaint community of lobster fishermen. We talked with the natives who spoke broken English and understood our broken Spanish. They offered us lobster; we gave their children our holiday nuts and candy. We communicated just fine. They were friendly, wholesome, healthy, clean people. We slept soundly among our new friends.

At no time did we feel threatened or in danger while visiting this country. We spent five days in Mexico, eating at restaurants when we wanted, camping in campgrounds or on beaches; we bought souvenirs and gas for the truck. We spent $100.00 for three people. If they cheated us, it couldn't have been by more than a peso.

December 29, 1983 Marlow, Craig, and I got through US customs smoothly at Tecate. We had eaten all our fresh fruit and vegetables, so we had no trouble passing California agriculture inspection.

We spent the day at the San Diego Zoo. We spent almost as much that one day as we did five days in Mexico. Anyhow, our resident photographer, Marlow, had a chance to get some great animal shots.

December 30, 1983 We took the back way north to avoid Los Angeles—we traveled up eastern California. We'd been on the road about four hours when truck trouble developed. Marlow had a hard time starting the truck after a restroom stop. He thought he'd better drive the whole way home rather than take a chance on stopping for the night somewhere and not being able to get the truck started in the morning.

December 31, 1983 It took fifteen scenic hours to get to Sacramento via Route 395 to Route 80. We had one bad patch of fog and a bit of drizzle. It was as though the weatherman was telling us the holiday was over and now we had to get back to normal. Bah, humbug!

Three

Wondrous East African Safari

1985

Travel had been a major topic of conversation between Marlow and me since our marriage in 1957. We both wanted to see the world. We had driven across the United States a few times and lived in Australia for eight years during the 1970s but still had a craving to see more of the earth. We decided that since our sons were grown and gone, and we had good-paying jobs, now was the time to start exploring more. We pledged to save diligently and make a trip to Africa our number one priority for 1985.

December 18, 1985 I awoke at four a.m. and was too excited to get back to sleep. I occupied myself by writing a letter to our son, Darryl, a soldier stationed in South Korea.

I verified that our plane was still scheduled to leave at nine thirty a.m. It looked foggy outside our suburban Sacramento home, and I wanted to make sure we wouldn't get to the airport and have to wait for an hour or two.

I knew we were in for an interesting taxi ride to the airport when we had only gone two blocks. The driver informed us that we were very lucky people. We had the privilege of riding in the same cab that Jesus had used just three days previously. Our driver, Jeremy, picked up Jesus at some unstated location and took him to jail to bail out a friend. Jesus and his friend intended to go to another planet as ours was too sinful.

I wondered which planet they could get to by cab but didn't ask. I didn't say anything the whole way to the airport for fear I would bring the wrath of God down on us.

After Jesus retrieved his friend from jail, they climbed into the cab and went to the location where the friend had left his Mercedes. Only then did they discover they didn't have enough money to pay the cab fare. Imagine that!

Needless to say, the cab driver wouldn't drive Jesus to another planet after that. He made his friend take him in the Mercedes.

When we arrived at Sacramento International Airport, the place was in turmoil. People rushed to buses and shuttles leaving for San Francisco's airport. They wanted to catch planes leaving for their original destinations. All flights from Sacramento had been cancelled until one thirty p.m. due to fog.

We exchanged our United Airlines tickets to New York for an American Airlines flight scheduled to leave Sacramento at one thirty for Chicago. At least we'd be closer to New York and have a better chance of catching a flight to the Big Apple.

We had a five-hour wait at Sacramento. I bought a newspaper and a magazine and read them from cover to cover. I was just starting to read the telephone book when the monotonous voice announced our plane was ready for boarding.

The Chicago flight was packed with families going home for Christmas. Children ran up and down the aisles, and babies cried. I felt sorry for the stewardesses as well as the parents.

A handsome gentleman about seven years old sat beside me most of the trip. He and I worked crossword puzzles together. He asked where we were going, and I told him we were going to Chicago, then to New York, then to England, and on to Africa. He told me he was going to England also. He told me earlier that he was going to Rhode Island. It took me a couple of seconds to realize he meant he was going to *New* England.

When he left his seat to visit a friend, a heavyset lady took his place, except she overflowed into my seat. She proceeded to lay out crocheting paraphernalia over both our laps.

The first thing she asked was, "Are you pregnant?"

I assumed she meant I was fat. I said, "No!"

"Oh, I thought maybe you were, since you're reading *Reader's Digest*."

Hmmm.

Then she asked if I was going to Chicago.

"Yes. We're just stopping there long enough to catch a plane to New York."

"Isn't that interesting? I'm going to Chicago too!"

I didn't tell her everyone on the plane was going to Chicago unless they bailed out.

At the Chicago airport, we retrieved our luggage, read departure schedules, and dragged our suitcases to a booking agent. We found a plane going to Newark, New Jersey. None were leaving for John F. Kennedy Airport until the next day.

The Newark plane was not packed to the brim with holidaymakers. Marlow, another man, and I had the five middle seats to spread out on the giant Boeing 747. The flight was a much more comfortable ride than the one from Sacramento to Chicago.

We arrived in New Jersey a little after midnight. We weren't worried since our travel agent in Sacramento told us we could catch a free shuttle to John F. Kennedy International Airport from Newark. The last shuttle for New York had left at eight thirty p.m., and the next one would leave at eight thirty a.m.

No problem. We'd take a taxi to our reserved hotel just outside Kennedy's gates. Whoops! Drivers wanted ninety dollars to take us to our hotel. The hotel would be another ninety dollars, and we'd have to check out by ten a.m. The ride was an hour and a half long, so taxi drivers weren't being unreasonable.

We decided to call hotels near Newark's Airport and make our way to Kennedy the next day (really later that same day). All the hotels were full—holiday season, you know.

I got a telephone book and randomly phoned hotels, but had no idea where they were or what class of hotel we'd end up getting. I was tired of dialing after a few fruitless minutes, and the trip had just begun.

A young African American took pity on us and said he was from Newark, and he'd help us get a nice hotel for a reasonable price. He also gave us a hint on how to handle taxi drivers. I felt there must be a sign stamped on our foreheads that said, "Novice Travelers!" The lad suggested we offer drivers a set price to a downtown hotel. He told us fifteen dollars was a fair price. He got us into a Quality Inn for $78.00, a fair price for that part of the world. He stayed with us until we were safely in a taxi, then he and his young friend left in their car. I was immensely pleased to find that such people do exist. He was only about eighteen or twenty years old and certainly had nothing to gain by hanging around the airport for an hour to help a couple of strangers in town—white strangers. He wouldn't accept a gratuity. When he flashed a pleasant smile at us, my mind played a trick on me, and I visualized him dressed in shining armor.

The Quality Inn clerk said we could stay in the room until noon if we wanted, as we were getting there so late. The time was three a.m.

The elderly porter brought us a couple of bottles of beer from the closed bar and said, "You look like you might need something to help you relax a bit before hitting the sack." He did accept a sizable tip, but his kindness was worth every cent.

What a different opinion I had of Jerseyites after meeting these few people! On the news we heard stories of crime and corrupt cops in New Jersey. The newscasters didn't tell us there were several kind, compassionate, normal people living among the scoundrels.

December 19, 1985 Well, so much for my plans of seeing Macy's dressed up for Christmas and visiting the art galleries in New York City. I had asked the travel agent to allow us a full day for sight-seeing. It took almost all day to get from Newark to JFK. The "free" shuttle cost us $20.00, but that was a bargain compared to taxi prices.

Along the way the shuttle went through the Bronx and other areas devastated by poverty and crime. I was distressed to think American children had to play on garbage-strewn streets and sidewalks when they left their apartments, where boards or steel bars replaced windows.

At the airport we got our camera equipment registered with customs. We didn't want to pay duty when we returned to the United States.

Marlow and I had a meal at the airport cafeteria before our flight to London, even though we knew the overnight flight would serve food. We had two hours to kill, and the temperature was six degrees outside, so we didn't want to go for a walk. We sat in the boarding section people watching. We met another couple carrying the same Maupintour travel bags our travel agent gave us. The people were part of our African tour group! We got acquainted and all expressed our excitement about our first trip to Africa. I hoped the rest of the tour group would be as pleasant.

Our British Airways flight to London was okay. The plane was worn and tattered, and the service passable. Dinner was served at ten p.m. amid clatter and commotion. An hour later trays were retrieved, people got refills of coffee or wine, and the noise was reduced to the continual drone of motors. I catnapped during the six-hour flight and got about three hours sleep. Marlow watched a movie and got about thirty minutes sleep.

December 20, 1985 We arrived at six a.m. and went through the usual airport fandangle—transferring papers, proving our passports were current, going through customs where the inspector wanted to see if we smuggled any tacos or decent-tasting hot dogs into England.

The Maupintour director met us and took us to a cluster of waiting passengers. Then he herded the whole group through the airport and onto a bus that took us to The Park Lane Hotel in Piccadilly to await our midnight flight to Nairobi.

On the ride through London to our plush hotel, we saw well-kept houses and emerald-green countryside. It was raining, of course, but the temperature was a pleasant fifty degrees.

While at The Park Lane Hotel, I was tempted to steal a towel for the first time in my life. The beach-size towels were about an inch thick. The hotel supplied us with a refrigerator full of drinks, the toiletries required for an overnight stay, comfortable beds, and a sitting room. We later learned the going rate for rooms was $250.00 to $300.00 a night, according to whether it was high-holiday season or not. Marlow and I had never paid more than $30.00 for a room before this trip. We had a package deal with Maupintour that included all land transportation, lodging, meals, and guides.

Marlow and I took a cab to see Madame Tussauds Wax Museum, which was nice, but not nearly as exciting as the taxi ride to get there. We were in a classic car chase from a Pink Panther movie. Our cab driver, as well as everyone else on the road, was speeding. The rule was every man for himself! A fire truck went by, and drivers that had moved out of the way tried to squeeze back into the spot just vacated by the huge red truck. I thought sure we were going to have a twenty-car pileup right behind the emergency vehicle.

After the museum inspection and lunch of fish and chips, we walked around Hyde Park and St. James's Park to Buckingham Palace and Piccadilly Circus. The palace appeared to be big, old buildings with high wrought-iron fences and Beefeater guards pictorially shown in advertisements. Piccadilly, like any downtown area, was gaudy and crowded with holiday shoppers.

We returned to the hotel in time to soak in the hot tub, use their giant-size fluffy towels, and rest before returning to the airport.

December 20, 1985 We crossed the International Date Line and repeated December 20. The group arrived in Nairobi, Kenya, at eight thirty a.m. African time. Marlow and I were now thirteen hours off Sacramento time. It was nine thirty p.m. in Sacramento. It would take a couple of days for our bodies to readjust.

A passenger from our tour group discovered at Nairobi that he had missing luggage. We sat at the airport for an hour while reports were filed and a search was put into motion.

Then we boarded a Gooney bird, a DC-3, for Arusha, Tanzania. Marlow was so excited to be riding in this classic plane. I immediately loved the pretty stewardesses that offered us hard candy to keep our ears from popping. During the flight the tour director, Ian, announced that the London agency had changed our itinerary and we would not be going to Mt. Kenya Safari Club. That caused quite a ruckus among the passengers. Many had been looking forward to spending a night at the luxurious resort formerly owned by actor William Holden.

In Arusha the weather was glorious—eighty degrees and sunny, with a slight breeze. What a pleasant change from Sacramento's fog, New York's cold, and London's rain.

Tanzania was lush green farmland around the base of a mountain. The vegetation was reminiscent of Australia—frangipani, poinciana, and jacaranda trees were in bloom—and bananas growing everywhere.

Mount Meru Hotel gave us a choice of views. We could either look at snowcapped Mount Meru or the golf course. We chose Mount Meru. Our second-story room had lovely big windows that opened and let in the pleasant breeze and the sound of music.

People strolled toward the hotel wearing colorful outfits and singing. I swung my camera out the window and took a couple of pictures before Marlow reminded me it was unlawful to take pictures of Maasai without their permission. Of course, I had no idea whether these cheerful people were from the Maasai tribe or not.

It turned out they were coming to the hotel for a wedding. I don't think anyone saw me take the pictures, as no one speared us for "stealing their souls." The singing was beautiful. The bride wore a long white dress, and the groom wore a tuxedo. Everyone else—handsome people—was wrapped in colorful cloths. We later learned the wedding party was from the Kikuyu tribe.

After breakfast at the hotel, Marlow and I walked into town. We went by European estates with beautiful landscaping on an acre or more of land. They were all well fenced. We later came to homes for average workers.

The general population lived in destitution reminiscent of Tijuana. There were few paved roads, even though the city had a population of twenty-eight thousand. The houses were dirty, the stucco was cracked, they had dirt floors, and few had windows. Stores had boards where windows should have been displaying the store's wares. Some had glass with wrought iron protecting the stock shown. Research before the trip informed me that the average income in Tanzania was equivalent to $200.00 a year, and the unemployment rate was 50 percent.

Dinner at the hotel wasn't edible, but the surroundings were most pleasant. The meat couldn't be cut with a knife, let alone chewed. I suspected what was called beef was wildebeest. I ate bread and cooked vegetables. I asked for bottled water and when the kitchen door swung open, saw the waiter filling a bottle at the water tap.

The black market on US money flourished in Tanzania. Banks offered fifteen to one exchange. The black market offered fifty to one. Marlow took advantage of the black market via our waiter. We signed and handed him a traveler's check wrapped in a napkin, and he brought us money wrapped in another napkin. I was afraid we'd be arrested on the spot, and then noticed that there were a lot of napkins being passed around the room, even by the hotel manager.

December 21, 1985 I used half a roll of film on Mount Meru at sunrise. Maybe it was the romance of being in Africa, but the view made my heart swell with happiness.

The group was divided into lots of six people to a car. I jumped into the front passenger seat so I could ply the driver with questions. On the way to Ngorongoro Crater, we passed several Kikuyu farms. The farmers were healthier, happier, cleaner people than those in Arusha. Many smiled and waved as we passed. They used oxen-driven plows and grew corn, tomatoes, potatoes, bananas, and melons. We didn't see any grain fields, but there were lots of cows. A different area supplied hay.

Our driver informed us the Maasai were nomadic cattle and goat herders. A Maasai man could afford one wife for every fifteen cows, thirty goats, or ten donkeys he owned. The cattle were Brahman. The owners rarely ate the cattle themselves, but drained blood and mixed it with milk for their protein. Only the men were allowed this treat. Women and children drank goat's milk. Some of the more affluent Maasai had donkeys. The donkeys were used to carry their belongings as they looked for water and grass for their herds.

Africa had an acacia tree called a whistling thorn. Ants ate channels throughout, and when they left, the tree was riddled, and the wind whistled through the branches.

There were lots of baobab trees, which had large trunks and contained moisture like North America's barrel cactus or Australia's bottle tree. Another tree was the yellow fever acacia. In the last century, people believed that the tree caused fever. The candelabra cactus looked like a candle holder with limbs pointing skyward. The limbs were a favorite place for lions and leopards to hide their catch.

The birdlife was abundant and colorful. Most of the birds were well named. The superb starling displayed iridescent shades of blue and purple, with a white belly and brownish-orange head. The black-shouldered kite had black shoulders on silvery wings with a white belly. Some of the other varieties the guide named for us as we passed them were the kori bustard, a bird about three feet tall; the secretary bird, almost the same size and dressed in black-and-white feathers; marabou storks, which were comical-looking scavengers, also three feet tall; and ostriches, taller still.

Oh yeah, we also saw things like Maasai giraffe, common zebras, Thomson's gazelles, Grant's gazelles, and spotted hyenas between the town of Arusha and Ngorongoro Crater.

We disembarked at Ngorongoro Wildlife Lodge, where the staff had set up a scraggly native pine and decorated it with tin can lids and twisted toilet paper in honor of Christmas. Bless their hearts. I love to see how other cultures celebrate this important feast day, but I think this tree was meant to impress the lodge guests more than the natives.

December 22, 1985 Ngorongoro Crater, a million or so years old, became an extinct, collapsed volcano seventy-five-hundred-feet high at the rim. Its floor was currently two-thousand-feet below our hotel. The crater's floor covered one-hundred-two-square miles, with a lake in the center, and was part of the Great Rift Valley.

In the crater we saw the "big five"—lions, elephants, cape buffalo, black rhinos, and hippopotami. We also saw wildebeests, hartebeests, sacred ibises, Egyptian geese, zebras, and monkeys—all within a few miles' drive.

We'd followed what represented a road into the crater in a Land Rover with a hole in the roof. Then we took off cross-country, bouncing around with very little self-control (no seat belts). Pat Britt was lucky there was a hole in the top, as she bounced so high off her seat when we hit a ditch that she stuck her head and shoulders through the roof.

We had wildebeest for lunch—yes, it was written on the menu—and something called pork chops for dinner. The pork may have been wart hog, but it was not noted on the menu. Every meat at both meals was served with a boiled potato, cabbage, and carrots.

December 23, 1985 Some hotel guests woke up, opened their curtains, and discovered a cape buffalo munching on the grass outside their window.

Marlow and I arose early so we could catch the sunrise over the crater. We went for a walk around the lodge, not knowing there were buffalo in the area. We didn't come across any, which was just as well, as they're the third most frequent killer of humans in Africa, after crocodiles and hippos.

We found a group of marabou storks and got some interesting pictures. They appeared to be waiting for the opening whistle of a soccer game on the sport's field.

After the rest of the tour group awoke, we ate bread, scrambled eggs, papaya (paw-paw to those familiar with the same fruit in Australia), and drank something that was supposed to represent coffee. From now on, I'd drink tea.

After breakfast we headed for Olduvai Gorge, where the Leaky family did so much archeological digging.

On the way we spotted a brilliant orange bird and were told it was called beautiful sunbird. What a perfect name! The guide/driver, Ali, pointed out his favorite bird, the lilac-breasted roller. The bird was stunning lavender, blue, and beige and similar in structure and size to our scrub jays. Another bird we saw was the white-bellied-go-away (and it did before we could get our cameras out). We saw a goshawk and a couple more kori bustards, which were the world's largest flying birds. Believe me, you don't want one flying over your picnic!

At Oldavai Gorge we visited the Leaky Museum and listened to a ranger tell us a bit about their archeological findings. I wondered if earlier examples of man would eventually be found in other parts of the world, or did we all start our family trees in Africa? I'd leave that to scientists and creationists to debate. I was just glad I was here right now.

We met a group of Maasai warriors who agreed to let us take their pictures. If we paid them shillings, that removed the curse of losing their souls. They were dressed in traditional red or brown blanket-like capes. I was thinking of trading my clothes for a red blanket. I really didn't want the Africans to look like Americans on our next visit, so I kept my clothes on. I didn't want to start a trend.

Marlow played a trick on the warriors by paying them a set amount for pictures of the whole group, and the amount could not be divided evenly. He was amused watching them figuring who got how much.

From Oldavai we drove to the Serengeti, a fifty-six-hundred-square-mile savannah with rivers, acacia stands, and immense rock formations. The national park was even more spectacular than we had hoped. It was thrilling to see the wildebeests (brindled gnu) migration. There were two million in East Africa. They migrated in herds of a thousand or more, believing there was safety in numbers, going from the Serengeti in Tanzania to the Maasai Mara Plains in Kenya. We saw lions, gazelles, zebras, and hyenas by the dozens. This was definitely one of the best days of our lives.

We stayed at the Lobo Wildlife Lodge located near the center of the Serengeti. The lodge could have been designed by Frank Lloyd Wright. It was magnificent. It blended into the rock-strewn savannah.

December 24, 1985 We spent the early morning cruising around the Serengeti, looking for animals. Being a morning person, I enjoyed the trip immensely. Ali found a new bird to add to our list—a crested crane, a regal-looking bird, two feet tall, proud and straight. It's the national bird of Kenya.

We kept our eyes open for animals at all times. Ali said he was bitten by a green mamba snake at the lodge last year. That's normally a fatal encounter. He was in a coma for two days before the antidote took effect. He was lucky the bite occurred while he was with people who had radios to notify the flying doctor service, who rushed him to a hospital. A green mamba is a tree snake. Look up when walking through the woods in Africa.

So far all we'd seen on lodge grounds were baboons (which would steal shiny things like watches from rooms if windows were open) and harmless rock hyrax, a cat-size mammal that looked rather like a possum. They evidently liked the habitat, as they were running all over the place. Their main predators were eagles and hawks.

The van bottomed out on a rock while crossing a dry creek bed. Everyone got out while the men tried various methods of getting the spring free from the rock.

I decided to take a picture of their efforts, and when I discovered I had my telephoto lens on the camera body, I backed away from the van so I could get the whole picture. I was fifty yards up the creek before I realized I had moved quite a distance from the safety of the van. We were in cobra habitat!

Later we had a flat tire. We disembarked, and everyone huddled close to the bus except another rock hound and me. We walked a hundred yards with our heads down, looking for interesting rocks. I was mildly reprimanded by Ali and vowed I wouldn't wander off into the wilderness again.

On our way back to the lodge after the evening drive, a tourist wanted to take a picture of the hotel from a couple hundred yards out. Ali pulled to the side of the road and stopped. We were all looking at the lodge when we heard a noisy yawn coming from an adult male lion snoozing under a tree beside the van!

Additions to our list of animals viewed included impala, one defassa waterbuck, and two klipspringers, which were antelope about twenty-inches high and weighing about thirty pounds.

The impala were so elegant. I wondered what went through a hunter's mind as he shot one. To me it would have been like shooting a ballerina during a performance of Swan Lake.

December 25, 1985 I was the first person awake, so I walked about looking for a cup of hot tea and the perfect spot from which to watch the sunrise.

As I left the room, there was rustling in trees beside the path. I looked up to see several monkeys stretching and yawning. I awakened them. They glared and chattered in a language I'm fortunate not to understand. I don't think they were saying kind things.

Ascending a set of stairs, I saw a dark figure coming toward me. I thought a worker was approaching, so I greeted him with the Swahili word for hello. *"Jambo!"* There was no reply, which was most unusual. When he got closer, I realized the figure was a very large baboon. He didn't greet me, the rude animal. He stuck his nose in the air and completely ignored me. Guess he didn't speak to just any old animal he happened to pass.

Our game drive wasn't until nine a.m. I could never sleep late on Christmas! There were myriad birds singing. There were hyraxes playing tag on rocks. Other tourists missed the sights and sounds; they were snuggled in their beds with visions of sugarplums dancing in their heads.

We had been in Africa one week. Here are a few details about our tour group. We had twenty-four people, ten were single women, one was a medical doctor, and three were PhDs. The age range was from thirty-five to seventy-nine years old. All were Americans except two elderly sisters from Winnipeg, Canada, and the tour director, Ian, who was English. All were seasoned travelers. Two women traveling together, Gwen Moore and Pat Britt, had been to Africa nine times. Lucky ladies! We took four minibuses on each game drive. Each van held six passengers. We had a window seat and room to stand up and take pictures out the "pop-top." We took turns riding shotgun so we could converse with our knowledgeable drivers. The drivers were excellent at spotting animals and stopping for as long as the photographers desired. Of course, there was one annoying passenger, a man who had a large, cumbersome video camera. He chatted to his camera at every stop. Passengers sharing his van pleaded with other tourists to trade places with them. It got so bad, Ian assigned him to a different van each game drive.

Our Christmas morning game drive consisted of slowly riding through the Serengeti as we transferred from one hotel to another. We found a pride of lions—a couple of adult females, eight young females, and two young males. They were handsome and healthy. The youngsters were about a year old and weren't the least bit frightened of the vans. They wandered around us as though parading their grandeur. I continued to be amazed to find myself physically partaking in all this splendor. I felt so honored.

We added Kirk's dik-dik to our animal sightings. They're the smallest of the antelope family, weighing approximately ten pounds and standing fifteen inches tall.

We got some good shots of klipspringers mounted on rock formations. They had round hooves made especially for hopping from rock to rock.

We passed a couple of hippopotamuses blowing bubbles in a rainforest pond and giraffes nibbling tree tops. After we broke out into the plains, we saw hundreds of gazelles, dozens of hyenas, a few wart hogs and jackals, and thousands of wildebeests.

I realized why wildebeests were called the clowns of the Serengeti. They loved to dance, prance, spin, and jump. It was good fun watching them.

I didn't go on the afternoon game drive but stayed at the Seronera Wildlife Lodge and got acquainted with some little humans, children of the staff. The boys received "trucks" for Christmas presents—one toy per child. The trucks were made of tin cans with bottle caps for wheels. Some had half a tin can attached to the rear with the open side up and a quarter of a can attached sideways to the front, which made them dump trucks with a bucket on the front. The girls each received a doll made of rags and sticks. I added candy canes to their booty and was rewarded with bright smiles and a mumbled thank you in Swahili *(asante sana)*. Imagine what an American child would have said if he or she had received only one toy for Christmas.

Marlow and the rest of the gang on the afternoon game drive experienced a lion chase in a herd of zebras. The huntress was distracted by a vehicle and lost her prey. The boss of the pride consoled her but gave her a little nudge as if to warn her that he wouldn't tolerate her losing his dinner too often. The group also saw a herd of elephants. We hadn't had the privilege of seeing too many elephants so far (how many is too many?). The drivers kept telling us we'd see lots later.

We had rice curry for Christmas lunch and barbecued something-or-other for dinner. We had the usual potato, cabbage, and carrots, which we had for every lunch and dinner in Tanzania. I don't think I've mentioned the soup we were served every day. It was delicious, no matter what they named it. It was different every day. I remember one called mulligatawny, which sounded Irish to me. I loved it. I felt guilty about the amount of food prepared for us, as I'm sure each meal would have fed a village.

We heard easy-listening western-style music, and singers sang a variety of Christmas songs in English and Swahili. "Jingle Bells" or "White Christmas" sung in Swahili while we're sitting on the equator sounded silly, but we knew they were trying to make us feel at home. Well, sort of; we didn't hear much Swahili at home, but their intentions were good.

Ian broke out champagne bought at the airport, and we celebrated the holiday. Our group dwindled to half a dozen good-natured companions, and all had a bit too much bubbly. We found one another's jokes incredibly funny. It was the best party I've attended for a long time.

December 26, 1985 What a miserable ride we had this morning! It consisted of four hours of rough, dusty roads. That was the first time I broke out a bandanna and wet it with drinking water to tie over my nose to breathe. Marlow braved it without a mask, but he was the only one in the van who did. The roads were washboards, and I talked Ali into driving off-road on the plains. That gave us some relief for a while, but we got into hilly areas where visibility was poor, and he didn't want a breakdown.

We got another break from the dust when we came around a curve and were face-to-face with a bull elephant. The magnificent creature preferred frightening us to giving up his right to the roadway. Ali backed away, lunged forward, and then backed away again in a game of chicken, trying to scare the pachyderm. Elephants do attack vehicles, so Ali accommodated the elephant's wish for us to stay out of his way. The elephant eventually tired of toying with the van and went back to pulling saplings out of the ground. Ali waited until the bull got a few feet off the road before making a run for it.

After the rough morning ride, we were treated to our best meal of the trip. We were invited to lunch on an English matron's coffee plantation called Gibb's Farm. She set a lovely buffet, and we ate on the manicured lawn overlooking acres and acres of coffee plants. The flowers were tropic exotic. Mrs. Gibb conversed with each of us. She told of her family's history in East Africa. Her ancestors first arrived in the late 1800s and were given land by the English government on which to carve out a living. She didn't mention England compensating the tribes for the land.

I bought my first souvenir. Ali stopped at a roadside stand where natives sold local wares, including ivory. I bought tanzanite in the rough, a precious stone that's only found in Tanzania. It normally sells in the same price range as emeralds or sapphires.

Marlow and I had a verandah attached to our hotel room at Lake Manyara Hotel, so we spent a pleasant evening sitting in lawn chairs on the porch, watching birds fly off into the sunset. The day had been long, and we were glad to snuggle into our mosquito-netted nest soon after sunset.

December 27, 1985 On our morning game drive, we went down the side of a crater to Lake Manyara, which was supposed to be covered with pink flamingos. Lions were supposed to hang out in trees. I had seen many pictures of lionesses draped gracefully over limbs.

The lake had almost evaporated a couple of years ago during a severe drought, and the salt had crystallized around flamingos' legs, making it hard and sometimes impossible to move. Many died due to starvation and/or thirst. We couldn't drive onto the beach to see the survivors, so we settled for viewing them with binoculars. We saw no lions. We were reminded we were in the wilderness, not a zoo.

What we did see was an unbelievably beautiful forest of mahogany trees and herds of elephants of various sizes, and they were glorious to observe. I loved the little elephants trotting below their moms and the teenyboppers bellowing at us for intruding. The adults appeared resigned to our presence.

We saw a large herd of cape buffalo and a stinky pond of hippos. That was the first time I'd noticed a bad odor associated with hippos. Perhaps the water was stagnant.

On our way back to the hotel, the driver stopped at a market in a small town. Ali told me the stones I bought were amethyst, not tanzanite, so he wanted to help us shop, Tanzanian-style. There was a law against importing clothes into Tanzania, even though people were crazy for American goods and willing to trade their artistic handicrafts for American clothes. The native costumes were colorful and looked especially nice with all the Maasai beadwork. I hoped they didn't get so many of our clothes, they looked like they were from Chicago.

Anyhow, Ali told me to pick out what I wanted and bargain the price down to half the asking price. I did that, and then he came along and asked the vendors if they would consider taking clothes instead. I felt so bad giving them a pair of Marlow's old trousers and my old sneakers for their wonderful wood carvings. It would have taken them ages to create the art. The driver said that if I offered them money on top of the clothes, it would be an insult—charity. They were a proud people and didn't want our charity; they wanted to feel they were clever enough to get the clothes away from us for the mere price of their handiwork. We got an ebony and steel spear, a hand-carved replica of a warrior about twelve inches high, an ebony elephant, and two teak impalas. I threw in a denim skirt and two T-shirts. Hope the vendors overcame the insult before bedtime.

This was our last night in Tanzania, so I thought I'd tell you what I'd learned about the Tanzanians. First impression was poverty. One-third of the people were Christians, one-third Muslims, and one-third traditional tribal religion believers. The Christian factor was growing the fastest. The reason for that, according to Ali, was that the Christians built churches that were great for singing and festivities. The Christians built schools, and Kikuyu loved having somewhere to send their children during the day so they could work in the fields. Next, they built hospitals, and people got medical help they ordinarily didn't receive. The government supported the hospitals as the country was Communist. The Muslims told the people to pray five times a day. Tribal religions threatened people with curses and taboos.

The people in town had homes of stucco, clay bricks, or wood. Houses were built on the edge of dusty walking paths; there were no yards, flowers, bushes, or trees. There were very few paved sidewalks or even paved streets. The vehicles we saw in the countryside were donkey-drawn carts, and those were for wealthy farmers. Kikuyu farmers were the wealthiest we saw. They had homes of hand-hewn logs, stucco, or clay and lived among their plowed fields or orchards on rolling hills. Farms looked neat and well ordered; the people dressed in western-style clothing. Farmers plowed fields with strips of grass or rows of trees separating them, showing they had been schooled in conservation of the soil.

Of course, there was the occasional Englishman who owned a coffee or tea plantation, and they exuded wealth. The English had a knack for beautifying the neighborhood with lots of flowers, trimmed hedges, and ornamental trees. The plantations had been taken from western owners when Communists took over the government in the 1960s, but when politicians saw that such plantations failed, they were sold back to private owners. At least their government was willing to learn from their mistakes.

The Maasai herdsmen lived a primitive life. They were nomads; their houses were built by women and were made of cow manure and grass mixed into clay. There was no ventilation except from the door, and a fire in the middle kept the insides warm and humid. One lady kindly let me walk into her home to look around. The entry was like walking into a snail shell with curved walls on both sides. The room was so dark, I took flash pictures so I'd have light to see the layout. The furnishings consisted of a few grass mats, a small stack of folded blankets, eating utensils, mortar and pestle, and three or four cooking baskets. Goats and chickens were kept in the home at night to protect them from lions. That made great growing conditions for germs. The Maasai mortality rate was high, especially among children.

The men ate meat on special occasions. If a woman looked at the men's meat, it was considered contaminated and was thrown away. They practiced polygamy. Few men remained bachelors because such a large number of the men and boys had been killed in the Mau Mau uprisings from 1952 through 1963. All Maasai men were needed as fathers.

The Mau Mau was a political group fighting the English for independence and tribesmen for political power. Mau Mau doesn't exist anymore. It was abolished when independence from England was obtained.

A Communist/Marxist government was formed in Tanzania, a dictatorship in Uganda, and a democracy in Kenya in 1963 when the Brits relinquished control. Tanzania was leaning toward capitalism after seeing the progress of Kenya.

December 28, 1985 We rode around the base of Mount Kilimanjaro to the border of Kenya. It took an hour to get everyone in our tour group through customs. No one hassled Marlow and me, as our papers didn't show we transferred US money into Tanzanian money. Marlow did it on the black market.

We said good-bye to our drivers, as they were not permitted to drive in Kenya without special paperwork. Our van occupants gave Ali all the Tanzanian money we had left among the group—a nice tip. One lady, named Sharon, gave Ali a private all-night farewell party. I was horrified at the thought of AIDS, but she said humans didn't get AIDS, just monkeys. I didn't think that was true, but it was none of my business anyhow.

Our new guides in Kenya greeted us cheerfully. I wondered if they would be as knowledgeable as Ali. He went to college for two years to learn the native fauna, flora, geology, native customs, and politics of Tanzania before being eligible to become a guide.

The border had only been open to Kenyans and other tourists a short time. Idi Amin had stirred up so much trouble among the three countries of East Africa that no one was allowed to cross from one country to another for several years.

Kenya had an unemployment rate of 25 percent, mostly the Maasai who didn't want to stay in one place. Kenya was more prosperous, and we saw more forms of transportation. Some people had bicycles; some even had cars. In Kenya the first eight years of school were free, secondary school was expensive, college was free, and students took an entrance test to determine which college they attended.

The road from the border to Amboseli was washboard clay (just like in Tanzania). We had our first rain—a real cloudburst with thunder, lightning, and lots of water—which dampened the dust and cooled the air.

Inside the resort grounds at Amboseli Serena Lodge was like a rainforest. There were flowers everywhere. There were ferns, acacia trees, waterfalls, and lily ponds. My goodness! What a few garden seeds and a lot of money can accomplish.

The rooms had hot water and electricity. Glory be! Our first hot water since we left London. I took a shower, scrubbed my hair, and did laundry. After the afternoon game drive, I soaked in a full tub of hot water just to be decadent.

The food, oh, the glorious food was a buffet of salads, cold meats, fruits, breads, and desserts. We overate. Dinner was real roast beef (chewable cow meat), Yorkshire pudding, cauliflower, carrots, asparagus soup, quiche Lorraine, rhubarb pie, and ice cream. No one was hungry after our big lunch, but everyone managed to overeat again.

The game drive was like being in Disneyland's bumper cars. There were so many buses that we got into traffic jams. Several lodges had been built around this small national park, and all of them were booked to capacity. Very few animals were near the road, and the ones we saw were surrounded by buses.

We saw two lions mating. Poor things, with all those people gawking and hooting every time he mounted her, I don't know how they could concentrate.

We saw a mother cheetah and cub, but she was soon scared off by rude, noisy people. As we headed back to the hotel, our van occupants agreed that we'd plead with Ian, our English tour director, to let us have one more good meal in the morning and one more hot bath, then head back to the beautiful wilderness of Tanzania. We went to Africa to see animals, primitive people, and scenery, not to eat, bathe, and turn on lights.

Ian didn't take us seriously. He said our itinerary was set and reservations made at parks in Kenya, and no reservations were made for us in Tanzania. He was right, of course, but no one liked it. The agency in London changed our itinerary without consulting us. Why couldn't we change it without consulting them? I knew that didn't make sense. It was just what the disappointed customers were saying. What it is, is what it is.

We went on another game drive in Amboseli at sunset. Our driver spoke very little English and didn't understand our questions about animals or the scenery. I'll say one word about the drive—depressing.

December 29, 1985 After a delicious breakfast, we poutingly packed up for a drive to our next Kenyan destination. The driver assured us there wouldn't be as many people, and the park was larger than the Serengeti.

Marlow and I changed vehicles to try a new driver. What a difference! Wilson was intelligent, charming, and conversational. I sat in the front seat and plied him with questions.

Wilson was married to one woman and had ten children. Four of his children were presently in high school. That's very expensive, and he said he couldn't do it without the help of friends he made as a tour driver. I took that to mean customers financed the children's schooling. He had one daughter going to a Japanese school and learning all of her classes—math, history, and so forth—in the Japanese language. A son was in technical school (whatever that meant); one was in a school that specialized in engineering. Secondary schools specialized! I mentioned Wilson had one wife, while our previous Kenyan driver had four wives and seven children. Maybe that's why he was reluctant to speak; he wasn't used to getting a word in edgewise.

Wilson told us about the golden weavers we saw frequently. Male birds built lantern-shaped nests of fresh weeds and grass. Several males worked on the same tree at the same time. Then they flew to another tree where females were waiting. The males courted several females until they convinced one to fly back to the newly constructed nest. If she looked the nest over and didn't like it, the male immediately built her a new nest. Sometimes they built several before one suited their girlfriend's fancy, and they got to mate.

December 30, 1985 Kilaguni Lodge was in the largest national park in East Africa, twenty thousand acres. There were several volcanoes in Tsavo West. The last one blew two hundred years ago, so it wasn't considered extinct. The area was lush; the rains had been good. The grass was two to three feet high; a profusion of wildflowers existed. Mammals were hard to spot, but the birds were abundant and gorgeous.

We saw two male giraffes fighting—"necking," it was called. We saw a lesser kudu, a grayish-brown antelope with white stripes and elegant, long, twisted horns. We stopped to take pictures of a brilliantly colored kingfisher and didn't notice the kudu in the bushes right behind the bird until she wiggled her ears. We found oryx, gazelles with long, straight horns, and even saw pink elephants. The elephants were reddish from rolling in the clay soil. It took one by surprise to see pink elephants first thing in the morning. We couldn't even attribute it to alcohol the night before.

We passed *one* other vehicle. The drive was wonderful after yesterday's madhouse at Amboseli. We were relieved to learn Amboseli wasn't typical of all Kenyan parks.

December 31, 1985 The early-morning game drive gave us a lion chase. We also saw a herd of defassa waterbucks, a herd of oryx, three jackals, giraffes, and zebras. Wonderful, wonderful sights! Our hearts sang with joy!

Our room had a balcony, so I enjoyed the tranquility and birdsongs while entering notes in my journal. I was so glad there were no utility poles obscuring my view of the grand surroundings. I realized humans liked electricity, but tourists were glad to get away from the ugly lines and poles. This lodge was run with a diesel-powered generator, and we had lights for a few hours each evening, unlike Tanzania, where we had power for one hour after dinner—not that that bothered us.

We saw a newspaper for the first time on the trip. News was as bad here as anywhere else. Dian Fossey, the scientist studying gorillas in Rwanda, had been murdered on December 26. We hadn't seen television nor heard a radio since London. I loved being away from reality.

We spent two days and two nights at Tsavo West, where everyone caught up on laundry, hair washing, and such. After lunch I went for a swim in the pool and strolled around the gardens admiring the flowers. It sounds strange, but we communicated with other tourists in Swahili; many didn't speak English. Some of us had learned a bit of Swahili for this trip. I'd become acquainted with people from Germany, France, Italy, England, and Switzerland during the course of this vacation.

We first met the Swiss group when they rolled into a hotel right after us in a four-wheel-drive vehicle that looked like a Jeep. Their gearshift had broken off when the car was in second, and they had driven several kilometers in that gear. They were glad it had not happened when the car was in reverse!

The afternoon drive was to Mzima Springs, famous for its hippos and crocodiles. We didn't see either. The Kenyan Park Department built a viewing building in the spring where we could walk downstairs and look through windows to see underwater. All we saw were fish. The building process probably scared away the bigger animals. It was a nice idea anyway.

We saw a sausage tree; the fruit of the tree was used for making beer. Did you know the Egyptian pharaohs gave beer to their slaves? They thought beer was a punishment. The slaves never told them different. That is just one of the tidbits I learned from Ali.

The passengers in our van saw a pale-chanting goshawk with long, bare, yellow legs and gray-and-white striped thighs. He had a two-toned gray body and a long black tail. He was a very handsome bird of prey. We viewed an African fish eagle, which had a white head, shoulders, and tail feathers like our bald eagle, but had a shorter wingspan than a bald eagle.

Crowned plovers and flocks of Fischer sparrows flew in groups looking like clouds. They choreographed turns the same way at the same time, as though they had practiced the maneuvers for generations.

We found a long-tailed Fiscal shrike posing in his feathered tuxedo in a tree just before we reentered the lodge grounds. He strutted up and down the branch until he heard cameras, then he promptly flew away.

After dinner Marlow and I sat in the open-air bar with Pat Brit and Gwen Moore and watched animals come to a flood-lit water hole. We had the rare pleasure of seeing a genet, which was a member of the mongoose family. The genet was light colored with black spots, a long body, and a fluffy, long, black-and-white striped tail. We would never have seen him in the wild without the hotel leaving bait to entice him within the circle of floodlights.

Impala approached the water hole with such trepidation, we were afraid they would die of thirst before they got a drink. In the morning we saw a lion eating an impala, so we understood their caution. One evidently didn't heed the others' warning.

We'd become accustomed to the long, dusty, bumpy rides from hotel to hotel. We weren't in Kansas anymore. The one to Mountain Lodge was no different. The day was New Year's Eve, so folks took naps upon arrival, anticipating a party in the evening.

The lodge was built on stilts overlooking a water hole. The water hole was 70 percent mud. Buffalo and elephants loved to roll in mud, as it was a good mosquito repellent.

Marlow and I didn't nap; we watched wildlife. We could sleep at home. One teenaged elephant was so amusing; he trotted to the edge of the opening and pulled a little tree out of the ground, then turned and chased geese away from the water before returning to destroying trees. He pretended he was coming up to the horse tank of clean water for a drink, and when he got a trunkful, he squirted it at the geese and ducks on the pond. Such squawking! They couldn't take a joke. Another of the elephant's games was to chase the forest hogs away from the water. They were ugly and mean looking, but that didn't deter the brazen young elephant. One of the funniest series of events was when the elephant harassed some storks; they set up a commotion in protest, then in frustration harassed the monkeys. The monkeys in turn climbed the hotel walls and balconies, harassing the humans. For once, humans were on the bottom of the hierarchy chain.

We weren't allowed to leave the hotel, as it was in the midst of Aberdare Forest with no visible means of protection from animals. We had an underground bunker with an opening at eye level to the water hole. Marlow and I spent most of the afternoon there watching the parade. The hotel staff dumped food scraps in front of the bunker, and each animal came by and sorted out its favorite treat. We saw giant forest hogs, and also defassa waterbucks with white ellipses under their tails as though they sat on freshly painted toilets. There were black kites and a lot of monkeys that came into the bunker to investigate us. The bunker window had no glass, but had X-shaped bars to keep larger animals out. The monkeys had no problem squeezing through. Actually, they added to our experience. I was glad we didn't share the bunker with squeamish, squealing, human females.

The rooms were miserable by Western standards. They had no insulation, so we heard everything that went on in the rooms above us, next door, or in the hall. We shared a bathroom with everyone else on the same floor. The bathroom was filthy. We barely had enough room to walk between the twin beds and had no closet; there were just two beds and a washbasin in our tiny room. We stored our suitcases and camera bags under the beds. The stench in the hotel was overwhelming with body odor from the unwashed workers. Still, it was one of our favorite places because of the animal sightings.

Ian sponsored a cocktail party to celebrate New Year's Eve. Marlow and I thought we'd have a couple of beers and call it a night; we didn't trust the sanitary conditions of the kitchen. After having the beer, dinner tempted us, so we ate the usual "beef," boiled potato, cabbage, and carrots and washed that down with another beer. We were in bed by ten o'clock; so much for ringing in 1986.

January 1, 1986 The group caused such a stink about the London Agency cancelling Mt. Kenya Safari Club that the home office managed to get us reservations after all. Today was our day to see what the famous Hollywood movie star retreat/hunting club looked like.

Classy! That's what it looked like. I mean every one of the staff was bathed and had been introduced to deodorant and clean Western-style clothes.

It was a glorious hotel with long, open hallways that had taxidermied animal heads over every door. That dated back to when William Holden, the owner, ran it as a hunting lodge for his Hollywood cronies. The heads made us sad after seeing these creature's descendants in the wild. Mr. Holden later became a conservationist and built an orphanage for animals and held no more hunts.

There was an enormous swimming pool in a Roman setting, a golf course, and ponds with swans and a variety of exotic birds imported from other countries. There was a tennis court, an equestrian trail, and miles of hiking trails fenced off from animals and natives.

Some of our group had been given hotel suites in the main building, and some had Victorian cottages set in Old English gardens. Marlow and I had a modern cottage about the same size as our home. It had a bedroom on either side of a large lounge with a fireplace and wet bar. We shared the house with the sisters from Canada—Madeleine and Jacqueline, both in their seventies. Our bedroom was thirty feet square, with one wall made of glass to overlook the golf course and ponds. Mt. Kenya, with an elevation of fifteen thousand feet, was the backdrop. Our closet was eight feet wide by twelve feet long, and the bathroom had a walk-in tub five feet square and three feet deep, with seats.

A uniformed man came to the door soon after our arrival and announced he was our man servant. He was there to start a fire in the fireplace. He wanted to know if we wanted a bath started, or did we need our beds turned down. I told him we didn't want either, as we were going to have friends over for cocktails before going to dinner. The next thing we knew, he appeared with ice, glasses, liquor, and Chukka dancers to perform on our front lawn. It was the most successful party Marlow and I ever threw!

Needless to say, dinner was decadent. We started with smoked sailfish and caviar, clear broth, croissants with honey, and asparagus with

Béarnaise sauce. Later we were served salad, lamb, prime rib, French-style potatoes, cauliflower, and chocolate mousse for dessert with delicious rich coffee and liqueur. It took three hours to eat, and no one minded, as we had soft music behind lively conversations surrounding us. No wonder the resort prices ranged from $500.00 to $1,000.00 per night.

January 2, 1986 We opened our floor-to-ceiling drapes to find an Indian stork staring at us. He was silver-gray with a bright pink patch on his face. He was the height of an ostrich but more graceful and handsome. He was a first cousin to Australian brolgas.

No one was the least bit hungry after last night's dinner but partook of the hedonistic display of food served buffet-style for breakfast anyway. Name any fruit, and it was there, plus a wide assortment of meats, breads, and egg dishes.

Marlow and I walked to the William Holden/Stephanie Power's animal orphanage and spent a couple of hours playing with the bongo, an antelope with twisted horns that weighed about five hundred pounds. The bongo was on the endangered species list, and the staff was hoping to breed it at the reserve.

We also wandered among giant forest hogs, dik-diks, various caged cats, a giant tortoise, and a newborn wildebeest (part of the umbilical cord was still attached). The tortoise was estimated to be a hundred years old; I didn't know how they could consider it an orphan.

When other tourists left the orphanage, the attendants let Marlow and I get in cages with animals. Marlow took some terrific pictures of the serval, a cat with black spots on a tawny coat. In Marlow's picture the cat was snarling with his ears back. In actual fact, he was yawning.

Then it was time to get on the road again. We drove four hours to our lunch break at Lake Navisha, a popular place to view birdlife. After an English lunch and a walk on the manicured lawns, we went on a boat ride to a privately owned island, where we viewed a handful of Kirk's dik-diks and Defassa waterbucks, but that was the only visible animal life. On the return boat trip, we also saw a fish eagle eyeing the lake fish. There were so many, the eagle would have licked his chops if he had any chops to lick.

The boat ride to and from the island was the best part of the resort experience. We went through great flocks of wild flamingos and other waterfowl. In some areas the cormorants on the trees were so plentiful, they made the tree look to be in full foliage even though it was nearly bare. Just before we docked, we stirred up submerged hippos. That took us by surprise, as we had seen people on sailboards in the same area. Did I mention that hippos are second to crocodiles for killing humans in Africa?

Our next lodging was in beehive-shaped bamboo cabins at Lake Nakuru. Marlow collapsed onto the bed while I unpacked. He mentioned he could see through the ceiling. I lay down on the bed and looked up. Sure enough, it was evident that if it rained during the night, we'd get a good soaking. The ceiling looked like a giant spider web made of bamboo branches tied together with reeds. There were candles on a ledge, which meant we'd be without electricity after dark. There were also sulfur mosquito coils beside the candles. They were there for a reason.

It was too early to sleep, so Marlow and I wandered the dark path to the lounge to watch a nightclub show. The show consisted of four young men doing acrobatics by candlelight. The lighting man waved a flashlight around, trying to keep at least one performer in view at all times. The athletes had white stripes painted on their bodies, which added to the eeriness of the performance.

I tired of the amateur show and made my way back to our cabin to take a shower by candlelight. Fortunately, we brought flashlights on our trip. I had mine turned on to look for creepy-crawlies before stepping into the shower.

I heard children laughing outside our cabin before we went to the show. While preparing to shower, I heard rustling in the brush against the see-through cabin wall. I assumed the children were playing near our cabin and wanted to sneak a peek at an old white lady naked. I yelled, "You kids get away from the cabin. Go on now." I was mildly concerned the interloper was a man and not children, as Marlow was still at the floor show.

When I flushed the toilet, the handle broke off in my hand, and the water wouldn't stop running. I made my way to the floor show and found a maintenance man, whom I asked to come fix the toilet. He did, and we had no more problems during the night.

The next morning we learned the plumber had borrowed a part from someone else's toilet, and they had listened to water running all night. They couldn't understand it. When they went to dinner, the toilet was working fine. When they came back to their cabin, the water was running and never stopped. We looked innocent, whistling through our teeth, and acted surprised that such a thing could happen.

At breakfast the manager said there had been some lions roaming around our cabin in the evening. He mentioned a time, and I knew it was while I was in the shower. He hoped they hadn't disturbed us. Oh no, I just yelled at them to be on their way, and they left.

January 3, 1986 We headed for the Maasai Mara north of the Serengeti. We were back among old friends, viewing multitudes of species the last two hours before we arrived at the Mara Serena Lodge. Nobody was in a hurry. We knew this was to be our last game park and wanted to relish every minute of the experience.

On the afternoon game drive, we finally got to see a leopard. Like the cheetah, it was a highlight on the trip. What a glorious, muscular, keen animal. We didn't see a single battle scar. He must have been the winner in any battles incurred. He snuggled against a tree trunk for an afternoon snooze but awoke and posed for our cameras. We stayed there half an hour to enjoy his presence. He kept a wary eye on a candelabra cactus behind our bus. As we left, we learned why. He had hidden a Thomson's gazelle corpse in the candelabra for later consumption. He snarled when we stopped to inspect his catch closer, so we drove off and left him to his domain.

At the lodge we learned the staff overbooked and didn't have enough rooms to accommodate our whole group. They needed four couples to volunteer to sleep in tents. Would I??!! That was what I'd expected during one week of our tour anyhow. I volunteered Marlow and me for a tent before anyone else got a chance to speak up—including Marlow. Once more, I was lucky Marlow was so tolerant.

It would be another exciting experience, sleeping in a tent in the wilds of Africa just like Gregory Peck and Ava Gardner in the movie *Kilimanjaro.*

Our tent was quickly erected in the parking lot next to the generator. Men worked on vans and trucks until the wee small hours, and the generator growled all night long. It was about as primitive as camping in Times Square. No self-respecting animal would get near all that commotion.

We didn't go to bed early anyhow, as we had an entertaining show of dancers after dinner, and I went for a swim to wash off a layer of dirt rather than use the *MASH*-style shower set up next to our tent. We rested on army cots until our four a.m. wake-up call for the long-awaited balloon ride.

January 4, 1986 It took an hour and a half to drive to the balloon ascension site. It was pitch black outside, except for the occasional streak of lightning. We were afraid the balloon ride would be cancelled because of the storm. After a lot of twisting and winding around on dirt roads, we arrived at a location to see balloons being inflated in the glow of early dawn. When it was fully daylight, we realized there wasn't a cloud in the sky; I don't know where the storm went, but it was nowhere near us.

We were up in the air before the sun rose over the horizon. I took half a dozen pictures of the sun coming up. When we ascended out of the clearing and could see over the trees, the first thing we saw was a large pride of lions, including some very young ones. They ignored us, the littlest ones chasing one another, wrestling and quarreling just like all brothers and sisters do first thing in the morning. Mom hunted for breakfast, and Dad reclined regally out of reach of the children. The teenagers groomed and flirted.

We floated over trees and across the valley to a stream. We followed the stream, watching crocs and hippos taking an early-morning dip. We stirred up monkeys and baboons, and they told us off in no uncertain terms. We took pictures of the tops of giraffes and elephants (the elephants were the only ones that showed any fright of us). We cast our shadow over herds of Thomson's gazelles, impala, and cape buffalo.

The balloon ride was surreal! It was superb, fantastic, and far too short. We were in the air for an hour and a half when we ran out of fuel and landed near a stream in an open field. Four chase trucks had been told where to meet us, and they were waiting when we arrived. Breakfast preparation was started with the dregs of fuel from the balloon's tanks. Champagne for breakfast, along with sausage, eggs, and toast while viewing nearby herds of elephants and giraffes. We were really in Africa! We were sitting right on the ground in East Africa. It was no dream. If it was, I didn't want to wake up.

We paid no attention to what direction we had been serenely floating above the landscape and were surprised to learn we were only ten minutes from the lodge. We hoped to see the lion pride once more. Do people who live here get tired of seeing the magnificence? I suppose it becomes background scenery for their lives, and they don't notice it any more than we do a new house being built on our block.

Back at the lodge, we went for a swim and took a nap. In the late afternoon, we went for our last game drive. Everyone was pensive and moody. We saw spectacular wildlife everywhere. I hoped our children and grandchildren would experience this someday. It had been a trip of unequalled splendor.

January 5, 1986 We rode to Nairobi and checked into Ernest Hemingway's favorite hotel, The Norfolk, which was colonial-style set in the center of town near the university. We saw hamburgers on the menu, and twenty three out of twenty four of our group ordered them. They were English-style, thick, greasy burgers with beets in place of tomatoes, not Burger King-style.

After lunch Marlow and I walked through the Nairobi University to the natural history museum and saw dozens of paintings Joy Adamson had done of tribesmen in Kenya. She did fine work. She was the author of *Born Free* and *Elsa.* It must be nice to be multitalented. She was murdered in Kenya in 1980. Stubborn, independent white women evidently didn't get along well with African natives. I would not get along well.

We walked downtown, talking about getting a drafting job and moving to Kenya. We were told at the US consulate that the Kenyan government didn't want Americans to come there to live. They wanted the jobs saved for the natives. We'd have to give up our American citizenship to hold jobs unless we could get a job through a US contractor doing temporary work in the country.

We priced cars; they cost twice as much as in the United States. We priced clothing, which was somewhat cheaper than the United States. The price of souvenirs in stores was outrageous. At least they were outrageous compared to what we paid the originators in the bush.

January 6, 1986 We left early after breakfast to visit Kiambetu Tea Estate, which was started in 1909 by an Englishman who bought three-hundred-fifty-six acres from the government (British, I presume) for ten shillings an acre. He cleared most of the rainforest off the land and planted a few tea plants. They flourished at this elevation, much to many people's surprise, and created a handsome estate. He built the first tea-processing factory in Africa, an Anglican church (Richard Leakey was buried in the cemetery behind the church), and a school so that his four daughters could have proper English educations. The school now enrolled three-hundred-fifty young ladies taught by imported English teachers. The current matron of the estate, Mrs. Mitchell, took us on a personal tour and told us the history of the estate. She was the very proud daughter of the original owner. She had her servants prepare a buffet for us and joined us at tables set up on her lawn.

After lunch we bid Mrs. Mitchell farewell, left the civilized settlement, and went to a primitive Maasai village. I had studied about the Maasai while researching a story I wrote about the Mau Mau when I was a teenager. I had been waiting for the opportunity to converse with the fascinating Maasai most of my life.

The Kedong Maasai Manyatta was originally mapped out on an English ranch in the nineteenth century and bought by Mr. and Mrs. Mayers in 1947. It consisted of six thousand acres spreading out from the lower slopes of the escarpment into the Great Rift Valley about thirty miles from Nairobi.

Villages existed throughout the ranch. Each village consisted of four to eight families with their herds. They lived in typical cattle dung homes surrounded by a barrier of briar bushes to keep small animals, women, and children safe from predators.

The warriors let their hair grow and wove it with sisal to protect their necks during battle. The women never had long hair. The shaved head was a sign of beauty.

I took a few pictures before running out of film. It started to rain; I quickly changed film, while protecting my camera from water, and took thirty six more pictures. I went to change film again and discovered the last roll had never caught on the sprockets. The film had never been exposed. I had no pictures on the second roll. Haste makes disappointment.

The village was our only encounter with topless girls in Africa. They ranged in age from ten to thirteen and were dancing with the warriors. We were told they were the warrior's girlfriends. The warriors ranged in age from twenty to thirty. We had naively expected to see rural natives wearing nothing but skins to cover lower body parts.

Marlow conversed with a couple of elderly men, mostly through sign language, who were fascinated with the way he combed his long, wavy, blond hair. One traded Marlow a plastic comb for a hardened, seasoned root with a natural bulb on the end used for hunting. It was hard to believe people could live such a primitive life so close to a major city. The Maasai didn't want to join the twentieth century and would fight against it as long as possible.

We returned to the Norfolk Hotel in Nairobi for a gourmet French meal and a concert by a classical pianist. The contrast between cultures was enough to make us dizzy.

The evening ended with a film and lecture by a member of the East African Wildlife Society, who acquainted us with problems the rangers had in their fight against poachers. In 1970 there were nine thousand rhinos in Kenya; now there were less than five hundred.

Cat numbers had come up since the ban against importing skins to the United States, but now they needed to convince the Japanese and Chinese that black rhino horns were not an aphrodisiac. Of course, ivory was one of the prime prizes of poachers, therefore elephants were being decimated.

January 7, 1986 A long, long day starting at three a.m. Our driver had a flat tire on the way to the airport; our plane left Nairobi *six* hours late; we just barely made our connection in London, and kept flying into the sun. Finally we landed in Denver long enough for night to catch up with us. We arrived in Sacramento at midnight and barely kept our eyes open long enough for the taxi to get us home.

Now, if you had really been smart, you would not have bothered reading this long dissertation. Why didn't you wait for the movie to come out? I heard Brooke Shield was considering playing me. She isn't quite as cute, but…When Marlow heard Brooke might play my part, he generously agreed to play himself—for free.

Four

Meleese and Scott's Wedding in Australia

With Side Trips to New Zealand and Fiji

1986

Our middle son, Scott, couldn't readjust to living in the United States after living in Australia for eight years in the 1970s. He was twenty years old when Marlow and I decided to return to California. After two years Scott was on a plane back to Queensland, where he intended to live the rest of his life.

When he fell in love with Meleese, he proposed marriage. The two were considerate enough to plan their wedding for late December when our employer, Aerojet, traditionally had company shutdown for the holidays. Marlow and I were able to go to the wedding and then on to New Zealand and Fiji for a glorious vacation.

December 13, 1986 At our home in Citrus Heights, California, it was cold and foggy. Darryl, our youngest son and chauffeur for the day, called the airport to see if planes were departing in the fog. All planes were running on time. Darryl confirmed our reservations on the flight to Los Angeles, and the Western Airlines agent said we had been booked on a "milk run" that would stop a few times between

Sacramento and Los Angeles. It would take us four or five hours to get to Los Angeles. Normally, it would take an hour via an express plane. That was strike one for the Citrus Heights' travel agent, who had impressed me as a bit flaky.

Darryl changed our flight to an express flight leaving thirty minutes earlier than the "milk run." We arrived in Los Angeles in time to watch the Washington Redskins/Denver Broncos football game. Good game. The Broncos won, thirty-one to thirty. That helped kill some time. We landed in Los Angeles at a quarter after one, and our next flight left for New Zealand at eight p.m. Almost seven hours was spent on our first layover. We were tired of sitting before we started the long trip across the Pacific. We were scheduled to land in Auckland at eight a.m.

We stopped for fuel in Honolulu, a stop our travel agent forgot to tell us about. She said it was a direct flight to Auckland; that was strike two. It had taken five hours to get to Honolulu. Air New Zealand staff served cocktails at nine p.m., which I thought was a nice way to put us to sleep. They rolled dinner trolleys down the aisle at ten. After dinner we were wide-awake, so we watched a movie, *Running Scared*, and then I read for an hour.

We had a fuel stop in Honolulu. I thought I could get some shut-eye after other passengers disembarked for a two-hour layover. I stretched out on four seats in the middle section and pulled a cover around my neck. All of the sudden, the plane was inundated with noise! The cleanup crew came onboard and picked up trash, vacuumed, took out the remnants of dinner, and loaded carts full of food and drink for the next leg of our journey. I got no sleep.

December 14–15, 1986 We were enroute over the Pacific; it was night most of the way. We crossed the International Date Line and lost a day. We would get a day back on our way home.

After we left Honolulu, we were served more cocktails, followed by a midnight snack the size of a full meal. We were supposed to sleep after the snack. Great! My watch said it was four in the morning. I distinctly remember the last time I ate two large meals between ten p.m. and four a.m.—*never.*

During the night I groggily staggered to the restrooms. The lights on five doors indicated they were occupied. I wasn't surprised after all the food and alcohol the patrons consumed. I cautiously opened the "vacant" one and saw the backside of a man. I quickly closed the door.

A young New Zealander standing behind me said, "See there, that does happen to other people. I thought I was the only one that got caught by that old trick. That man didn't lock the door on purpose. He wanted to give you a thrill."

When the man emerged, we saw he was well into his eighties, had a vacant stare on his face, and his mouth was hanging open. Obviously quite harmless, in my opinion.

After he walked past us, the young man said, "Did you see that smug look on his face? He was quite pleased with himself for giving you a tingle." Tee-hee.

Marlow and I got a few hours of fitful catnaps. We passed the bottle of antacid pills back and forth between naps. We awoke to sunrise over thick, fluffy, white clouds.

We had a ten-hour layover in Auckland, so we spent it sight-seeing rather than sitting in the lovely airport decorated with islands of tropical plants and waterfalls. Auckland was on a strip of land located between the Tasman Sea and the Pacific Ocean and was quite a pleasant temperature and very green. The peninsula was three miles wide. The population was one million—incredible, as there were only three million people in the whole country.

Marlow and I took a city bus downtown, and then caught a taxi to an aquarium, which had been recommended. The aquarium was unique, as we stepped onto a conveyor belt and were carried through a Plexiglass tunnel with fish swimming on three sides of us. (Over our heads was the third side. I wasn't saying we are triangle shaped; Marlow and I are sphere shaped.) The aquarium had a good selection of saltwater fish, and it was a rich experience.

We took a ferryboat ride to see the various suburbs located around the shore. Once we were away from the industrial docks, the residential areas were lovely and inviting. The British colonists had a knack for turning barren land into landscaped gardens.

Marlow and I were eventually on a plane to Australia. When we arrived in Brisbane, Queensland, Australia, thirty-six hours after our takeoff from Sacramento, we looked horrible and smelled worse. Marlow had a two-day growth of beard, and my hair looked like I had gotten caught in a lawnmower. We wore winter clothes that had two cocktails, three meals, and a snack spilled on them. Our breath smelled like the bottom of a birdcage.

We waited an hour for our suitcases to show up on the turntable, then dragged them from baggage claim through customs and out to the waiting room to pick up our prearranged rental car and head for a nearby hotel, a vibrant tooth-brushing, a shower, and sleep.

No such luck. Our Brisbane friends, Pat and Christine Nugent, met us in the waiting room wearing spotless, fresh, matching pink-and-white summer outfits. They looked like they had just stepped off a magazine cover. I'd made arrangements to visit them the day after our arrival. I forgot to allow for the International Date Line crossing. They helped drag our heavy suitcases to the car rental station. Pat drove Marlow in the rental car, and Christine drove me in their car. We went to their home.

They lived an hour away from the airport on the outskirts of Goodna, where we had lived from 1972 through 1977. Christine chatted away, telling me family gossip, and I could hardly understand a word she said. I guess it was a combination of tiredness and the accent, but I really could not understand this dear friend who was speaking a foreign language.

It was a delightful summer evening, and they lived in the country, so we chatted for a couple of hours. The Australian vernacular was coming back to me by the end of the evening. Thank goodness! We could get away with looking stupid our first night and blame it on jet lag, but I didn't think we could use that excuse the whole week we were scheduled to be in Australia. Chris and Pat fixed up their travel trailer as guest quarters, so we had privacy and should have been able to sleep for at least ten hours. It had been forty-six hours since we were last in bed.

December 16, 1986 Tuesday in Goodna, Queensland, was warm and sunny. At five a.m. the kookaburras cackled, which woke up the dozing magpies, which woke up every other bird and wild creature within ten miles of our trailer. What a wild, wonderful place Australia was! I lay there listening to the cacophony for thirty minutes, then decided to sneak out before I woke up Marlow. He slept until eight. I heard Chris moving around in the house, so I joined her in the kitchen. Pat had left for work a couple of hours earlier. Fancy his going to the airport to pick up friends and entertaining them when he knew he had to get up at three a.m. to go to work! What incredible friendship! What marvelous hospitality!

Chris babysat her grandson, Patrick, so she had a darling baby to entertain. Chris fixed us coffee, tea, and great slabs of thick toast for breakfast. I had Vegemite, a toast topping found in Australia. It's a rich, salty, beefy-tasting spread made of yeast.

After breakfast and a bit of a visit, Marlow and I drove across town, stopping at familiar spots to see what had changed in the seven years since we'd resided there. We lived in Brisbane's suburbs from 1972 to 1980. The current operators of Marlow's former real estate office knew who he was. Brian, Marlow's chief salesman, worked down the street from this office and evidently visited them from time to time. My former real estate office was now a furniture store. There was a freeway through the suburb of Tingalpa, just a block from our former home. We were glad we moved before it got noisy. Our house looked exactly the same, still needed the trim painted and the lawn mowed. We sold it for $45,000.00 in 1980. The home was now up for sale for $95,000.00. Wages had not doubled, so real estate was currently a slow game. I was glad I wasn't playing that game anymore.

We had Chinese food on Wynum Bay with our former next-door neighbors from Tingalpa. They filled us in on the gossip from that side of town. They're in the cabinet-making business, so they didn't like the current Socialistic government. The business owners were heavily taxed to pay for the government giveaways to those who didn't want to work, or couldn't work. Australia had practiced apartheid, not allowing anyone of Asian or Black descent to immigrate until the mid-1970s, when Vietnamese boat people showed up on their northern shores. Then world pressure made the nation open its borders to the war victims. Some of the newcomers from Southeast Asia brought their prejudices with them, and soon gang warfare broke out in the cities where Laotian, Cambodian, and Vietnamese families settled. Supposedly, they were given several thousand dollars per family to get them started in their new homeland.

Marlow and I felt we were doing something sneaky having the government pay half our airfare when we migrated to Australia in 1972. It amounted to about $2,500.00 for the six of us. (Macon, Marlow's dad, immigrated with Marlow, our sons, Craig, Scott, and Darryl, and me.) Australia encouraged Caucasian immigration from North America and Europe by subsidizing their fares. White people from the United Kingdom paid a total of ten dollars fare to the Land Down Under. We were all allowed to stay in immigrant hostels for a minor amount of money for up to two years, or until we had gotten jobs and were self-sustaining. The hostels even provided three meals a day. The six of us paid $60.00 a week for the pleasure of a private apartment and cafeteria-style meals.

After Marlow and I toured our old haunts, we went back to Pat and Chris's house, where we had a delicious home-cooked dinner with all the trimmings. After dinner two other couples arrived. They were mutual friends, and we had one of the best evenings of our lives—laughing and telling jokes just like when the eight of us used to get together. We had sore ribs and were having second thoughts about going home to the States by the time we finally made our way to the trailer and sleep.

December 17, 1986 Wednesday in Goodna was warm and sunny. I was up with the kookaburras at five thirty. Kookaburras are birds that sound like they're laughing. The name *kookaburra* means "laughing jackass" in Aboriginese. I lay in bed savoring the sounds until Marlow stirred. I couldn't hear noise emanating from the house, so I assumed today was one of the days when Chris did not babysit, and Pat was already at work. Marlow and I took advantage of the privacy for an early-morning swim. The temperature was already warm enough that the pool felt refreshing.

It wasn't too long before the Nugents stirred, and by the time we finished our swim, they had breakfast fixed. Pat had stayed home from work. He and Marlow visited while Chris and I did laundry so we could arrive in Rockhampton with a fresh wardrobe.

We went for a walk through the bush to Pat's brother's house. John was the local shire councilman we'd campaigned for, and we knew his family. His children took care of wounded animals, and we went to see their collection of possums and birds. In addition to rescued animals, the youngsters had beautiful peach-faced lorikeets that they bred.

Far too soon the time to head for the airport arrived. I was eager to see Scott and meet Meleese but hated to leave these dear friends.

Meleese and Scott met us at the airport in Rockhampton. What was my first impression of my future daughter-in-law? She was beautiful! She had auburn hair, blue-green eyes, a fair complexion with freckles, and was a fragile, dainty, five-foot-tall size six. She was shy and let Scott do most of the talking.

We went to Meleese's parents' house, where her brothers, sister, and parents were waiting to meet us. The boys were scrubbed, polished, combed, and displaying their best manners. Meleese's sister was another beauty. Coreena was sixteen years old, Meleese was eighteen. Rod and Merle, Meleese's parents, had tea, ham sandwiches, and cake set out for us. I love those thin Australian ham sandwiches with no mayonnaise and strong tea! We stayed a short time, and then Rod left to go back to work as a tree lopper (pruning and/or removal). We tagged along with Scott and Meleese on some prenuptial chores. Merle said we'd all meet at her mom's house for a barbecue later that evening.

When we arrived at Meleese's grandparents' house, they greeted us charmingly and invited us in. Her grandmother—"Nan," as the grandkids called her—said she had just baked a meat pie and made a caramel tart for their dinner. I thought that a bit unusual, but decided that maybe they didn't like barbecue food.

Then she said, "I was told about the barbecue five minutes ago. I don't know what we have on hand, so you folks will just have to take potluck." How embarrassing! Of course, we could go to a restaurant, or eat nothing at all, as we had those nice sandwiches earlier. I wanted to get out of there!

The high-set house, set up on wooden columns, had a lower level used as a garage, laundry, and general gathering area in the hot summers. Everyone went downstairs where there was a breeze; we sat on an array of chairs gathered from hither and yon, talked, and drank soft drinks we had brought. Nan was one of the most entertaining, lovely people we could ever hope to meet. We thoroughly loved our visit with her and "Grang," Meleese's grandfather. Our embarrassment dissipated with their charm.

By and by, Merle, Rod, and their youngsters showed up, bringing cartons of food, and within a few minutes, we had a banquet spread out before us. I couldn't believe how quickly everything was on the table and the steaks and sausages cooked and served. The meal was fantastic, and we all had a nice visit. Scott was uniting us with a great extension to our family.

After an evening of getting acquainted, we drove to Mount Morgan, Queensland, with Scott to spend the night in his newly completed, self-built house. He was still talkative, so I left him and Marlow sitting on the only bit of furniture in the house, the bed, and took a blanket and pillow out to the living room and slept on the carpet. I was asleep within moments and woke up at six thirty the next morning. Imagine a full eight hours of sleep all at one time!

December 18, 1986 Thursday in Queensland was hot and humid.

Meleese arrived at Mount Morgan from her home in Rockhampton at seven thirty. We woke the men and drove to the grocery store that was in the process of opening for business. We bought a few groceries, but not much, as Scott's fridge was the tiny type made for offices to keep lunch and a quart of milk cold. We rummaged through engagement presents and found enough equipment to make coffee, using a funnel with a paper-towel filter. Some people had cereal, and some had sandwiches.

Scott and Meleese took us for a three-hour tour of Mount Morgan and environs. Mount Morgan was a small town in a hilly setting with a history of gold mining and lots of character. The last stop was a real surprise.

Scott showed us a block of land he had just bought! It was two-and-a-half acres, with three-hundred-sixty-degree views. He told us he bought it with part of the money we sent himas a wedding gift. I thought he meant he had used the money as part of a down payment. No, he meant that he had bought the land, paid in full for—are you ready for this?—for a grand total of $165.00. No, that isn't a typing error. I don't mean $16,500.00. I mean he pulled off another deal like only Scott can do. He heard there was to be an auction held by the shire council (equivalent to county), but he was unable to attend.

The next day he asked his friend, a builder, how the auction went, and the builder told him that only a couple of people showed up. The builder bought the blocks of land right in town, but wasn't interested in the acreage blocks. Scott's land was surrounded by "Crown" land, government land, which he had the option of buying at a later time, if he so desired. All he had to pay for this block was the stamp duty to transfer the title deed to his name. It was being sold on a first come, first served basis at the shire office, so Scott bought it sight unseen, as there was a line forming behind him, and he didn't want to lose out. He knew what the general area was like, but didn't know what a beautiful block he had until after he bought it. Scott had the Midas touch. We expected him to discover gold while digging the foundation for his home.

Scott and Meleese's house in Mount Morgan was small but livable. It was a two-bedroom, high-set, and there was room underneath to put a garage and a playroom. The view from the big kitchen window was of the town swimming pool and park. The house was up so high that the view was over his next-door neighbor's trees. The view out front of the house was of a bank—a mud-bank, not a money bank. I suggested they plant bougainvillea there so they'd have something pretty to look at. There was a nice bright bathroom with an enormous sky light in the ceiling—I loved that. I like lots of sunshine in a house. Scott paneled his double closet door in the master bedroom to match one wall, which made the room look larger. He had an air conditioner in the living room and recessed lights in the ceiling. The house was decorated in earth tones and would be quite comfortable for newlyweds.

In the evening Scott treated us to dinner at *the* classy restaurant in town. He knew all the customers: the town doctor (a woman), the hardware store owner, and the only real estate man in town. The restaurant owners came out from the kitchen after our meal to congratulate Scott and Meleese and wish them well. They were typical good-natured country folks with only half their original teeth intact.

We went back to Scott's house, and the two young people opened Christmas presents from us. Meleese was a delight to watch. Her eyes lit up with each gift. I could tell we were going to get along famously. She liked getting pretty, feminine, scented things, and I loved buying them for young ladies. I was impressed that she carefully removed the ribbons and paper and neatly folded them for future recycling. Thrifty. A girl after my heart.

I bought Scott's presents when I thought he was coming to the United States to spend the Christmas holiday in the snowy mountains. Therefore he got lots of warm, woolly clothes. The air was sweltering, so we didn't ask him to try them on to see if they fit. He could wait until next July when it cooled down. The kids gave us a beautiful book on the Barrier Reef. We would make good use of that by showing friends the coral we had seen while snorkeling.

I forgot to mention one of the highlights of the day. Scott took us to a factory in Mount Morgan that was owned and operated by Aboriginals. We got to watch them making and painting boomerangs and other sundry decorative pieces to sell to tourists. We got a wall decoration and I took a picture of a darling baby who was sitting in a stroller next to where his mom was painting designs. He had a smile a mile wide. What a little doll.

December 19, 1986 In Mount Morgan, Queensland, it was sultry, sultry, *sultry*! We finally had a kick-back day. Marlow and I drove to Scott's vacant land just for the fun of it, did the laundry, and went to the Olympic-size swimming pool. I walked about town enjoying the sights, sounds, and aromas. Scott went into Rockhampton to greet out-of town wedding guests as they arrived at the airport.

December 20, 1986 The Wedding Day! Mount Morgan was extremely hot, humid, and sunny.

Scott was cool, calm, and collected early in the morning, but the closer the hour to the wedding got, the more tension built. We started for town reasonably early so we could meet some of Scott's friends. A group went to Scott's place of employment, a building construction firm, and went for a swim in the owner's pool. Yes, the owner and his wife joined us. Marlow and I hadn't thought to take swimsuits to town the day of the wedding, so we sat in the shade chatting with the new arrivals. Scott bought lunch of tasty reef fish and chips for one and all, the typical Australian meal. Then he took me to Meleese's house to get dressed with the bridesmaids and Meleese while he and Marlow went to a groomsman's house to dress.

Meleese looked gorgeous. She had one of the most beautiful wedding gowns I'd ever seen. She was the vision of an angel dropped to earth. The bridesmaids and flower girl were dressed in matching dresses of pink lace over taffeta. They had their hair done in French braids. Meleese and her mom had their hair done at the beauty shop. I combed my hair. The house was in a cheerful uproar as the photographer patiently waited for everyone to get organized for the pre-wedding pictures. It was so hot; I felt sorry for the girls trying to look cool.

Scott got to the church on time; he was there before I arrived. It was a closed wedding, so only invited guests were there. Scott and the groomsmen were seated in the front row. They didn't escort people down the aisle like in the United States. When I walked in, Marlow and Scott stood in the front of the church waving their arms, telling me to come down front and sit with them. I felt conspicuous walking down the aisle by myself with all eyes watching me. I carried my camera bag as well as my purse, as Scott had asked Marlow and me to take pictures. I ended up with my camera on the wrong setting, and none of the indoor pictures came out anyway. There were so many gadgets on the new camera Marlow got me for the trip. Oh, for a good Brownie Hawkeye! Marlow took pictures, and we had copies of those to distribute to our family. I'm sure the guests thought the parents of the groom were mad.

The reception was a formal sit-down English dinner of roast beef and all the trimmings. Two of Scott's friends—Maoris from New Zealand—sang beautiful songs after dinner, and a pianist played music through dinner, as well as playing the wedding waltz afterward. Speeches were made by groomsmen and fathers before we went to various places and changed clothes. I bet the bride, groom, and attendants were glad to get out of their formal wear. The temperature was well over one hundred degrees, with high humidity.

Scott, Meleese, Marlow, and I headed for Yeppoon on the coast, where Scott had made reservations at a hotel. We were on one of the top floors, so we had beautiful views of the bay.

December 21, 1986 The four of us arose early and left for Great Keppel Island on a huge catamaran. We made one stop at an aquarium in the bay. We walked down a spiral staircase and found windows all the way around the room. We had views of the coral and colorful fish without getting wet.

On Keppel Island we looked over the plush resort where Scott and Meleese would spend their honeymoon. It was a tropical setting with beautiful flowers and birds as well as miles of walking paths and beaches. There were also the usual things such as tennis, golf, and of course, a freshwater swimming pool. It looked like a super place to relax and unwind after all the trauma of wedding preparations.

We were surprised to learn Scott had booked us into a room at the resort for one night. We had expected to take the return boat to the mainland and bemoaned the short visit with our middle son.

December 22, 1986 The day was spent on Keppel Island. Marlow and I made use of the recreational facilities and left the honeymooners to themselves until we met for lunch. Then they were on their own again until joining us for a gourmet dinner.

They said they were exhausted from the buildup to the wedding, and they'd spent the day lying by the pool or sleeping.

We hated to say good-bye to the kids, but they had to get on with their adult lives, and we had to get to Rockhampton for the next leg of our journey. We did lots of hugging, dropped a few tears, and wished them years and years of happiness.

Scott and Meleese stayed at the resort. Marlow and I caught a ferry to Yeppoon, a bus to Rockhampton, and a flight to Christchurch, New Zealand.

December 23, 1986 Christchurch, New Zealand, was cool and cloudy. I got up and went for a walk in the overcast, comfortable weather. I returned to the Travelodge and woke Marlow at eight thirty. We had an English-style breakfast of sausage, eggs, and cooked tomatoes, then picked up our motor home. We stocked it with groceries and toiletries and left town by noon.

Every hour the weather and scenery changed—very windy with bright blue skies, slightly windy with cloudy skies, no wind with rain, then the skies cleared and started all over again. The scenery changed from cityscape to suburbia, to farms, to stations (cattle, sheep, and red deer stations (ranches)).

After the stations came the deserts, high tumbleweedy lands like Nevada, and from there we entered the green zone. Lake-strewn foothills, green fields, and green mountains with hundreds of waterfalls and rivers lay before us. Wonderful, just wonderful. A fantasy unfolded before our eyes.

We drove until nine thirty p.m. and settled into a campground at sunset. The long southern twilight began. I had a shower before dark, as the restrooms only had one light bulb each, and that was located quite a distance from the showers. I didn't want to reach for the soap and pick up a creepy-crawly instead. I cooked dinner of tasty New Zealand beef with vegetables in the motor home. Then we were off to bed by midnight.

December 24, 1986 It was cold, windy, and cloudy on Wednesday morning in a quaint, nearly deserted campground between Christchurch and Queenstown.

No blue skies were in sight or even forecast for the day. We drove to Queenstown, one of the most beautiful resort areas in New Zealand. We planned a jet boat ride, but everything was closed because of the impending holiday.

I was tired, maybe coming down with a cold, or just not getting enough restful sleep with the continual change of beds. All I wanted to do was sleep. Marlow wanted to take a bus tour of Queenstown while I slept in the camper parked on Main Street next to town hall.

When I first lay down, I thought, *I'll never sleep with all this traffic noise.* That was my last thought for an hour and a half, until I heard Marlow unlock the camper door.

He had been the only passenger on the tour bus and had plied the driver with lots of questions, so he had an interesting history tour of Queenstown, which used to be a gold rush town. He related the story to me as we shared hot drinks at our tiny kitchen table.

Not much sense sitting in town during a heavy rain, so we headed toward our next destination. We got to Te Anau, and it was still pouring. The glowworm caves were flooded, so there went that idea of a way to spend a rainy day. The park keepers were allowing no admittance to the caves. We bought our Christmas all-day boat ride tickets for Milford Sound—the main spot I wanted to see in New Zealand—reputedly one of the most spectacular places in the world. We also got tickets for another all-day boat ride in Doubtful Sound for December 26.

We drove to Milford Sound through some of the most glorious scenery (and remember I've been to Yosemite and Yellowstone, so I know what "glorious" means). Milford Sound was a rainforest; the area got over three hundred inches of rain a year. Ferns, moss, pine trees, three varieties of beech trees, lots of wild flowers, and even a few cacti lived side-by-side on the hillsides and gorges. We drove through a gorge with mountains towering on either side. Looking through the rain to higher elevations, we saw snow accumulating on the ground.

Marlow caught a cold our last day in Rockhampton. The night was so hot, we slept with the air conditioner blowing cold air directly on our prone bodies. I started sneezing and blowing today and was shivery and achy. We loved the scenery, but felt miserable by the time we got to Milford Sound. There was no electricity available for our camper, which meant we had no heater, so we checked into the fancy hotel. We had our choice of a room with a view for $140.00 a night or sleeping among the hotel staff for $70.00 a night. There was no view in the rain anyhow, and we just wanted somewhere warm and quiet. We took the cozy room among the staff's quarters, had hot soup, took a hot shower, went to bed, and slept through the gala dance celebrating Christmas, that was being held in the lodge ballroom.

December 25, 1986 Christmas Day at Milford Sound, South Island, New Zealand, was very cold, with snow flurries and rain. It was wonderful holiday weather, good for singing around the hearth with family and friends and drinking hot toddies while opening gaily wrapped gifts. Indeed, there were a number of hotel guests clustered at dining tables near the roaring hearth eating delectable Christmas breakfasts that probably cost $40.00 apiece.

I cooked Christmas breakfast in our camper, did the laundry at the hotel, and then we took our boat excursion on Milford Sound. This was truly a gorgeous place with pointy granite islands, a plethora of waterfalls cascading down cliffs covered with green, green undergrowth anywhere there was soil. There were ferns growing on moss, and I was told there was very little topsoil. The moss was breaking down the granite and adding some nutrients, which took hold and fed the tiny plants. We were actually among fjords like in Norway, where the mountains go from the water to the sky. The mountains in Milford Sound also went under the bay's surface for an estimated thousand feet. I wish we could have seen it on a sunny day. With three hundred inches of rainfall, a sunny day was a rare occasion. I was disappointed; I really wanted to see this particular spot without the rain that pelted us 99 percent of the time. Our colds had us sneezing or blowing our noses in between every camera shutter snap. Of course, there was no chemist open to get Sudafed or nose drops.

The camper ride through the valley was equally impressive. We stopped a few times, once at a place called Chasm River, which had worn smooth holes through enormous rocks and rounded every granite edge. We took a wonderful walk on a trail. We each wore a garbage bag over our clothes as did some other tourists. No sense coming all this way and missing the beauty because of the rain or disease.

We stopped at Mirror Lakes, another gorgeous, green place. The vegetation was unique and indescribable. I wish I had a year to study the botany of Milford Sound. You will have to take the trip yourself, to understand the overwhelming feeling of beauty.

We drove past Te Anau and up to the point where we were to catch our boat for Boxing Day's tour of Doubtful Sound. We found a pleasant little motor camp and settled in for the night. We could get a lot of sight-seeing done when the day started at sunrise, five a.m. and ended at dusk, ten p.m.

December 26, 1986 Doubtful Sound, South Island, New Zealand, was resplendent with *sunshine and no wind*! Hallelujah!

We awoke to find ourselves in a very nice campground, trees and flowers galore, plenty of space between sites, and lots of open grassy areas for children's play. I loved the colorful foxglove growing in profusion. The restrooms had no hot water, so I stayed dirty and hoped no one got too close.

We threw crumbs on the ground and watched local birdlife while eating our breakfast. We saw mostly sparrows, a couple of thrushes, and one goldfinch. We also saw another kea, the twenty-inch-long green parrot found only on South Island, New Zealand. There are few of these omnivorous birds left in the world, and we had been fortunate enough to see two. The first one was a clown in the hotel parking lot at Milford Sound. He hopped from person to person looking for handouts. When he flew to a car roof, we saw that he sported bright-orange feathers on the underside of his wings.

We were only half a mile from the boat dock for the trip on Doubtful Sound. I was in a much better mood with the sun shining, and was sure we were going to see the beauty we expected, with blue skies as a backdrop.

First we traveled by boat across Lake Manapouri ("mournful heart" in Maori), then toured a power station, which meant we had to go underground in a bus. After the powerhouse, the bus took us to another boat dock, where we boarded and toured Doubtful Sound. The bus trip was a scenic twenty kilometers across a mountain.

The bus driver told us the average rainfall on the first side of Lake Manapouri, where we camped, was fifty inches a year. The other side of the lake, where we caught the bus, was a hundred-fifty inches a year, and Doubtful Sound averaged three-hundred-thirty inches, even more than Milford Sound! The weather was so changeable from one hour to the next, the only accurate way weathermen could forecast was to look out the window. If they saw the mountains, that meant it was going to rain. If they couldn't see the mountains, it was already raining. Hah! The natives maintained a sense of humor.

On the boat we learned Lake Manapouri was one of the deepest lakes in the world. At some spots the depth had been recorded as being two miles deep. Hang on—Marlow looked over my shoulder and corrected my journal writing. He said the captain said the lake was two thousand feet deep…Who's telling this story anyway? Well, would you believe me if I told you it was pretty dang deep?

The hills were emerald, covered with pines, which were introduced to the country by pioneers. Palms and ferns grew on vertical moss-strewn escarpments. Every once in awhile, we passed a spot where there had been a tree avalanche, where the rain had gotten under the moss and uprooted a tree. When one tree fell over, it slid all the way to the water, taking everything in its path with it.

When white men first arrived in New Zealand, there were no four-legged animals, only birds and ducks. White men introduced many species. The English loved to hunt, so they brought wild critters and encouraged them to multiply for hunters to kill them. Go figure. Many of the animals escaped the hunters' bullets and have become pests. We saw hedgehog and skunk carcasses littering the highways in the early morning before the vultures had breakfast.

We saw many waterfalls on the strip of land between Lake Manapouri and Doubtful Sound; one was named Matilda after that famous waltzing Australian.

The boat ride was delightful! The good weather held all day long. We were able to snap pictures of sheer cliffs dropping into deep gorges filled with crystal-clear water. There was fresh water about eighteen inches deep on top of salt water because of the heavy rainfall, which kept rainwater from mixing with the seawater coming in on the tides.

After our boat/bus/boat tour, we drove our camper toward Queenstown. We traveled through ranchland. New Zealanders raised red deer for human consumption. The Kiwis had developed a taste for venison. I wanted Marlow to figure out how we could raise deer for venison in Northern California. That would be a good way to live, except on sale day. I hated the thought of selling our deer to a butcher. Marlow thought we'd have problems catching the first pair of deer. And he didn't think they'd like living in our little backyard. Well, it was just a thought.

December 27, 1986 In Queenstown, it was another sunny day! It was windy but clear, and the temperatures were comfortable. We drank a quick cup of coffee and headed for the Kiwi Wildlife Park to be there when the kiwis woke up and started foraging for food. One of the first things we learned after arrival was that the birds were nocturnal. The zoo keepers had the room dark so the kiwis would think it was night when customers arrived in the morning. It took awhile for our eyes to adjust to the darkness, but we soon spotted two birds about the size of a six- or seven-pound chicken. They were much larger than I expected. I was searching for sparrow-sized birds.

We were the only people in the zoo, so we had our faces pressed against the window and our hands shading our eyes for better views when two birds came right up in front of us and started mating. I felt like I was intruding; the twenty-year-old guide said it was rare for anyone to see kiwis mating, they were so secretive. That was embarrassing.

There are three different species of kiwis and only about a total of a thousand birds left in the wild. Zoos are trying to get pairs to multiply. So far zoos had produced approximately three hundred birds to turn lose in the wild. Kiwi couples normally only raise one chick a year.

After a couple of hours at Queenstown's bird sanctuary, we went for a jet boat ride. We skimmed across the top of the water and could go dangerously close to rocks before turning away. Now, *that* got my adrenaline pumping! It was the most exciting ride I had had since we went on the airboat in the Everglades in 1970. Marlow felt it was the most exciting ride he *ever* had. It was a roller coaster on water.

When we got safely to shore, I asked a member of the crew if they ever had accidents. She said they had been very lucky; they had not had a single accident *all week*. She did say that sometimes they messed up the boats a bit, but no customers had ever been injured—the day was coming when that record would fall.

We took pictures of the beautiful area and of other people in the jet boats, and then headed on up the road to Haast Gate. We spent the night on a mountain pass with glaciers around us. It was a lovely campground with plenty of trees, shrubbery, and flowers to admire. I wanted to stay there a week. There was even a ranger talk, which was one of our favorite forms of entertainment, but we were too tired from our colds to go. I'd really like to return to New Zealand with no time restraints. I would spend a week or more at each place we spent a night.

December 28, 1986 On Sunday, Haast Gate weather greeted us with heavy pouting clouds and strong winds. Glorious glacier scenery and alpine lakes set among rainforests were ours to be admired. We traveled west to the Tasman Sea, then north. The scenery was reminiscent of Route 101, without any traffic. Route 101 is a road that winds along the coast through California, Oregon, and Washington. In both places there are scenes on both sides of the road—seascapes on one side and mountains on the other worthy of being pictured in calendars.

There were only three million people in New Zealand in 1986, and two million of them lived on the north island, with one million in Auckland, so we drove for an hour or two without passing another car while on South Island. It was also a far piece between gas stations.

We hiked on Fox Glacier, which was busy receding uphill, creating a new Yosemite in its passing. The difference would be the jungles growing in the gorges and clinging to the cliffs instead of alpine forests.

December 29, 1986 Fox Glacier was very cold, and rain descended in torrents. We cancelled our flight to the peak of Franz Josef Glacier and planned walking down the glacier-side trail. A few minutes on the wet, muddy trails were enough to change our minds. Instead we drove north on the highway, trying to find a warm, sunny spot again.

December 30, 1986 At Inangahua Junction, we were still in rain and gloom. The restroom showers at our campground were freezing. The camp was occupied by a group of kayakers who were playing games on local rivers and didn't notice the cold rain or the cold showers. Miserable weather, beautiful, beautiful country. I wanted to go home and sit in my own living room in front of a roaring fire for awhile and come back better prepared with proper winter clothes. It was midsummer in New Zealand and as cold as midwinter in Sacramento.

We drove all day. We got our interisland ferry tickets changed to an earlier ride and went to North Island. The crossing was lovely and smooth once we were out of South Island's rain pattern. We drove fifty more miles before settling into a camp for the night. The matron said they needed rain! It hadn't rained on North Island for two months. Bah, humbug! They could wait until we were on Fiji for their rain.

December 31, 1986 Southern North Island, New Zealand, was sunny and warm. God smiles on New Zealand! Neat, clean farms, neat, clean towns, warmth, and sunshine—what more could anyone want? I loved North Island. We drove through pleasant scenery with stops at a geothermal power plant and a lovely calm lake, and the most glorious aquamarine-colored waterfalls imaginable. They were called Huka Falls, and I was very glad Marlow made a U-turn and went back to them after I, as navigator, missed the turnoff the first trip past.

On to Rotorua. We lucked out and got the last campsite available in a campground, and then were told that the owners were having a New Year's Eve party starting in about thirty minutes. They had a barbecue with live music and good company. They offered all the beer we wanted. That first one tasted good in the warm summer air. The night before, it would have been torture to drink. Plus, our campsite for the night was $11.00 (US$5.50). They even had steaks, as well as the usual burgers and snags (sausages) for meat. That evening completely revived our spirits.

January 1, 1987 Thursday at Rotorua, North Island, New Zealand, was heavenly, warm, and sunny. We slept until nine o'clock. Both of us felt better; our colds had passed their peaks.

We drove to a viewpoint where we saw two lakes, one blue and the other green. They were side-by-side; the locals said the difference in color happened at the time of the 1886 volcanic eruption. I figured it was because of different algae in the water.

We went to Whakarewarewa, a Maori village and a thermal area with boiling mud for which New Zealand was famous. We threw some coins into a cool river where local youngsters were diving to retrieve them. When they got enough coins, they ran to a thermal pool to warm up, then took their loot to a store to get ice cream. We talked to some of the boys at the hot pool, and they said they made an average of $2.00 a day. Hardly worth the effort, but it kept them off the streets.

We walked around the village snapping pictures of the unique architecture. The Maori designed place of worship was decorated with spiritual designs. The museum of art was British Victorian. The graveyards were interesting; they couldn't bury their dead underground, as the steam tunnels were so close to the surface. Each grave was a concrete mausoleum. Most Maoris were Christian; there were crosses and statues of saints by many graves. We went to a concert and listened to the history of the Maori people, then went through their arts and crafts school. The men do wood carving, and the women do weaving. No woman was ever allowed to carve, and no man was ever allowed to weave reeds.

We spent four hours at Whakarewarewa, then went to a fauna and flora park. We spent a couple of hours looking at the plants and animals that had been imported to New Zealand. We topped off the day by going to a *hangi*, a traditional Melanesian/Polynesian feast.

The hangi food was disappointing, as we were served plain old English foods, lamb, roast beef, chicken, and the usual roast potatoes and pumpkin as the vegetable. It was the same meal Australian families had once or twice a week. The Maori concert was most enjoyable. Everyone was related, and they sang traditional songs and danced very well together. The people had such melodic music.

January 2, 1987 Friday, northern North Island presented us with variable clouds and spring-like weather. It was our last day in New Zealand, the most beautiful country we had seen in our travels.

The people were great. They were fond of Americans in spite of our nuclear submarines plying their waters. The older ones reminisced about World War II and how grateful they were the Yanks saved their hides from the Japanese. The younger ones loved our neat cars, music, and clothes. The Maoris were rapidly intermarrying with Europeans, so few were a race apart. New Zealand had some racial problems. The Melanesian/Polynesian people arrived in 1350 AD, and the Europeans arrived with Captain Cook in 1760 AD. All went well until gold was discovered in 1886, and the Europeans got greedy and took land from Maoris. Maoris wanted the land back. That sounded familiar.

New Zealand didn't have much crime. We saw a couple of policemen outside of Auckland. We'd seen two fender benders, one in Queenstown, where kids were driving faster than they should and didn't get stopped for a red light. The police arrived on foot to take the report. That happened while I was getting ready to take my nap in the motor home parked on Main Street. The second accident was at one of the multitude of one-way bridges. We were halfway across, going slowly, when a car approached from the opposite side and didn't get stopped in time. He hit the corner of the bridge. We stopped to see if everyone was okay. We asked the owner of the new Volvo if he was all right and he said yes, but he was sure surprised; it was his first accident in twenty five years of driving. He was towing a big boat, and the boat trailer brakes had been grabbing, so he stopped at a garage to get them fixed. The garage people said they couldn't help him, but all he had to do was disconnect the brakes on the trailer and drive slowly to the next town where he could get help. The boat was too heavy to be pulled as fast as the driver was going as he approached the bridge, and after the car stopped, the boat pushed the car forward into the bridge. Poor man.

The economy was not to the liking of most Kiwis (nickname for the residents). Everything cost twice as much as in America, and the average man made half as much. That meant they could buy a quarter as much as Americans. The only time I saw any bargains was on fresh vegetables as we were driving through small towns set in farm country. The average house cost $100,000.00; the average car was $25,000.00. Imagine paying a quarter of what you would pay for a house—which you'd live in for most of your life—for a car you would use for four or five years. Regular T-shirts started at $20.00, and jeans started at $50.00. We ate in restaurants a couple of times and paid NZ$40.00 for what we would have paid US$20.00 U.S.. With the exchange in money, we came out even. It didn't work that way for the natives. No wonder so many were leaving their beautiful homeland to move to Australia.

January 3, 1987 Saturday we left Auckland, North Island, New Zealand, and went to Fiji—it was warm and sunny both places.

We had a seven-twenty a.m. flight to Fiji, so we were up with the birds to check out of our hotel and get a shuttle to the airport. We looked forward to Fiji, with our scheduled cruise to outer islands. Everything was paid in advance. We gave the money to our US travel agent; we wouldn't have to spend any more money except on souvenirs. We'd get glorious suntans in January and make our California acquaintances jealous.

We arrived in Fiji to learn that the tour agency at the airport had no notice about our cruise. They said that maybe the cruise ship people had left word at the hotel where we were to spend the first night. We went to the hotel. No one knew anything about our cruise. They phoned the cruise ship company, who said they never received money from our agent, so they never confirmed our trip. We called our agent in Citrus Heights, California. They had mailed our money to their home office in Los Angeles, but had not done so until *late November*, even though we had given them our check in September. The agent in Los Angeles said he learned the cruise was full at the time he received our check in November. He hung on to our check instead of mailing it to Fiji in case there was a cancellation that we could fill. The home office never told our agent in Citrus Heights any of this. What I had in mind about this time was justifiable homicide, or rather genocide, starting with the twit who originally took our trip orders and messed up so much. We checked to see if we could get an earlier flight home. No such luck; everything leaving Fiji was booked until January 15.

We had a couple hundred dollars in traveler's checks and our Master Cards, which we had never used. Supposedly, we had credit up to $3,500.00. We would find out how well those cards worked. We stayed in the hotel where we had expected the cruise ship shuttle to pick us up the next morning.

It turned out to be the same hotel we used during our 1980 stop on our way to California from Australia. We had asked our agent to book us into the Regency, a super-luxurious hotel, as we planned on only being there one night. For once I was glad the twit didn't do what we asked. The Dominion Hotel was glad to have us stay with them until our plane left on the eighth, and we could pay with our plastic money. It would only cost us a third of what the Regency would have charged.

They had put in real air conditioning since we were there in 1980. Marlow was so frustrated; he wanted to take a nap. He did. I put on my swimsuit and headed for the pool. I met two other couples from the United States who had been visiting children in Australia. Both had similar frustrations with their travel agents, so we passed an hour whining and complaining while submerged neck deep in tepid pool water. I told them my husband didn't even have his swimsuit; he left it in Australia. They told me the stores in Nadi (pronounced *Nandee*) were staying open late that night to do inventory. I went to the room and woke Marlow, and we headed for town to get him swim trunks.

We stood at the bus stop. It cost $.25 to ride the bus downtown. A taxi pulled up and offered us a ride for $2.50. We said, "No thanks, we will wait for the bus and save $2.00." He then offered to drive us for $.50. We got in and had the comfort of a taxi. He wanted to be our private chauffeur while we were on the island. We took his telephone number and said we would call him whenever we needed a cab. There was so much competition among taxi drivers that some drivers got customers' names and bugged them at their hotel every day to see if they wanted a ride.

We walked from one end of the commercial district to the other and got the swimsuit, toiletries, and other sundries we felt we needed to stay for the next week. We went to a restaurant off the tourist's beat and ate among the natives. We had delicious all-you-can-eat Chinese food for a mere $2.00 per person. What a difference from New Zealand!

I saw the four people I met at the pool earlier. They were eating in the same restaurant, and we spent the evening together. Good company and good music from the band at our hotel. We sat at the pool and listened to music and talked until midnight.

January 4, 1987 In Nadi, Viti Levu Island, Fiji, it was warm and sunny. We booked passage on a ten-passenger plane to Plantation Island. Plantation Island was paradise. We spent the day snorkeling. It was my first attempt, and I loved it, although I thought I would surely drown from all the water coming in around my mask. Marlow went windsurfing, but I stayed with the snorkeling, as the tide had gone out and I could swim closer to the coral. It was another world. The beauty was unbelievable! There were so many types of corals—which are animals, not plants, in case you didn't know that. I didn't know that. Most were white or muted pastel colors. The colors of the fish were unrealistic—red, orange, blue, green, bright yellow, and every combination of those colors.

I could lie flat on top of the water for hours and watch the world pass beneath me. When my mask filled with enough water that the fish were invisible, I treaded water and emptied it. The trick was to empty the water out of the mask without tipping the end of the breathing tube into the water behind my head. When I emptied my mask and put it back on the first time, I choked on a mouthful of seawater coming down the tube. I had to touch things to see if they were soft or hard. Marlow said that was silly, as some of those things bit or stung. It was so hard to be a kid in a candy store and not touch. I didn't get bit or stung or even sunburned, so I was eager to try again the next chance I got.

We had a delightful scenic flight back to Viti Levu Island. The bus trip to Nadi for pizza was noisy. Bus drivers played loud Indian music, which clashed with the melodic Melanesian ukuleles we heard on the beaches, in the resorts and restaurants, and on Plantation Island.

January 5, 1987 *On Fiji it was hot, humid, and sunny on January 5*! Marlow got sunburned, so he wanted to stay out of the sun. We caught a bus to Suva, a hundred-twenty miles away on the north coast of Viti Levu. We wanted to see if the route was still the same as in 1980. It wasn't. Progress had caught up with Fiji. There were cars instead of pedestrians and donkeys.

The children didn't run out to the street to shout, "Bula!" as our bus passed. They kept right on with their games and ignored the mundane sight of a vehicle passing. Men didn't stop their game of soccer on vacant lots to smile and wave a cheery "Bula" as we passed; they sat in sad-looking groups staring at the ground.

In 1980 most of the roads had been dirt, and we had driven very slowly through small villages and yelled, "Bula" to everyone we saw. They had waved and returned a cheerful greeting. Many had grass huts that looked so romantic. Now the government had given them money to build ugly cement-block and corrugated-iron buildings, and the roads were paved.

We whizzed through towns too fast for even a wave, let alone a "Bula." The people looked poor instead of romantic and bored instead of idyllic. Traffic was intense and plentiful. Television was supposed to arrive on the island the next month, and that would end any chance of the people being quaint and cheerful. They would learn that they were supposed to hate tourists and Americans in particular. They would also learn they needed a lot of nonsense they never knew existed.

January 6, 1987 I did an end-zone victory dance each time I woke up and it was hot and sunny.

We caught a boat to another island. There were three-hundred-thirty islands in the archipelago, and one-hundred-eighty were occupied. Eighty-three percent of the land belonged to the Melanesians for as long as they existed. They could pass it on to their sons (not daughters) or grandsons. There were very few interracial marriages between the Indian (from India) population and the Melanesians. Indians were brought in as slaves or indentured workers for the British sugarcane fields in the last century. The Indians were smart, energetic, and motivated; they built businesses when freed from slavery and ended up owning most businesses on Fiji.

Our destination was called Daydream Island; the tour company was new and went all out to entertain us. They organized singing and dancing on the way over and back and had snorkeling, volleyball, and fishing planned for our stay on the island. Marlow and I went fishing with a couple of local men and three boys from Down Under. Marlow, the Melanesians, and I each caught a fish. I caught a rock cod—the ugliest fish I ever saw. Marlow caught a leather jacket—that's the name of a reef fish. The Australians caught nothing. I said that meant we got to take the America's Cup home. That started a bit of bantering, and the Fijians looked at us as if we were nuts, arguing over a cup.

On the way to the main island, we drank *kava*, which tasted like muddy water, from a shell and then passed the shell to the next person. They didn't have germs in Fiji. We sang or tried to sing a song for each country represented on the boat—Australia, Canada, France, Sweden, Germany, Fiji, New Zealand, and the United States. The last song we sang was "We Are the World." We certainly got a full day's entertainment.

One of the crew caught a thirty-pound Spanish mackerel by trolling on the way home. That meant we had to dance to celebrate. It was amazing, but Marlow and I could country swing to Melanesian music.

January 7, 1987 Eureka! We found them, the real Fijians we remembered from our 1980 trip. We rented a car and drove into the mountainous interior of the main island. What roads! I swore that some of the hills were forty-five degrees, but Marlow said he didn't think the car would climb that steep an angle. He reckoned the angle was a mere thirty degrees. They were curvy dirt roads, so we drove slowly and yelled, "Bula" to lots of smiling faces working or resting in front of their little grass-thatched huts. Hallelujah! Real people! Happy people!

We came to one village where men were playing in a muddy river. They waved to us. I tried to talk Marlow into joining them while I chatted with the women and children. He didn't like the condition of the water; he'd rather see the bottom. I thought the men and boys were skinny-dipping, and that was the real reason Marlow didn't want to join them. We stopped to ask directions and were surrounded by small smiling faces. I asked if I could take their picture, then got so excited when they posed for me, I focused on the horse standing behind them, and the children were fuzzy figures in the foreground. Dang. The women were busy preparing the *lovo*, a dinner where they wrapped meat, yams, and vegetables in banana leaves and buried them in an earthen oven of hot rocks. We chatted for a few minutes, then went on our way. The whole town waved, smiled, and chanted, "Bula!"

We saw a road that said something about a dam, so we went there. We were on a road that descended just short of free fall and ended up at the lake that supplied Nadi with its drinking water. I was so thirsty; I wanted to fill our empty soft drink cans with the water. Marlow would have none of that, so I swam out and filled a couple of cans for myself. We ate lunch, then attempted to find our way back to Nadi.

It took me three different stores to find the ingredients for sandwiches. I wanted lunch meat, cheese, mayonnaise, and bread. Presliced lunchmeat was nearly impossible to find, and when I did find some, I had my choice of ham-flavored mutton or mutton-flavored beef. The second confused me, so I picked the first. Why would someone want to make beef taste like mutton? I found mayonnaise at the third store, which was very proud of being "almost like American store." It was about the size of our living room and called itself a supermarket.

Who am I to criticize mutton-flavored beef? At home everything we ate was turkey flavored to taste like something else—ham, pastrami, bologna, or whatever.

The average Fijian's English left something to be desired. I asked a man at the dam if we were on the correct road to get to Nadi. His answer "Yes, but it doesn't go to Nadi." Or how about the sign in the restaurant that had in big red letters, "We are happy to being welcome you!" If they had just said, "*Ni sa bula*," we would have known what they meant. I loved what they meant. When somebody didn't have a clue what we said, he smiled from ear to ear and said, "Where you being from?" Everyone knew California even if they weren't sure of the location of the United States. California was where videos were made. Anyone with an income of $200.00 a month or more had a video-playing machine, which was amazing, since they didn't have electricity outside of the cities in 1980.

In the evening we went to the Regency Hotel and watched fire walkers. They built an enormous brush fire on top of a pile of rocks, and we watched that burn for thirty minutes; when the fire was down to embers, the program began. A lovely lady told us the history of fire-walking and the meaning of chanting while men took the embers off the rocks. There was more chanting and praying while they turned the rocks to just the right position for walking. I figured they were praying for rain. The little girl behind me thought they were looking for frogs, which she thought would be horrible to step on—much worse than hot rocks. After thirty minutes of turning the rocks and chanting, they were ready to show us how brave they were. After the ceremony some skeptics in the audience felt the rocks. Oh, disillusionment, the rocks were barely warm. They looked brave walking on them anyhow. I couldn't walk barefooted on cold rocks; inch-thick carpet is the extent of my bravery.

January 8, 1987 Our last day in paradise. We cleaned out the refrigerator for breakfast—ham-flavored mutton, vegemite, and crackers. Oh well, it was filling. We returned our rental car, checked out of the hotel, and left our luggage in the hotel "safe" (closet, really). We booked a last trip to one more island, for one more day of fun in the sun, then sat down to wait for our bus.

The hotel telephone operator said I had a call from the security officer on Plantation Island. Someone found my watch and turned it in! They said they would put it on the next plane to Viti Levu, and I could pick it up at the airport on our way to the United States that evening.

Now, I know I never mentioned that I lost my watch on Plantation Island. I didn't want you to know that anything had gone wrong in paradise after I spent so much time complaining about the cruise mix-up and the weather in New Zealand. Yes, I had really lost the beloved watch Marlow gave me on Valentine's Day in 1969. I lost it at the beach on the first day after our arrival in Fiji. I didn't expect anyone to turn it in to security, but had left a description and my name and hotel, just in case.

Finding the watch made the last day on Fiji so much more enjoyable. I had been really bummed about losing the keepsake. I asked the security guard what I could send him from the United States as gratitude for retrieving this special watch.

He thought for a minute, then said, "You could maybe send me just a little peanut butter?" I surely could do that! He had heard of peanut butter on a video; he wondered what it tasted like.

We enjoyed our day on the three-masted schooner and on Beachcomber Island. At Beachcomber we went snorkeling with equipment that actually fit, which made a big difference. I loved it so much, I forgot all about being afraid of deep water and swam in thirty-foot depths. We also enjoyed the *lovo* we had for dinner back at the hotel in the middle of a blackout.

When we got to the airport, no one knew anything about my watch. What a low blow. I left my name and address with everyone who would take it in hopes we could get the watch back. I called the owner of the island-hopping airliner we had used to fly to Plantation Island, and his wife answered the phone; she assured me that she would track down my watch and make sure it was returned. We spent about two hours going from one person and department to another, trying to get the watch. We had the time to spend, as our flight was two hours late taking off. We were supposed to leave Fiji at eleven p.m. on January 8 and arrive in Sacramento at ten p.m. on January 8 after flying all night.

We ended up in the smoking section of an overcrowded airplane (the seats were chosen by our ditsy travel agent) and missed our connection in Los Angeles because our agent had booked us on one airline with the flight number from another airline. We booked our own flight home from Los Angeles.

Darryl met us at the airport and drove us to Citrus Heights through the gloom of foggy Sacramento. Gone were the delicious hot, sunny, humid days of Fiji and Australia.

Epilogue: I received my watch in the mail about a month later and sent the security guard the largest jar of Skippy Peanut Butter I could find. I wanted to make sure he had enough to share with the people involved in the return of the precious keepsake.

Five

Hawaii, The Big Island, or The Sierra Club, Ya Gotta Love 'Em

1988

I joined the Sierra Club in 1980 when we returned to California after living in Australia for eight years. The Sierra Club offered wonderful hikes in the mountains with knowledgeable guides to explain the fauna, flora, geology, and history. They were conservationists and agreed with me that man's responsibility was to take care of the earth for future generations. Marlow thought they were a bunch of crackpots. However, when I read their travel brochure and found they offered a lovely trip to the big island of Hawaii for a ridiculously low price, he was willing to put his opinions aside and join them for a couple of weeks.

December 19, 1988 All arrangements were confirmed. Darryl, our youngest son, took Marlow and me to the Greyhound Bus Station an hour before our departure time of four twenty p.m. Brian, our three-year-old grandson, jumped out of the car when his dad left us at the front door of the station. He wanted to look at the "biiiiiig buses." We didn't see anything wrong with that. He could tag along with us while his dad parked the car. I took him to admire the buses parked in the terminal garage while Marlow waited in line at the ticket counter.

When Marlow reached the front of the line, I joined him. We found there was a bus leaving at three thirty. We had ten minutes to make it to that bus if we cared to leave earlier than four twenty. The bus was only a hundred feet away. We could make it, no problems. Yes, we chose to buy our tickets for the earlier ride. We might as well, instead of hanging around the depressing bus station.

By three thirty Darryl had not appeared in the lounge, and the long line of people was migrating toward the bus. Marlow saw Darryl drive past the open doorway behind the bus loading San Francisco-bound passengers.

I told Marlow to take Brian and see if Darryl got stopped in the downtown traffic. Sure enough, Darryl was stopped at a red traffic light beside the bus station. Marlow, carrying Brian, hurried to the car, told Darryl about our change of plans, and quickly buckled Brian into the backseat.

Poor Brian didn't have a clue what was going on. He thought since he was in line with us, we were going to take him for a ride on the bus. I apologized when we got home, and Brian said, "It's okay, Grandma, I didn't cry." That made me cry.

We were on our way by three forty-five. The earlier departure saved us no time at all. We had an hour layover in San Francisco before catching the connecting bus to San Francisco International Airport. Our lodging for the night was two miles from the airline terminal. I never, never book hotels that close to noisy airports, but made an exception this time because of the convenience of bus connections.

December 20, 1988 We were up at five thirty, the normal time we arose to get ready for work. We drank instant coffee, compliments of the establishment, as we prepared for our day of travel.

Marlow was still in the shower when I was ready to leave. We were quite a way from the hotel office, where I understood the airport shuttle would meet us. I decided to make two trips getting our luggage to the office, so I dragged the heaviest suitcase down the long sidewalk first. I vowed once more to invest in a suitcase on wheels. I struggled into the office and checked out of our room. The clerk said the shuttle would pick us up at our bedroom. I was dismayed, but took hold of our suitcase handle and started for the door.

The clerk said to leave the luggage, and he'd have the bus driver load it into the cargo space before he picked us up. I happily agreed.

I wandered to our room past the gardens and swimming pool, wondering if foreigners from snowy countries would be tempted to use the pool. After all, San Francisco was in sunny California! The air temperature was forty degrees Fahrenheit.

The driver arrived ten minutes later and packed us into the vehicle beside two sleepy people. He drove to more rooms loading passengers and luggage. When he was satisfied the van looked like a can of sardines, he took us to the airport. People unloaded at different airlines. We were the third couple to disembark.

The driver off-loaded our luggage and sweetly smiled while waiting for his tip.

"Where is the big green suitcase you picked up at the hotel lobby?" I asked.

He didn't know what I was talking about. He said the clerk had not radioed him to stop at the lobby, so he'd driven directly to the rooms where he knew he had waiting customers. He radioed the hotel and confirmed my story. He told me to go ahead and check in, and he would have the suitcase onboard before we left. I was so glad I'd chosen a hotel close to the terminal.

The driver was true to his word; he brought the suitcase to the airline counter just as we were ready to embark. We gave him an unusually handsome tip.

Our flight to Honolulu lasted four hours and thirty minutes. It seemed longer, as our travel agent had accidentally booked our seats in the smoking section of the plane. We quit smoking cigarettes in 1982, and our bodies weren't used to inhaling the nicotine-laced air. Our chests felt like we had smoked a full pack by the time we arrived in Hawaii.

At nine a.m. the steward offered cocktails. I thought alcohol was a strange drink for that hour of the day, but soon understood his logic when he came down the aisle with dinner, chicken Kiev. I had a talk with my body and tried to convince it that it would have to be adaptable. Vacations were that way, it would have to go with the flow. "When in Rome…" and all those other clichés.

After this unusual breakfast, I opened my new book, *Outback Woman,* about an Australian Aboriginal lady who lived partly in the real world and partly in "dreamtime." The book sort of went along with the atmosphere of people deliberately sitting in a poisonous smoke-filled container plummeting through the air, drinking a controlled substance, and eating rich food first thing in the morning.

By the time we arrived in Honolulu, I had read half of the book. I tucked it in an outside pocket of my camera case, thinking I'd read more on the next leg of our trip. Wrong! There was way too much to see and do from the moment of touchdown.

We rode a wiki-wiki from the international airport to the Interisland Terminal and took a very scenic ride over the blue, blue ocean to the big island of Hawaii. After an enjoyable thirty-five minutes, we arrived in Hilo.

The Sierra Club leader was there to greet us. Jan helped us find the car rental agency, where we had a reservation. She clued us in on the fact that rental car agencies would not let us have the car if they knew we'd be camping. One of the questions on the form to be filled out was, "Where will you be staying while on the island?" Jan gave us the name and address of an acceptable hotel.

Jan asked if we'd mind giving two other members of our troop a ride to camp. No problem. One passenger arrived on our plane; the other landed the day before and had spent a night locally. We agreed it would be a good opportunity to get acquainted with fellow travelers.

The four of us squeezed into the compact two-door car, the more limber women in the back with the camera cases.

Dora was from Nevada, a health consultant for the government. Joe was from New York, an accountant for a hospital. They had several things in common; they were amiable and good-humored, they were active hikers with the Sierra Club, in their late forties, and single. I could see where this was headed.

We enjoyed the trip to our first campsite at Namakani Pa'io on Kilauea (killo-WAY-ah) in Volcanoes National Park. We arrived an hour before sunset; Dora joined Marlow and I on a half-mile walk to peer into the steaming caldera. The plants along the walk were decorated for Christmas with a lot of red and green leaves. The wind blew up a storm, and we got cold and wet from the drizzly rain. We headed back to the campground.

Marlow and I put our belongings in a cabin, which had a double bed, plus two single beds built into the walls. We made up the double bed and unpacked what we would want for that evening and the next morning.

Before long other members straggled into camp. Another married couple joined us in our cabin. Marlow was upset, as he thought we'd have a private cabin. Loran and Joyce were from Los Angeles. They were embarrassed to find they were to share a cabin with other people, but soon adapted. This excursion was the first time any of us had traveled with the Sierra Club, and we didn't know their policy (and secret for having cheap trips) for sleeping arrangements.

The four of us went to the cooking shelter, which was like any park shelter you find on the mainland—a big, open place with half a dozen picnic tables. The cooks decided on sandwiches for the evening meal, as people would be arriving at various hours.

For appetizers they had sashimi, raw fish dipped in a very spicy sauce and eaten with grated carrots and daikon. I thought the dish was delicious and hoped I wouldn't get stomach bugs from the raw fish. The cook assured me the fish had been marinated in lemon juice, and that killed germs and parasites. I took her word for it.

Marlow passed on the sashimi and made himself a hardy Dagwood sandwich. The Sierra Club certainly didn't scrimp on food that first meal.

Jan suggested a moonlight walk, as the sky had now cleared and there was a full moon. The lava flows were delightful to see as were the occasional islands of shrubbery we missed seeing earlier. The trek was on an elevated boardwalk where it was easy to see into the molten lava.

In spite of the fact that we were in Hawaii, the month was December, and by the time we returned to the cabin, I was cold. I decided to take a hot shower and hop into our cozy warm bed. The showers were cold water only. I really had chills by the time I finished, slipped into my muumuu, and darted to our unheated cabin.

I was surprised to find an additional man in there unpacking his belongings. Were we expected to sleep three people in the double bed? I told him that four people already occupied the cabin and obviously there were only four sleeping places. He looked like a forlorn beagle, and I felt like a rat having to tell him he'd have to find somewhere else to sleep. He'd already unpacked most of his clothes as though he thought he was going to spend two weeks lodging in this cabin.

Joyce and Loran returned and said they'd sleep in the top bunk and let the fifth person have the lower bunk. He looked happy again. He was bouncing on the lower bunk when Judy, the trip organizer, arrived at the door and announced she'd found an empty bunk. He'd have to repack and move to another cabin. Once more he portrayed a dejected puppy as he repacked his belongings. I could see we were going to have quite a scope of personalities in our group.

My three cabin mates were smarter than me. They unpacked warm flannel sleeping bags. I felt I should use the cool sheets since that's what housekeeping provided. Hawaiians evidently felt the temperature was warm on their islands year-round, and I didn't want to disappoint them by not using the equipment supplied. Fortunately, they did supply a blanket, so I stopped shivering enough to get to sleep by midnight.

Both men were terrific snorers, and I coughed all night from a combination of the airplane cigarette smoke and being chilled to the bone most of the evening. Joyce must have had a miserable night trying to rest. Of course, in the morning she politely claimed she didn't hear a thing all night.

December 21, 1988 Marlow and I were up at six thirty due to people wandering into our cabin by mistake, apologizing, then leaving. All of the cabins looked alike, and the numbers were hard to see in the dark. The doors had no locks.

We were off to breakfast, a great one of scrambled eggs, homemade date-nut bread, fruit juice, and Kona coffee. We made our lunches from a buffet setting of meats, cheeses, vegetables, fruit, and cookies. I normally ate a hard-boiled egg or a carton of yogurt for breakfast and cottage cheese and fruit for lunch to maintain my current state of fluffiness.

Dora and Joe joined us as we started an all-day tour. These two people got along great. We took turns sitting in the front seat so that we each got a turn at better viewing.

Our first stop was at Waiohinu, an old town bursting with flowers and unique architecture. We snapped pictures, visited a church built in 1841 that was being repainted, and went through an old cemetery.

Our second stop was at Ka Lae, the most southern point of the United States. The day was extremely windy; high, choppy waves beat against the lava cliffs. Hawaiians were fishing off the cliffs like it was perfectly wonderful weather. I took a couple of pictures and climbed back into the car to get away from the wind. Thirty minutes later Joe joined the rest of the group, and we got back on the road.

The third stop was for lunch at a botanical garden reminiscent of Australia. My favorite flower trees from Down Under were there, as well as that prickly beauty called a bunya tree. The Moreton Bay fig trees were my favorite.

Our fourth stop, Pu'uhonua O Honaunau National Park, had Hawaiians building grass huts and weaving baskets in the lovely, well-kept park commemorating a refuge spot for the explorer, Captain James Cook.

By this time I was tired of listening to the meaningful chatter of our car mates, who were into collecting absolutely everything. Marlow evidently was also sick of hearing the rewards of collecting expensive art, calligraphy, Oriental china, stamps, coins, crystal, books, and even old newspapers. He and Joe started arguing. I think after crawling into and out of the car so many times, all of us were ready for a hot shower, a warm meal, and solitude.

The fifth stop was a filthy, trashy, black-sand beach filled with slovenly looking people. We were invited to go for a swim or snorkel and were told the coral was great. That was supposed to be a forty-five-minute stop, and it would take me fifteen minutes to find the right size bush to hide behind while I changed into my swimsuit. Some folks didn't bother with proper-sized bushes and hid strategic parts of their body with other parts prominently in view of God and the whole world.

Marlow and I said, "No thanks," and walked to a shop for a soft drink and souvenir shopping. No souvenirs enticed us so we bought Cokes and went to the car to be protected from the wind, listened to gentle Hawaiian ukuleles on the radio, and waited for the group to travel on.

When the leader announced where our sixth stop would be, we asked her if she'd give us directions to our next campsite so we could get there and relax. She did, and we left the group along with our car mates, after being assured they would get rides, and headed directly for Hapuna Beach.

The beach was glorious, just the kind of beach that people traveled long distances to see in Hawaii—clean, white sand fringed by palm trees and tropical flowers. Hapuna was going to be a terrific place to stay!

We looked at our accommodations. By now we knew what to expect. Marlow was hoping for better than our last lodging. We found the cabins without any problems. They had one room with two long wooden benches down two sides and a little picnic table in the middle. The walls were solid wood up about four feet from the concrete floor, with screened openings at the top. No windows to close against the constant wind, no privacy, just a roof over our heads.

I took the head of a bench and Marlow took the foot. We knew at least two more people would be joining us. I unpacked a clean change of clothes and toiletries and headed for the showers, praying for warm water.

Pasteur would have loved the showers; they consisted of a large, open room made entirely of concrete, covered with a paisley print of mold growing on the walls, ceiling, and floors. The toilet and lavatory sat in one corner of the room. Am I the last human being in the world who wanted to do some things where no one could see me?

I was glad we came back early so I could take a quick shower, slightly warmer than cold, and change into clean clothes without sharing the space with three other people. There were four showerheads protruding from the walls.

When I returned to the cabin, two men were unpacking on the opposite side of the room from our sleeping bags. We greeted each other like it was a common occurrence for us to be sharing bed space. Marlow wasn't there, so I was less self-conscious about getting acquainted with these men I'd be sleeping with, so to speak.

The meals were gourmet! We had a delicious chicken dish with pineapple, papaya, and coconut. The two cooks, both from Sacramento, were enjoyable to be around. Debra sang Girl Scout camp songs while she cooked, and Caroline told stories. Each tour member had to take turns helping in the kitchen. I knew we wouldn't mind working with these ladies.

December 22, 1988 The wind was relentless throughout the night. I wasn't unbearably cold, but my mind told my body I was because of the wind. I snuggled down inside a warm sleeping bag and was lying on top of a brand-new air mattress. The glue in the ribs at the bottom of my mattress broke loose and created a large bubble under my feet. I habitually slept on my stomach, and this bubble gave me the feeling I was lying with my head downhill. It felt even stranger when I turned on my side.

I got up at five forty, went to the restroom, dressed, and headed for the beach. The moon was full and gave me plenty of light, and sunrise wasn't far off. It was glorious at the beach. I walked the full length of the beach and started up the path leading into a tropical forest. Who should be coming out but one of my cabin mates!

We passed the time of day and went our separate ways. The forest was beautiful; the birds were singing their good-morning songs. The mongooses skittered hither and yon looking for breakfast. All was at peace with the world.

As the sun rose, the wind died down. It was going to be a perfect day in paradise. I walked for an hour before turning back toward the cabin.

The others were heading to the cooking shelter as I arrived. This morning we were treated to coconut and macadamia pancakes with coconut syrup and lots of fresh papaya and pineapple—yummy.

We built our lunches and split up into little groups to pursue our separate interests. A lot of the people headed for hiking trails. Marlow and I went snorkeling. We rented equipment in town and got directions to snorkeling coves. We relished the clean, clear waters with colorful fish. We snorkeled for a couple of hours, went to a shady park, ate lunch, then rode through the Parker Ranch estate looking at lovely homes built on rolling green hills with unobstructed views of the ocean.

What the heck, we might want to move to Hawaii. We stopped at a real estate office and inquired about land and/or houses for sale in the estate. Three acres, the smallest lots for sale, started at $200,000.00. Ten-acre lots started at $500,000.00. We looked at homes—a three-bedroom, three-bath home on ten acres for a "mill-six." The property was a nice place—comparable to homes in Sacramento selling for $175,000.00 to $200,000.00. We thanked the agent but explained that we required something larger.

From there we went to the Laundromat, which was a good way to get back to reality after fantasizing about living in a house worth more than $1.5 million.

Back at camp, I showered the salt out of my hair while I studied the flora on the walls. There was such a variety. It made showering much more interesting than at home.

After bathing I showed Marlow the tropical grove at the end of the beach. We strolled along until we were well into the grove. I spotted a picnic table overlooking the ocean, and we sat down for a short time. A very short time! We looked down at the cove shoreline and realized it was a "nudie" beach. It was a family beach, and the kids had suits on. Just the adults were naked. A lot of ugly fat was congregated in one spot. At other beaches I'd seen clothed adults and naked two-year-olds, and they were a delight to watch running free in the sunshine. Not so with this group.

We headed toward camp, passing a man with a gray beard down to his bellybutton and gray hair hanging the same distance down his back. He was doing some sort of a slow motion dance like he was mimicking the waves or practicing the martial arts (later I learned the exercise was called Tai Chi). We walked by as though we passed people in the state of "Yo" every day of our lives.

I wanted to take his picture so badly, but didn't know what his reaction might be. He was possibly an aged hippie wacky from drug use. I asked Marlow to casually look back and see if he was facing away from us. I took a picture of the ocean.

I put my telephoto lens on the camera while Marlow whistled and casually looked around. With the man's long, gray hair, it would be hard to tell for sure which way he was facing.

"He's staring at you with a menacing look on his face," Marlow said.

We walked a few more yards, and I asked Marlow to check again. "He looks like he's about to pounce on you. We'd better get the heck out of here." I never got my picture but had a fun encounter.

We hurried toward the beach. As we reached the start of a paved sidewalk around the perimeter of the beach, we saw a pair of pretty young ladies walking toward us speaking German. They were about thirty feet in front of us when suddenly one girl flipped her muumuu over her head and dropped her knickers. We were flabbergasted; we didn't know what to do. We stopped dead in our tracks and momentarily contemplated heading back toward the "guru." We chose to keep on walking past the girls while the naked one retrieved a swimsuit from her bag and proceeded to put it on, all the time chatting away to her friend.

Later that evening I told Caroline, the cook, that I had seen more naked bodies that day than I had seen all the rest of my life combined. After relating our experiences, she educated me to the fact that there were indeed several "sun worshiper" beaches in Hawaii, and it was common practice in Europe to change clothes on the beach. It had no moral implications. She also explained the art of Tai Chi. We were so naïve! We really needed to get out more.

After dinner Jan, the Sierra Club leader, gave one of her talks about the local environment and culture. She mentioned that there were a lot of leftover hippies living on the big island, and drug-related crime was prevalent. I felt she was quoting the Eagles song: "Call someplace paradise, kiss it good-bye."

During the windy night, Jan heard screaming and commotion on the beach. When she checked it out from a distance, she saw six police cars and an ambulance and suspected that someone had overdosed.

December 23, 1988 Marlow and I were on our way to a snorkeling cove as soon as possible after breakfast. What a great sport! I'd been afraid of being in water over my head all my life and now enjoyed doing that as a hobby. Last night at dinner, Marlow and I told our companions how much we liked the snorkeling. Today half the group joined us.

We had to wear a mask over our eyes so we could keep them open in saltwater, stick a breathing tube in our mouths, remember to breathe in and out through our mouth, and float on our stomach. A panorama unfolded beneath us. There were rainbow-colored fish, coral, eels, shellfish, anemones, and sea slugs going about their daily lives.

Marlow and I stayed at the beach for three hours before racing back to camp to shower off the salt water and changing into nicer clothes.

The Mauna Kea, a fancy resort, was a beautiful place, like something out of the movies, with plants growing beside indoor waterfalls and pools. There was wicker furniture so that guests could sit quietly and enjoy the colorful atmosphere. We were there for a group lunch.

I felt sure it was the type of place movie stars and other wealthy people went to play; there were golf courses, tennis courts, and swimming pools. I had to inquire about staying in this place for just one night. I checked with the hotel clerk—yes, we were lucky, there were a few rooms available. The starting price was $469.00 per night! The Sierra Club cabin wasn't that bad after all. With two night's stay, we would have spent as much as the cost of our Sierra Club trip.

Our scrumptious meal at the Mauna Kea was valued at eighteen dollars $18.00 per person, but had been part of the all-inclusive cost of our tour.

Marlow and I walked the grounds for thirty minutes and drove around the golf course looking at privately owned homes. The homes were pretty fancy places, with lots of bougainvillea brightening every nook and cranny. Ferns and palms sprouted up as islands on lush green lawns.

We went to our screened-in cabin, reorganized our belongings, and relaxed the rest of the day. I read more of my novel about an Aboriginal's meandering—such a weird story, but so compelling. I'd be glad when I finished the book.

December 24, 1988 Marlow and I separated from the group once more. They were going to see an electrical powerhouse run by seawater and then visit "The Queen's Baths," which had been covered with flowing lava and turned into a "sun worshiper's beach" for homosexuals.

Marlow and I went to Pu'ukohola Heiau, Kamehameha's fort and home. "God" told him that if he built a temple to the god, he would become king. Heck of a deal. Kamehameha built the temple and invited his last remaining adversary to join him in the completion ceremony. The adversary was captured upon his arrival and offered as a human sacrifice to the god. This sanctified the heiau as a place of worship and made Kamehameha the first king of all the Hawaiian Islands. That was a warning to check invitations to parties before accepting them.

We drove to the newest resort on the island. The Hyatt Regency opened in September 1988, had 1,240 rooms, and it defied description, but of course I'm going to try anyhow.

It took us five hours to tour the grounds, and the only reason we quit then was because our leg muscles told us to do so. We'd not yet seen the shops and art galleries. I always liked visiting art galleries and had convinced Marlow we needed to return another day. He agreed that we would come back there to stay for a week just as soon as we won the California state lottery.

The rooms ranged in price from $200.00 per night for a single person on Monday through Wednesday to $2,500.00 a night for the honeymoon suite. The most popular way to reach a reserved room was via one of the boats in the picturesque moats winding about the complex. The hotel consisted of a series of buildings spread over several hundred acres of manicured, landscaped grounds.

If you tired of floating among the lovely aromatic flowers, you could take the monorail to one of the many pools, beaches, or sporting centers. One of the pools was three-quarters of an acre of freshwater, with waterfalls and a shady island bar reached by swimming (serviced via a bridge). The second pool, which I personally fell in love with, was a saltwater pool in a natural rock and sand setting that contained dolphins. Imagine, swimming in an enclosed area among dolphins! What a concept! I had to do that! I didn't have a bathing suit with me, so I couldn't do it at that time but vowed to return.

We ate lunch in the Cascade Dining Room. Marlow had stir-fry with chicken and octopus, while I had a fruit bowl (love those papayas and melons) with macadamia nut bread. As the restaurant name indicated, we sat beside a pond with cascading waterfalls, lushly landscaped rocky escarpments, and a pond with swans that floated within two feet of our table. We spotted mandarin ducks—seen for the first time in our lives—on one of the islands, but they kept their distance from the diners. All the man-made ponds that we'd seen in Hawaii contained koi, the colorful fish developed in Japan. Some koi grew over two feet in length.

That evening we told the others in our group about our find. They wanted to see the place. Jan announced that the Hyatt was one of the decadent places the Sierra Club fought valiantly. They had protested the fact that "those people" were putting in "that playground for the rich and famous" over a lava pond that held an endangered species of shrimp.

Many Sierrans voted to visit the place anyhow. They wanted to see if it was worth taking a chance on losing, or moving, the shrimp.

Judy, a Sierra Club member from San Diego, did a lot of tongue clucking about the décor, but she had to admit it was outstanding. The whole area had been desolation from the volcano's flow before Hyatt bought it.

The Hyatt organization hauled in topsoil and planted emerald-green grass and tropical flora for golf courses, leaving part of the pitch-black lava exposed. The contrast was a feast for the eyes. We showed our traveling companions some of the points I've already described and did make it to the art galleries. A few ladies were interested in shopping, so they went their own way. The rest of us admired and critiqued the Oriental and Polynesian art in the galleries.

We spoke of going to one of the nightclubs for a Christmas Eve drink and a few dances. Marlow and I were too tired for that and retired to our open-air lodging for a sound night's sleep. Humans did adjust to distractions like wind and bubbly air mattresses. I flipped my mattress around so that the bubble was under my head instead of my feet. The bubble was only eight inches wide.

Sleeping with three men in my room was tolerable after I adjusted to the snoring interrupting the sound of the wind in the shrubbery and vice versa.

It was really an excellent, educational vacation. I was going to be so broad-minded by the time I got home.

December 25, 1988 We slept in late, almost missed breakfast, God forbid—a Kilpatrick has never been known to miss a meal before! The cooks fixed a strange breakfast for Christmas morning—bagels and cream cheese, and omelets. They served taco salad last night, so I had an omelet with sour cream and salsa. Marlow had fruit. He may have been getting tired of eating three large meals a day.

The group packed belongings and moved to the next campsite, Kalopa State Recreation Area, in the rainforest that was at two-thousand-foot elevation. I had just gotten used to the idea of sleeping with three men when we moved. At the next campsite, we had three cabins to serve the whole group. One was reserved for single women, one for single men, and one mixed. We were in the mixed cabin. Loran and Marlow made a duet out of the snoring. Loran had something else in common with Marlow; he liked to stir things up. Loran wore an NRA cap to irritate our hosts. The National Rifle Association and the Sierra Club were archenemies.

We loved the two hikes we took through the rainforest before going to the snug, warm, enclosed cooking shelter where someone had built a roaring fire in the fireplace. The large cabin had been decorated with colored lights, and the cooks were busy fixing Christmas dinner with all the trimmings.

After another wonderful meal, the group sang songs around the fire and told stories of Christmases past. Marlow told about the one we spent in the Serengeti, Tanzania, Africa, in 1985. I compared two Christmases we had experienced, 1971, when three feet of snow fell on Christmas Eve. We were in Shrewsbury, Massachusetts. The second Christmas was 1972, one year later, when it was a hundred-five degrees, and we went to the movies so we could get the relief of air conditioning. We were living in Wacol, Queensland, Australia.

December 26, 1988 What a day! I went off to breakfast early. As other cabin mates arrived, they complained vociferously about Marlow's and Loran's snoring keeping them awake all night. The youngest woman on the trip complained the loudest and longest. I ignored her, but she finally came up and asked me directly what I intended to do about the situation.

I flashed my most endearing smile and said sweetly, "Not a thing, sweetie." Did she expect me to say I would get a divorce? Suffocate my husband? What?

Marlow slept through breakfast, so he missed the brouhaha. He would have added insult to injury. I must admit it was embarrassing when the single women from the cabin next to ours arrived complaining about our men keeping them awake.

We made lunches and headed off for the day. We were supposed to stop at a woodworking factory and then hike to Wapio Bay. The factory was still celebrating Christmas and was closed.

We arrived at Wapio Bay in our rental car and were told that only four-wheel-drive vehicles were allowed down the steep road to the beach. We parked at the top and walked a mile down the thirty-degree slope. My legs were complaining when we reached the bottom.

Everyone made it to the bottom in reasonable shape. The leader asked who wanted to hike two miles up a crevice to see a waterfall. Marlow and I were among the group that chose to play on the beach instead.

The hiking group was gone over four hours. They returned about two thirty, the same time a four-wheel-drive vehicle arrived to take us weaker people to the parked cars. The hikers were willing to walk to the parking lot. We lazy beachcombers climbed aboard the vehicle a few at a time.

As we waited our turn for a ride in the vehicle, Jan told us about the road being so treacherous that there had been a number of fatal accidents. One happened recently when the driver coming down didn't yield to the driver going up. The driver going up stopped his car, and when he shifted into gear again, the car slid backward and went over the cliff.

After hearing that story, we were relieved to see Jan climbing behind the steering wheel, as we assumed she was experienced on this grade. She grumbled about the other driver quitting with the job half done. She ground the clutch a couple of times before she got the car in gear. She swore under her breath and lurched forward, hitting the embankment.

Marlow volunteered to drive. She declined and said that getting us to the top was her responsibility, and she and the other driver were the only ones allowed to drive. She backed the car onto the road and lurched forward again. The car died. She complained that she didn't know why they had to make these vehicles so hard to drive.

Hmmm. I was thinking of volunteering to walk to the top just as she righted the vehicle and started grinding up the dirt road in second gear. I knew it would take me at least an hour to walk to the top, but was wishing I had taken the time to do that.

The totally silent passengers had white knuckles by the time we reached the crest. Jan cheerfully greeted hikers on our ascent. In hindsight I thought she'd been playing a trick on us at the bottom of the hill to add a little excitement to our day. We made it to the top without any further incidents.

The companions in our rental car had been on Jan's second trip up the hill. They told a harrowing story of how she had ground the gears and then lurched backward, hitting a tree and scaring the pee out of the assembled passengers.

At dinner that evening, Judy did a head count and found we had two people missing. No one knew of anyone saying they had other plans. The cabins and local area were searched. No one was camped in the park but our group, and there was no sign of the two missing people. We had left them at the beach.

The leader headed back to the site and found the two walking along the road in the dark. The woman had taken her wet hiking boots off and put them in one of the cars when she first reached the parking lot. Then she and her male companion walked to a cool shady spot to enjoy the view while waiting for the balance of the group to ascend the hill. No one noticed them sitting there when we piled into our cars and took off. They hadn't seen the cars leave. They waited until dark for someone to return to get them, and then the man took his socks off and gave them to the woman to wear to protect her feet a bit as they started the walk back to camp. They were sore and exhausted when they reached home base.

Loran and his wife, Joyce, chose to sleep in the cooking cabin on the floor. The rest of our cabin mates glared threateningly at Marlow as he innocently prepared for bed.

I told you we were in the "mixed" group. Mixed is right. What a crew! You already know a bit about Marlow, Loran, Joyce, and me. Here's a brief description of the balance of the people. There was a darling schoolteacher who fussed over people and things wherever she went. Each rock, plant, and animal was something special to learn about.

There was a workaholic named Ethel. She made me look lazy, and people have accused me of creating dirt so I could clean it up. If Ethel was not hiking with a group, she was in the kitchen making holiday candy or creating macramé candy canes as gifts for each of us. I thought she was a sweet old lady and was surprised to learn she was a year younger than me.

Lynn was twenty seven, an exhibitionist and a contortionist. It was really amazing how much time she spent putting lotion on her feet and ankles without bending her knees. Her ass always seemed to be at eye level with one of the men who happened to be sitting on his bunk. In the morning she completely stripped and redressed very gymnastically while two men were in the room. Both were gentlemanly enough to ignore her.

Single man number one was Bill from St. Louis. Marlow and I shared a cabin with him at Hapuna Beach. He was a super-quiet gent in his late thirties. He loved everything about nature and was a willing team player for any activity. The one time he separated from the group was when he chose to stay behind and admire the moonlight on the water while the rest of us ogled the decadence of the Hyatt Regency.

Single man number two was Bob, a computer specialist from San Jose—very intelligent, well-spoken, and good mannered. He was the gent we left at Wapio Bay who gave the lady traveling companion his socks when she had no shoes.

December 27, 1988 Today was moving day. We drove back to Volcanoes National Park where we had started. We were in the cabin closest to those restrooms with cold-water showers. Fortunately, someone must have complained, as we now had blessed hot water.

Our passenger on the trip from one campsite to another was Bill. He was the only one who would ride with Marlow now. Marlow had argued with almost everyone over Sierra Club polices and beliefs.

After we left Kalopa State Park, we drove to Laupahoehoe Tidal Wave Memorial Park. It was a memorial to a town that lost most of its young people when a tidal wave washed over the schoolhouse. What a horrible, tragic event! The park was beautiful. The ocean ferociously pounded the shoreline as though it were angry with itself for what it had done.

Next stop was Nanue Falls at Waiehu Point. They were one of the dozens of high falls we'd seen rushing to the ocean through lush tropical gorges. We took a hike through one of the gorges to see Akaka Falls and Kahuna Falls. Gorgeous, gorgeous, gorgeous!

The shoreline drive brought us to Hilo, a major city, where we did laundry, then drove to our new/old campsite. For this lodging place, Marlow got to share the cabin with three women. Two New Yorkers joined us under great vocal protest. The cabins were assigned on a first come, first choice basis, and they arrived last.

December 28, 1988 A movie and a lecture on a volcano's behavior preceded a twelve-mile walk for most of the group. We chose the less strenuous two-mile hike up to the edge of a crater of a dead volcano.

We drove to several more craters and peered inside. They all began to look alike, holes in the ground lined with black, gray, or brown rocks. We went to a museum and learned what the natives thought caused those holes in the ground. They blamed it on the goddess Pele.

We walked the shoreline to see steam at the water's edge way off in the distance. That was where an active volcano was busy adding real estate to the island by streaming hot lava into the sea. I told Marlow I'd love to see that closer and that we should inquire about a boat ride.

We couldn't get closer than five miles away from the actual flow via a boat, so all we would see was steam. Marlow and I agreed on a helicopter ride over the park so we could see what the volcanoes really looked like. The Sierra Club was against airplanes and helicopters flying over national parks; I hoped Marlow wouldn't tell them our plans.

That evening Marlow joined the Sierrans while they attended another movie and lecture on the scientific cause of volcanoes. I bought a book, Mark Twain's *Letters From Hawaii,* and chose to stay at the cabin and read.

Our younger cabin mate, Saundra, bought the same book and chose to stay in and read also. It was like having a slumber party with just us "girls" eating cookies, drinking tea, and sharing quips as we read by light of our flashlights. It was an enjoyable way to end an active day.

December 29, 1988 We had hot Malt-O-Meal with dried fruit for breakfast; it was one of my favorite breakfast combinations, but for Marlow, not so much. The group prepared for an eight-mile hike across the desert in the cold rain to peer into a crater that you could see by driving ten miles.

You guessed right, Marlow and I drove. Thank goodness our airline ticket included the price for a rental car on the holiday. Another nice thing, the Sierra Club said they would supply us with transportation as part of our tour price; they were buying the gasoline that we used.

We drove to Hilo and made our reservations for the helicopter ride. Then we went to Kapa'ahi to try to walk closer to the lava flowing into the sea. No such luck. I wasn't game to cross lava and take a chance on falling through thin crust into an active flow. There were warning signs about the dangers. I believed them. We drove the coastal route several miles through rainforest, which brought us to the edge of a beautiful black sand beach. The black sand was from the surf pounding the lava to bits.

We looked at house lots for sale; these were only $3,000.00. They were so thick with vines and undergrowth that we couldn't walk thirty feet off the road. My kind of place! The problem with buying one was that they were possibly in the path of oncoming lava. It might not get to our chosen block of land for a couple of years, but sooner or later it would.

We drove to the Mauna Loa Macadamia Nut Factory and picked up samples to take home. We walked through a gorgeous orchid farm. I went through a thirty-six-frame roll of film really quick in there. We "ooohed" and "aaahed" over each and every bloom.

We continued our tour down Chain of Craters Road to reach the beach and watch the sunset. There were red and gold rays of sunlight shooting out from behind giant, fluffy cumulus clouds piled on the horizon of the deep blue ocean.

Back at camp I snuggled up with Mark Twain while Marlow joined the Sierrans for a slide show.

December 30, 1988 We moved to another campsite high on the mountain. One thing I have learned the hard way—always take a winter coat with you when you go to the tropics. The day was cold, windy, and rainy. Snow wasn't far off. Some of the avid hikers took off to find the snow. They found it. Now they'd be able to tell their grandchildren they had thrown snowballs on Hawaii. We were at seven-thousand-foot elevation on the highest mountain in the world. Didn't know that, did you? If the mountains in the Himalayas were measured from their base to their top instead of from sea level to top, they would not be as tall as Mauna Kea. If Mauna Kea was measured from its base, instead of from sea level, it would be taller than Mount Everest. Its official height, as with all mountains, is listed on maps from sea level to peak.

As the day went on, we noticed many people were grouchy. I think everyone was getting burned out on the continued bad weather and long wet hikes. There was a general rebellion going on. No one wanted to do any of the scheduled activities. They stayed huddled around the fireplace and engaged in boring conversations. A few people went to Hilo to a movie.

December 31, 1988 New Years Eve! We left camp right after breakfast to keep our appointment with the helicopter pilot. He promised to show us inside a volcano before we left the island. It was still pouring down rain at camp, and we wondered if we were going to miss out on our ride. All the way off the mountain, the weather alternated between heavy fog and heavy rain. At Hilo city limits, we could see a patch of blue sky approaching land from the ocean. By the time we got to the airport, it had stopped raining, and the patch of blue was almost overhead. The pilot, a Tom Selleck look-alike, had already done his preflight on the helicopter and suggested we take off immediately before the weather closed in again. I was glad we had gotten there an hour early for our appointment so we could take advantage of that patch of blue.

The flight was so exciting! Marlow let me sit in front with the pilot, and I had a window at my feet as well as three-hundred-sixty degree views at eye level. The first five minutes, I was concentrating on the instruments as though I was the pilot. It looked like helicopters were easier to fly than Cessnas, but I was a long way from taking lessons in helicopters. Better stick to getting my regular pilot's license in 1989 and instrument rating the following year.

The conversation the pilot was having with Marlow made me realize that Marlow had not only stirred up trouble by telling the Sierra Club people we were going on the helicopter ride, but he also told the helicopter pilot we were traveling with the Sierra Club. The pilot was giving us his dissertation on how he had taken thousands of people over active volcanoes in the same period of time that fourteen Sierra Clubbers hiked to the closest spot allowable by law. Of course the hikers didn't get to see nearly as much as the thousands of airborne visitors.

We flew right to the rim of the boiling, bubbling, popping cauldron. The air was filled with sulfuric smoke. I wondered if Dante had visited such a sight before he wrote *Inferno*. It was easy to see where early Christians had gotten their idea for Hell. We saw many skylights, which were places where the hot lava had broken through the surface as it flowed through underground tunnels. The new layers of shiny black lava built on older layers, gave the area a waxed look. We weren't supposed to fly over the crater because of the explosions, but the wind shifted, and we were being engulfed in sulfur smoke. The pilot made an exception, and we flew out over the red and black lake where the air was clear. We were about twenty yards above the rim. What a stimulating feeling it was to be so completely involved in this violent work of nature.

From there we flew over the town that had been buried and reburied this past couple of years. I was sad to see that Father Damian's famous church, part of his leper colony, had succumbed to the lava. Somehow the lava had been flowing around it the first year.

We could see inside a home. The beds were neatly made up. The furniture was all in proper places. It was a high-set house built up on concrete posts to take advantage of the sea breeze to cool the residents. There was three feet of lava beneath the house.

We made our way over the shoreline and saw where the volcano was adding land to the island. It added seventy acres of lava to the island last year. The hot lava was extruded through tunnels, and then the ocean waves washed in and cooled it, and more lava flowed out on top of the just-cooled lava. Sometimes the lava was so porous, the surf pulverized it into black sand in a matter of weeks.

The flight back to the airport took us along the shoreline, where we admired the azure waters, ferocious, white waves pounding against the pitch-black cliffs, the tropical rainforest slowly being overtaken by the creeping lava, and the optimistic people who had built their homes perched perilously close to the forces of nature. The lofty view was totally enchanting.

Within minutes of landing, the rain returned. We knew this would be our last chance to see the botanical gardens, so we decided to tour them under an umbrella. When we got to the ticket tent, the clerk told us there was a crew in the gardens trying to rescue the last group that had gone down. The waves were washing over the paths, and it was extremely treacherous. Naturally, they were not allowing anyone else to enter.

The weather was miserable on the trip back to camp. It progressively got colder and windier as we ascended the mountain. We came to the conclusion that we no longer wanted to camp out with the Sierra Club. I was sure our presence would not be missed if we left. The leader wished us well and said she was sorry we would miss out on the New Year's Eve festivities. They were going to play charades after dinner.

We had been told that the Hilo side and the mountains usually had bad weather at the same time the Kona side had warm sunny weather. We told the leader we had chosen to spend the balance of our trip on the sunny side.

When we got to Kona, the sun was shining, and there was no wind, just a slight tropical breeze. We settled into the King Kamehameha Hotel, which was a hundred dollars per night. That was more than we usually paid, but it was a very nice place. It had several restaurants, a pool, tennis courts, and beaches. The whole town had already begun to celebrate New Year's Eve. Bands were playing, firecrackers and fireworks blasted away. It was so festive and fun to stroll along the sidewalk and watch the revelers. They started celebrating when it was midnight Eastern Standard Time (seven p.m. in Kona). Then they celebrated Central Standard Time, then Mountain, then Pacific, then Hawaiian. That gave them a lot more midnights than we had on the mainland.

Marlow and I had T-bone steaks in an open-air restaurant that overlooked the beach and the children with their fireworks. It was a great, warm evening. It was one of the best New Year's Eves we had ever celebrated. Unlike most celebrants, though, we were eager to enjoy our cozy, clean, *private* bedroom and were sound asleep by ten o'clock.

January 1, 1989 What a nice hotel! We luxuriated in long hot showers, the quiet privacy of our bedroom, and the balcony that overlooked a lagoon with wild ducks. We could have spent the day right there in the hotel, but chose not to.

We went to the parasailing concession for an hour-long ride in the calm sea. Marlow went parasailing. I was running out of money and wanted to save my play money to pay for a swim with the dolphins at the Hyatt Regency. I got to ride along on the boat and watched the other five people parasail. We saw half a dozen dolphins, but they wouldn't let our noisy boat get too close. Oh, maybe some of you landlubbers don't know what parasailing is. It is being tethered to the back of a boat with a five-hundred-foot cable while you float along in a harness attached to a parachute. When your time is up, the boatman winches you back onto a platform on the back of the boat.

When we got back to terra firma, I phoned to make my reservation for the dolphin pool. Their schedule was full, and all parties had confirmed. Darn! I could have gone parasailing after all. I ended up missing both thrills. Oh well, now we had more reasons to return.

Next we joined nine other people in a submarine and went a hundred feet below the surface to play among the coral. We got to see lots of fish we would not normally have seen by snorkeling. The submarine company had scuba divers feed the fish, so the marine life flocked to our windows. The submarine had only been in operation since August, and I predicted a bright future for the company. I could see this type of treat being popular in Australia and Fiji as well as the Caribbean.

The balmy breeze felt so good. We looked at Mauna Kea, where our compatriots would be breaking camp and getting ready to depart for Oahu. Mauna Kea had a fresh dusting of snow and was shrouded in heavy clouds. Those poor folks didn't know what they were missing.

We traversed the four-hour drive to Hilo and checked into a lovely hotel that only cost $35.00. It was clean, quiet, and private. It had a pool and lots of flower gardens.

Our suitcases seemed to have shrunk while we were in Hawaii, and we spent a couple of hours trying to pack our belongings for the trip home. Then we bought a six-pack and settled into watching a James Bond movie.

January 2, 1989 Our plane was scheduled to leave Hilo for Honolulu at nine-thirty a.m. Marlow returned the rental car, and we ate breakfast. We shared a traditional Hawaiian breakfast—an order of *loco moco*, which was Japanese-style rice (sticky) with gravy, a beef patty, and a fried egg. Oh boy, my digestive tract would be glad to get back to yogurt or an egg for breakfast. I was sick to my stomach before I left the table; I had Pepto-Bismol for dessert.

Our plane departed right on time. I shared my little corner of the airplane with a short, round, Hawaiian schoolteacher who giggled a lot. I bet her students loved her. She was pleasant, and I wished I had more than thirty-five minutes to get to know her better. She happily pointed out landmarks on the scenery floating below our plane.

We had a four-hour layover in Honolulu, so we headed for the bar to watch the Notre Dame football game. Notre Dame was so far ahead by half time that we changed seats so that we could watch a different ball game.

Our plane was due to leave at two o'clock. We started rolling at two-forty-five, not too bad a delay, but we knew we had already missed our Greyhound Bus connection in San Francisco. Wait a minute! What was happening? A truck rushed toward our rolling plane. The plane stopped, and a mechanic got out of the truck and started working on the plane. Not a pretty sight when you are about to fly over a great big ocean. The mechanic worked for thirty minutes, then we started rolling again. The plane taxied slower than normal, and at the end of the runway, the pilot announced that the hydraulic system was not working properly and we would have to return to the terminal.

We did that, and the passengers sat in the plane for an hour listening to mechanics thrashing about beneath us. The pilot announced that the air conditioner would be turned off, so the passengers would have to disembark. He said we should stay close by, as the mechanics felt the plane would be ready to leave within an hour.

At seven, five hours after scheduled takeoff, nine hours after our arrival at that airport, the airline issued dinner vouchers and told us not to leave the terminal, as the plane would be ready to leave by eight thirty. At ten p.m. the airline told us they were issuing vouchers for a night's lodging at a terminal hotel. We could not have our luggage; however, they would supply transportation to the hotel.

We were bused to a Holiday Inn and told we would be phoned when the plane was ready to fly. Marlow and I went to the lounge with some fellow passengers and had a beer before retiring. It was midnight when we got to bed.

At twelve thirty the phone rang; the caller announced that we had fifteen minutes to catch the shuttle back to the plane. Departure was scheduled for one a.m. We rushed through showers, dressed quickly, and caught the shuttle.

Back at the airport, one a.m. came and went as we groggily sat in the departure lounge. At one thirty the loudspeaker announced that Hawaiian Airlines had sent for a crew to fly us to the mainland, and the crew was on its way to the airport. Why in the name of heavens had they called us at the hotel before a crew was organized? I could not imagine. The airplane left thirteen hours late. I'm not superstitious, but that "thirteen" did make me a bit nervous this time.

There had been three hundred forty people on the original flight. A hundred of those people didn't want to take that plane anymore and scheduled other transportation. That left us with several vacancies. Once aboard I quickly grabbed an aisle seat in front of Marlow. There was a vacancy in the seat between the lady sitting at the window and me. I thought I might be able to curl up on two seats and catch a bit of sleep after takeoff.

The man sitting in front of my companion had a broken seat back. He kept falling into her lap. She got up and moved to a different row. That left me with three seats to use for a bed!

I stretched out full length, trying to maneuver the seat-belt buckles to the least intrusive spots. I could not get comfortable and flipped end over end, and around and around. No luck.

The stewardess came down the aisle offering complimentary cocktails. I decided that maybe a beer would relax me enough to dose off. I was half finished with that beer when the same young lady started serving breakfast. I couldn't face scrambled eggs with my beer at three thirty in the morning, so I passed on breakfast and relaxed with the headphones tuned to the comedy station. I planned on sleeping some night in the future.

I laughed once more at Bob Newhart's interpretation of Sir Walter Raleigh and Bill Cosby's stories about him and his brother, Russell.

Somewhere over the Pacific, I fell asleep, because the first thing I knew, a stewardess was shaking my shoulder, asking if I would like some fudge before we landed in San Francisco. What was wrong with those people? Of course I didn't want to wake up and put fudge in my already sticky mouth. I wanted to sleep. As I was about to answer her inquiry, I realized she was also telling me to buckle up for landing in San Francisco.

Fifteen minutes later we still had not landed. I remembered that I had put the orange juice container from the three-thirty breakfast tray in the seat pocket, and I decided to wash the foul taste out of my mouth with that. The orange juice dissolved the morning-mouth fuzz, I felt a bit more human—tired, but at least human.

We arrived in San Francisco at seven thirty a.m. Hawaii time, nine thirty California time. I hoped I'd remember this night the next time I booked a trip to Hawaii.

We dragged our heavy suitcases to the Greyhound Bus Station and had no problems getting to Sacramento. In Sacramento we hailed a cab to take us to our home in Citrus Heights. I was so flaky from the strange sleeping, drinking, and eating habits of the past few hours that I was hallucinating.

I felt like I was sitting in the middle of an arcade game. The taxi driver was never satisfied with his position on the crowded freeway. He constantly changed lanes, gaining speed all the time. At one point I looked at the speedometer and it was between ninety-five and a hundred miles an hour. The driver started to take the wrong turn off the freeway, and Marlow communicated this fact to him via hand signals. The Iranian driver quickly jerked the car back onto the freeway at the last possible second and proceeded to speed through the truck-weighing station normally occupied by two or three highway patrolmen. We safely made it to our front door in a time that even Ripley wouldn't believe.

Would I go to Hawaii again? In a New York minute! Would I go with the Sierra Club on other trips? Oh, I hope I have future opportunities to do that. Would I fly with Hawaiian Airlines? No. Would I pack warmer clothes for trekking in the tropics? You better believe it!

Six

Australia

1989

A woman phoned our home every other day for a week before I was scheduled to leave for Australia, asking, "Is Macon there?" I figured she wanted him to take wedding pictures, as Macon, my husband, was a part-time photographer. Macon is called by his middle name of Marlow by the family and his friends. Only businesspeople call him by his given name of Macon. Marlow said he had no idea whom the woman might be."No, not right now, can I take a message for him?" I asked.

"Thank you anyhow, but I have to speak to him personally."

"Can I give him your phone number and have him phone you?"

"No, he can't reach me at this phone, so I'll call him later."

The following Monday it dawned on me the young-sounding woman called on the days when I'd normally be going to school in the evening. I was currently on a semester break and had temporarily been laid off from my job at Aerojet. My evil little brain immediately turned nasty. I'm the suspicious type, you know. That comes with the territory when one marries a handsome man.

Dang their hides, they must be setting up meetings to fool around while I'm out of town. I'll fix their wagons; when I change the bed the day I leave, I'll put crunched-up crackers on the bottom sheet. They might fool around, but doggone it, they won't enjoy it.

On Wednesday when she phoned, I was exasperated. "Just call him at work; he's never here during the day." I gave her his phone number at work.

Thirty minutes later she called back again and said she couldn't reach him at work. She cleared her throat a couple of times and asked, "Are you Mrs. Kilpatrick?" I affirmed that.

She cleared her throat a couple more times and said, "A month ago we sent you a telephone survey to ask who your long-distance carrier was. Did you receive that survey?"

"Yes, and I threw it away."

"We just wanted to let you know that you have options. At AT&T long distance—"

"Do you mean that all this time you have been calling for my husband, you wanted to sell him long-distance telephone service?"

She stammered a bit and said, "I wanted to let him know about Sprint."

"Why didn't you tell me that the first time you called?"

"We aren't supposed to talk to anyone except the person whose name is on the bill."

I won't write what I told her, but I bet she turned in her resignation soon after I hung up.

The trip preparation had already had a few twists and turns. Two weeks before the scheduled departure, Scott, our middle son, whom I was going to visit in Australia, phoned to inform me that he checked with the airlines, and I wasn't listed on any flights arriving in Rockhampton. There was a "M. Kilpatrick" scheduled earlier, but that reservation had been cancelled.

I had reserved tickets for Marlow and me in June; in August Marlow decided he couldn't afford to go, so I cancelled his ticket. I phoned Qantas (Queensland and Northern Territory Airline Service) in Los Angeles and relayed Scott's phone call. Qantas dug into their computer records to discover Scott was correct. I was rescheduled.

I got the airline reservations straightened out, but was glad Scott forewarned me. I normally confirm reservations forty-eight hours before the flight. I would have been frantic.

December 23–24, 1989 A day was lost crossing the International Date Line.

Of course, the US side of the Pacific had its own transportation problems. My departure point, Sacramento International Airport, had been socked in with fog every evening so far in December. No flights took off between sunset and noon the next day. I changed my seven p.m. flight to Los Angeles, where I was to pick up my Qantas flight, to four thirty, just to be on the safe side. Even at that time, I saw fog rolling in while waiting for takeoff. Our departure was an hour late, but at least we made it off the ground.

The American Airlines plane circled Los Angeles a couple of times to get into the landing pattern behind numerous other planes. I don't know why the pilots say they are circling when they are actually flying a rectangular pattern. I learned that while taking flying lessons this past year. I'm now and empowered passenger.

I shared the ride with a five-year-old girl, who was flying alone, on her way to spend Christmas with Daddy. She pointed out his house as we rectangled: "The one with the green porch light!" I'm not sure I ever picked it out; I saw lots of green lights but didn't know what they represented. She found Daddy's house, even though we were flying at two-thousand-feet elevation. I loved flying with children.

I had a five-hour layover in Los Angeles, so I didn't fret about the hour delay in leaving Sacramento and the hour and a half we circled Los Angeles before landing.

I went to baggage claim in Los Angeles to make sure my luggage wasn't going around on the turntable. The bags had been checked through to Rockhampton, Queensland, Australia.

Next, I asked the information desk clerk for the location of Qantas's terminal. The clerk answered in some combination of English and

Pakistani. I asked her to repeat the answer again more slowly, and this time I picked up the word *shuttle*. I went out the front door and asked the shuttle driver if he went to the Qantas terminal. The driver answered in French/English. I understood "Shuttle A." I waited for a shuttle with the letter *A* on the front and hopped aboard. I told the driver I wanted to go to Qantas, and he said something in Vietnamese. I asked him to repeat it again but still didn't discern any English expressions indicating a location. I got off the bus at the next stop, looked around, and realized I was still at the domestic terminal.

I boarded the next shuttle marked *A* and asked the driver if he went to Qantas. He said, "*Si*." Thanks to Mr. Beery, my high school Spanish teacher, I knew that was an affirmative answer, and not a directive to look out the window. I watched for international airlines' marquees before exiting, and then walked half a mile to Qantas.

I was proud to think that people from all over the world wanted to live and work in the United States. I wondered why they all wanted to work at LAX. Did they just have enough money to make it that far and were working to get taxi and motel money to make it further into America?

The Qantas flight left Los Angeles an hour late due to holiday air traffic. I was ready for sleep. As soon as the plane leveled off at thirty thousand feet, I switched seats from a window seat to the middle of the plane where there were four vacant seats with arms that lifted up. I fantasized about stretching out on those four seats for eight hours of sleep. A young lady from Melbourne, South Australia, joined my row of seats. Dang! I was down to three seats. That was okay; I could lie on three seats and let my knees poke over the edge.

After dinner the staff started the movie *Honey, I Shrunk the Kids*. I gathered my pillows and blanket and turned to put them on the seats next to me. My dinner companion was stretched out on three seats with her eye mask and earplugs already in place! She was fast! I stood and looked at the other middle seats, and all were occupied with drowsy people stretched out, covering any vacant seats.

Of course, the man who was sitting on the aisle beside my former window seat was already curled up on the two seats snoring serenely. I dozed fitfully in contorted positions in my ever-shrinking single seat.

At dawn travelers stirred, so the stewards served coffee, tea and a snack of club sandwiches, cookies, and fruit. I looked at my watch; the time was five in the morning in California. I hadn't eaten anything they served at the one a.m. meal, just drank a glass of the red wine, and so I thought I'd eat the sandwich. It would be a shame to pass on all the free food, and regulations wouldn't let me exit the plane with food in my possession. There was a $10,000.00 fine for such a dastardly deed.

After devouring the sandwich, my traveling companion went back to sleep stretched out on three seats, with her feet occasionally in my lap. I gave up on sleep and watched the movie *Traveling Man*, a man's story, but not bad. At least that killed a couple of hours.

The flight was smooth all the way across the wide Pacific, and I had an easy transfer from one Qantas plane to another in Sydney. My seat from Sydney to Brisbane was upstairs in a bubble on the same level as the pilot. The bubble held thirty people, and we had our own private stewardess. She offered us breakfast, but we had been served the snack an hour before landing in Sydney, so not many people were interested. A Japanese man sat next to me and farted all the way to Brisbane. I presume he had eggs or beans on his flight to Sydney. Thank goodness that leg of the flight only took an hour.

Passengers slowly wended their way through customs in Brisbane. Lucky for me we were delayed in the passport/visa line; I automatically looked at the turntable for my luggage, and there it sat, big as life, even though it had been booked through to Rockhampton. If I had gone through quickly, I'd have stepped outside and caught the shuttle to the domestic terminal before the ground crew had time to unload cargo.

After customs' inspection of the luggage, I was left with fifteen minutes to catch my connecting flight. I took a taxi to the domestic terminal instead of the shuttle. The taxi driver promised to get me there on time, and he did. He even carried my bags to the check-in station.

The serene flight was scenic up the coast. The weather was perfect, with blue skies and a few little clouds. The next day I read in the newspaper that Brisbane had tornadoes blow through three hours after I departed. The tornadoes did $10 million damage.

An hour after takeoff, we landed in Rockhampton. It had been twenty-seven hours since I checked in at Sacramento's airport. I needed major grooming.

Scott, my middle son, met me at Rockhampton and introduced me to a couple he knew who had been to a wedding in Brisbane. They arrived on the same plane as me. They were dressed ready to pose for a magazine cover. After the introduction Scott explained that the gentleman, Keith Wright, was a member of Federal Parliament. I kept my distance, as I'm sure my deodorant wasn't the twenty-seven-hour kind, and my teeth had green algae growing on them. We chatted until our luggage arrived and then went our separate ways, possibly ruining any chance Scott had for becoming a politician.

We arrived at Scott's small grocery store/sandwich shop, with its attached apartment, and I had my first meeting with Joshua Marlow Kilpatrick. My four-month-old grandson really was perfect, just as his parents stated on earlier phone calls. He was full of smiles, gurgles, and coos. He entertained us all evening, and once he dozed off, he wasn't heard from again until morning.

Meleese, Scott's wife, Scott, and I opened Christmas presents, as it was Christmas Eve. We turned in for the night at ten o'clock. Sleep, blessed sleep in a horizontal position.

December 25, 1989 It felt good to wake up to the myriad birdsongs of tropical Australia. I distinguished lorikeets, honeyeaters, giggling noisy miners, plovers, and cockatoos. I later heard the red-tailed black cockatoos flying toward farmers' grain fields in search of breakfast.

Meleese and Scott kept the shop open from six thirty a.m. to eight thirty p.m., except for the two hours they closed to go to Nan's house for dinner. Nan was Meleese's grandmother. Meleese's parents and five siblings were there and had brought food, so we had a traditional

Australian buffet under the high-set house, where the temperature was cooler. A high-set house is one built on stilts for ventilation. Festive tables were set, and "Grang," Meleese's grandfather, played his accordion for entertainment.

December 26, 1989 Boxing Day is another holiday in Australia brought from the motherland, England. Business was a bit slower for the shop. In the evening Meleese's family arrived for a barbecue in the yard behind the shop. I had spent the day playing with Joshua, so I gave his other grandparents and great-grandparents a chance to enjoy his company in the evening.

December 27, 1989–January 3, 1990 The days flowed quietly and comfortably. I don't remember when I spent so much time doing so little. I studied my machine shop textbook, as I'd be starting a class on that subject in late January. I also read a novel, slept, played with the baby, and walked around the neighborhood. Once in a while, Scott or Meleese would take an hour or so away from the shop, and we'd go to one of the local tourist attractions.

We went to Gangalook, a museum set in the country with old buildings on the perimeter of an emerald-green lawn. The museum was especially pleasant as we were the only visitors and could take our time looking and asking questions. We also went to Glenmore Estate, the first sheep station in central Queensland. The original owner was a man from the United Kingdom who married a Mexican woman and had nine children. The current owners showed us musical instruments the Mexican lady had mastered. I asked how she had time to learn music with nine children. She had slaves, Mexican slaves.

January 4, 1990 Merle and Coreena, Meleese's mother and sister, took charge of the shop so Scott and Meleese could have a holiday. Meleese, Scott, Josh, and I went to Yeppoon on the coast, where Scott had reserved an apartment facing the beach.

Scott rented a catamaran, and we had a great time skipping across the waves. The sailboat was like a Hobie Cat that held two people.

Sailing was a surefire way to stay cool. Meleese and I took turns staying on the beach with Josh. He loved swimming, but he preferred the pool at the apartment to the waves in the ocean. If the adults had the nerve to let go of him in the pool, I bet he would swim on his own. None of us had the gumption to try it.

We took a tour of Iwasaki's Capricorn Coast Resort. Iwasaki had three nice hotels with swimming pools and golf courses. What most impressed me of the twenty three thousand acres were the native groves of trees and the wetlands where migratory birds spent part of the year. We were honored to see the state bird of Queensland, a jabiru, a three-foot-tall stork. Jabiru was a Portuguese word for "wood stork," and was named by early explorers. Brolgas (cranes) had come to the wetlands for the mating season. Their ballet was a show well worth seeing; it was much more intricate than the jitterbug Marlow performed to impress me.

We went to a petting zoo, where we got to play with kangaroos, emus, and koalas. Josh was most impressed by the baby bunnies. He sensed they were babies like him.

January 5, 1990 We juxtaposed the allures of Iwasaki's modern new resort with a trip to Mount Morgan, a nineteenth-century gold-mining town where we took a trip on a steam train and explored a cave with dinosaur footprints on the ceiling. That part of the world had been turned upside down by the forces of nature a hundred-sixty-million-years earlier.

January 8, 1990 Meleese, Scott, Josh, and I went to Keppel Island on the southern tip of the barrier reef. We caught the ferry at Yeppoon, crossed the blue expanse of water, and arrived on the tropical island where Scott checked us into a cabin surrounded by sweet-smelling flora.

I unpacked and took a walk on a sandy trail.

Meleese and Scott napped, as Josh had kept them awake most of the previous night. I read for a couple of hours and then took a dip in the cool, clean, clear Pacific. Keppel had powdery white sand beaches around half the perimeter and rocky outcroppings with waves breaking over them on the seaward side. The interior of the island was wild bush, except where man had interceded.

Mankind was doing a good job decorating the island with a resort, cabins, and camping areas spaced so people had privacy, no matter where they chose to stay. It had greatly changed from the time Marlow and I took the family there in 1973. At that time the only improvements were a few private cabins and a small shell shop that doubled as a hot-dog stand.

After dinner Scott and I went possum hunting armed with flashlights and cameras. We found a few and captured them on film. One possum was a tiny baby, a darling little creature (like all babies).

January 9, 1990 Scott, Meleese, Josh and I spent the morning exploring the land and the afternoon on the water. Scott rented a motorboat and found a perfect coral reef. Just as we were ready to throw the anchor over, a man in another rental boat came by and told us he had seen a shark swim past. We debated on whether to forgo snorkeling. We rode around the cove for a few minutes and didn't see any sign of sharks, so we went into the water.

The plan was for one adult to stay in the boat with Josh and keep an eye out for the shark. I'm not sure what we were supposed to accomplish with that plan, but we did it anyhow. I knew if someone yelled, "Shark!" while I was in the water I wouldn't be able to hear them, let alone swim faster than the animal. I also knew that if I yelled anything at anyone, even on dry land, they eventually looked at me and said, "Huh? Did you say something?" I swam for about half an hour and then climbed into the boat to give Meleese a chance to see the watery wonderland.

I enjoyed playing with Josh for the next half hour, and when Meleese returned, her first question was, "Did you see any sharks?" Whoops, I forgot all about being the lookout!

I went back into the water and took some bread with me. The bread immediately turned to mush when it hit the water. I kept it in my fist and let little bits leak through my fingers right in front of my snorkel mask so I could see the colorful fish close up when they came for a feed. We saw sea slugs, anemones, brightly-colored coral, and one illegal spear fisherman on the ocean floor. We'd gotten life jackets with the rental boat and used them to prevent sunburn as well as to keep us afloat. I hadn't thought about doing that before as I normally float easily, but the life jacket worked out well when I had to turn over on my back and clean my mask or empty sand out of my flippers.

January 10, 1990 Sadly, it was time to catch the ferry back to the mainland. A thirty-minute drive from the ferry had us back in Rockhampton, and the rest of the day was spent doing laundry and other mundane chores. I knew Scott and Meleese felt they were back to reality, but for some reason, I still felt I was in paradise.

January 14, 1990 I had one last visit with Meleese's family before I caught the bus to Darwin.

The bus left Rockhampton at eight thirty p.m. and showed videos as we trundled through the darkness. I watched part of a movie and fell asleep in the roomy, cushy seat with my feet proper up on the vacant seat beside me. I woke up at six just as we were pulling into Townsville. We had a breakfast break and picked up a new driver. I was in the second seat and chatted with the lady in the first seat.

The driver said he detected an accent and asked where I lived, and I told him. He had lived in Citrus Heights, California, in the late 1970s. Citrus Heights was the suburb where Marlow and I currently lived. We lived in Brisbane, Queensland, in the late 1970s, which was the driver's hometown. Small world. We had exchanged residences for a few years of our lives.

The scenery was surprising. I thought outback Queensland would be all desert and dried pastures. The landscape was green all the way from Rockhampton to Darwin. Some areas were hilly, and some were flat; some places had lots of trees, and others had few, but it was always green. I expected to see lots of animals, but only saw two emus, an occasional herd of cattle, and a few sheep.

We stopped on top of the Warrego Mountain Range for a "smoko," as there was no smoking allowed on any public transportation in Australia. I figured it would take the smokers ten minutes for a cigarette, so I grabbed my camera case and headed for the edge of the escarpment to get some shots of the panorama. I walked about three minutes behind the bus and was over the crest of a hill when I heard the bus start up. I rushed back over the hill and ran toward the moving bus, waving both arms just as it went around a curve in the road. Well, I knew the next bus wouldn't be along for twenty-four hours, so I stopped running. I took a slow three-sixty-degree turn and saw no signs of civilization.

I took a preemptory inventory of the contents of my camera case. I didn't relish the thought of spending the night in the wilderness with no water and no insect repellent. My camera case held nothing but a couple of mints and camera gear. I started toward the escarpment to scope out a good place to spend the night.

A few minutes later, I heard a bus coming up the grade from the Darwin side of the range. One of the last passengers on my bus had seen me running toward them and alerted the driver. The driver said he didn't realize I had walked away from the bus, and since no one wanted a cigarette, he decided to travel on. Glad that passenger saw me. The lady in the first seat hadn't noticed me depart the bus.

The bus had motor trouble about an hour before our dinner stop in Mount Isa. The driver said the engine was overheated, so he pulled over and tried a few tricks. The motor wouldn't restart after he turned it off. We waited for it to cool down. That gave passengers further opportunity to get acquainted. We walked up and down the aisle introducing ourselves and exchanging destinations and plans. Nice group, mostly Europeans, several backpackers, all tourists, all loved Australia. A mechanic arrived, changed some engine parts, and had us on our way again.

When we arrived in Mount Isa, the mining town looked unique sitting in the middle of nowhere. I knew we had an hour stopover, so I dashed through town to take pictures of the well-lit mine scaffolds at twilight. The mine that produced iron ore, lead, and silver was decorated for Christmas all year-round.

Dashing across the lawn at city hall, I observed a group of Aboriginals sitting in a circle passing a bottle around. No one else was in sight. It was Saturday evening, so stores were closed. Only the pubs were open and doing a booming business. All of a sudden, I stepped into a hole and hurt my foot. Pain shot up my leg. I let out a yelp and fell to the ground. One picnicker turned and looked at me sprawled on the grass. He waved his bottle and went back to the "picnic." Ten minutes passed before the pain subsided enough for me to try to get up.

I was on one knee struggling for breath when I heard a car coming up behind me. I knew there was no street there. I turned and saw a policeman driving along the wide sidewalk I had just crossed. I waved to him, and he gave me a look of disgust and shook his head. I'm sure he thought I was drunk. He kept going and left me striving to become erect. It took me half an hour to hop to the bus station three blocks away. I floundered into the station snack bar and asked the waitress if she had any ice. My ankle was swollen to twice its normal size.

"No, but we do have ice cream," she said. I figured eating an ice-cream cone probably wouldn't reduce the swelling, but it might reduce the self-pity, so I ordered one scoop of lime.

I staggered to a news agency (where newspapers and magazines are sold) and bought a couple of postcards of the town and mines lit up at sunset and a bottle of aspirin. The postcards would serve to show Americans why I was running across a lawn looking up instead of watching my feet. I wobbled onto the bus as it was ready to leave. Once I was seated and knew I would be on the bus for the next twenty hours, I took off my hiking boot. The foot ballooned out. Fortunately, I only had to hop to the back of the bus to use the restroom. A fellow passenger brought me food and bottled water at the next two stops.

I had to decide what to do when we arrived in Darwin. It would be late Sunday, so I could catch a taxi to my hotel, then arise the next morning and take a taxi to the hospital for x-rays, or I could book tours in the national parks and hope I wouldn't be expected to walk. A booking agency was visible in the bus station, so I opted for the latter. A couple of young Swedes from the bus virtually carried me to the booking office since they were headed there anyway. We booked the same tours. There were three parks I wanted to see, and three and a half days before I had to catch a plane to Brisbane. I tucked my shoe under my arm, leaned on a counter, and ordered four-wheel-drive tours of wildlife reserves and a Greyhound Bus trip to Katherine Gorge. If I couldn't get a shoe on Monday morning, I'd cancel the tours and go to the hospital.

The name of the hotel the bus driver recommended was Air Raid Lodge. When I got there, I realized the reason for the name was because it had no windows. It had been built during World War II and had been used as an air raid shelter when the Japanese flew over town. The lodge was immaculately clean, had a private bath for each room, and was very quiet. It also had a common room for cooking meals and doing laundry. Perfect. My kind of place.

January 15, 1990 I slept with my foot elevated on four pillows and awoke on Monday with a swollen foot displaying lovely Easter shades of lavender, purple, green, and yellow. I took two aspirins before attempting to squeeze my foot into the boot. With extreme pain the foot was forced inside, and I laced the shoe as tightly as possible. With the shoe in place, I hopped from the bed to the bathroom for morning ablutions.

The four-wheel-drive tour vehicle arrived in front of the hotel just as I scooted to the bottom step on my derriere. The guide helped me into the front seat. There were two bench seats behind me, which held five more tourists; we headed toward Litchfield National Park. I plied the driver, Rod, with questions that he respectfully answered as he wended his way to the outskirts of Darwin. Then he turned on a microphone and made a prepared speech about the area, and left me with no unanswered questions. Rod was delightfully smart and witty.

Litchfield had only been a national park for two years; few tourists knew about it, and we practically had the place to ourselves. The park was glorious, certainly much better than sitting in a hospital waiting for x-ray results (I already knew what they would reveal).

Rod's daughter was traveling with us, and she brought her boyfriend from Melbourne. The boyfriend wanted to impress the young lady; he had the driver stop several times so he could catch lizards seen along the road. The other tourists probably would never have had the opportunity to see the bearded dragon and frilly lizard up close if not for this young man. I became acquainted with them in the seventies while living near Brisbane.

The land varied from hilly to flat, but was always vibrant shades of green. The driver said the grass grew three feet a month in the wet season, and got up to twelve feet high by the start of the dry season. Then it turned brown and fell over. The packed dead grass caused spontaneous combustion, and 80 percent of the area burned during the dry season. The trees and insects survived the tortures of the seasons. The trees were mostly eucalypts, palms, and grevillea (a type of conifer). I especially enjoyed seeing the cycads, pandanus, and Livingstone palms. Snuggled down in the grass was a multitude of flowers peeking out.

I couldn't complain about the lack of wildlife that day. We saw a black-tailed kite with a six-foot wingspan, pheasant cookals by the dozens (the driver said they tasted like barbed wire), spinifex termites (a closer relative to cockroaches than to ants) building castle-like mounds, a golden-orb weaver (a spider with a white speckled body and black legs, which stretched three inches in diameter), king parrots, red-wing parrots, rainbow lorikeets, sulfur-crested cockatoos, red-tailed black cockatoos, white egrets, cattle egrets, white-faced herons, wallaroos (large reddish-brown kangaroos) and half a dozen different kinds of lizards.

The tourists went swimming at three different places, any of which could have been used to film a movie about Adam and Eve before they discovered apples. There were waterfalls feeding crystal-clear pools. One of the young Swedes helped me down the grassy slope to the water's edge at the first pool. I went into the water at Wangi Falls wearing my hiking boots, hoping the cool water would reduce the swelling and pain.

Rod warned the women that Wangi was where the Aboriginals swam when they wanted to have children. It had only been the past three hundred years or so that some tribes had associated sex and pregnancy. Before that time they thought the gods made women pregnant. On that same subject, the women used to eat chunks of termite mounds when they were pregnant. Scientists later discovered that spinifex termite mounds were very high in calcium and magnetic mounds high in iron. How did the women know that? How did they know they needed extra amounts of those elements?

After our dip in the billabong, we had a delicious lunch of roast chicken, salad, homemade rolls, and cake. We sat on the grass by the falls, and a goanna wandered out of the reeds looking for leftovers. He didn't mind us eating on his lawn, but he didn't want anyone to pet him. One man tried and learned how fast a lizard's tail can whip around.

We rode to an abandoned tin mine. The family that had been running it had been attacked by Aboriginals in the 1940s and burned out. I didn't realize there was such ferocious animosity that late in history. But then, look at the hatred aroused in America's South in the 1960s. Sadly, humans will never abide by the Golden Rule.

We saw fields of termite mounds of various heights. Gray magnetic mounds looked like cemetery headstones, as they were elliptical, all pointing north and south. The spinifex mounds resembled castles, some of them twelve feet high. Aussies ground up spinifex termite mounds, mixed them with water, and rolled the mixture out on the ground to make tennis courts. Once they dried, they were as hard as concrete.

The second swimming hole was a short distance from the car, maybe a quarter mile, and another young man helped me to a shady spot to watch the others frolic. I hated being helped around like an old invalid. Hang on, I *was* a fifty-two-year-old invalid! I didn't want to sit in the hot car either, so I graciously accepted the gentleman's assistance.

The third water hole was at the bottom of a mile-long trail, so I sat in the cool, shady stream at the top of the grade with an elderly lady. She was fifty-five if she was a day. I kept my eyes open for leeches, as it was a rainforest, and I hated those creepy-crawlies. The animals I found disgusting were leeches, ticks, snails, and slugs. Snakes and spiders didn't bother me, but I did respect their territory. Australia had several deadly species.

We were treated to a twilight display of lightning in huge cumulous clouds as we headed for Darwin. It was the end of a wonderful day. I wondered what on earth I had ever done to deserve the happiness I felt.

January 16, 1990 Have you ever noticed that the things you think you want the most turn out to be the most disappointing once you have them? That summarized my trip to Katherine Gorge. When we lived in Brisbane, I kept asking to go to Darwin, and one of the main reasons was that I wanted to see Katherine Gorge. I had read novels about pioneers finding this heavenly oasis. The gorge was pretty, but not spectacular. I visualized it as being Grand Canyon II. Perhaps my painful foot clouded my judgment.

I took a four-hour Greyhound Bus trip from Darwin to the town of Katherine, then a half-hour van ride to the gorge. After an hour wait, passengers were herded onto boats for an hour-long ride through gray and brown canyons, a painful, painful mile-long walk over rocks and around rapids, then another hour-long boat ride. Thank goodness I'm not allergic to aspirin; I consumed three getting over the rocks. Then I reversed the above to get back to Darwin.

Before I caught the boat, I hopped along the short flat, grassy trail to the campground where there were only two groups of campers. Also two tame kangaroos and an emu were present. An obnoxious emu! Why obnoxious? Well, every time I tried to take his picture, he turned his rear to my camera. I gave up and took pictures of the roos.

A young lady approached and said she had lost a gold necklace, so I helped her look for it in the grass. I heard a "cluck" behind me and knew the noise was the emu. He was following so closely that my nose hit his beak when I turned around to see what he was doing. I hobbled faster, he walked faster; I stopped, and he stopped. I went around a big tree fast enough to come up behind him, and he pretended to be busy eating something off the ground.

The girl with the lost necklace said she'd been watching us before I became aware of the emu, and that he mimicked me step for step. She asked if I wanted her to take his picture with me, and I said yes.

As soon as I handed her my camera, the emu turned his rear end to her, and kept it there—no picture. I took the camera back and kept it in plain view while I looked for the necklace. The emu wandered off so he wouldn't have to worry about me getting an unexpected picture of his humorous face. What a character!

On the way back to Darwin, I shared the Greyhound Bus with a group of women, and we bonded—a woman my age, two ladies in their twenties or thirties, and two youngsters in their preteens. I suggested we take a cab from the bus station to our hotels together, as it would be close to ten o'clock when we got back to Darwin. They weren't worried since they were all staying at the same hotel. There were so many drunks on the streets, I felt uneasy walking alone.

Do you know what the bus driver did? Instead of taking us to the station, he took us to a point that was a two-block walk each way to our hotels, and he sat there until he saw that we were all inside safely. I turned around and checked after hobbling a block, and he waved, waiting for me to stagger the last block. The group of ladies had already reached their destination, and there was no personal benefit for the gentleman to keep an eye on me. The driver was a healthy thirty-five years old, so I felt that if I had been accosted, he could have saved me. I'm glad he didn't get any bruises on my account. I should have been keeping a log of all the exceptionally nice people I dealt with on this trip. My sister, Nancy, could have added them to her nightly prayer list. She prays for everyone who is nice to her or someone she loves. My list would have kept her up all night reciting names.

January 17, 1990 Six a.m. was bus-boarding time for a day at Kakadu National Park. Our four-wheel-drive vehicle held seven passengers. Our group consisted of an Australian sheepshearer, an Austrian youth, the handsome Swede from the Greyhound Bus ride to Darwin, a married couple from Scotland, and a Vietnamese lady.

The driver, Max, had been a Darwinite since 1948. At one time he had leased a three-thousand-square-mile station (ranch), which we drove through on the way to Kakadu. He could buy a ninety-nine-year lease from "the Crown," which was renewable or could be inherited by his children, but it would always belong to the federal government. "The Crown" referred to the Queen of England, and although Australia gained its independence in 1903, the people still tended to think of federal land as the Queen's land or Crown land. Australian banks only loaned 10 percent on agricultural purchases because farming and ranching were such dicey businesses.

Max raised water buffalo that he sold for pet food. He also raised cattle and lost his shirt when the United States and Japan stopped importing beef from Australia in 1976. He claimed that happened because Australia wouldn't allow the United States build a missile base near Darwin. Maybe so; I don't know about that, but I wished there was someplace Americans could get jobs near Darwin. It would be a fun place to live. Both Max and Rod, the man who took me to Litchfield, had been on trips around Australia, and when they got to Darwin, they never left. Both had been in Darwin for many, many years. I was tempted to do the same.

Anyhow, after Max lost his station, he went into crocodile shooting for the skins. He told stories about the "good old days." If movie moguls wanted to do a *Crocodile Dundee III*, they could use some of his stories in the movie. Max worked on the first two *Crocodile Dundee* movies; he located the places for shooting the films and organized camps for the movie crew. He said Paul Hogan was a wimp. I found that hard to believe.

We drove miles and miles through scrub that looked exactly the same inside and outside Kakadu Park. The passengers were a jovial crew, and we had a good time singing and listening to Max tell stories. The Vietnamese lady rode shotgun and slept the whole time we were in the car. I wondered if she suffered from jet lag.

Five hours later we reached our departure point for the boat trip on the Yellow Waters (yes, it really was) Bird Refuge. We were warned not to dangle any body parts in the water, as the river was highly populated with crocs. We believed the boat driver. Two tourists had been killed by crocs while I was in Darwin. They didn't heed the signs warning about swimming in rivers.

Kakadu was bursting at the seams with beauty. The birds were outstanding—snowy egrets, cattle egrets, white heron, jacana (called the Jesus bird because it walked on hyacinth leaves, and it looked like the bird was walking on water), magpie geese (they were black and white like their songbird relatives with the same name) and squawking corellas (parrots) by the dozens. We were even lucky enough to see the occasional sea eagle and jabiru.

Rich mimosa grass looked like velvet in fields populated by *brumbies* (wild horses). Pandanus lined the river with its palm like fronds. When we got into the water lilies, I felt like I was floating through a Monet painting, a very unreal serenity. I could have spent days at this spot, but unfortunately we eventually went back to shore and to a bistro to eat. I spent the second half of my lunch hour in the resort swimming pool with my shoe still on my foot. I hadn't removed it after the first night, and that time was a mistake. The only other swimmer told me that a goanna had just left the pool. I guess he felt a need to cool off also.

That refreshed me for our tour through a uranium mine and a town built especially for its employees. It was a most unusual town; anyone caught possessing a house cat was immediately fired from his job at the mine and evicted from his rental house. Only one dog was allowed per household, and it must be kept on a leash at all times and inside a closed building from sunset to sunrise. The reason for the laws was because the town was built in a national park, and politicians were trying to protect the bird and animal life. Bless their hearts. The town hotel was built in the shape of a crocodile, supposedly so it would fit into the surroundings. Didn't fool me; I knew it wasn't a real croc.

From there we went to the airport for a flight over Arnhem Land, the Aboriginal Dreamland. The weather was miserable; it started to rain, and I was afraid our plane ride would be cancelled. The pilot figured out how far away the lightning was and took off.

What a panorama! Row after row of rocky escarpment fell into deep ravines and hidden rivers. The rivers flowed into wide grassy plains that were inundated in "the wet." Soon every valley and low spot would contain at least three feet of water.

I thought about how I had begged Marlow to join a group of naturalists who were walking from Cairns to Darwin across this country back in the late seventies. At no time in my life have I ever been fit enough to walk ten miles across that terrain, let alone a thousand miles. Thank goodness Marlow didn't allow me to do all the things I thought I wanted to do. He's not only my better half, but he's also my common sense.

When it was time for us to land, the airport was having a terrific electrical storm, so we flew around for an extra twenty minutes. I didn't have any problem with that. I was next to the pilot's seat, so I had the best view and enjoyed every inch of the land.

We landed after the rain had stopped, and we trundled off in our four-wheel drive to early Aborigine caves. The rain had cooled the air a tad bit, so the short walk was pleasant; we went back twenty thousand years. Max gave us explanations of the cave paintings, and we learned a little about the earth's earlier inhabitants.

We had dinner of water buffalo steaks and headed for home, hotel, or air-raid shelter, whatever the case was for each person.

January 18, 1990 I left a "Do Not Disturb" sign on my door and slept until nine o'clock. I took a taxi to the airport, dropped off my bags, and took the same taxi back to Darwin's museum to kill a couple of hours. I viewed Vietnamese boat people's conveyances at the museum. Several boats had floated from island to island from Vietnam to Darwin in the mid and late 1970s. I saw a terrific display of animals that live in the "North End" and a history of Aboriginal paintings. I took a few pictures and acted like Ms. Innocence when the docent told me, "No pictures allowed." Thought I'd better get out of there before they arrested me, so I went back to the airport and awaited my plane to Brisbane.

When the boarding call was made, I got in line, and the airline clerk mumbled something about steps. I said "Okay," and walked onto the tarmac. Only then did I notice that there were two sets of stairs up to the plane. Being lazy, I naturally took the closest one. Halfway up it dawned on me that I was using the steps for the first-class passengers.

To heck with it. I'd walk through first class to my seat, and no one would notice me.

"Ah, here she is now!" the stewardess exclaimed as I passed her. I mumbled a "Good morning" and moved a bit faster. I wondered how she knew I didn't belong in first class. They must be trained to identify people's paying capacity. My seat turned out to be in the first row behind first-class passengers, and I slunk into it.

A few minutes later, the same stewardess came up to me with two other ladies in stewardess uniforms, and I heard one of them say, "Her?"

I thought that was a bit much for just having used the wrong stairs, so I put on my most indignant voice and said, "Yes, can I help you?"

The three stood smiling. Finally the first lady said, "You don't remember us, do you?"

"No, I'm sorry, have we met?"

"We were on the bus to Darwin from Katherine Gorge together. Remember, I told you we were taking the same flight as you to Brisbane?"

Oh my heavens, these couldn't be the same ladies who were barefooted, wearing shorts, and had their hair in braids. I wished I had some of that stuff that *shrunk the kids*. Did I ever feel silly. Rude and silly. The ladies were as nice as ever to me the whole trip back to Brisbane, and I was very humble the same length of time.

Back in Brisbane, Scott and Meleese met me at the airport, and we went downtown Brisbane and "ooohed and aaahed" at all the changes that had been made the past ten years. Brisbane was no longer a cow town proud of its drinking habit. It was a cosmopolitan city, with ladies wearing hose and high heels and men in suits. I was impressed! When I owned my own real estate office in Brisbane in the seventies, it had been a chore to get my office clerk to show up for work wearing all her clothes. Sometimes she showed up barefoot, other times she forgot to wear underwear. Australian working women had since become sophisticated.

We eventually found the correct freeway to suburban Goodna, where we wanted to go. It took Brisbane four years to put in two miles of freeway while we lived there in the seventies. Now freeways went everywhere. The government called in some outside help before the Expo and the bicentennial celebrations and put up several miles of freeways as well as a couple dozen glass and steel skyscrapers.

In Brisbane we visited friends and neighbors and had a nice time. I always felt sad when a vacation came to an end, and this time was no different. I wanted to drag out one more conversation with our beloved friends, the Nugents, travel down one more road, see one more renovation, but eventually it was time to board Qantas and fly back to reality.

Epilogue: At home in Sacramento, I made an appointment with my doctor, as my foot still hurt. She concurred that the foot was broken, but was mending. The only thing she could do was either rebreak the foot and put it in a cast, or offer me a prescription for pain-killers until it healed completely. I told her I'd continue with my aspirin-as-needed regimen.

Seven

Europe

1993

I went to night school at Sierra College near Sacramento, California, to take classes in machine shop and welding to aid my work as a manufacturing engineer in aerospace. My welding teacher told me about a class being offered at San Francisco State University, where the students were going to Europe to tour factories to see how they were preparing for joining the European Union. I decided to join them. I invited Marlow to sign up for the class, but he rejected the idea, saying he knew I'd spend all my time outside of class tours looking at art and architecture. Well, duhhh. Of course! Europe was my first vacation without some family member involved.

June 22, 1993 Finally, after months of working two jobs to pay for my next adventure, departure day arrived. I left for Europe.

Those of us from Sacramento left on US Air for a flight to Los Angeles, where we transferred to Alitalia Airlines for our flight to Rome. We had all stewards, no stewardesses, on our twelve-hour Alitalia ride to Roma (that's Italian for Rome; see how fast I pick up foreign languages).

Our plane left Los Angeles and we had two hours of daylight before sunset. We flew northeast over Nevada, Utah, and Saskatchewan, Canada, in daylight. Then the sky dimmed into twilight, and folks settled down for sleep. By eleven thirty California time, the sun rose again.

The seats were organized in a three/four/three configuration, with two narrow aisles separating the four seats in the middle. I'd been assigned an inside seat in the middle. The girl on the aisle wanted to trade so she could sit next to her friend. That suited me just fine. I had more legroom and could leave my seat without disturbing her.

We flew the polar route. I went to the door opposite the galley and peered through the window with awe. We were over Greenland. We had spectacular views: icebergs, glaciers, black volcanic mountains, icy blue water, and grayish-blue skies.

June 23, 1993 We arrived in Rome at five thirty in the evening their time, on Wednesday. There were so many guards in the airport sporting Uzis, we thought the country was under attack, or that we had been hijacked and taken to a hostile nation. We learned from Professor Taylor, our teacher, that was typical Italian security.

A charter bus met us at the door beyond customs and took us to Hotel Delta. The four-star hotel was comparable to an eight-story Motel 6. My roommate, Jamie, and I each had a single-size bed with a cement column at the foot of one. We bumped into the column while using the closet. We were located on the fifth floor with a mini-balcony and view of the Coliseum. I felt giddy when I first opened the balcony door and verified I was actually in Rome, the real Rome of ancient history and uncountable items of classical art.

Fortyish Jamie was traveling with her daughter, Karen, who had just graduated from the University of California at Davis. Karen wanted to share a room with her college roommate, Nancy. Jamie and I were glad to room with each other rather than someone half our age.

Jamie and I unpacked, then joined a group of girls in the lobby for our first meal in Italy. The girls, Nancy, Ellen, Ayudi, and Marianne, thought they knew where others from our class had gone for pizza.

We walked to the first traffic light and pushed the button signaling we wanted a green light to cross the street. The light turned green, the little sign lit up saying, "*Avanti*." I didn't see any traffic, so I stepped into the crosswalk.

Beep, beep! If the driver hadn't honked, causing me to take a step backward, he would have creamed me! Yes, he ran the red light. We managed to make it across the street in one piece in spite of motor scooters buzzing past. They hardly slowed for the red light.

We never found the other students, but we did find a presentable pizza parlor. We each ordered different ingredients, then traded slices, just like college kids do in the States.

Marianne ordered a salad made of extremely bitter green leaves, olives, and tomatoes. A couple of people ordered beer or wine, and a few ordered gelatos (Italian ice cream). I stuck to pizza and water and had more than I could eat; my bill was US$12.50. We discovered that tap water cost US$2.00.

We were confused about directions when we walked into the very dark street but muddled our way up one street and down another and arrived at the hotel at eleven.

June 24, 1993 Overwhelming, magnificent, awesome, glorious—I don't know enough adjectives to describe the beauty seen my first full day in Rome.

Karen called our room at nine o'clock. Otherwise, Jamie and I would probably have slept for another four hours. We dressed and joined Karen's friends for the continental breakfast. Our choices were croissants, hard rolls, canned fruit cocktail, and canned orange juice, coffee (thick enough to make a spoon stand up), or tea.

Jamie and I learned that Ellen was Greek and spoke Italian, Greek, German, and English. We made a mental note to invite her on as many excursions as possible.

Jamie, Karen, Nancy, Ellen, and Ayudi joined me for a taxi ride to the Vatican (we took two taxis). Our driver pretended he didn't know where we wanted to go and took us to the Vatican *hotel*, which doubled the price of our ride.

At the real Vatican, we followed the arrows directing us to the Sistine Chapel. Room after room, hallway after hallway, we gawked at awesome splendor. Every space was filled with glorious art. The frescoes, the tapestry, the furniture, the floors, the walls, and the ceilings kept us saying, "Ooooh, aaaaah" all the way. Finally we reached the Sistine Chapel.

The "oooohs" and "aaaaahs" stopped. We gaped in stunned silence. Slowly, one by one, we regained our voices as we studied the incredible artistry.

"Is that a sculpture or a painting?" Some of Michelangelo's figures looked three-dimensional. Muted pastels made the figure's skin lifelike. We spent an hour in the chapel and could have easily spent a day. Unfortunately, the chapel closed at one thirty so artists could get on with never-ending restorations.

Wandering through hallways on our way out, the group accidentally split up. I looked away from an exceptional midnight-blue porcelain vase about twelve feet high and realized that Karen was the only person I knew in the room.

Karen, a beautiful tall blonde in her early twenties, got the two of us into the Hall of Caesars after it closed to the public. The guard agreed we could snap a couple of pictures. He tried to strike up a conversation with Karen, who completely ignored him.

He asked where we were from, and I answered, "California."

He asked if we knew what California meant, and I said no.

His eyes never left Karen as he explained "Cali" came from *caliente* or "hot," and "fornia" came from "firmament" or "earth." I didn't know that! California meant "Hot land!" The man who named it hadn't been in the Sierras in January.

We waited by the front entry for thirty minutes for the rest of our group. We later learned they waited thirty minutes at the back door.

Karen and I walked around the perimeter of the Vatican walls until we found the entrance to St. Peter's Square. That gave us access to St. Peter's Basilica. Pictures could never do this building justice. Every square inch was opulent. The Papal Altar had a canopy that took nine hundred men and three hundred horses to erect.

We attended Mass, a Mass recited in Latin with the traditional chanting and phrases of my youth. *Kyrie Eleison, Christe Eleison...* It was wonderful to hear Latin recited once more.

The Basilica was the final resting place for Saint Peter as well as sixty-six other popes. It took one-hundred-eighty years to build. Every detail was designed by an artist. I wished every Catholic, and every art lover, could see the magnificent edifice.

Karen and I reluctantly pulled ourselves away from St. Peter's so we could meet the class for our first scheduled event—a bus tour of the city. Rome offered so much to see, I enjoyed every single minute. I understood the youngsters who got bored; they declared the guide really said, "On the right we have an old building, and on the left we have a very old building, and on the right we have a very, very old building..."

Both older and younger people enjoyed our stop at Trevi Fountain and the Spanish Steps, beautiful spots hidden among the back streets of Roma. I'm not sure who made it more famous, the original sculptor, Nicola Salvi, who designed it in 1732, or the 1950s movie *Three Coins in a Fountain*. At any rate we threw our coins in the fountain in hopes we would one day return to Rome.

The tour lasted four hours, so by the time we got back to the hotel, we were ready for dinner—my little clique had skipped lunch. The girls wanted to go to one of the romantic piazzas where there were restaurant tables outside around a fountain. That sounded lovely, and Jamie and I agreed to join them. Jamie and I put on another layer of deodorant and a new layer of lipstick, and we were ready. We hadn't counted on it taking the girls until ten to get ready.

Ellen instructed the two taxi drivers to take us to the Trastevere, which was like a movie set. Small round tables with white tablecloths, flowers, and candles rimmed the piazza, which had a lovely fountain in the center. Young lovers strolled from restaurant to restaurant reading menus. They were tourists, but that didn't detract from the romance.

We chose a restaurant with a cheaper menu. Being a nickel squeezer, I resented it when the waiter put a bowl of bread on the table when he handed us menus, then added 21,000 lire to our bill, the equivalent to US$14.70. He added 6,000 lire to the bill for the use of the tablecloth and napkins (laundry fees, I guess). Of course, we figured the waiter's 20 percent tip on those items as well as the food we ate. Again, a glass of tap water was $2.00. (We later learned from the professor that the tip was included in the bill before we received it. We had paid the waiter a 40 percent tip! Live and learn.) For a plate of tasty, meatless pasta, a glass of water, a piece of bread, and a taxi to the hotel, my meal cost US$25.00. I had to find a way to be more conservative, or I'd run out of money before we left Rome.

The girls and Jamie wanted to walk back to the hotel. My legs were tired and wanted me to catch a taxi. I agreed with my legs.

June 25, 1993 The class had a ten a.m. appointment to tour the American Embassy, so Jamie and I rolled our aching bodies off the cement slabs called beds at seven thirty. We showered, ate hard rolls, and canned fruit cocktail, and drank a brew of equal parts coffee and milk in the breakfast room. For lunch I snitched an extra hard roll to fill with peanut butter brought from America.

Upon arrival at the embassy, we were treated like suspected terrorists. We made it past the submachine-gun-toting US soldiers and arrived at the visitor's center. Our passports were examined and sent to a supervisor. We had sent photocopies from home a month before our trip, so we thought we would be buzzed right through. We were eager for the tour described by the engineering professor. Now, if we could just make it past US security…

I'll digress for a minute to tell you about Italian security. At the airport there were soldiers armed with submachine guns, regular police with revolvers, and a variety of uniformed, armed security guards hired by the airlines. At the bank where Jamie and I cashed traveler's checks, there were armed guards at both the entrance and exit. Also, there was a security system on the doors—I had to ring the doorbell, the first door opened, and let me into an anteroom where my picture was taken. I pushed another doorbell to open the second door and gain entrance to the bank. The exit door had a push button release. Only one person at a time could enter or leave the bank.

Back to the embassy story—an unsmiling secretary met us at the visitor lobby and marched us around the building to a back door where we were ushered up a narrow staircase to the third floor and into a stuffy little room with four chairs. Four people sat and the rest stood and politely listened to three clerks tell us about their jobs.

The first gentleman was interesting. He spoke on the Italian government, the Mafia, and the Church for fifteen minutes, and then excused himself, saying he had a meeting. The second man was unsure of himself and gave a rather boring fifteen-minute speech about America's place in Italy. He then left; he had a meeting too. A very, very boring woman spoke for fifteen minutes on her duties as a file clerk and paper shuffler, then excused herself (had to clean up her desk to go on vacation). We were left in the room with the original secretary who met us at the visitor's center. She announced she was ready to take us back to our bus.

Professor Taylor asked where his good friend, the ambassador, was.

"On vacation."

"Well, could we still take the planned tour of the embassy?"

"No," she said, mumbling something about the Pieta and David being vandalized, and they couldn't really take a chance. Those statues were vandalized by non-Americans years ago and were in a church/museum, not the embassy! What did that have to do with us touring the embassy? Did they have precious art stored in the embassy? Well, no, but still, they just couldn't take any chances.

We left disgusted with our treatment and felt the trip had been a complete waste of time. Professor Taylor babbled gaily about what an excellent experience that had been. I suspected we were *not* going to have fun, educational factory tours, if that was his idea of a good time.

Jamie and I walked around the Coliseum, reading plaques and taking pictures before cooling off in the hotel pool located on the roof. Thank goodness the hotel was air conditioned; the weather was hot and humid.

The young ladies planned a romp at local nightclubs; Jamie and I declined their invitation to join the fun. We found a quiet, inexpensive place to eat and were in bed by ten, just as the kids were leaving their rooms.

June 26, 1993 We went to the Roman ruins and checked out the exterior of Mussolini's palace, which looked like a giant wedding cake. By one thirty Jamie was ready for a rest, so we returned to the hotel, where she napped.

I roamed around Nero's palace. Most of his place was underground. I don't know if that was for security or because of the heat. The roof could have been a nice park, but it had been neglected and had deteriorated into a home for derelicts.

Jamie was awake and ready for a swim when I returned to the room. We cooled off in the pool, ate dinner the same place as the night before, and retired to our room to catch up on journal and postcard writing.

June 27, 1993 The charter bus, driven by Joseph, left Rome at eight. Thought I'd use the bus trip to take the time to give you my opinions about Rome and Romans. I never got pinched. I never saw anyone else get pinched. I never felt uncomfortable because of unfavorable attention from men. Some of the girls received catcalls from passing motorists, and that was the extent of flirting. People looked at us if they heard us speak, just as many Americans look up when they hear someone speaking a foreign language. Men greeted us in passing, "*Bona sera, señoras.*" That certainly wasn't disconcerting; it was most pleasant.

Older women didn't speak to strangers, but everyone else did. Many people offered a "*Bona sera*" or "*bon giorno*" when we passed. People were friendly and helpful.

Romans drove fast, recklessly, and disregarded traffic signs. They showed no regard for road rules and paid a dear price. Sirens roared past our hotel continually, day and night. The law said vehicles were supposed to honk at all intersections; some did and some didn't. The honking added to the stressful city noise and did little to prevent accidents. Romans drove minicars or motor scooters. We rarely saw a full-size car or truck.

City dwellers lived in apartments, of course. I didn't see more than a dozen single-family residences anywhere in Rome, the suburbs, or on farms near Rome. Farms were a cluster of apartment buildings with fields radiating out in all directions. The gray homes looked ancient.

The people were thin to average build; I expected them to be overweight from eating pasta and pizza. They got a lot of exercise walking up and down steps. I kept thinking about all the famous people who had preceded me in such places as the Roman ruins—Julius Caesar, Augustus Caesar, Nero, Saint Peter, Charlton Heston. Now, I'd been there also! Amazing.

There were buildings from the eighteenth and nineteenth centuries that were still occupied. We saw a two-thousand-year-old building—yes, 2,000, not 200—that was occupied. It was called the Theatre of Marcellus and was built at the time of Christ's birth.

Our bus arrived in Florence (Firenze) at noon. The driver took us directly to the Acadamie Galleria so we could see Michelangelo's *David* before the museum closed.

David was incredible. It was much larger than I expected—the statue, that is. David was twelve feet tall and was on a pedestal about six feet tall. Every detail was so perfect, I expected the eyes to blink. The paintings in the museum were dark Botticellis, Monacos, Lippis, and the works of other Renaissance painters. (A car bomb exploded at the entrance to this museum a week after we returned to the United States. The bomb killed five people.)

When the museum closed, our kind bus driver took us to Michelangelo's Pizzale, a park on a hill overlooking Florence. The lovely old city had red tile roofs stretching as far as the eye could see up and down gently rolling hills. There were multiple church steeples standing guard over neighborhoods. The *Duomo* or *Dom* (Italian for cathedral) was prominently visible protruding above all other roofs.

Jamie and I wanted to see Santa Croce (Holy Cross Cathedral) where Michelangelo, Leonardo di Vinci, Galileo, and others were buried. We took a taxi from our modern Florentine hotel with an English-speaking driver, so we got a mini-tour of the city and were exposed to the narrow passageways called streets. We couldn't get all the way to the church, as there was to be a soccer game played in the piazza in front of the church, which was cordoned off.

We walked to a different piazza and heard drums approaching. The sound indicated a parade, a very colorful parade of men dressed in all the various costumes of Italian armies past and present. They were escorting the soccer teams to the playing field. They were accompanied by a series of drummers as though being led to the gallows. Italian viewers cheered wildly when their team appeared. What fun to see the enthusiasm!

Jamie and I drank enormous glasses of delicious peach-flavored iced tea. This was my first experience tasting peach tea, but it won't be the last.

We headed for a bus stop and spotted the postgraduate student who was assisting Professor Taylor. We asked if we were at the correct spot to catch a bus back to our hotel. He confirmed our choice and introduced us to his friend. Naturally, the four of us chatted until our bus arrived.

When we got on the bus, there were just two vacant seats. They were in the back of the bus. Jamie and I sat in them. Soon a seat emptied on either side of us, and the boys joined us. We chatted and giggled the rest of the way to the hotel. Passengers looked at us disapprovingly. I couldn't understand why until it dawned on me that we appeared to be two middle-aged women who had just picked up two young men. When one woman my age was about to disembark, she gave me a particularly nasty look and clucked her tongue. What else could I do but say, "Eat your heart out, toots!"

June 28, 1993 The class went to the Gucci plant to see how this factory was preparing to operate under the European Union rules. We watched employees make purses, belts, and suitcases. Almost everything was done by hand. Men cut patterns on large tables with templates and tossed the scraps into a stack to be used for smaller items like change purses and key chains. The bamboo handles on the purses were heated on a Bunsen burner and bent to a template by hand. It seemed like a slow job, and we were told that it took sixteen man-hours to make one purse.

The foreman claimed all the company's leather came from farm animals, even the elephant and ostrich skins.

Workers were making a suitcase for Francis Ford Coppola, the producer of the *Godfather* movies. His old suitcase was lying on the floor, and we could see that the handle was slightly worn. We figured that if Gucci's purses cost between $700.00 and $2,000.00, the new suitcase must cost $15,000.00. Coppola must trust it to different baggage handlers than the ones I'd encountered at airports. I offered to buy his old suitcase for twenty bucks, but that was an offer Gucci could refuse.

Greco Gucci started his company in Florence in 1920; he opened his first store in New York in 1960. Currently the company owned sixty-four stores, where they sold the most expensive merchandise; they had sixty-four franchises where medium-priced items were sold, and Gucci sold to seventy duty-free shops around the world.

Joseph drove downtown after the city tour. Only the oldsters got off the bus. The youngsters went back to the hotel to sleep; they had been nightclubbing the night before.

I say *oldsters*; I assume you thought I was the oldest person traveling with college students. Wrong! There were two couples in their seventies; the professor was in his late sixties; Jamie and a physician were in their middle forties; then came me at age thirty-nine; after me was the physician's consort in her thirties, and the students ranging from twenty one to thirty one. What? You don't believe I was thirty nine in 1993?! Well, okay, maybe the seventeenth anniversary of my thirty-ninth birthday was fast approaching, but I felt thirty-nine.

Karen told her mom that drinks at the nightclubs were 21,000 lire each. No one became inebriated. The clubs played sixties American and English music. Karen said men out-numbered the women about twenty-to-one, but they didn't ask the girls to dance. Everyone danced by themselves, and if a man wanted to dance with a certain woman, he maneuvered himself into position dancing in front of her, but avoided looking at her.

Jamie and I toured the Basilica di Santa Maria del Fiore (also known as "the Dom") begun in 1296, and completed in 1436, with the huge brick dome designed by Brunelleschi. We saw San Giovanni di Baptiste (John the Baptist) church with its sculptured brass doors by Andrea Pisano and Lorenzo Ghiberti. The building was built between 1059 and 1128 and showed no signs of deterioration. The doors have a very interesting history which can be found on the Internet, as does the building of the Dom. We visited Santa Croce that had sarcophagi for Michelangelo, Leonardo di Vinci, Machiavelli, Caravaggio, Galileo, Raphael, two Bonapartes, Rossini, and a great deal of art and history in an irreplaceable building. I couldn't believe I was actually viewing those historical priceless art forms.

From those sacred masterpieces, we went to the Arno River with its colorful restaurants and boats and walked to Pointe Vecchio, a two-thousand-year-old bridge. I remembered reading in novels about people taking their diamonds to Pointe Vecchio in northern Italy to sell to goldsmiths. It seemed incredible that I could actually be in the very place that I'd read about. Pointe Vecchio was a bridge with jewelry stores along both sides; there must have been at least thirty stores. It was fun to window-shop among all that gold and those precious stones.

We saw American actors Rhea Perlman and her husband, Danny DeVito, on the bridge. They returned every greeting sent their way and cheerfully signed autographs upon request.

There weren't as many fountains in Florence as in Rome, but there were plenty of statues and sculptured walls. Jamie and I walked along the streets admiring different works of art and dodging zillions of motor scooters. The drivers weren't as rude and lawless as in Rome, but we still had to be cautious.

We shopped until our legs refused to go forward anymore. Then we went back to the hotel. Another day crammed to capacity.

June 29, 1993 Today was a travel day through the Italian countryside. The scenery between Florence and Bologna was grassy rolling pastures and fields of sunflowers. The people lived in old tenement housing clustered on the edge of plowed fields. We did see a few single-family residences and wondered if they were the landowner's homes, while the tenements held the farm laborers. After we got to Bologna, the land flattened. It remained flat until we were between Udine, Italy, and Vene'zia (Venice), Austria. From Udine to Villach, Austria, we climbed into the mountains. The Alps were so pretty, green and piney, with jagged granite peaks. We could see the occasional castle on a peak to remind us that we were not in California.

We got to our hotel in Villach, Austria, at a quarter after five. Jamie needed a nap, so I left her in our room and went for a walk. I walked as fast as I could, to make it exercise, and it still took me an hour and a half to walk the perimeter of a city park. I saw three soccer fields, all occupied, a playground occupied by mothers and children, well-used bike trails, and fishermen along the banks of the Drau River. For the first time this trip, I saw people exercising. Joggers and cyclists were plentiful. It was a lovely walk, such a pleasure to get away from the sound of traffic for a while.

The students noticed the farther we got from Rome, the larger the cars got. In Austria the people were considerably wealthier. Single-family homes were the norm. Everything was neat and clean, the traffic was orderly, and rules were obeyed. Most of the buildings looked like they were built after World War II.

June 30, 1993 On the road to Vienna (Wien) we saw beautiful villages set among farms ripe with a variety of crops. Each village had a backdrop of mountains to set off its charm.

I was surprised to see the landscape getting flatter the closer we got to Vienna. For some reason I thought all of Austria was in the Alps. I'm like the foreigners who think all of California looks like Los Angeles.

Vienna was an enormous city in a valley. There were no mountains the last twenty miles going into the city. There were 190,000 people living in Vienna; two-hundred years ago there were 200,000. What a stable population!

We checked into the hotel and rushed to the concierge desk to see if we could get tickets to an opera. Good luck! There were a small number of seats left. We paid $60.00 per seat to see *Don Giovanni*, written by Mozart, in Mozart's hometown. How special is that?

This evening was my first time seeing an opera in an opera hall (the other operas I'd seen had been in a circus tent at Bear Valley, California). The opera house was red and gold, just like in the movies. There were tiers and tiers of seats and little boxes on the sides close to the stage. We had ideal seats. Perhaps cheaper seats sold first, and that's why there were a few tickets left; we had the most expensive seats in the house. The singing was glorious (in German). It didn't really matter what language they used; it was the music itself we came to hear. Jamie and I read the story before the opera started, so we could follow the action. The scenery, the costumes, the orchestra, all were perfect.

A group of us took the subway, a clean, reasonably priced, fast form of transportation for the masses. The subway ride to the hotel at midnight felt safe. The train was filled with cheerful music lovers after a night in town. The city had been the home of so many musical greats such as Liszt, Schubert, Strauss, Haydn, Beethoven, and Mozart. Everyone was taught to appreciate fine music from the first grade onward. They were also taught to relish the fine architecture of their city, and there was very little graffiti or vandalism.

July 1, 1993 We went on a tour of the General Motors plant that made Opel cars. The plant was five-eighths of a mile long and two hundred yards wide. Parts traveled from one point to another via overhead conveyors and elevators or via robotics. One big room was filled wall to wall with computers. Lights came on if a machine or robot was malfunctioning. There were four-hundred-fifty maintenance men at the plant, and they were dispatched immediately to the malfunctioning machine (not all of them, just a couple, according to their specialty).

Conveyor-belt assemblers started at $6.00 per hour and were company-trained on the whole line over a three-year apprenticeship. When they graduated, they were making up to $12.00 per hour. They received benefits, including free lunch at the company cafeteria.

We students were invited to join the employees for lunch. I didn't care for the lunch, but that was my own fault. I poured what I thought was vinegar on my salad, and it turned out to be syrup. Oil and syrup do not make good salad dressing. We had a choice of "hot plate" or "cold plate" lunch. I ordered the hot plate, which consisted of a quarter-inch-thick slice of pot roast (that was delicious) and a quarter-inch-thick slice of fatty, salty ham—I ate one bite. And a dumpling the size of a lemon sat in creamed cabbage. The dumpling was very rich with butter and cream, and I could only eat a couple of bites. We received a hard roll the size of a saucer with cheese and liverwurst sealed in tinfoil. I wrapped those items in a paper napkin and stuck them in my purse beside the hard roll with peanut butter taken from the hotel breakfast room. There was a variety of desserts to choose from, but I had no problem passing on them. Imagine eating like that every day for lunch! One meal's quantity was a two-day supply of food.

What a city! We left the plant and did a city tour. The architects were artists who loved scrolls and curlicues, flowers, and faces. It was Rococo and colorful. There were lots of statues on buildings and decorations inlaid into the brick, marble, and stucco walls. When the tour guide announced, "That was Schubert's winter home" or something similar, it turned out to be a seven-story building with two hundred or more rooms. Johann Strauss the Younger's pink-and-white stucco and brick home was now an apartment building with a McDonald's on the ground floor. Incidentally, there were as many McDonald's in Vienna as there were in Sacramento.

Schoenbrunn, the summer castle of the Hapsburgs, was a golden-colored palace of 1,200 rooms. One wing of the home was just for funeral paraphernalia such as horse-drawn glass carriages. The gardens were expansive. I only covered about a quarter of the back garden during my half-hour walk. There were so many flowers, bushes trimmed into ornamental shapes, a variety of huge, ancient shade trees, and ponds with statues.

World wars had been fought in this beautiful city—how sad. It was evident, though, when we traveled through downtown and the guide pointed out buildings that were austere and modern. They replaced buildings covered in Rococo figures and flowing lines that were destroyed by bombs. It had taken the Austrians through the 1950s and into the 1960s to clear the rubble in order to build the current buildings. It also took that long to stabilize their economy. The country was currently second to Germany as an economic leader in Europe. It was hard for me to comprehend why any country would ever go to war again after seeing the devastation of World War II.

July 2, 1993 I should correct the impression given of the American Embassy in Rome. We just learned today that the strange treatment we received was due to impending events. The United States was preparing to bomb Baghdad, Iraq. President Bush didn't tell us he was going to do that before we left home. Perhaps there was someone in the embassy building we weren't supposed to see. Ellen, a fellow student fluent in German, read about the bombing in the Austrian newspaper.

Professor Taylor warned us that Saddam Hussein had put out a contract on all Americans traveling abroad. We were told to keep a low profile. That wasn't possible while traveling with an exuberant group of young people. The excitement of seeing new things kept everyone hyped. None of us were able to disguise our citizenship.

After a six-hour bus trip, we arrived in Budapest, Hungary, at two p.m. and Jamie took her nap. I took off to explore Budapest and look for genuine Hungarian goulash. The desk clerk told me to take bus number 1 to get to the American War Memorial Park, and art gallery. He told me to catch the bus by walking through the lovely park adjacent to the hotel. I waited at that bus stop for about ten minutes and noticed only buses numbered 7, 7a, and 7b were stopping. I asked the fourth bus driver if I was at the correct stop to catch bus number 1. I could tell he didn't understand my question. After pointing to my bus ticket and to my map, he suggested I wait across the street at another bus stop going the opposite direction.

Buses with numbers 53 and 127 were stopping. When in a non-English-speaking country, it is good to remember younger people know English, not older people. I looked for a younger person. I watched a well-dressed young lady walking toward me from two blocks away. When she was near, I asked if she spoke English.

"Nein." I then pointed to the bus stop sign, my ticket, and my map showing where I wanted to go.

"Aah," she said and took hold of my elbow and escorted me three blocks in the direction from which she had just come. She stood at the bus stop holding my elbow, waiting until bus number 1 came along and I was safely boarded. *Fancy that*! What thoughtfulness from a perfect stranger.

As soon as I boarded the bus, a gentleman stood and gave me his seat, though the aisle was full of standing women. I think it was because I was wearing slacks; that gave me away as a tourist. Other ladies wore dresses or skirts and blouses.

We passed a beautiful building, and I asked the lady sitting next to me the name of it. She smiled and nodded. I ask the man who had given me his seat. He smiled and nodded.

I decided to play a game. I asked loudly if anyone on the bus spoke English. There was silence for a minute, then one man sheepishly spoke up, "Mickey Mouse." Another minute and a lady said, "Hollywood." That broke the ice. Different people all over the bus started saying words they knew in English: "hamburger, McDonald's, hot dog." They tried to teach me a few words of Hungarian. That really got folks laughing.

I turned to my seat partner, pointed to my chest, and said, "Marilyn." She smiled, pointed to herself, and said a word that I repeated. There was a snicker behind me. The lady said the word more slowly and louder; I mispronounced it slowly and louder. Someone laughed. I got so involved in the fun, I almost missed my debarkation point. We had been stopped for a few minutes before I woke up and saw the War Memorial on the opposite side of the bus. The lady who had helped me board the correct bus must have told the driver where I wanted to go. All occupants waved cheerily as I departed. One older woman hugged me. That brought tears to my eyes as I waved good-bye.

An engineering student told me that evening he had seen me on a city bus, and it looked like there was a party going on. I agreed it had been a very nice party.

I went about ten miles into town and found much of the architecture was similar to Austria and that steel and glass buildings replaced bombed buildings. They looked out of place.

I went to a park surrounding a castle that had been turned into a museum. The park was enormous and filled with people—men playing chess, ladies were doing needlepoint, young mothers playing with children, lovers walking hand in hand, people playing with their dogs. It was the first place on the trip I remembered seeing people with dogs.

There was a statue of George Washington in the park, and I heard a lady telling two children something about the statue. All I understood was the word *Washington*, but it was an admirable story, judging from the looks on the children's faces.

The park had a lake with paddle boats and fountains and of course, lots of statues of soldiers from various wars. I went from one to the other, admiring the sculpture and attempting to pronounce the names.

Then I went to the art gallery and found a statue by Rodin called *Sirens*, which I'd studied in art history at San Jose College, and a painting of a young lady dressed in black filmy curtain material done by John Quincy Adams in 1785 when he was eighteen years old and a student in Europe. The picture was no Michelangelo, but it was very good.

July 3, 1993 The students were scheduled to visit a graphic arts studio and learn how Hungarian businesses advertised. We drove to our meeting place, and a nice young man greeted us. He apologized, saying that when the appointment was made, he hadn't realized we would arrive on Saturday. The company was closed. He took us up five flights of stairs to a conference room to tell us facts about advertising in Budapest under current conditions.

The young man told us about problems that businesses had while they were trying to change from Communist to Capitalist. The country had been ceded to Russia as part of the Allies treaty with Germany at the end of World War II. Europe had been divided between east and west, and that started the Cold War. Hungary first revolted against Communism in 1956 and overcame it in 1989.

People in Hungary earned an average of $200.00 per month. There were no polls—such as Gallup—because people couldn't bring themselves to offer opinions. Communism taught people to keep their opinions to themselves. They wouldn't answer questions. That made it hard for businesses to target specific groups with their advertising.

There were a few billboards, but not much other public advertising. The advertising executive talked for an hour and a half, and then caterers served sandwiches and Coke.

Professor Taylor told us afterward that the young man rented the room and paid for the sandwiches out of his wages because he made the mistake of booking a tour on Saturday. We felt bad and wanted to refund his losses. Professor Taylor said he'd take care of it. We took up an impromptu collection and hoped it covered the expenses.

Joseph, the bus driver, dropped the students off downtown. Jamie and I shopped at a craft fair for a few minutes; indoor stores were closed Saturday afternoons. Then we took a taxi to Fisherman's Bastion on top of a hill overlooking the city. It was a castle replica. We watched a wedding party, including a gypsy with his violin. Oh, how romantic!

The temperature was near one hundred degrees. Jamie felt ill from the heat, so we caught a bus to the hotel. On the way there, we crossed the Danube, and I saw a church carved into a mountain. I mentioned that I really wanted to see that. There was supposed to be a labyrinth with apartments where people hid during wars.

Right away Jamie said, "Okay, let's get off at the next stop and walk back there." What an incredibly good sport she had been throughout the trip.

The caves were fascinating. We walked through a few passages in the labyrinth but were afraid to wander in too deeply for fear we'd get lost. They had been occupied since 4000 BC and were continually expanded as need arose. The Catholic Church had been in continual use for several centuries.

At the hotel we took advantage of the swimming pool. It felt wonderful. Later we went to an outdoor restaurant on the river and ate delicious pork steaks and salad. I never did find a restaurant that served Hungarian goulash. People said they ate it at home, not in restaurants.

July 4, 1993 During the seven-hour trip from Budapest, Hungary, to Salzburg, Austria, everyone told about having a good time in Budapest, but the stories were so different that it was hard to believe we were visiting the same place.

Austria was cleaner, neater, and more prosperous than Hungary. The people were not as friendly—not unfriendly, but just more conscious of proper behavior. We traveled the width of Austria. Hungary was on the eastern border. Salzburg was on the western border with Germany.

We ascended into the beautiful Alps with quaint villages, high granite escarpments, and alpine lakes dotted with sailboats.

Our hotel was in a quiet neighborhood, not the middle of downtown. Jamie and I caught a public bus and rode the full circuit, admiring the architecture and picturesque streets decorated with flower boxes and flags. We got off the bus at a *Gasthof* with a *biergarten* that looked shady and inviting.

There was only one customer in the garden. The waitress arrived at our table after a few minutes. We felt sorry for her as she had elephantiasis and shouldn't be working a job requiring so much walking. We asked if she had a menu, and she said, "Nein." We asked if the beer garden had food. She said, "Nein, just bread and sausage." We said that sounded great. We would each have an order of bread, sausage, and Spaten Hell (beer).

She brought us our beer immediately. Thirty minutes later she brought us two hot dogs on a plate with three hard rolls. It took three minutes to devour the food, and then we asked for our bill. The waitress disappeared into the kitchen. We waited and waited. We wanted to leave, so we went to the kitchen to ask for the check. There were four women standing in the room with a large shaggy dog—one of those dirty-minded male dogs. I smacked it hard three times before it kept its nose out of my business. We received our check, paid, and left. We wondered afterward what had taken so long for four women to cook two hot dogs and decided it was because they were busy fighting off the dog.

We sat in the front seat of our return bus so we could see our stop as we approached it. Jamie, like me, smiled a lot and generally enjoyed life. Our giggling and smiling set us apart from the stern-faced Austrian women. A gentleman handed each of us some edelweiss (flowers). We thanked him; he bowed and got off the bus. We later asked our hotel clerk what it meant when a man gave a woman edelweiss; she said it meant he admired her. She asked what it meant when a man gave a woman flowers in America. I realized how stupid my question had been.

We went to bed early. Jamie was asleep by eight thirty, and I was by ten. About eleven we were awakened by a terrific thunderstorm. The thunder was extremely loud, and there were bright flashes directly outside our window. The light show lasted about ten minutes, then it poured, and the wind blew violently. We considered that our Independence Day fireworks.

July 5, 1993 I wanted to see as much of Salzburg as possible before our ten a.m. departure. I was up at five thirty and off to the river for a walk, going the opposite direction as the previous evening. Everything looked and smelled freshly scrubbed after the rain.

About eight o'clock, our little clique of young women, plus Jamie and me, took the bus downtown. Jamie wanted to walk up a steep hill to a fortress. I opted to take the tram. We went our separate ways.

Karen joined me as I walked toward the tram. We toured the local basilica and its gardens. The walls had so much sculpture, they looked like lace. The church was an elegantly beautiful place of worship, and we wished we had more time to explore the nooks and crannies.

Karen didn't want to go to the fortress, so we parted company as she headed for the shops and I entered the tram. I saw Jamie exiting the fortress as I entered. We waved in passing.

There was a whole city inside the walls! Walkways and roads went in all directions. I felt like I was walking on a gravel spider web. Some of the roads were compacted dirt; men swept them with oversized brooms. It was easy to let my imagination run wild and picture Renaissance living in this setting. There was the usual butcher, baker, and candlestick maker, as well as the busy blacksmith. Customers were tourists. Salzburg had concerts and plays in the main *platz* (square). At nine thirty I took the tram downhill and returned to the hotel.

At ten o'clock we students piled onto our bus for the trip to Munich. A lengthy stop at the border delayed our progress for an hour. Giuseppe

(Joseph), our bus driver, said Italian buses were inspected more closely and charged higher border taxes. He didn't elaborate, so we were left to surmise why.

We arrived in Munich after another gorgeous trip through the Alps. Some of us decided it was time to hit the laundry. We had been rinsing things each evening in our hotel bathrooms.

The laundry *(waschsalon)* was challenging. I brought detergent from home. Jamie and I put our clothes in together, and I put a package of detergent into each washer. We then tried to figure out which German coin would fit into the slot to start the machine. None fit.

I asked a young man with a ponytail and a ring in his nose to show us how to use the washer. My first question, of course, was, "Do you speak English?"

His answer: "A bit. I'm from Liverpool."

We needed a five deutsche mark coin and a one deutsche mark coin to put into the token dispenser, which would then emit a coin for the washer *and* a cup of soap. The machine wouldn't give me just the token. I poured two cups of detergent back into my plastic bags; we could use that later.

The Liverpudlian was about to leave, so I asked him about coins for the dryer. He said, "One deutschmark for each twenty-minute cycle." That made sense, but I couldn't figure out which one of the slots on the token dispenser was marked "dryer." One slot was marked with a word that had "*mangle*" in the center. I remembered that my employers, when I was a teenager, had an industrial iron in their home called a mangler, so I figured that slot must have been for the pressing contraption in the corner of the room. We already eliminated the *"was-serauto,"* where we had gotten tokens and detergent for the washer. We had three more slots to choose from. The boy from Liverpool said he used one slot to get a token for the wringer-dryer. I thought that must have been his term for the dryer.

Just as soon as I bought two tokens, I heard an awful noise behind me. I knew immediately what it was. In Australia, where I had lived for eight years, there was a special cylinder on washing machines where wet clothes were put and spun around so fast that everything inside was wrung almost dry. It also tore clothes, ripped off buttons, broke zippers, and permanently wrinkled your clothes. That was the wringer-dryer the boy had used for his dungarees. I gave those tokens to Karen for her jeans after forewarning what might happen.

Now, we were down to two slots to choose from. I asked a German man to show me which machine used the tokens that came out of the slot marked *"wasserspheil."* He sounded out the syllables slowly and loudly in German as though that would make me understand. I said, *"Danke,"* and tried someone else. The second man handed me a little cup. He opened a lid on top of the washer and showed me where the wasserspheil went. I smelled the cup. "Bleach! *Danke, danke."* That left us with one slot. I purchased one token, and it fit the dryer's coin slot perfectly. Yea, success!

Of course, we did have to make three trips to the sweet shop for change to get coins for the token dispenser, but that's a whole different story.

After two hours in the steamy laundry, we were drained of energy. The temperature outside felt like one-hundred degrees. Inside it must have been a hundred-fifteen degrees. I was sick to my stomach from the heat, and Jamie had a headache. We dragged ourselves and our clothes to our hotel room, drank a quart of water, and rested for an hour.

That's when we observed the street noise, which was so loud, we could hardly hear each other. We turned on the television to get the news and had to jack the volume up as high as it would go to hear the announcer. We called the front desk to see if they could give us a quieter room. No rooms were available for people in our group except the ones assigned.

When we were revitalized, we went to the garden dining area and ordered Hungarian goulash (we were in Germany, so they had it in restaurants). It was a packaged meal with little slices of bread covered in a tasty cream-cheese spread, sliced tomatoes, and a red wine similar in taste to Chianti. The goulash was lean steak with potatoes in chili gravy. It was wonderful!

We returned to our room after dinner and took cool showers (no air conditioning, pool, or fly screens at this four-star hotel in modern Munich). We closed the windows to make the street noise tolerable for sleeping, took sleeping pills, used earplugs, and dropped off to sleep.

I woke up two hours later drenched with sweat. I opened a window and was immediately assaulted by noise. It was raining and cooler outside. There was a breeze, and it felt so good. I left the window open and took another cool shower.

I think it was a combination of the sleeping pill and the wine from dinner, but I was suddenly gripped with panic. I couldn't remember taking my passport out of my pocket when I came home from the Laundromat.

I searched my bags as quietly as possible. Of course, I still woke up Jamie. I turned on the light and found my passport on the bedside table where I left it. Then both of us rolled and tossed the rest of the night. I expected Jamie to request a different roommate the next day, but she didn't. I thought no one in the world would put up with all my nonsense, except Marlow, my sweet, tolerant husband.

July 6, 1993 Coffee, strong coffee, that's what everyone needed to start the day. The kids had been sampling *biergartens* until two in the morning. The oldsters fought heat, humidity, and noise all night. We were scheduled for the most interesting factory tour of the trip—Ziemersteins.

What an enormous plant! The building was twice the size of the General Motors plant in Austria. It would be hard to surpass the educational opportunity offered at General Motors, but the potential was there. Ziemersteins in Munich made computer hardware components.

We were led into a dimly lit room and asked to sit at a U-shaped table. Franz asked what questions we had about Ziemersteins. He collected a dozen questions and took an hour to answer them. I took copious notes as a ruse for staying awake. I eagerly awaited the anticipated tour. I glanced around. There were three alert faces; the rest looked like zombies. A couple had their eyes closed and mouths hanging open.

Franz introduced Kirk, whom we hoped would show us the factory. Students started to rise; he motioned us to sit down. He flicked a switch and a slide show of charts and figures was revealed on the flat screen at the open end of the table. The fiscal year of Ziemersteins was impacted by declining economic growth, but they managed to eke out thirteen billion deutschmarks profit.

Students settled back into semi-reclining positions in preparation for another snooze.

"Every company has problems to overcome," he said. "People everywhere have their Africans."

No one's eyes were closed anymore.

"You in America have the slave descendants to hold you back," Kirk continued as students sat upright in their chairs.

"Here in Europe, our Africans are the Italians and Greeks."

Joseph, our friendly, smiling bus driver from Rome, and his bride were in the room. The smile faded from Joseph's face for the first time on our European tour.

We had four Greek descendants and two Italians in the student group. Clenched jaws twitched, but they said nothing.

I held my breath and hoped someone who spoke more eloquently than me would tell Kirk to shove his personal opinions up his lily-white Aryan bodily aperture. No one spoke. Perhaps we had too much class to say what we were thinking. Perhaps we were cowards. I was ashamed I held my tongue.

After Kirk's financial dissertation on the company's prognosis for the coming year, we were asked to wait in the foyer. There was a lot of mumbling, and one person after another approached Professor Taylor.

Many of us were heavy water drinkers and most felt dehydrated after perspiring all night. I asked the girl at the information desk where we could get water. She said she thought there was a fountain on the third floor but wasn't sure. About that time Kirk announced there were drinks awaiting us in the dining area. The drinks were various colors, and we assumed they were fruit juice. Wrong! They were alcohol! Just what we needed. Jamie thought she had carbonated grapefruit drink and took a long drink before she heard someone say it was a champagne and vodka. Mine turned out to be orange juice and champagne. I drank it, took the glass to the nearest restroom, and downed three glasses of water.

Kirk and Franz swung open double doors to display an elegant lunch set on fine china dishes, with fluted crystal glasses sparkling by each silver set of utensils. The company had gone to a great deal of trouble to impress the visiting Americans.

Professor Taylor walked to the open door and said quietly, "It is by unanimous decision that we have chosen not to partake of any further hospitality. We came here to learn how your plant was being prepared for joining the European Union. Obviously, your plant will have to wait until your personnel join the twentieth century in their attitudes toward others."

With that, Mr. Taylor headed for the exit, followed by twenty eight smiling students. A short distance away, we obtained enough McDonald's hamburgers and fries for everyone to eat their fill, including Joseph and his wife, who were beaming from ear to ear.

We had an hour's rest before our scheduled city tour of Munich. The tour was a bit different. Ninety-five percent of the buildings in downtown Munich had been destroyed by Allied forces in World War II. Amid all the rebuilt structures stood Hitler's quarters, which had escaped unscathed. How very sad that reminder of the cause of the destruction must have been to the many citizens who lost loved ones and their livelihood during the war.

The government gave prizes to owners of buildings that were reproduced as close as possible to the original historic architecture. The population was currently 1.3 million. People looked and acted affluent. In general, they were rude, like they really wished tourists would leave their money and go home. People displayed a noticeable frustration with our lack of knowledge of their language. (Had I inherited my brusqueness from my lovable, ornery German paternal grandmother?)

We were at the Glockenspiel, the chiming clock tower, in time to watch the puppet dance. That lasted ten minutes. I wondered if locals came to see the show. It seemed like a pretty big deal to go through to change from one hour to the next.

Jamie wanted room service for dinner and an early night. I went to the hotel restaurant alone and had real German sausage and sauerkraut (cooked until it was brown) with new potatoes. A gypsy played his violin just for me. I felt self-conscious but didn't know how to politely tell him to go away. There was only one other customer in the restaurant, so I guess the musician felt he had to play for one or the other of us, and he chose me because I was female.

July 7, 1993 I skipped the class's brewery tour. I'd been to a brewery in Washington State, and the most interesting thing there was the salmon runs in the Columbia River outside the plant.

Instead, I bought tickets for a tour of Bavarian castles. Bavaria is a state in Germany. The countryside was adorned with prosperous, neat farms and postcard-perfect villages. The people loved flowers, and there were flower boxes at most windows. The houses and barns were joined. Each end was painted a different color; usually the house was white and the barn was brown, and each end had a different type of roof. I was told they were joined because of the inclement weather. Animals were kept in the barn most of the winter, and farmers didn't have to go outside to care for them. I inquired if people had problems with mice and insects because of the close proximity of animals, manure and fodder but got a shrug as a response.

The bus passed many, many planted forests with old growth standing proudly among the young trees. I wished the timber industry from our Northwest would learn something from the Germans about running their businesses, instead of destroying everything, regardless of age or scarcity, and leaving us with naked mountains, followed eventually by new growth of bushes and deciduous trees.

No snow was seen on the Alps. I thought they had glaciers. They were glorious granite peaks scraping the blue sky. The skies were dotted with hang gliders, parasails, and gliders (motorless airplanes) gracefully choreographing performances.

One hunting lodge castle was owned by the Bavarian bachelor king called Mad Ludwig II in the late 1800s. It had so much gold, it was gaudy, but the gardens were beautiful. They were filled with Bourbon kings' busts (he really admired the Bourbons), flowers, and ponds. Europeans had a special affection for swans, and the graceful white birds seemed fitting in a regal pond. Ludwig had men carve a grotto out of the side of the mountain, complete with a subterranean lake, stalactites, and stalagmites. That was an idea he got from Wagner's opera, *Tannhauser.* Being king was a lucrative business in those days. He had lots of money to spend, and he loved spending it. He had massive parties with Europe's royal elite in attendance, hunting parties that lasted several days, and gambling parties where wealthy people ate, drank, and lavishly threw money at games of chance.

Another of his castles was Königsschloss Neuschwanstein, which he didn't care for much after building it, so he spent very little time there. I thought Königsschloss Neuschwanstein was outstanding! Walt Disney used it as a model for the iconic Disneyland castle. The original was designed by a stage-set designer, not an architect. It had enough gold and art to pay off the national debt. Neuschwanstein was decorated with beautiful paintings from various operas as well as religious themes. I loved the rich woodwork, marble, and paintings. I climbed to the top of the highest parapet, a real accomplishment for me, and soaked in the atmosphere. I hugged myself and laughed out loud at the thought that little Marilyn Leddy from Columbus, Ohio, who wanted to grow up to be a gypsy, was actually standing on top of a castle in Bavaria. I was so glad the Allies didn't destroy this decadent example of extravagance.

European nobility certainly lived lavishly. Ludwig II was the son of Maximilian II, who was science-minded and did a lot of good things for his people. Unfortunately, he never took the time to train his son in politics and kingdom ruling. When Maximilian died unexpectedly, the people were left with a nineteen-year-old king who only knew how to play.

Oberammergau, the next stop on the tour, was a Bavarian village, where there was a plague in 1634. The people promised God that if he'd spare them, they'd recreate the crucifixion on a regular basis. The whole town participated in an eight-hour passion play once every ten years. The actors playing the part of Jesus endured hanging from a cross suspended by real nails through their hands.

The commercial buildings downtown and the residences in town had biblical murals or scenes from Grimm's fairy tales painted on their walls. Almost everyone in the village was artistically talented in one way or another—woodworking, lace making, landscaping, cake decorating, or clock manufacturing.

I made friends with two Australian couples on the tour bus, and we had a great time together. They were touring Europe on a shoestring and found interesting ways to save a "quid" and still see the major points of interest. I felt good when I got back to Munich because I'd spent the day among beauty and happy people.

Then I met Jamie and Karen, who had spent the afternoon in Dachau, the concentration camp. They were really bummed.

July 8, 1993 On the long and scenic road to Zurich, I changed my mind about the Germans. They weren't just frustrated with the tourists' lack of knowledge of their language; they were rude. Can't say I blame the Munich citizens for being upset with the Allies for destroying 95 percent of their buildings, but we tourists didn't personally do it. Our fathers and uncles did it. We didn't start the war, and neither did our fathers and uncles; the Germans did. And of course, all military men were just "following orders."

I spent time on the bus contemplating the pros and cons of today's world if there had never, ever been any wars. Would the world be a better place? Just think of a utopia where everyone only takes what he needs and shares whatever he has—where everyone is tolerant and respectful of his neighbor's choice of beliefs, and no one considers himself more important than anyone else. I know, that sounds like I'd been smoking funny mushrooms.

Al and Delores were a thoroughly charming couple from San Jose. Al left his wallet on the counter when he checked out of the hotel in Munich. When he called to see if anyone had given it to lost and found, the clerk made rude remarks and hung up on him. Nancy left her purse with her passport and credit cards in her room. She called housekeeping, and they confirmed finding it. They said they'd send it via DHL (European Federal Express) and it should arrive the next day. It didn't. Nancy phoned again and was told she'd have to go back to Munich and get the purse. The catch was that she couldn't cross the border into Germany without her passport. Karen volunteered to go back on the train and retrieve the purse. We were afraid the desk clerk wouldn't release the purse to her. Thank goodness she did. Karen lost a day with the group, but all ended well for Nancy. It took Al four days to get his American Express traveler's checks replaced, and several long-distance calls to report his lost credit and other identification cards.

In Munich, when Jamie and I ordered something in a restaurant, the waiter asked us a question. We didn't understand the question and asked him to repeat it. He slammed his order book closed, turned on his heels, and marched back to the kitchen without repeating his question. Now, that's just plain rude! Our food and check were curtly delivered without another word.

Would I return to Munich if given the chance? Absolutely. I'd just know what to expect and wouldn't spend any more time in the city than necessary to book tours of Bavaria.

In Zurich, Switzerland, the hotel staff was polite and friendly. The room was luxurious and large. There was air conditioning (the first time since Rome) and a pool. We received real food for breakfast (in Germany, we were offered a hard roll and a cup of coffee, nothing else).

Jamie, Al, Delores, and I checked into the hotel, then headed for the station to catch a train downtown. We got separated in the busy terminal and spent a while looking for each other. Al and I were together, and Jamie and Delores were together. We looked for Jamie and Delores for about fifteen minutes with no luck. I said I thought Jamie would have gone across the street to the museum when she got tired of looking for us. Al and Delores had been married over forty years, and he felt sure Delores wouldn't leave the station until she found him. He was right, of course. We took the routes Al thought Delores would follow and soon met the lost ladies.

The financial district of Zurich exuded money. There was an open tram that served sushi and cocktails as it transported workers home in the evening. There were expensive sidewalk restaurants and pubs and exquisite stores lining the streets. We ate at a hotel dining room overlooking the street and watched the people parade. It was a most enjoyable evening. May the Swiss live long and prosper.

July 9, 1993 All the students had a good breakfast, which included a variety of meats, egg dishes, breads, cereals, and juices and courteous service—what a treat!

We were off to Migros, the giant food producer in Switzerland. The corporation was started in 1920 when Mr. Migros bought five trucks and carried six products—rice, pasta, coffee, soap, sugar, and coconut oil. The owner and his employees traveled around city neighborhoods and country towns in company-owned trucks selling Migros products more cheaply than the stationary stores. A year later he built his first store, which stocked one thousand items. Suppliers were jealous of his immediate success, so they boycotted delivery to Migros. That was when Mr. Migros and his family decided to build their own factories to supply his store. The project became a co-op and expanded to include clothing, banking, and insurance, plus all the items you would normally find in the most modern American supermarkets. They produced 95 percent of their own products. Hurrah for entrepreneurial enterprise!

After the factory tour, we went back to the luxurious hotel. Many students relaxed and used the hotel's pool the balance of the day.

Al, Delores, and I went to town, where we caught a boat on the Zurichsee. The trip was four hours of fun. We ate sausage and bread, drank beer, and made friends with local folks.

One man introduced himself, saying his brother taught English, and he had learned a bit of our language. He wanted to practice. We started out with basic questions, such as, "What is your name?" and "Where do you live?"

When I said I lived in California, the Swiss gent's children joined us to ply me with questions.

"Are Mickey and Minnie Mouse married?"

"Is Pluto Mickey's friend or his pet?" The twelve-year-old daughter was more interested in Tom Cruise.

I asked the father what type of work he did, and he replied he was a baker. I thought about all the hard rolls I'd eaten the past couple of weeks, but didn't comment on them.

He asked me if I worked. I told him, "Yes, I'm an aerospace manufacturing engineer."

A totally blank look came over his face, so I said, "You know—missiles and rockets sending communication devices into outer space."

He still looked at me with glazed-over eyes.

"I had a teensy, tiny bit to do with the production of the space shuttle."

He immediately jumped up and talked to several other people in the vicinity. They came forward smiling and wanted to shake my hand.

I heard the baker telling one man, "This lady made the space shuttle!"

I didn't correct the impression. It would have been too complicated to translate.

Each town we passed along the emerald shores of the lake had a white building with a clock tower. I thought they were churches, but later learned they were municipal buildings. There were a few single-family residences in towns, but mainly white, austere (after Rococo Budapest, Vienna, and Munich) apartment complexes. Farms on the outskirts of towns had quaint gingerbread homes. They were what I expected to find throughout Switzerland. They looked like something Heidi might pop out of at any moment to go in search of a goat or to hang a load of clothes.

July 10, 1993 In the early morning, the class was off to Lugano, Switzerland. We made it about ten minutes into the trip when an alarm went off in the bus. Joseph tried for about half an hour to get the buzzing to stop. We were parked in a gas station a few blocks from our last hotel. He came to the conclusion we were having brake failure and he couldn't fix it himself. He called a mechanic, who showed up shortly and worked on the brakes. It was three hours before we got back on the road.

We drove an hour and arrived in Lucerne. Some people wanted to shop for Swiss chocolate, Swiss watches, and/or Swiss army knives. We stayed in Lucerne for three hours.

I walked to the top of the hill and went around a fortress. I could hear faint music and decided it was wind chimes. After I got over the crest of the hill, I saw several cows and goats wearing various-sized bells. I was located somewhere in the middle of the book, *Heidi*. The joy overwhelmed me, and tears welled in my eyes. I wished I could share the feeling of beauty with all the Americans who never travel further than their own neighborhood.

It started to rain, our first rainy day on the trip. I reluctantly headed toward the commercial section of town in search of shelter. Looking down on the river, churches, stores, and all the colorful umbrellas was like looking at a live Pissarro impressionist painting. I worked my way down to a long pedestrian bridge built in 1333 that crossed the swan-studded river. There were flower boxes filled with pansies along the sides of the bridge. The interior had historical events depicted in paintings, and accordion players entertained the pedestrians. I mean, really now, doesn't that sound just too, too European? It was like a fairy tale. The town was magical.

I found a flea market and bought a suitcase for two francs to cart home some of the souvenirs I'd picked up during our travels. Two francs is equal to about $1.25. I didn't know if the suitcase would hold up until I got to Sacramento, but it was worth the try.

When we piled onto the bus, people displayed their bargains—jewelry, dolls, knives, and lots of postcards. Jamie was sitting a couple of seats behind me and shouted, "Marilyn, show them the bowling bag you bought!" How embarrassing, she was right! My flea market suitcase was actually a bowling bag! I never owned a bowling ball. How the heck did I know what a bowling bag looked like?

We made it to Lugano, a touristy ski resort located on a lake. Jamie, Nancy, Ayudi, Ellen, and I had dinner at the hotel. It was an Italian restaurant with checkered tablecloths and a big fireplace. Very cozy. Europeans like Italian food as well as Americans do. That was the most prevalent type of restaurant we found in each country we visited. I loved Italian food, so that suited me fine. I had minestrone, and it was excellent.

July 11, 1993 Happy birthday to me! The day started out perfect. Jamie ordered room service for breakfast and shared with me. We sat in bed, propped on pillows like we were Mrs. Astor, leisurely ate and read.

I looked out the window and saw a cable-car track going up the side of a mountain. I suggested we take that to the top. Jamie wasn't enthused, but agreed to my idea when I told her, "That'll be my birthday treat to myself. I'll pay for both of us."

A ferry took us across a pristine lake. We went by cable car to the top of Mount San Salvador and walked the trails. We could see snow on the Alps from the previous day's storm. We saw alpine lakes all around us.

Jamie and I had a cup of tea in a glassed-in coffee shop and enjoyed the warmth. That was the second day I required a jacket; the previous day had been the first. We started the decline in a cable car. Lugano, lakes, forests, and mountains spread out before us. I told Jamie to look at the incredibly beautiful scene. She said she couldn't. I asked why not. She said she was afraid of heights. I looked at her, and she was hanging on so tight, her knuckles were white, and her eyes couldn't have been pried open. Why didn't she tell me she was afraid of heights before we started up the hill? She didn't want to spoil my birthday. Wasn't she amazing?

We went to the shore of Lago di Lugano and took a ferry from Paradisio to Gandria. At Gandria, there were no vehicles; there were no roads; there were only sidewalks with lots of stairs. The buildings were constructed of stone with clay tile roofs and of course, had flower boxes wherever possible.

The boat trip got us back to our hotel just in time for our meeting to summarize the educational part of the trip. Jack Taylor, the professor, had gotten me an ornament that said "Happy birthday" in Swiss. I didn't expect that! He presented it to me at the end of the meeting. It certainly had been a happy day.

July 12, 1993 The day arrived to head home. I knew it was the last day by looking at my supplies. I had $100.00 in traveler's checks and one roll of film left. The class rode from Lugano to Milan in a subdued manner. Some people were extending their tours, and some were heading home. We knew we might not see one another again.

On the flight I slept soundly for three hours, awoke refreshed, and spent the balance of the trip chatting with neighbors or looking out the galley window to view polar ice caps.

After a smooth twelve-hour flight, we rushed through customs and dashed to catch our flights from Los Angeles to our final destinations. Out of the original twenty seven people, there were only six on the final leg of the trip to Sacramento. It was sad to say good-bye to my new friends. I'm sure I'll think of them many times in the future.

Eight

Alaskan Inside Passage Cruise

1997

I don't like eating in restaurants unless they have unusual ambience, such as Japanese chefs chopping, slicing, and dicing at the table before searing the food to perfection on a tableside hibachi. I abhor calling dinner at a restaurant a celebration of a special event like an anniversary or birthday. Therefore, Marlow and I usually plan unusual activities for our anniversaries. We have been on hot-air balloons, shark fishing expeditions, white-water rafting trips, and so forth. Things we wouldn't do on an ordinary day. We eat every day; that's no way to celebrate a once-in-a-lifetime event like a fortieth wedding anniversary. I suggested a cruise, and Marlow said he'd like to see the Inside Passage of Alaska. Plans were made, confirmed, and carried out.

June 15, 1997 Most writers would call day one uneventful, meaning everything went as planned. It was Father's Day, so Marlow opened his presents from me, a hummingbird feeder and a cassette of elevator music. I'm into heavy metal or classical myself. He filled the hummingbird feeder and hung it on the front porch. We put the cassette into the truck tape player and started toward our first destination—Margo and

Ben's house. Our daughter-in-law's parents consented to our leaving our truck parked at their house during our cruise.

We transferred luggage from our truck to Ben's, and he delivered us to Princess Cruise Line's shuttle stop. We arrived thirty minutes early, so we were able to get acquainted with two other couples taking the same trip. I mentioned that we were celebrating our fortieth wedding anniversary. Both couples were also celebrating their fortieth anniversary! It must be a popular way to celebrate.

The bus arrived. The driver emerged and greeted us while lifting a huge door on the side of the bus. We put our suitcases next to the open luggage compartment and climbed onboard. Since we were the first people on the bus, we sat in my favorite spot, the front seat opposite the driver—the best place for viewing the scenery. We'd have more legroom and wouldn't have someone lowering a seatback into our faces.

Traffic was normal for Sunday morning, and we cruised along smoothly from Sacramento to San Francisco. I read a brochure on Victoria, British Columbia. Victoria would be our first cruise port, and I wanted to discuss shore plans with Marlow.

I had finished that task when the driver started telling us about the history of the area we were riding through. He told how much of San Francisco Bay had been filled-in to use for building houses and commercial buildings. The structures were built on unstable, unnatural surface and therefore were subject to structural damage from earthquakes. The bay was only about 40 percent as large as it had been a hundred fifty years ago. Fortunately, it's no longer permissible to dump debris into the bay to build up land for construction. The cities around the bay had learned the hard way about liquefaction.

By the time the driver had completed his interesting speech, we were pulling off the freeway onto the Embarcadero, and up to Pier 35 where our beautiful cruise ship was docked.

We climbed the stairs to the highest deck, which meant going twelve stories, and took pictures of the ship and shore. We wended our way back to our cabin on the fourth floor. Our bags had been deposited inside, so I unpacked and wrote two letters while Marlow napped.

He awoke when the captain announced over a loudspeaker built into our headboard that we were ready for departure. We joined the portside supervisors (similar to "sidewalk supervisors" at a construction site). We dutifully helped direct the tugboats as they maneuvered the ship away from the docks and into lanes of ocean-bound vehicles. Sailboats and pleasure cruisers joined us in a parade as we left beautiful, sunny San Francisco. We went past dark, dismal Alcatraz and under the gleaming Golden Gate Bridge.

The wind was strong and cold as we approached the open ocean. Soon after passing beneath the Golden Gate, we were enveloped in fog. I was chilled in a matter of minutes.

We went to our room and tidied our windblown bodies in preparation for dinner. We met our dinner mates, Gene and Janet, a retired couple from Long Beach, who were pleasant people.

After dinner we attended the first stage show. We were introduced to entertainment personnel and enjoyed short singing, dancing, and comedy acts.

Back in our cabin, we snuggled into warm beds. The room temperature was cooler than I liked, so I asked our room stewardess, Lynn, a lady from the Philippines, for an extra blanket. We read and let the mild boat movement rock us to sleep.

June 16, 1997 When I awoke at seven thirty, Marlow was arriving back from his first trip topside. He had drunk morning coffee and watched the foggy day arrive.

I leisurely dressed, and we went to our assigned restaurant and to our assigned table for breakfast. Gene and Janet were already there. The dining room was quiet, and we got acquainted. Gene and I had a hard time hearing individual conversations in a noisy room, so we agreed that at dinner, when the room was filled with chattering people, we'd just nod and smile. Marlow got an evil-looking grin on his face, but I thought it best to ask him in private what thought had popped into his head. What was he going to ask me to do, when he knew I'd just nod in agreement?

Marlow and I strolled along the decks in the morning gloom looking for whales, land, or points of interest. The day was windy and cold, and nothing was in view, so we checked out enclosed public areas and found the casino, where people were busy depositing coins. I wondered if they'd been there all night. Marlow joined them and quickly went through twenty dollars. We meandered through shops trying to entice us with overpriced merchandise. We checked out the game room used for playing cards or board games, or building picture puzzles. We went back to our cabin, where Marlow watched television, read, and napped. I wrote the previous day's happenings in my journal.

After dinner we took in the Las Vegas-style stage show called *New York, New York*. There were lots of bright-colored costumes, singing, and dancing. The show was almost, but not quite, professional.

We ended our day by going to the movie theater and seeing a delightful movie called *We the People* with Jack Lemmon and James Garner.

June 17, 1997 Marlow and I awoke to fog. By the time we had eaten breakfast, the weather deteriorated into rain. We went wildlife hunting on deck and spotted our first animals—orca whales. They came close enough for people with really good cameras to photograph them. My photos would have shown little black spots on a whole lot of water, so I just admired them through binoculars.

We walked through the public passageways of five stories for a bit of exercise, then went back to the room and read until lunch. Marlow read science fiction, and I was reading a biography of Queen Victoria. I daresay his book was probably much more exciting.

We went on deck and found the rain had stopped. The ship sat in Victoria Harbor; we disembarked and explored Victoria, British Columbia. We took a shuttle from the ship to the city center in front of the wonderful Old World Empress Hotel. I loved European architecture with massive staircases, natural wood, ornate ceilings, and crystal chandeliers.

Around the corner from the Empress, we found the Crystal Gardens, a glass enclosure of tropical plants and a few animals. One section was devoted to butterflies, and that was delightful. The plants, waterfalls, birds, and landscaping were exotic and entertaining. After over an hour of viewing those treasures, we were ready to sit down for a while.

We hopped onto a public bus and went for a ride through the suburbs. Victoria was known as a garden city. They had potted plants hanging from lampposts. Lawns were manicured and decorated with a great variety of colorful flowers. Victoria received an average of a hundred eighty inches of rain a year to water those plants.

On the return trip, the bus got very crowded with locals on their way home from work, and we missed seeing our landmark, The Empress Hotel. We went twelve blocks too far before we realized we were seeing some places for the second time. We walked an hour against a cold, damp wind. I was chilled once more and tired by the time we arrived onboard.

I soaked in the hot tub and went to bed. Marlow went to dinner and the show, where he saw a comedian and a harmonica player.

June 18, 1997 We slept in late, really late—eight o'clock, too late for breakfast in the dining room. The ship ran on schedules. There were two seatings for meals, and if we were fifteen minutes late for our seating, we could not enter the dining room. Food was available in other restaurants, so it didn't matter.

As I dressed, I fantasized about a plain bowl of oatmeal and a glass of orange juice on a sunny deck. The cafeteria I had in mind was enclosed with picture windows. I told Marlow I'd meet him in there. I planned on relaxing over a cup of hot tea before obtaining food. I thought by the time Marlow dressed and joined me, everyone else would have gone ashore in Vancouver.

Wrong! As soon as I got to a place on the ship where I could see outside, I saw it was pouring rain. We had an inside cabin with no windows. People who should have been spread throughout the ship, or on shore, were crowded into the cafeteria. After waiting in line fifteen minutes, I managed to get a bowl of oatmeal, but had to eat it in the bar. Marlow and I never saw each other in the melee.

The crowds of noisy people were beginning to stress me. The weather didn't help. I felt like I was being held prisoner in a restaurant.

I gladly returned to our tiny room, thinking I'd crawl under the covers and read until Marlow returned and switched on the television.

When he did arrive, Marlow suggested we get off the ship in spite of the weather and see what we could find on shore. We gathered our cameras and rain paraphernalia and were ready to leave the ship when the sun came out. It was a glorious, fresh, clear day.

We toured Canada Place, built for a World's Fair, a Vancouver landmark designed to look like sailing ships. We spent thirty minutes listening to classical violin music performed by a twelve-year-old boy and his father. The beauty of the performance made our hearts sing.

Canada Place had an IMAX theatre, so we bought tickets for two movies, *Alaska* and *Underwater*. Those three-dimensional movies were scheduled for later in the day.

We walked a couple of blocks to the Skytrain terminal, another World's Fair feature, and took the elevated train several miles into the suburbs and back without a chance of getting lost. The only other people in our car were a couple also looking for a cheap way to see the city.

We arrived back at Canada Place with five minutes to spare before the first movie started. Our seats were reserved, so there was no problem walking right in and getting the best seats in the packed house. The seven-story screen made the mountains and glaciers of Alaska real. We reignited the excitement of being on a cruise headed to that beautiful state. While in the warm theater, the wind blowing across the glaciers looked lovely, and we didn't think about how cold it would be standing in that wind.

The movie on underwater life off the coast of Northern California was not only informative but beautiful. The three-dimensional effect gave the illusion that people seated in front of us were underwater with the fish and plants. I had no idea we had so many wonderful sea creatures in Monterey Bay. When I had seen the title of the movie, I took it for granted the movie would be about the Great Barrier Reef in Australia. It was a most enjoyable way to spend a couple of hours.

After the movies we walked through Gastown, the oldest section of Vancouver, to the tallest building in western Canada. The building closely resembled the Space Needle of Seattle, with a revolving top.

We snapped lots of pictures as we walked the circumference of the exterior of the restaurant.

Later on the cruise ship, I photographed our departure from Vancouver, a lovely, sophisticated city. The setting on the bay with the Cascade Mountains as a backdrop was picturesque. We passed under a bridge designed by the same group of men who designed the Golden Gate Bridge—Leon Moisseiff, Joseph Strauss, Irving Morrow, and Charles Alton Ellis—and were soon on our way up the Inside Passage to Alaska. The sun playing among the clouds and the long lingering twilight made for a pleasant evening. We sat outside after dark and watched the little towns of Vancouver Island slide by in the night.

We went to the floor show. I have to tell you a joke that we heard tonight. It's immature, just my level of humor.

Two men were traveling throughout England. They chose to eat fish and chips as much as possible, as that was one man's favorite meal. They came to a tiny town that was famous for its fish and chips restaurant run by the Catholic Church.

The fish and chips gourmet was overwhelmed with the deliciousness of the meal and asked to give his compliments to the chef.

The waitress said he could find the cook behind the dining-room door, down the hall on the right, the second door on the left. The travelers followed the directions and came to a room with a man standing at the stove wearing a brown wool robe tied at the waist with a rope. He wore sandals and a funny haircut.

"Excuse me," said the gourmet, "are you the fish fryer?"

"No," the man answered, "I'm the chip monk."

June 19, 1997 We were scheduled to be at sea all day; it would have been a good day to sleep in late. But instead we went topside and were treated to entertainment by schools of porpoises. We saw Dall's porpoises, which were black and white, and had been mistaken for small Orcas.

We lunched among the hordes of starving, chattering passengers who pushed and shoved to make sure they got their platters filled with enough food to feed a family of five. Marlow and I ate twice as much each meal as I would have at home. Maybe the tendency was contagious. We had each gained nearly ten pounds since the beginning of the trip. I found that disgusting and vowed to cut back on food consumption.

Passengers were definitely distinctive groups. Ninety-five percent were Caucasian, 4 percent Asian, and 1 percent other. Ninety percent were over sixty, 75 percent were couples, 24 percent were single women. Those were statistics scientifically calculated by me at lunch.

There were perhaps twenty youngsters out of twelve-hundred passengers. There were six-hundred crew members, mostly third-world residents supporting families; the officers were European.

Since Marlow didn't want to pack enough clothes to last the whole trip, I asked him to help me with the laundry. Next time he'll be willing to carry a heavier suitcase with enough clothes to last the whole excursion. The laundry was steamy hot and crammed with people wanting to take advantage of the day at sea. We had three loads of clothes and had to wait in line for both washers and dryers. That killed a few hours. The dryers didn't work well, so we took damp clothes to our room and hung them on hangers.

There was no sign of dinner preparations in the aft deck cafeteria where Marlow chose to eat. I told him everyone was expected to partake of the formal party in the dining room. He didn't believe me until almost five thirty, when he finally asked a deckhand. We dashed to our cabin, showered, and dressed formal. We made it just in time for the six fifteen p.m. deadline to be allowed to sit at our assigned table. I felt thrown together. Of course, that was the night everyone was expected to pose for pictures. I thought, *Yeah, right. Those will be memorable.* Believe it or not, they were the best pictures taken in years. Marlow was progressively getting more handsome with maturity. I noticed that before seeing the proof on film.

I wanted to make sure we got to the show early so we could get seats down front. The showroom had several columns to block people's view, and the seats in the back were not conducive to short folks. If we weren't one of the first hundred people in the room, we didn't get good seats. We went to the theater at seven forty five p.m. for a scheduled eight-fifteen show. An usher at the door said we couldn't enter until eight-ten. We went upstairs to watch the twilight for twenty minutes. When we returned, five-hundred people were in line.

I skipped the show and went to bed. My book would tell me what Victoria and Albert were up to. Marlow had a couple of beers in a small pub and came to the cabin about midnight.

June 20, 1997 We turned the clocks back when the captain announced we were passing into a different time zone.

Marlow dressed and left the room to stake out his favorite viewing spot on deck. I folded clean clothes and organized for the day. I wanted to take everything upstairs I needed for our trip into Juneau. In Vancouver I had made three trips to the room to get forgotten paraphernalia.

We whale watched with a bit of luck—saw a couple of humpbacks fairly close to the ship. Marlow saw another school of porpoise while I was still in the room. We sailed up Steven's Straight past Admiralty Island, which had the largest concentration of brown bears in the world. We didn't see any bears, but saw Tracey Arm and Endicott Arm and our first viewing of magnificent glaciers and icebergs.

Juneau, the country's smallest capital, was off in the distance. What a gorgeous setting for a capital city! The towering mountains plunged into the bay. Peaks still had snow on the upper elevations, and the lower elevations were covered with greenery. About five or six tall buildings stood in the center of town.

There was a bridge stretching across the bay and private homes along the edge of the water on the far side. Even in little Juneau, they had rush-hour traffic, with people living on one side of the bridge and working on the other. Of course, that helped keep the touristy riffraff out of the residential area.

We disembarked as soon as possible and chose to start our tour with a tram ride two thousand feet up the side of the mountain. The tram terminal was located at the boat dock, so required very little walking. The line waiting to board the tram consisted of half a dozen people from our boat. A few minutes passed before we were floating skyward.

The sky had low clouds and haze, but our spirits were soaring. Finally setting foot in Alaska was exciting. The tram stopped at a modern terminal that had souvenir shops, plus a restaurant and a theater, where they showed videos about local inhabitants and environment.

We skipped all the man-made entertainment and headed outdoors. There were trails leading several directions, and we chose the one that looked like it went along the rim of the mountain facing the bay. The day before summer started in the Northern Hemisphere, wild flowers were in profusion, the deciduous trees had new shoots sprouting, and the air smelled super clean. We walked for an hour and rarely passed another tourist. Life was good.

That didn't last long enough. Marlow was soon ready to explore the town. We took a sight-seeing trolley. The driver was a college student working in Alaska for the summer. He let everyone go through town twice. The first time he showed what was available, and the second time, people got off where they wanted. That double trip consumed fifteen minutes.

We went to a store so I could purchase an *ulu*, a knife Eskimos used for scraping skins, chopping, and slicing. They were crescent shaped, with the handle reaching from one end to the other. They came in five-, seven- and nine-inch lengths. I tried one and discovered my arthritis was too far advanced for me to grip the handle. The fingers on my right hand didn't close anymore. I got one for our son, Darryl; he did a lot of slicing, dicing, and cooking.

We came to the famous Red Dog Saloon and went in for a beer at four dollars apiece. We only had one each. The place was crowded with tourists. The walls were decorated with antiques from gold rush days, cutesy signs, and pictures of past patrons. The furniture was rustic, and there was sawdust on the floor. Since the customers were people from our ship, and the workers were college students from the Lower Forty-Eight, it felt like a tourist trap instead of an old-time saloon.

We caught the shuttle to the heliport, where we had tickets for a sight-seeing ride over glaciers and ice fields. The bus trip through the suburbs gave us insight into the type of housing in Juneau. All were small, and most looked temporary. I suspected most people packed up and went south in the winter.

The helicopter ride was spectacular. We rode with one other couple and the pilot. Glaciers came in all sizes and shapes. Some looked like whipped cream, others were craggy and rough. It would have been impossible to walk ten feet without falling into a crevice. Some were blue and white; others were packed with rocks scoured from the mountains and were gray to black. The snowfields were pristine with no footprints. The ice fields were forbidding. We saw a student camp where geologists were studying the whole phenomenon.

We landed on a relatively flat glacier (they all sloped). The wind blew fiercely, and I hadn't dressed warmly enough. The temperature was in the seventies in Juneau. Now I wished I had the army coat with the wolf-hair hood that Darryl and Sandy had gotten me for Christmas. We were supplied with boots for walking on snow, and a vest in case we landed in water. The boots kept us from slipping on the ice. I got cold in no time, even though the vest did cut the wind a bit, and I was glad when I ran out of film and had to hop back into the warm helicopter to put a new roll in my camera.

I was also glad I braved the temperature and went outside again, as the pilot had taken Marlow and the other couple to look at a crevice in the ice. The ice further up the slope was melting and running into the crack. We looked into a beautiful blue waterfall with no bottom. The further down you looked, the deeper blue it got. The pilot said he'd hold on to my vest so I could lean over and take a picture. I wondered what made him think he wouldn't slide in with me if I started to slip. Perhaps he planned to let go. I didn't lean over the edge. I took my picture about four feet from the edge, which was close enough. We spent about twenty or thirty minutes playing on the ice before the helicopter took off again. As we took off, the pilot said that last year the company lost a helicopter when it parked on a slope too close to a crevice.

We saw bald eagles, lots and lots of bald eagles. They were playing gracefully in the sky around us. They probably had good thermals rising from the warmed ground at Juneau's elevation. We didn't see bear, moose, or caribou. I guessed we would have to go farther inland to see those animals. We flew over glaciers, ice fields, snowpacks, forests, and lakes. Alaska was unspoiled nature at its best. What good fun to see it from an eagle's viewpoint.

We landed at the heliport and were invited into the office for a cup of hot cider, which was most welcome. We took the shuttle to the dock and arrived in time for a late dinner and to watch the crew maneuver the ship out of Juneau's harbor and up the next leg of the Inside Passage. The twilight showed the mountains in silhouette as we gradually sailed into darkness.

June 21, 1997 We watched Skagway drift into view past the dining-room windows. Graffiti! I couldn't believe it. All along the granite boulders on the far side of the docks was graffiti! I wondered if Skagway had gangs marking their territories. The population of Skagway in the winter was about one thousand. In the summer it expanded double or more, but how could the town have enough teenagers to form gangs? This was going to be a disappointing town to visit if there were turf wars going on. When we disembarked, I saw that the graffiti was actually the names of *cruise ships and their captains* and what dates they visited Skagway. Shame on them for defacing nature.

Marlow and I walked along a wharf and through a campground to the steam train station. We had prepurchased tickets to take a scenic ride following the famous Chilkoot Trail used by the Argonauts in late 1898. So many died trying to survive in the Yukon that the Canadian government made a law that each person had to take two-thousand pounds of supplies over the Chilkoot Trail, which was on US soil, in order to be allowed into Canada. For the miners, that meant they had to make several trips up and down sides of icy, snow-covered mountains with large packs on their backs. Out of the two hundred thousand who made the trip, about two-hundred found enough gold to be considered wealthy by the standards of the day.

The train left late, as the organizers waited for two other cruise ships arriving in port. That gave me time to chat with the staff and learn the best place to go for picture taking. They told me we would be taking a diesel, not a steam train, as advertised, but suggested I go to the first car and sit as close as possible to the front. That way I could go onto the platform between the diesel and the first car and get good shots. Also, the engine would switch ends for the descent, and I'd have a clear view of the mountains behind us.

After I got that scoop, I settled on the bench beside Marlow to wait for departure. The tardy ships were just arriving. I was too antsy to sit still, so I went sight-seeing. I knew it would be at least thirty minutes before passengers left the ships. I found a golf-cart rental establishment and told Marlow about that. He agreed we could rent a cart after the train ride.

The train eventually got underway. It was a good way to see the treacherous grounds the miners climbed over. Of course, we got to see it in comfort, and it was spring rather than the dead of winter. Not that all the Argonauts made the climb in the dead of winter, people were on the trail year round. There weren't as many waterfalls as expected, but the scenery was glorious for mountain-loving people.

The sun played hide-and-seek among the clouds, but we never got rain, and the temperature was perfect. I spent the whole ride to the top of the grade (about an hour and a half) standing on the platform between the diesel and the first car. No one else was interested in doing the same, so I had the whole place to myself. Crystal-clear streams, granite boulders the size of skyscrapers, marbleized snow on the peaks—I got to enjoy it all in solitude. Even Marlow stayed in the cozy car looking out a window.

I sat in the train off and on for the return ride. I mentioned to Marlow that I'd be surprised if I made it all the way through the trip without catching a cold or getting a sore throat. I pushed the envelope breathing in diesel engine dust. My adrenalin was pumping; I felt exhilarated. I had long been a Jack London fan and could picture the characters he wrote about. The ride took three hours, and I enjoyed every minute of it.

We got off the train, rented a golf cart, and drove thirty minutes to see all of quaint little Skagway, and another thirty minutes following the river road to the historical cemetery. It was pleasant slowly riding along in the sunshine and looking at the river and evergreens. The cemetery was built in the foothills and had a nice waterfall and stream named after Skagway founder, Tom Reid.

After we returned the golf cart, Marlow was ready for his afternoon nap, so he went back to the ship. I went through the town museum, reading every placard on every display. I mentally created a new story to write about the Alaskan pioneers on my walk to the ship.

I got back thirty minutes before departure, and Marlow and I chose good seats on deck to watch Skagway slip out of view. I felt I was saying farewell to a friend and regretted the cruise ship crews defacing the entrance to the harbor with their graffiti even more vehemently.

At dinner Marlow remarked that I had picked up a bit of sunburn. I confessed I didn't think that caused the blush; I was running a temperature. I managed to eat some soup, then went to the drugstore and bought cold medication, dosed myself, and went to bed. I progressively got worse as the night wore on. I couldn't get the fever to stay down. I'd take a couple of Tylenol, and the fever would alleviate for half an hour, then return. My throat was sore, my chest congested, and I had a headache and a cough.

June 22, 1997 I was much too ill to think about breakfast. I stayed in bed until nine, and then dressed and headed for the ship's doctor. I got there a few minutes before the doctor opened for business. By the time his doors opened, about fifty people were waiting to see him. Many of the people were coughing and complaining of the same symptoms I had. I wondered if there was a virus floating in the air-conditioning vents.

The doctor declared I had bronchitis and was on the verge of pneumonia. He gave me medication for congestion and cold symptoms, an antibiotic, and stronger Tylenol. He said to take two Tylenol every four hours for the fever and headache, and to take the other medication as prescribed. He felt I'd be fine in a week. A week!

What a way to celebrate a fortieth anniversary! I had brought it on myself; getting chilled so many times and breathing that train smoke didn't help. The stronger Tylenol knocked my temperature down for about an hour, but then it came back. Nothing helped the congestion and sore throat.

The stewardess came into the room four or five times. She felt she had to put clean towels in the bathroom every time I used one to dry my hands. I thought there must have been a wire attached to the toilet handle that turned on a light in her room telling her I had used a towel. She wanted to straighten up, which meant removing my drinking glass, bucket of ice cubes, and the washcloth I wrapped around an ice cube for my head. She felt my wastebasket needed to be kept in the opposite corner of the room from my bed. Each time she left, I staggered about replacing the things I needed.

While I was in the bathroom on one of her forays into the room, she made my bed with the sheets pulled so tight, I didn't have the strength to pull them loose. I learned later, when Marlow couldn't pull the sheets out, that they were caught on bedsprings. Marlow lifted the mattress and disengaged them and tucked me in with blankets up to my chin.

Marlow enjoyed his day topside. He stopped by to check on me every couple of hours. I was getting exhausted; I needed to be left alone so I could sleep. I alternated between chills and fever and got progressively crankier as the day went on.

By seven o'clock that evening, I was ready to kill the next person who came into the room. It was Lynn, the stewardess. She wanted to know if I'd like a cup of tea with some honey. I was going through a chills stage at the time, and that sounded like the most wonderful idea I had ever heard. I was so happy and so weak from the long, long day, I cried. I had an overwhelming urge to hug her.

When Lynn brought the tea, she also brought a menu and said I could order room service for breakfast. My throat was sore; I knew I couldn't eat much, but ordered yogurt and hot tea.

June 23, 1997 This day was better than the previous one. I was wise enough to tell Marlow I needed to sleep and asked him to check on me every four hours, instead of every two. I hung a "Do Not Disturb" sign on the door right after my yogurt arrived, and Lynn stayed away several hours. I slept—having feverish nightmares—for almost twenty-four hours.

June 24, 1997 I had yogurt and tea for breakfast. My other symptoms were much the same, but now I was weak and dizzy when I got up to go to the bathroom. I was forcing myself to drink as much water as possible to avoid dehydration, a condition I got fairly easily.

It dawned on me that I'd only had two containers of yogurt and one bowl of soup in two and a half days. I asked Lynn to bring me some soup. She said no. No explanation.

That evening I asked Marlow to bring me some soup from the dining room. He returned and told Lynn to bring me soup. That was what his waiter in the dining room had told him to do. Lynn brought no soup, but instead presented a menu consisting of three sandwiches that I could have with my choice of coleslaw or potato chips. She said if I wanted any of those sandwiches brought to the room, I'd have to order them twenty-four hours in advance.

I told her my throat was too sore to eat a sandwich and asked for soup or bananas. She said she'd see if she could find any. She was irritated with my disruption of her routine.

That evening Lynn brought a bowl of fruit. The lights were out in the room except the bathroom light, and I could see the silhouette of the fruit. I took a banana out of the bowl and realized it was very soft. I knew I needed to get some nourishment, so I ate it anyhow. It tasted terrible and didn't stay down long. I later tried a dusty-feeling grape; I washed it off in my drinking water. It tasted terrible; I spat it into the wastebasket. I took the bowl of fruit to the bathroom and looked at it in the light. The other banana was brown, beyond edibility and the grapes were dirty, had cobwebs, and some were split, with mold growing on the exposed pulp. I threw the banana away, as well as the bad grapes, and washed the six grapes that looked edible. There was an orange in the bowl, so I cut it in half with the ulu I had gotten Darryl and drank the juice. That wasn't much nourishment. I was shaking and sweating from the effort of getting from bed to bathroom and back.

June 25, 1997 I was too weak to disembark on my own, and Marlow had to pack for both of us. The ship loaned me a wheelchair to make it from my cabin to the shuttle bus taking us back to Sacramento. It was so good to get off that ship and out into the warm California sunshine. The bus trip home went well, but I did notice there were several coughing passengers.

Epilogue: Keep in mind that while I was sick on days eight, nine, and ten, Marlow was still able to partake of the meals, shows, and shipboard activities, so Princess did earn his share of the fare.

My story was not typical of cruise ship experiences. I lost twelve pounds—twenty-two, if you count the ten I put on the first few days of the trip. I was sick in bed for a week after returning home. I regained strength once I got chicken soup, dairy products, and fruit juice into my system. By the fourth day, I had enough energy to get to a doctor. He said I had pneumonia and severe bronchitis. He gave me a stronger antibiotic and medication for the symptoms. They started working within twenty-four hours, and I progressively felt better.

Two weeks after I got home, on the advice of our travel agent, I wrote to Princess Cruise Lines and told them of my travails. I didn't want Lynn to get fired; she was probably supporting a family of ten in the Philippines. Still, I thought they should change their policy so that ill people could get nourishment as needed.

Princess sent a basket of flowers and a note saying they hoped I felt better. I thought that was the end of the story.

A week later we received a letter offering us a $1,500.00 discount if we wanted to take another cruise. That sounded like an invitation to a masochism convention, but maybe as time passed, my memory would dull, and another cruise would sound inviting.

Nine

Caribbean, Panama Canal, and Acapulco

1998

It is amazing how easy it is to forget bad cruise experiences when the cruise line offers you $1,500.00 off your next trip. It took a little over a year for Marlow to talk me into a cruise with land extensions on either end of the excursion. What with the discount and other advertised bonuses, it would have been more expensive for us to stay home over the Aerojet shutdown during Christmastime.

December 12, 1998 The airport shuttle driver was due to arrive at six a.m. He called at six fifteen and said he was at Folsom Dam and wanted directions to our home. Fortunately, he was lost only two blocks from where we lived.

The trip to the airport was uneventful; check-in at the airport went smoothly; we waited thirty minutes and boarded the plane that arrived and left on time; we got good seats and sat near bright, cheerful people. The skies were clear. We saw Folsom Lake and even picked out our home in the mobile home park. If this kept up, we were going to have an unusually dull vacation.

The skies over my beloved Sierra Nevada and Lake Tahoe were clear; the partly frozen lakes shimmered among majestic granite peaks and snow-bedecked forests. The flight to Dallas/Fort Worth International Airport was smooth and scenic, with the pilot announcing various landmarks as we approached them—Lake Tahoe, Colorado River, Bryce Canyon, Lake Powell, and Ship's Rock. When we crossed over West Texas, the pilot was silent. I guess he didn't see anything interesting.

Marlow took his first ride on the robot-controlled train that ran on tracks from gate to gate around DFW Airport, and was as delighted as I was the first time I used this unique reminder that we lived in the computer age. We arrived at our transfer gate just as our plane to Puerto Rico was boarding passengers.

The Boeing 757 had every seat occupied. The ride from Dallas to San Juan was over puffy clouds; we saw no more scenery on the ground. We hit a few shallow potholes in the sky, but nothing to disturb the tranquility of the ride. We were served a mini-lunch of lasagna, a roll, and a cookie midway through the flight.

Marlow and I worked on crossword puzzles together or read to pass the time. I brought my Aerojet homework along, thinking I'd have lots of time to study new assignments I had recently acquired. Our landing in Puerto Rico coincided with my boredom peaking from reading the Delta Configuration Management Plan.

The conveyor belt was broken in the airport, and instead of transferring the luggage to another belt, the airport authorities introduced us to the laid-back atmosphere of Puerto Rico by making us wait while they repaired the original belt. It took an hour to get the luggage from the plane to the passengers.

The taxi driver agreed to take us to our hotel for $12.00; they use US dollars, as Puerto Rico is a US territory. I paid him with a $20.00 bill. He gave me folded bills in change, which I accepted with my left hand, and I handed him two ones with my right hand as a tip and thanked him. He smiled brightly.

Like a tourist ready to be scalped, I didn't count my change until we were in the hotel, and the taxi driver was long gone. Dummy alert! Don't act like a tourist unless you want the natives to take advantage of you. He had given me $4.00 change instead of the $8.00 I was owed. He made a $6.00 tip on a $12.00 fare.

The hotel was a nice little place with a pool and clean, comfortable rooms. We deposited our luggage and walked down the main street to a Burger King for dinner. The time was eleven at night in Puerto Rico, seven p.m. in California. We ate our burgers, which tasted just like the ones in California, and walked back to our hotel in gentle tropical rain.

Traffic was gridlocked, with horns honking. We assumed there was an accident, but the hotel clerk told us traffic was like that all the time because tourists were visiting casinos.

We watched a comedy hour in English on television. My favorite joke (I thought of my cat-hating brother at the time) was when a comedienne said she thought cats were a perfectly foolish waste of good fur. Marlow went quietly off to sleep while I made my first journal entry.

December 13, 1998 The clock read one a.m. by the time I dozed off; that was my usual nine o'clock bedtime in California. An hour or so later, I was awakened by loud noises from a party. There were lots of people talking and laughing. It was frustrating having a party within hearing range, and we weren't invited! After listening to them tell their jokes in Spanish, not having a clue what the punch line meant, I was irritated enough to call the front desk and ask them to contact the partygoers and ask them to either tell their jokes in English, invite us to join them, or turn the volume down on their voices. No invitation arrived. The jokes were still told in Spanish, but an hour later, everything got quiet, and I went back to sleep.

I slept soundly until eight a.m., close enough to consider my biological clock in working order. I won't bore you any further with the time differences.

Marlow woke up just as I was exiting the bathroom. Good timing. He took his shower and dressed while I packed our belongings, ready to check out of the hotel and start our grand adventure. I asked a hotel employee in English if he knew the weather forecast, and he looked at me blankly. I asked in Spanish if he thought it would rain during the day. He answered in Spanish, "Of course!" His expression said, "What else would it do?"

We had a continental-style breakfast consisting of cornflakes, orange juice, and coffee on the patio beside the pool. We finished just as a tropical shower came along. The young employee looked at me, shrugged his shoulders, and grinned from ear to ear.

I called four car rental agencies, all closed. The day of the week was not only Sunday but also Election Day. The island was deciding whether or not they wanted to petition Congress to have Puerto Rico admitted as the fifty-first state. We told the desk clerk at the hotel that we'd spend an extra night.

We began a walking tour of Old San Juan at the beach, which was littered with broken glass and empty beer cans. Access was over broken blocks of concrete. We gave a walk on the beach a miss and went down Condado Avenue, where the casinos were located. We had just gone half a block when we came to a car rental agency. We peeked into their windows to see if they posted rental charges. The place was open! They had a car available, a Chevy two-door, so we took it and went back to the hotel and checked out. Yea! We escaped the city.

We drove east to El Yunque National Forest, a lush rainforest reaching into the clouds. The park was officially closed for voting day, but a volunteer at the gate informed us that meant we could drive through free.

It sprinkled from time to time as we drove along, enjoying the scenery and looking fruitlessly for local fauna. We debated on whether or not to hike. We had an umbrella, and the weather was in the eighties and humid, so a shower wouldn't hurt us. We took a route to a cascading waterfall. The trip was uphill, with lots of concrete steps. We left the falls on a different route so we could experience more of the jungle. We took our time and enjoyed the luxuriant display of tropical flowers in bloom, vines that held the trees together in groups, and lots and lots of ferns and palms.

The only fauna we saw was a lizard, a tiny one, and a snail that looked more like a sand dollar standing on its edge than the fat, round snails we see at home. We saw lots of broken trees and couldn't figure out what happened. We had seen that in the Sierras when the trees get burdened by snow, and then a strong wind comes along and breaks them off at snow-pack height. A ranger later told us the cause in El Yunque was the recent hurricane season.

The hike took three hours. At the street I collapsed onto a stone bench and let Marlow walk to the car parked a mile away. He picked me up, and we drove until we came to a roadside vendor selling food. Everything was deep fried except the rice and the fresh coconut milk. I chose the rice and was given a heaping dinner plate full. I hadn't expected that much for the few pennies the vendor charged, so I ordered a *relleno* (ray-YEAH-no) *papa,* which turned out to be a meatball surrounded by mashed potatoes, dipped in batter and deep fried. Marlow ordered a *carne y queso burrito* (meat of some sort and cheese inside a tortilla), which was also deep fried. The young lady took out a machete and chopped the top off a coconut, leaving a hole in the center. She stuck a straw in the hole and handed it to me. Now, that's fresh coconut milk! The liquid was just barely more flavorful than water, but it helped wash down the greasy food.

We drove through Luquillo, an oceanfront town that supposedly had the most picturesque beaches on the island. We got lost and ended up in residential *barrios* (neighborhoods). Lots of people stood around listening to blaring loudspeakers. We presumed they were announcing election results. Several police and armed soldiers leaned against trucks and jeeps, laughing and talking to people. We never found the white-powder sand beach lined with swaying palm trees advertised in brochures.

Marlow and I made our way back out to the "highway," a pothole-strewn four-lane road with traffic lights every mile or two. We went further south to the fishing village of Fajardo and found a lovely inn on top of a hill overlooking town and the seashore. We checked in. Fajardo Parador was the nicest and newest building we had seen in Puerto Rico. Most of the commercial buildings, casinos, and hotels seemed to be built by amateurs who didn't have to adhere to building codes.

We enjoyed a leisurely swim in the large pool, ate dinner in the modern, tastefully decorated dining room, and sat on the verandah with other guests watching the sun set. Soon after dark we saw a parade of trucks and cars—emergency and military vehicles among them, with sirens wailing and horns honking—winding up and down the streets of town. Their side won the election.

The vote was 46 percent in favor of statehood, while 50 percent said to rewrite the conditions of petitioning statehood. I felt these warm, friendly people would be an asset to our melting pot.

December 14, 1998 We dressed and drank coffee. I ate my leftover half a sandwich from last night's dinner and walked around the quiet hotel patio, taking pictures of the sunrise. We packed the car and were off down the road before the hotel employees arrived.

We were pleasantly surprised that our legs weren't sore from hiking in El Yunque National Park. We decided we could take another hike if the opportunity arose during the day.

Marlow stopped at Burger King in Guyana for his breakfast. I plotted highlights on the map while he ate. We drove the coastal route, which took us through fishing villages and adjacent to sugarcane fields. The houses looked middle class, and the countryside and villages were cleaner than the big city (just like in the Upper Forty-Eight).

In beautiful Ponce, the second-largest city on the island, we parked and walked, admiring their colonial buildings. Some looked like pastel-colored wedding cakes with white flourishes. We toured a red-and-black striped firefighter's museum originally built in 1878 and the central plaza and government buildings.

By noon I was ready for lunch. We found a little downtown diner where we could sit. Many were made for customers to stand at a bar running the length of the room. I couldn't think of the Spanish word for bread, so I ordered a *pollo y panderia*. I knew that meant chicken and bakery. What I got was a delicious chicken salad sandwich. Marlow ordered a *chorizo papa* and a *pizza*. What he got was a chorizo sausage ball surrounded by mashed potatoes, dipped in batter and deep-fried, and a deep-fried beef turnover, which he said was very bland. I hoped he brought lots of Tums. We almost never ate fried food at home.

We found ourselves in a town named La Parquera on the northwest side of the island and walked to the waterfront. There were no beaches; there were mangroves. We bought tickets for a night ride on a motorboat to an area that had phosphorescent creatures living in the water.

The stroll in the heat of the day zapped our energy, and we went back to our little family-run *parador* for a nap. The old-fashioned hotel was originally a two-story home. The owners lived upstairs and ran a grocery store next door, which was a local hangout for elderly men. The benches in front of the store had men chatting and watching passersby from dawn to dusk.

We changed into bathing suits and were off for our boating adventure. There were two other couples plus the driver and his assistant sitting knee to knee in the fourteen-foot metal rowboat. The boat motor needed some serious attention and chugged along slowly. I wondered if we might not have to swim back and inquired about sharks in the water. I was told not *many* came inside the mangrove islands where we were going. Well, that was good. I could probably only fight off three or four at any one time.

Marlow said the boat reminded him of the *African Queen,* except the *African Queen* had a better motor. The three-hour ride only cost five dollars per person. What could one expect to get? The balmy night air was wonderful, and the twinkling lights on shore gave us a cheery reminder that it was Christmastime.

Our copassengers consisted of a pair of three-hundred pound honeymooners who were so lovey-dovey, they didn't notice whether we had a motor or not. Ain't that sweet? The second duo was teenagers on a date. The boy spoke good English; I suspected he might be stationed on the island with the US military. He was our interpreter. His girlfriend was a cute local lass who squealed with delight every time we saw anything interesting. We saw a minor meteor shower, Christmas-decorated boats coming into harbor, and phosphorescence in the water.

We dragged our hands through the warm water, and gradually more and more creatures glowed. When we got to the magic spot, Marlow and the driver's assistant jumped into the water. Their whole bodies glowed as they swam around the boat. Everything else was black—the water, the sky, the mangrove islands, the shoreline. It made the luminescence brighter. We played in the water for thirty minutes. I didn't jump in because there was no ladder to get back into the boat, and I didn't want to be dragged over the side like a bag of potatoes.

December 15, 1998 Marlow was worried about getting to our cruise ship on time—we had to be onboard by nine ***p.m.*** We stuck to the highways for the balance of our trip around the island, so we didn't slowly roam through fishing villages along the shore. We did get to see the mountainous backbone that runs down the center of the island. We did see the cultivated lands and green, green foothills.

We arrived in San Juan by noon and couldn't board the cruise ship until three, so I talked Marlow into doing the tourist thing and seeing the forts that protected the island from hostiles between 1539 and the mid-1900s. Fort El Morro and Fort San Cristobal were fascinating. The island had been owned by half a dozen different European countries before it became a US territory. The museum showed military uniforms for each country, along with the usual memorabilia of colonial life in the tropics. The construction of the forts took over three hundred years, including the modernization done during World War II.

Downtown traffic was bumper to bumper through narrow, pedestrian-strewn streets. I enjoyed the architecture and window-shopping from the passenger seat. Marlow enjoyed nothing while driving five miles an hour with his eyes glued to the road ahead.

The rental car was returned, and we took a taxi to the cruise ship. Boarding went without a hitch, and we were soon ensconced in a nice little cabin. The ship was more modern and spacious than the one we had taken to Alaska eighteen months earlier. An outside deck surrounded the floor, where there were shops, making it unnecessary to go through the mall for every meal, like on the *Sky Princess.* Hip, hip, hooray! This was much better.

We toured the ship, went through our emergency exit drill, did laundry, ate dinner, and went to a stage show. By midnight I was ready for sleep. Marlow stood on the deck and watched us depart Puerto Rico. We made it safely past the cannons mounted in Fort El Morro.

December 16, 1998 The inhabitants of St. Thomas, American Virgin Islands pay taxes and collect welfare but can't vote. The residents were mostly descendants of African slaves brought to the islands to work in the sugarcane fields. The islands were originally owned by the Spanish, then by the French, then the Danish. The United States bought the islands from Denmark in 1917 for $25 million. The US government felt Denmark might fall to the German Kaiser and didn't want Germany to have a foothold so close to the United States.

Our three-hour tour purchased through Princess Cruise Lines was supposed to be through the rainforest and mountains to see the scenic spots around the island. Instead, it was a bus trip from one shopping mall to another. Very disappointing. Supposedly, the main reason US citizens went to St. Thomas was to shop without having to pay sales tax or import duty.

The afternoon tour of St. John island was much better. The island had a great deal of land that was purchased by Laurence Rockefeller between 1950 and 1956. He turned most of it over to the government to use as a national park. There were beautiful rainforests leading to mangroves or palm-lined beaches. Our fellow shipmates spent the day on one such inviting beach called Magan's Bay. Maybe we could do that on our next trip.

Our driver didn't know how to shift smoothly. Every change caused a grunt, groan, and squeal of the transmission before we jerked into gear. He drove on the correct side of the road about 50 percent of the time. The law said to drive on the left, but the pullouts for scenic views were on the right. The speed limit was ten miles per hour in the city and twenty miles per hour in the country, where the roads had many hairpin turns and steep, steep drop-offs. Our driver drove twenty miles per hour in the city and forty miles per hour in the country, where he honked his horn at every curve to let other drivers know he was driving on their side of the road. We tourists hung on tightly and gritted our teeth as though on a roller coaster.

Back onboard the ship, we watched St. Thomas sink into the distance as night fell. We topped off our day by going to the nightclub shows, a banjo soloist and a comedian. Both were very good. We then sat in the atrium and listened to soothing piano music until we were ready to sleep. It was good to be away from the blood and guts television shows that filled our living room every evening at home.

December 17, 1998 We slept in late, ate breakfast, then sat in deck chairs and read until it was time to leave for Martinique, a French colony.

We learned from a Princess staff member that everything on Martinique was expensive ($6.00 for a canned soft drink), so we didn't plan on buying anything. I only shopped out of absolute necessity at home. Some Princess passengers got off the ship as soon as we docked so they could hit the stores. We practically had the ship to ourselves in the morning.

Our afternoon tour was divided into two segments, one part conducted from a taxi, the second from a bus. We shared our taxi with a non-English-speaking Asian couple. Our driver spoke a little bit of English. He drove safely and sanely and pointed out vegetation and geological features of the island. He told us that Mount Pelee had erupted in 1902 and buried the city of St. Pierre, which had been known as the Paris of the West. Everyone in the city except one person died. The number of people killed ranged from 30,000 to 40,000, according to which source you believed. The one survivor was a prisoner in an underground dungeon. Rescue workers heard him trying to dig his way out when they looked through the rubble for survivors. The prisoner had been in jail for being intoxicated and using foul language in public. Who says swearing isn't good for you? It could save your life!

The bus driver spoke no English. He and his colorfully dressed companion picked us up at the butterfly farm—a greenhouse built on the oldest sugar plantation on Martinique. The guide told us rum was made from fermented sugarcane parts called muscovado. She wore a native costume of brightly flowered material with a bandanna wrapped around her head. She explained that if only one point stuck up from a woman's bandanna, it meant she was single. If two points stuck up, it meant she was married. If three points stuck up, it meant that she was married, but willing to fool around. The tour was fun, the island beautiful, the butterfly farm serene.

The majority of the population of Martinique was Creole—a combination of Spanish, French, and African. Their skin was dark, and most had predominately African features. Their language was French and/or Creole. Their nationality was French, and they were not interested in independence because of the unemployment benefits that France sent to 35 percent of the people. Worker's compensation, social security, or welfare was sent to many other people. Why worry, be happy. The French taxpayers were willing to support the islanders.

We went to the ship's dining room for the first time and met our table mates—four elderly (in their eighties) people from New York who always traveled together. They were pleasant people, but we had nothing in common.

We went to a stage show called *America's Music*. The singers and dancers did a couple of World War I songs, then went right into rock and roll. They did no country, jazz, bluegrass, folk (as by Stephen Foster), marches (John Philip Souza) or World War II melodies. They missed an opportunity to display a variety of good music.

December 18, 1998 We left the ship for an early morning tour of Grenada, a former English colony. We were in a minibus that contained eleven people. Three of those eleven were youngsters; it was good to hear young people giggling and having a good time. The tour operator was a Caucasian, one of the few on the island. "One Time" said his grandparents came from England and had eleven children. His parents had eight children; he was the eldest and the only one of his siblings still living on the island. He had four children of his own, and only one of them stayed on the island as an adult. Leroy got his nickname, One Time, when he first started driving taxis as a young man. He tried to break into the tour-operator business by proving he could get along with tourists. He met the ships and airplanes that arrived on the island and pleaded with passengers to give his taxi a try just one time. He said there was a younger generation on the island who thought One Time was his Christian name. Sure enough, everywhere we went, we heard people of all ages calling out, "One Time!"

The unemployment on Grenada was 50 percent; they became an independent nation in 1974. In 1983 the Communist from Russia and Cuba tried to take over the island, and Uncle Sam sent some troops to dissuade them. The Grenadines were grateful.

Spices grew everywhere. They had nutmeg, a seed inside a fruit that looked like an apricot. The seed was covered with a red hull that was dried and ground into mace. The fruit split when it ripened, and natives knew it was time to pick and put the seeds on large drier trays for the sun to process. The trays were on rails and could be slid inside a building when one of the frequent tropical showers started.

Cinnamon was taken from the barks of trees, dried and ground, or shaved into sticks. Cloves grew as a cluster of flowers on the ends of tree branches. The clusters were ripe when they were bright red, and were picked and dried to a deep brown. Curry and mustard came from the saffron tree. Coffee beans were the seeds of small fruit that grew on short trees. Citrus and all vegetables except potatoes, onions, and garlic grew prolifically on the island.

Grenada had no flat land. The elevation ranged from sea level to 2,400 feet. The roads were narrow, with winding, steep, hairpin curves. Our tour was like a ride through an amusement park fun house, with people and animals darting out onto the road unexpectedly. The driver continually braked, swerved, sped up, and then swerved around another hazard.

Approximately 100,000 people lived on Grenada, which was twenty-one miles long and twelve miles across at the widest part. People didn't rent houses; they rented the land and built their own frame house (usually from twenty feet to forty feet square, according to how many inhabitants there were). If they didn't pay their rent, or the landlord decided to sell his land, the tenant tore down his house and moved it elsewhere. The landowner-occupied houses were built of brick and stucco. There were approximately 20,000 cars on the island, two of which were Pontiacs, and three of which were Chevys. The rest were Japanese made. The people spoke Pidgin English or French patois.

Grenada was the most southerly island in the windward Antilles. The tour was enjoyable and educational, though the driving was a bit scary.

December 19, 1998 A four-wheel driving tour along the mountainous coast of Venezuela showed us where there were people, there was filth. Graffiti was displayed on everything; even the "For Sale" signs on houses were spray-painted on house walls. People appeared both poor and unwashed. Litter was strewn along highways, around homes and businesses, on beaches, everywhere. The countryside shouted a lack of self-respect or respect for other people.

The guide drove over steep mountains with escarpments going straight down to the sea. We tourists were taken to a special reasonably clean beach where locals were not allowed. It wasn't inviting, as it had rough seas, sharp rocks to climb over approaching the sand, coarse sand. It had no restrooms, so there was toilet paper, newspaper, or napkins at the base of each bush. It cost two dollars to sit on a lawn chair under a straw sunshade. Marlow and I walked along the beach until it was time to get back into our vehicles. No one went swimming.

We left the beach and went to a waterfall of fresh water. The tour guide said we were there so we could wash sand and salt off our bodies. Two or three tourists got into the brown, foaming suds at the base of the waterfalls to get cooled off. The jungle was hot and humid, and the trucks were not air conditioned.

We met nice people from our cruise on this trip—Anne and Robert, a young married couple from Denver. Anne worked in some sort of job where she traveled to Mexico City frequently. She spoke fluent Spanish and was able to communicate with our non-English-speaking driver. Gail and Dick were a married couple in their late forties or early fifties traveling with their daughter, Tracy. I misjudged Tracy to be the type of young woman I wouldn't like because she had a safety pin in her navel, tattoos on her limbs, and greenish-yellow hair. I was wrong; she turned out to be perfectly charming, entertaining, and highly educated (majored in Spanish literature). I chastised myself for jumping to conclusions. I'd be proud to count her as a friend, if she would have me. Tracy chatted away with the driver about the recent elections in Venezuela and was able to translate all our questions and requests. We were lucky to have two translators in our car.

Marlow rode shotgun—next to the driver. That was the only good seat in the vehicle, as the rest of us sat on benches in the bed of the pickup shell and struggled to catch glimpses of the landscape out the little windows behind our seats, or bent to look out the front windshield. Our seats were perpendicular to the driver's seat. Marlow said he'd trade places with me after we stopped for lunch, so I could see a bit of the countryside. Great!

We were taken to a clean restaurant for a lunch of fish, steamed rice, and cooked vegetables. The tables were on an open patio, so each had an assortment of cats and dogs begging for food. The food was tasty enough, and the service was excellent. There was a small souvenir shop attached, and I picked up a little candle holder made of clay. The trick would be getting it home unbroken.

We rode to a village where schoolchildren entertained us by playing drums and dancing. They were darling; we really enjoyed watching them. The children later invited us to join them. Each little boy asked a woman to dance, and each little girl asked a man. Marlow and I tried to do country-swing to the drumbeats, but it didn't work too well. The children were the highlight of Venezuela.

In general the Venezuelans we met were friendly, dirty, and careless. Our driver was safe and thoughtful; some of the other drivers took unnecessary chances with people's lives. The roads often had foot-deep mud or were washed away on the escarpment side, and our driver made sure we made it through without a mishap.

Onboard the ship that evening, we heard horror stories about tourists that went into Caracas, Venezuela's capital. It was a cesspool, and one man from the ship was assaulted by would-be thieves who were chased away by hordes of irate tourists.

December 20, 1998 The day started out with a snorkeling trip up the coast from Willemstad, Curacao (KYOOR-a-so), an island of the Nederland Antilles. That was a good way to start the day. Anne and Robert were on the boat with us for their first time snorkeling. They had trouble with their equipment. I remembered my first time being miserable and sympathized with them. I hope they would try it again with better-fitting equipment.

Marlow and I carried our own snorkel gear on our trips after learning the hard way that one size does not fit all. The water was calm, and it was easy to get in and out of the boat. The few fish we saw were colorful, and we got to feed them bread, which brought them up close. The fish had to get within arm's length to eat.

There was nice coral—not anything like we'd seen on the Barrier Reef, but all in all, it was a delightful experience. The crew fed us fresh, sweet pineapple and bananas on the ride back to our cruise ship.

We showered and went to Willemstad. We were told that everything on the island would be closed, so we planned on admiring the architecture and window-shopping in the beautiful, colorful, clean city. We found an art dealer who was open, and I bought some postcards. I asked her if the domestic bus was running on the island. She said yes. She was a bit surprised that we'd ride on the same bus that transported the locals to and from work and school. She wrote out a note to the driver in Papiamento, a creolized Spanish with admixtures of Dutch and Portuguese, spoken by most of the natives, telling him what we wanted to see and what time we had to be back on the ship. She said the trip around the perimeter of the island should cost us two dollars.

The bus only ran once an hour, so we dashed to the bus station three blocks away and caught the bus just as it was ready to depart. We were the only Caucasians on the packed bus. The dark-skinned natives and three Hispanics were clean and dressed in their Sunday best. They were courteous and friendly. The homes on the island were clean and well kept. Some were obviously more expensive than others, but there was no litter, garbage, or graffiti anywhere. Finally, an island where the people did not foul their own nests. We wished we had another few days to spend in this tropical paradise.

December 21, 1998 Yea! A day at sea, total relaxation, which was what cruises were supposed to be about. I lay in bed without a care in the world and then spent an extra five minutes in the shower, knowing I didn't have to rush anywhere. Marlow and I ate a leisurely breakfast topside and watched the placid sea.

We went to a slide show and lecture on the Panama Canal so we'd have proper respect for the wonder we'd be experiencing tomorrow.

I went to a classical music concert by four people from Sydney, Australia. Two of the girls had been playing together since they first started lessons at the age of three. The boy joined them two years later, and the final girl joined the group when they were six years old. They were currently in their early thirties.

I sat on a deck chair and read my novel, *Caribbean*, by James Michener. Marlow wandered the decks looking for flying fish and dolphins. We had seen each of these animals on our trip, plus a couple of sea turtles.

We watched two artists carve ice mermaids and a swan before taking in the children's matinee, *Antz*. I expected us to be the only adults in the theater, but 90 percent of the audience was adults.

There were several Mexican families onboard because Princess ran an ad in a Mexico City newspaper, "two for the price of one and children free." Older people onboard had problems with the children's rambunctiousness.

We listened to other Princess patrons list the antics they'd observed—children putting shampoo, conditioner, and lotion on the banisters; a water fight in the dining room (started by the father of a family of ten); dancing and standing on the dining-room tables; sitting and standing on the exterior railings; running and sliding into people in the swimming pool areas. There was a fistfight between two fathers because children shoved each other into the deep end of the pool. One man indiscriminately threw whomever he could grab into the pool one afternoon. He wasn't taking time to ask people—man, woman, or child—if they could swim.

In a strong wind where we had twenty-foot swells, we saw a Mexican man trying to get a little girl to sit on the ship's railing. The wind was too strong for me to walk outside. We were sitting in the dining room, and he was outside the window beside our table. He looked at us each time he tried to get the girl placed on the railing. She jumped down as soon as he let go of her. I figured he was trying to upset us, so we thought he would stop if we didn't look at them. Fortunately, he did stop before there was a disaster. I wished there was a way we could have him jailed for child endangerment. He'd have been long gone by the time we could get Princess security staff on deck to stop him.

After dinner we went to the stage show called *Pirates*, a lively song and dance performance with lots of bright-colored costumes and pyrotechnics. They also worked some acrobatics into the show. Those were performed by a troop from China.

December 22, 1998 *Sun Princess* made a transit of the Panama Canal. We set our alarm clock for five thirty so we wouldn't miss anything. We were due to enter the first lock at six-fifteen.

The first thing I did was throw on my bathrobe and drag our dirty clothes to the laundry at the other end of the hallway. It wasn't an option; we were out of clean clothes. I thought I'd be the only person to think of doing laundry on such an important day for cruise customers.

When I got to the small, humid room, one person's clothes were in the dryers, and a second person's clothes were in the washers. Princess put four washers and four dryers on each deck occupied by customers. I don't know how many were on the decks occupied by staff. We had sixteen washers for over two thousand people. The first week I thought we only had eight washers and eight dryers but learned differently from the man removing his clothes from the dryers. He said he set his alarm for four a.m. to do his laundry that day. Two hours and fifteen minutes later, I was finished.

I missed the first three locks we went through, but was able to see the ship leave the last one and enter Gatun Lake, the second-largest man-made lake in the world. The largest is Lake Mead, Nevada. The locks were a hundred-ten-feet wide; our ship was a hundred-six-feet wide. Four train engines guided our big ship through the locks. The train engines were called "mules" and were attached to the ship by cables.

It took four hours to cross the beautiful lake. I wished we had our pontoon boat to explore all those half-hidden canals and islands. I knew they must have been teeming with wildlife. We saw a few birds, frigates mainly, but that was all. The *Sun Princess* made its way through the Gaillard Cut, a channel that cost 20,000 men their lives to build. Most of the deaths were due to yellow fever and malaria. The cut still required continual excavation to keep the mudslides dredged out. We were told during the slide show that enough dirt was removed to fill four trains circling the earth. That was hard to perceive. Wouldn't the mountains on either side erode back so far the mudslides wouldn't be a problem?

US crews were currently widening the Gaillard Cut for two-way traffic. When the cruise ships went through, cargo ships had to wait. The United States would be turning over control of the canal to the government of Panama in July 1999. I hoped the operation continued to move well.

It took eight hours to cross the three sets of locks, a large lake, and a deepwater channel, and make it to the Bridge of the Americas at the western side. There were several cargo ships sitting in the Pacific waiting their turn to traverse.

We were greeted by a truly placid ocean living up to its name—Pacific.

December 23, 1998 A day at sea, a day at rest. We ate and read, and Marlow napped. We watched the movie *The Horse Whisperer*. Then we read, and Marlow napped some more.

We toured the ship's bridge, completely run by computers, but still interesting. We asked a dozen questions that I'm sure the captain had answered on every cruise. I read all the notices attached to the walls and admired all the pretty flags stored in their separate little bins.

We ate again—lobster tonight. Not Maine lobster but still good. All of our meals had been good. Our dinner mates sent something back every night, claiming it was ill prepared. We felt it was just posturing, as everything had been just fine.

December 24, 1998 Another day at sea. This could be habit-forming! This was the perfect way to end a vacation where we had been running over islands trying to see and do everything.

The crew hit the brakes at one stage; it took us another three miles to get the ship slowed down enough to make a U-turn. The crew wanted to go back and investigate a small overturned vessel they saw. When we got back to the thirty- to thirty-five-foot boat, crew members found it had no markings and no signs of humans. The Panamanian Coast Guard was notified, and they sent a crew to recover the boat. Princess had no hoist to winch the boat onto our ship. The captain announced that he thought it was a boat broken loose from its mooring or from a yacht during a hurricane. Some passengers on the Princess thought it was more likely a contraband-running boat that had lost its way in bad weather. Of course, we wanted it to be mysterious so we'd have something interesting to put in our journals.

We toured the ship's galley. There were no people working. I was surprised; I thought they hustled about twenty-four hours a day to produce the gourmet selections offered at each meal. The rooms were immaculate and filled with enormous refrigerators, stoves, and cupboards made of stainless steel. A couple of big stainless steel pots simmered on one of the stoves—probably our dinner soup.

We ate in the quiet Horizon Court dining room, a sit-down restaurant where you could order from a menu, and it rarely had more than a dozen customers. I much preferred the quiet to the larger selection of fancy food offered in the noisy dining room. Tonight the Horizon was especially empty, as it was formal night, and many people preferred to get decked out in glitz and glitter and eat in the dining room.

The sea got rougher and rougher as we ate. I had had a hard time standing on deck because of the wind before we went into dinner. Our table was at the front of the ship, so we watched the waves roil up over the deck. Fortunately, there were no crazy men trying to get children to sit on the railing.

December 25, 1998 Did laundry at five in the morning. While waiting for clothes to get clean and dry, I filled out Mexican customs forms, debarkation forms, customer comments forms, post cards, and my journal.

Once on land we took an organized tour of Acapulco, a nice touristy city—at least the part we saw was good. It had a population of two million during the nonholiday season and had the main Naval Academy and fleet for Mexico. We saw three used US ships left over from World War II; that's all. The tour guide said Mexico knew if they got into trouble, Uncle Sam would bail them out. They didn't need to spend their money on defense. Acapulco was the vacation spot for Mexico City inhabitants. Many were in Acapulco to celebrate the Christmas holidays.

We saw La Quebrada cliff divers that climbed up steep precipices and dived into a tiny inlet of the ocean. Timing was critical with the waves coming and going. I remembered saying over forty years ago that someday I hoped to be rich enough to go to this exotic port and see these daring young men. Acapulco seemed a lot more exotic than Columbus, Ohio, when I was growing up. And I was still amazed to see men take their lives in their hands to perform that incredible feat. I wondered if they had an adrenaline rush every time they did it, or did it become old hat after half a dozen dives. We were told how many men had died, but I forget the number—relatively few anyhow, maybe two or three men in fifty years. Occasionally a woman took up this form of employment. They made $5.00 for diving from the lower cliffs, and $10.00 for diving from the highest cliff. What a way to pay the rent!

For dinner we skipped the hoopla of the ship's traditional Christmas dinner (turkey, ham, lamb, lobster, caviar, baked Alaska, and cherries jubilee) and went to Señor Frogs for Mexican beer, enchiladas, loud rock music, singing, and a gorgeous sunset. It was great!

Our taxi driver, Manuel, gave us a bit of history on the thirty-minute ride to the restaurant. He waited for us while we ate, drank, and sang. Then he took us back to the ship. Marlow tipped him ten dollars. In a country where the minimum wage was three dollars *per day*, I wondered what Manuel would buy with Marlow's tip.

December 26, 1998 What a mess trying to communicate with Princess shore personnel. We were not doing the typical thing of getting off the ship, getting on a bus, and going to the airport to catch a plane to the United States. We wanted to take the bus to the airport to pick up our reserved rental car. We didn't want to catch a plane.

We received a notice from the ship's personnel that our bus would be leaving for the airport at eleven thirty a.m. Marlow was anxious that we might not meet it on time, so he set the alarm clock for six a.m. Yikes! I told him to wake me up at eight, which I felt would give me ample time to shower, dress, and eat breakfast. Our luggage was delivered to the holding area the night before.

No such luck. Marlow woke me at ten after six and told me to hurry and get ready to leave. We left the ship at a few minutes after seven and waited and waited and waited in a large humid warehouse that was smelly from the diesel exhaust of the buses coming and going. Marlow walked to a nearby store to buy maps for our drive to the pyramids near Mexico City. He told me to arrange a ride to the airport on an earlier bus going that way. I tried a couple of times, but felt I was just getting in people's way as they organized the correct passengers with their luggage for bus rides to the airport or to a hotel. I thought about taking a taxi; the drivers were harassing us to use their service. They charged $25.00 plus tip, and we had already paid Princess for our bus transportation. I hated to pay twice for one trip.

Right at eleven thirty, we were called to board a bus. When we arrived at the airport, we found that our tour agent in Folsom had ordered an open Jeep. Just exactly what I had told him we definitely did not want. People only listen to half a sentence before leaping into action. Jeeps were fine if you don't have luggage to store while sightseeing. Fortunately, we were able to trade that car for a Ford Escort.

Marlow told the lady at the Avis counter that we were going to see the pyramids on the other side of Mexico City. She immediately whipped out a piece of paper for me to sign (I was putting the car charges on my credit card). I could read enough Spanish to realize that what she had given me was a waiver on our insurance, saying that it was null and void if we took the car near Mexico City. I told her I wouldn't sign the paper as we were going to drive around Mexico City. I sure didn't want to drive through it. Marlow took the side of the agent and told me to just sign whatever the lady wanted. He said she knew how to do her job. He never reads forms or papers before he signs them. I later explained that what the lady was offering was a statement that we would be responsible for any and all costs of any citation or accident that we had, if it occurred within so many miles of Mexico City center. He just said, "In that case, I'm happy you won that argument. I'm glad I married a bulldog." Grrrrrr.

We were eventually on our way eastward. We didn't have to drive into Acapulco to get on the turnpike; the western terminus was near the airport. Once on this beautiful highway, we relaxed and enjoyed the scenery. We saw acres and acres of coconut palms planted in orchards. Some had cattle grazing beneath the palm fronds; some had shorter crops growing under the trees. We began our climb into the Sierra Madres. They were a combination of jungles, pastures, cultivated fields, and occasional fruit trees. When I say cultivated fields, I don't mean the type we see from Nebraska through Pennsylvania. These fields were clinging to the sides of steep hills and had to be cultivated by donkeys or manual labor. We saw people riding donkeys or walking them as they both carried loads. We saw women doing laundry in the creeks or carrying jugs or baskets on their heads. Such a short distance from resplendent Acapulco, we were in a third-world country.

The country homes were poor structures of adobe bricks or hand-hewn logs. Many had no windows, and a few had dubious-looking roofs. I doubt they were much shelter from the rain. Each seemed to have a handful of dogs and chickens in the yard. We took the occasional side trip to see a small town here and there. The turnpike was one of the best roads we've ridden on; the side streets were some of the worst. Many were slightly more than one car wide, full of deep potholes and just a bit of asphalt now and then. People walked in the streets, with kids and dogs trailing behind, so it took close attention to maneuver the car safely.

We looked for somewhere to buy lunch but didn't find a regular restaurant. With my weak digestive track, I wasn't game to try the vendors cooking in wagons parked in the gutters.

We hoped to find a place to spend the night before sunset, as driving after dark would be doubly nerve-racking. Just as the sun set, we saw the first sign on the turnpike that indicated a hotel. We took the next off-ramp and discerned that somewhere down the deserted road, there was a hotel of some type. We drove a mile and saw another sign directing us to turn onto a smaller road. We were visualizing spending the night in a partially constructed adobe building, with or without a proper roof. Suddenly we saw a lake with buildings around its perimeter. Our first attempt at following the hotel signs led us down a dead-end road, where the smiling locals delighted in watching Marlow maneuver around sleeping dogs and playing children.

Further down the road, we saw a large white building with a sign on the side that said, “Master Club Hotel.” The sign was well lit, which was encouraging. As we pulled off the road onto the steep brick-paved driveway, I looked up at the building containing the sign and realized that it was a corrugated iron barn with some of the iron missing. I hoped that wasn’t the hotel!

Marlow maneuvered around the two hairpin curves heading toward the lake’s edge. We came to a parking garage with a sign that said, “Private Property, No Trespassing.” I convinced Marlow the sign meant not to park there unless you planned on staying at the hotel. He pulled into the garage and looked for a way across the steep ravine to the hotel.

We found a lovely flower-bedecked pedestrian bridge that led to a beautiful hotel. We walked through the corridors to the lakeside of the hotel and found we had happened upon a wonderful resort. There were several swimming pools, a restaurant, and tables with thatch-covered umbrellas sitting strategically on a lawn that led to a boat dock. The building itself was five stories high and had balconies for the rooms and bougainvillea blooming everywhere among the manicured landscaping. What a find! Now if they just had a room. My first thought was, *We can’t afford this.* My second thought was, *We’ll take it anyhow.*

We located someone who could speak some English, and he helped us register at Master Club Tequesquitengo. I gasped when he said the price was five-hundred-thirty. Then I had the presence of mind to ask, "Do you mean pesos?"

He said, "*Sí*," and showed us to a marvelous big room with two king-size beds, a great bathroom where the shower was about four feet by six feet, a dressing room, and a full-size closet. There was a second door in our room that opened into a kitchenette, dining room, and patio. The American price for this incredible find was $53.00.

We truly enjoyed our stay in serene, secure surroundings. The people were friendly and helpful and used their few words of English. We used our few words of Spanish to communicate just fine. The club was a time-share for wealthy city residents to get away once in a while. A small part of the building was set up as a public hotel.

December 27, 1998 I got up early so I could stroll around the hotel grounds. The landscape was pretty and quiet, with only the early birds singing their morning greetings. They were different birds than we had back home, but I didn't have a book to identify them.

Soon Marlow was up and ready to get on the road. We drove toward the pyramids of Teotihuacan, which were located thirty kilometers northeast of Mexico City. The trick would be to get there without getting into Mexico City (population twenty-one million, more than we had in all of California).

We left our delightful hotel and found our way back to the toll road, the most expensive in the world, we were later told. We worked our way through Cuernavaca (KWEHR-na-vaca). We got slightly lost when we got off the toll road to take the "highway" that skirted around the edge of Mexico City. We stopped and asked directions a couple of times, and people were glad to help. We followed their gestures more than their words and finally got onto the right track.

I enjoyed the mountain scenery, volcanic cores, and Shotover Jet boat ride. We had taken a similar ride in New Zealand. For some reason Marlow decided at the last minute that it was too expensive and didn't go. I went with a group of Hispanic tourists. I sat up in front with the driver so I could see better. This jet-propelled boat could make a three-sixty-degree spin on a dime. We got soaked with the water spewed airborne by our own boat. The sun was shining brightly, and it was over eighty degrees, so watching the rainbows in the boat spray was well worth the cost of getting wet. The boat could travel on only four inches of water; we buzzed through the bulrushes, pulled into a cave and spun out, missing rocks by inches. I loved the thrilling ride!

We skirted the suburbs of Mexico City without having an accident, an incredible accomplishment! There were no lane lines painted in the streets. Sometimes it looked like we were on a three-lane road, only to have someone create an additional lane between us and the vehicle beside us. People didn't stop at red lights; they slowed down to see if they could safely make it across the traffic that had the right-of-way. Other times they'd keep jerking their car a few inches at a time into the intersection until the cross traffic gave up and let the offending car through. Every time we stopped at red lights, people honked at us. The police drove as crazy as everyone else, and we didn't see a single driver getting a citation.

By two o'clock we were at the pyramids. What an awesome sight! Eight square miles had been uncovered. Anthropologists were still guessing what went on there. They thought the city inhabitants disappeared around 150 AD, possibly due to the lack of food. The area surrounding the pyramids was desert. Anthropologists surmised it was jungle 2,500 years ago and then desert 2,000 years ago. The Pyramid of the Sun was the third-largest pyramid ever uncovered. It had two-hundred-forty-eight steps to the top, over twenty stories. I made it to the first landing. Marlow made it a bit farther, but his fear of heights got to him when he turned around to see where I was. The steps were only about six inches wide, so he made his way down very carefully. Thousands of people were climbing the pyramids, and no one fell.

I don't know if it was more popular on this first Sunday after Christmas because *Time* magazine had done an article on Teotihuacan the week before, or maybe it was more crowded because it was holiday time in Mexico. We viewed the grounds. I'd have spent a whole day reading the plaques and asking questions, but I knew that was just the type of behavior Marlow hated. The pyramids were not large cut blocks of stone like the ones in Egypt, but rather a variety of sizes of stones put together with lots of mortar or cement. Archeologists were exploring tombs at the site, and we may have more answers on the original inhabitants in the next few years.

December 28, 1998 We ate a leisurely breakfast at the Master Club at Tequesquitengo Lago, enjoying the tranquility and the friendliness of the people. We were lucky enough to spend a second night in their company. Then we headed toward Acapulco.

We got off the turnpike to explore coconut farms and to get a better look at the volcanic plugs. I hoped to see more of the jungle, but we couldn't find a road that we dared use with our little Escort. The coconut farms were interesting anyhow. The coconuts were cut off the trees with machetes and then split open and left lying on the ground to dry out. I'm sure the bugs were removed and it was all purified before it hit our stores in the United States. Right?

The sun was setting when we reached Acapulco; we had spent almost $200.00 on turnpike fees and gasoline for our side trip to the pyramids. Seeing them was worth every cent.

We searched and searched for a place to stay. We hadn't made reservations because the agent in Folsom couldn't find anything for less than $200.00 a night. I didn't want to pay that much for a bed to sleep in for one night.

We couldn't find a vacancy at any price!

I happened to see a neon sign saying, "Hotel" down a side street a couple of blocks off the main drag. I told Marlow to circle around and go down that street. Such a simple maneuver took some doing, as the blocks weren't square; they were triangles and pentagons.

We found the place and pulled into the courtyard looking for the office. A young woman walked toward us, motioning us to pull into one of the garages. I thought that was pushy, but we did it anyhow. Zap, everything turned dark. The woman pulled a thick rubber drape across the opening. What strange behavior! We paranoid gringos thought we were about to be robbed!

We got out of the car, opened the drape, and asked if she had a room for two for the night.

"*Sí, sí*." She pulled the drape closed again with a jerk; we jumped out of the way. We asked if we could see the room, being very suspicious by now. She directed us to the opposite corner of the garage and opened a door that led up a flight of stairs. She switched on a light, which had about a twenty-watt bulb. I felt my way to the top of the stairs and found another light switch. Another twenty-watt bulb came on. The room looked clean, had a king-size bed made up with clean sheets, and had a bathroom. That was all we needed.

I asked her how much, and she said five hundred, which meant US$50.00.

I said, "Okay, will you take a traveler's check?"

"No, no checks."

"Will you take MasterCard?"

"No, no cards. Cash only. Mexican money." We said we'd take the room, but we'd have to go to a bank and cash a traveler's check. She said it was all right to leave the car in the garage.

We walked to Walmart, where we found an ATM and got the cash, then returned to the motel. I suggested Marlow register while I carried luggage upstairs. I wanted to get our bags sorted out to take to the airport in the morning and wanted to take a shower. The air was so humid, I was dripping with sweat.

When I got my chores done and was ready to take my shower, I realized the clear glass shower was located at one end of the bedroom, not in the bathroom, where there was only a toilet and washbasin. I told Marlow I was much too old and fat to undress in front of him. He promised he'd keep his head turned away from the shower. I didn't know if he could be trusted, so I waited until he volunteered to go get some beer, then I quickly took my shower. I was rinsing off when I heard him back in the room. I turned to get the towel. He was sitting on the bed with his back to me. He had a big grin on his face. I could tell because there was a floor-to-ceiling mirror in front of him.

We commented that with a few changes, such as hundred-watt bulbs, frosted glass in the shower, a closet, and air conditioning that got the temperature below seventy-eight degrees, this would really be a good motel. It was nice to have a garage, and we were off the main street far enough that it was quiet.

After Marlow had taken his shower, we settled in bed with our beer and sandwiches for dinner. I switched on the television to see if we could get *Monday Night Football.* Pornography! Of course, now it all made sense. It was one of *those* motels! Boy, are we naive or what?

"Oh, so that's why the girl didn't want to know my name when I tried to register," Marlow said. "She just wanted the money, no forms to fill out. I handed her the money, and she handed me a key."

December 29, 1998 The plane was scheduled to leave at ten a.m.; Marlow figured we needed to get up at six to get to the airport by eight to return the rental car and secure our seats. All planes were overbooked at holiday time. Oh well, I'd sleep late when we got home.

No traffic. Everyone else was sleeping late, so we got to the airport by ten after seven. No one was scheduled to man the check-in counter for the car or the plane until eight. We put our bags first in line at the plane check-in desk, parked the car in the rental return lot, and looked in the souvenir store windows until a worker arrived about twenty after eight.

We returned the car and were second in line for the airline clerk. Another man had gotten in front of us when his taxi driver put his luggage on the scales. He apologized, and we assured him there was no problem. I was sure there were at least three seats on the plane.

"I guess you want to change your ticket," the clerk said as she examined our tickets.

"No, it's fine," I said. "We just wanted to make sure we had an aisle seat and a window seat. I hate sitting in the middle seat when there are three seats across."

"Okay, I'll reserve your seats for tomorrow's flight," she said. What! Tomorrow's flight! Yes, we showed up at the airport a day early. We had lost track of what day of the week it was. We could have spent another night at Tequesquitengo Lago! We decided to go on standby and see if we could get back to the land of air conditioning, Monday night football and television shows where the actors spoke our language. Several plane rides and lay-overs later, we arrived in Sacramento.

Ten

Adventure in Australia or Hooray for Retirement

1999

I retired from Aerojet on June 1, 1999. I had been planning a post-retirement circumnavigation of Australia for five years. Marlow didn't want to join me on the six-month trip, as I wanted to spend as much time as possible camping in the outback. When the weather was inclement, I planned on staying with members of a peace organization called Servas, or staying in hostels. Marlow hated visiting anyone and would never consent to staying in the home of strangers. He told me he was going to continue working until I got all this "roughing it" out of my system. Then he'd retire and we'd take civilized vacations together—cruises. Yuck!

I found a traveling companion in my friend, Annabel, who had been a draftsperson at Aerojet for the same twenty years as me. She was married to an Aerojetter who thought similar to Marlow. Cruises were vacations; camping trips were torture.

August 3, 1999 Annabel and her husband, Jonathan, picked me up at three fifty a.m. at our home in Folsom, California, for our drive to San Francisco International Airport. At that time of morning, we thought we'd have the freeway to ourselves. Not so; lots of people drove at night. The traffic consistently got thicker as we approached San Francisco.

As we arrived in the town of Pinole, we saw a flashing road sign reading, "Freeway Closed Ahead." Jonathan, who was driving, and Annabel discussed alternate routes to get to the airport. None sounded feasible; we'd have to travel a hundred miles out of our way, whichever route was chosen.

By the time the decision was made, we had no option but to go straight and hope for the best. We coasted to a stop along with four other lanes of traffic. We were in the left lane and inched our way forward when possible. The right lane began moving faster, but we quickly discarded plans to work our way across four lanes of freeway to get in that lane. Those people were heading for the Appian Way off-ramp.

The lane next to us moved slowly forward. The highway patrol had just opened the left two lanes. Yea!

Annabel tuned the radio to the local news station. The main story was the freeway closure. The freeway had been closed since eleven p.m. The newscaster reported that police chased a suspect in a drug-related crime quite a long way. The involved personnel ended up on Route 80 West.

The suspect started up the Appian Way off-ramp. Seeing police at the top, he swerved back onto the freeway, changed his mind, and charged up the embankment. His pickup was not able to reach the apex. He shifted into reverse and backed down the embankment, hitting a highway patrol car. The bed of the pickup ended up on the roof of the car.

The perpetrator could not proceed, so he pulled out his gun and started shooting. In the ensuing exchange of gunfire, he was injured. He was taken into custody and airlifted to the hospital. The story sounded like a fictional television drama.

As we arrived on the scene, police were taking pictures from all angles and recording any evidence found. The whole melee delayed our progress by fifteen minutes.

We arrived at the airport, and drove around three times before getting into the correct lane for Air Reno departing passengers. Annabel and I arrived at the check-in counter at six forty five, and the clerk asked if we'd like to take the six-fifty-four a.m. flight to Los Angeles rather than our scheduled nine-twenty-two flight.

In my usual impulsive way, I said, "Sure, why not."

Annabel gasped. "What about Jonathan? He won't know what happened to us." He was outside looking for a parking place. He planned on joining us inside for a leisurely breakfast.

It also had not dawned on me that I was only leaving nine minutes for us to complete check-in and arrive at the departure gate. I surely was not athletic enough to sprint the half a mile between the check-in counter and the plane.

Annabel more wisely suggested we take the next available flight that was scheduled to leave at eight twenty a.m. That made more sense. It would be good to have someone with common sense to keep me under control on our adventure.

In Los Angeles we needed to transfer from the domestic terminal to the international terminal, and being naturally lazy, I suggested we take the shuttle to the international terminal. Annabel pointed to the building a hundred feet away that said, "International Terminal" and suggested we walk. She not only had common sense, she could read! That was going to be a real plus! I'd have charged out of the domestic terminal and hopped on the shuttle and ridden around for an hour looking for the Qantas departure terminal.

Our luggage was routed from San Francisco to Sydney, so we sauntered to our departure gate for some people watching. People watching has always been an interesting spectator sport in Los Angeles.

Qantas (Queensland and Northern Territory Airline Service) left the gate right on time at one p.m. We joined other planes in the queue for departure. We taxied for ten minutes and then waited for tower clearance. To entertain us during that period, the stewardess made announcements. She said it was expected to take us fourteen hours and forty minutes to travel 12,054 kilometers (7,473 miles) to Sydney.

Eventually, we were free of the bonds of earth, floating serenely over the ocean. Homeward-bound Aussies were easy to recognize. By the time we cleared the coastline, they had their shoes off. I settled in and watched *Walk on the Moon,* a silly, depressing movie about infidelity and its effect on the family. A few minutes into a second movie, *Molly,* I got bored and turned to my novel. Annabel, who had an aisle seat across from mine, watched a bit of this and that and snoozed from time to time.

By ten p.m. I was ready for sleep, and dinner had not yet been served. I knew I'd never sleep through the hustle and bustle of feeding the multitudes, so I forced my eyes to remain open. Qantas served a roast beef dinner at eleven California time, as the sun slowly sank from view out of the plane windows. We were heading west into the sun.

There was a vacant seat between me and the Sydneysider sitting next to the window. The young man said he had been on tour of the *whole* United States. He had flown from Los Angeles to Portland, then worked his way down the west coast to Tijuana via land transportation. He then flew to New York City (oh cringe). Yep, he had "toured" 30,000 feet of sky above the United States.

When I asked if the residents in New York were rude, he remarked, "Only until I said something. Then they mellowed out."

I found it sad that he hadn't visited the national parks, the mountains, the colorful deserts, or the heartland, but I guessed twenty-one-year-olds with pierced eyebrows and dreadlocks weren't interested in that sort of thing. He said people were very friendly everywhere he went on the West Coast. Bless their broad-minded, tolerant hearts.

You realize, of course, that the reason the first day of my journal is long is because I had little else to do but read, write, or watch boring movies on the plane. I won't go into so much detail later in the trip.

August 4, 1999 We lost a day crossing the International Date Line. See, I told you each day's entry wouldn't be as long as the first day.

I'll fill in the extra space with a song, one of the interpretations of Banjo Patterson's poem. I was so glad that Annabel agreed to go waltzing Matilda with me.

Waltzing Matilda
By Banjo Patterson

Oh, there once was a swagman camped by a billabong
Under the shade of a coolibah tree,
And he sang as he watched and waited till his billy boiled:
"Who'll come a waltzing Matilda with me?

Waltzing Matilda, waltzing Matilda
You'll come a-waltzing Matilda, with me"
And he sang as he watched and waited till his billy boiled:
"You'll come a-waltzing Matilda, with me."

Down came a jumbuck to drink at that billabong.
Up jumped the swagman and grabbed him with glee.
And he sang as he shoved that jumbuck in his tucker bag:
"You'll come a waltzing Matilda, with me."

Waltzing Matilda, waltzing Matilda
"You'll come a-waltzing Matilda, with me."

Up rode the squatter mounted on a thoroughbred.
Down came the troopers, one, two, three.
"Whose is the jumbuck you've got in your tucker bag?
You'll come waltzing Matilda with me."

Up jumped the swagman and sprang into the billabong,
Drowning himself 'neath the coolibah tree
And his ghost may be heard as you pass by that the billabong,
"You'll come a waltzing Matilda with me.

Waltzing Matilda, waltzing Matilda,
You'll come a waltzing Matilda, with me."
And his ghost may be heard as you pass by that billabong:
"Who'll come a-waltzing Matilda, with me?"

Glossary: Swagman = tramp, itinerant traveler. Billabong = pond, water hole. Billy = tin can with a wire for a handle used for making camp tea. Waltzing = traveling. Matilda = swag, belongings tied in a cloth. Jumbuck = male sheep. Tucker bag = lunch box. Squatter = wealthy landowner.

August 5, 1999 We arrived on schedule to the very minute, picked up our luggage, went through customs without a delay or hassle, and taxied to the reserved lodging in two hours. The time was a bit after midnight, so we bathed and gladly snuggled into our beds. It had been at least twenty-seven hours since we last lay in a bed.

I got a sound six hours of sleep in our nice, clean, little cabin in suburban Sydney.

In the morning Annabel and I took our time reorganizing our luggage. We were only allowed two bags each while airborne, so they were crammed. We packed empty bags inside our suitcases so we could arrange things better once we arrived in Australia. We put camping gear in one bag, things needed for home stays in a second bag, and used the third bag for things we would need on the cross-country train ride.

I cooked breakfast—tea and granola bars.

We phoned our respective husbands to let them know we arrived safely. On the way to the phone, I was drawn to the tree where the caravan (trailer) park managers fed the rainbow lorikeets. They were such beautiful birds. It sounded as if they were yelling. "Welcome back, welcome back," but it may have been my imagination.

I wanted to wait at the caravan park until the office staff arrived. I paid for the reservation with my MasterCard and didn't know if the office deducted the full payment or just a deposit. I didn't want to start out with the police on our tail for nonpayment of a bill. The lady arrived at eight thirty and reassured us everything was paid. She called a taxi and arranged for the driver to take us to the train station so we could see Sydney sights unencumbered by luggage. Had we not waited for the office lady, we would have thought it necessary to drag our belongings wherever we went.

Annabel waited for the taxi at the caravan park driveway so she could show the driver to our cabin. The driver showed up at the cabin sans Annabel. Said he had not seen anyone at the entrance to the park. He loaded Annabel's luggage, and I loaded my own; I double-checked the room for left-behind socks, and we drove to the front of the caravan park, where we found Annabel standing by the curb. She hadn't seen the taxi enter the park and was surprised to find that we were ready to leave. It was easy to get distracted on one's first visit to the tropics. Trees and bushes were in bloom, colorful birds could be seen everywhere, and the architecture was geared toward keeping cool, with houses built on stumps high off the ground and surrounded by open verandahs, which confirmed we were in a foreign country.

The train station attendant showed us a room where other tourists had their luggage stored awaiting the two p.m. departure. We put our cumbersome bags into the room. After the train business was sorted out, we made our way to Circular Quay.

I took the tour of the Sydney Opera House and learned:

- The Chamber Music Theatre seated four hundred.
- The Opera Theatre seated three thousand.
- The Chamber Music Orchestra usually sold approximately twenty-five hundred tickets, so it played in the Opera Theatre.
- The original Chamber Music Theatre became a playhouse.
- Architecture was done by Jan Utsea, who was awarded the 1954 contract for design of the exterior.
- Peter Hall completed the interior design.
- $7 million was set aside for the construction in 1954. The cost came to $123 million at completion in 1973; that was paid with the sale of lottery tickets.
- The Drama Playhouse was the busiest section, as there was an average of three-hundred-eighty plays a year.
- Sydney Symphony Orchestra performed in the Orchestra Hall, where the acoustics were incredible because of the Austrian wood and the design of the seats surrounding the orchestra pit.

- One hundred and thirty-seven organ pipes were seen by the audience, but the actual number of pipes was ten thousand five hundred, the second largest number of pipes in the world (Mormon Tabernacle in Salt Lake City took first place).

We had a minor hassle with luggage when we were ready to leave on the train. The baggage claim man said the bags were too heavy to lift, and we would have to dispose of part of the contents. I asked if we could take our gear if I lifted it onto the train. The embarrassed gent decided he could put it onboard for us. We climbed on the Indian Pacific Train at two o'clock and learned that our seats were preassigned. Annabel and I had the first seats in the economy class car. We had heaps of legroom between us and the restroom wall, plenty of space for our six bags. A table was supposed to be set up in that space, but the bracket was broken.

We got acquainted with our friendly neighbors, then listened to a tape telling us about the area between Sydney and Broken Hill. The Blue Mountains were blue because of the haze. They consisted of eucalyptus-covered sandstone, shale, and basalt. Just lovely.

August 6, 1999 I slept fitfully, as the train slowed down or stopped every hour or so. As it turned out, there were stations (ranches) along the railway line that were considered potential train stops. The engineer had to slow down to see if any passengers were waiting to board. We awoke in the morning to see landscape had changed to Chihuahuan-type desert.

Our first full stop was at Broken Hill, New South Wales. We toured Broken Hill, where we saw the silver/lead/zinc mine. We saw miner's housing and mining equipment. In the 1970s six mines hired six thousand people. They now had one mine that hired nine hundred.

We viewed the Flying Doctors' Facility. Stations were supplied with medicine trunks approximately eighteen inches square with layers of trays filled with hypodermic needles and paraphernalia for setting broken bones or assisting in other maladies such as birthing children. Everything in the box was numbered so the doctor could dictate which item was to be used when talking to the caregiver at the scene of the medical emergency. Many times the agriculturist or a child performed medical chores while awaiting the doctor's arrival in his plane.

The Flying Doctors' Facility consisted of a museum, a lecture hall, an administration office, a hangar for three planes, a mechanic's shop, and a radio room where two women monitored calls on their two-way radios.

Leaving Broken Hill, we saw a group of prepubescent boys dashing down a hill toward the train. I thought, *How sweet, they've come to wave good-bye.* As they neared the slowly moving train, they turned and dropped their drawers. I'd never been mooned before! I knew this trip would be a learning experience.

We arrived in Adelaide one and a half hours late, and our Servas hostess, Joyce, cheerfully greeted us. Servas was the name of the organization Annabel and I had joined so we could stay in private homes in Australia to exchange cultures. I loved learning about other cultures. The organization was started by Bob Luitweiler after World War II. His thought was that if people understood one another better, they wouldn't go to war. Nice idea, but our government decides if we're going to war, not individual citizens. Anyhow, we were screened by an interviewer who decided we were honest, upstanding citizens who would not rob our hosts or murder them in their beds. We looked like the type of people who would share our California culture with the Australians in return for lodging and listening to their stories.

Joyce helped load our heavy bags into her station wagon and took us to her beautiful home in the suburb of Athelstone, which backed against a national park. She had a low-set (built at ground level) brick home with a rainforest setting for landscaping. Even her garage was filled with hanging pot plants and was decked out like a patio. The tools had been hidden in a storage shed somewhere. Annabel and I were shown to private bedrooms tastefully decorated with warm colors and natural woods and smelling of potpourri.

August 7, 1999 Joyce drove us to a zoo for close encounters with Australian fauna. Of all the exotic foreign animals such as emus, cassowaries, kangaroos, Tasmanian devils, wombats, and so forth, the ones Annabel liked the best were the dingoes, as they reminded her of her dogs at home. The zoo was a lovely walk-through park where kangaroos bounced merrily among the tourists and allowed themselves to be petted or fed.

Joyce took Annabel and me on a historical tour of the town, pointing out statues and architecture, and explaining the usage of various buildings. She dropped us off at a shopping center so we could experience Adelaide's form of mass transit. She told us where she'd meet us and how to get there. We took the super-modern monorail from the shopping center to a park set among skyscrapers. From there we caught a streetcar, called a tram, with antique equipment, and we rumbled through the suburbs to the beach on the ocean.

Joyce was waiting with a picnic basket when we disembarked, and we ate homemade Dagwood sandwiches and cake at a picnic table. She escorted us to a local casino where she knew hot tea and coffee were served free to all. The weather was cold, wet, and windy, so the warm refreshments were welcome. June, July, and August were winter in Australia.

Back at Joyce's home, we huddled in front of a space heater and traded travel stories. Joyce had belonged to Servas for some time and loved to travel. She promised to stop and see us on her way home from the Middle East and the United Kingdom in March 2000.

Joyce was a football fan, so we joined her watching an Aussie Rules game on television. I'm a football fan, also. We debated the pros and cons of the two different types of football. Of course, she held the opinion of most Aussies that American football players were sissies for wearing so much armor.

After the game she served a fantastic Italian dinner, and then we gladly retired to our respective beds laden with warm comforters. Annabel and I were happy we were not yet camping—it was *cold* outside.

August 8, 1999 It continued to rain heavily, so we aborted our plans to go to Kangaroo Island. Joyce told us the highlights of the island entailed lots of walking outside.

Joyce took us to Adelaide Botanical Gardens, which had a hothouse of rainforest plants. We enjoyed the twenty five degree Celsius (seventy eight degrees Fahrenheit) warmth and the lush display. We tried to remember as many plant names as we could. We knew we'd be seeing them again.

We went to a commercial tourist attraction called the Woolshed, where we watched shearing and wool-spinning demonstrations, as well as played with baby animals. Most of the animals were domestic, but there were some stubby-tailed lizards also. Holding the subspecies of reptiles, I realized the lizards' scales were as hard as a turtle's shell. The tourist attraction was a delightful place to spend a rainy day.

Later that evening Joyce took us to our next Servas host and hostess's home on the other side of Adelaide. We said our good-byes to Joyce and told her we'd look forward to seeing her after her camping trip across the Middle East and the United Kingdom.

Ron and Elly, our new Servas hosts, had two sons, Jared and Merlin. The sons were twenty-one and twenty-five years old and were six foot four. Annabel and I are both five foot two. The boys gave Annabel and me their apartment in a separate building in the backyard for our sleeping quarters.

Ron and Elly had many of the same hobbies and collections I've had over the years, such as shells, dried plants, family photos, traveling, camping, bird-watching, and feeding wild critters. It was obvious they were nature lovers. The only cultural exchange was the different ways we spoke English.

The parents were in their mid-forties. Ron worked for the phone company, and Elly was a nurse. The boys were extremely intelligent university students. They had a fellow student staying with them. The three boys were eager to question Annabel and me about the aerospace business. I wished I had been a real rocket scientist so I could answer their questions in depth.

Ron and Elly had gone to lots of trouble to fix a typical Australian dinner for us: barbecued lamb chops, pumpkin, peas, potato casserole, and sweets—all things that I would normally relish. I was still full from breakfast and lunch; there was no way I could handle another meal. I apologized profusely and drank tea instead.

August 9, 1999 We had a reasonable-sized breakfast—cereal and tea. My stomach was glad. Ron left for work installing phones. Elly went to the dentist. Merlin and Jared went about their business. Annabel and I walked to the train station only to discover that the transport workers were on strike.

Annabel and I walked around the neighborhood, admiring the brick and stone homes adorned with wrought-iron decorations. Most of the homes dated from World War II. A lot of them had fences made of uniform-sized branches about a quarter to a half inch in diameter, bundled together into packs about a foot in diameter. They were called brush fences.

When Elly returned from the dentist, she took us to Bel-Air National Park, where we walked along the trails viewing spring flowers beginning to bloom. We admired the birdlife, shrubs, and flowering wattle trees. Elly pointed out carnivorous plants (that dissolved insects) and anything else she thought we'd find interesting.

She then drove us through downtown, where we admired the multitude of churches and parks. Adelaide *was* a beautiful city, just like the travel brochures said.

August 10, 1999 Merlin drove Elly, Annabel, and me through the world-famous Barossa Valley for wine tasting. Merlin didn't taste, so we felt confident we'd make it back to Adelaide even if we got a bit tipsy. That didn't happen, as we were only offered a thimbleful of various wines before we chose a bottle to buy.

We relished our first sunny day in Adelaide. The valley was scenic, with baby lambs frolicking in pastures, vineyards budding, and spring grass glowing with health and dew. The people were pleasant and conversational when they heard our accents.

I was glad to get into the country after several days in big cities. Annabel enjoyed chatting with fellow grape growers. Servas hosts certainly did an excellent job of entertaining us. We hadn't expected that. We expected a bed to sleep in, possibly a meal, and an evening of chatting around the dining-room table.

Elly helped us load our bulky baggage into her Holden (GMC car comparable to a Chevy) and drove us to the train station for the next leg of our trip. Night had descended when the Indian Pacific left town, so we watched the city lights disappear into darkness.

August 11, 1999 I had about two hours of sleep. Annabel had more. She had a real knack for sleeping under any condition and in any position.

The gray dawn revealed beige sandy gravel as we approached the infamous Nullarbor Desert. We soon learned how the desert got its name. Mile after mile of sandy soil was seen from the window without the sign of a tree (null arbor). I found it interesting to watch the geology as well as look for animals. Only the occasional emu was seen and an occasional sandstone sculpture broke the flat plain.

We were entertained by the Indian Pacific crew, who ran a couple of films on the video machine and played soft background music during the day. Economy class was just that; a car adjoined ours with a ten-foot counter where we could order sandwiches, meat pies, or hot meals served in Styrofoam. At the other end of our coach, we could walk across the platform to the smoking room, which was about ten by eight feet, with hard wooden benches along the walls. The space was depressing, and we only made one trip there out of curiosity; we weren't smokers. Our car was filled with passengers, so we didn't have the option of sitting in seats with empty adjoining spaces to prop up our feet.

First-class passengers paid double the price to have an eight-foot-square room in which to sleep or sit, and a dining room that consisted of tables and benches designed like 1950s diners. The dining-car decor was various shades of gray. They had a lounge car that held well-worn plastic sofas of the same colors, with a bar at one end. It looked uninviting.

Our third stop was in Kalgoorlie, which was larger than I expected. The population was about 30,000. Kalgoorlie was the location where there was a gold rush in the 1890s that brought in approximately

200,000 people, mostly miners. It is still considered the richest square mile on earth, and most of its occupants had mining-related jobs. We had a three-hour layover, and I planned on touring the gold mine, where I thought we would walk into a mine itself. Not so. It would have meant going from sitting on the train to sitting on a bus, so Annabel and I decided to do some walking instead. The day was Sunday; we found no shops open except one chemist (pharmacist) and a couple of fast-food restaurants.

Back on the train, I collapsed into an unoccupied double seat after the former occupants disembarked at Kalgoorlie. I took a sleeping pill and curled up for six restless hours. I awoke each time the train slowed for a station. I felt somewhat refreshed in the morning.

August 12, 1999 I passed the morning watching the pleasant scenery of the York and Avon Valley agricultural districts, which was like riding through Iowa, and Illinois.

Annabel and I were scheduled to arrive in Perth at seven in the morning. Instead, we arrived at eleven thirty. I was glad no one was waiting for us. Annabel stayed at the train station with our bags while I took a taxi to the Avis office, where I had a rental car reserved.

Annabel navigated while I drove through the beautiful, modern city of Perth and out to Coogee Beach, where we had a cozy cabin reserved. The cabin slept six, the only one available at the time of booking six months previously. We had all of the appurtenances needed for a comfortable stay, including separate bedrooms. We spread out and made ourselves at home.

A path led through a sand dune between our cabin and the beach on the Indian Ocean.

August 14, 1999 We went to Fremantle, the town where the America's Cup yacht race was held in 1987. The town had been renovated for the event, and many historical buildings had been restored to their original "splendor." I put that word in quotes because I don't think the original insane asylum for women had ever been "splendid."

The women were committed for signs of insanity such as talking back to their husbands, swearing in public, wearing suggestive clothing, wearing men's clothing (Egad! Not trousers!), and lying. What would they have done to women who held male-dominated jobs such as drafting and engineering? Or those who had the unmitigated gall to travel in a foreign country without the protection of their husbands?

The building was later used as a women's prison. A padded cell was installed for the women who were truly mentally ill and might do harm to themselves.

Dark dreary rooms with tiny windows and an iron bed with no mattress were added for solitary confinement of the women who were uncooperative with the warders. The remainder of the prisoners slept in dormitories. A sign on the wall said that people in the men's prison, who were uncooperative were denied cigarettes for several hours.

The massive stone structure later became a refuge for indigent women and was probably marginally better than living on the streets, except, of course, when epidemics hit. Then the women would have been better off living on the beach or in the woods.

In present-day Australia, indigent women have a pretty good life, thanks to the welfare system. I didn't know what their mental institutions or prisons were like, but I'd guess the women were treated considerably better than they were a hundred years ago.

The complex was now an enlightening museum and art gallery.

Fortunately, we saw many bright, ornate, cheerful buildings in Fremantle to offset the women's facility atmosphere. In fact, it was the law in Fremantle that facades had to maintain their original design. New government buildings were located inside the old building's facades. The old buildings looked like a movie set built a few feet in front of modern brick structures.

We went on a bus tour, a walking tour, and shopping. I got three rolls of film developed ($48.00) and bought used books on trees and birds of Australia. Annabel bought an ice-cream treat. Fremantle merchants would never be able to retire if they were counting on big spenders like us.

August 15, 1999 A public bus transported us from Coogee Beach Caravan Park to the pier in Fremantle, where we caught the ferry to Rottnest Island. I planned on cycling around the island to prove to Annabel that I could be athletic. She was fit as a twenty-something athlete. I'd bought a bike a year before the trip to practice. I wasn't very good. I wasn't really athletic at all. The weather was rainy and windy, the bike seats were narrow and hard, and the roads had many steep hills. I joined Annabel on a bus tour instead. That was far more sensible. Maybe Annabel's sensibleness was contagious!

The limestone and quartzite geology created a spectacular shoreline. The unique flora consisted of grass and weeping Rottnest tea trees, rather like a combination of a weeping willow and a cypress tree. We learned that the island had been a penal colony for Aboriginal men from the 1800s and up until 1930. I don't know why we were touring historical penal establishments. It just happened. Aboriginal men committed suicide if confined in a cell, so the government thought that keeping them on an island away from their families was punishment enough. By the 1900s white people became jealous of the lovely island on which the Aboriginals were being held, and the prison was closed and the land converted to resorts.

We walked about the island and ducked into the museum to wait out a thunderstorm that blew past. I was so happy Annabel was there reading display-case label after label like me. Many people couldn't tolerate the slow pace of a good museum visit.

The island was now a resort frequented by 400,000 people annually. We were there in the off-season. I tolerated rain and cold better than throngs of people. There were presently about two thousand other people on the eleven-mile-long island.

The highlight was seeing the quokkas, cat-sized kangaroos. There were approximately 15,000 on the island. A few had been found on the mainland, smuggled there as pets. Outside of those few, quokkas were found nowhere else on earth. Annabel came alive when able to feed the little, furry animals and was downright enthusiastic when she discovered a joey (baby) in a mama's pouch. When Annabel showed signs of enjoying herself, I got ecstatic.

August 16–19, 1999 Three days were spent car shopping. I finally bought a 1993 Toyota Land Cruiser with 111,000 kilometers (approximately 70,000 miles) on the odometer. It was petrol driven as opposed to diesel; it had a power transmission as opposed to manual. I paid $29,900.00 for the car and then spent an extra $450.00 putting in a new windshield and buying tools in case of an emergency. The registration was $1,175.00, and insurance was $450.00 for a total of $31,975.00. To rent a comparable vehicle would have cost us $175.00 to $200.00 per *day* (between $32,000.00 and $36,000.00 for six months). I planned to sell the vehicle when I got to Rockhampton, Queensland, before taking a bus to Sydney for my flight home to the United States. Annabel didn't agree with my choice of vehicle, so she didn't want to pay half. Instead, she agreed to pay for the fuel used. In the end we probably spent close to the same amount, except I would get part of my money reimbursed in Rockhampton.

August 20, 1999 We spent the day taking care of car insurance, grocery shopping, buying camping equipment, and appurtenances required for our circumnavigation of this big sunburned country. Anticipation was building...

August 21, 1999 This day marked the eighteenth day of our trip. We felt we were finally getting underway. We went in search of a petrol station where we could use the $.06 a liter discount coupon we had obtained from Woolworth's grocery store. A liter is approximately the same amount of liquid as a quart. We learned Woolworth's petrol stations were the only places the coupon could be used. The car held over a hundred ten liters in its two tanks. After the discount our petrol cost $78.00!

Annabel tried the single-burner gas stove she brought from home on the new propane tank we purchased at Big W (Woolworth's variety store). It didn't fit; the tank had a metric-sized nozzle. We found a Kmart that carried the Australian version of single burners. Annabel packed her American model to be taken home at the end of the trip.

It was eleven thirty by the time we were actually on the road. I told our next Servas hosts we'd be at their home between three and four o'clock. That was going to be a bit of a push, but we still made a stop at the beach at Bunbury, where we expected to swim with dolphins. Not a single dolphin or human was in sight, so we didn't bother getting into the wintry water.

We stopped in Australind, a site mentioned in the historical novel I was reading as the second place that England developed an agricultural center (after Fremantle) in Western Australia. The name of the novel was *To Be Heirs Forever* by Mary Durack. The site was now a pleasant seaside town with a park stretching picturesquely along the shore. We ate lunch there and watched children chase sea gulls and pelicans.

We arrived at our Servas hosts' house soon after four. Francis and Janet's home was located in the beachside community of Busselton. Janet took us for a walk on the fenced paths of the shoreline and through the exclusive neighborhood. Most of the homes were valued starting at $750,000.00 ($1.5 million in the United States). Many were on canals with yachts anchored at private piers.

As soon as dinner was cleared away, we scurried off to their country club tennis player's fund-raiser called Quiz Night. Marlow could have guessed some of the songs from the forties and fifties. Annabel and I were no help at all. The game was played like the *Name That Tune* television show, where one or two notes were played, and then the participants tried to name the song. Our table came in fifth. I never heard of most of the songs or artists—they were Australian. After the games tickets were sold for chances on various prizes, and drawings for winners were made. We cheered each winner though we went home empty-handed. The evening was topped off with some DJ music and dancing. Annabel was too reserved to dance, but I had no problem making a fool of myself. I would never see those people again.

We arrived back at the Servas hosts' home after midnight and chatted for another hour. Once in between the crisp, starched, ironed sheets of my bed, I rolled and tossed for a couple more hours. I couldn't get warm. The temperature dropped to three degrees Celsius (about thirty-six degrees Fahrenheit). At home on such a night, I'd have had flannel sheets and an electric blanket.

August 22, 1999 We slowly began moving about eight o'clock. I offered to *shout* (treat) the hosts to breakfast, so by nine thirty, we left the house to go to a nice restaurant attached to a beach resort, which was lovely and classy. I expected the bill to come to at least $50.00 and was pleasantly surprised to see it was only $28.50.

We said our farewells and told Francis and Janet we'd come back and spend more time with them if we got a chance. They promised they'd come to California and visit us. Francis and Janet owned a car parts store in Busselton and were actors in live theatre. They were hospitable and entertaining. They had three grown sons, whom we did not have the opportunity to meet. Annabel and I each have three grown sons. They also had several tennis awards on display in their home, so *they* must be athletic, unlike half the people on our excursion.

Being on the road, basking in our third day in a row of sunshine was appreciated. We played soft music on the radio and talked very little as we cruised down the highway of Western Australia heading south. We made stops at Cape Naturaliste National Park, Leeuwin National Park, the Eagles/Raptors Wildlife Park, the Bentonbrae Winery, and Mammoth Caves.

Cape Naturaliste and Leeuwin had rugged cliffs, and rock-strewn shores stretching from the western side of Australia around the corner to the southern side. The parks were therefore the meeting place for the Indian and Antarctic Oceans. The landscape had been formed by the natural forces of wind, rain, and waves. Back a short distance from the oceans, we found trees protecting pastures of rich green grass and wildflowers. Calla lilies grew in profusion in sheep paddocks, along with buttercups, daisies, and violets.

The Eagles/Raptors Park was the type of place that made me feel sorry for the penned-up animals, but at the same time, I realized I'd never otherwise see those animals close up. If they weren't in pens, I could never have stood ten feet away admiring the delicate colors and textures of their feathers.

The winery was set among rolling sheep paddocks (pastures), interspersed with several acres of vineyards. We could tell we were not in Napa Valley, California, by the presence of kangaroos and emus among the sheep.

Mammoth Caves were the usual fare of stalactites and stalagmites. If you'd never seen them before, they would strike you as awesome. The time consumed to create the wonders always fascinated me—one drip at a time. Stalactites cling to the ceiling. Stalagmites grow up from the ground.

We settled in for the night at Prevelly Beach Resort and ate delicious sandwiches made with Janet's homemade bread. We caught up on our journals and then snuggled into warm sleeping bags on top of the comfy beds provided in our seashore cabin. The sound of waves lulled us to sleep.

August 23, 1999 I awoke at seven thirty and went off to the ablution block. There were two other people in Prevelly Beach Resort, and they were boys, so we had the ladies room to ourselves. By the time I returned from my shower, Annabel was up and dressed. We ate a simple breakfast of cereal, orange juice, and tea and were quickly on the road.

We drove along Prevelly surfing beach and marveled at how no one was taking advantage of perfect surfing waves. Even though it was winter, the water would have been dotted with wet-suited surfers in California.

We visited the community of Margaret River in the developing wine country. The green countryside was decorated with dairy farms, vineyards, and tree farms. The pastures were sprinkled with black and white Friesians (Holsteins). We were later told the grass would turn golden brown by October. In that part of the continent, the rains came in the winter. Western Australia's climate mirrored California's. The eastern shores' humidity was like America's eastern coastline. But the difference on both of Australia's coasts was that the north was the hot climate. The southern part of the country was farther from the equator.

Our next stop was at Cape Leeuwin Lighthouse, which warned ships of impending hazards in two oceans.

In Augusta we refueled the main petrol tank. A lady insisted on doing the labor for me. At $.86 a *liter*, I let her. The petrol came to $64.00 and we had traveled five hundred twenty five kilometers. That could get expensive with the amount of kilometers we'd be putting on the odometer (they are called odometers in the United States also).

In Pemberton we went to see the Gloucester Tree, which was a karri tree standing over ninety meters high. There were steps made of twelve-millimeter rebar (twisted reinforcement steel bar used to anchor concrete) that spiraled up the tree to a platform at the top. I climbed a short distance and realized I didn't have the strength in my arthritic fingers to hang on to the rebar. The platform was used as a fire lookout before more modern ones were constructed.

We meandered on trails through the karri forest, viewing the tall, smooth, gray trees with their luxuriant foliage clustered at the tops. The forest floor was covered with acacias and grass trees. We learned that Aboriginals took offense to the short black-trunked trees being called "black boys," and I'd call them by their new name, grass tree, from now on. The taller trees were filled with songbirds as well as noisy, colorful parrots.

We arrived back at the start of the trail just in time to see the ranger feeding parrots. He let us hold out food for the beautiful western rosellas, and they landed on our arms and shoulders. That brought smiles from Annabel and me too.

Our last stop near Pemberton was at Cascades National Park. We bought an annual "all parks" pass at the Gloucester Tree ranger station and wanted to make maximum use of it. We walked five hundred meters down to the cascades and admired the foaming, swirling water before starting off on an alleged circuitous trail. Once we were a good distance along, we faced forks in the path and saw no maps showing where we were or where the trails led. We ended up getting hopelessly lost.

At one point I heard a logging truck drive by and suggested we head for that road and walk to our car from there. Once on the road, we flagged down a *ute* (pickup truck) and asked the driver where the parking lot was for Cascades National Park. He had never heard of the park, but pointed, with his beer can, to a trailhead that he thought might be in the park. We took that trail, which put us back on the maze where we had originally gotten lost. Fortunately there was another couple on the trail, and they pointed us in the right direction. We found our car just as it was too dark to go any further on foot without flashlights. At least we now had the hazard of getting lost accomplished and could cross it off our itinerary.

Back on the road, we located a caravan park with on-site vans (rental trailers). At $40.00 a night, we said yes without looking inside. It turned out to be a poorly maintained trailer with the last occupant's trash still in the basket. It was shelter from the elements, we were tired, and I didn't want to drive further. We stayed.

August 24, 1999 I took a shower in the clean communal restroom and was on my way back to our van when a chocolate-brown baby llama ran toward me. He stayed so close, it was hard getting a picture. Yes, I carried my camera to the ablution block. I never knew when a picture opportunity would present itself. I managed to get far enough away by walking quickly in a zigzag pattern. When I walked in a straight line, he thought I was playing a game, and he butted me like he was a goat.

He had a family that stayed a bit of a distance from us. The llamas were part of the park owner's menagerie. He had goats, sheep, kangaroos, emus, dogs, and cats running around the property. What a fun way to live. He said the kangaroos appeared on public television. We had slept near media stars and didn't have to pay extra for it!

The owner complained about the kookaburras being introduced into Western Australia from "the east." I managed to keep my big mouth closed about llamas, dogs, sheep, goats, and cats not exactly being indigenous to the area. And I certainly didn't want to say anything about the owner's decided *Pommy* accent! The word *Pommy* came from the term "Pome," which stood for "Prisoner of Mother England" and was a derogatory term used to describe any Australian immigrant from England.

The original European settlers in Eastern Australia were prisoners sent from England along with their warders.

We packed the car and headed for Mt. Chudalup, the oldest part of earth above water, according to an Australian geology book I read. We were the only climbers, as the weather was cold, windy, and rainy once again. Let me emphasize the windy part. I had a dickens of a time keeping my balance on the granite outcroppings of the mountain, with no trees to cling to. When I got to the top, I found the view would have been spectacular on a clear day. The hazy rain made picture taking useless. I checked out the three-hundred-sixty-degree views and scooted down the granite. Annabel waited for me on a lower plateau, once more proving she was the smarter of the two of us.

We walked through the forest of three-hundred-year-old karri, jarrah, and grass trees. A few wildflowers were blooming in well-protected crevices. I had no idea what their names were, but they were very pretty pinks, yellows, and whites, and a welcome reminder that we'd get into spring-like weather any day now.

Annabel and I drove to Windy Harbour, which lived up to its name. The holiday cabins were deserted. I used the Toyota's four-wheel-drive capacity climbing up the limestone and shale creation called D'entrecasteaux, which meant "entrance to the castle" in French. The enormous waves of the Antarctic Ocean pounded the jagged shore and were a bit frightening with their awesome power. The air smelled freshly scrubbed.

We retraced our path to Route 10 and drove through Shannon National Park. The Shannon River was the largest we'd seen since leaving the Swan River behind in Perth. We picked up Route 1 which followed the rugged Antarctic coastline. We rode it from the town of Shannon to the heavily forested Walpole-Nornalup National Park.

That took us to the Valley of the Giants, a forest of karri and tingle trees with a treetop walk. Some of the trees reached forty-six meters in height. The walk consisted of traversing a series of steel-mesh bridges high above ground. I loved it. It reminded me of hot-air ballooning. Annabel followed some distance behind with her video camera. I learned that Annabel didn't like to get her feet off terra firma. She saw almost nothing on the trip except the back of the person in front of her. It must have been terrifying when rain started and the bridges got bouncy with scurrying people.

We both survived and were soon back in the car on Route 1, driving through dairy farms and sheep stations on our way to Denmark—the town, not the country.

Once there we filled our thirsty petrol tank and left the coast behind to start our northward trek. We spent the night in a wonderfully clean, well-furnished cabin with a private bath connected to our bedrooms.

August 25, 1999 It rained most of the night. By the time we were on the road, the rain began to slacken. Blue skies peeked through large, fluffy, cumulous clouds.

We retraced our route for eleven kilometers, as Annabel wanted to take a video shot of a picturesque winery. It had been too dark when we passed it the evening before. By the time we got to the winery, the rain stopped, and Annabel got pictures, tasted the local Shiraz, a very dry burgundy wine, and had a lovely conversation with the vintner on the growing of grapes.

Back on the road, the clouds dumped on us. So far we had been lucky with the weather giving us a break when we wanted to go for a walk or take a picture. The storm gave me an excuse to try the windshield wiper on the rear window. The Toyota Land Cruiser had so many cute gadgets on it. We were soon on a dirt road, so after a few kilometers, I tried the rear window washer. So far everything worked well on the vehicle.

The rain stopped as we approached the trail for the *Tree Growing in a Rock*. We saw the tall karri tree growing from enormous granite boulders. It managed to get its two-hundred-year-old roots through the cracks and into the soil for nourishment. After observing the wonder of the Tree Growing in a Rock, I walked up the trail for thirty minutes before getting cold and returning to the car. I've always chilled faster than people around me. Thin blood, I guess. Annabel, who walked considerably faster than me, was well ahead when I decided to go back to the parking lot. She walked for another two hours while I sat in the warm car and read *To Be Heirs Forever.*

We drove through the Stirling Ranges, which caught me by surprise; I wasn't expecting them to be so beautiful. We first saw them off in the distance as purple hills behind yellow canola flower fields. When we stopped to admire the beauty, a flock of red-tailed black cockatoos flew up from the yellow blossoms with their wings beating to the time of the Tchaikovsky music on our tape player. The combination of sight and sound was mesmerizing. The mountains held a wild variety of plants, eucalypts of all sorts and sizes, chaparral, and flowers. We took a walk to a scenic lookout and then drove every road in the park. We didn't feel like walking anymore because of the weather.

We treated ourselves to dinner at a country cafe across from the caravan park where we stopped for the night. The owner had some artifacts made from grass trees. Only Aboriginals were allowed to cut down those rare, ancient trees. Annabel bought a bowl, and I bought a vase made from the rich, dark wood. We paid nominal amounts for them; my vase was $12.00. (We later saw similar artifacts selling for $100.00 and more when we got to larger cities.)

August 26, 1999 I was sick all night from the fish and chips eaten at dinner. I felt far too woozy to handle a car properly, so Annabel got to do her first extensive drive. Driving on the left side of the road made her nervous, and not being used to narrow, shoulderless roads didn't help. The sound of the tires hitting gravel kept me from sleeping soundly, but I did get a few short naps in during the ride to Hyden, where we saw Wave Rock.

I was able to get out long enough to see the rock formation fifteen meters high and one-hundred-ten meters long. The rock was estimated to be 2,700 million years old. The age of rocks never ceased to amaze me. The granite had been undermined by wind and water flow to make it look like a cresting wave. The dark and light vertical striping was made from water runoff containing carbonates and iron oxide.

August 27, 1999 I was still too ill to take the wheel, so Annabel drove through the farmlands east of Perth. The fields were green, green, green, and many were topped with golden canola flowers. Such a sight should cheer the most depressed person. My spirits were raised, but my body was weak from dehydration. I nursed oral electrolytes and dozed throughout the day. We spent the night on the outskirts of Perth.

August 28, 1999 We replenished our supplies, as Perth would be our last city for many kilometers. We stocked up on fresh fruits, vegetables, and dairy products, and then treated our faithful car to a good scrubbing.

We drove the Great Northern Highway and detoured to the Indian Ocean shoreline to see Yanchep National Park. We walked past a couple of pens of kangaroos and approached the koala cage as the ranger arrived to give his daily speech about the behavior of the cuddly animals. I had seen that a few times before when we Kilpatricks lived in Australia, so I only spent about ten minutes listening to the ranger before I wandered into the botanical garden.

It started to sprinkle, so I whipped out the compact raincoat that Joyce, our first Servas hostess, gave me. By the time I was buttoned in, it was pouring. Annabel and I raced for the car. We skipped the rest of the urbanized zoo and headed into the wilds of the thick vegetation growing between Yanchep and Pinnacles National Park. Pinnacles was a must-see on my itinerary.

We looked unsuccessfully for an on-site caravan to rent. We decided to try the backpackers hostel before we resorted to pitching our tent in the pouring rain.

What a find! My first experience at a backpackers lodge was a gem. We had a clean, quiet bedroom with two sets of bunk beds, a lounge with comfortable couches and chairs, and a television for those who cared to watch it. The kitchen was well stocked with all the needed electrical appliances and kitchen utensils. We ate our dinner in the company of people of all ages, nationalities, and backgrounds. It was a safe, family atmosphere.

August 29, 1999 The best day of the trip so far! It started out with rain dumping on us as we packed our overnight cases and food into the car. Usually, the clouds had been kind enough to wait until we were on the road.

We searched for stromatolites, living fossils. I know that's an oxymoron. The cyanobacteria expelled oxygen that made it possible for oxygen-dependent species to evolve on earth. When one layer died, a new layer was formed by the accumulation of carbonates in the water. Therefore, the interior could be up to 3.5 billion years old, with layer after layer added on top of one another. The outer layer held living organisms of blue-green algae (cyanobacteria). The stromatolites were beneath ten feet to twenty feet of floodwater from recent rains, so we didn't get to see them. I was disappointed but knew I had one more opportunity to see stromatolites at Shark Bay. Stromatolites are mostly found in lakes and marine lagoons where extreme conditions due to high saline levels exclude animal grazing. One such location is Hamelin Pool Marine Nature Reserve, Shark Bay in Western Australia, where excellent specimens exist today.

Rain still fell when we arrived at Pinnacles, but the little blue spot in the sky was expanding and stretched until we had a beautiful day. We went through the limestone pillars protruding up to five meters from the sand. At first it looked like we had entered a giant cemetery where each of the headstones was slightly different. There were only two other cars in the park. The park was awesome! Haunting pinnacles were still being uncovered by wind.

I saw one pillar that looked like petrified wood. Some had seashells imbedded in them, and some were like porous lava. We viewed the different formations and then drove on every available road (sandy path) available in the park.

One road had a sign that said it led to a fishing village called Grey. We drove the distance. That was so much fun. It was four-wheel driving at its best for an hour. We found a deserted village of shacks made of corrugated iron on a lovely, secluded bay. We sat in the sun enjoying a peaceful lunch.

The solitude was disturbed by a couple of boys on dirt bikes buzzing up and down the streets of the village and playing tag with a third boy on a quad (four-wheeler). They soon bored with their machismo game and left us to delight in the sun, surf, and sea gulls.

After lunch we slowly bounced back along the deserted sand track, taking pleasure in the wildflowers that consisted of lilies, daisies, leschenaultia, grevillea, banksia, kangaroo paws, and orchids. Wild kangaroos and emus made appearances from time to time. We took another driving tour through the pinnacles before leaving the park. I would have loved to camp there and watch the changing colors on the pinnacles. They went from dark gray in the morning when the sky was cloudy and threatening to golden yellow in the afternoon sunshine. I had a feeling they would have gone from gold to pink to purple with the sunset. The lichen on the stones also caused a variation in color. Annabel felt we should put some mileage behind us and get further up the coast.

We drove through Badgingarra National Park and on to Jurien, where we spent the rainy evening and night in a huge cabin built to sleep eight people. The cabin cost $30.00 a night, the same as the backpackers' hostel the previous evening. It had a kitchen that was about fifteen feet by twenty feet, perfect for a big family.

August 30, 1999 We drove most of the day. We stopped at a museum in Greenhough that was a converted farmhouse originally built in 1836. As the family expanded, so did the stone and plaster house. The couple became prosperous sheep farmers, and the old barn was still used to house sheep and shearing equipment. The original family ended up with fourteen children, so the house had lots of big rooms. A descendant showed tourists through the home and told a bit about his ancestors.

We were treated like welcome guests and invited to eat our lunch in their front garden after our tour. The wife took us to see the oldest living river-red-gum tree in Australia. I don't know who verified that it was the oldest tree. The river-red-gum was indeed a knarred and enormous specimen. The hollow limbs housed a variety of creatures that look for such spots to build their nests.

While I was admiring the tree, Annabel caught sight of a herd of sheep being brought down the road. A middle-aged man was walking behind the herd, and a young woman was on a motorbike bringing in the strays. I asked the girl where her famous Australian sheepdog was. She answered that she was its equivalent. She chatted with us for a few minutes until the man called her name. She immediately bid us farewell and went back to work. Good doggy.

We saw enormous flooded gums in the paddocks north of Greenhough and learned those trees grew parallel to the earth because of the strong salt-laden wind coming from the ocean. I had been to a lot of seashores and seen the juniper branches bent in the wind, but had never seen L-shaped trees before. They would surely make neat places for little boys to play.

We went through the small city of Geraldton as quickly as possible and on to beautiful Kalbarri National Park, which was reminiscent of the Grand Canyon. No camping was allowed in the park, so we pitched our tent in Anchorage Caravan Park on the shores of the Murchison River, in the town of Kalbarri. It felt good to finally be in weather conducive to camping. We didn't worry so much about the rain now that the weather was warmer, but it would still be a nuisance to take down a wet tent and pack it in a car filled with clothes, cameras, and food.

August 31, 1999 Annabel and I started our day with a tour of a wild flower reserve. It was easier to appreciate the blossoms when we were on foot rather than in a speeding car. I liked the lamb's tails, kangaroo paws, and stinky socks the best. I didn't smell the stinky socks blossoms; I believed the Australians. They were interesting, as they consisted of bushy-looking shrubbery about six feet high, with blossoms on the ends of ten-foot stalks waving like miniature sock-shaped flags. The banksias, with their dried seed pods—shells looking like chimpanzee's lips—were a close second in favorites. I could see where people could make fun sculptures—like a rock group singing—from the pods.

We saw Hawks Head and Ross Graham lookouts on our way into Kalbarri Park. They overlooked river gorges I wanted to hike. My itinerary allowed for a week at this park. Today we planned the three- to five-hour walk through the gorges along the river. Unfortunately, the road leading to the trailhead was closed due to flooding from the recent rains.

Instead, we drove along the rugged coast, stopping at each scenic lookout and walking the short distance to the overlooks. The names included such descriptive places as Red Bluff, Rainbow Valley, Island Rock, and Natural Bridge. The cliffs were startling colors—reds, oranges, browns, and grays against turquoise seas and brilliant sky-blue heavens.

We drove up Mianarro Hill to the lookout, where we could see miles and miles of coastline, definitely a place I could spend time exploring. It would be good to sit still, watch, and listen to the determined surf pound the cliffs, watch the soaring seabirds, smell the damp, salty air, feel the warm rays of the sun. Alas, Annabel was ready to move on after a ten-minute walk along the crest.

On the outskirts of the park was a commercial parrot reserve that was well kept with big cages—some walk-through cages. The mating pairs' cages were separated by fish ponds and brick walkways lined with tropical plants. At lunchtime we relaxed in the shady picnic area beside a waterfall into a koi pond.

We went to the pelican-feeding demonstration on the Murchison River. I sat down on a bench beside a young couple and a boy who was "almost three." I chatted with them for a few minutes and played with the baby. After fifteen minutes or so, our conversation ran out of speed, and we quieted down, waiting for the arrival of the pelicans. The baby started playing with something on his mother's lap. I noticed that each time he reached, his mom pushed his hand away. I thought it was a game they played. Finally the boy got frustrated and said very loudly, "I want to see your baby-maker."

The mom kept her cool and quietly said no.

The boy sulked and went to his dad and started grabbing for his dad's zipper and repeated again, "I want to see your baby maker." The dad quietly picked up the boy and held him on his lap and gave him a cookie.

I would have died of embarrassment and exited stage left quickly, especially as there was a group of twelve-year-olds sitting on the bench behind us, cracking up over the scene. The adults in the crowd studiously stared out to sea, praying that a large flock of pelicans would descend upon us.

We spent our second night in the Anchorage Resort Caravan Park. It had a screened-in camp kitchen with ample fridges, stoves, sinks, and tables for several families to prepare meals simultaneously. The ablution block was next to the kitchen, and our tent was close by but away from the paths vehicles would use. There were no marked sites for tents. We could set up anywhere on the lawn.

September 1, 1999 We tried to take the hikes to the Loop and Z Bend first thing in the morning. We got to the Loop and walked to the overlook. I took a trail admiring the gorge scenery. I wondered if someone standing at a similar site had put the word *gorgeous* in our vocabulary. Annabel, being leery of heights, didn't take the trail. She got as far as the overlook.

We went back to the car, and the electronic device called an immobilizer wouldn't disconnect so I could start the car. Western Australia had a law that every car sold must have an immobilizer installed to prevent theft. What we needed to find was a car thief. I'm sure they knew how to override the gadget. Several people tried to help, to no avail. One group said they would notify the Royal Automobile Club (Australian equivalent of AAA) when they got to Kalbarri town. We waited and waited.

Finally, at two o'clock, a Nissan Patrol, an SUV, showed up pulling a trailer. Without any prelude he started preparing my car to put it on the trailer. I thought maybe he was the car thief I had been hoping for.

His first words were, "Right, we need lots of muscle to push the car back away from the stone wall so it can be winched onto the trailer." Annabel immediately flexed her muscles and started pushing the car.

"Excuse me, who are you?" I asked.

He mumbled, "RAC Kalbarri" as he got into the driver's seat and steered the car toward the trailer. Annabel pushed the car and man forward.

"Wait a minute, wait just a minute," I said. "What makes you think the car needs to be hauled somewhere?"

"We will take it to my station and decide what to do from there," Mr. Mechanic said.

Dollar signs flashed before my eyes as I blustered and fumed. "The immobilizer is stuck; can't you just disconnect it so we can be on our way?"

"Nope, don't know what kind of immobilizer it is," Mr. Mechanic explained as he lined up the tires with the ramp on the back of his trailer.

"Didn't know what was wrong with the car, so all I brought was the trailer to haul it in. I got the message third hand from people passing through town. All I knew was that a car with this license number was stuck at this lookout."

We were soon ensconced in his Nissan, traveling twice the speed I traveled to get from Kalbarri town to Loop Bend on the bumpy dirt road. But this time my car was on a trailer behind the driver.

About four kilometers down the road, he said, "Right, the deal is, RAC pays the first thirty minutes of my time, and the car owner pays the balance. I left my office at one p.m."

I visualized the bill skyrocketing and was very quiet the rest of the trip to Kalbarri. The driver talked incessantly. Annabel shouted her opinions of world affairs from the backseat so that she could be heard over his voice and the car noise as it bounced and jiggled.

He educated us on all the wrongs of the world and how to solve them, and got around to asking what was wrong with the car. I told him about the immobilizer. He said he had seen "hundreds" of cars with the same problem.

"So, you know how to fix it?" I asked.

"It could be any one of twenty-five hundred combinations," he said. He would have to learn the make and call the manufacturer with the combination number I got when I bought the immobilizer.

I told him I hadn't bought the immobilizer, I bought the car used, and the immobilizer was already installed. I had no paperwork on the immobilizer and didn't have a clue where the owner bought it or had it installed. Mr. Mechanic informed me that we would be better off to drive the car off a cliff and claim the insurance loss. My heart sank;

there went the balance of the trip. I'd have to spend the rest of my time and money trying to straighten out a problem with an immobilizer.

When we got to his shop, he said to "go have a *cuppa* with the missus" while he decided what to do. His girlfriend put the kettle on, and as soon as our back was turned, Mr. Mechanic talked to other mechanics about the jobs they were working on. I waited about ten minutes for him to complete his conversations and then screwed up the nerve to tell him since I was paying for his time, I thought he should be working on my car.

He said my car was fixed! He had taken a little box out from under the dashboard, connected another little box to it, and started up the car. He was letting it idle for a few minutes to make sure it ran okay. He told me to never, never lock my car with the immobilizer. Annabel and I both took the electronic gadgets off our key rings and tossed them into the glove box. I promised him I would never use it again and asked how much I owed him.

"No problem, RAC will fix me up. You girls be on your way and have a good time."

Hip, hip, hooray! We were out of there. I was so full of relief; I was on the verge of tears. People like that sure made it hard to keep a chip in place on my shoulder.

Annabel didn't want to stay in Kalbarri any longer. We dismantled our campsite and packed the car. We drove about two and a half hours away from magnificent Kalbarri National Park and pulled into a roadside rest where camping was allowed.

We had just pitched our tent when a neighbor announced he would be running his generator until nine thirty to make a loaf of bread. I told him we could tolerate that. We cooked our rice and vegetables and ate a leisurely dinner before reading ourselves to sleep.

September 2, 1999 First thing in the morning, our neighbor showed up with hot coffee, hot tea, and advice on where to buy cheap fuel (he told us we could bargain with the petrol station when buying 100 liters or more at a time). He told us where to get cheap camping between Kalbarri and Alice Springs, which Aussies call "the Alice." His wife chimed in with where to get cheap food and which tourist sites were worthwhile. They ended their recitation by telling us they had been on a camping trip to the US national parks and that Americans had been so friendly, they were glad to be able to pay back a bit of the help they had received. Comments like that were always welcome.

We got out of camp by nine thirty and went merrily along the highway, enjoying the plethora of wild flowers in the wide-open spaces. Spring had sprung! We started to see mulla mulla—lavender-colored, triangular blossoms on top of fifteen- to eighteen-inch stems. We saw a variety of grevillea, including stinky socks.

The man who owned the caravan park at Northrup told us that a group of citizens wanted to get rid of all introduced animals in Australia. There were poison baits set for feral cats, foxes, dogs, and rabbits. We had seen signs warning pet owners not to let their pets run free. The signs had been everywhere we had traveled so far. We had seen two foxes along our routes, which was a lot, considering that's a month's time. I had probably not seen more than three foxes in the wild in my whole life in the States.

I wondered if "they" would eventually ask people to euthanize household pets, as cats, dogs, and goldfish were introduced to Australia by Europeans. What about the two hundred thousand camels running loose in the central desert? There was a company rounding them up and exporting them to Afghanistan. Gold miners had brought them to the Australian deserts from Afghanistan in the 1800s. What about cows, horses, and sheep? I didn't give the movement much hope for success. Someday we would have to accept that what man did to the earth was part of the evolutionary process. How's that for a statement from a lifelong greenie? I was not going to condone the changes man caused to nature without protest, but I was aware everything couldn't be reversed.

We filled our petrol tanks in Denham on the Monkey Mia Peninsula. The car took a hundred eighteen liters and petrol was selling for $.94 cents a liter. Even after the discount, it cost $108.56 to fill both tanks. Our discount was only two bucks.

We went to Hamelin Pool and saw the 3.5-*billion*-year-old stromatolites. I was rewarded with spectacular views from a boardwalk.

It was incredible to think that these fossils were living, growing, and increasing. During daily photosynthesis the vegetation waved around. At night the microbe folded over, often trapping calcium and carbonate ions dissolved in the water. The sticky chemicals they exuded added to the concretion of another layer on the surface of the stromatolite. The interiors were fossils, the exteriors were alive. Can you imagine being able to see something that was 3.5 billion years old? I was immensely happy.

Our next stop was Shell Beach. Believe me, the name was descriptive. The tiny coquina shells were ten meters (over thirty feet) deep. Coquina was another name for "cockle." More shells came in on each high tide, so they were being used for commercial purposes. A pharmaceutical company bought them for use in calcium pills, and a concrete company used them in cement. The shells under the top layers were compact and were quarried for building blocks.

We arrived at Monkey Mia in time to set up camp, eat dinner, and attend a terrific slide show narrated by Dr. Amy Samuels, an American zoologist who studied the dolphins.

Some of the things I learned:

- Dolphins were identified by the notches and scars on their dorsal fins.
- The males helped one another to mate with the female of their choice.
- Dolphins needed to breathe air, so they only slept with one-half of their brain at a time.
- The half that was awake told them when to surface for air, when there were sharks in the vicinity, and other news needed for survival.
- The dolphins had a definite language that was being learned by scientists one word at a time.
- Dolphins at Monkey Mia should not be touched because the ones that came into shore to be fed were nursing mothers. Their genitalia and nipples were super sensitive. Those parts were located between the dorsal fin and tail. The mother could get agitated and swat people with her tail.

- Outside of the genitalia, the way to tell the difference between males and females was that the males were more aggressive.
- One youngster had been coming in with his mom on a daily basis from the time of his birth. He occasionally brought the ranger a fish. The dolphin was now two years old and had taught his new baby sister to bring little fish up to the ranger. The ranger then gave the fish to the mother to eat.
- Rangers never fed babies.

September 3, 1999 We ate breakfast quickly so we could be the first people on the beach to greet the dolphins when they swam in for a morning feed. Within half an hour, we were up to our knees in the cool ocean, wading among forty or fifty other tourists while waiting for the dolphins to arrive. The dolphins swam right up to the people. The ranger arrived, and the dolphins followed him as he walked from one end of the stream of tourists to the other, answering questions, making educated guesses, and telling dolphin stories. Sometimes the dolphins rubbed against the people. If that happened, we were supposed to stand still and let the dolphin make the contact.

I was hoping a dolphin would choose me. No such luck. Maybe tomorrow morning I should rub fish oil on my legs as an enticement. The rangers were working to keep the dolphins wild, so they only allowed a handful of people to feed them their maximum limit of two kilos a day. The ranger chose people who could prove today was their birthday, and children between the ages of ten and twelve. No one was allowed to feed the babies or youngsters. It was a magical experience being so close to those beautiful creatures.

Annabel and I took a nature walk after the dolphins bored with entertaining us and swam out to sea. I strolled along tasting, smelling, and touching plants, so I had a good time. Annabel walked for exercise, so she went fast and didn't notice the plants at all. The only animals we saw, and those were from a bird hide, were sea gulls and swallows. Annabel appeared disappointed in the walk and showed no interest in attending the video about the area shown by the rangers. I saw the video and liked it so well that I bought a copy to take home.

Annabel had been melancholy since our car problems. I waited for her to say she had had enough of Australia and wanted to go home. We had been in Australia exactly one month. I knew that was normally the length of time Marlow could stand to be away from the comforts of home, so was familiar with the attitude.

September 4, 1999 We both had a restless night, as a generator ran all night to keep the street and restroom lights going. Also, the wind whipped the tent about. We had clothes on the clothesline (tent string), and I worried about them blowing away, rather than climbing out of my warm sleeping bag and bringing them inside the tent.

At first light we rushed down to play with the dolphins. The dolphins must have had a rough night also; they didn't show up until nine fifteen. By that time about a hundred fifty people were wading in the water. Tourist buses had been disgorging people for thc past hour. We knew there was very little chance either of us would be one of the nine people who would be selected to feed a fish to three adult dolphins. We still waited until the dolphins had come and gone before we left the beach. It was thrilling to wade among them, even though we never made physical contact.

The pelicans entertained us while we waited for the dolphins. One pelican waddled to the lawn as soon as the sprinklers were turned on. He opened his mouth wide and caught the fresh water in his pouch, then swallowed each time the pouch filled halfway. Other pelicans strolled up and down the beach, hoping a fisherman would toss them leftover bait. They greeted each fishing boat as it arrived and followed the people carrying fishing poles. It took a pretty smart animal to recognize a fishing pole. The pelicans didn't follow any other people.

I telephoned to wish my brother, Walter, a happy birthday while Annabel packed us sandwiches for lunch. We deflated our tires a bit and drove onto a sandy track on Useless Loop Peninsula, which pointed toward Dirk Hartog Island. Dirk Hartog was a Dutch sea captain that landed in the area about a hundred-fifty years before Captain Cook landed on the eastern shore. Captain Hartog left a plaque dated 1616 nailed to a tree. The plaque is in a museum in Amsterdam.

The drive was beautiful, with wildflowers, green shrubbery, and occasional glimpses of turquoise water. A stubby-tailed lizard about a foot long, with hard, dark-brown scales, reluctantly posed for pictures on the shoulder of the road. He was the same species we'd seen at the Woolshed in Adelaide.

We stopped, brought out our new wooden TV table and two little stools, and ate lunch behind the car. We were at Eagle's Bluff to view sea eagles (osprey) on an island a short distance offshore.

We took the turnoff to Little Lagoon, which looked like something off a postcard, with azure water, long white beaches, and no people. It turned out that the beaches were made of rocks and shells and were not the least bit inviting to walk on, let alone throw down a towel and take a snooze.

September 5, 1999 Annabel and I decided to skip the dolphin scene so we could take off on a four-wheel-drive adventure in Francois Peron National Park beside Shark Bay. Annabel drove. Four-wheel driving took some experience, and we were learning as we went. It was good fun bouncing down the sandy trail.

We ate lunch at a picnic spot on a pearling cove where oysters had been seeded and put back in the water so the seed—a grain of sand or tiny pebble—could be made into a cultured pearl by the oyster. Pearls are made of the mineral aragonite.

It amazed me that plants got nourishment from sand. There were vines, shrubs, and trees growing everywhere on the dunes. We sat under a shade tree admiring the teensy flowers blooming like a pastel-colored carpet underfoot.

Further down the road an emu scooted out of tall, toasted brown grass and across in front of the car. It felt like we were in Jurassic Park seeing one of those enormous birds dart in front of our bumper. We also saw goannas, stubby-tailed lizards, lots of pretty birds, and a couple of kangaroos.

We camped on the beach at the end of the peninsula. Three other couples were within view, but not close enough to be heard. I savored the sunset in peaceful solitude.

Annabel said the loneliness made her realize how far from home she was. Uh-oh, will she leave at the next town? Will she make it to Broome?

September 6, 1999 It was good to sleep soundly in our quiet corner of the world. I slept ten hours, Annabel slept eleven. We awoke to a concert of birdsong. After watching the surf lapping the shore during breakfast, we dismantled the tent and headed toward Carnarvon.

I drove from the far end of wild, sandy Francois Peron Peninsula. What an experience to be bumping along an expanse of land deserted—except for birds and animals—and listening to didgeridoo music on the cassette player.

We stopped at abandoned Peron Homestead and took a nice, long soak in the cooling tank from the bore (well). The windmill pumped water up several feet from below the earth's surface. Some bores went down as much as five hundred feet. The water in our "hot tub" was probably about thirty-nine degrees Celsius (one-hundred-two degrees F)—perfect for a bath. Cooling tanks were used to chill the water before it was given to livestock. Geology books said there was a huge basin of fresh water lying under much of Australia. It went to a depth of three thousand meters and ranged in temperature from thirty degrees to one-hundred degrees Celsius.

From the tub we were able to watch a real-life nature show. Several emu families with various-aged youngsters were squabbling over water rights at a pond a few meters from us. It looked like a play. There was plenty of drama. One adult male chased a male and female out of the water, then went into the bushes and came out with a female and three midsized chicks. They had settled into the water for a few sips and a bit of a splash when all of the sudden, there was a third male on the scene.

The second and third males chased each other up and down, around and around. The third one won the contest, and the second female and her chicks ran off into the bushes.

The third male then brought his family of a female and a handful of chicks to the pond. The victory was short-lived; the original pair reappeared, wanting their turn at the water. I didn't know why they couldn't all swim and drink together. Anyhow, the thrilling spectacle with all the chasing and posturing involved at least twenty animals.

When the emus had their fill of water, and we resembled raisins, we got out of the tub and proceeded on our excursion. We drove into Denham, and reinflated our tires to maximum pressure for use on the bitumen (asphalt) roads. The petrol station was located next to a bakery, so naturally we had a hot meat pie.

As we approached Carnarvon, we saw a large satellite dish on a hill. It turned out to be a NASA relay station used for communication with satellites. The operation was closed, and the only signs of life around the facility were the occupied housing units. It looked like a good place for a military assignment. The housing was on a hill with ocean views.

Our housing for the night was a campground on the edge of a banana plantation.

September 7. 1999 We tried for an hour to find someplace in Carnarvon that would do a lube and oil change on the car. The mechanics couldn't get to it for four or five days. I asked if I could borrow their tools and do it myself, as it would only take me twenty minutes. Their insurance wouldn't allow me to work in their garage. Of course, I knew that; I was just being a smart aleck. I felt so empowered since I knew how to change the oil in a car. I took a yearlong course in automotive engine repair in preparation for this trip (and hoped I wouldn't have to use the knowledge).

We went on a banana plantation tour at Munros. I learned that:

- Each plant grew one stalk of bananas straight out of the center of the plant.
- The outside layers carried water up the trunk.
- The roots were only six to eight inches deep.
- The parent plant's stalk was cut off at ground level as soon as the bananas ripened enough for removal.

- A "sucker" grew in the same spot to produce the next stalk of bananas.
- Most bunches weighed thirty to fifty kilos (seventy-five to one-hundred-twenty-five pounds). Last year Munros got one bunch that weighed 80 kilos (200 pounds), a record for that plantation.
- The bananas had to be harvested by hand. A man slashed the bunch loose from the rest of the stalk, and the bunch rested on his shoulder while he carried it to a shed for storage. A machine had not yet been invented that could do that carefully enough to prevent bruising and could maneuver around the disarray of trees. They were not planted in rows in Western Australia.
- In Western Australia the trees were grown in dense clumps, with as many trees as possible growing on the government-allowed ten-acre plots.
- The plantation owners were limited by their allotment of water.
- In the semidesert of Western Australia, it took twelve months to produce one bunch on a stalk. In Queensland it took nine months.

In Queensland the agriculturalists got plenty of water from the wet season rainfall and could grow bigger bananas in less time. On the east coast the plantation owners could plant their crops in straight lines as there were no land restrictions and no water restrictions. That also meant that Queenslanders could use mechanized harvesters. Some Queensland plantations consisted of thousands of acres.

We ate lunch at the plantation—smoothies and muffins. I had a mango smoothie and a mango/coconut muffin; Annabel had a banana smoothie and a banana/date muffin. Talk about heavenly food! Yummy!

We spent the afternoon driving through desert between Carnarvon and Cape Range Peninsula. We saw several emus and one fox (our third for the trip). We stopped for a break at Minilya Rest Stop and discovered hundreds of small-beaked corellas singing love songs to each other in the trees lining the dried riverbed. Small-beaked corellas are from the cockatoo family, and their song was not really pleasant to the human ear. The sound was loud, though.

We camped in Cape Range National Park at a fisherman's retreat.

September 8, 1999 We started out early in the morning so we could explore Cape Range Peninsula, which ran along the shoreline of Ningaloo Reef coral beds.

The land was flat between the shore and the convergent boundary of the continental crust and the Indian Ocean tectonic plate. The land mass pushed up, forming mountains. Where rivers used to cut through the mountains, now gorges decorated the range. What will they become over the next million years? Valleys among rolling hills?

We drove to the far end of the park on corrugated dirt. Yardie Creek Gorge was worth the trip. Annabel and I walked along the trail next to the river. We saw reef herons—unique because the males are deep blue and the females are white—nesting on the far side. The trail over rough lava dropped off to the river below.

Annabel announced she wasn't feeling well and went back to the car. I went down one more gorgeous gorge and up the other side, then started to worry that Annabel might be seriously ill and turned back. Annabel said she had digestive track problems from eating mangoes the day before and wanted to stay close to the restroom. I knew how miserable I was between Stirling Range and Wave Rock. I empathized with her before remembering she hadn't eaten mangoes the day before. I did. I thought perhaps the height of the embankment bothered her.

When I reached the picnic area, she convinced me that she'd be fine, but she wanted to stay in the shade and rest. She said she didn't mind waiting while I took a boat cruise up Yardie Creek. Thank goodness she didn't stop me from exploring.

The tour guide on the boat cruise pointed out black-footed wallabies living along the cliffs and the multitude of small-beaked corellas. He informed me that they mate for life and live in the same nest forever after their first mating. He also pointed out the blue and white reef herons and said they never produced mottled youngsters.

The predators on the peninsula were foxes that killed baby wallabies and stole bird eggs. The wallabies lived in caves on the cliffsides and could bounce up and down the precipices like mountain goats. The foxes had not yet developed that trick.

Annabel felt better when I returned, so we stopped at each of the other turnouts between Yardie Creek and our campsite except at the mangroves. I had been warned about an illness humans could get called Ross River virus, which was prevalent at that particular mangrove site. The disease was supposed to cause livers to deteriorate. I didn't want to see mangroves badly enough to take the chance of picking up a bug like Ross River virus.

At one turnoff we found several kangaroos; at the next one, we saw half a dozen emus, including babies; at the third turnoff, we saw a pair of bustards. Now we were really having fun!

One stop had rocky shores along a pounding azure sea, the next was white sands beside a calm turquoise bay, and the last turnoff took us to sand dunes, where we climbed to the top. That gave us respect for the nomads who crossed the Sahara. Climbing sand dunes was no easy feat.

We went to the information center, where I asked the correct name for the bustards, telling them that in Africa, they were called kori bustards. The ranger told me that in Australia, they were called "bustards" with no "kori" in front. Within twenty-four hours, I saw a sign about the birdlife in Cape Range that said "kori bustard." Whatever. They were interesting-looking birds, larger than a goose, which would rather run than fly. They walked with their beak in the air like they were either looking through their bifocals or were really snooty.

We ended our tour by climbing the hill (in the car) to the lighthouse. From there we could see whales migrating south. They were way, way out to sea, and we could just detect the waterspouts and flipping tails with our binoculars. We would never have known they were there if a tour guide had not stopped to chat with Annabel while I was on the boat trip up Yardie Creek. The lighthouse was near the end of the peninsula, so we could see the shore on three sides—the perfect spot to watch the sun set.

We went to our friendly fishermen's campground and cooked dinner. Night had descended by the time we finished, and we decided to take our torches (flashlights) and walk the mile-long driveway leading to the highway. We hoped to find wildlife on the prowl. Unfortunately, our batteries were so weak, we could barely see the path in front of our feet.

The evening was pleasant, and we heard critters with bouncing footsteps in the fields. The cicadas chirping and the distant sound of waves swishing ashore assured us that all was well with the world, at least with our little corner of the world.

September 9, 1999 We went snorkeling in Turquoise Bay on Ningaloo Reef. We were told by other campers that we could walk two kilometers up the beach, catch the water current back down, and we'd be over the reef the whole time. Supposedly, we would end at our parked car.

Being such a poor swimmer, I was constantly fighting fear when in water over my head. I was bound and determined to get over this weakness, and decided this was as good a time as any to conquer my fear. I put the snorkel gear on, tied my tennis shoes to my swimsuit shoulder straps, and entered the water at the same time as Annabel. Our plan was to swim out to the reef, catch the current, and float face down, admiring the coral. We would be swimming side-by-side.

I swam and swam and swam and saw nothing below me but sand. When I looked up, I had been swimming ninety degrees away from Annabel, a hundred eighty degrees away from our car and parallel to the beach. I was only a few meters from dry land. No wonder there was no reef! I turned out to sea and swam as hard as I could. I began to see fish and various signs of coral. The colors were getting better and better, and there was more and more coral. I felt the current pick me up. I floated along, entranced in the wonderland below me.

I looked up to see if I was close to our car yet. I felt that the timing was just about right; I'd be within twenty meters of Annabel and pointed toward our car. Instead, I was way, way out to sea! I couldn't see Annabel, I couldn't see anyone! I could see that the current was taking me farther out to sea. I instantly panicked!

I turned toward the beach, put my face back down so I could see which way I was swimming, and stroked and stroked. The coral below me barely moved. I got nowhere. My heart pounded like crazy. The best thing to do was to stop fighting the current, to turn onto my back and float until I got my heart and lungs functioning correctly.

As soon as I turned over, the snorkel tube filled with salt water, and I choked. I had enough presence of mind to take the tube out of my mouth and breathe normally as though I was in the pool at home. When I finally finished coughing and regained normal breathing, I put the tube back in my mouth and kept the tube pointed toward the sky, instead of wrapped around my head facing behind me (underwater). I kicked as hard as I could with the fins. Somehow, lying on my back with the sun shining on my face was reassuring.

Suddenly it felt like I made a sharp right turn. The current switched directions and started pushing me toward shore. It probably wasn't long, though it felt like an hour, before I floundered onto the sandy shallows near Annabel. She said she was starting to worry when I swam out so far that she couldn't see me anymore. I was a bit worried myself. Maybe tomorrow I'd work on conquering my fear of deep water.

We went back to camp and took hot rainwater showers. I had a lot of sand in my hair. After the shower life looked bright and sunny again. We dismantled the campsite and headed toward Coral Bay.

We drove through desert landscape on the landmass side of the range and admired the handiwork of termites. There were mounds of all sizes and shapes. One of them had a ball on top of a narrow neck. I wondered if that was the penthouse section.

At Coral Bay we found ourselves in an obvious tourist trap. People, people everywhere. The campground looked depressing with its rows of trailers, motor homes, and tents crammed against one another. We chose a campsite as close to the sand dunes as we could get. There were other campers on either side of us—close enough to be disturbing when they snored. Oh well, it was just for one night.

September 10, 1999 We were the only customers on the glass-bottom boat. The educated driver took us out to the reef, let us snorkel over the coral and take pictures with underwater cameras. We were in pretty deep water that was murky in spots. Not the best coral viewing in the world. When the guide moved to a different location, Annabel rejoined him in the boat.

He tossed me a rope and told me to hang on. That was really, really neat. He drove slowly enough that I could see the coral, and I had my head underwater enough that it muffled the boat noise. I had a private viewing of the reef without any effort or stress. I could enjoy the scenery without worrying about getting lost at sea or having to propel myself forward.

When we were in more shallow water with lots of colorful fish, Annabel joined me, and the boat operator gave us bread to feed the fish. We got close and personal with them.

The weather was perfect; the ride back to the harbor was relaxing and scenic. Fortunately for the operator's business, there was a line of people waiting for the next tour. We learned that better snorkeling was at low tide, as it was possible to swim closer to the coral and fish.

We showered, packed, did our postal and photographic business, and left for Karijini National Park. The landscape started out looking like Nevada, except that we saw a couple dozen emus along the way. Then the soil got redder with oxidized iron as though we had driven from Nevada to Southern Utah. By late afternoon we were on the outskirts of Karijini in deep-red soil, with hills of reddish-purple rock, green scrub, snowy-white ghost-gum trees, and lavender mulla mulla flowers. What a feast for the eyes!

We pulled into a roadside rest and startled a wallaby (a small member of the same family as kangaroos) that went bounding off into the brush. He had been the sole occupant of the campground. In the twelve hours that we spent at the campsite, we heard five or six cars go by on the roadway. No one stopped to use the picnic tables or inspect the camping facilities. The site was heavenly. I was a hermit at heart. The cicadas sang us to sleep, and the magpies gently crooned us out of sleep in the morning. Their song was so sweet and melodic. It gave people time to get awake before the corellas and black cockatoos came squawking and arguing overhead.

September 11, 1999 A day of travel. We drove slowly over the red-dust roads under deep-blue skies. We arrived at Karijini early enough to be choosy about a campsite. We viewed a few campgrounds that catered to motor homes or caravans (trailers) and opted for the primitive campground for tents only, which was several kilometers away.

We set up our tent under a ghost-gum tree for shade from the early-morning sun. We had happy hour, dinner, and went to bed.

We wrote our journal entries. Annabel finished rather quickly, and I asked if she didn't have anything interesting to say for the day. She said she wasn't keeping a journal; she kept an expense account. When she got to a set dollar amount, she'd go home. Ohhhh, so that's why she never wanted to go on any of the paid excursions like the Yardie Creek tour.

September 12, 1999 We left camp at seven forty-five in the morning to go to the town of Mount Tom Price to take a tour of Hamersley Iron Ore Mine. We made it about three-quarters of the way when the wall of my right rear tire blew out. I was on a curving grade with side rails preventing me from pulling over. Then, at the end of the guardrail, I had to go a few more meters to get to a spot flat enough to jack up the car. Annabel did all the hard work. She got under the car to locate a good spot on the axle to put the jack. Annabel proceeded to change the tire. The jack was a real struggle to use, but Annabel overcame the problem. The only help I accomplished came from unloading the paraphernalia in the rear of the car and helping to restack it on top of the blown tire.

We were back on the road an hour later. I missed the tour, but booked it for the next day. It was Sunday, so the town's petrol (gas) station mechanics were not working. The petrol pumps were operating, and a lady was collecting money for that.

We turned back to Karijini and saw several gorges. I had never seen rocks such a deep-red color. They were startling against the bright blue of the sky. The white ghost-gums and gray-green spinifex grass were a stark contrast to the land. The wild flowers were trying their best to show off, but looked pallid next to the earth.

We went for a short hike and got to a point where we could have climbed a hundred feet down to cool water. Neither of us felt like climbing back up the gorge walls, so we skipped our bath for the day.

While back at camp, we discovered that one of our neighbors was an Aboriginal with a group of didgeridoo groupies from Germany. Two young men were learning to play the instrument from George. The benefit to us was that we had a delightful free concert while sharing the campfire with a congenial group, and a good time was had by all.

September 13, 1999 Monday morning we left the campsite intact with our supplies inside the tent while we drove into Mount Tom Price. Our first stop was at the Shell Station, which had two mechanics and two tire repairmen on duty. We asked if the tire repairmen could replace our blown-out tire. They had no tires the right size. After asking if there was another tire sales place within driving distance, the repairman directed us to Tyrepower.

Those people had the correct tire—for $280.00. For an additional $70.00, they could do a lube and oil change. Finally! I had wanted to get that done for several days. Each place I asked required an appointment three or four days in advance. I paid to have both jobs accomplished while I was on the Hamersley tour.

Annabel didn't want to take the $10.00 tour of Mount Tom Price Iron Ore Mine, so she did the laundry while I absorbed the interesting information imparted on the tour.

The company was started after geologists, including an American named Tom Price, discovered iron ore in the vicinity in 1962. Tom felt they could extract at least a million dollars worth, and after a lot of talking, he convinced the Australian government to invest in the venture. Within two hours of being told that the mine had hit a mother lode of iron, Tom Price, who was seventy-one, died of a heart attack. In 1966 they sent their first trainload of ore to Karratha, a town on the Indian Ocean, to be sold overseas.

The company had been in operation ever since and sent three trains, consisting of two-hundred-twenty-six cars each, of iron ore to Karratha each day. That iron was loaded on ships and sold to the Orient to be made into steel.

The company started out as a conglomerate of five organizations, including Kaiser Steel of the United States. The mine was now solely owned by Hamersley Iron of Australia, and they had six mines in Western Australia. Hamersley was a subsidiary of Rio Tinto, mining giant of South America.

The town of Mount Tom Price, one of five towns built by Hamersley, had thirty-two-hundred people, including twelve-hundred school-age children. The mine currently hired six-hundred-twenty employees.

They hired Aboriginals, but had not had good success getting those employees to stay on the job any length of time. Aboriginals would not work underground. Their supreme being, the Rainbow Serpent, lived there.

The company did occasionally hire women engineers, but had no female equipment operators or laborers.

Annabel and I went to the local pub for a "counter lunch," we had a broiled chicken sandwich and chips. It seemed like chips (fries) were served with every meal in restaurants.

We drove to the Auski campground in hopes of finding George, the Aboriginal who made didgeridoos. Annabel bought one of his creations to give her son, Eric, and his future wife, Felicia, as a wedding present. The young lady obtained her doctor of philosophy degree in indigenous music law. Felicia loved music from natives around the world.

We didn't find George—he was off having a swim—but his friends were there, so Annabel gave them $300.00 for the didge, and we took the freshly painted instrument with us.

We arrived back at our campsite exhausted from the strain of hours and hours of driving on rough dirt roads. The last hour was after dark, and my headlights were not as powerful as I would have liked. I knew a lot of kangaroos were waiting for the chance to jump in front of my car. Other campers were using our picnic table, and we chatted with them while dining on cheese and crackers and a can of beer and calling it dinner.

September 14, 1999 Annabel wanted to make one more effort to talk to George to find out what the paintings on the didge meant. We toured gorges on our way to Auski campground.

We swam at Kalamia Falls, which was wonderful, as it had been three days since we had a bath. We were the only swimmers in the large secluded pool at the bottom of gentle waterfalls. Only two other hikers intruded on our solitude the whole time we were there. We were able to get in deep enough that we could swim and float in cool, clear water. The flat rocks at the water's edge made an ideal place to dry off after our "bath."

We drove to Fortescue Falls near the entrance to the park. From the overlook we observed about thirty school kids doing cannonballs into the pool below the falls. There were half a dozen adults running back and forth trying to keep the kids reasonably safe on the rock overhangs. The crowd was probably on a school trip from Mount Tom Price. We were glad we had chosen Kalamia Gorge for our swim.

We admired the two and half-billion-year-old striations of iron, limestone, silica-rich quartz, and other minerals that lined the gorges. Imagine those layers of rocks accumulating as sea beds, being compacted with more silt collecting on the surface and being compressed into rocks from the pressure of weight from above. Movement from hot magma under the sea had caused the striations to buckle and crack before lifting to the surface to form dry land after a sharp drop in sea level over the next few million years. Then rivers formed and ran through cracks to cut gorges. The sediment washed out of the gorges, forming alluvial fans on the surrounding plains, much the same story as at Cape Range National Park and probably the US Grand Canyon.

Those plains were covered with yellow cassias, acacias, as well as bluebells and purple or white mulla mulla. In some places the flowers were so numerous; they were threatening to reclaim the dirt roads. The soil must have been the perfect combination of nutrients needed by those little beauties.

We found George and ate lunch at his camp while he answered a multitude of questions. He traveled around the country camping out. He had more time than us as he planned on spending the rest of his life doing this. He was able to stay at each campsite for however long he wanted. When he needed money for car expenses and food, he made and sold a didgeridoo or two. George was a fun-loving, congenial Aboriginal about fifty-five years old. He currently traveled with four young people who shared their food, cooked for him, and did car repairs on his ancient van in return for music lessons and lessons in Aboriginal culture. George said he preferred eating beef to witchetty grubs (a caterpillar that looked like a tomato worm that the Aboriginals living in the wild ate as a source of protein).

Time arrived too soon for us to be on the road again. I didn't know whom I envied more, George or his entourage. I would love to stay at Karijini for a month and take every hike available, and have time in between to sit and listen to the waterfalls and look at the scenery. Then again, I would love to listen to George tell about his people and their beliefs, and hear stories about their survival in the wilderness.

We were on the road to Millstream Chichester National Park. I saw a little clump of Sturt's desert peas, a brilliant scarlet flower, and stopped to snap a picture. As soon as I stepped out of the car, I heard a loud hissing sound. My first reaction was to back up onto the running board and look for a snake. I didn't spot any creepy-crawlies, so I stepped down again and found the source of the sneering hiss was our brand new $280.00 tire as it deflated before my eyes. I won't repeat the language that I used, but I will tell you that I was upset.

Annabel immediately started the procedure familiar to vacationers of unloading the storage containers and luggage from the rear of the car, so that the tire-changing tools could be accessed. She had the tarp on the bull dust under the car and was wrestling with the contrary jack when another car came down the road. I waved to them in hopes that a gallant man would know that we were two weak, helpless females in distress. The lady smiled broadly and waved back. As they drove on by, I lowered four out of five of my fingers as my salute of gratitude for their help. They immediately pulled over, and I thought that maybe they had seen my salute and were going to punch me in the nose.

They turned out to be the folks who had shared our dinner table the evening before. They didn't mention my salute so, hopefully it went unnoticed. The man tried valiantly to get the jack away from Annabel. He was more than willing to do the labor for us. Annabel eventually relinquished the tools, and the man changed the tire in no time. He did mention that our jack was broken, as the handle had been turned so hard against its will that the square corners had been rounded. Was Annabel aware she was that strong? She was really fit and enjoyed hard labor. Probably the jack had been broken at the time we bought the car.

I realized how lucky we had been that those people came along and helped us after I counted the number of cars we had seen between when we left George and when we arrived at Millstream Chichester Campground—a total of four cars during a six-hour drive on rocky roads.

We pitched the tent beside a river in Millstream and ate leftover cold rice and pineapple for dinner. I loved that I didn't have to provide meat, a starch, a green vegetable, a yellow vegetable, and a beverage every night like I felt required to do at home. Neither Annabel nor I felt food was very important, and water was suitable as a beverage. We knew we weren't going to die of malnutrition if we skipped a few dinners.

Mother Nature sang us a lullaby as we dozed off to sleep.

September 15, 1999 We decided to spend the day at the tranquil riverside retreat. There was no one there, and we had a nice swimming hole in the river. The melaleuca trees shaded us from the sun, birds and lizards entertained us, we had a barbecue pit, picnic table, and an outhouse—all the comforts of home. It seemed like a good place to relax for a couple of days.

Annabel suggested we go to the visitor's center, where there was a phone, and report our flat to Tyrepower. It seemed logical that we would get a refund of some sort on a tire that went flat within twenty-four hours of purchase.

We took the road to the visitor's center, which was a homestead from a former sheep station. The park was no Karijini, but nice. We were definitely camped at one of the most picturesque spots in the park.

I phoned Tyrepower with no beneficial results. The only way they would refund any part of our money was if we had only been driving the car on paved surfaces. Of course, there was no way to leave town other than on dirt roads, so they knew we had been driving on rough gravel, as they knew we were calling from Millstream. They told us the tire was not faulty, and that it was probably driver error—going too fast on rough roads. They didn't know that I'm one of the slowest drivers in Western Australia, as I'm forever dodging rocks in the road, watching scenery, or looking for animals.

The homestead at the visitor's center was well preserved and set up with displays of local Aboriginal artifacts and last-century European agricultural appurtenances. We took the time to read the signs at all the displays, and then took the short walk around the outbuildings and through the garden of water lilies, pandanus, and palms along the edge of the stream coming from a spring.

A surprise awaited us when we returned to the car. Another flat tire! Egad, the same wheel as the previous two flats. Thank goodness, the car dealer had given us a second spare tire, "just in case." We unloaded the tools that were now located in a handier spot so we didn't have to unload the back of the car.

A couple of wallabies wandered up the road to see what we were doing. The larger of the two was very aggressive and wanted to know what we had in the car; she checked out each open door. Then she checked out each bag and box we had removed from the car. Too bad she didn't know how to change the tire. As it was, she was just in our way. But how could you get mad at someone with such a cute face? Women would kill for those long lashes.

We read the car manufacturer's instructions on how to dismantle the second spare that hung from a chain and bracket underneath the car. Three men arrived to tour the homestead. One young man in military fatigues asked what was wrong. We explained that we didn't know how to release the spare from its mounting. He came over and looked at the instructions and explained how we were supposed to put the jack handle through a tiny hole in the back bumper to unwind the chain. Annabel did that, and it worked.

The man was willing to tell Annabel how to change the tire, but he didn't want to get dirty. The other two made no attempt to offer advice or help in any way. Annabel put the tarp on the ground, crawled under the car, and attempted to use the broken jack to elevate the car. I loosened lug nuts on the flat tire.

Finally, the man in fatigues offered to turn the jack handle for Annabel. As he got down on his knees, I heard the older man behind me say to his acquaintance, "I don't know why he's bothering to help a couple of old Yankee dikes."

I avoided the urge to use the tire iron in my hand to teach him some manners. I said nothing and did nothing. He was the first rude Australian we had met; we could tolerate his ill breeding.

The young man raised the car far enough to get the tire off. He then dusted off his knees and proceeded to tell Annabel how to change the tire. He offered no further physical help. His friends had gone into the visitor's center. I didn't tell the young man that Annabel knew how to change a tire; we were hoping he'd be chivalrous enough to do the labor.

He did end up helping us in one important way. He told us a shortcut to Karratha, the nearest town. We would have to trespass on Hamersley Mine's private road, but we would save about a hundred kilometers of dirt road driving.

We went back to camp, packed up, and took off for the city. I hated to leave our lovely campsite, but felt we really didn't dare take a chance on waking up in the morning and finding that we had flat number four and no spare, as we were so far from civilization.

We took the Hamersley road and drove for a long, long way before we came to another vehicle. At a distance I could see that a truck was parked diagonally across half the road. I wondered if Hamersley had a roadblock to catch trespassers. We were too far along to turn back and take the public road. I decided to play dumb and take my chances. I'd tell them I didn't notice the huge billboard that said, "Private Road, No Trespassing."

When we got to the vehicle, we saw five men wearing bright orange vests, and realized they were working on the railroad track beside the road. We waved to each other as we passed, and then Annabel and I released a sigh of relief. I put our campsite permit in a prominent place on the windshield and hoped any law enforcers would mistake it for a Hamersley permit to access the private road.

Several kilometers down the road we saw another vehicle, a utility (pickup truck) with "Hamersley" printed in large letters on the door. We waved to him, and he nodded and waved back as though he was used to seeing two old women driving out there on the private road.

In the next ten kilometers, we saw three more Hamersley Mine vehicles, and each time the driver just waved to us as we passed. No problem; being criminals was a piece of cake, we were naturals. We were glad when we met the Great Northern Highway and turned toward town.

I phoned a tire dealer in Karratha from the Millstream visitor's center to see if he had my size tires. He said he'd save two for me. We arrived at ten minutes until five and knew that he would not want to change two tires ten minutes before quitting time. The proprietor checked the brand-new flat tire and said it was totally destroyed by the heat that had built up inside. The walls had warped and separated. He agreed that we had been sold cheap tires that didn't handle Western Australia's roads very well. He'd not give us any credit toward new tires, as he knew Yokohama wouldn't reimburse him. I told him I didn't want any more "cheap" Yokohama tires, as I couldn't afford $280.00 a day for tires. I said I wanted Michelin All-Terrain tires as I was familiar with their quality. He looked up those tires in his book, and found that he'd have to order them shipped from Perth, and they would cost $500.00 apiece when they got to Karratha.

I feigned a heart attack at the cost and told him we were just beginning our trip and had a lot of rough road ahead, so he had better order me four Michelins. He double-checked and found that Michelin didn't make them for my size rims. Thank goodness, I really didn't want to put out $2,000.00 for tires. The dealer ordered Bridgeports, which he assured me was what the locals, who were smart, used. He said he'd have them ready and waiting to mount at eight in the morning. We came to an agreement on price at $260.00 per tire.

September 16, 1999 The morning was spent at Tyrepower. The serviceman put four new tires on the car and balanced them. He fixed the salvageable old tire that had been mounted under the car (it was a different width than the other tires, but would work in a pinch). He remounted it under the car. Then he sold me the extra rim I needed to give me three good spares (the usable tires he removed from the Land Cruiser) with rims and one without a rim. He sold me a used roof rack, mounted it, and placed three spares on top of the car. We used my bicycle cable and lock from home to attach the spares to the roof rack. I drove out of there $1,500.00 poorer but with a sense of security that we'd not have to worry about future flats. There was no way we'd have five flats before we could get to civilization and get the flat tires replaced. Right? Right.

No sense having such an expensive car with shiny new tires and a roof rack covered with all that iron dust. I took the car to a drive-through car wash that advertised the job would cost $10.00. It ended up costing me $27.00, as the operator had to manually lift the sprayers high enough to drive the newly extended height through. It was quite a procedure, and by the time I had vacuumed the interior, I had been at the car wash for an hour and a half.

We did a quickie tour of Dampier Peninsula. Dampier was one of the towns built by Hamersley for exportation of iron ore. We saw the enormous Liquid Natural Gas plant and made reservations to tour Hamersley waterside operations the next morning.

September 17, 1999 Annabel joined me on the free wharf tour. We saw how the iron ore was stored after being off-loaded from the daily trains and how the ore was loaded onto the ships. We were told it was shipped to Asia, where it was made into steel. The tour was not as good as the mine tour, but it was like seeing "the rest of the story," to paraphrase Paul Harvey.

We learned that the roadside rocks we thought were iron were actually oxidized basalt that cracked and broke due to the heat of the summers in the Pilbara Region. We thought someone purposely piled heaps of iron ore rocks ranging in size from oranges to grapefruits. Mother Nature had been doing it all along.

We went for a hike looking for Aboriginal petroglyphs in an area where there were supposed to be 10,000 rock carvings. We didn't see any at all. We did see an explosion of wild flowers and half a dozen kangaroos.

We made a trip into the shopping center to pick up my developed film that we had left while grocery shopping the previous day. While there we had lamb souvlaki for lunch. In the restaurant a young man smiled and said, "*G'dai*" (Australian for "hello"). I didn't recognize him, but Annabel refreshed my memory. He was the fatigue-clad man who had "helped" us change our flat at Millstream Chichester.

We thanked him again for his efforts and told him we had used the road he suggested and were grateful to make it to the city without further car problems. I couldn't resist; I smiled sweetly and said, "Tell your old friend that we are not a couple of dikes. We are both quite happily married to males."

The fellow turned six shades of red and walked away. Poor boy, I shouldn't have embarrassed him. He had no control over his acquaintance's rudeness.

Annabel was flabbergasted and asked, "What was *that* all about?"

I told her what I had heard at the visitor center in Millstream. Being naturally easygoing, she just shrugged her shoulders. Do you think that some of her niceness will rub off on me by the end of this trip? Can a leopard change his spots?

At three o'clock we got out of Karratha. We only drove two-hundred-thirty-two kilometers to Port Hedland and set up camp in a caravan park on the edge of town. Annabel decided to drive back into town to buy something and got properly lost. When I drove and she navigated, I traditionally turned the wrong way automatically, and she had to correct me. I made a lot of U-turns. I was glad she finally made a mistake, but it sure made her nervous. She was gone for a couple of hours trying to find her way back to the campsite. She forgot that women were allowed to ask directions.

We were now two weeks ahead of schedule. We had left Kalbarri, Karijini and Millstream Chichester earlier than planned. We skipped some of the national parks near Perth, as we were tired of the cold, wet weather and were eager to get up north, where the weather would be more conducive to camping.

September 18, 1999 From Port Hedland to Pardoo Cattle Station, where I wanted to stay next, was a very short drive, only one-hundred-fifty kilometers. We planned on driving from Millstream to Pardoo, and that would have been one full day's drive. I had not proceeded further the night we stayed in Port Hedland, as I was afraid of hitting kangaroos or loose cattle when driving after dark. Kangaroo eyes do not shine red like deer eyes in the headlights. Also, I was afraid that I would miss some neat scenery.

We were greeted at Pardoo Station by a middle-aged lady who showed us around the homestead, the camping area, ablutions, and laundry. She told us to camp wherever it suited us. We chose a spot away from fishermen, but close enough to the restrooms to be convenient.

The homestead dated back to 1869. It had changed hands many, many times over the century. Some of the owners added more land to their holdings. There were now 500,000 acres, including beachfront and a few islands offshore. Part of the shoreline was covered in mangroves and was a good place to go fishing or mud crabbing. We asked if they had problems with Ross River virus in the mangroves, and they assured us they did not.

We arrived at ten thirty and spent the day relaxing, reading, drawing, and enjoying the domestic animals. Annabel played with the kelpie dog; I played with calves and a baby emu.

The station ran Brahman cattle, and it had a couple of horses in the campground that were just pets used to keep the grass down. The mustering was done by four-wheel-drive vehicles and helicopters. The owners expected to take a road train of cattle to Broome to be sent to Indonesia. They said we could help with the loading, if we wanted. Of course, we—errrr, I mean, I—wanted to help with the cattle. Annabel wanted to videotape the episode. That was her opportunity to make it on *America's Funniest Home Videos.*

September 19, 1999 The station owners got a telephone call from someone at midnight and were told they had to get their cattle to Broome immediately. They were loaded and gone before four in the morning. Annabel and I slept through the whole loading process.

The magpie larks didn't wake me up until five. The magpies ushered in a full day of birdsong, which was the predominant noise heard. You know I loved that. Magpie larks were known as mudlarks in Western Australia, as peewee magpies in New South Wales and Queensland, and as Murray larks in South Australia. It was neither a magpie nor a lark. Just thought that was interesting; I won't give you an overdose of information on each bird we see.

Kristy, a young lady who worked on the cattle station, took us mud crabbing. She drove us to the beach in a four-wheel-drive ute that had no extras whatsoever. We were lucky to have seats to sit on. It had no seat belts, no paneling on the interior, a couple of missing windows, manual transmission with the gearshift on the floor, no cavities filled with a radio or any such nonsense on the dashboard—you get the idea. It was one fun ride.

Kristy had thrown a burlap bag and three poles about seven feet long in the bed of the ute before we left the homestead. The poles had curves on one end. They reminded me of a Halloween costume I had as a child where I dressed up like a fairytale character who lost her sheep. Oh yeah, I remember—Little Bo Peep.

Kristy stopped the vehicle when we reached the mangroves. We trudged across the sand and slogged our way up the muddy river carrying the bag, poles, and our cameras. I was glad I had worn my ten-year-old sneakers. I brought them for walking on coral that cuts shoes to pieces. They were the perfect apparel for this trip. Kristy was barefoot, of course. Annabel wore shower shoes. We were all covered with mud. No problem. The dirtier I am, the happier I am. Before long, you're going to get the idea I loved this whole danged trip. Annabel and Kristy had no problem with mud either. We were all having fun.

Kristy showed us how to use the hooks to pull mud crabs from their holes under rocks. We poked around under several rocks in the exposed mud of low tide. It didn't take long to learn the type of hole where we were most likely to find a critter.

I was lucky enough to find the first crab. I was upset with my effort to get the crab out, as all that I retrieved was a large claw. The second attempt produced a second large claw. I got squeamish at the thought that I tore the poor animal apart. It didn't take too much instruction or work to get the crab out of her hole. She was intact! Kristy explained that the two claws I had first retrieved were the ones the female had taken off of a fellow crab and took into her hole for food as she waited for her eggs to hatch. Kristy reassured me that the producer of the claws would grow new ones. The law forbade taking females, so she was only out of the hole long enough for Kristy to show us how to tell her gender. She had a load of eggs and was needed to produce little mud crabs to feed all the critters waiting in the evolutionary chain.

Kristy found a second crab in a hole in the mangrove bank. She and Annabel worked at retrieval for about an hour. They managed to drag out two enormous claws, but no body. I wasn't squeamish this time, as I felt that Annabel was probably not the perpetrator who had removed them from a living crab. Kristy said she thought the hole held a giant male monster because he knew how to fight the hooks. She and Annabel were tired of his game and tried to find a different crab for our dinner.

We slipped and slogged in the oozing mud for another hour without any further luck. We started back toward Kristy's truck with our meager catch of two claws (the two I retieved were returned to the hole along with the female), and then Kristy decided to try to get the monster out one more time. This time she and Annabel were successful. What a beauty he was! He was about ten inches in diameter across the shell on his back. The claws were huge, large enough to snip off a human finger, as Kristy warned us.

My job was to carry the crab in the burlap bag, the hooks, and my camera the two kilometers to the ute. Annabel took videos and plied Kristy with questions about life on a cattle station. Kristy was a town girl who went to school with one of the station owner's sons. He offered her a job, and she took it. She was only going to work on the station for another year or two and then go to the "big smoke" (Perth) and study to become a tour guide. She was energetic, patient, and pleasant. I was sure she would be a success.

Annabel did the hard work when we got back to camp. She cleaned the crab and claws and boiled water to pour over them while they were in a bucket. Our little cooking pan was half the size of the crab. It took Annabel an hour's work to get the crab ready to eat.

By that time I had had a shower and felt refreshed. Then I fixed rice and salad for our gourmet meal. We had enough crab for four good-sized meals.

We spent the balance of the day reading, doing laundry, and lazing around the homestead. I could stay there and share the station chores for a week. It would have been good to ride a horse out looking for cattle, bottle-feed the *potties* (calves), feed geese and the baby emu and other animals. I was sure they had chickens somewhere out of our sight. It would have been *great* to help with the mustering. Well, at least it always looked like fun in the movies.

Annabel wanted to get on up the road. She lived in the country at home, so she was not as impressed with tranquility as I was. Have you noticed how often I wanted to stay put for a week or so and Annabel prodded me to move on? If I had been on my own, I would not have seen and done nearly as much. I probably would just be leaving Pinnacles about now. My six-month visa would have expired before I got to Darwin.

September 20, 1999 We were only on the road for two hours when we saw a sign saying, "Eighty Mile Beach." We remembered that a fellow camper in Karratha told us that Eighty Mile Beach was a nice place to camp. We drove ten kilometers off the highway and found a glorious white sand beach devoid of people.

My watch said ten a.m., but never mind; we were home for the night at the caravan park in the palm-treed paradise. We went for a shell-gathering walk, then took our loot to the tent, changed into togs (swimsuits), and went for a swim. We ate an easy lunch of hard-boiled eggs, carrots, and Granny Smith apples. We knew we'd be having a big crab dinner in the evening.

September 21, 1999 We spent another day at Eighty Mile Beach. I loved the days when we didn't have to drive. We walked the beach and swam in the ocean. I tried to find the ultimate seashell by using my snorkel outfit. That way I would find the shells before they washed up on shore. All I saw was sand. Annabel found a nice cone-shaped shell about eight inches long.

September 22, 1999 We drove as far as Eco Tourist Resort. That sounded like somewhere we'd enjoy. George, the Aboriginal we met in Karijini, recommended it.

The first thing that irritated me was that we could not drive up to the resort. We had to park in a parking lot next to the sad, dirty, bug-infested horse stables. We then had to call reservations to arrange transportation to the resort. The second thing that irritated me was that the reservations clerk told me on the phone she didn't know the price of accommodations. Give me a break. Of course she knew the price. I was ready to move on as soon as I hung up. Annabel wanted to look it over. We might learn a new way to conserve something. Well, golly, she didn't request much. I sure wasn't about to say no.

Reservations sent a car for us; actually, they sent two cars. We had no idea why, since each car had open seating for six passengers. I guess they didn't believe in conserving fuel. Each driver wanted one of us to ride with them. I was apprehensive about the request to separate us, but we did it anyhow. We rode through typical wattle bush we had seen for miles and were dropped off at a lovely open-air restaurant filled with pretty people eating lunch. There were open-air bars, shops, and a closed-in reservations office.

Reservations wanted to show us the "chalets." My first question was, "What is the starting price for these chalets?"

"Well, they start at $100.00 a night, but those chalets don't have water. You probably want something a little more convenient."

I asked Annabel if she wanted to pay $100.00 for a bed to sleep in, and she said, "No!"

"Thank you, we're ready to be driven back to our vehicle," I said. The clerk said transportation to the parking lot only took place at one p.m. I informed her that we'd be leaving immediately, with or without transportation.

I had no patience for scams, ecological or otherwise. We'd be expected to pay extra to eat their food, drink their wine, ride their horses, or anything else we cared to do.

Annabel was outside admiring the luxury of the resort's public facilities. She didn't understand why I had steam coming out of my ears when I told her we were leaving. I explained on the way to Broome. She agreed with my decision.

Annabel and I checked out the beautiful Kimberley Klub Hostel that had the same appurtenances as the Eco Lodge, but had a parking lot beside the building. I would have been happy to stay there, even though it was more expensive at $55.00 for a private room for two, than the $30.00 we had paid at hostels previously. I looked longingly at the tiki bar and restaurant one more time and joined Annabel in the Toyota to look further.

We opted for Cable Beach Caravan Park, $15.00 per night for a tent space among friendly tourist, and we had amenities—a lovely shaded pool in a tropical setting and access to the beach a short walk away.

Eating in Broome's Chinatown beckoned, though finding a Chinese restaurant was no easy feat. After dinner we bought two lawn chairs, sat outside our tent and split a bottle of wine. I could see those lawn chairs were going to add to our enjoyment of camping considerably. We had been using a couple of little three-legged stools I brought from home.

September 23, 1999 We explored glorious Gantheame Point. The rocks were exquisite layers of oxidized sandstone, limestone, ochre, and quartz that had broken and been smoothed by the pounding surf and constant wind.

A house fenced off from tourists stood next to a lighthouse. There was a love story told on a plaque about a former lighthouse keeper who loved his crippled wife so much that he carved a sitting pool in the natural sandstone. The pool filled with water at each high tide. The keeper carried his wife to and from the sitting pool so she could enjoy the seawater and scenery. Awwww.

When we left Gantheame Point, we drove to Broome Jetty and walked the length of the pier. We watched a sea eagle in its nest keeping an eye on the fishermen lining the long pier. Perhaps he was waiting for them to turn their backs on their bait. The jetty was built for the export of cattle, the pearling industry, and as a fishing spot for tourists. The main business in town was definitely tourism.

Back downtown, we went to Chinatown and walked through twenty or more pearl jewelers' shops. We saw one Chinese general store and one Chinese restaurant. Those were the only places that told us we were in Chinatown.

We spent a relaxing evening in the delightful Sun Pictures open-air theatre. We watched the movie *Runaway Bride* from canvas lawn chairs. The theatre was built in 1916 and had been flooded a couple of times over the years, but managed to get back into shape and continue to entertain.

September 24, 1999 We drove two hundred twenty seven kilometers to the end of Cape Leveque Peninsula. The rough road was four-wheel drive all the way. On the way out, I averaged forty kilometers per hour, dodging holes and rocks and trying not to slide in the sudden sandy spots. We passed deep potholes with tree branches sticking out of them as a warning sign to drivers. The scenery wasn't picturesque, as most of the ground cover had been burned off to encourage new growth during the impending wet season. It traditionally started raining in November, with hurricane season arriving by December and running through February.

We stopped at two Catholic Aboriginal missions. The first one, Beagle Bay, had an atmosphere of hostility toward tourists. No one could be bothered to talk to us, or even smile. We went into Sacred Heart Church, built by the Pallottine monks in 1918; it was stunningly decorated with mother-of-pearl shells. Each altar—there were three—was beautifully designed with ceramic tiles and pearl shells. The Stations of the Cross were also made of pearl.

The community was filled with houses built by the government within the past twenty years. They were quite large, with nice verandahs where occupants sought refuge from the noonday sun.

The second community was much friendlier. Lombadina had a young mother running the information office. She had a baby on her hip and a boy about ten wandering in and out. She told us the community consisted of one family of sixty people. The people rotated chores so that everyone had an opportunity to learn different jobs. She had taken turns working in the bakery, grocery store, and now it was her turn to learn the operation of the visitor center and craft store.

We went to the gift shop, but there was little left for sale. No tourists went that far north during "the wet" (monsoon season), so artisans stopped bringing their work to be sold. They would bring in a new supply of didgeridoos, paintings, crafts, and clothes at the start of the next tourist season in late March.

The community was built around the perimeter of a park. From a park bench, we were able to watch boys playing ball, men working as mechanics in a garage, and women working in a laundry, the bakery, and the store. The grocery store, with a petrol pump out front, looked like the gathering place. Just like little country towns in the United States, it had a bench where elderly men passed the time.

The Catholic school had nonindigenous teachers, with Aboriginal teacher's aides.

The Catholic Church had been built by the Aboriginals under the direction of a Western contractor. Construction consisted of corrugated iron on the exterior, and the interior was lined with the bark from melaleuca trees (one species of eucalyptus, also known as a wattle or tea tree). Perhaps that tree bark was chosen because it was naturally waterproof. The lining was held in place with mangrove tree limbs nailed to the frame. The confessional was a matter of the priest sitting inside the church, and the confessant kneeling outside the back door on the verandah. The church was decorated with drawings and paintings done by schoolchildren. The children had written prayers requesting peace in East Timor. I wondered if Aboriginals served in the Australian Army stationed in East Timor.

We left this pleasant community and drove to Cape Leveque lighthouse, where gorgeous red-and-orange sandstone coastal cliffs led down to white sand beaches and azure water.

The trip to the end of the peninsula had taken almost eight hours. We had to choose whether to sleep in our car there in the campground or drive back to our tent in Broome. Annabel chose to return to Broome, so we started out at four o'clock and made it to the camp ground in three and a half hours, as we made no stops along the way.

September 25, 1999 This was a kick-back day. We went to Chinatown and picked up my developed film. We found that all of the one-hour film development places in Australia took twenty-five hours. I inquired about a camera repair service, as my "point and shoot" camera was broken. The telephoto lens would not work. There were no repair shops north of Perth. My big, heavy, expensive camera stopped working properly at Kalbarri. That camera was putting a dark strip across a third of the picture on about a third of each roll of film. I couldn't possibly make the rest of the trip without a good working camera. I was down to my Polaroid, which I brought to give the Aboriginals photos of themselves. I also had a couple of little throwaway underwater cameras. I had thought I was well prepared for this trip, but only seven weeks into the trip, I had to buy a new camera. It cost $385.00 for one like Marlow bought me for $200.00.

We went to the tourist bureau and got information on the tides for seeing the original dinosaur footprints off Gantheame Point, and for seeing the Staircase to the Moon. I bought a couple of books—Aboriginal children's stories. I read mine while enjoying a spinach and feta cheese pasty at a local bakery. I got an extra book for my grandchildren.

There was a pearl shop in the residential district that reputedly had the largest collection of Australian shells in the country. When we arrived, we were not disappointed with the beautiful collection. I had no urge to pay $150.00 for a little pearl to hang around my neck, but had no qualms about paying that much for a carved shell. I fell in love with it at first sight. Sure hoped I could get it home unbroken.

We went to a mango winery for wine tasting at a private home, and there were kids standing around watching the expressions on our faces as we tasted the various offerings. I was not a gourmand, I didn't know a good wine from vinegar. I drank winc to make my toes tingle. Annabel said she particularly liked one of the wines, so we went halves on a bottle for $18.00. We would never have another chance to buy mango wine; it was one of those oncc-in-a-lifetime expenses. The whole trip was one of those expenses.

We rested at our campsite for a couple of hours while waiting for low tide. Then we went to Gantheame Point to see the dinosaur footprints. I was so frustrated with myself. I couldn't find a way to climb down to the level of the footprints without endangering myself, and I didn't want to take a chance on breaking a limb in a fall. Annabel was quite capable of making it over the jagged rocks, down the cliffside, and out to the exposed engravings. She said she took videos so I could see them. Not quite the same.

September 26, 1999 I woke up at five thirty and thought of calling Marlow to wish him a happy birthday. Decided he'd be too hard to locate at two thirty on a Saturday afternoon. I'd do it later when he'd more likely be home. I phoned him at twelve fifteen, which was a little after nine on Saturday in California. He was home and said he had been at a movie earlier to celebrate his sixty-third birthday. The theater had changed the age for senior rates from sixty to sixty-five that very day. He was disappointed to have to pay full price. I chided him about going from watching television to watching a movie, and calling it a celebration. He said he'd continue to celebrate his birthday on Sunday. He was going to watch football on television. That was the same thing he did every Sunday between August and January. I was glad I lived a more exciting life.

I went on a bird-watching expedition in the morning. Well, for me, that was more exciting than watching television. The birds were nice to see, but the weather was too hot to enjoy the beach trail, and the trail through the scrub had been burned away. The Broome Bird Observatory was closed down for the summer. They had cabins, campgrounds, and a big screen in the kitchen/meeting room where they taught about local and migratory birds. Over 2,000 species of birds spend the northern winter in the Broome area. It would be neat to come back here for a couple of weeks during bird migration season.

I returned to the tent just as Annabel was departing for the beach. I didn't care to join her on the hot sand, so I spent the next couple of hours alternating between sitting in the shade reading and taking the occasional dip in the campground's shaded pool. The pool was in a landscaped garden, and was such a pleasant place that I was surprised to see only a couple of other people taking advantage of the luxury.

In the evening we went to Cable Beach to watch the camel safari return from their hot trek along the shore. We watched the sun set from the fancy resort, then went to the park, where we were told we would be able to see the phenomenon known as Staircase to the Moon. When the full moon rose at low tide, the glow on the rippled mud flats looked like shiny stairs leading to the moon.

September 27, 1999 We provisioned for two weeks at the one store we found open in Broome. It was the Queen's birthday, as well as Sunday, and Australia was celebrating by staying away from work. Most stores were closed, as it was a long holiday weekend. The locals had left town. Where do people who live in a remote resort town on a world-renowned beach go? I asked, and was told, that many go "bush." Others take advantage of the time to visit friends and family.

We drove northeast to Derby, which had been a cattle-processing town years before and was old, tired, and dusty. They had one tourist attraction, a thousand-year-old boab tree that had been used as a jail during the last century. The tree was hollow inside, and a single prisoner would have had more room than a lot of today's prisoners do in properly constructed jails.

We arrived at Windjana Gorge off the Gibb River Road, in the Kimberleys, at sunset. We set up camp, ate, and visited with the friendly ranger for half an hour. After he left, we enjoyed the cold-water showers, went to bed, and read. The temperature was forty-one degrees Celsius (one-hundred-six degrees Fahrenheit). We had been having uncomfortably hot weather for the past three days.

September 28, 1999 We walked the trail through Windjana Gorge soon after sunrise while the air was reasonably cool. The walk took us along the Lennard River, which was currently a series of puddles, one of which housed freshwater crocodiles. Only their eyes could be seen above the murky water. There were sulfur-crested cockatoos eating eucalyptus blossoms in waterside trees, and fruit bats hanging upside down, wrapping their translucent wings around their bodies.

The outstanding geology was entirely different from Karijini; it was predominantly dark-gray limestone, one hundred meters high, with a bit of orange sandstone thrown in for contrast. The rock was very porous, with large holes and caves—habitats for critters.

The trees were mostly melaleucas (paperbark eucalyptus), but other types were thrown in for variety. There were river red-gums with their hollow limbs harboring a variety of birds and small animals. There were also native fig trees and Leichhardt trees.

We spent the heat of midday relaxing in the campground. Annabel and I enjoyed drawing. I did birds, and she did trees and landscapes. We took turns playing solitaire with our single deck of cards and spent several hours reading. I loved having all that time to read novels. I haven't been able to do that for years.

Before sunset we walked the gorge trail again and watched the crocodiles watch us. Annabel wandered farther than I did. She was back shortly after hearing something hissing at her from the bushes—probably a goanna; they hissed at intruders.

At sunset the ranger came by for another visit and told us the temperature was forty-two degrees (108 degrees Fahrenheit). Annabel had wondered before the trip if she'd be able to tolerate the heat. She was finding out.

September 29, 1999 We drove to the town of Geikie Gorge outside of the town of Fitzroy Crossing. The gorge itself was only accessible by boat. Fitzroy River was currently about thirty meters wide, but reputedly got to be seven miles wide by January. We made the short walk to the jetty. The boat ride schedule seemed terribly unorganized. One notice board said one time, another said another time, and the tourist bureau gave us a third time for departure. The prices on the different announcement boards ranged from $17.50 to $85.00. In the tourist office in Fitzroy Crossing, the clerk told us the boat rides were conducted by Aboriginals, and they'd sometimes cancel if they didn't feel they had enough customers to make the trip worth their while. We decided not to wait around to see if there would be a boat trip or not.

We drove the rocky, scenic road between Fitzroy Crossing and Tunnel Creek. There we took the hike down a riverbed that went through a mountain in the 350-million-year-old Napier Range, a barrier reef from an ancient seabed. At least it would be cooler inside the mountain. The trail was underground for seven-hundred-fifty meters. Walking there was a surreal experience. The only light was from the entrance or from our flashlights. There was an opening in the cave about midway that gave us a glimpse of vines, trees, and bushes outside. Annabel waited at this opening while I went the remainder of the way.

The cave had stalactites as well as lots of bats hanging from the ceiling. I did have to traverse knee-deep water from time to time and tried not to think what those bats were doing to that water. I would take a shower as soon as I returned to base camp. In the wet season, which had not yet started, there were saltwater crocodiles in the tunnel, but we were assured by the rangers that they left with the receding water, and the only kind of croc we might come across would be the freshwater crocodiles that don't like the taste of nasty humans. I walked until I came to the rear exit, then rejoined Annabel.

On the way between Tunnel Creek and Windjana, where we were camped, we got flat tire number four. Annabel changed the flat with minor help from two men. When our new tires were installed in Karratha, the mechanic told us what tire pressure we should use on rocky roads and what we should use on sand. We followed his recommendations to no avail.

September 30, 1999 I loved this glorious Kimberly country. It represented the Australia of my dreams. I drove slowly so I wouldn't miss a single scenic view. We left Windjana Gorge campground and traveled Gibb River Road to Bell Gorge.

Sometimes the surrounding landscape looked unreal—the escarpment of orange and pink rocks set against a deep-blue sky. Halfway down the escarpment, the talus started, with sandy orange, pink, and beige soil supporting gray-green spinifex grass. The alluvial fans were dotted with deep-green eucalypts and stately baob trees. Other times we saw black, ominous-looking cliffs with the odd pandanus hugging a crevice, or ghost-gums with their startling white bark.

We saw areas where there were no hills, no escarpments, nothing but waist-deep grass, golden brown at this time of year, and gently waving in warm breezes. Those areas were usually speckled with termite mounds. I thought of termites as being in areas where they had wood to eat. Out here they existed by eating mud.

We saw another bustard, our first since Cape Range Peninsula. Kangaroos were so plentiful, sometimes Annabel didn't even turn her head when I called out a sighting.

We trekked the rocky trail at Bell River Gorge to the waterfalls, and were so glad we made the effort! It was a fantastic spot. A steep cliff face had to be descended to get to the best swimming hole. There was a group of pubescent Aboriginal children having a great time jumping from the cliffside into the refreshing water.

Families with small children were playing in the shallow pools at the top of the waterfalls. Those pools were within easy access, so that was where I washed off. The water was only slightly below body temperature and fuzzy (algae). It still felt good.

I survived the uphill trek back to the car. I got distracted by trees, bushes, bugs, lizards, and flowers. There was so much to see along any trail, and it was wonderful to know I was retired and had time to stop and enjoy every little thing.

We made a stop at Galvan's Gorge, which was totally different from Bell River Gorge or Windjana. There were giant sharp-edged boulders strewn alongside water lily ponds. I wished I had the talent to paint a picture with words like James Michener. You just have to see this place for yourselves to understand why I loved it. One site after another was named "Gorge," and no two were alike. The one thing they all had in common was that they were gorgeous.

The sun was setting by the time we returned from Galvan's, and we debated on whether to camp next to the sign that said, "Absolutely No Camping Under Any Circumstances." There was another couple with a tent pitched there, and it looked so serene. I wondered if they had posted the sign. We chose to leave them in peace and go on down the road.

We pitched our tent at Manning Gorge. It was dark when we arrived, so no one collected our money. We were the sole users of our dunny, which was almost as good as a private motel room. Western Australia's dunnies were different than any we had seen before. There was a bucket of disinfectant in water beside the toilet. There was a long-handled wire toilet brush in the bucket, and the brush was chained to the toilet. Each user was expected to slosh some water around the stainless-steel toilet bowl after use and put the lid down when finished. Believe it or not, those toilets did not have the usual outhouse smell like our lime-coated ones in the States. There was practically no odor.

After dinner we settled in for a good sleep and dozed off while watching the lightning in the distance and listening to the far-off thunder. We were soon wide-awake as the blinding lightning struck near us; thunder drowned out any efforts at communication. After several loud claps of thunder, it finally started raining.

Once the rain started, Annabel fell into a sound sleep. She didn't even roll over during the night. I rolled at least twenty-five times every hour and woke up feeling like I'd been in a wrestling match. I spent that night mopping up the puddles beside my sleeping bag. My air mattress was punctured early on the trip across the Gibb River Road, and didn't hold air for more than an hour, so I'd been sleeping on the ground until we could get to the next city, where I could buy a new one.

Annabel remained melancholy and hadn't shown much interest in the scenery since Kalbarri. I kept expecting her to tell me she was going home. Maybe she'd leave when we got to Darwin, our next reasonable-sized town for catching an international flight. I expected her to make that announcement in Broome when the weather started getting hot.

I felt frustrated that she wasn't having fun, and I didn't know how to help her. I knew it was a major financial decision to come on the trip. The only time she appeared to enjoy herself was when she was bargaining on the didgeridoo with George, when she was able to play with dogs, and when we saw someone who was traversing the country on a motorcycle or bicycle. She related to those people, as her sons had made such trips. I, on the other hand, was ecstatic over every rock, plant, and animal. That probably added to her depression. I would have liked to stay a week or more each at Pinnacles, Kalbarri, Pardoo Station, Karijini, and now, the Kimberleys.

October 1, 1999 We started a walk from Manning Gorge campground to the actual gorge. By seven thirty a.m. my head was splitting from the exertion of climbing uphill over huge, flat rocks that were reflecting the sun's rays into my face. There was no shade in view. I asked a lady hiking past my resting spot if she knew how far it was to the gorge. She said she was told to expect to hike for one and a half to two hours to get there. Good grief! I had only made it thirty minutes. I possibly could have made it to the gorge, but someone would have to carry me back to the campsite. I didn't work hard enough on getting fit for this trip. I didn't think that Annabel would be willing to give me a piggyback ride back to camp, though she had agreed to every other request except spending more time at any one spot.

Annabel was way, way ahead of me. I shouted, but didn't really expect an answer and didn't get one. I figured she'd complete the circuit and be back at the starting point within half an hour of me, if I turned around right then.

Reversing down the trail and along the creek, I found a place to cross. I knew it wasn't the same crossing spot I used before, but figured I could find the campground once I was on the correct side of the creek. Finding the campground was no easy trick, as the grass and bushes were so high. I was lucky that a busload of tourists came by to cool off in the idyllic swimming hole. I followed the sound of their voices and was soon joining them in the water.

The bank was undercut, and when I finished my swim, I tried to gracefully exit the water by hanging on to a rope from a tree like I had seen the German tourists do. My arthritic hands were useless in holding up my weight, and I looked totally absurd. The tourists cheered when one of their group felt sorry for me and pulled me from the water. How embarrassing!

Europeans amazed me with their lack of modesty. Those people changed clothes, into and out of swimsuits, right at the water's edge. A couple or three had someone hold a towel up so that only half the people could see their nakedness. The age of the group was from forty to eighty, so it wasn't as though they were trying to flaunt their beauty; it was just their natural way of getting into a swimsuit.

I was concerned to find that Annabel was not back at the campsite. I decided she had stopped to take a dip at the waterfall shown on postcards of Manning Gorge. Another half hour passed. I walked along the trail a short distance to see if I could see her in the tall grass, where it was easy to get confused. No luck. I yelled her name as loudly as possible to no avail.

After another half hour passed, I visualized all the warnings I had read over the past five years—broken legs, snakebite, spider bite, dehydration (she rarely drank water when hiking), sunstroke (she refused to wear a hat).

The day tourists left in their four-wheel-drive bus, and just a couple of kids were still at the campground. I formulated a search plan. It would certainly do no good for me to look on my own. Then both of us would be lost, and no one would notice for days and days. I got lost if I blinked twice without noting my whereabouts.

I'd leave a note tacked to a tree at the trailhead, and another at the campsite, in case Annabel returned and found the car gone. I'd drive the dirt road out to the roadhouse and admit we had camped the previous night on their property without paying. After they had collected their fee and forgiven me, I'd ask them to notify State Emergency Services of a lost person.

Annabel walked out of the bush just as I was climbing into the car. Thank goodness! I was so glad to see her. She had been lost within a hundred yards of where I was sitting writing the notes. She was beside the stream, but couldn't find the campground. Spinifex grass grew in clumps, so it was hard to distinguish a regular trail. Each clump looked like it had a trail all the way around.

We went to the roadhouse and paid our rent. The rest of the day was spent at leisure in the campground. We caught up on our journals (or money-spent list, in Annabel's case), swam in the billabong (yes, there were crocodiles, no they didn't threaten us; they were the freshwater kind), read, and sketched.

When I asked Annabel if she'd help me emerge from the billabong if I went in for a swim, she said, "Sure." When I was ready to get out, she was standing there with her video camera going. Big help she was.

I had searched for the hole in my mattress with Dawn liquid soap. No luck in finding it, but now I had a very clean, flat air mattress to sleep on. Another problem with the mattress was the velour finish on it. That acted like Velcro with my pajamas. Every time I flipped over, the air mattress came with me. Then I was lying on the bare plastic tent floor with an air mattress on top of me. Every night I'd say that I was going to scrap the air mattress and just sleep on top of my sleeping bag. Then I'd decide to give the mattress one more try because the sleeping bag was a very slippery material—Dacron maybe—and I knew I'd have it wadded up in a ball before daylight.

October 2, 1999 We left Manning Gorge in good shape. We packed the car and went for one last swim. That way we started out feeling cool and refreshed. That was what I meant by "good shape." I wasn't trying to trick you into thinking that we now looked like Raquel Welch.

At the roadhouse (gas station/convenience store), we filled the fuel tank ($1.14 per liter, about $5.50 per gallon US!). We got our sweets for the day and chatted with the manager. He told us a bit about the history of the Aboriginal Community across the road from the roadhouse.

They were the new owners of Manning Gorge Station. The previous Australian/European agriculturist had been raising cattle on a hundred-year lease of the land. The Aboriginals decided they wanted to use their prerogative and reclaim the land. The family who had been cultivating the property for several generations had to move. The roadhouse manager didn't say whether they were compensated.

The Aboriginals were being trained as cattlemen, store clerks, teachers, and general laborers as required in maintaining a station, school, and roadhouse. They had been in training for two years. As far as the roadhouse went, one girl had learned enough to be an assistant to the bookkeeper. There was a school set up in the community, and one girl learned to be a teacher's aide.

The government tried a scheme of sending Aborigine children to the city to go to white children's schools, and the children had been so traumatized, they not only didn't learn anything, but they also came home with psychological problems. That scheme was discontinued in the 1970s. The United States did the same disgraceful thing with Native Americans starting in 1870 and continuing for almost a hundred years.

Annabel and I went to Barnett Gorge, which was five-kph driving most of the way, and I frequently made choices about which rock to hit. I figured tires were easier to replace than oil pans, so I tried to keep the biggest, nastiest-looking rocks out from under the center of the car. We ended up pulling the car off into the grass at a reasonable spot and walking down the "road."

Annabel drove out of the gorge. She didn't have the problems I did going in. We bounced merrily along. I asked her how she was able to choose which rock to dodge, and she explained it.

"The hood sticks out in front of the car so far, I can't see the road." She just put the two left tires up on the edge of the grass and drove. We made it to Durack River Station before nightfall.

After setup, Annabel walked to the restroom and was back in two minutes. I asked what was wrong.

"You have to see this." I trailed up the hill to the pink wooden building. There were no signs saying "Men" or "Women" or any of the cutesy derivations of those meanings written on the doors. Annabel opened the first door and aimed her flashlight at the toilet.

"Go ahead, you go first," Annabel said with a smile in her voice. I knew she wouldn't suggest that if I were in danger, so I walked across the fully furnished bathroom and lifted the toilet lid. There were beautiful little green frogs in the bowl. We tried each of the other rooms and found the same animals in every toilet. No, we did not flush them away. We picked them up and put them outside. We learned to check before we sat on camping toilets in the future.

October 3, 1999 We slept in late. I had another bad night, as I gave up my leaky air mattress and slept on the ground. Every once in a while, my downward side would start throbbing, and I would shift positions. I was okay as long as I stayed on my fluffy stomach, but I kept rolling over on one side or the other out of habit. Annabel said she slept soundly, except for one period when she heard something eating right beside her head. She got awake enough to check outside the tent and found a cow eating grass adjacent to her pillow.

We walked to the Durack homestead to pay for two more nights camping. Yea! We got to enjoy the scenery for a while longer. We talked to the nice Dutch lady who operated the campground and store. She said the saltwater crocodiles would have to swim up waterfalls to get to the dammed part of Durack River. That made us more comfortable about swimming.

The manager's home was made of corrugated iron with screen for windows. The floors were paving rocks set very unevenly in concrete. The "tearoom" had a built-in steel oven set under a rock counter. It was a charming place exuding pioneer know-how!

Australia had colorful birds. I enjoyed seeing the following: ever-present cockatoos, both black and white, masked-lapwing plovers, dollar-birds, red-backed kingfishers, blue-winged kookaburras, black-fronted dotterels, black-winged stilts, willy wagtails, snowy egrets, blue herons, star finches, and my favorite, the rainbow bee-eater.

The rainbow bee-eater was teal on his head and back and iridescent bronze on the underside of his wings. He did spectacular aerobatics while chasing flying insects.

October 4, 1999 We walked the tumbled rock-strewn shores of the Durack River in hopes of finding elusive Aboriginal art. We started out at seven in the morning while it was as cool as it would get for the day. I drank a gallon of water, and it ran right through me and out my pores.

Once we discovered the art on the cliffside, we tried to figure out if the drawings were authentic or not. We couldn't tell. They consisted of the outline of a crocodile and the outline of a snake. The hike was fun getting there anyhow. We did a lot of climbing over boulders the size of trucks that looked like they were thrown willy-nilly at the bottom of the banks. They probably were thrown there by rushing water before the river had been dammed.

The manager said her husband had marked the way with cairns. The only problem was that the next cairn was never in sight when we were standing at one. Annabel walked ahead in one direction, and I went in another, and whoever found the next cairn would call out. There wasn't much chance we'd get lost as long as we stayed between the cliff and the river. I was wringing wet with sweat when we got back to the campground, and I walked past the tent and straight into the lake-sized river to cool off.

In the heat of the day, we lounged in the shade beside our tent and read or drew pictures. The biographical novels I'd read so far on this trip were *We of the Never-Never, To Be Heirs Forever, Sons in the Saddle, Kings in Grass Castles,* and *Keep Him My Country.* The last four were about the

Durack family and written by Mary Durack. They drove cattle across country from Queensland and settled in the Kimberley range in the late 1800s and early 1900s.

October 5, 1999 I had to face the facts. Sooner or later we'd have to leave the Kimberley region. We loaded up and were off down the road by seven thirty. I wasn't sure whether it was tears or sweat running down my face. I wanted to stay—just one week.

I knew the heat must be driving Annabel buggy. Before the trip I might have said something really silly like, "When it gets too hot, we'll just ride in the air-conditioned car." That sounds like a lie I would have promised. Of course, we couldn't drive twenty-four hours a day.

The landscape changed dramatically as we approached the eastern entrance to the Kimberleys. The road remained corrugated, trees were scarcer, the escarpment was closer to the road, and the general landscape was created by a desert lover.

We planned on making our last Kimberley overnight stop at El Questro Station, the campground run in conjunction with Emma Gorge. We were early, so we decided to take the hike before checking into the campground.

Emma Gorge was a shock. A sign said to stop at the office to register before proceeding on the trail. We didn't do that before at any gorge. My first thought was that it must be a really hazardous trail, and we needed to let someone responsible know when we expected to return. No such thing. El Questro charged $5.00 to walk to the gorge. No thanks; it was a matter of principle. If this had been our first gorge, we would have paid without a second thought.

The "office" was at a fancy-smancy restaurant where we were required to reserve a seat even though there was not a single person in the establishment except the reservations clerk. The office rented tents on platforms for $70.00 a night. There was no place for us to put up our own tent. Hotel rooms ran from $350.00 to $750.00 per night. No food was allowed to be brought on the premises; we had to eat in their restaurant. We skipped El Questro. We left the tropical, unspoiled paradise and drove to Wyndham.

While filling the fuel tank, we saw a jabiru, Queensland's state bird. It stood about four feet high and was white and iridescent black in color. We took a few pictures of him. He decided Annabel's camcorder looked like something to eat. He walked toward her; she tried to shoo him away by waving her camera at him. He thought she was offering food, so he came closer. She managed to get away from him by running into the garage. The mechanic told her not to carry things in her hand, and the stork would not chase her. She put her things down and came back out to have her picture taken with the stork. She stood twenty feet away from him to pose.

I asked the garage man to fix our spare tire. He wanted to keep it overnight, as he was busy on another job. It was forty-four degrees Celsius (one-hundred-ten degrees Fahrenheit); it would be cooler in the morning. It was a logical request.

Annabel and I went to a bookstore/art gallery that had a sign saying, "Open," but they were just teasing. We went to a guesthouse that had a sign saying, "Air Conditioned Rooms." The house was really a hostel, with a guest kitchen and laundry. We were ready for a place to clean out our food containers and do laundry. Unfortunately, the place did not respond to our door knocking or "Yooo-hoooing." The guesthouse was such a pleasant-looking place with a nice pool in a landscaped yard and mango trees full of ripe fruit. Darn it. Was it siesta time in Wyndham, or was everything closed for the impending wet season?

We located an open museum where I found factual historical information about the Durack family. I had read about them before I left home, and I read Mary Durack's novels, but I was beginning to think they were fictional characters, as no one along our route knew whom I was talking about. Supposedly, Patrick Durack was one of the first pioneers to bring cattle into the Kimberley. Tales of heroism, hard work, and tenacity inspired me. Mary Durack, Patrick's granddaughter, the author, was made a Dame of the British Isles, the English female equivalent to being knighted (women are not knighted). Wyndham was founded as an abattoir, a meat-processing plant, to handle Durack cattle before shipping it off to Indonesia and east coast Australian cities.

The best part of the museum was the water cooler in the corner. The kind man let us fill our water jug, after we had our fill from his cups. He used a couple of ceramic cups for everyone who wanted a drink. I thought the water tasted like nectar; Annabel thought it tasted like rubber hose. It had been a long time since we had ice water; she probably forgot how good it was.

It started to rain, so we decided we'd better find lodging for the night. We drove out of town to a place called Parry River Farm. The campground was advertised as a good place for bird-watching. Annabel was driving and chose our campsite. We pitched our tent right next to the water lily-covered stream. I was concerned about saltwater crocodiles, as there was no waterfall for them to climb to reach us as there had been at Durack Station. Annabel asked the proprietor if they had problems.

"Heavens, no, it has been weeks since we've seen one."

Annabel slept in the tent. I slept under the stars a hundred meters away from the water. Before sleep, I luxuriated in a long, cool shower in the wonderful ablution block built of natural stone. As I exited the restroom, the manager called out, "I hope the tree python didn't bother you. He just goes in there to catch the frogs." We knew to watch for frogs in toilets as well as snakes. From now on, we'd inspect the shower before undressing.

October 6, 1999 Annabel had the charming habit of saying, "Goodbye, thanks for letting us stay with you," at every public campground. Today was no exception. I waited in the car. She was gone an unusually long time. I walked to the office and saw her taking pictures of something on the ground.

Upon approach, I saw it was a snake. It was the tree python, a pretty grass-green snake about four feet long with a yellow belly. It stopped its swaying crawl and raised its head up three or four inches to look around. I lay down on the ground and was lucky enough to get a couple of good closeup shots of his face.

We finally left and went to Marlgu Billabong, where "five hundred brolgas" (cranes, like sandhill cranes) had been seen earlier in the week.

We didn't see a single one. We watched the beautiful selection of water and shorebirds playing hide-and-seek with a saltwater croc, and we took a few pictures. I used up the last of my roll of film and changed it. In the process I dropped the finished roll of film, and it went through the grading of the steel mesh walkway and into the billabong. There went my good snake pictures. I'm sure they would have been prizewinners.

Annabel and I went to an Aboriginal Memorial Park—an unkempt, rocky plot of ground, with no grass or greenery of any kind, but with gorgeous bronze sculptures of an Aboriginal family, a kangaroo, and a dog. I didn't learn if the sculpture was done by a native, as there were no signs.

We picked up our repaired tire, bought some goodies at the bakery, and left Wyndham. We drove along the Great Northern Highway that was under construction from Wyndham to Kununurra. Once in Kununurra, we went to a gallery where zebra rock was cut and polished. The only place the primordial beige and reddish-brown striped rock was found was in the eastern Kimberleys. We bought some to take home.

The two of us ended up at a place called Kimberley Caravan Park located on a lake that sported ducks on the surface and birds on snags at the water's edge. I did laundry and went for a swim in the shade-covered swimming pool, then watched the sun set over the peaceful lake.

October 7, 1999 Annabel's fear of flying kept her at our campsite while I flew in a six-passenger plane. On my all-day tour with Slingair Airlines, five Englishmen and I flew over enormous Lake Argyle. Lake Argyle was forty-two times larger than Sydney Harbor. The lake was small right now because it was the end of the dry season; at the end of the wet season, the lake was much larger. There were places in the lake where you could sit in a boat and not see any land. The dam was completed in 1972 with the prediction that it would take eight years to fill. It took three years of intense wet seasons. Forty-two times larger than Sydney Harbor, imagine that.

We landed on a private airstrip and toured Argyle Diamond Mine. Argyle was the largest diamond mine in the world, as they claimed to have overtaken De Beers in Africa in production. Argyle produced 25 percent of the world's industrial diamonds and did find gem-quality stones also. The tour was conducted in a bus, and we were only allowed to depart the bus when we were in the employees' lodging compound, where we were served a cafeteria-style lunch and permitted to shop for diamonds in the company store that was attached to a one-room museum. After the delightful light lunch of salad, fresh rolls, and fruit, I spent most of my time in the museum. Diamonds were found in corundum, as was sapphire. Argyle removed an average of a ton of dirt to find one gem-quality diamond. They were finding pink and champagne-colored gem-quality stones among the dust used as industrial diamonds (for saw blades, other cutting tools, and sandpaper).

The planeload of tourists flew over the Bungle Bungles, which was a national park founded in 1983. Very few white men had seen the phenomena of the silica- and iron-layered mounds before it became a park because it was located on a private cattle station. The Bungle Bungles—called Purnululu by the natives—looked like beehives in some cases, as the mounds were well rounded by the wind and water erosion. The area had been a sea bed in olden days, like millions of years ago. I had been looking forward to seeing the Bungle Bungles, as I had read so much about them in planning this trip. They were unique, but did not possess the beauty of Karijini.

Annabel spent most of the day washing the car. I couldn't believe how good it looked when I got back. She said she had to wash it several times. I believed that! Our chariot was tidy inside and out. She must have left two inches of Kimberley bull dust in the campground gutter.

October 8, 1999 Annabel joined me on a two-hour boat tour of one-fifth of Lake Argyle. We saw a man catch a catfish with his bare hands, using his thumb as bait. It was a pleasant trip as long as the boat was moving. The motor stopped for a while so people could go in for a dip, and it really warmed up inside the canopied boat. The temperature had ranged between thirty-seven and forty-four degrees Celsius this past week.

We went to the shopping center, where I bought a new air mattress. Aren't you glad you won't have to read any more whining about my sleeping accommodations?

The gent camping next to us suggested we would enjoy seeing Ivanhoe Crossing. He was correct. The pleasant half-hour ride went through lush farmlands. When we got to the crossing, I pulled into the parking lot where fishermen parked. There was no way I was going to drive our clean, packed car across a road covered with two to three feet of water along the edge of the waterfall. Granted, the weir was only a six-foot drop, but it would make a mess of the car that went over the edge of the crescent-shaped dam. We were fascinated watching car after car plow through the water. Many utes had a bed load of people. To them it was an everyday occurrence. Occasionally, a driver worked his way around fishermen trying to catch barramundi.

Children swam upstream from the weir wall and roadway. I was afraid they would be washed into traffic. The thought didn't appear to bother their caretakers.

We went to Kelly's Knob, Kununurra's scenic lookout. Damming the Ord River to make Lake Argyle was a fruitful move by the government. From the top of the Knob, we could see miles and miles of farmlands. They wouldn't exist without the Ord River irrigation plan. A sign said that sixty different crops could be viewed from the outlook. I took their word for it.

We finished off the day at Mirima Hidden Valley National Park, where we went on a nature trail with little signs telling us about trees. The trees we had seen with cotton balls were called kapok. The geology was a miniature Bungle Bungles. As we were there at sunset, we watched the colors turn from flame to purple. Isn't it amazing how much beauty there is in this old world?

October 9, 1999 We bought a new part for our broken tire jack, lots of batteries for reading at night, and then started off to spend a week in the beehive-shaped Bungle Bungles. We drove down the highway listening to our new cassette series—*Award-Winning Australian Country Music*. The songs were about who was doing whom wrong, just like American country music.

We passed through Turkey Creek, where we planned on spending time with an Aboriginal woman who taught white women survival in the bush. We stopped at the office and found a heavyset woman watering plants. The office was closed, and I inquired of the gardener if there was somewhere else we could make reservations for the following week. The third time I asked, the lady finally answered in the negative. She had a cigarette dangling from her mouth and looked very bored. I didn't pursue the issue, as I was afraid she might be the person who would take us out bush to teach us how to catch our own meals. She didn't appear to be someone I'd feel comfortable living in the bush with for a week. She might leave us stranded somewhere, as she obviously didn't want to talk to us.

We looked for the turnoff to the Bungles and found it on our third pass. The turnoff was in a construction zone, and we missed it the first couple of tries. We drove ten kilometers down the roughest dirt road we'd encountered. I was afraid I'd do permanent damage to the car if I continued. It was even worse than the road we drove into Barnett Gorge. I stopped and looked at the map. We were destined to stay on this road for one-hundred-fifty kilometers. At the rate we were traveling, it would take us two days to get to the Bungles. Then we'd have to walk a long distance to get to the *start* of the trails leading through the mounds. The two trails I had planned on taking were a hundred kilometers apart. See why I needed to travel with someone with common sense? This plan looked good when I was back in Folsom looking at books.

Annabel suggested we drive back to Turkey Creek (Warmun in Aborigine) and sign up for a helicopter flight over the mounds. Once in Turkey Creek, we learned the next helicopter was due to leave in twenty *hours*. We found a grassy spot under a tree and pitched Annabel's tent. She was tolerant of my venturing off into the wild blue yonder as long as she didn't have to do it. Now she'd sit at the campsite and wait for me to return from yet another flight. The only entertainment at the campsite was watching the Aboriginal community dogs, which Annabel loved to do, and swimming in the pool, which didn't interest her in the least. Fortunately, she shared one of my idiosyncrasies; she could strike up conversations with strangers. That would keep her amused while I was slipping the surly bonds of earth.

October 10, 1999 My flight was scheduled for eleven a.m. I reported in at ten-forty-five so I could get weighed (I'd lost weight on the trip!) and fill out paperwork. The second person had not shown up by eleven o'clock. The office clerk said the pilot would wait fifteen minutes, then would cancel the flight, if no one showed up. Eleven fifteen, no passenger arrived, so the young woman who was going to pilot us left for Kununurra. What a disappointment.

At eleven twenty, I went to the office to get a refund, and a young man held the door open for me. As I finished with the clerk, the young man asked about a ride. The clerk informed us that a second pilot was about to land who was more than willing to take us for a flight over the Bungles. Yea! The clerk said to get out to the landing pad when she landed.

I ran back to the campsite and got my camera. Annabel handed me her video camera and gave me a couple of quick instructions on its use. At the pad I heard the pilot ask the young man if he wanted to sit up front by the opening where a door would normally be mounted. He said, "Absolutely not." My lucky star was shining brightly. I definitely wanted to sit in front next to the opening so I could see better and take pictures without the glare of window glass.

What a ride! What a sight! The brown and golden country was a study of the torment the earth had gone through to form the existing topography. We saw earthquake faults, horsts, and grabens, where the earth's surface had been stretched and pulled apart. The portion of the plate that sank was called a graben. The uplifted structures on either side were called horsts. (I remembered which was which by thinking of climbing up on a horse (horst). If I fell down, I would be grabbing (graben) for something to stop the fall. There were synclines and anticlines, where tensional stresses had elongated the crust into blocks and tilted them. I was flying over a geology lesson. Then we flew over the beehives for a close look at the sedimentary stratas of silicates and iron that were swirled and shaped for my personal enjoyment.

I was hyper from excitement when we landed. The helicopter was a much better ride than the airplane because we were able to get much closer to the ground. Of course, the fresh wind blowing through the helicopter cabin added to the feeling of freedom, and it cooled the occupants.

Annabel had the car packed and lunch made (Granny Smith apples, crackers, and peanut butter, my favorite). I wolfed down a couple of crackers in between sentences about the wonders of the earth's movements. Annabel patiently listened to my ranting.

I was still excited three hours later when we arrived back in Kununurra and didn't feel like setting up a tent and going through our mundane chores of evening preparation. I treated us to a stay in an air-conditioned cabin right on the lake's edge.

I was too wired to sleep. We watched two movies on television. The movies were *The Silver Brumby* about wild horses in Australia, and *Ransom* with Mel Gibson. Who would have thought I'd want to sit and watch television? I finally unwound enough to sleep by midnight. Remember, we had been going to bed at seven or eight o'clock.

October 11, 1999 Back to normal, we made a quick trip to a Toyota dealer to buy an air filter, filled the tank with fuel, and we were off across the dull, flat, bitumen (asphalt) road to Katherine.

We arrived at Katherine Gorge, which was reclaimed by the Aborigines in 1989 and renamed Nitmiluk. The park was completely changed from the way it was ten years earlier when I last visited. Now it was commercial, and the campground had expanded to six campgrounds, an office, a store, a museum, a marina, and a restaurant.

Annabel found a quiet place to camp way down in the back forty (that means "behind the black stump" to you Australians). It was forty-five degrees Celsius (a hundred-twelve degrees Fahrenheit) and humid. I heard the breeze blowing in the treetops, but it was deadly still on the ground. The inside of the tent felt like a sauna. I took my new air mattress and lay outside. To heck with night critters; they'd think it was too hot to eat a fat old lady.

October 12, 1999 We took the scenic boat trip through the gorge, went through the museum, ate in the restaurant, and spent the rest of the day in our campsite.

We watched the fascinating mating ritual of the bowerbird. He flirted, danced, and did aerobatics for his ladylove. He presented her with presents of white scraps he'd stolen from campsites; he did acrobatics on tree limbs and flashed bright puce head feathers at her. She finally flew to the entrance of his neatly constructed, grass, U-shaped nest. He flew to the opposite end of the tubular nest and peeked in to see if she was inside. She was busily inspecting the white presents on the ground. She flew back to the tree, and he took off to look for more enticement. She was playing hard to get. He was determined. It was thrilling to watch love progress. He brought a shiny, blue piece of tinfoil and won her heart (or something).

We took pictures of the agile wallabies that came to eat the campground's lush green grass. No emus were seen, but there were hundreds of fruit- and blossom-eating birds about.

Annabel wrote postcards, and I labeled ten rolls of film that had been developed. I sent them home to Marlow every time I got a collection of ten rolls. That way he could share the excitement of the trip.

At five that afternoon, a school bus loaded with high school kids pulled in next to us and pitched their tents. They were on their way to Darwin to enter a vehicle in the Solar Car International Race from Darwin to Adelaide. The kids were from a Catholic high school located in Redcliffe, near Brisbane. I chatted with a senior driver. She introduced me to her teacher, who was in charge of their race car. He went to all the trouble of unlatching the multiple locks on the trailer and showing me their car. I was thoroughly impressed by the minilecture on the mechanics of the car and was caught completely off guard when the teacher asked if I'd care to be one of their sponsors. For $5,000.00 I'd be considered one of their primary backers. He was disappointed to learn I was on a budget trip; I was not one of those famous "rich Americans." What would I be with a hundred-dollar donation?

October 13, 1999 We drove from Katherine Gorge to Darwin and took a quickie stop at Edith Falls. The pool of water at the bottom of the falls looked so inviting.

I walked to the pool, took a quick dip and a few pictures of the pandanus, and then rejoined Annabel at a sign describing the trails available. I asked if she wanted to go for a hike. Fortunately, that was a negative.

We stopped for lunch at the Adelaide River Hotel, where the progeny of the water buffalo, Charley, from the movies *Crocodile Dundee I* and *II* lived. Supposedly, one of the creatures was the original bull, Charley. That would make him at least fifteen years old. Was Charley like Lassie? There were a whole bunch of dogs named Lassie between the time Elizabeth Taylor and Roddy MacDowell made the first Lassie movie and Tommy Retig made the last TV show.

October 14, 1999 Scott, my son, was due to arrive at Darwin International Airport at one that afternoon for a three-day visit. I straightened up the tent so that it looked cozy and homey. We had unloaded our food and cooking utensils from the backseat, so the third person would have room to sit. Everything was stacked in the tent.

I did a load of laundry and hung the wet clothes on the clothesline just as it started to rain. I left the clothes to be rerinsed and dashed for the tent. The tent leaked. We moved items away from the leak, and then the dry spot leaked. It took less than five minutes for the interior of the tent to look like a garbage tip (dump), with plastic bags piled everywhere. So much for impressing my son with what an efficient homemaker I was while on the road.

Scott's plane arrived at one thirty. He brought me a surprise—Joshua and Rhys—his two oldest sons. That was just great! The visit was going to be especially fun. I had been eager to see the family; now I was getting a preview.

The boys sat in the backseat with Annabel, while Scott and I got reacquainted in the front. We did a mini-tour of Darwin. We went to the botanical gardens, and the boys and I played hide-and-seek among the trees. That gave the boys a chance to run off some pent-up energy. The plane had taken the long way around to get to Darwin. It went from Rockhampton in the middle of the state of Queensland, south seven hundred kilometers to Brisbane, before heading north to Darwin in the Northern Territory.

Scott got a cabin in the caravan park where we were staying. Thank goodness we didn't have to figure out how to sleep five people in a soaking tent. I slept in the backseat of the car and found it comfortable. I knew there was an advantage to being short. The backseat width was five feet, two inches, the same as my length.

October 15, 1999 It was so much fun to show the enthusiastic youngsters some wonders of their country. We went to Litchfield National Park for hiking and swimming. Josh and Rhys got wet in Bluey's Rock Pools, a series of short waterfalls cascading down the creek.

Everyone except Scott went in the water at one of my favorite places, Wangi Falls. At Wangi, a twin set of falls went over a high cliff and cascaded down to a picture-perfect pool. Josh was very adept at swimming, so he and I swam across the pond to the waterfalls. I had no idea why it felt great to have water falling on our heads when the rest of our body was in deep water, but it did. I asked Scott to keep Rhys on his side of the pond, as Rhys dog-paddled instead of swam, and I knew I was not strong enough to rescue him, if he got into trouble.

When I had been at Wangi Falls ten years before, the tour group of five people had walked to Wangi on a dirt path through eight-foot-tall grass. We were the only ones there, and we luxuriated in the setting while swimming within sight of freshwater crocs in the reeds at the water's edge.

Now we shared my secret paradise with a couple hundred people who were eating at the modern kiosk, swimming in the pond, or lounging on the well-tended lawns. Oh well, the best places never stayed secret very long. I was happy to be sharing it with my grandchildren. The boys loved it and could hardly wait to see what we were going to do next.

We ended this wonderful day with a steak dinner at Sizzler, Scott's favorite restaurant. I shouted (paid the bill) and called it a birthday party for both Scott and Annabel, who celebrated birthdays in October.

October 16, 1999 We were miraculously on the road to Kakadu by eight. I was amazed Scott was able to get the boys up, fed, and dressed so early.

Kakadu was a three-hour drive from our campsite. At the entrance to the park, we asked the ranger which boat ride to take to see the most animal life. He suggested we go to Yellow Water, the boat ride I took ten years earlier and loved. We went to Frontier Kakadu Village, where Scott booked our boat tour for one o'clock. We had two hours to get two hundred kilometers (one-hundred-twenty-four miles) through the park to Yellow Water. Scott drove, and we didn't do any sight-seeing on the way. He parked the car, and we walked directly onto the boat at one o'clock.

Joshua sat with me on the right side; Annabel, Scott, and Rhys were on the left side. The crocodiles showed no partiality; some appeared on our side, some on theirs. Both grandsons got to see the enormous "salties" up close. That was exciting.

We saw jabirus, magpie geese, jacanas, whistling ducks, azure kingfishers, and representatives of every species of heron and egret. What a sight! To top it off, the ranger told us that the beautiful horses we saw in the meadows were brumbies (mustangs). The boat trip was a complete success; everyone had fun.

It was two thirty when we docked, so we ate lunch at the boat-ramp hotel's outdoor cafe. As with most outdoor eating places, there were a few animals around. In this case the pied herons grabbed crumbs as they hit the ground. The pied heron was an elegant-looking shorebird about two feet tall. He had a white head and neck and a shimmery gray-blue body.

Nourlangie Rock was next on our list of places to explore. There was a well-defined path through the bush up the hill to the cave paintings. Those were the best Aboriginal paintings I had ever seen, and I was happy to find that they had not changed one iota in ten years. I was afraid I'd find brand-new ancient paintings with all the other new stuff that had sprung up at the national parks.

We walked two and a half kilometers to the lookout. The scenery was worth the effort. We saw the escarpment along the Koongarra Mineral Lease and for miles around Kakadu National Park. No wonder the Aboriginals considered Kakadu a sacred place. I did too. I hoped it would stay a pure wilderness forever.

Scott drove to our caravan park while Annabel took a turn in the front seat to get acquainted with him. I sat with the boys in the backseat. Annabel had set the precedent of playing games and reading to Josh and Rhys, so I followed suit. She had the right idea. Brothers didn't squabble when they were being entertained by an adult.

October 17, 1999 Scott needed to catch his plane home at one o'clock; we didn't have a lot of time to play. We squeezed in a tour of Howard Springs Park, where the boys saw a variety of fish, turtles, and lizards—all favorites of youngsters.

From there we went to Darwin City Park on the bay. There were many forms of entertainment to choose from: bike trails, hiking trails, equestrian trails, picnic areas, and playgrounds. There was a World War II plane display, as Darwin had been bombed by the Japanese and was a staging ground for Yankee forces fighting in the South Pacific.

Scott and his crew got to the airport on time. It was really, really quiet in the car as Annabel drove to Manyallaluk Aboriginal Community seventy-five kilometers south of Katherine. The speed limit was a hundred kilometers per hour (sixty-two mph), so she had to be on the lookout for solar cars in the race. They traveled considerably slower, more like thirty kph (eighteen mph). The high school groups that built the cars started out from Darwin and were on their way to Adelaide on the only highway that connected those cities.

We arrived at the Aborigine community at dusk and found a campsite. There was only one other family camped on the grounds; we had plenty of privacy.

October 18, 1999 We spent the day with the Manyallaluk people. Manuel, his wife, Jessica, and granddaughter, Justina, were the first people I met. Manuel was holding the baby while his wife made *damper* (bread cooked on hot coals in a pit). I asked Manuel if I could take his picture.

He said yes with a resigned tone of voice that told me I was like all the other tourists who visited. I whipped out my Polaroid camera and took his picture. When it dried, I handed it to him.

"That's for you to keep." He was flabbergasted. He had never in his fifty years seen a picture of himself.

He asked shyly if I'd take one of his wife and granddaughter for him to keep. Of course, I agreed. That was why I brought the Polaroid. Larissa, Justina's mom, came by, and Grandpa wanted her picture also. The first thing I knew, I was taking pictures of everyone in the community. It was rewarding to watch the expressions on their faces when they saw their own image and found out they got to keep the pictures.

A twelve-year-old girl asked if I'd take her picture.

I said, "Sure," and Larissa started to hand her baby Justina, whom Larissa had been holding. The girl looked at the ground and dug a hole with her bare toe.

"Can I have one without the baby? I want to give it to my boyfriend."

I told the group when I was down to the last picture on the third roll of film and asked who should be in the last picture. I had taken pictures of several family groups. There was no contest; they had a conference. Heads nodded up and down in unison, and they told me they thought the last picture should be of Justina and *me*. I was no longer just another tourist, I was their friend. What a nice feeling.

Annabel and I spent the next two days learning to paint with ochre, weave with pandanus leaves, throw spears, blow didgeridoos, and appreciate native plants. I learned I had no talent for weaving pandanus, throwing spears accurately, or blowing didgeridoos. Thank goodness I didn't have to catch my own food!

Manuel's son, Daril, and Daril's cousin, Quentin, took us on a walk in the woods. Here are some of the things they taught us:

- Ironbark trees (doobah) leaves were used to flavor fruit bats for eating. They were also used to burn like incense at a funeral (the aroma scared away evil spirits).
- The size ironbark tree we can easily cut with a chainsaw these days took two to three days with manual tools. The time depended on the diameter of the tree. The wood was used for tools and blades before white men introduced the Aborigines to steel. In the olden days, when they were cut with sharpened rocks, it took several weeks to fell one tree. The termite-resistant wood was still used for house stumps.
- The custom forbade saying a person's name for two weeks to three years after he died. The time period varied from one tribe to the next.
- Earth ovens (*garris*) were dug in the ground, and kangaroo meat or *barramundi* (fish) was wrapped in wet eucalyptus paperbark and placed on the hot coals to cook.
- The evil spirit, Boulga, was supernatural and tried to make one afraid or to do foolish things.
- Pandanus roots (*mulafiti*) of very young trees were radish red and could be used to cook a vat of dye for the women to use as makeup.
- Snakes wouldn't crawl over the rough woolly butt tree bark. Put bark around sleeping bags for safety.
- Emu apple tree bark was put in ponds to poison fish; fish were stunned and floated to the top of the water. Aboriginals gathered them with a net. The fish were degutted to get rid of the poison. Emus could eat the apples without being poisoned, but people could not.
- Wild white apple trees' fruit was good to eat. Wild red apple trees' fruit tasted like spicy-hot chili.
- Wild sugarcane's (*gilly-jill*) sweetness was concentrated, much sweeter than cultivated sugarcane.
- Green ants (*potperung*) were caught by breaking off the leaf they were on, and quickly folding the leaf in half and smashing it between your palms. The aroma was good to clear a

stuffy nose. The ants were also used to create a drink that reputedly tasted like lemonade.

- Paperbark (*coolagong*) was used as utensils, for roofing, and for making boats, as it was waterproof. Daril demonstrated by pulling a piece of bark off a tree and holding it in a canoe shape, dipping it in the creek, and drinking some water before passing the vessel to the rest of us. I presumed they didn't have the parasite giardia in Northern Territory.
- Carrigon tree was used to make fire sticks (sticks to twirl on a block of wood to create enough heat to catch kapok on fire). The bark was used to make fishing nets; it could be peeled in strips.
- Sandpaper (*yetting-yetting*) tree leaves were used as sandpaper on fire sticks, other tools, and musical instruments.
- White clay (*yal-can*) was used as deodorant by painting the skin so the kangaroos couldn't smell the hunter.

In the evening I taught Daril's six-year-old sister some of the rudiments of swimming. She had been following me around like a shadow, and when I went swimming, I turned around in time to see her flailing and gasping for air. As a reward for my efforts, her brother gave me the board he had used to teach us Aboriginal painting with ochre. It pictured a wild carrot. He later said he lost a young cousin to drowning. The sculpture I saw beside the pool had been a memorial to the cousin.

The ladies cooked a buffet meal for us. I tried a few bites of kangaroo and barramundi, but stayed away from anything exotic enough to cause my touchy digestive track to explode. There were vegetables and fruits that looked familiar, but didn't taste like I expected, because of special seasonings. These people worked hard to make our stay a most pleasant one. I wish I had more of a reward for them than Polaroid pictures, books on Native Americans, and plain old money. They liked the books the best and pointed out similar rituals practiced on both sides of the Pacific. Everyone in the community knew how to speak, write, and read English as well as their own tribal language.

One of the camp dogs adopted Annabel and me; he slept at our tent door to protect us. He barked raucously each time he heard a noise. In between barking episodes, he coughed as though he had a fur ball or bone caught in his throat. I would rather have taken my chances with burglars.

October 19, 1999 I caught yet another cold and chose to use antihistamine rather than bitey green ants. The antihistamine made me drowsy, so Annabel drove us to Tennant Creek, the next town on our route. I relaxed and read Durack family biographies or snoozed most of the day.

We made a couple of stops—one at Mataranka, the homestead of Mrs. Aeneas Gunn, author of *We of the Never-Never.* I read that book about pioneering station hands earlier on this trip. The station was now a resort, with people using the cool, shady springs for medicinal purposes as well as for relaxation. There were wooden walkways through tropical gardens to each pool.

A second stop was made at the Roper River, the main source of water supply for central Northern Territory. The park along the river was not conducive to hiking or picnicking, so we spent a very short time there. We were there long enough for me to close my eyes and hear the jackaroos (cowboys) of old herding cattle to the river to drink before they made their way further out to the Kimberleys.

October 20, 1999 I went on a tour of a gold mine and stamp mill in Tennant Creek. The gold in that area was powder fine and found in iron ore. There were approximately twenty ounces of gold per ton of iron ore. Remember that when talking about ounces of gold, people are talking about Troy ounces, which consist of twelve ounces to the pound, rather than the normal sixteen ounces to the pound. I remembered that by thinking of gold and silver being heavier than flour, so it takes fewer ounces to make a pound. You probably couldn't care less, right?

The iron ore was two billion years old, too old to contain fossils. Lassiter, the famous explorer, said there was no gold in Tennant Creek because he was looking for the more common kind found in quartz. The gold was discovered by a pair of men, one blind and one crippled, in the early 1920s. No, I don't know how the blind man detected powdery-fine gold. I'm just repeating what I was told by the tour guide.

The iron ore was broken down into sand-sized granules by the noisy stamp mills that were made from manganese. Those stampers' cams moved up and down ninety-six times a minute. Believe me, that was a lot of pounding, which converted into a lot of noise. Did they have earplugs in the 1920s? The guide ran the stamp mill for about two minutes, and the ringing in my ears didn't let up for several minutes afterward.

In searching for levels of gold-bearing ore, geologists knew magnetite was found below the hematite, and both were found below the water table. The gold was encased in magnetite. That meant the gold was pretty far down in the earth. The top water table was salt water of no use in this arid land or for cooling mining equipment. The salty water was pumped off into a reservoir and left to evaporate and the salt sold as a preservative.

The gold was impossible to extract manually. People who arrived with mechanical devices from the 1930s through to today were the only ones who made a living; very few made a fortune.

The Chinese smuggled gold out of the fields by putting it in dead bodies that were being shipped back to their families in China. It seemed to me they couldn't pack too much into a body without the customs officials getting curious about the way Chinese gained so much weight in the gold fields of Australia. Wouldn't they be curious about a five-foot-tall Chinaman that weighed two hundred pounds?

The weather took a most unusual turn. It became chilly and rainy. The locals were astounded. They welcomed the cool weather as much as we did. The rain limited our activity, though, so we spent the afternoon in the cooking shelter at the campground reading and writing.

I kept my eyes open for birds and was lucky enough to identify the following:

- Magpie lark (also known as the pee wee lark or pee wee magpie)
- Black kite
- Grey-fronted honeyeater
- Little (or lesser) corella
- Galah

- Spinifex pigeon
- Willy wagtail (one of my favorites because they were so cute wagging their tail feathers like a happy puppy)
- Zebra finch (another favorite; oh heck, why not just admit that some of my best friends are birds)
- Rainbow bee-eater (I already told you they were super gorgeous, my absolute number one favorite! Really!)

October 21, 1999 For Annabel and me, it was a day on the road between Tennant Creek and Alice Springs. What a surprise the scenery was. There were bushes, trees, and grass the whole way. Granted, some areas were the type of landscape where it would take fifty acres to support one cow. I expected the whole center of Australia to be desolate. The soil was red here and there because of mineral content, but we had been seeing that ever since we landed in Sydney. Instead of calling central Northern Territory the "Red Center," the Aussies should just call their country the "Red Country." Oh, wait, they do call it "The Sunburned Country." Never mind.

We stopped briefly at Devil's Marbles. Some of the enormous round granite boulders were sitting on top of each other. Others were strewn helter-skelter across the plain. Geologists concluded this area was the tip of a granite mountain. The rest of the mountain was under dirt. Erosion washed away, or blew away, dirt and sand, exposing the "marbles." I enjoyed climbing on the rocks and watching more daring people try stunts on them. I wondered how young men standing on top of a marble that was twenty feet in diameter were going to get down. One couple climbed to the top of a rock by bracing themselves against one rock with their back and another rock with their feet. It looked way too tricky for me. I'd probably get six feet off the ground and fall and break my back. This was another one of those times when I was glad I was female, a sixty-two-year-old female, and didn't have to prove anything.

In beautiful, clean, friendly Alice Springs, we camped in Alice Creek Caravan Park on the outskirts of town set against the beautiful MacDonnell Ranges.

October 22, 1999 I started the day with a camel safari down the Todd River. The Todd was completely dry, and it was where the annual Alice Springs Boat Races were held. Folks built boats that had no bottoms; several people got inside, picked up the boat, and ran down the river. It must have looked like something out of Fred Flintstone's day.

On the camel safari, I was fortunate enough to get the front camel, right behind the guide. The guide's name was Luke. I was able to hear every word he said.

Some of the things Luke told us were:

- Water in the river came when there was runoff from the MacDonnell Ranges. The Aboriginals knew when there would be water in the river a day before anyone else. If you visited the park along the dry riverbed and there were no Aborigines lying in the sand, don't set up your tent. It would get washed away.
- Hibiscus had more vitamin C than oranges.
- People who use moisturizer on their skin attracted insects.
- The river red-gums were hollow, and when a branch broke off, animals moved into the trunk. Sometimes they got trapped inside by predators or floods.
- Many river red-gums along our trail were over five hundred years old. They were found along riverbeds and had white bark with olive-colored leaves. The first year a new branch grew, it had rough, dark-colored bark.
- The weather got colder than I thought. Alice had snow last winter.

The ride was easier than riding a horse and was fun and educational. The weather was perfect. The guide had a good sense of humor and entertained us with stories. Luke stood on the seat of his saddle facing the tourists when he talked. He said he learned to do that by being a surfie. I was wishing I had signed up for the overnight camp-out. I wanted to see more, learn more, and hear more stories.

I tried to keep my side tours to a minimum length of time since Annabel didn't care to go on any that cost money, and I felt guilty about leaving her in camp while I was out having fun.

In the afternoon Annabel and I toured Alice Springs. It was cleaner, greener, larger, more modern, and more expensive than I anticipated. The average house sold for $200,000.00.

We went to the cultural center and natural history museum, which was one of the best I had ever visited. Maybe I liked it because it had different information than American museums.

The two of us stopped at a pub downtown for happy hour—buy a beer and get a free sausage sandwich. Heck of a deal! We were entertained by watching the characters at the pub while listening to live folk music. People had fun flirting, dancing, and singing along with the band in their native tongue—be it German, French, Japanese, or American.

We learned from a newspaper that our young solar car racers from Redcliffe had to drop out of the race, as they got too far behind during two days of rainy, cloudy weather. There had to be sun to charge the solar panels that operated the car motor. The kids would have been disappointed, but I bet they had one heck of a good time.

Annabel settled down under a sheet, and I had on summer pajamas inside my lightweight sleeping bag when night fell. We both got up during the night and put on jeans and a heavy shirt. Annabel got inside her sleeping bag, and I put on an extra blanket. It got "high-desert cold" during the night!

October 23, 1999 The MacDonnell Range was a strip of mountains stretching about two hundred miles on either side of Alice Springs. We went to the East MacDonnell and traversed the very short Emily and Jessie Gap Gorges. They were sedimentary sandstone pushed up by earth's inner turmoil and fractured during past ice ages (not the one last night). We found a couple of ochre paintings on the walls, Aboriginal, I presume.

Trephina Gorge was a bit wider and longer. Annabel took the Panoramic Trail and climbed to the top of the rise for views over the surrounding area. I took the Riverbed Trail and watched crested pigeons dig in the sand until they got down to water. Lizards came to the tiny hole and dug it larger. The water didn't look palatable to me, but the animals were glad to find it. I watched swallows bringing nest supplies to holes in river red-gums. For my last bit of pleasure, I climbed on the purple and orange dolomite and quartzite rocks and enjoyed the solitude.

Annabel and I drove further east to the Arltunga Historic Reserve, which was another gold mining area from the late 1800s. The government buildings were rebuilt and/or restored, making them look ten years old rather than a hundred and ten years old. There were shored-up mines for people to explore. We climbed down the wooden ladder provided and looked for a lost gold seam. We didn't find gold, just squeaky little bats. There were a lot of tunnels; I felt like Huck Finn. Some of the tunnels were only two feet high, and others were eight feet high. I traced quartz veins as far as I could crawl. My knees yelled at me to act my age, so I climbed out of the mine and went back to the car.

In the evening we cleaned the dust and dirt off ourselves, dressed up like ladies, and attended a didgeridoo concert in downtown Alice Springs. The main artist was Andrew Langford. He and his two companions, one on keyboard and one on drums, played intriguing music while showing slide shows of Australian landscapes (many familiar to us now).

On the way to our campsite, Annabel announced she felt there was a McDonald's
ice-cream cone in her future. She was right.

October 24, 1999 We explored the West MacDonnell Range along Namatjira Drive. Namatjira was a famous Aborigine painter. The first stop was Stanley Chasm, which had a pleasant walk along a narrow creek bed filled with eucalyptus trees and native pines, some of which looked like our evergreens. Most Australian native pines are scraggly. Stanley Chasm was about twenty meters (sixty-five feet) wide, and the sheer crimson walls stood a hundred meters (three-hundred-twenty-five feet) tall.

On down the road, we came to Ellery Creek Big Hole. It had a permanent pond, very deep and very cold due to the lack of sunlight, because the hole was enclosed in more hundred-meter-high walls. It had narrow beaches and river red-gums strewn along the banks, clutching the orange and purple walls.

We traveled on to Ochre Pits, which were quarried and mixed into paints used for Aboriginal ceremonies. What beautiful colors those soft stones possessed—everything from light yellow to dark orange, pink to crimson, and white to black. The area was small, but the Aboriginals got enough ochre for trade with tribes from other areas.

In Glen Helen Gorge, Annabel spotted a wild dingo. He wandered through the sharp spinifex grass across from the homestead. Annabel was thrilled to see the dingo even though he was quite a distance away. I got excited about seeing coyotes in Nevada, so I could relate.

At Ormiston, our last sight-seeing site for the day, Annabel went for a walk by herself, while I sat in the shade and rested. A skinny, sad-looking mother dingo came by to beg for food. Other tourists fed her human snacks. I thought she'd be better off if she found a healthy rabbit for her dinner.

October 25, 1999 We went south through the red center of Australia. Annabel agreed to a side trip to Coober Pedy, the opal mining area in the state of South Australia. I read so much about the miners' underground homes and the pioneer spirit; I wanted to meet some of the miners themselves. Okay, I really wanted to do some fossicking (prospecting) myself also.

Today was another of those unusual rainy days, so I offered to pay for us to stay under cover for the night rather than pitch the tent. We stayed at an underground hostel and had the private room next to the shared unisex bathroom, with one toilet and one shower. In other words, we lived like cavemen with amenities.

We met interesting people in hostels. They were friendly, sharing, caring people. In hostels people helped one another have an enjoyable stay. There were usually half a dozen people cooking meals in the kitchen at one time, so if someone had a missing item from the meal they were preparing, there was a good chance someone else had what they needed. Those same people worked as a team to clean the kitchen after use and would sit together at tables. They shared experiences they had during the day or during past travels. They were willing to tell of good places to see and things to do.

Annabel and I went to abandoned mines and scoured the potch-detriment left around the hole after truck loads of opal bearing material had been removed. Eureka! I found a pint-sized jar of opal bearing material to take home. Yippee! Whooo-ooo.

October 26, 1999 I had two tours scheduled for the day. The first one ($5.00 Australian) was two hours long and took us through two versions of where opal came from—the Aborigine mystic version and the Westerner's scientific version. Two professionally done videos with special lighting effects were shown. A walk through a former mine, now used as a commercial entity for tourists, showed us how the walls were sprayed with a fixative to keep the powdered dirt from caving-in. By the end of that tour, I thought that both versions had elements of fact and fantasy intertwined. Annabel joined me there, but not on the second, more expensive trip.

For $25.00, I got a bus tour of the city and learned:

- The population of the town was currently four thousand; 60 percent of the people lived underground.
- Ten percent were Aboriginals; they wouldn't live underground, as that was where their Rainbow Serpent God lived.
- Three hundred miners were currently working the opal fields.
- The fields were on Mount Clarence cattle station.
- The opals originated 120 million years ago as silica filtered through other minerals in the bottom of the inland sea. Each opal molecule had a drop of water in it that acted as a prism. The colors were picked up from the minerals the silica drained through (that's the Western version of origination).
- There were many opalized fossils found in Coober Pedy.
- Coober Pedy was an Aboriginal expression for "white man's burrows." That came from the early miners living in their mines during the one-hundred-twenty-five- to one-hundred-forty-degree summer heat.
- Some mines were thirty meters below sea level.
- The Gibber Desert surrounded the fields.

We toured a beautiful Serbian church (underground), a mine, a home, and a house under construction. The tour went to The Breakaways Reserve, which was used for movie making. Some of the films made there were *Mad Max I, II, III*; others included *Priscilla, Queen of the Desert* and *Mission to Mars*. There was a Val Kilmer picture being filmed presently.

We visited an eccentric desert rat called Crocodile Harry, who was drunk and grabbing at women and girls. He proudly displayed a list of over two thousand girls that he supposedly deflowered. The signatures on the lists were allegedly the girls' own. He had pictures of himself in the 1950s, when he worked as a croc hunter out of Darwin, and he was built like Tarzan.

He claimed to be one of two men used as a model for the character, Crocodile Dundee. The second person was shot and killed by police two weeks ago—early October 1999—during a drug-induced shootout near Darwin. Both models were adventurous young men who later became reprehensible due to abuse of drugs and/or alcohol, nothing at all like that cute Paul Hogan.

The bus drove along the 9,000-kilometer Dog Fence, built to keep dingoes away from sheep stations. The fence ran from South Australia, near Adelaide, up to Queensland, near Brisbane. The dingo fence was patrolled regularly for damage from hopping kangaroos and running emus. What a project! Australians claimed it worked.

We went to the cemetery, where the tombstones, all except one, looked similar to ones found in any US cemetery. The unusual one was an aluminum beer keg. On it was printed a man's name, date of birth, date of death, and the inscription, "Have one on me." At the time of the funeral, the keg had been full. The memorial belonged to the town drunk, who had mooched free drinks off miners for years. When he became ill, he went to Adelaide to see a doctor. The doctor told the man he had six months to live, as cancer had eaten most of his liver.

The patient immediately applied for a credit card, and since he had been on the dole for many years, he was considered to have a permanent income. He was granted a card. His card arrived in Coober Pedy a month later, and the patient maxed it out, buying everyone in town drinks, meals, and other goodies. He arranged his own funeral and paid the director a handsome sum to conduct a party at the gravesite with music, dancing, and booze. Three months after the man died, the credit company came looking for their first payment on his $8,000.00 debt.

October 27, 1999 I showed Annabel some of the sights I had seen on yesterday's afternoon tour and managed to find the homes being built underground. Never found the cemetery or the beautiful church before it was time for us to leave unique Coober Pedy.

We drove to Uluru, Ayers Rock, as it was known to non-Aboriginals. I was surprised to learn that Annabel had never heard of Ayers Rock. Being a lifelong Australophile (is there such a word?), I thought everyone in the world knew about Ayers Rock, the world's largest monolith.

We found the only campground within driving distance of the sacred site, and Annabel started dinner as soon as the tent was pitched. We missed sunset on The Rock, but I didn't worry about it, as I expected to camp there for at least three more sunsets.

October 28, 1999 It rained most of the night and was still raining when we got up, dressed, ate breakfast, and drove to Ayers Rock (the campground was five kilometers away). Our arrival coincided with a ranger starting her tour. No geology was discussed, only Aborigine legends about the birth of Uluru and how different spirits caused different features on the face of the rock. We were told that Aboriginals preferred that no one climb the rock, as it was sacred. The rangers didn't allow tourists to climb the rock after a rain, as it was slippery and steep. Annabel was disappointed; she wanted to make the climb her sixty-second birthday celebration.

Annabel and I walked the base trail. We walked together about a quarter of a kilometer, and I was winded from keeping up with Annabel. I suggested she go on her own so I could take pictures along the way. She made it around in two hours; it took me three. I stopped to admire the sandstone formation, the oxidation left by waterfalls after a rain, the exfoliation, the highly porous caves, the scalloped ridges, the birds' nests. What a nice experience! The rain stopped when we joined the ranger at the start of her lecture, and it didn't start again until we were in our car after our walk.

We drove around the perimeter of Ayers Rock and then down the road to the Olgas. It rained pretty hard along the way. We stopped at a viewing site, and the rain stopped. We were able to read the signs about the vegetation, the geology, and the legends and stay perfectly dry. We got back into the car, and the rain started again. I loved the chiaroscuro as we approached the Olgas. Their colors changed from beige to brown to gray to purple, according to how much cloud cover there was. The wind kept the clouds blowing to and fro between us and the sun.

The Aboriginals had reclaimed 30 percent of Northern Territory. They took over cattle stations, and then the government hired Westerners to train them to support themselves on the stations. No one mentioned the white families being given compensation for having built the stations up over the past two hundred years. It would be great for Aboriginals to be self-sufficient, but was it necessary to drive generations of immigrants off the land? I was glad I didn't have to make the decision about the fair thing to do.

In the afternoon we got a short break in the weather, so I took my anticipated Harley-Davidson motorcycle ride around The Rock. A handsome young man drove the tour cycle, while I sat behind him. On the way down the road, I was a bit tense as we got up to a hundred kilometers per hour, and the wind whipped around inside the oversized helmet. A couple of times, I thought I might lose my head. When the driver slowed to turn around, I was able to tighten the chin strap. The ride back to the campground was much more comfortable. It was a good experience, and it convinced me that I didn't want to become a Hells Angel.

Rain poured at sunset, so there was no colorful sight of Ayers Rock. It rained all night, the tent seams leaked, and puddles formed on the floor. My new air mattress kept me above flood level. We slept just fine, thank you.

October 29, 1999 The long-range weather forecast called for continued rain for the next week, so we packed our wet equipment into plastic trash bags and headed back to Alice Springs. It actually took several hours to drive that distance. On PBS shows, it looked like Ayers Rock was in suburban Alice Springs.

October 30, 1999 We toured Desert Park in the West MacDonnell Mountain Range, a well-laid-out park with walkways depicting desert, riparian, and woodlands environments. One building was dark inside with special lighting so we could watch nocturnal animals at work and play behind glass. I was delighted seeing animals like the bilby and numbat that I'd never have seen in the wild. The park had enormous walk-through birdcages where we could get close to parrots, songbirds, and waterfowl. The rangers put on a raptor show that was educational and entertaining. I wondered if we were keeping the owls awake. Don't they sleep during the day?

We walked through a fenced area filled with kangaroos and emus and learned that kangaroos were different colors to blend in with their surroundings. Red kangaroos only lived in sandstone and ironstone country. Gray wallabies lived in forests. We completed the tour by watching a movie on the geologic formation of central Australia. You know I loved that. Have you ever contemplated the multiple changes the ground under your feet has gone through? The movie ended by asking the question, "What will happen to this landscape next?" The screen was lowered, and a window the size of the screen appeared. The stunned audience stared at the glorious view, deep in contemplation.

October 31, 1999 The caravan park had a free pancake breakfast for its customers. We called that a birthday party for Annabel.

We headed for The Mud Tank, a zircon and garnet fossicking area. We saw our fourth dingo and some wild camels along the way. The weather was perfect, and we took pleasure in our ride through green fields speckled with wildflowers. The breeze kept the air clear, and we were surrounded by lavender and orange ranges to admire along the way.

November 1, 1999 I looked for zircons. Annabel sorted a couple of buckets of dirt, but soon lost interest and went for a walk. Of course, she spotted the biggest zircon on her walk. Her zircon would make a nice piece of jewelry. I ended up getting several cuttable stones, so I was happy as a lark.

A flock of zebra finches kept me company. They were one of the few birds that were not only pretty but also sang pretty songs. The rule was usually the prettier the bird, the uglier the song, such as galahs and lorikeets.

We ate lunch in the fields, so I could continue prospecting among the serenity and scenery. The purple Hart Range displayed miles and miles of flowers after the recent rains.

November 2, 1999 Annabel finally said out loud that she was too homesick to continue.

We drove from Mud Tank Fossicking Fields to Tennant Creek in a subdued, contemplative mood. I don't remember what the scenery looked like.

Annabel searched for a tour agent to book her flight home. She found none. She decided to leave from Cairns, so she could see the Great Barrier Reef. She chose November 9; that would give us one week to make the next segment of the trip and see the Barrier Reef. I had planned on taking two to three weeks to drive that expanse. I knew once we got to the east coast, traffic would pick up, and we'd have more tourists to deal with.

November 3, 1999 Annabel spent an hour on the phone with Qantas. I sat in the car in Camooweal, Queensland, wondering what people in town did for entertainment. I knew that Camooweal was a major beef exporter and reminisced about the days of old when cowboys brought the herds (mobs, they were called) overland to the train depot. I thought about the famous overlanders—Nat Buchanan, Matt Savage, and the Duracks. I imagined many a cow had walked on the same route we had just driven. It may have been more romantic getting cattle to market a hundred years ago, but it was quicker and easier with road trains.

Western Queensland was desolate from suffering a long drought. We passed areas where there was no grass at all, just flat, hard-baked mud with six-inch-deep cracks.

We drove as far as Mount Isa, took a mini-tour of the fossil museum, which was not worth the $5.00 entry fee (or was it that I felt depressed about Annabel leaving).

I booked a five-hour tour of Mount Isa Mines. Lead, zinc, and silver mining took place deep in the earth below the town.

We checked into the caravan park and pitched our tent under the red poinciana trees. Lavender jacaranda and yellow wattle trees tried to outdo each other in their splendor.

November 4, 1999 My mine tour bus left the fossil center at seven thirty a.m., precisely on time. The mines employed 3,500 people. There were two women who worked in the mines—one was an engineer and the other was a geologist. Two Aboriginals did menial aboveground work.

After donning bright, white overalls and hard hats, we toured twenty kilometers, starting at level nineteen and working our way back up.

The big D7 Caterpillar dug the blasted ore out and dumped it in train cars. This machine was run by remote control from a booth where a miner operated two computers, working from what he saw on screens. It looked like a video game in progress. The D7 moved to the next designated area after the first had been cleared.

Next a giant drilling machine looking like a large Gatling gun was brought to a specific site. The machine was water cooled, so the area had water on the ground, and tourists were not allowed to walk close for fear of slipping. The machine drilled holes for bolts to be inserted to hold up the heavy mesh screening that kept the walls and ceiling in place. Each bolt had the capacity of holding seven tons of weight.

Miners who performed the blasting made $110,000.00 per year. The "muckers," the men operating the D7s, came next on the pay scale at $100,000.00 per year. There were various other jobs underground, such as plumbers, mechanics, and engineers that made between

$65,000.00 and $100,000.00 per year. That was not nearly enough to entice me to work there. As fascinating as the tour was, I was glad when we were out in fresh, clear air again.

The work schedules were: two days from seven a.m. to seven p.m., twenty-four hours off, two night shifts from seven p.m. to seven a.m., four days off. How could men stay alert on a schedule like that? It looked like a good place to open up a Sominex concession.

There were over 1,200 kilometers of tunnels. thirty-two levels, with sixty-five meters of ground between them. They extracted lead, zinc, and silver. There were sublevels of short passages used as equipment repair shops and storage. One of the early levels, eleventh, I think, was filled with fresh water. The company harnessed the water and used it for equipment cooling and air conditioning. The environment got hotter, the deeper the tunnels were dug. Was Hell at the bottom? Or was it hot magma? I bet there was more than one miner who thought working there was hell. That was the most comprehensive mine tour I had ever taken, and I ended the tour wired with excitement.

Mt. Isa Mines, known as MIM, used Toyota vehicles exclusively because of their reliability. Other brands had been tried, but were not as reliable. The vehicles were modified so the exhaust was purified to avoid buildup of carbon monoxide.

MIM also had a copper mine in the area, but tours were not available. Australia had a wealth of minerals in its soil, and I wished I could tour all the sites. It amazed me that men had learned to dig various types of rock out of the ground and turn it into machinable metal.

Annabel was in a hurry to put in the mileage. I drove three hundred kilometers after the tour, and we spent the night in Richmond, Queensland. Richmond was home to a dinosaur museum. Bones were found in the area. The museum was closed when we arrived, but a co-camper said that Tyrannosaurus rex used to live near there. Well, I hoped he moved to the suburbs. I didn't want him wandering into our tent.

We had an electrical storm at sunset, and then the wind blew like crazy. The air soon smelled fresh scrubbed. Good for deep breathing, sleeping, and good for the thirsty land.

November 5, 1999 I drove five hundred six kilometers (three hundred fourteen miles) from Richmond to Cairns. It looked like a piece of cake on the map. Not so. The Queensland roads were the worst asphalt roads we had seen on the trip. They were so lumpy and bumpy that by the end of the day, I felt as though I had been riding a *brumby* (mustang). Passing a road train was a steering-wheel-gripping experience because of the narrow width of the road. In many places the bitumen (asphalt) was one and a half cars wide. When there was oncoming traffic, or when passing another vehicle, each car was supposed to put two wheels on the shoulder.

We stopped in Townsville long enough to climb Castle Rock, a protrusion in the center of town that was about five hundred meters high (the Great Dividing Range was only five hundred fifty meters high). The views were great, and the road break was appreciated.

We made a quick stop in Ingham when we saw a sign saying to watch for cassowaries on the road. Man, oh man, would I ever love to see one of those avian remnants from the dinosaur days. We searched for them from an overlook but saw none. The view was nice, though, with rainforest down the mountainside and around the bay.

We wove up the coast through rain and mist. By eight p.m., I was tired and stressed. I pulled into a motel and adamantly refused to leave. Whatever the price, we would pay it.

November 6, 1999 Annabel went to the Cairns Airport and got her tickets exchanged for the earlier departure date. She was originally scheduled to leave January 17. We drove to Yorkey's Knob Beach north of Cairns and rented a *bure*, a self-contained cabin with screens for windows. The word *bure* was Fijian for a wood and straw hut, but in Australia it meant a cabin made of local materials. The bure was perfect; we were in a rainforest setting. We had ceiling fans in case the night got too warm, and a pool to cool off in during the day. We were on the coast, so we could walk the beaches for a breeze. No way would I swim during that time of year. The November/December north coast was known for its stingers (poisonous jellyfish), sharks, stonefish, and sea snakes. Any one of those could kill you. Why ruin a perfectly good vacation?

There were only three bures rented in the complex. We had plenty of privacy. The guinea fowl, peacock, and wild turkey kept it from being our quietest place of residence, but I loved their voices. The price was right at $45.00 a night. I couldn't imagine why the place was not packed.

November 7, 1999 We took the Super Express tour—a one-day tour of Cairns, The Great Barrier Reef, and The Tablelands. A bus picked us up at eight a.m. and took us on a mini-tour of resorts while the driver picked up other passengers.

We were marshaled onto a sleek catamaran that ferried us to Green Island, where we had a choice of renting snorkel equipment or taking the glass-bottom boat ride. I took my own snorkel equipment, so was told I could snorkel off the beach for an hour and then catch the glass-bottom boat at eleven a.m. I made arrangements to meet Annabel on the boat and scurried to the dressing room to get into my swimsuit the minute we docked.

I threw my clothes into a locker and was in the surf within ten minutes after docking. I knew it would take at least fifteen minutes to shower and dress after snorkeling. That would give me exactly thirty-five minutes to snorkel. I must have looked like someone who escaped from a Charlie Chaplin movie, the way I dashed around getting into the water and swimming out as far as I could as fast as I could. It took me approximately ten minutes to swim to decent coral. I frantically tried to see as much coral and as many fish as possible. I held my underwater camera out in front of me and snapped the shutter while aiming the camera in the general direction of the fish whose image I hoped to capture. When I got home, I'd figure out what I'd seen.

There was a bit of brain and cabbage coral, and lots of staghorn coral. There were also some fish, although not many. I did see a few trevally-black fish about two feet long. Hopefully, I took some recognizable pictures of them. Not having a watch on, I tried to estimate my time on the safe side of thirty-five minutes.

I thought I'd get to see a lot more fish and more colorful coral on the glass-bottom boat, as they should go deeper onto the reef. I made it to the boat with five minutes to spare. We rode to the same depth I had been swimming and saw a couple of giant clams, a little bit of colorful coral, lots of dead coral, and a few fish. Several trevally swam around the tour boat, waiting to be fed. We went a short distance and then turned around and went back to the catamaran. The time restraint was just ridiculous. I felt there was no way Annabel could feel she had seen the real reef. Having been to Heron Island and other reef areas in the past, I knew how much she was missing. She didn't, though, so she was satisfied she'd seen reef beauty.

We were taken back to the mainland, put onto the bus, and slowly made our way through traffic to the Skyrail that took us to the Tablelands. The Skyrail was an overhead cable-car system with little cars that held four people. There were no open windows, so it was not possible to hear the sounds of the birds as we floated above the rainforest. The Skyrail was not Annabel's favorite part of the day; she was glad when we landed at Kuranda, the town on the Atherton Tablelands.

We had thirty minutes to see the town and catch our train down the mountain. We opted to go to the first reasonable eatery we saw and order sandwiches. We ate breakfast at seven in the morning, and it was three o'clock when we got those sandwiches. We gobbled them down and dashed to the train just as it was ready to depart.

The train slowly rolled along, taking two hours to get back to the Cairns's bus stop. We went through the rainforest and stopped to take pictures at waterfalls. The train was relaxing after the hectic day. The bus was waiting to take us on the thirty-minute ride to our bure. Whew, now I knew how those tourists who take organized week-long European trips felt. They saw a whole different country each day.

November 8, 1999 Annabel wanted to do last-minute souvenir shopping. We went downtown Cairns, where she got her souvenirs, and then she helped me find a camcorder to record the balance of my trip. I wanted a camera like hers, as I was a bit familiar with it. We found a Sony with all the features on Annabel's camera. By the time I bought the batteries and battery charger, I was out almost $2,000.00 Annabel later told me she paid $500.00 for her camera at home. Oh well, I didn't want to just have four months worth of film of the trip, and I sure didn't want the responsibility of taking care of Annabel's camera. She offered to let me borrow it. I didn't have a good track record with cameras.

November 9, 1999 I dropped Annabel off at the airport departure lounge. I felt sad that she was going, but also felt she'd have no fun if she stayed, considering her present state of mind. She said she had a nice time, but she'd appeared melancholy 90 percent of the trip. I hoped the adventure would look better in hindsight. We hugged, and neither of us explained our tears as we said good-bye.

I went back to the camera store to find out why the battery charger wouldn't work. I assumed the problem was my lack of knowledge. It took two hours to get an answer. The store clerk called the manager, the manager called the manufacturer. They were back and forth on the phone while I was back and forth pumping coins into the parking meter. I still had a parking citation on the car when I left the store, as I had stayed in the same spot too long. I presented it to the camera store and asked them to pay it for me. I don't know whether they did or not.

Driving to the serene bure, I mentally made plans to unload absolutely everything from the car, wash everything washable, and reorganize the car so I could sleep in the backseat. Annabel took her tent home, as I didn't want to erect it by myself. I put suitcases and the rectangular water jug on the backseat floor and my air mattress on top of those and the seat, so I ended up with a three-foot-wide and five-foot-long bed. Next I put the new bedding purchased in Cairns on the bed and put a battery-operated reading light on the hand grip located on the ceiling over the door. It was a cozy mini-bedroom.

I arranged the trunk into a kitchen and breakfast bar (the tailgate). That left the front seat available for camera gear, a tape recorder, maps, and tourist books.

I debated about heading west and spending more time in the Kimberleys and Northern Territory. Lordy, I loved those places. I'd be willing to live out the balance of my days anywhere along the way. I knew "the wet" was descending on the countryside and felt I'd better not retrace my steps. I might get caught by some of those seven-mile-wide rivers I'd read about. I made the determination to stay on the east coast and still see new country at a leisurely pace.

November 10, 1999 I helped the managers of Yorkey's Knob Beach Bures look for their lost peacock. It departed their premises on the night of November 8, after they accidentally left the cage door open. They only had the bird for a week and hoped it was used to its new home. We looked for two hours with no luck. At least the neighbors were alerted to where it belonged.

After the car was packed, I hopped into the pool and floated on my back until I was completely cooled. It was easier to plan the day's strategy while lying on my back watching fluffy white clouds float overhead. The pool was private, surrounded by a natural rainforest and next to a lagoon where we had found snakes and a ton of dime-sized (baby) cane toads.

That was a good way to start a car trip. I hit the road heading north. Destination—Cooktown. I planned on going the coastal route, which looked more primitive on the maps but was sure to have pretty scenery.

A picture opportunity soon appeared, and I pulled off the road. I was vaguely aware that another Toyota Land Cruiser was parked in the same turnoff with the bonnet (hood) up. By the time I alighted, a man was standing outside my driver's door.

"Do you have jumper cables?" he asked *in American.*

I told him I did, but that they were given to me by the man who sold me the car and had never been tested. I dug them out of the toolbox and gave him a jump-start. The cables worked just fine. That was good to learn.

The man pointed to the logo on my T-shirt and asked, "Is your Aerojet the one located outside Sacramento, or the one in Azusa?"

In a state of amazement, I answered, "I worked at Sacramento. Folsom, California, actually, for twenty years."

Peter Yates, the stranger, said he worked there as a contractor from Synergy. He was on a six-month temporary assignment in Australia. His home was at South Shore, Lake Tahoe (about a hundred miles from my home). He worked on Sad Arm and F22 military equipment. Imagine meeting someone in Australia who worked at Aerojet! We both worked on F22, the super-duper fighter jet. We chatted a few minutes, and then I took a picture of the scenery and was back on the road.

I stopped at a post office to mail pictures to Marlow. The lady in front of me in line was picking up her holiday mail. She spelled her surname for the clerk, "C-O-A-K-L-E-Y." I gasped, and she turned to look at me. I explained that my mother's maiden name was Coakley. As the clerk looked for her stack of mail in the back room, the customer and I discussed the possibility of being "cousins." She said her husband's family, the Coakleys, went from Ireland to England. His parents had immigrated to Australia. I gave her my name and address and said I'd be happy to send her husband info I had collected on Coakley genealogy, if he was interested.

What a day! Is this a small world, or did I cross into the *Twilight Zone* after leaving Yorkey's Knob Beach?

I went to a sanctuary of rainforest animals, tropical flora, and other fauna of northern Queensland. I was enthralled with the place and spent three hours wandering around. Most of the animals were free in big, open areas with plenty of vegetation for nests and shade for daytime rests. The birds were in an enormous walk-through enclosure with streams, waterfalls, and the vegetation they would have been used to in the wild. I shot three rolls of film plus some video. With my cameras going on the fritz from time to time, I didn't want to take a chance on not getting this place recorded.

Up the coast further, I came to the town of Port Douglas. The last time I had been there, it had been a sleepy fishing village. Now the four-lane highway was lined with palm trees and golf courses leading up to Hilton- and Hyatt-type resorts. I went to a scenic lookout on a knoll and then for a stroll along the beach before heading toward Daintree National Park. I didn't belong in this perfectly manicured city.

A ferryboat took the car and me across the Daintree River and dumped us off in a jungle with a paved road. The pavement lasted for a few miles before it deteriorated into gravel, then sand, then muddy corrugation. I felt peacefully at home once more. It wasn't long before I was in total solitude. The rain started, and I drove along at my own pace, watching for animals in the dense underbrush. I came to rest at a campground that advertised itself as a sanctuary with hiking trails. I was the sole occupant. I ate leftover spaghetti directly from the storage jar and drank a glass of wine before retiring to my cozy backseat lodging.

November 11, 1999 I had a restless night—no, not air-mattress problems again. I opened the windows all the way down. I was the only occupant of the campground; it was safe enough. The weather was too warm for a sheet. I was lying on my side with my feet positioned toe to heel. Something fell through the window and landed across both feet. I figured it was leaves because of the soft texture and light weight. The object slowly moved off one foot and was creeping up my leg. I swung both feet toward the back of the front seat in one swift movement. Then I turned on the light to look for the intruder. I should have done those two things in reverse order. I looked and looked but found no snake (tree snake was my first guess), lizard, or bug. I thought that whatever it was had probably crawled under the seats to get away from the violent throwing machine.

I eventually dozed off again, but woke several times thinking I felt something crawling on me. Just nerves. I heard movement outside from time to time, but saw nothing when I sat up to look, as it was pitch black. Heavy clouds blocked out all light from the sky. The electric lights at the restroom were manual, and I had turned them off before retiring (dang).

I got up at six and dressed. The morning was drizzly, so I put on the raincoat our first Servas hostess had given me, and went for a walk along the "marked" trails in the rainforest. It soon became very confusing. I couldn't tell the difference between the trails made by man and those made by kangaroos or some other larger animal. I was only gone a half an hour. I didn't want to get lost and have to spend hours and hours trying to find my way out. I did get to see bright copper-winged doves, a small number of other birds, and lizards. I also spotted a tea plantation off in the distance. I didn't know that tea grew in Queensland.

I drove through Daintree Rainforest National Park and took a seashore trail at Cape Tribulation (where Captain Cook wrecked his ship, the *Endeavor*, hence the name). The dark, dismal day made the beach seem dreary, so I didn't spend much time there. I stopped at the ranger station to inquire about the condition of the road between Cape Tribulation and Cooktown. The ranger assured me that a Land Cruiser could get me there with no problems.

The road was incredible, with steep hills that the car climbed with effort and then narrow spiraling declines. The trees' canopy grew over the road, and it was like driving through a tunnel in a fun house. I crossed three rivers of running water up to the axles. The gravel and mud road deteriorated into a track with grass growing in the middle. Some steeper grades had tire-wide tracks of amateur-laid concrete. As soon as I got to a wide spot in the road, I pulled over to study the map to figure out where I had gotten off the road to Cooktown.

Another human drove up behind me. It was a lady, a pretty lady, dressed for visiting the city. I asked about the route. She was the local mail lady and assured me that this was indeed the road to Cooktown. She told me to keep on keeping on, and I'd get there by and by. She said it was about fifty kilometers further and should take me about two and a half to three hours. I felt much better. Now I could relax and enjoy the ride.

The rain stopped, so I rolled down the windows to hear nature's serenade. Kangaroos were plentiful along the road, as were squawky parrots. Mossy "grandfather's whiskers" hung from vine-covered trees. Orchids and staghorns grew in proliferation.

I made it to Cooktown, filled the fuel tank, and settled into Pam's Hostel. The hostel's main buildings were concrete block around a courtyard. That sounds bleak, but it was anything but bleak. The exterior walls were colorfully painted with scenes of landscapes and animals. The furniture was hewn out of beautiful wood and left in natural form as much as logical. There were picnic tables, lawn chairs, and cement-block barbecues in the courtyard that overlooked the swimming pool. The pool could barely be seen for the flowery vegetation surrounding it.

The dining area served as a place where workmen gathered for a beer before heading off to their homes. It turned out that several of the men lived at the hostel. The stainless-steel kitchen was buzzing with activity and held a variety of tantalizing smells when I went in to boil water for my Cup-a-Soup.

One of the men asked if I wanted to get in the betting pool for the final score of the ball game. I had no idea what sport, or what game, or when it was being played, so I said, "Sure!"

Half a dozen people were shortly gathered around the "telly" to watch a cricket game. I watched the caretaker catch pet birds and stow them in cages for the night. He told me that during the day, the birds were turned loose, and two dogs were responsible for tending them.

I was too tired for a swim, so I stood in the hot shower for several minutes, then collapsed into bed. About midnight another lady checked into my dormitory room. She was the only other occupant and left by five thirty. I don't think she got her $15.00 worth.

November 12, 1999 Rain was forecast to last all day. This would be a good time for a kick-back day off the road. I sat on the wide verandah in a chair made of vines and read, wrote postcards and journal entries, and was about to get out my colored pencils to draw when the rain stopped.

I drove to Endeavor Falls, twenty-four kilometers out of town and spent an hour yarning with the proprietor of the kiosk, as he had just returned from the United States and wanted to tell me about our wonderful places and people. Whew, I was always glad when I heard tourists had a good time in the United States. It's like having a teacher tell you your children are "so well behaved." Or, at any rate, I imagine the feeling is about the same—not that I ever experienced a teacher saying that about my sons.

I dropped eight rolls of film off for developing and bought postcards. That took an hour, as the proprietor was a native of

Cape York Peninsula. I was heading that way at the worst possible time of year, so she wanted to give me some pointers on travel. She was very positive about the trip and thought I should enjoy the experience, if I used common sense and took plenty of supplies. She suggested taking a three-month supply of fresh water and food. I drank a gallon of water a day. I guessed she thought I was driving a road train. Just kidding; I could pack that much in my enormous Land Cruiser. She said it was quite possible I'd be stuck in the outback until the next "dry."

I went grocery shopping and loaded up on items that needed refrigeration and a large block of ice. I got a two-month supply of groceries, as I knew I'd be going to Scott's house, and then home to California before the three months were up. It was tempting to contemplate spending "the wet" in far north Queensland and becoming an illegal immigrant. It would have added some interesting tales to this journal. Northern Queensland had hurricanes, floods, and wild electrical storms during monsoon season.

The mail lady walked up to checkout and said, "Glad to see you made it."

I looked at her blankly before the light bulb came on, and then I asked if I could buy her a cup of tea or coffee to express my thanks for the peace of mind she gave me. She had a date, so she declined. I assured her the Daintree route had been delightful.

The James Cook Museum was next on my agenda, and I spent an hour and a half looking at the displays, and then another hour and a half chatting with the sole occupant of the museum. The curator told me the history of the town and the local gossip from the past thirty years (the length of time he had lived in town). I loved small-town museums!

At the hardware store, I bought four broom handles, four tent stakes, and heavy-duty twine so I could make two tarps into verandahs extending from the roof rack. That way I could leave the car windows open without worry of getting wet or having critters drop in uninvited.

I arrived at the hostel just as the sky opened up with another downpour. I ate some meal—a combination of lunch and dinner—would that be called "lunner" or "dinch?"

November 13, 1999 On the road into Cape York Peninsula, I experienced the usual corrugated dirt and powdery fine bulldust. The scenery was eucalyptus scrub. I saw at least two-dozen kangaroos hip-hopping along. Some were not much more than a foot high. I inquired about pademelons in the area, and the ranger at Lakefield National Park said what I saw were probably young agile wallabies. Their mother kicked them out of the pouch when she was ready to start nursing another joey. Or maybe thc ones I saw were young agiles with a mother nearby.

I saw one goanna, one frilly lizard, and heaps of birds, ducks, geese, and brolgas when I stopped at Horseshoe Lagoon.

The ranger said no one was allowed to travel farther north than the park because of high-water conditions. He suggested I stay at Kalpowar Crossing campground for a few days and see if the rivers receded.

Kalpowar was a wonderful campground! Rainwater tanks supplied the restrooms with delightful soft water for showering and drinking. There were flush toilets, mowed lawns for tents, heaps of animals, and only one other campsite occupied. I used the tarps for shade and rain protection and slept like a baby.

November 14, 1999 A breeze was blowing gently, with variable cloudiness and temperatures in the twenties (Celsius). In other words it was a delightfully cool spring day. I thoroughly enjoyed the cool-water shower in the clean restroom and shared my breakfast with a bush turkey. I gave him uncooked oats, and he loved them. I could tell because he showed me his colorful wattle expanding and contracting and groaned a low bellow of appreciation. I don't know how girl turkeys could resist such a magnificent masculine display.

I organized another package of pictures to send to Marlow. He told me last week that he was not opening them. They were just pictures with no meaning. I had sent him over a dozen packages, thinking I was sharing my excitement with him. He said the packages were just lying on the dining-room table waiting for me to come home and take care of all the mail received since August 3. When the electricity to the house is shut off, maybe he'll open mail and pay some bills.

I would enjoy the pictures for years to come whether Marlow cared to look at them or not. The $2,000.00 video should also keep pretty good records of the trip.

The other occupants of the campground stopped by on their way out of the park. They saw the bonnet of my car up and wanted to know if I needed help. I was just topping off the water. It evaporated in the heat. They told me there had been a saltwater crocodile outside their tent when they returned from a hike the evening before. They thought he was probably after the chicken scraps they left in a trash container. Still, they were camped about three hundred meters from the river bank. I didn't expect crocs to travel that far from the water or up a steep embankment. They didn't say how they got rid of it or if they were worried about sleeping in the tent. They just mentioned the croc among the wildlife they had seen in the park.

I took a late-afternoon stroll to the river but saw no crocs, just a pretty sunset. I felt great satisfaction in spending a pleasant evening with my new best friend, the turkey.

A couple of crows hung around the campsite hoping to be fed. They turned up their beaks at the oatmeal. The crows did me a favor by dislodging a paw-paw (papaya) from a wild tree when it was within twenty-four hours of being ripe. I grabbed it and wrapped it in newspaper and stored it in the car. The crows resented that, even though I pretended to believe they had picked it just for me and thanked them profusely. I paid $2.50 for half a paw-paw in Yorkey's Knob Beach. There was another paw-paw fifteen feet off the ground on the same tree that would be ready for picking tomorrow, and I was hoping the crows would knock it loose.

I knew the rain would keep the water tank full for the next couple of months, so I took another luxurious shower before bedtime. While I was gone, the crows went in the open window of the car and dragged out the garbage bag and spread the contents around the campsite. I think that meant there was no way in hell they'd pick the second paw-paw for me tomorrow.

Throngs of fruit bats flew over the campground. Dozens chose to spend the night with me. They only wanted blossoms, not my personal paw-paw. I watched their aerobatics and listened to their grinding conversations until I fell asleep.

November 15, 1999 The live alarm clock in the trees woke me at five thirty. The parrots were after the nectar in the blossoms on the gum trees—the ones the fruit bats had not sucked dry. In the rainforest there was a bountiful supply of blossoms and berries to attract a plethora of animals.

My ice from Cooktown was almost melted, so it was time to consume refrigerated foods quickly. I had a grilled ham and cheese sandwich for breakfast, along with copious quantities of black tea. I continued reading the biographies of the Duracks while taking two hours to eat breakfast and hydrate with tea. Gone were the days when I had to grab a piece of toast or a bagel on my way out the door to go to work. I loved retirement!

By eight a.m., I decided I had better get dressed just in case the ranger wandered by or fishermen arrived at the river crossing. There was nowhere to go, so I took myself on a four-kilometer walk along the Normanby River. I spotted a few agile wallabies; I actually saw more staying in camp than I did by going into the wilderness. I saw some beautiful, delicate honey-eaters (birds). I later learned that their name was fairy gerygone. Musical-sounding name, isn't it? I saw two wonderful specimens of the monitor lizard family; one was about five feet long, and the second was about seven feet long.

For some reason my back had been getting tired on long walks. It could be the air mattress, it could be the heavy camera equipment, and it could be my age. Anyhow, I stretched out on grass to rest when I got back to camp. Did I tell you there were a bazillion ants in Australia, and they all had sharp teeth?

No one had come into camp, but people used the roadway to cross the river for traveling further north for fishing and boar hunting. It was pleasantly isolated except for those few people.

Still, I decided to move north to a place called Hanns Crossing in hopes there would be less traffic. I'd stay there for three or four days and explore the area. It would soon be time to either get supplies to stay for the wet season or head south to Scott's house. I was eager to see Scott and his family, but it was a bit sad, as arrival there would signal the twilight of this heavenly trip.

While eating dinner I watched a dingo chasing a kangaroo. It looked like a game, not serious food search. I stood up to get the video camera; the dingo saw me and took off.

November 16, 1999 Another perfect day in paradise. My ice was now air-temperature water, so I ate dried-out bread fried with cheese for breakfast and lunch. I'd hate to throw out cheese or butter, you know. Broccoli or Brussels sprouts, I could throw out.

I gave Mr. Turkey bread, oats, and a few dried cranberries as a parting gesture before dismantling the verandahs and packing for the road trip. That took ten minutes. I found a broom in the restroom and managed to reach the ripe paw-paw and work it loose. The crows screeched at me the whole time, "Mine! Mine!"

After a long shower, I lit out for Hanns Crossing. The trip through Lakefield National Park was not particularly picturesque. There were signs of former occupants. Some of the station buildings didn't look that old. One place looked like it had been deserted within the past ten years. There were orchards of mangoes. I picked half a dozen to keep away the scurvy.

Upon arrival at Hanns Crossing—"crossing" meant there was another sizable river to cross—I looked for the ideal camping spot. The crossing was a raging torrent, and I couldn't tell how deep the water was or what was under the flowing muddy liquid. I stayed out.

I didn't find a camping spot that suited me. Some were surrounded by grass that was eight to ten feet tall. Too many critters like boars and crocs could hide there. Some were so isolated that no one would bother checking for inhabitants. In case of illness or accident, I'd be too far up the creek to signal for help. There were no restrooms, no showers, and no safe swimming areas. I didn't like the prospect of bathing in a cup of water for four days. I ate a leisurely lunch at a little waterfall in the river and turned back toward Kalpowar.

I went to several lagoons—Red Lily Lagoon, White Lily Lagoon, Blue Lagoon—sound patriotic, don't they? I walked about and took videos. No one would enjoy the videos but me. It would be hours and hours of birds.

Some of the birds I saw were:

- Brolga
- Jabiru
- Black-billed spoonbill
- Rajah shelduck
- Great egret
- Bustard
- Bush turkey
- Orange-footed scrubfowl
- Coucal

November 17, 1999 When I returned to Kalpowar, I found another camper in *my* site. I drove to the far end of the campground away from the intruder. After thinking it over, I decided I'd surely irritate the ranger if I stayed there. There were little signs saying "Company" campsites. I knew that meant reserved for busloads of tourists. I also knew there wouldn't be busloads of tourists coming north at this time of year, but I didn't want to upset the ranger.

I drove past *my* ablution block and *my* campsite next to it and parked two sites further down the lane. There were thick leafy hedges between the campsites, so I wouldn't be in view of the other camper.

An hour later, as I walked to the restroom, the other camper yelled, "Do you need any help setting up your tent?"

I assured him that I was set up. It took ten minutes to put up the tarps and get out my chair and TV tray.

Then he offered me a cold beer. *Cold beer*! It sounded familiar. I knew I had heard that expression before long, long ago in another life. What a concept! Cold beer, how could I refuse? We talked for an hour or so.

He was an agriculture inspector looking for illegal crops planted in Cape York by boat people from northerly islands. He had been married thirty-nine years and had two daughters and six grandchildren. The only one of the lot that he liked was his wife. I thought that sounded strange. Then he told me about his dingbat daughters and the men they married and his flaky grandchildren. Two grandchildren were into drugs and were thieves; a thirteen-year-old girl abused alcohol and was fooling around with a married forty-five-year-old man. A twelve-year-old and his ten-year-old sister rejected any present unless it cost over $1,000.00. They had extensive expensive wardrobes, their own home entertainment systems in their bedrooms, and anything else advertised on television they thought they needed. None of the grandchildren contacted the grandparents, unless they wanted money. He blamed the grandchildren's behavior on his daughters, as they were such poor mothers. I wondered why he didn't put any blame on the fathers, but didn't ask.

I told him my sons turned out just fine, married nice women, and my grandchildren were nearly perfect. That killed that conversation.

I was glad when the talk turned to music. John's cassette player sitting on the tailgate played Eagles music. John played in a band in the seventies and liked a lot of the same musicians I did—Black Sabbath, Deep Purple, Led Zeppelin, Pink Floyd, Eagles, Journey, and Bob Seeger.

He told me about his love of hunting. He said he carried a gun, a .357 Magnum, and used it on pigs, crocs, dingoes, and other "varmints."

One beer was all it took to make me feel mellow. I was ready to snuggle down in my private lodging with a book. The Duracks were awaiting my attention.

November 18, 1999 At six o'clock I trudged to the restroom with one eye open. John yelled that the coffee was done and breakfast was cooking. By the time I finished my shower and dressed, I could face a cup of coffee. It was much too early to think about baked beans on toast and greasy, half-cooked bacon.

After one cup of coffee, John packed up and left for work. I got my camera and went for my walk. The animals saw my camera and hid from view.

I returned at nine and was eating the last of my cream cheese on pan-fried toast when I heard a ruckus in the bush. A very young wallaby had just disappeared into that bush! Out he hopped going full speed with a dingo on his tail. Both made one circuit around my legs and returned to the bush. I don't know the outcome of the race, but feared the worst for the little roo. I think he was the one I videotaped. He had tried to get into his mom's pouch a couple of days ago, and the mother cuffed him away. She probably had a new baby in there. I later saw a lone female in the area where the mother and child had spent a lot of time the previous couple of days.

The campground became peaceful again, and I took another shower. The walk had been strenuous and dusty. The day was going to be a hot one.

I thought that a ride in the air-conditioned car was called for. I saw the ranger and asked about those giant-sized lizards. I thought they might be something unique. He said they were giant-sized goannas. They grew that big on Cape York because of good living conditions.

I revisited White Lily Lagoon and took some roads not yet traveled. I saw a blue-tongued lizard, a couple of undernourished dingoes, some very healthy brolgas, emus, cattle, brumbies, and of course, kangaroos.

I settled in a new campsite at the far end of the campground away from John's tent, drew pictures of some of the locals, and looked up to see John approaching.

"You should have been with me today. One mob of brolgas must have been at least a hundred strong. The rivers were running bankers, and cascades were at their best. There was lush greenery everywhere."

The night before, he had invited me to ride along on his route. I had added up the pros and cons:

Pros

1. Possibility of seeing new animals and scenery.

2. Learning more about the area.

Cons

1. I would be riding into a deserted area with a total stranger.

2. I knew the stranger carried a .357 Magnum.

3. I knew the stranger enjoyed shooting animals, so what about people?

4. I would be out behind the black stump (miles from anywhere).

I missed seeing the mob of a hundred brolgas take off in flight, and that must have been spectacular, but at least I still had my scalp.

He went on extolling the wonders of the bush, the lushness of the vegetation, the proliferation of animals, and so forth. His trip sounded great. He ended his story with the warning not to try that route on my own, as he had winched himself out of mudholes twice and hit some black-soil plains, which were slick as ice.

John left mouthing the invitation to stop by his house for a home-cooked meal and a free night's lodging when I passed through Mission Beach. The "missus" loved company and would be delighted to have me stop by. Yeah! I bet she would. Did she have a Magnum also?

The entertainment for the evening consisted of watching a road train, a semi with two trailers built for hauling cattle, cross the Kalpowar Crossing. It would have taken fifteen minutes of videotape to record the incident and would not have been interesting to anyone who had not tried to drive through fender-deep water with high embankments on either side of the river. The truck twisted and turned, moaned and groaned. The tires spun on slick spots, throwing water high into the air, and then caught hold to climb boulders hidden under the current. With a great deal of effort, the driver nursed the reluctant truck across the river and up the opposite bank. Surely he scared away any lurking saltwater crocodiles.

A young couple pulled into the campground and chose a space halfway between John and myself. The place was getting downright crowded. I walked over to say, "Howdy" (American for *G'dai*). The couple said they had to stop at Kalpowar for the night when they saw the green grass. They had seen nothing but burned-out bush for three days. The only thing that relieved the scenery was brown rocks and dust. I told them they'd love Kalpowar with its fresh, clean water. I pointed to the nightly migration of flying foxes (fruit bats) and said that Kalpowar was peaceful, but never quiet, and certainly never dull.

Later that night I was halfway through a sentence in my book when a strange thought entered my head. The young couple had come from the same place that John spent the day. They certainly had a different description of the environment.

November 19, 1999 The ranger stopped by to tell me there had been more storms up north, and all roads were closed until the beginning of the dry season—March or April. I sadly packed the car, ready to turn south. Farewell, my lovely, wild country. I'll think of you often.

I took the turn in the road at the Old Laura homestead. Old Laura had provided beef to gold miners who prospected nearby late in the 1800s. The road led to the roadhouse called Laura, located at the New Laura homestead. I didn't ask who the current owners of the New Laura cattle station were. There were Aboriginals sitting on the ground in the shade of many of the trees around the roadhouse and fuel station. I figured they were the landlords.

By eleven thirty I was thinking about brunch when I saw a sign saying I could buy food at a roadhouse a short distance down the road. Marlow and I had looked at a station near here when we went to Australia to become cowboys in 1972. We could have gotten a hundred-year renewable lease from the government for a hundred and fifty square miles of land for $40,000.00. We would have to come up with 90 percent of the money as cash. We needed to quickly sell our houses in California and Massachusetts. Marlow and I had left the two houses on the market in the United States. We didn't get our money together in time. We had second thoughts about living so far from civilization anyway. We were such novices at cattle handling. We decided to buy a little place on the outskirts of Ipswich, Queensland, instead.

Someone else bought the lease. They went bankrupt in 1990 (we could have done it in a shorter length of time), and the station was purchased as a freehold property by a corporation. That meant the government no longer owned it, so the Aboriginals could not reclaim it. The new corporation used it as farmland, growing grain, bananas, and cotton. They put in a roadhouse where they sold food and petrol. The increased traffic called for a caravan park. Now it was a small township, maybe two dozen houses, with the occupants running the various moneymaking enterprises and/or doing the farm chores.

There were proper bridges across the Annan River. I didn't have to ford the questionable waterways to get to Cooktown. When I arrived in Cooktown, I checked into Pam's Hostel and got my old room back. The dormitory had eight beds. This time two young women shared the room with me. The thunderstorm during the night convinced me this was a good choice of lodging.

November 20, 1999 Daintree National Park road south of Cooktown was impassable. I'd wait at the hostel another day and see if the water receded.

That gave me a free day in town. I went to the Botanical Gardens, which were first created in 1778. Imagine that! Two years after James Cook landed there. The gardens changed considerably in 1886 when there was a movement to make Australia look more like England. Trees, flowers, bushes, and animals were brought to Australia. Many had proliferated and were now considered a nuisance. The mango tree brought from Indonesia had become a mainstay and an acceptable import.

The gardens were very pleasant indeed, in spite of the forty-degree temperature (that's hot in Fahrenheit) and high humidity. I walked over a hill on the trail that led to the beach and spent half an hour in the shade of the forest, watching fishermen net fish. They were catching shimmering, silver herring to use as bait when they went reef fishing. They got a few mullets, which they kept to eat. Some of the live herring were thrown back into the sea, as they had caught fifteen or twenty dozen and only wanted about two dozen for bait. That was the story they told me. It didn't make sense that they kept fishing if they didn't want the fish. I guessed they thought I saw them pull in the last few nets full and were trying to convince me they got all those fish with one try. I suspected what they were doing was illegal, as they talked too much and too fast when I approached them from my shady lookout in the rainforest.

The lunch counter special at the Cooktown Hotel Garden Pub was chicken Kiev Hawaiian-style (Hawaiian-style Russian chicken). The meal was crumbed, baked chicken with pineapple. There was coleslaw on the side with chips (French fries) and an open salad bar loaded with vegetables and fruits. All for $5.50.

November 21, 1999 I drove from Cooktown to Mission Beach, Queensland. It took twelve hours the way I went. The sky dumped rain about fifteen kilometers out of Cooktown, so I didn't take the picturesque drive through Daintree. There were several river crossings that were a couple of feet deep when I was on my way north. I was afraid they would now be three or four feet deep. I'm sure a Toyota could handle that but didn't know if I had the nerve. I liked to see the bottom when I drove through water. I thought that was what Annabel would have told me to do—use some common sense.

Taking the inland route brought me back to the station roadhouse. I stopped and had a cup of coffee and chatted with the young waitress and cook again. They treated me like an old friend since this was my second visit.

I stopped at Split Rock Aboriginal Art Cave and hiked up, up, up to the indentation. That took well over an hour as I stopped often. My lungs couldn't get enough oxygen to walk any faster. Dang those years of smoking cigarettes. The art was several layers deep and truly looked ancient. The sign said it dated back 13,000 years. I wondered if we'd have to look at the graffiti on our downtown buildings for that long. The trail led to a lovely scenic place to live. The cave was cooler than the surrounding hillside. I'd get tired of the walk up to the front door if I were an Aborigine living there.

I was glad to get back to my air-conditioned car. I drove along the Palmerston Highway that eventually turned from dirt to bitumen. It rained intermittently all day. I timed my tours accordingly—stopping in Mareeba, Atherton Tablelands, for a tour through a coffee bean roasting and grinding plant, the best-smelling tour so far this trip. Then I went to see a few of the local sights like the Curtain Fig Tree, with its roots extending downward from the limbs spread out fifty meters. The tree was five hundred years old. One tree had fallen across the saddle of two major limbs on another, and roots grew from the trunk of the nearly horizontal fallen tree.

I made it to Mission Beach just after dark. I wanted to stay there because they reputedly had wild cassowaries nearby.

A young lady at the tourist information center gave me a map to local backpackers' hostels and told me which ones were for young people—those had a licensed bar, which meant they would be noisy—and which ones were for nature lovers, where people went to bed at sunset and got up at sunrise. She ended up by telling me that one resort in town set aside half a dozen rooms that it rented at hostel prices. She suggested I try there first. Mission Beach Resort had one bed available in a wonderful motel room. Occupants had a fridge, television, video player, and private bath. The sliding-glass door opened onto a patio facing landscaped gardens and a pool with waterfalls over natural rocks. The six hostel rooms had their own kitchen, dining room, and laundry. I couldn't believe my luck (again). Once I saw the room, I went right back to reservations and signed up for an extra night.

November 22, 1999 I tiptoed out of my room, where two women were still asleep. I pretended not to notice that one of them had a man sleeping beside her.

I drove to Licuala State Forest, which was beautiful, but I had not gone there to see trees and vines. I had gone to see cassowaries. I walked for two hours around the paths in the forest of fan palms, strangler figs, and assorted tropical flora. I heard a few birds in the trees, but mostly the only noise I heard was my own shuffling feet. My back started bothering me, so I went back to the car in a state of disappointment. I really wanted to see that magnificent specimen of giant birdlife.

I sat down at my dining-room table (the tailgate) and was eating my breakfast. I was sitting on my little three-legged stool when I heard footsteps approaching from behind. I thought it was about time for the ranger to show up to collect the park entry fee. I looked over my shoulder and came face-to-face with a full-grown cassowary!

I turned away from him and picked up my camera with slow, deliberate movements. He was more interested in the bowl of cereal than he was in me. I had heard stories about cassowaries gutting a man with their enormous claws. I was willing to share my cereal if that was what he wanted. I didn't try to stand up until he finished looking over the contents of the "kitchen." He didn't find anything that interested him, so he turned and wandered toward the bush. I snapped some pictures before his three-feet-long legs took him quickly out of view. As he was about to disappear into the bushes, he let out one long, low bellow as though he knew I wanted to hear his song. He sounded like a bull.

Had this been a perfect trip or what? Incredible! I asked myself so many times what I'd ever done to be rewarded with such a wonderful life.

When I came down off Cloud 9, I returned to the resort and enjoyed the man-made Mecca. My roommates had moved on. I had the room to myself. I swam when the sun was out and watched videos, compliments of the establishment, when it rained. One video was *The Wedding Singer*, and the other was *Analyze This*. There had been an hour's break between movies, which coincided with an hour's break in the rain. I walked on the beach. After the second movie, the sun came out, and I went for a second swim, playing tag with a child as we ducked under waterfalls and raced from end to end of the rock-lined pool. I got my $15.00 a night out of the place.

November 23, 1999 I drove onward to Townsville, intending to spend the night and check out tourist attractions. I arrived at eleven and cruised up and down the old section of town admiring the architecture. I ate Greek pasta at a quaint restaurant with newspapers on the tables for the patrons to read. Then I went to the Barrier Reef

Nature Center and learned from a ranger that tree snakes in Australia are nonpoisonous. From there I walked to the IMAX Theater and saw *The Living Sea.* The movie was great, as expected. It was a bit of a neck strainer, as the screen went from the stage floor in front of the audience up and over the seats and came down to the joint of the back wall.

All of the above took two and a half hours. I could think of nothing else I cared to do or see in the city, so I drove down Route One until I came to Queens Beach near Bowen and checked into a chalet. The roomy cabin was $35.00 for the night. The space and privacy gave me a chance to clean out my car. I kept stuffing things into corners "until later." After a few days of that, I couldn't find anything and had to reorganize.

November 24, 1999 I walked around a lagoon in Bowen's city park for my morning stroll and saw pelicans, black swans, purple swamp hens, masked lapwing plovers, Rajah shelducks, and magpie geese. I was getting faster; my two-hour walk only took me an hour and a half!

Driving until twelve thirty brought me to a roadside rest, time for a sandwich. A guinea hen, a butcher bird, and a magpie joined me for lunch. Fortunately, I had enough to share. I usually didn't give animals my processed white-flour bread, but I did this time. I hoped they wouldn't get sick or have their beaks decay from eating such food.

I decided to spend the night in Mackay, as I saw advertised tours of sugarcane factories and one for watching jeweler's facet sapphires. The tourist office couldn't get bookings on either tour. The sugarcane had all been processed for the season. No answer at the gem shop. The clerk thought the owners had gone south for the summer. The lady asked if I'd be interested in a tour of Eungella, (YOUNG-goo-la). I had no idea what that was. It turned out to be a national park where there were platypuses! Would I be interested? You bet! You guessed it, she was not able to get me on a tour there either. It cost $65.00 and was only running sporadically because of the decline in tourist activity.

It didn't seem logical to pay that kind of money to tour a national park, so I got out the central Queensland map and plotted my own way to the park. What a drive; it was almost as steep as some of the spots in Daintree, but this time I had asphalt all the way. The scenery was glorious from the seashore to the mountaintop. I kept pulling over to let other people pass me, as I wanted to savor the ride.

When I arrived at the beautiful Eco Lodge, I found the last reasonably inexpensive motel room had been rented to the last couple that passed me on the road. After the other customers left the reservation area, I told the clerk that I really could not afford the $120.00 rooms in the lodge. I asked if I could possibly sleep in my car in the parking lot, as I was too tired to drive back to Mackay. Absolutely not! They had standards to uphold. I asked if there were any dirt roads where I could pull off for a few hours of sleep without lowering their standards. He finally felt guilty about turning a little old lady out in the dark forest and said he could rent me one of their deluxe accommodations for motel prices. I took it.

The cabin was lovely, just lovely. It had natural light-colored wood interiors with lime-green accents. There was a wood burning stove in the lounge of my suite, a king-size bed in the master bedroom, a spa in the bathroom. It had all the comforts of home (not my home, but someone's). I could handle it (as long as I didn't have to pay for it). I stayed two nights.

I got to see several platypus—platypi, platypuses, whatever. You know what I mean—those cute little monotremes with duckbills and beaver tails. They fed for an hour before sunset and an hour after sunrise. I walked through the rainforest to get to the platform lookout and got a leech under the strap of my sandal. I didn't discover it for a couple of hours. Ooooh, guck! I knew they couldn't help being such sleazy characters, but I just didn't like them. I tried a new anti-leech trick learned on this trip; I sprayed the slimy thing with mosquito spray. He backed out of my skin, curled up, and bled to death. Maybe he was just spitting out my blood. I put disinfectant on my ankle, but still had an open sore for a month.

November 25, 1999 I arose at five to visit the platypuses before they returned to their underwater lodge for the day. I was rewarded with the sight of two of the little nippers on a foraging fest. They came up to the top of the water for just a few seconds and then jackknifed to the bottom of the river. I watched the bubbles to tell where they were likely to come up again and was able to get some video footage. Gosh, I'll be ready to apply for a *National Geographic* grant by the time I get home.

There were plenty of turtles and birds doing their morning chores. I was surprised at the number of purple swamp hens working the shoreline of the mountain stream. There was certainly no shortage of interesting birdlife in Australia.

I packed the car and headed for Rockhampton. I only got twenty kilometers when I saw a sign saying, "Finch Hatton Gorge." One more gorge, how could it hurt? I bet it would be different than any I'd seen on the trip. I took the turnoff. There was no mileage on the sign, so I thought the gorge was beside the highway. I drove twenty kilometers to the *start* of the trail. Still no mileage signs. A couple pulled into the parking lot soon after me. I asked if they knew anything about the gorge. They told me it was supposed to be a two-hour walk to a waterfall. The rainforest allegedly had lots of animal life. Sounded good to me. I needed my daily two-hour walk anyhow.

It was quite pleasant—shady, uphill, of course, but still the weather wasn't bad for an uphill walk. I came to a waterfall in two kilometers instead of two hours. I knew it was two kilometers because there was a sign saying, "Parking Lot—2 kms." Water fell over a granite cliff into a boulder-strewn creek with a good swimming hole. I didn't have togs (bathing suit), so I sat on an L-shaped rock, smelled the eucalypts, relished the cool spray and mossy scenery, and listened to the lullaby of water.

I went about a kilometer beyond the waterfall before turning back, and I was treated to the sight of a variety of lizards, including goannas ranging in length from ten inches to five feet. The ranger at the base of the walk reconfirmed that the big guys were goannas, not dinosaurs. They grew eight to ten feet long under the right conditions—lots of food and few predators.

A short drive took me back to civilization and traffic. The Bruce Highway, Route One, was littered with road repair crews, so going was slow. Yuck! I wanted to turn back toward Daintree and Kalpowar.

November 26,–December 4, 1999 It was Thanksgiving Day in the States when I arrived in Rockhampton, where Scott, daughter-in-law Meleese, and their family lived. That evening Meleese fixed turkey and cranberry-sauce sandwiches for the Yanks—Scott and me.

My family was glad to know I was back where they could keep an eye on me. I enjoyed getting reacquainted with Scott, Meleese, and the three boys. It was pure pleasure meeting my two granddaughters, Mikaela and Shinnay. The children ranged in age from one to ten. Even the two oldest boys were home from school, as it was summer vacation time. After a four-month camping trip, it was a bit of an adjustment to adapt to all the activity. Meleese and Scott understood that and left just one or two kids at home with me while they went to work. That worked perfectly. I went for nature walks and/or played games and/or played with toys, according to the age of the child of the day. The Australian Kilpatricks lived on a cattle property, so at least I wasn't pummeled by city noises twenty-four/seven.

December 5, 1999 I still had more touring and more visiting to do. It was time to give the Rockhampton Kilpatricks a break from my company. I left for Brisbane to visit friends.

The first stop was at the Ginger Factory, started by a group of five men after World War II. They came home from the war and couldn't find jobs, so they planted ginger, harvested, and sold it. They were soon exporting it to Asia. The farm grew into a multimillion-dollar corporation. They built a factory where they produced ginger syrup, candy, cookies, and dehydrated chunks.

There was an enormous store that sold everything imaginable made from ginger, plus any kind of souvenir sold in Queensland. They had restaurants, ice-cream shops, and a wonderful nursery where they sold tropical plants.

December 6, 1999 Next came a stop at the Big Pineapple, a tourist site near Nambour, where I took a ride through pineapple fields on a little train. We passengers looked over acres and acres of pineapples, and the guide told us that every single pineapple had to be planted by hand. He told us that starting a new plant meant cutting the top off a pineapple and planting it. Each plant produced one fruit. What a time-consuming process!

I managed to find my way through metropolitan Brisbane and out to the suburb of Goodna. Brisbane had grown so much since we lived there in the 1970s and was sophisticated, with freeways and more commercial areas. It had two miles of freeway completed when Marlow, the boys, and I left Australia in 1980. Brisbane had gone from an oversized "cow town" to a major cosmopolitan city during the past twenty years.

December 7–11, 1999 I visited Pat and Christine Nugent's home. They were good friends. Someday I hoped to return the hospitality they'd shown me on every visit I'd made to Australia. They ensconced me in an elaborate, immaculate, lacy, frilly guest bedroom and gave me an open invitation to make myself at home.

Pat and Christine built this house from the ground up after a devastating fire destroyed their last home, a two-story brick house. They carefully thought out every nook and cranny and made it beautiful and functional. Verandahs overlooked their thirty-two acres of pastures, pond, and trees.

I spent time with Pat and Christine's two grown children, Anthony and Kim, and their respective spouses, Nikki and Allen. It was a fun, sociable time. I was glad Marlow sent me an early Christmas gift, a nice new outfit to wear for "dress-up." My camping clothes from the past five months were threadbare and stained.

December 12, 1999 I headed north, stopping at Wivenhoe Dam, which used to be a primitive lake where Marlow and I took our half-cabin cruiser for a day of fishing. There was now an upscale community living in luxurious homes on the edge of the lake. The state government did leave a few areas primitive, but others were well-developed urban recreation areas with tennis courts, golf courses, and restaurants.

I went northwest to Bunya National Park in the mountains. My usual luck did not hold as far as rain was concerned. Rain was threatening when I wound through the mountains approaching the park. There was thunder and lightning as I reached the parking lot at the start of the trails. I put on my raincoat, tucked the video camera into a waterproof container, and started into the rainforest. At first the path looked like I was going the wrong way on a one-way street. Other hikers were dashing for the parking lot. I soon had the place to myself. The thunder and lightning passed, and it rained, it poured, it blew swirling leaves and branches around in the canopy overhead. Down on the path, there was only a sprinkle. The thick, thick canopy protected me from most of the water. I had a delightful hike to waterfalls along a rushing stream through Mother Nature's playground. The lack of other hikers didn't concern me one bit; it gave me a chance to observe old friends—lizards, snakes, birds, and insects.

It rained as I descended the northerly side of the mountain range in my car. The weather was soon back to variable cloudiness, and I was driving through a pastoral scene on my way to Proston, where I spent the night in a rented caravan.

December 13, 1999 I made arrangements with a farmer who owned land on garnet fossicking (prospecting) fields to return with my grandson, Rhys, to look for gemstones. The farmer told me most of the other farms nearby had sold their mineral rights to BHP (Broken Hill Proprietary, Ltd.), a giant consortium, who wanted to mine for diamonds. Those people didn't buy mineral rights as a hobby, so I went to Rockhampton thinking I might find a diamond!

I reminisced on the train stop at Broken Hill, New South Wales, Annabel and I made at the start of this trip. What wonders I've seen since that time.

I drove on to Hervey Bay and stayed at my first mixed-gender hostel. When I walked into my assigned room and saw two handsome hunks asleep in beds, I thought I had been assigned to the wrong room. I checked with reservations, and they looked at me like I was speaking a foreign language. They couldn't see why there would be a problem with me sleeping in a room assigned to seven men. At my request they reassigned me to another room that was currently only occupied by two men. They said they'd try to fill the other beds with women, if any applied for lodging. I accepted that. It ended up that the young Dutch and Swiss men and I were the only occupants. We got along just fine; they were complete gentlemen. They didn't snore. The next morning they invited me to eat breakfast with them on the patio next to the pool so we could get acquainted. The Dutchman was heading to Brisbane looking for work. I suggested he contact my friend, Peter, in Goodna. Peter, also from Holland, might be able to find him a job in the building industry.

December 14–16, 1999 I saw Fraser Island on an organized tour; a bus picked me up at the hostel and took me to the ferry, which crossed the Great Sandy Strait. A custom-made four-wheel-drive bus took the paying customers from the ferry to the scenic sites throughout the island and then back to our place of lodging on the island.

At the first site, we hiked through Yidney Rainforest. On the ocean side of the island, we journeyed south to see Yidney Rocks. From there we went to pastel-colored Rainbow Gorge.

Next on our tour was Lake Wabby (where did they get those names?), where we walked up a long, long sand dune to reach a swimming hole. That sounds crazy, but that's what it was, a lake encased in a sand dune. The guide said the lake did not drain into the sand and disappear because there was compressed sandstone under the dunes.

The island was 95 percent sand; it was supposed to be the largest island in the world composed of sand. It still managed to grow lots of vegetation.

Happy Valley Retreat, where we were taken for lunch and dinner, and where we were scheduled to spend the night, was a secluded group of cottages that originally belonged to fishermen. The cottages were now nothing but bedrooms and bathrooms. Our tour company arranged the sleeping accommodations. I had no idea how they decided who slept in what rooms. They managed to keep married couples together. Outside of that it was a hodgepodge. I shared a room with one woman and one man. None of us knew each other.

I was the first of the three to hit the hay, so I got first choice of beds. Naturally, I took a lower bunk. I carefully hung my clothes to be worn the next day on the headboard.

In the morning I was the first one up, so I quietly took my clothes off the bed to head to the shower. Just as I reached for my T-shirt, it moved. I cautiously picked it up by the shoulders and shook it vigorously. Out fell a huntsman spider about the diameter of a grapefruit. It scurried under my bed. I knew I couldn't catch it without waking the two late sleepers, so I didn't try. They were in no danger. Huntsmen hunt insects; they don't chew on nasty-tasting humans.

I went for a walk on the beach and watched the sunrise. I was gone for almost two hours and returned to join the rest of the group at the breakfast table on the patio of the restaurant. The bus driver noticed a carpet snake on a banana tree beside our table. He caught it and was telling us about carpet snakes. This beauty was about seven feet long. The guide wasn't too concerned about handling the constrictor. He asked for a volunteer to hold the snake while he climbed up on the patio railing. He wanted to put the snake into a different tree. I was lucky enough to get to hold the delightfully beautiful creature for a couple of minutes. After he put the snake into the tree, he told us that he knew the snake was a pet named Charley. The owner of the restaurant heard him say that and came out of the kitchen to tell the driver that Charley was still in his cage in the restaurant owner's cabin. The guide turned pale.

My roommates entered the restaurant about that time. I was finished eating, so I asked the owner if I could have an empty ice-cream container to catch a huntsman to show the group. He gave me a clear plastic container, and I went to the lodging quarters and caught the fuzzy brown spider. It was still under my bed, hiding in the corner where the wall and floor met. The tourists were fascinated to think that an old woman would hold a snake and catch a giant spider. One boy asked me what animals I feared. I didn't fear animals, but I had a healthy respect for their natural instincts.

We packed into the bus and started our sight-seeing with a trip to Eli Creek. The water was crystal clear and cool. We were allowed to swim, so I joined half a dozen mates in a game of tug-of-war in the creek. We lost, but we all got equally wet. I did enjoy traveling with cheerful young people. We walked the creek to the beach and had the best views of the flowers growing along the edge of the freshwater stream.

Some people kept their swimsuits on for the rest of the day. I changed back into street clothes and was glad I did, as the temperature dropped about ten degrees. The day was rainy off and on and downright chilly by nightfall.

I expected to be suffering in the heat from the first of November until I left in February. Instead, the weather changed frequently and gave me plenty of cool days.

The group climbed to the heights of Indian Head, which was at the end of a peninsula. We saw water crashing against the shores on both sides of us. The most fascinating part of this walk was that I found an unusual geologic feature. I found fragile stones shaped like straws. They had thin shells and a straight hole down the center. The guide told us they were caused by lightning striking the sandy beach and fusing the sand into glass. The hole was where the lightning bolt had passed through. I brought one home. The stone was called a fulgurite.

We went to Lake Allom, which was home to freshwater turtles. The roads were incredibly deep with dry sand, and I was glad I didn't make this trip in my car. We saw half a dozen people get stuck trying to make it uphill. Our bus got stuck once trying to make it up an incline leading to the comparative safety of the moist sand at the surf's edge. I say "comparative," as that stretch of beach was also used as a landing strip for airplanes and a highway for some crazy-driving tourists—and there were no white lines.

We had a barbecue dinner at the restaurant, and there was enough beer consumed that we all became buddies before the night was over. Actually, it was a friendly group before we started the beer. A couple of the young men realized I carried way too much camera equipment and insisted on carrying it for me on our hikes. Bless them!

We eventually went back to the mainland and were taken to our places of lodging, completely worn-out.

December 17, 1999–January 17, 2000 I drove to Scott's farm, where he had workers building a kitchen and bathroom addition to the hundred-year-old farmhouse. I was glad to see those improvements being made. I didn't know how women managed to cook in the ten-foot-square kitchen with a single sink and minimal counter space. The first owners didn't even have the single sink; they had a pump outside and a bucket. About a third of the kitchen space was taken up with a large wood burning stove. The new bathroom did not yet have water connected, nor did it have a toilet or basin, just a tub installed. That left room for Scott to put in a single bed. I had a private bedroom in the house for the rest of my stay.

The balance of my trip was spent enjoying my middle son's family on their section of land. Life on the farm was full of activity and never dull. With five children and two very ambitious adults, things were kept hopping.

I took ten-year-old Joshua on a fossicking trip to the sapphire fields near Emerald, Queensland, for a few days. Eight-year-old Rhys and I went to Proston to find garnets, and six-year-old Caleb joined me on a camping trip to Mount Hay to find thunder eggs. It was good to have one-on-one time with my grandsons. The girls were too young to go exploring with Grandma. Next time…

When it was time to leave for America, I sold the car for $20,000.00, $10,000.00 less than I paid, and caught a bus to Sydney. I had fulfilled my dream of circumnavigating Australia. It had been one heck of a trip—the trip of a lifetime filled with wonder, beauty, great people, and fantastic animal life. The trip cost me approximately $22,000.00 and was worth every penny.

I hated to leave, but I really needed a break to give me time to put seventy rolls of film into albums, type the handwritten novel called my journal, and see about translating the six VHS videocassettes into something that Marlow would view.

Eleven

Copper Canyon, Chihuahua, Mexico

2001

I spent last summer traveling "my way," via my Toyota Celica car, staying in a tent or with family or friends. On the occasional rainy night when I was not staying in someone's home, I stayed in a hostel, where I shared my bedroom with total strangers. I ate food brought from home, subsisting on granola bars, fruit, raw vegetables, canned tuna, and Top Ramen noodles. Marlow would abhor traveling in that manner. He is past sleeping in a tent and hates staying in someone else's home. He would never knowingly agree to sleep in a room with strangers.

For his Christmas vacation from Aerojet, I agreed to travel his way—by plane and train, staying in four-star hotels and eating restaurant food—well, mostly eating restaurant food. I packed a little food and said I'd eat in restaurants at least once a day on our travels. We were off to see the geological wonder of the Barranca del Cobre, Copper Canyon, in the state of Chihuahua, Mexico.

December 23, 2001 I requested the airport shuttle to pick us up at six thirty a.m. Surprise! The lady driver arrived at our front door at six twenty. She was a perfectly normal lady and drove safely. There was no adventure getting to the airport.

We arrived at Sacramento International Airport two hours early as suggested by the airline and checked in without a hassle. Security personnel x-rayed our carry-on belongings and passed them without a hitch. I had to take off my hiking boots to run them through the x-ray machine, as they had metal fasteners.

I noticed that with the added security personnel at the airport after the September 11 attack on America by terrorists, no one chatted or laughed like they had in the past. Security had become serious business.

Our plane filled with passengers and took off on time. With a tail wind, we arrived at Phoenix, Arizona, ten minutes early. We transferred to a plane flying to El Paso, Texas, and were on our way again forty minutes later. No drama there. This might turn out to be a boring vacation, with everything going so smoothly.

In El Paso we walked across the street to our reserved accommodations at the Hilton Hotel. We were two of maybe half a dozen customers staying in the maze-like hotel. The echo of our footsteps as we walked to our room was a bit spooky. The desk clerk told us breakfast in the fourth-floor dining room was included in the price of our room. He said that free hors d'oeuvres were served in the same dining area from five to seven p.m. It was dreary, foggy, cold, and uninviting outdoors, so we stayed in our hotel room watching television the balance of the afternoon.

At dinnertime we went to the fourth floor and found an empty dining area with a sign on the serving table saying that due to lack of patronage, there would be no service. A promise is a promise, so I went to the hotel desk and complained. They sent us to the lounge, where the bar tender gave us free hors d'oeuvres (quesadillas and a beer). Marlow hated it when I whined, but I noticed that he wolfed down three-quarters of the quesadillas.

December 24, 2001 Marlow wanted the hotel shuttle to take us across the street to the airport departure lounge. I don't know why; maybe he just wanted to show me how luxurious it was to stay in an $85.00-a-night hotel instead of $10.00-a-night campground.

We made it through El Paso International Airport's check-in and security in fifteen minutes, including x-raying both parties' shoes. The airline insisted that my camera case was too large to use as a carry-on and made me check it. I hoped it would arrive in Chihuahua City in good condition. I carried a video camera, a digital still camera, and a Polaroid, plus all the battery-recharging equipment, extra packs of Polaroid film, and so forth in one large, heavy bag.

We settled into the lobby listening to Christmas music while I read and Marlow looked at airplanes. The atmosphere was eerily quiet, with just one other family in the lobby. They were adults, so they didn't make much noise. Sacramento and Phoenix airports had been madhouses of noise and confusion.

Two hours later a Mexican turbojet whisked us ten passengers to Chihuahua in an hour's time. The trip between the two airports was neither scenic nor smooth. The flight was bumpy from turbulence, as we were over low mountains of brown, dried grass. There were no trees, no exposed rocks, no rivers, and no lakes, just hills.

We landed smoothly, and I was happy to see my camera equipment was still in working order. We were taken to our luxury hotel in a shuttle. The driver spoke minimal English but was pleasant and a cautious driver. What more could we want?

Our hotel room was better than the Hilton in El Paso.

Marlow and I spent the afternoon wandering around downtown Chihuahua. I had planned on seeing the Pancho Villa Museum but was told that it was closed because it was Christmas Eve. Naturally. How silly of me to think it would be open. There were throngs of shoppers hurrying from store to store with last-minute Christmas bundles. The mall had all the usual stores and fast-food restaurants we expected to see in any American city. Young people played rock and roll versions of Christmas carols in the pedestrian square. I found it hard to believe we were in a foreign country. The people looked, dressed, and spoke like people in US southwestern towns.

We went to the *zocalo*, central park, in front of the cathedral. I got my first glimpse of Tarahumara natives huddled in colorful blankets selling baskets and artifacts. I decided to wait until the return trip to buy souvenirs rather than carry them with us.

We ate lunch (tortilla soup) and dinner (chili relleños) in the elegant hotel dining room, where we were joined by a decidedly upper-class patronage. I felt grossly underdressed in jeans and a sweater.

December 25, 2001 The wake-up call from the desk jangled at four thirty. We were wished *Feliz Navidad* by a cheerful desk clerk. We bathed, dressed, and ate a breakfast of hot grits and coffee brought from home.

We were soon in the lobby, where our tour guide picked us up precisely on time. He loaded our suitcases in the rear of his van and took us to the train station to catch the Ferrocarril Chihuahua al Pacifico for a four-hundred-mile trip. This gent spoke perfect English and told us to walk straight through the station, which was packed with waiting passengers. We followed his instructions, and a footman at the train escorted us to our seats and helped us with our bags. We were the only people on the train for five minutes before others went through a security check and struggled aboard with their own luggage. I don't know why we were treated special with no security check and help with our bags. Perhaps the world has come to realize that Marlow and I are *speeeecial.*

The half-full train was luxurious, with comfortable, roomy seats, sparkling clean restrooms, tasteful decoration, and soft music. We had lots of legroom. Ninety percent of the people were well-dressed Mexican families obviously on holiday. The remainder of passengers was tourists speaking various languages.

We left exactly at six a.m. as stated in the brochure. We rolled along mile after mile and saw nothing but brown hills. There were defoliated trees at this elevation of 7,500 feet and skinny livestock. Occasionally, we passed through tired-looking little towns.

At noon the train made a fifteen-minute stop at a scenic overlook in Divisadero. After a couple of attempts to find the viewing area via paths followed by the locals, we discovered that the only safe way to traverse the rocky ground was through the arts and crafts mall. Even on Christmas morning, vendors manned every booth.

We recognized the chili relleños wrapped in flour tortillas being fried on open grills by vendors and thought they should be safe to eat for lunch. They contained no tap water, raw fruit, or vegetables. The dining car on the train would be crowded with families, so we opted for the local fare.

A large number of American tourists embarked at this point. The ratio of American/Mexican tourists on the train was now about fifty/fifty. We rolled along through the countryside, which had changed to scraggly-looking pines on hills.

We arrived at our overnight stop at Cerocahui. The Hotel Mission was quaint, comfortable, and remote. We were told it was fifty kilometers from the train station. We rode that distance in a dilapidated school bus along rocky, potholed dirt roads. This might be an adventure after all.

There were four Texans on the bus and many Mexicans. We got acquainted with the two Texan couples after checking into the hotel and sharing happy hour. They were polite, friendly, and pleasant. They spoke good Spanish and talked warmly and naturally to the Mexicans. One gentleman was a lawyer, and the other was a beer distributor. The Mexicans accepted our efforts to speak Spanish for a while before telling us they understood English.

Marlow and I visited the mission across the road from the hotel. We took a few video pictures of the three-hundred-year-old building being used for a game of hide-and-seek by small children. I took my stash of candy canes and walked around town. It didn't take long to pass out forty candy canes, as there was a soccer game in the zocalo. Children of all ages were playing, and more were watching.

Dinner was served family-style at long, heavy, dark-wood tables in the wonderful hotel. I was careful to eat only cooked food and brought my own bottled water.

Marlow built a fire in the wood burning stove in our room. I unpacked my electric hot pot and proceeded to boil water for my hot-water bottle to warm the bed. Marlow shivered after a lukewarm shower and snuggled down under the covers, thoroughly enjoying the hot-water bottle that he felt was foolish to bring on the trip. The room was picturesque, rustic, clean, and comfortable. We slept well.

December 26, 2001 What a day! Breakfast was included in the price of the hotel. Marlow had bacon, eggs ranchero, hash browns, homemade biscuits, and fruit. I was filled to capacity with two of the fluffy hot biscuits, papaya, and pineapple (peeled fruit). Yummy.

The Texans joined us on a spectacular tour of the Urique Canyon. The van driver was careful and thoughtful. Yes, you are right, I rode shotgun. I got the best view, though the road was much too bumpy to take videos. I didn't understand why no one else wanted to sit up front with the driver.

I took pictures when we stopped at various wide spots in the road. At the scenic overlook on top of a mountain (or was it the rim of the canyon?), I whipped out my Polaroid and entertained the Tarahumara with my magic trick. They had never seen anything like that before. Some had never seen images of themselves.

I chatted in Spanish to a lady weaving baskets. She said she was forty-three years old. I would have guessed her to be seventy-three. She lived a hard life. Most Tarahumara never saw a doctor their whole lives, as there was one clinic, run by the Jesuits, to care for forty thousand indigenous people. They had to walk to that clinic, which was located in a copper-mining town, so when they got sick, they were in no condition to make the trip over the mountainous terrain.

The Sierra Madre Occidental canyons made by six rivers were lovely, with green desert plants and copper-colored rocks. The temperature was in the sixties, the company was cheerful, the driver excellent. All made for a nice outing.

Lunch awaited us upon our return to the hotel—fried fish, hot potatoes with chilies and cheese, a fresh salad, and orange Jell-O topped with whipped cream. I ate the fish and potatoes.

The six of us (including the Texans) boarded the bus for the return trip to the train station. The Mexican folks were evidently staying on Cerocahui. We learned the road was seven miles, not fifty kilometers, as we were originally told, and it took an hour to drive. At the train station, I had time to fire off another roll of Polaroid film. I took pictures of the macho caballeros leaning on their pickup trucks. They turned giggly like adolescent girls when they saw their image. That was so much fun. I know that one of the first purchases the Texans will make when they arrive home is a Polaroid camera. They couldn't believe that grown men ran or drove home to get their children and/or spouse so they could have their pictures taken. Some just wanted pictures of themselves beside their prize possession—a twenty-year-old pickup. It seemed like a mini-party with the Mexicans at the station during the forty-five-minute wait for the train. There was lots of laughing and joking as some caballeros pushed shy men in front of my lens.

We were spirited off on our way to Los Mochis among shouts of "*Felicidades*" (Happy Holidays). We rode through a fairy-tale land of colorful canyons over thirty-nine bridges and through eighty-six tunnels.

December 27, 2001 During the train ride yesterday afternoon, I developed a temperature and felt like I was coming down with stomach flu. I took two aspirin. What could there have been in fried fish and cooked potatoes that made me sick? It was so frustrating.

We arrived in Los Mochis at nine thirty in the evening, and I was achy, nauseated, and tired. We checked into the lovely Santa Anita Hotel. Our travel agent had booked us a suite. The place was nice and clean but had the odor of bug spray, which added to my nausea. I had nothing left on my stomach and suffered dry heaves for an hour or so. By midnight, my old nemesis, diarrhea, hit with a vengeance. I fished the Imodium out of the suitcase. For some reason that broke my fever, and I no longer had chills and sweats to go with the digestive tract distress.

By morning I was weak and had cramps from early dehydration. I told Marlow to enjoy the scheduled bay tour on a yacht by himself. I would stay in bed until he returned.

He chose to eat breakfast in the hotel restaurant, and in our room, I cooked hot oatmeal and chamomile tea, made with bottled water. I also boiled enough water to mix with the powdered oral electrolytes needed for twenty-four hours. I put that fluid in our emptied water bottles to nurse during the day. I was careful to brush my teeth and take medicine with bottled water, but came to the conclusion I was getting the bug by eating off dishes washed in tap water.

Marlow returned after breakfast and said the boat tour had been postponed until two o'clock. I flushed my system with electrolytes, and by the time we were scheduled to board the shuttle to the bay, I felt alive again.

It was a nice bus trip through the modern town supported by a sugarcane factory and agribusiness. There were as many hair colors on the ladies as there were in Sacramento. I didn't know if that meant there were many Americans and/or Europeans living in Los Mochis or that Clairol had arrived.

The cost of living was similar to Sacramento. We saw Nike shoes in store windows for US$100.00 plus. The bus driver said the average house rental was about US$600.00 a month. That did not compute with the stories we had heard in Chihuahua that the minimum wage was $3.50 per day and factory workers made $40.00 a week. I suspect the town was made up of retired non-Mexicans or that there were technical or manufacturing industries that paid higher wages.

The bay ride on the hotel's yacht was lovely. The weather was perfect and the water calm. Carlos, the tour guide, was good at his job and pointed out brown and blue-footed boobies, bottlenose dolphins, cormorants, pelicans, and a couple dozen graceful frigate birds. The shore was rocky desert with numerous caves, and we saw myriad shorebirds taking up residence there.

December 28, 2001 Another bad night, doggone it. For some dumb reason, I only brought one quinine pill with me. Quinine gets rid of muscle cramps. I know better than to just bring one, and have no idea why I didn't bring half a dozen pills. I tried to decide whether to take the one pill or wait and see if my condition got worse. It was kind of like the cyanide pill that spies carried. Then the spies had to decide whether they could tolerate the torture or did they need to kill themselves rather than spill the beans. Fortunately, my problem was not that bad. I held off taking the pill for one more day.

Marlow lugged the luggage (is that where the word *luggage* came from—lugged?) to the hotel foyer for our five fifteen a.m. departure. I trailed after him feeling like a wet dishrag. My brain was definitely not firing on all eight cylinders. When we got to the train station, I handed him the wrong ticket and got everyone confused. The train personnel finally allowed us to board, I eventually found the correct ticket in my suitcase, and we sorted out the error. The good part of that story was they changed our seat numbers, and we were able to sit on the side of the train we wanted with the best views of Barranca del Cobre.

Once everyone was content with his location, Marlow moved to an empty seat so I could stretch out and look at the insides of my eyelids for an hour. The sky was still dark.

At seven o'clock Marlow and I went to the dining car. After tea and toast, I was ready to face another day. I was weak but had no cramps. I might make it all the way home with the quinine pill intact.

We reviewed the canyons we had passed on our trip west; there were several branches with different names, and I soon gave up trying to memorize the titles. The train traveled along Canyon Urique. They all looked alike to me. I would hate to get lost there. I read that the vegetation was ever changing with the elevation but didn't notice a difference. It was oaks and pines and occasional cacti among brown grass. The brochures said the canyons had twenty-three different species of pine and two hundred different species of oak trees, in addition to alder, palm, and fig trees. I suspect it was lovely in the spring and summer. There were cliffs of limestone and granite. If I had been well, it would have seemed much better. We had gone from sea level at Los Mochis to 7,874 feet at Divisadero, where we disembarked.

We took the five-minute shuttle to Barrancas-Posada Mirador Hotel. The hotel was built into the rim of the canyon. Each room had its own balcony. The exterior was painted a bright peach color, and much of the interior was natural wood. The doors and doorframes were hand-carved wood that would surely have brought big bucks back home. The rooms were painted lovely southwestern US colors of peach, aqua, and cream. The hotel was so serene—no road noise, no train noise, and no aircraft noise. There was happy chatter from tourists and occasionally soft Christmas music wafting through our open patio door.

The views were wonderful. I sat on the balcony and enjoyed them while Marlow went on a walk. He was back in ten minutes, huffing and puffing from the exertion. When I read the brochures of this place, I planned on hiking down to the river and seeing the Tarahumara homes, palm trees, and huge fig trees lining the river. I was looking forward to walking the trails with my handy-dandy Polaroid camera. In my weakened condition, I could have made it maybe five minutes on a flat trail. Instead, we looked at native artifacts ladies brought from their homes in the canyon to sell at the hotel.

Marlow ate dinner with other tourists in the hotel dining room. Again, the meal was served at long, heavy wooden tables. The family-style dining encouraged strangers to talk to one another. He then attended a video about the area, how it was geologically formed, who inhabited it, what minerals were mined, and all that good stuff. He had a couple of beers in the bar with newfound friends. I went to bed at seven after cooking myself a Cup-of-Noodles.

When soaking in hot water would not release the cramped leg muscles, I broke down and took my quinine pill. I got a much better night's sleep. I dreamed that sinister people were trying to extract information from my demented mind. Little did they know, no information resided there.

December 29, 2001 Marlow and I spent the morning taking Polaroid pictures of natives. That was the highlight of the trip for me. They had no idea what was happening. I went from vendor to vendor asking permission to take their picture. Each nodded, although Marlow told me he had learned in the video the night before that the Tarahumara had their own language, and only a few spoke Spanish. I took the pictures and then handed them to Marlow until they dried. One baby about a year or fourteen months old squealed each time the flash went off. I didn't think until later that it might have been from fright rather than delight.

As the images became evident, I asked Marlow to give them to the person portrayed and to explain, "Por usted, Feliz Navidades" (for you, happy holidays). Marlow loved doing that, as each time he was rewarded with smiles and giggles. I went through a roll of film quickly, and Marlow volunteered to walk to our room on the second floor and get more. I told him to bring two packages. He did and soon wanted to walk around the hillsides taking pictures of folks I didn't have the strength to reach. He went through the film and came back beaming.

We finished off my last roll of Polaroid film at the train station and were soon on the train bound for Chihuahua.

I was so glad I had gotten a decent night's sleep and was able to enjoy the scenery and the company of the children on the train. I sipped electrolytes instead of eating train food. Marlow had a delicious-looking cheeseburger with lots of fresh vegetables on it. My intestines were under control; I wanted to keep it that way. Nothing phased his insides.

It was dark when a train employee came down the aisle explaining something very exciting to passengers. Unfortunately, he was speaking Spanish. We didn't know what he was talking about. We asked him to repeat it in English, and he valiantly tried to explain that we would disembark and return the rest of the way to Chihuahua by bus. There had been a train wreck up ahead. As a response to our first question, he said no one was hurt.

I haven't mentioned anything about the dreaded *Federales* that were traveling on the train. Those legendary lawmen looked like our sweet grandson except they had dark hair and eyes. They were polite and friendly. During the transfer from train to bus, an observant Federale handled my part of the luggage transfer, as well as his own. He didn't speak English and smiled tolerantly at my amateur attempts to communicate in Spanish. I wanted to hang on to my camera bag instead of having it tossed under the bus with loads of suitcases piled on top.

The bus made it to the Chihuahua train station an hour earlier than the tour-train's expected arrival. Fortunately, the shuttle driver from our hotel had gone to the station to learn if the tour-train was due to arrive on time. He didn't know anything about the accident. He learned the facts and quickly had our bags stowed in his van and returned us to Hotel San Francisco.

Marlow inflated my air mattress and put it on the floor in the corner of the room. I fell onto the air mattress and slept soundly. Marlow had the bed to himself, so he too got a decent night's sleep.

December 30, 2001 Marlow and I had a long, long, long day of airport inspections and sitting in waiting rooms. The total flight times were less than five hours, but we left the hotel at eight in the morning and arrived home fifteen hours later. Each airport had to inspect us, our luggage, and our shoes. In Chihuahua we didn't have the right papers, and it looked like we were going to have to immigrate. There was no way around it. We had to have the paper someone had given us when we arrived in the country. We finally gave the lady every piece of paper from our suitcases, and she found the one needed to let us leave the country.

While waiting to leave Chihuahua's airport, I read a newspaper. Yes, it was in Spanish, so I had to skip most of the words. The gist of the story said three men had been killed and four additional men injured the evening before when a train hit an agricultural truck headed for Chihuahua. That was the second train accident on our route during the week. The first train was overloaded with agricultural goods and overturned on a curve. No wonder the tour-train traveled so slowly.

I wore my hiking boots; I sure didn't get any use out of them on this trip. It meant a lot of lacing and unlacing at each airport. Mothers had to take their babies' shoes off and put them through x-ray. Would someone really plant a bomb on her own baby?

"Yes," the security officer informed me.

We arrived at El Paso an hour after takeoff from Chihuahua and immediately went to see about getting our scheduled flight to Sacramento changed. Otherwise we would have a five-hour layover in El Paso. The clerk told us that she could get us to Phoenix, but there was no plane space for us to fly from Phoenix to Sacramento. I talked Marlow into taking the earlier plane out of El Paso and hoped someone would not show up at Phoenix so we could get on an earlier flight there.

He agreed to that as long as our luggage could be checked through all the way to Sacramento. The airline agreed to that. We were on the flight that left El Paso in thirty minutes. Perfect timing. Then we arrived in Phoenix and immediately tried to change our flight to Sacramento. No chance. The one and only earlier flight was booked full and had over twenty people on standby. We stood close to the counter along with twenty or thirty other people until that flight took off an hour after our arrival. We all were still standing there as the doors closed. Our shoulders slumped, and we dejectedly wandered off. We were in the United States, land of the free and home of the drinkable water. I wanted to eat vegetables, lots of vegetables.

We went to a steak-house restaurant in the airport, and I had a veggie sub sandwich and ate about half of Marlow's French fries. I usually have about four French fries, and that is all I want. Oh my, everything tasted good. My malady wasn't terminal! I would live after all!

Eight hours after arrival in Phoenix, we were on a plane to Sacramento. Whoops! Now what was happening? A young man asked to check my ticket, as I was sitting in his seat. What a sinking feeling. My ticket was a duplicate of his. The woman sitting next to Marlow spoke up and said, "Well, this man is sitting in my seat, so I'm going to stay right here." All the seats in the plane were taken, and we still had four people standing in the aisle. The stewardess announced a $400.00 coupon toward another flight to anyone willing to give up his seat and take the one a.m. flight to Sacramento. Another five hours in that airport? No way! The delay was not worth four hundred dollars to me. Gratefully, it was worth it to other folks. We left the gate ten minutes late, and Marlow and I were still onboard.

The only turbulence that we experienced was going over the Sierras, and it was violent. I was looking toward the front of the plane and saw the insides torque first to the right and then to the left. It looked like the plane was going to be twisted in half right behind the wings. My stomach did a little flip-flop, and I thought it would be better to look out the window. This was one of the rare times I had a window seat. It was raining, it was snowing. It looked so pretty and sparkly in the plane's lights. It didn't look the least bit threatening. I kept my eyes glued to the window until we were beyond the Sierras and gliding toward home base.

Our baggage made the earlier plane from Phoenix, so it was sitting outside the America West office when we arrived. We didn't have to wait for the luggage to come off our transport plane. We picked up the suitcases and walked to the door where the shuttle was waiting. The husband of the lady who had driven us to the Sacramento airport on December 23 drove sanely through the rain and cold of a typical Sacramento winter night. He asked if we had bad weather on our trip. We told him it had been perfect. He said Sacramento had had rain every day for a week, and there was record snow in the Sierras.

Twelve

To Alaska or Bust, From Alaska Busted

2002

Marlow worked at Aerojet as a contractor, and his current contract had come to an end. Aerojet had a new policy that contract employees had to take a break after eleven months on the job. He was sixty-six years old and eligible for Social Security, so why not quit work altogether? He'd retire! To start his retirement, he wanted to go on a trip. We discussed it and decided on an extended trip to Alaska. We'd take our travel trailer and drive to Alaska, leaving Fort Jones, California, the first week of June and returning in October. I researched British Columbia, the Yukon Territory, and Alaska and made up a schedule of sights to see along the way.

June 2, 2002 The odometer reading was 13,528 on Marlow's Toyota Tundra when he and I left Fort Jones, California, for his first postretirement trip. We spent the day leisurely driving through lush rural areas and the mountains of Northern California and Southern Oregon. The sun was shining, the temperature was perfect, and the roads were good.

Marlow was in an especially good mood, as he had taken a handful of lotto tickets to the store to verify that we were not millionaires.

That proved true, but he had won an incredible $59.00! We were sure that was the sign we would have good fortune on our vacation.

We pulled into our first destination, Diamond Lake, Oregon, and took a lakefront pull-through campsite. Marlow didn't have to go through the hassles of unhooking the trailer after parking it. There were no other campers in the spacious grounds; we had our own private lake. We spent the twilight hour walking around the campground, inhaling deeply, as the air was pine-scented after a recent rain.

Over years of camping, we had developed evening entertainment we both enjoyed. We played Chinese checkers, or I read aloud from the classics. For this trip I brought Jack London stories and Robert Service poems. Tonight's story was *To Build a Fire* by Jack London. Marlow raised the temperature on the thermostat twice during the reading.

June 3, 2002 Marlow decided the lake water was too cold to put the inflatable raft in the water. He bought the raft especially for the trip to Alaska. I didn't expect the water to warm up as we traveled north but said nothing.

We were out on the lake in a rental boat before ten. Marlow left the marina with the required safety equipment, a thermos of coffee, a Styrofoam container of night crawlers, his tackle box, a fishing rod, and high hopes. I had a good book, a thermos of cinnamon tea, an inflatable pillow, and no optimistic expectations.

Marlow got a couple of bites before landing his first fish. The little trout had hardly enough meat on it for a single sandwich. Marlow tossed it back.

An hour later he was thrilled when "the big one" took his bait. The pole flexed into the water. It was at that moment Marlow realized he hadn't brought the fishnet. He played the fish so it would be worn-out and easier to get from the water into the boat.

He landed the fish! What a beauty! The flashy bright hues glimmered in the sun as the eighteen-inch rainbow trout flopped about on the boat floor. I whipped out my camera and took a picture of Marlow holding his prize. The fish didn't appear the least bit worn-out. He was full of fight and bound to get even with Marlow for tricking him with that juicy worm. The fish succeeded.

Marlow started to remove the treble hook. He was holding the fish in place on the floor with his foot; the fish was strong enough to throw his head to one side at just the right moment to drive a barbed hook through Marlow's finger.

Oh my gosh! I was instantly nauseous. The fish writhed wildly, freeing itself from Marlow's foot. Marlow told me to take the hook out of his right hand or out of the fish's mouth, as he needed his left hand and both feet to control the muscular animal.

I tried, really I did. I was also being cautious not to get caught by the third barb. I was at the point of panic thinking of the pain the two caught animals were going through. Of course, the barbed hook would not go back through Marlow's finger the way it had gone in. The second barb was imbedded in the fish's jawbone.

Marlow said to hit the fish in the head and knock it out. I looked about for a weapon and found the oar. I thought better of swinging the oar at the united pair.

I emptied the tackle box looking for a blunt instrument. Nothing in the tangled mass of fishing line, lures, lead weights, and little jars of smelly goo would suffice. I looked for pliers to cut the hook or pinch the barb and found none. I did find a penknife and bravely suggested that I stab the fish.

Marlow agreed, and I held the two-inch knife in two hands in the fashion learned from the movie *Psycho*. Marlow had second thoughts about me stabbing the fish. If I missed, he might come up missing a finger. He suggested I cut off its head.

I couldn't do that! Marlow was sure I could and convinced me I had the ability to decapitate an animal. I held the knife an inch behind the pulsating gill, apologized profusely to the fish, and inserted it. I kept saying, "I'm sorry, I'm sorry" aloud. Silently I was saying, "Don't faint. *Don't* faint!"

"For heaven's sake, cut his head off," Marlow said. "Don't just sit there mumbling." I didn't realize my hand was motionless.

The sight of blood on Marlow's hand gave me the incentive I needed. I started cutting. There was suddenly blood everywhere. I carefully avoided looking at the accusing eye staring blankly at me. Marlow's hands were covered with blood. My hands were covered with blood. The fish was covered with blood.

The fish's head was soon free from the body. The hook was still imbedded in both the head and the finger. With more gumption than I knew I possessed, I cut the hook out of the mutilated fish head.

Marlow told me to cut the Rapala lure from his finger. My gumption was totally depleted. There was no way I could deliberately cut a human being.

"Do you have any pliers?" Marlow yelled.

"No!" I yelled back. "I would have used them if I did."

I realized Marlow was looking past me. I turned to see a boat about thirty feet away. Where had it come from? It was a miracle! There wasn't another boat on the whole lake.

The fisherman did have pliers and squeezed the barb flat so the hook could retrace its path through Marlow's finger. We expressed our gratitude and headed for shore. The fisherman called to our departing boat, "You're not going to call it quits now, are you? It looks like you're having good luck." We said nothing in return.

What an ordeal! I was totally drained. Fortunately, our campsite was nearby, and we docked the boat there. Our travel trailer never looked so inviting.

Inside the trailer I offered Marlow a Vicodin pain pill left over from my last dental surgery. He said he didn't need it. I held the pill for a few seconds trying to decide whether I should take it myself or not. Decided "not."

Marlow stood in the tiny bathroom washing his hands. I stood behind him suggesting that I take him to the hospital for stitches and a tetanus shot. I suspect he thought about his brand-new Toyota Tundra attached to the new travel trailer (which I had never towed), the mountainous terrain between us and the hospital, and emphatically rejected my offer.

I felt I should at least flush the open wounds with peroxide and tape them closed so they would stop hemorrhaging. That suggestion was rejected also with the statement that he'd need the pain pill, if I did that.

He turned and showed me two teensy, tiny black holes on either side of his finger. I gasped at the pinprick-size wounds in awe. All that blood belonged to the fish!

Marlow put on a Band-Aid, changed clothes, and took the rental boat to the marina. I showered, changed clothes, and drank a glass of wine while visualizing the emergency room staff's expressions if we had rushed into the hospital seeking assistance for Marlow's wounds.

June 4, 2002 Marlow didn't want to go fishing for some reason, so we spent the day in the campground. I wrote four letters and made a malachite pendant. Lapidary and jewelry making are two of my many hobbies. We walked six kilometers. Distance in the campground was in kilometers rather than miles. It was lovely, sunny weather, a near-perfect day.

June 5–7, 2002 We rode through scenic, selectively cleared pine forests dotted with fishing lakes on our way from Diamond Lake to Interstate Five, the West Coast's main conduit between Mexico and Canada.

Once on the freeway, we went along with the flow of traffic on our way into Portland, Oregon, where we stayed with my cousin, Susan, and her family for two nights and one full day.

June 8, 2002 We awoke at five and made our way to Port Angeles, Washington, to catch a ferry to Victoria, Vancouver Island, British Columbia, Canada. We departed from the ferry after a smooth, pleasant hour-and-a-half crossing of Puget Sound.

The tour book I received from British Columbia said it was all right to take a rifle into Canada, as long as we declared it at the border. Marlow wanted to take his .22 rifle for when we were camped in the Alaskan wilderness in case of bear or wolf attack (he had seen movies showing how dangerous it was to visit Alaska). The book said we would have to fill out a registration form and would then be on our way. Not so folks, not so.

The young man who worked for Canadian customs quizzed us extensively and was immediately suspicious when we told him we wanted to register a rifle. He told us to drive to one side and park, blocking perpendicularly parked cars. We were still in the lane of off-loading traffic from the ferry. Five minutes later a second customs officer told us to park at the curb, which made more sense. We sat there thirty minutes before Marlow went to the customs officer and asked if they had forgotten us. A twentyish female officer told him to return to his vehicle and not to leave it again. A bit rude, we thought.

Fifteen minutes later the same young woman came to the window and asked another series of nonsensical questions, such as did we have any automatic weapons, exactly how long were we going to be in Canada, exactly where were we going to be spending nights. We answered all her questions to the best of our knowledge. We explained that we were taking a leisurely tour of the country on our way through to Alaska.

She announced she'd have to see the gun. Marlow got the unloaded gun out of the trailer closet. He told her the bullets were in the glove compartment of the truck. The officer told him to return to his truck. He did so, wondering why she stayed in the trailer.

Fifteen more minutes went by, and nothing happened except we saw a second woman enter the trailer. I got out of the truck and went to the trailer door and asked if there was a problem. One woman left the trailer without speaking to me and went to the driver's side of the truck to tell Marlow to get out of the truck; she wanted to search it.

The woman in the trailer asked me how much wine I had told the customs officer we had. I replied that we had a two-liter cardboard box in the refrigerator. It had been opened some weeks before, and I had no idea how much was left inside. She said she had found a second container in overhead storage, so they had to search every inch of the trailer. She had been going through the trash when I entered the trailer. Did she think I hid a can of beer or bottle of wine under the coffee grounds and eggshells? Later, I discovered they had unwrapped frozen meat from the freezer. I had no idea where the second container of wine came from, or why the customs officer looked in the overhead storage bin in the first place. Perhaps our son Darryl left it there as a surprise for us. He had used the trailer just before our departure. At any rate it was only wine, not heroin.

What nonsense! They would not allow us to be present when they were searching our belongings. Pretty scary; they could have planted narcotics in the trailer, stolen our belongings, done any number of things. We were there two hours, had to fill out several forms and pay a $35.00 registration on a $100.00 gun.

Marlow told the customs officer that we had not planned on accessing the gun in Canada, just when we were in the wilds of Alaska. She responded that was good because it was against the law to use a gun to defend yourself from bears or wolves in Canada. Say what?

We tried to tour Victoria, a beautiful city, but found we were too upset over our treatment at customs. We decided the best thing would be to get out of town before we took out our frustration on some innocent Canadian.

When we reached Duncan, we stopped at the Cowichan Indian Cultural Center and took their tour. The aborigine explained the meanings of the various totem poles. The poles consisted mainly of carvings of mythical thunderbirds, salmon, bears, and frogs. Women or gods were represented by thunderbirds. Men were bears, frogs represented the surrounding mountains, and salmon depicted the sea, lake, or river. Since I was interested in cultures of the world, I found this tour interesting and informative.

We found a campground at Quinnell Lake and backed our trailer against the waterfront. Quinnell Lake was just what we needed—calm water, blue skies, green trees, wild flowers, and tame bunnies hopping around the campground.

June 9, 2002 It was so peaceful at the campground that we chose to stay an extra night. It was good to be retired. We rented a rowboat (it was "too far to carry the raft to the dock"). Marlow did install the motor he brought to go with the raft onto the rental rowboat. The morning was spent riding around on the lake observing Canada geese, ducks, and a few jumping fish. We didn't try to catch the fish.

The afternoon was spent walking trails and playing with the rabbits encountered everywhere. Marlow socialized with the campground host while I read my novel, *Carry the Wind*, a western.

June 10, 2002 The route across Vancouver Island from Quinell Lake to Tofina was through thick forests and along large lakes. The weather went from sunny blue skies and warm temperatures to gloomy, cold fog.

We saw many spots of clear-cut forest and hoped Canada wasn't depleting its forest to feed the appetites of Yankees.

June 11, 2002 Today was our day to play with whales. Marlow and I were two of the four passengers on the small sight-seeing boat. It was an hour-long boat ride to the whale area. The ride itself was worth the price of the ticket.

We were given full-length, heavy-duty suits that doubled as flotation devices, and it was just as well we wore them. The swells were ten to fifteen feet high. The boat occasionally left the water after cresting a swell. My stomach left its allotted space in my abdomen at the same time and jumped into my throat. Then both the boat and my stomach crashed as we hit the bottom of the next dip.

We saw several gray whales but kept our distance. The blow of a spout alerted us to the fact the whale was about to surface. We observed the slow-motion curve of the graceful back as it came out of the water. We saw one tail flip but didn't catch it on film, as the choppy waters made picture taking impossible. The adult whales were up to forty-five feet long and barnacle encrusted. We were thrilled to be close to these gentle giants in their own element.

On the boat ride back to the harbor, we stopped along the shore to visit with a pair of nesting bald eagles. The boat driver said they had a little one in their nest, but we didn't see it.

After the tour Marlow and I drove through the oceanfront rainforest to our campground. We parted company there—I took a hike along the beachfront and through the forest while Marlow napped. What a wonderful day!

June 12–14, 2002 Marlow deviated from the itinerary. Heck, that was what retirement was all about. Instead of touring the rest of Vancouver Island, we went back to the mainland.

On the way there, we stopped at Sproat Lake to view the enormous flying tankers used to douse forest fires. A crew climbed in a boat and motored out to a floatplane. We watched the plane for thirty minutes, hoping to see it take off. No such luck; it remained stationary.

We caught the ferry from Discovery Bay, Vancouver Island, to Horseshoe Bay, Northern Vancouver City, then slowly wended our way through town in rush-hour traffic and headed to Cultus Lake, where we stayed at a wonderful Thousand Trails Campground for three nights.

There was a heated pool where we could float on our backs and view surrounding mountains. There were lots of leafy green trees and spacious campsites. The campground was attached to an emerald-green golf course. We ate at the clubhouse and watched golfers do their thing. I strolled around the perimeter of the golf course. There were times when I appreciated mankind's efforts to create a beautiful environment. This golf course was like a botanical garden, with green grass separating other foliage.

June 15–16, 2002 We dazzled our senses on a self-guided tour at gorgeous Minter Gardens in the Fraser River Valley. There were hybrid flowers planted in neat little gardens with different themes from Oriental to Victorian. We walked the forest trail to view Bridal Veil Falls through deciduous/evergreen mixed forest.

We drove on to Lac la Hache (LACK-la-clash). The English translation for the French was "Ax Lake." I presumed that referred to its shape and not to a sinister murderer wandering the area. The friendly German proprietor of the campground gave us a full hookup site for US$15.00 a night for two nights. Wow! I was going to like camping in Canada.

We rented a boat, attached our motor, and toured the large lake surrounded by spruce forests. I forget what excuse was used for not using the raft carefully stored in the back of Marlow's truck. There were delightful homes well spaced, perhaps on hectare-sized blocks, scattered around the lake's edge. A hectare equals about two and a quarter acres, but Canadians, like Englishmen and Australians, didn't use acres as a measurement of land.

I was able to take walks each evening, which was such a pleasant way to spend the long twilight. Each time we moved further north, the days got longer. The sun rose about five thirty and set about nine at Lac la Hache. The sky was light for an hour to an hour and a half on either side of the sun's appearance.

Marlow went fishing, so I guess he was over the fishhook scare. He got a couple of bites, but didn't catch dinner.

June 17, 2002 Today was a day on the road through lush forests and picturesque farmland. The construction material of choice was logs. We saw all manner of log homes and outbuildings.

We also saw our first moose of the trip. Marlow saw a gray fox, and we both saw a couple of deer. The deer were much larger than the ones around Fort Jones. We looked forward to seeing more wildlife as we went north.

As I write this, it is nine at night, and the sun is still well above the horizon. We have settled into a free municipal campsite in the town of Burns Lake, British Columbia. The little lakeside park is in town, but I suspect they will roll up the sidewalks within an hour. It'll be quiet enough for sleep, if not dark enough. I use eyeshades to block out the light.

June 18, 2002 After much searching and getting directions from three different people, we found the 'Ksan Historical Village, a native village tourists could visit. We enjoyed a wonderful tour and learned much about the Gitxsan people. There are approximately 11,000 in the world and 3,500 in the Hazelton, British Colombia, area. They are a handsome, friendly, educated people willing to share their culture with curious tourists.

We enjoyed the tour so much that we decided to stay in their campground.

After my walk along overflowing Kispiox River, I tried something new. I took our videos and audiotapes around the campground to see if anyone wanted to trade with us. We have watched most of the videos we brought along. We have also listened to two books on audiotapes. I was hoping someone else would have tapes they had seen or heard. No such luck, but I did have enlightening conversations with several people.

June 19, 2002 Today was a red-letter day for wildlife viewing. We saw a black bear. We also saw two moose, two ptarmigans, a fox, a rabbit, and a bald eagle.

We took a side trip, Route 37A through the Canadian countryside until we came to the border of Alaska. We went across to Hyder, the most southerly point of Alaska accessible by car. The village was like a ghost town, so we didn't get out of the truck. We drove through town, and everything was closed. We made a U-turn and went back into British Columbia. The crossing guard made no commotion about the gun or wine, just looked at the paperwork and welcomed us to Canada. We learned later that there were some nice parks out of Hyder where we could have seen grizzlies fishing for salmon.

Driving through the gorge on Route 37A was the best part of the trip so far. The scenery was spectacular. Many times we could see half a dozen cascading waterfalls in the same scene. We saw several glaciers, rushing torrents of water in every stream and river, an escarpment of solid rock and mile after mile of spruce forests. Early explorers called Alaska "the Land of Little Sticks," because of all the straight spruce trees.

June 20–26, 2002 We rode through mountainous scenery along the Cassiar Highway, a well-graded gravel road with very little traffic.

Yesterday, June 20, sunset was at eleven twenty and sunrise this morning was a few minutes after four o'clock.

Marlow had cut a week's worth of touring from the itinerary. We were now at the place I thought we would arrive at on July 2. He didn't want to disconnect the truck and trailer, so basically the only sight-seeing we did in the evenings was within walking distance of the trailer.

On July 20 we ate the worst Chinese meal ever. The "garlic barbecue ribs" were strange tasting, and I suspected we were eating dog tail, as the bones were little discs. Marlow thought perhaps the round cylinders called ribs were actually oxtail from mighty small oxen. We each tried two bites and left the rest untouched. The ultra-greasy noodles had no flavor and barely stayed down when they hit my stomach. I was nauseated for four hours. Marlow said it was my imagination at work after eating dog tail. I wished he hadn't said that.

Yesterday, the twenty-fifth, we did have something good to eat—homemade rhubarb pie. The nice lady manager of the campground baked it.

Each evening we played Chinese checkers or read. If we had electricity, we watched a video brought from home. At bedtime one or the other of us always said, "How can a person get to sleep when it is still so light outside?" Within two or three minutes, Marlow was snoring away. Lucky guy. I eventually dropped off with the help of eyeshades and the towels I'd draped over the windows.

We saw a moose yesterday and a couple of elk today. We also saw a couple of bald eagles each day. We were always delighted to see animals in their natural habitat. Marlow reacted like a kid on his first trip away from the big city—not that Fort Jones is a big city. The current population is 660 people.

The place where we were waiting for mail to catch up to us was called Destruction Bay on Kluane Lake. It got that name in 1942. The base camp set up there for workers laying the Alaska Highway was destroyed by strong winds. Sixty years later we spent most of the day inside our trailer because of wind. Combine that with temperatures hovering around fifty degrees, and it was downright uncomfortable outside.

The owner of the RV park promised she would go into town and pick up mail on Wednesday. That meant we would be staying put until we saw if our forwarded mail arrived. It was addressed in care of the RV park. Marlow was expecting his final paycheck from his employer. We had a lady in Fort Jones forwarding our mail to certain places according to the original itinerary. It took ten days to two weeks to get mail from Fort Jones to Canada.

I phoned Linda in Fort Jones and told her to send our next package to Anchorage. Everything would have been okay if we hadn't deviated from the original itinerary. Marlow agreed with all the stops I had listed. Once we were on the road, he got antsy and wanted to start making better time. He didn't realize he would get tired of traveling so quickly. Now he said he wanted to hurry up and see Alaska so he could get home to his recliner, television, and his own bed. The original trip was supposed to take four months. We had only been on the road twenty-six days, and he was homesick.

June 27, 2002 We left the RV park without our mail and drove to the post office, which we then learned was only open Monday and Wednesday from one to five. I tacked a note on the front door asking them to forward our mail to General Delivery in Anchorage and hoped the note wouldn't blow away.

Then we left Kluane Lake. We never did see a grizzly, though we took several short walks along the lake. Grizzlies were supposed to be plentiful. We had seen a bite one took out of the corner of a cabin. Thank goodness it didn't taste good, and he didn't eat more.

We drove to Tok, Alaska, and had no problems whatsoever crossing through American customs with our gun in the closet and wine in the kitchen. The mature customs inspector merely asked if our gun shot more than one bullet when we pulled the trigger. It was a .22 rifle, not an automatic assault weapon.

We camped by the Tok River in a $10.00-per-night state park. Our site was a nice double-wide, with the river flowing past our back windows.

The RV and truck were filthy on the outside from the dusty Cassiar Highway. The gravel roads were flatter and smoother than the paved roads with all of their frost heaves and potholes. I suspected the trailer would stay dirty until October, when we returned to Fort Jones.

June 28, 2002 Sunset last night was at eleven-forty-five, sunrise this morning was three-twenty-one. I know the announcement of sunrise and sunset is getting trite, but it amazes me every day.

We had an incredible day for scenery! It started out being merely beautiful from Tok to Glenallen. Then the views from the Richardson Highway up and over Thompson Pass became absolutely spectacular. There weren't pullouts every five hundred yards, or I would have used up all my film.

The glaciers were young and active; the melt-back created multiple waterfalls. Some mountains looked like they were covered with velvet, the greenery was so uniform in size and color. Other mountains were a riot of color. The rest were just magnificent granite protrusions sculptured by working glaciers.

Soon after entering the Alaska Highway at Glenallen, a semitrailer passed us. We were driving forty-five miles per hour, which was reasonable for the load we were hauling and the dipsy-doodle condition of the road. The road had frost heaves—sudden depressions where the ground had sunk under the pavement. It happened when the ground thawed, froze, and thawed again. There were a lot of curves also.

The semitrailer was probably going sixty-five. A half mile further down the road, we reached a long straight section; the truck was not in sight. I mentioned to Marlow he was really barreling along to get that far ahead of us. The driver was an accident waiting to happen.

Sure enough, an hour later a policeman waved us around the overturned semi. The driver had lost control, went up the embankment on the far side of the road, and rolled the truck onto its side. It didn't look like there were any other cars involved, thank goodness. There were no tire tracks to show he had hit his brakes.

We walked to the base of Worthington Glacier and admired its blue-ice, gray-gravel-filled moraines, and rushing silt-filled streams.

We limped into Valdez (val-DEES) exhausted from exhilaration. We stayed at Sea Otter RV Park on Prince William Sound. Our camping spot backed onto the boat channel. We could watch various yachts, fishing, and tour boats come and go from the popular marina. Prince William Sound is the most southerly ice-free port in Alaska.

Marlow and I went to the community center and watched a video on the devastating Good Friday 1964 earthquake. The quake registered 9.2 on the Richter scale.

Valdez lost thirty-one people out of a population of four hundred. The lives that were saved were spared because of community spirit. The few cars in town were used to carry the population up Thompson Pass and away from the enormous tidal waves. Every able-bodied man, woman, and child became heroes for the injured, trapped, infants, and elderly. What a horrific story! They lost all the town's buildings to tsunami waves. One wave tipped a ship on its side, and then the receding water righted the ship again.

June 29, 2002 Marlow and I experienced another totally wonderful day entirely different from yesterday. We scheduled a five-hour tour of Prince William Sound. The *LuLu Belle* boat tour went over the area affected by the *Exxon Valdez* oil spill. The captain told us there was a very small area actually affected, that oil had drifted to three islands. There were dozens of unaffected islands in the sound. He also said it was absurd for the tanker to go aground on the well-marked shoal. There was no logical excuse for the accident. But the captain said the harm done was greatly exaggerated in the press. The Sierra Club claimed they spilled one hundred million gallons of oil. I didn't know who was telling the truth. The ship was banned from entering Prince William Sound in the future. The *Exxon Valdez* was repaired at the cost of $30 million and sold to a company that hauled oil from the Middle East to Europe. Exxon built the town of Valdez, a huge community center and sports complex as compensation.

On our tour the captain entertained us with excellent stories of the area—historical, geological, and biological. He knew where the animals were and showed us Steller sea lions, harbor seals, tufted puffins, bald eagles, and sea otters. When we were among the animals, he stopped the boat and allowed the animals to approach as close as they wanted. We had not seen whales when it was time to return to port. The weather was perfect; we had seen so much beauty and so many animals. I felt we certainly got our money's worth ($75.00 each).

The captain didn't share my opinion. Captain Fred Rodolf of the *LuLu Belle* took us beyond the Hinchinbrook Islands and searched and searched until we came upon a pod of whales. Then he cruised into their oncoming path and shut off his motors. He let the whales swim toward us. They played around and under our boat with no fear. There were some great photo ops. I got excited trying to take pictures so fast that I broke my camera. The extra effort of the captain added two hours to a wonderful experience.

I was sure he would cruise past the scheduled stop at Columbia Glacier since we were late returning to shore—not that we had to worry about darkness overtaking us. No way, man! Captain Rodolf slowly crept into the iceberg-strewn water until we were as close as was safe, stopped the boat, and let the crew take pictures of people in front of the glacier with their own cameras. He said we would want to use the pictures as Christmas cards. I bought a disposable camera from a crew member to take pictures of the glacier and icebergs. I did get some wonderful video footage of the glacier calving—that's where big chunks of ice break off and slide into the water with a thunderous crash.

On Glacier Island Captain Rodolf came within two feet of the rocky cave walls so we could see the tiny eight-inch-tall puffins roosting in the crevices. I'd expected them to be the size of penguins. What am I saying! Maybe penguins are eight inches tall. I don't know. I haven't been to Antarctica (yet). The five-hour tour took nine hours, but I didn't hear a single person complain.

Valdez had moderate temperatures compared to other places in Alaska—average December and January daytime temperature was twenty-two degrees. The snow accumulated throughout the winter. We were told by the museum docent that they frequently had twenty-feet of snow in town, and it sometimes didn't melt completely until July. On Thompson Pass, east of town, the *average* snowfall accumulation was eighty feet. No wonder there were so many glaciers, over 100,000 in Alaska.

June 30, 2002 Marlow and I spent a few hours visiting museums. I admire the hardy people who trek into unknown wilderness and set down roots. Here in Valdez, early settlers were men making their way to the Klondike gold fields. There were half a dozen fishermen living in tents on shore when the first shipload of miners landed. The miners forged a trail over Valdez Glacier and ice fields to get to the gold discovery areas. Of more than four thousand people who attempted the trek, four hundred made it. No one knows how many found gold, but the museum suggested that perhaps forty were lucky enough to make a living off prospecting. Many others set up supply stores for miners who were on their way to the fields and made enough to live out their lives comfortably. Most miners went home broke, some died in their attempts to obtain a fortune.

July 1, 2002 We were on the road again, over Thompson Pass in dense fog, with visibility at about fifty feet. Marlow crept along at a reasonable speed. Every once in a while, someone passed us. I didn't understand why drivers felt it was necessary to take a chance on losing their lives and destroying someone else's life to get to the other side fifteen minutes before us.

As we descended the mountain, visibility gradually improved. We were able to resume normal speeds. The day remained gray, and the awesome scenery we saw on a clear day while approaching Valdez was shrouded in fog or clouds. I was so glad we were privileged to see that splendor a few days earlier.

We were soon on the outskirts of Palmer headed for a musk ox farm. We spent a delightful hour learning about the shaggy beasts. They had changed little in 600,000 years. How did the owners know that? From discoveries made by archaeologists, I guess. Anyhow, we had good fun seeing them and learning a bit about their habits. At one time hunters had decimated all the musk oxen in Alaska. The animals stood in a straight line or in a circle around their babies when faced by a predator. It made them easy prey for men. Some oxen were imported from Norway about thirty years ago. They are protected now in Alaska and are gradually making a comeback.

July 2, 2002 It was holiday time, and we were lucky to get a parking space for our trailer in Seward. Our neighbors told us someone had left the site we chose five minutes before we pulled in. It was just a parking lot, but at least it was on the waterfront (no mosquitoes) and had public toilets and showers.

I made friends with the neighbors and plied them for information on the area. They lived in Palmer, a hundred miles away, so they had the "scoop."

July 3, 2002 Marlow and I went to the Sea Center in Seward, which was comparable to Monterey Aquarium except it didn't have as many tourists. We got to see those darling tufted puffins up close, I mean like ten feet away. They were in a controlled environment of rock walls with a waterfall and a large, glassed-in pool. I loved learning their behavior, and they wore such cute costumes. I had fun watching them in the water with the kittiwakes-a gull that couldn't dive. When food was thrown in the water, both the puffins and kittiwakes swam like crazy to get to it. If it sank, the puffins won. The Sea Center had to be considered one of the highlights of a trip that started out good and was getting better and better.

July 4–8, 2002 We took the neighbors' advice and booked a tour on a boat with a ranger onboard. We saw Kenai Fjords, which were grand. The wildlife—otters, puffins, harbor seals, and Steller sea lions—were wonderful. We shared a table with a young personable couple from Michigan. Every person was assigned a table. Ours was on the upper deck with window seats. I spent most of the time running around on the decks trying to see everything at once.

We had chosen to take our trip on the fourth, as we knew there was a lot of hoopla scheduled in town. The town holds an Independence Day Marathon. Racers ran up a hill, around the top, and back down at an elevation of about 1,700 feet; the angle looked to me to be about thirty degrees. The record time for men was forty-five minutes. The record set by a woman was sixty-six minutes. It would have taken me three days.

We went to the races in the morning before catching our tour and saw the six-to-sixteen-year-olds group take off at nine thirty. There were about two hundred kids in the race. They had to reach different levels of elevation according to their age.

There were vendors as usual at such an event. The difference was, this time the hot dogs were made from reindeer or caribou. It was too early in the morning to try this exotic delicacy.

Due to the crowds, Marlow found a parking space a half mile from the boat dock. I was tired, I couldn't carry my camera equipment that far, and Marlow was loaded down with his own paraphernalia. I protected his camera gear as well as my own and waited for him to retrieve the car and bring it to me.

A live band was doing an excellent imitation of the Eagles, my favorite band on a bandstand near me. It took Marlow forty-five minutes to get the car and drive back. His driving time was twice what it took him to walk to the car. The roads were jammed with holidaymakers. The town's population was normally 2,100. This weekend they expected 10,000 visitors.

Marlow said when he started his truck, a woman came out of the motor home parked next to him and asked if he was going to return. He told her no. She said, "Oh good." He told her he didn't feel they had known each other very long, so how could it have been that bad? Hopefully she laughed as she put a folding chair in the vacant space.

We made it to our trailer through the jubilant crowd. It felt good to be in the comfort of our little home away from home. Boat passengers had a late lunch of prime rib and salmon included in the tour price, so Marlow and I didn't want dinner. As it was ten at night, we showered and went to bed. I ached all over, so I took two aspirin before retiring, hoping I was not coming down with a cold or influenza.

Fireworks were scheduled at sunset after midnight. The blasts awakened me. My *left* shoulder and arm hurt. I couldn't lift the arm. I thought perhaps I had slept on it and shut off circulation. After waiting a few minutes to see if the arm would move and the pain go away, I took a couple more aspirin and went back to sleep.

At two o'clock I was awakened by the pain in my *right* shoulder and arm. I figured I had picked up a virus. I could move my right arm a minimal amount, but my left shoulder and arm were paralyzed. I took two more aspirin—which was six aspirin in six hours. I slept restlessly, as the pain came in waves. The pain floated from the shoulders, to the elbows, to the wrists, and then back to the shoulders.

In the morning I could move the left arm a small amount, but not the right one. I got my left thumb hooked over the belt of my pajamas, but didn't have the strength to push them down. Marlow helped me go to the bathroom and get dressed. I wondered if I had had a stroke. Marlow accepted my opinion that I couldn't go to the hospital in case the illness was multiple sclerosis or muscular dystrophy. I didn't want to establish a record of having a preexisting ailment the week before I was eligible for Medicare. I didn't know if Medicare would pay for months and months of hospitalization if I got an ailment the week before I turned sixty-five.

Marlow helped me climb into the Tundra, and then he secured the inside of the trailer by putting everything on the floor that could have fallen en route. Securing the interior was normally my job, and he couldn't figure out where things went.

In spite of how badly I felt, Marlow said it was mandatory we get on the road so we would get to the post office in Anchorage before they closed. He really wanted that paycheck. I wanted to stay in Seward another day and recover from my ailment.

The pain was excruciating, so Marlow fed me a Vicodin. I couldn't lift a glass of water with either hand. The Vicodin and exhaustion helped me sleep after we were on the road. I dozed off and on until we got into Anchorage traffic.

As we approached the post office, Marlow asked, "Can you just jump out and run in and see if our mail is there while I drive around the block?"

I told him no. I didn't even swear. I couldn't move either hand enough to reach the door handle, let alone have the strength to depress the lever, jump out, walk to the post office, attempt to open the door, wait in line, and then ask for the mail I couldn't carry anyway.

Marlow parked, went into the post office, and waited in the long line to ask for his mail. The package mailed to us on June 20 had not arrived. That put Marlow in a bad mood. He made arrangements for the post-office to forward our mail to Fairbanks General Delivery.

By mid-afternoon, I was almost out of my mind with pain. Marlow fed me another Vicodin. If it had been Marlow who was in that condition, I would have raced to the nearest emergency ward.

I told Marlow I couldn't stand to ride any farther. We needed to stop so I could lie down. He pulled into a recreational vehicle park and helped me get from the truck to the trailer. He lowered the table, making it into a bed.

I existed on nothing but water and pain pills for the next two days. I couldn't sit up by myself, so Marlow pulled my legs over the side of the bed and lifted me by my armpits. He helped me to and from the bathroom, washed my face and hands between my naps, and tipped glasses to my lips for frequent intake of water.

On the seventh of July, some movement returned to my limbs. I had no idea what was wrong. Marlow said he thought I'd had a heart attack! So, if nothing else, I did learn how Marlow would react if he thought I had a heart attack. Scary.

Marlow decided we had better get back on the road so we could get to the Fairbanks Post Office, our next scheduled mail drop. We both wanted to see Denali, so he made reservations for the twelve-hour tour and booked a camping space just outside the park for two nights.

We toured Denali on July 8 in an old school bus with hard seats. I felt like I was recovering from influenza—tired and achy. I could use my arms and hands minimally. I quit taking pain pills on July 7, so I was able to stay awake. The tour was disappointing to both of us. I thought it was just my imagination because I felt punk. We saw very few animals. The scenery didn't compare to the beauty we had seen along the way. There was just one road, so we saw the same scenery coming and going. We were sixty miles from Mount McKinley. We saw a quick glimpse of it before the cloud cover hid the mountain.

Maybe we needed to go back when we were both healthy. I would do the tour and camping differently. I'd take a hiking tour and camp in the park.

July 9, 2002 We drove the twelve miles permitted by private vehicles into Denali looking for wildlife and saw one moose with a collar on. She must have been the ranger's pet. We saw no other animals.

We watched a fun show by lady rangers. The ladies showed us the care and feeding of their blue-eyed sled dogs used for delivering mail in the winter, as well as for rescue. They were great animals—an Akita mix—and definitely people friendly. The rest of the day, I spent catching up on this journal—celebrating the fact that I could write. I finally had the full use of my hands and shoulders again.

The ranger told us that only about 30 or 40 percent of the people who come to Denali actually get to view Mount McKinley. It is in cloud cover most days.

July 10, 2002 We drove from Denali to Fairbanks and picked up the mail! Hip, hip, hooray! There was no paycheck in the package. Boo, hiss. We settled into Rainbow RV Park on the Chena River in downtown Fairbanks. The brochure the park sent us last March didn't mention that the park was located between the airport and the freeway. The noise was like being in any large city in the Lower Forty-Eight. I was sorry we'd made reservations and paid in advance for this campsite. I would rather have been parked in the wilderness outside of town.

July 11, 2002 We went to the Alaska Bird Observatory and saw several lesser sandhill cranes. What magnificent birds they were to watch. We took a walk through the fields, interrupted by a trillion mosquitoes. In the evening we went to a theater and saw a special show on the aurora borealis, waves of light that form around the Arctic Circle in winter due to an atmospheric phenomenon. When we were buying tickets, and the agent repeated the date, Marlow got a funny look on his face and said, "Is it the eleventh? Well, happy birthday." Scott, our middle son, had sent me enough birthday cake before we left on this trip to last all year. He sent seventeen cakes from a bakery near our home to make up for the cakes he hadn't gotten me before he grew up and left home. That was enough celebration. I was glad to have reached the age where I had Medicare. It was comforting to know I could go to the hospital if I needed to, as long as it didn't interfere with mail pickup.

July 12, 2002 We toured a gold dredge, a historical company village that had been home to the dredge workers, and the machine shop where parts were made and repaired for the dredge. That brought back memories of my days working for Natomas Manufacturing Company in Folsom in the early 1960s, when I was in my early twenties. Natomas shared the same type of business. It had been one of my favorite jobs. I loved listening to the older men tell stories of the early days when dredges ran twenty-four hours a day and the company hired a band to play for community dances on Saturday night. The company owned the houses the men and their families lived in, the water and power to those houses, and the store where the workers spent their paychecks.

I called the Destruction Bay Post Office to see if they had forwarded our package of mail. They said no, they had not. Canadian post offices did not *forward* mail to foreign countries, so they *returned* it to the sender. Excuse me, they couldn't forward it to the United States, but they could return it to the United States? Well, at least we didn't have to look for the check anymore. It would be at home waiting for Marlow.

July 14-15, 2002 It took sixty-five minutes to fly to Barrow, Alaska, from Fairbanks in a Boeing 737. Barrow was the most northerly town in America. The landing strip was the only pavement in town. We saw the marker where Wiley Post and Will Rogers had died in a plane crash. We also saw Barrow Point and the surrounding area on a tour.

Bunna, our Inupiat bus driver and guide, told us:

- The area "enjoyed" eighty-two days of daylight without sunset in summer.
- In winter they had sixty-three days of dark with no sunrise.
- The temperature in the summer had highs in the forties and lows in the twenties. In the winter the range was minus-seventy degrees to minus-forty degrees. Yes, that says minus-seventy degrees and minus-forty.

- o The average annual snowfall level was fourteen inches, and rain was eleven inches.
- o The Eskimos, who preferred to be called First Nation or the Inupiat, had the right to kill six or seven whales a year.
- o The permafrost went three miles deep.
- o Alaska was divided into boroughs. The North Slope Borough consisted of 90,000 square miles. The borough was a corporation. The natives ran different businesses, and the profits were used for the betterment of the borough.
- o They lived on subsistence rules. They had the right to hunt and fish for anything, anytime. They killed bowhead whales, walruses, bearded seals, polar bears, and any fish that came their way.
- o The tide in Barrow was four inches high.

We watched people butchering seals and walruses. We saw a lady scraping the fat layer off the sealskin with her ulu, a special knife with a crescent-shaped blade and a wooden handle between the tips. Marlow and several people on our tour bus tried dried seal meat. Marlow said it tasted fishy.

We went to an Eskimo hunting camp and saw sealskins, polar bear skins, walrus skins and meat hanging on racks to dry. I didn't learn how they kept the wolves at bay.

Marlow and I stayed overnight in Barrow, and I spent time chatting with the desk clerk at the hotel while Marlow caught up on televised news. Rachel was a charming, educated, First Nation woman. She was expecting her fourth child. She had three sons. Two of the sons attended grade school. They were learning their native language, culture, and history, as well as "readin', writin', and 'rithmetic." Her husband worked in construction, and she worked at the hotel five evenings a week.

The Eskimos were big on education and had turned the deserted Quonset huts left by the air force into college classrooms.

Back to the killing of whales, Bunna quoted the following statistics:

- o There are approximately 7,000 bowhead whales in the world. They are increasing in numbers annually by 5 to 8 percent (thirty-five to fifty-six whales).

- The Inupiat will not decimate the population by taking six or seven whales a year. (I wondered what they could possibly do with all that meat, blubber, skin, and so forth in a town of 2,000 people.) But if each borough took six or seven whales…

The Inupiat were close-knit, family-oriented, educated Christians. I wished them well in their quest to keep their culture alive. I hoped they would develop a tradition of killing fewer whales.

The Arctic Ocean was calm on nonwindy days. Both days we were there, the ocean was very smooth. The waves were ripples an inch to two inches high as they tickled the shore. We could see reflections off the multiple small icebergs floating on the surface. Children played on the gravel beach, and in the edge of the water, even at three o'clock in the morning. I watched them from the warmth of our hotel room.

The flight to and from Barrow was clear and calm. We got good views of the Brooks Range and the tundra. We did not see the multitude of caribou as I had hoped. I enjoyed seeing the patterns of streams and rivers as they started and stopped. Sometimes the rivers bent into a U shape, and then the water flow was cut off, and an oxbow lake was formed. There were lots of kettles—ponds formed from melting icebergs of millenniums ago. I later learned some of the lakes were formed from the melting of the permafrost in exceptionally warm spells.

One of the prettiest sights we saw was from the air. We were over rain clouds and saw rainbows—full-circle rainbows of brilliant colors. Marlow said they were a rare weather phenomena he had read about. This was the first time I had seen them, and I was fascinated.

The following morning Marlow and I left Fairbanks and drove to Tok, Alaska. We loved being in a quiet campground once more.

July 17, 2002 We left Alaska via the "Top of the World" route between Tok and Dawson City, Yukon Territory, Canada, and stopped on the way at a settlement called Chicken, Alaska. The miners that founded the town wanted to name their new settlement after the state bird—the ptarmigan. No one knew how to spell *ptarmigan*, but they knew the bird tasted like chicken, and they could spell chicken.

We skillfully made it past the Canadian customs officers without any hullabaloo and drove peacefully into Yukon Territory. We found a nice government campground on the banks of the Yukon River. Marlow and I took our evening stroll on trails along the fast-moving, deep, muddy river. I could almost hear miners working and laughing. My imagination works overtime when I think about pioneers.

We traveled across the Yukon River via a ferry and saw the quaint old town of Dawson. Dawson was in the heart of the Klondike Gold Rush. Some of the houses in the old section of town had sunk a couple of feet. The windows were almost at ground level, and the front doors were only about four feet high. It turned out they were built on the surface of the ground. The heat from inside the home melted the permafrost, and the houses sank.

We ate dinner at Klondike Kate's restaurant. Then we attended a cancan stage show at Diamond Tooth Gerties. There really was a woman who had a diamond imbedded in her front tooth back at the turn of the century. She owned the casino and theater. The building was still operating with the same venue, but was run by the Canadian government.

July 18–19, 2002 Marlow announced he wanted to get home as quickly as possible. He cancelled the rest of the vacation and took the most direct route, stopping only for necessities. For two days we drove and drove and drove. The scenery was nice, which alleviated the tension in the truck cab.

July 20, 2002 Okay, Marlow changed his mind again. He decided we would go the long way around, but not doing extra touristy stuff.

An hour later, he asked if I wanted to stop at Liard Hot Springs. We walked to Liard Hot Springs from the parking lot. The springs were in the far north of British Columbia. The Indians and miners welcomed a stop there for hot baths year-round. The water came out of the ground at one hundred forty degrees, so it was best to stay downstream from the source and let it cool down a bit before it reached the body. Hot tubs set about one hundred four to one hundred six degrees suits me, but I wouldn't want it hotter than that. We didn't go in the water because of Marlow's new time restrictions. We watched other people enjoying themselves as we walked along the creek on a path.

I understood Marlow's problem. He was homesick for beautiful Scott Valley and tired of being on vacation. But at the same time, he didn't want to miss anything. Both made sense.

We camped at Stone Mountain. After we settled in, I was sitting at the dining-room table looking toward the lake. A young man came out of the water naked. He was soon joined by a second naked man. I guessed they were in their early twenties. Completely oblivious to campers, they started snapping their towels at each other. I casually mentioned that there were a couple of young Germans outside who were swimming in that cold, cold water. Marlow asked how I knew they were German. I said because they didn't have any clothes on. Marlow jumped up off the bed and looked out the window.

When he saw the well-built young men playing, he said, "Well, you don't have to look!" That reminded me of Ray Steven's song, *The Streak*—"Don't look, Ethel!" Too late, I had already been incensed.

July 21, 2002 We drove ten hours with no stops for entertainment. We left Stone Mountain and went within ten miles of Dawson Creek, BC. Two good things did happen—we saw some wildlife, and we camped in a provincial park (instead of an RV parking lot). The wildlife consisted of Stone Mountain sheep and bighorn sheep who posed for pictures, a few caribou (yea!), a female elk, a deer, a coyote, a hawk, and a darling little squirrel who entertained us at the campground. The squirrel was a tiny thing not much bigger than a chipmunk and was a deep reddish brown in color. I love feisty, cheeky little animals.

Last night just as we were closing the blinds to go to sleep, we saw another moose strolling down the road. How wonderful to be so blessed with wildlife viewings.

We also saw the winner of the Asshole of the Year award. A jerk in a silver-colored motor home pulling a "toad" (passenger vehicle) passed us on a curve, causing Marlow to hit his brakes hard to let him back in the correct lane in time to prevent a head-on collision. Instead of pulling back in, the driver stayed in the opposing lane, and the three oncoming cars had to hit the shoulder to avoid ramming into him. Fortunately, no one was hurt.

July 22, 2002 We clocked eleven hours of riding with stops for necessities only. Marlow asked me to call Linda, our mail contact in Fort Jones, and tell her to forward our last mail package to Leavenworth, Washington. She said she would do that on the twenty-third. That meant it would arrive in Leavenworth on the thirtieth. The mail only took a week since it didn't have to cross the Canadian border.

July 23, 2002 Marlow looked at the maps. I showed him how we could go a short distance further east and drop down through Jasper-Banff National Parks. He agreed to make the detour. Now if I could just get him to stop for a walk in the woods, I'd be one happy camper.

We were both so glad we experienced the Canadian National Parks of Jasper and Banff. The scenery was spectacular, with towering granite peaks, glaciers, and ice fields surrounded by evergreen forests containing aqua lakes fed by aqua-colored rivers and many waterfalls.

We spent the night inside Jasper National Park at Whistler Campground. The campground had seven hundred eighty one campsites. I expected parties, noise, loud music, and inconsiderate campers and drivers. Instead, each site had fifteen to twenty meters of space around it. People drove slowly and respected the peace of the surroundings. The campsites were laid out in a series of cul-de-sacs off a main beltway. Only campers located in our circle had any reason to drive past our site. The camping sites were hidden in trees, and there was an open field in the center of the cul-de-sac. We realized how many other campers were around us when we went to the ranger lecture at the amphitheater. There were hundreds of people in attendance.

July 24, 2002 We saw a pika, a tiny, round-eared mammal weighing about six pounds, with a loud voice. We also saw a handful of chipmunks and several of those darling little red squirrels today. That was the only wildlife we observed except for a couple of Clark's nutcrackers (birds).

We started the day with a tram ride to the top of a mountain near our campground. I have already told you that every scene in the park was postcard gorgeous. The morning was clear and sunny, and we were there before the crowd. Even Marlow enjoyed it, and he normally hates aerial trams—it's that height thing. Flying machines are fine; doesn't bother him a bit to be in an ultralight with a lawn mower motor keeping him aloft. Trams and high places with railings at the edge make him queasy.

We wended our way south, stopping frequently for treks to outstanding waterfalls, icy-blue glaciers, or crystal-clear lakes. That was the way I had visualized spending the whole trip.

We found another national park campsite in the evening. It was spacious, quiet, and located on pristine Sun Lake, which was fed by a fast-flowing stream from a melting glacier. I walked halfway around the lake while Marlow caught a nap.

I talked to some young folks in swimsuits and asked if they had been in the water. They said they stuck their toes in and it felt like it just melted five minutes ago. Could be. I talked to an older couple who were there on a day-trip from a nearby town. They told me some of the history of the park and the road building. The road was quite a feat, and we were grateful for the men's hard and dangerous work done for our benefit.

After dinner Marlow and I went for a walk along the river until we came to a second lake. We were searching for moose. We found none. We did talk to a man fly-fishing. The water was like a mirror reflecting the surrounding peaks. The man was fishing where that lake emptied into the stream that fed Sun Lake. *Outdoor Magazine*'s photographer would have loved to come across such a scene.

July 25, 2002 We toured the Columbia Icefield at the southern end of Jasper National Park. Saw Peyto Lake, which was turquoise colored like the stone. So was Bow Lake. That was due to milky silt coming from the glaciers.

I took pictures of wild flowers around Peyto Lake, including Barrets willow, which was fuzzy, the hairy-looking anemone, Indian paintbrush, and bell-like alpine heather. During that walk we saw two snowshoe hares.

The most highly touted lake in the area was Lake Louise in Banff National Park. Banff was a continuation of Jasper National Park. Lake Louise was beautiful, to be sure. The area around it was extremely crowded. Tourists were everywhere—in canoes, on walkways, in every hallway and room of the elegant hotel. Negotiating the walk through the hotel was reminiscent of Los Angeles International Airport, with all the foreign languages being spoken and swarms of people. Lake Louise was a stop on every tour sold—plane, train, bus, or auto.

The scenery throughout Banff was as spectacular as Jasper. Both were breathtaking, the prettiest mountain scenery in the world. Imagine me saying that, after years and years of going on about Yosemite.

July 26–28, 2002 We made a mad race through British Columbia and crossed the border into the United States. Customs had no concern with our gun (we were out of wine). It was an emotional cooling-off period after all the excitement of Jasper and Banff. We were racing to Leavenworth, Washington, to pick up the mail. It wasn't due until the July 30, but Marlow hoped it would arrive July 27. We arrived a half hour after the post office closed, much to his disappointment. Now we had to wait over the weekend for the post office to open again on Monday. Thank goodness for the break.

July 29, 2002 We walked from shop to shop in the mountain village of Leavenworth. There were several streets where the architecture mimicked the lacey trim and pastel paintings of Bavaria, Germany. We saw beautiful clocks that would drive a person cuckoo with their chiming. We went to an art show, which encouraged me to get back to painting. I'm almost as good as some folks trying to make a living from their painting, and I'm not very good at all.

We ate lunch in town. I had sauerbraten, spaetzle, and red cabbage—all yummy. After we cleaned our plates, we shared the best apple strudel I've ever eaten.

Then it was back to the trailer for Chinese checkers.

July 30, 2002 We picked up the mail as soon as the post office opened and went down the road through forest-fire-smoky central Washington and Oregon. There were eighteen forest or grass fires in progress. I was glad for the air conditioning in the truck to filter our breathing environment. We spent the night in another lovely Thousand Trails Campground near Bend.

July 31, 2002 When we stopped for gas, the man asked us which way we were going. We told him south. He said that was good because the road north had been closed by the forestry department because of fires.

We arrived home at one thirty p.m. and surveyed our property. The landscape was dry but alive; the house was fine. The air was smoke filled.

Linda brought us the balance of our mail. There was no paycheck. Marlow had not submitted his time card! It was lying on the dining-room table under the pen he used to fill it out.

Odometer reading, 21,847.00. We had traveled 8,319 miles in two months. The approximate cost was $6,000.00. Would I recommend the trip? You betcha, but please, please, leave the mail at home and leave at least three months time for the trip so you can savor the atmosphere.

Thirteen

Hawaii

2003

Hi ho, hi ho, it's off to Hawaii we go. Marlow went back to work at Aerojet as a consultant after we returned from Alaska. So much for retirement. He lived in our travel trailer in the Sacramento area and came to our retirement home in Fort Jones to visit me every other weekend. I went to Sacramento to spend a few days with him once a month. By the end of the year, he was ready for another trip. He wanted to go on a cruise of the Hawaiian Islands during Aerojet's Christmas shutdown. I wanted to go camping. We compromised. I scheduled the boat tour and added a stint of whale watching with the Sierra Club onto the end. Marlow and I both loved our niece and nephew who were living in Honolulu and wanted to spend some time with them. We could combine the three.

December 15, 2002 I winterized the house in Fort Jones—unplugged all electricity except the Monitor heater and the timer on the living-room light and turned off the hot-water heater. Don, our next-door neighbor, was kind enough to crawl under the back deck to turn off the water.

I was on the road to Sacramento by nine thirty. I was due at a Christmas cookie-baking party with friends at two thirty. I've made the drive from Fort Jones to suburban Sacramento often enough to know it takes five hours.

The weather forecast was for six to ten inches of snow at a 4,000-foot elevation. Forest Mountain pass between Fort Jones and Yreka is 4,070 feet, so I called the Siskiyou County Transportation Agency to see if I could get over the mountain without chains. The recorder told me the road was clear and had been sanded, but warned me to watch for rockslides. The lady on the recorder also said there were gusty winds between Yreka and Weed, plus snow mixed with rain. In other words I was in for nasty weather. I could handle those conditions, so I headed out.

I had a premonition something bad was going to happen on this trip. I told Marlow about my feelings earlier in the week. He said to put a yellow sticky note on my driver's license telling the highway patrol where he was. That way they could notify him in case of an accident. He was staying in our travel trailer in Folsom, near Sacramento. He had no phone in the trailer and would have to be contacted in person after work hours. He did have a phone at Aerojet, so I put all that information on a yellow sticky attached to my driver's license.

I had no problem getting over Forest Mountain. Interstate Route Five between Yreka and Weed, a twenty-five-mile stretch, was a tense ride because of gusty winds. It felt like someone was trying to push my car from one side of the road to the other. I saw a huge gray cloud hanging like a dirty sheet in front of me. As I approached Weed, rain was added to wind. I climbed in elevation and snow mixed with rain and wind. I didn't drive over fifty-five miles per hour to avoid hydroplaning.

Those conditions prevailed until I was south of Dunsmuir, about seventy miles south of Yreka. Then the precipitation was intermittent, and I had only wind to worry about.

I was concerned about the length of time the ride was taking, since I wasn't able to maintain a steady sixty-five to seventy miles-per-hour like I did in normal weather. When I was about thirty miles south of Redding, I glanced at the clock on the dashboard. There were no numbers showing! I figured I must have blown a fuse and thought nothing of it.

I put a cassette in the player, and Igor's Jazz Cowboys sang, "Yah, yahh, yahhhhh..." It sounded like a record at the wrong speed. His singing coasted to a stop. At the same time, I realized the car was slowing down.

I saw an off-ramp coming up, swung onto it, and rolled to the top of the hill before the car stopped. I tried unsuccessfully to restart it. Darn it, a dead battery. How could that happen when I was rolling down the freeway?

I looked about for a building and found nothing but empty fields in all directions. I dug out my Good Sam Emergency Road Service card and prepared to walk to the nearest telephone. Just then a Toyota Tacoma filled with a family came up the off-ramp.

I waved at them, requesting they stop. I shouted above the roaring wind, "Do you have a cell phone?" I could see one between the bucket seats, so I ventured on with my shouting, "Would you please phone this number and ask them to send a tow truck to this location?"

The adults stared at me blankly, and it dawned on me that they didn't understand English. A girl about ten was in the backseat with three smaller people, and I asked her if she spoke English. She nodded. She interpreted to her parents what I needed. The man dialed the number on my card and handed me the phone.

I listened to the recording about the next available operator helping me. I had no idea where I was and asked the ten-year-old if she knew the name of the street. She shook her head.

I hung up the phone, thanked the Hispanics, and explained I would have to go back down the off-ramp to find a sign telling me the name of the street. I said I would stop the next car that came up the off-ramp. At the time I was shouting this, I was thinking it might be hours before another car used that off-ramp.

I returned to my car to put on a hat and gloves before starting down the off-ramp while my interpreter explained to her parents what I had said. I was about a quarter of the way down the ramp when the Tacoma passed me, going in reverse. They stopped at the street sign for a few seconds, then came back to where I stood. They offered a ride. I presumed they wanted me to sit on Mom's lap. I rejected the offer and asked the girl for the name of the street. She enunciated the answer slowly, like she was speaking to someone who spoke a foreign language.

Dad dialed the phone again and handed it to me. I gave Good Sam my name and address and started to tell the operator where I was when she asked me for my membership number. The number was on the card on my car seat a quarter of a mile uphill. I explained that I had laid it down when I put on gloves and forgot to put it in my pocket. Thank goodness, they accepted the call anyhow.

I told the interpreter that all was well; someone was on the way to start my truck. I thanked them profusely and walked back up to the warmth of my own Tacoma. I was no sooner inside the car when Dad walked up to my window and motioned for me to lift the hood. He worked under there for a few minutes and told me to try to start the car. Nothing happened. He finally shrugged his shoulders and went back to his truck.

About five minutes later, I looked in my rearview mirror and saw my benefactors still sitting in their truck. I went back and explained that they didn't need to wait, Good Sam would be along in half an hour, and all would be fine. The interpreter said their truck wouldn't start, and Dad had phoned a friend. What the heck? Toyotas never break down! Did we enter the Bermuda Triangle? Was there a Western Bermuda Triangle between Fort Jones, Redding, and the coast?

Good Sam arrived, attached my car to the rear of the tow truck, and jump-started my benefactor. The tow truck driver and I were wheeling north toward Redding within fifteen minutes. I told the driver my battery was four years old, and it was a seven-year battery. I was surprised it had left me afoot. He asked where I bought it.

"Sears," I said, so he said he would take me to the local store to see if they would replace the battery at a discount.

I felt we were lucky to find the Sears garage open and operating on Sunday afternoon in a little town like Redding. Four hours later I drove out of Sears with my original battery intact and a new alternator. I was

$328.00 poorer, but enriched to know that there was still goodwill in the world. What a miracle to have a nice family like the Hispanics help a total stranger sitting at a deserted corner in the middle of vacant fields in a storm. I was glad my premonition of doom was such a minor event, and I could now relax and enjoy the rest of the trip.

I made it to Sacramento at eight thirty. My five-hour trip had taken eleven hours.

December 16–19, 2002 On Monday I went to the Toyota dealer who had done $2,471.00 worth of repairs on my car in September. I complained about their replacement of the starter when the problem had been a faulty alternator. They said they would research the problem to consider giving me a refund on part of my money. Later in the week, they gave me a $165.00 check—half the cost of the alternator. That was better than a kick in the shins. Now I knew I'd have no more electrical problems.

Thursday I ate lunch with friends from Aerojet—Robin and Debbie. I apologized to Robin about missing her cookie-baking party, and she forgave me.

December 20, 2002 Marlow and I were up at three in the morning. Our airport shuttle driver had a hard time finding the trailer park where Marlow and I were waiting. She was to pick us up at three thirty. At four o'clock Marlow walked to Folsom-Auburn Road, and watched for a van to pass by in the scarce traffic. Fortunately, the driver saw him wave at her. She made a U-turn and came to our trailer with Marlow in the passenger seat.

We arrived at the airport thirty minutes later than planned, and it was jammed with holiday travelers. What a mob scene! There must have been two hundred people in the United Airlines queue. The plane was scheduled to leave at six, and it was now five. We would never make it through airport security in time to catch the plane. Everyone else felt the same way. The United crew opened multiple windows and herded us into various groups. We were checked in by five thirty and boarded our small, thirty-person turboprop plane leaving Sacramento directly at six. We took the forty-five-minute flight to San Francisco International Airport.

United had overbooked the flight to Honolulu and was looking for volunteers to stay behind. Marlow and I did not volunteer; we were in a hurry to get to the tropics. Our giant Boeing 777 left the gate on time at nine. There were approximately fifty rows of seats. Isn't it amazing that the plane could lift off with all that weight? Some of the carry-on luggage looked like it weighed a hundred pounds by the way people dragged their bags.

The efficient staff kept everything humming right along, with beverages, breakfast, and a snack served during the six-hour flight. They said they were going to show us television shows. They showed a billion commercials, just like TV at home. Most people dozed. I read a mystery novel. The movie was made for teenyboppers, so it was of no interest to me. It had lots of sixteen-year-olds in bikinis, so it held Marlow's attention. The movie was about surfing in Hawaii. Really, I think Marlow would watch anything that was shown on a screen. The time passed, and we were eventually on the ground in Honolulu.

The airport was hectic, with lost tourists being herded from place to place. Marlow and I were running from one conveyor belt to another, trying to gather our five pieces of luggage. With such a large airplane, there were four conveyor belts for removal of luggage. Once we had everything, we shuffled along with others to an inspector to show that ID tags on the luggage matched our driver's license. I was glad to see this new security detail in force. It had worried me in the past that someone could make off with our luggage. I would hate to have a suitcase full of size-six bikinis to wear the whole trip. I'd have to sew three or four of them together to avoid arrest for indecent exposure of fat.

A Norwegian Cruise Line shuttle driver met us at baggage claim. He took our bags and told us to board the bus. At the dock we had to identify our luggage to security inspectors working among the piles and piles of bags. There had to be a better system. We were not allowed in the luggage area. We had to stand outside a rope and try to identify our black bags among all the other black bags. It eventually all worked out, and we were in line to prove we had paid for tickets to enter the ship. I cannot imagine how eighty-year-olds can stand all that stress and hassle, and yet many of them take cruises.

Marlow and I were walking toward the gangplank when an effeminate little man ran up to me and scrunched up my hair.

"Oh, you have such beautiful hair. You must tell me who does your hair." I told him I cut it with a butcher knife, as well as doing all the other torture required to keep it looking like it does. The fellow explained that he worked in the onboard beauty shop and would love to "do me." I don't think so.

Our room was comparable in size to our travel trailer. We had a little sitting area with a convertible love seat, ottoman, easy chair, coffee table, and TV/bar/buffet stand. There was a king-size bed, a closet, and a bathroom. For the first time on a cruise, we had portholes—two of them. It would be nice to look out at the water or shore. No outside deck existed at our level, so no one walked past our windows. Some people paid extra to have picture windows, many of which opened onto a public deck, so the travelers kept drapes pulled while in the room.

Marlow and I unpacked and acquainted ourselves with the ship. There were lots of bars and restaurants and a few sporting areas, plus the large theater. We could eat in any restaurant and were not confined to one formal room, and stuck with the same group of people at our table for each meal. We could even have a private table, if we so desired. I was going to appreciate that sooner or later on the trip.

I drank a fruity, tropical concoction made with pineapple juice and bearing a little umbrella sticking out the top that was offered by a white-coated gentleman carrying a tray of drinks. When I found out the drink cost $7.00, I vowed not to drink any more. Cruise ships made a good income off their bars.

For dinner the first night, we had barbecue steak and salad while watching a show of Hawaiian dancers. I talked to one of the young ladies later and learned this was her first cruise. I asked where she lived and was surprised to hear she was from Ventura, California. She was pretty with olive skin and almond-shaped eyes. I don't know why I assumed the entertainers were from Hawaii. Silly me.

Marlow and I stood on deck to watch our departure from Honolulu a little after eight p.m. The coast guard put on a nice water show with their fire-fighting equipment for the benefit of the departing cruise ship.

December 21, 2002 Our schedule for today started with a Zodiac (inflatable) boat trip twelve miles to a snorkeling area. We were off the coast of the big island of Hawaii. It was exhilarating to ride the waves in our sturdy raft. For snorkeling we pulled into a quiet cove and watched the colorful show put on by fish playing around the coral. We snorkeled for an hour, enjoying the serenity of being in a private show of nature. A ladder was attached to the side of the raft for entering and exiting the water, much to my pleasure. I hate being dragged up and over the side of a boat. The captain took us for a short tour of the coastline on the way back. He showed us lava tubes also known as caves. What a great way to start our holiday.

On our way between the snorkeling shop and the cruise ship in a taxi, Marlow stopped at a store and bought himself a dozen cans of beer. The dozen cost $8.00. The beer onboard the ship was $4.00 each.

Once on the crusise ship we showered the seawater off our bodies and went to the first nightclub show. We had never seen an act like Steve DePass before. He would ask people in the audience their names and ask them for a noun or subject, and then he would make up a song about the people in association with the subject they had chosen. The song rhymed and made sense. He was an incredibly creative, talented poet.

We went for a late dinner and were joined by a trio: Michael, his wife, Cheri, and his sister-in-law, Lynne. They loved to travel, and we had shared many of the same destinations. The other guest at our table was a man in his late seventies who had lived in Victoria, Australia. We could carry on an intelligent conversation with each of them.

December 22–23, 2002 We were at sea all day. I saw the older gent from last night's dinner carrying an infant and commented on the child's beauty. I asked if it was his grandchild, and he replied, "No, he's my son." Second day of the cruise, and I'm already hopping around with my foot in my mouth.

The temperatures were in the eighties, and we had smooth sailing. I walked the promenade and found a little sign saying that three and a half times around the ship equaled one mile. I would put in two miles each day.

I spent a couple of hours sitting in a deck chair reading, just like the ladies in commercials. What decadence. This could be habit-forming.

December 24, 2002 The weather got warmer as we approached the equator. Sunset was later.

We visited Fanning Island, an atoll in the tiny country of Kiribati. The population was Polynesian. They lived in thatched huts made from palm fronds on poles or sheds made of corrugated iron.

I went inside a wooden structure near the dock that had stalls separated by chicken wire. I asked if the post office or bank was open. The response was yes, and the speaker pointed to two different cubicles. I found a woman sitting in the "post office" stall selling Kiribati stamps. I bought some. There was a man asleep on a wooden plank balanced on two rocks in the stall that was the bank. I couldn't get him to wake up to ask if I could get some Kiribati coins for my collection. A nice lady who spoke some English told me they no longer made their own money; they used Australian money. She did find one old coin in the bottom of her handbag that I bought for US$2.00.

We had crossed the International Date Line, so it was actually Christmas Day, making it even more unusual for the post office and bank to be occupied. I saw one child with one toy, and it was a block of wood with four wheels nailed to it. I wondered if the people were Christians. Maybe they didn't celebrate Christmas. Maybe they didn't have Santa Claus. They seemed to be poor and a bit sad. The only smiles I saw were when they were entertaining the tourists with their singing and dancing or when they (the children) were asked to pose for pictures. And they didn't always smile then.

Marlow and I walked away from the glitzy beach area owned by the cruise line and went to a little village. There were a few pigs, dogs, and chickens wandering around freely. Almost every person from the village was at the Catholic Church singing their hearts out in celebration of Christmas. That answered the question about being Christians. The church was a pole building with an iron roof (no sides). Women were cooking around the edges of the building, and there were sleeping mats for the children. Older children and adults sitting on the ground occupied the center of the church. Everywhere we went, the people were friendly but unsmiling.

Among the beach shops built by the cruise lines, we saw baskets asking for donations for the building of a stone block schoolhouse. It seemed like the cruise line could have built them one without putting a dent in their profits.

The cruise line was paranoid that a stowaway would sneak onboard. Passengers had to show Norwegian Cruise Line picture ID cards and a driver's license every time they got on the ship. I ended up dropping my new Kiribati coin in the ocean when I dug out my ID. That was disappointing.

December 25, 2002 During the night and our second Christmas Day, we had rough seas. People onboard who had read the history of the ship were nervous. The ship had been cut in two to add an extension. The boat was then welded back together. As a manufacturing engineer, I had seen how strong a good weld could be, so that didn't bother me. Our room was in the far forward (bow) of the boat, so we felt every slap of the water as we crested waves and then hit bottom. The seas washed over our fifth-floor portholes.

No one was allowed outside. The seas were treacherous and unpredictable. There was room indoors for people to learn crafts, play games, read, listen to lectures or music, or eat, eat, eat. At the request of the Hawaiian government, the casino was never opened. That area was used as an art gallery, much to my delight. I ogled the Kincaids and other modern painters' works. I took a class in lei making with ribbons and/or kukui nuts and a class in making decorative fish from pandanus tree leaves. Lessons were something to do and an excuse to get out of our room.

The wonderfully funny comedian, Rex Havens, who had a show in the evening, kept us in stitches for thirty minutes straight. We enjoyed it so much, we bought one of his CDs to share with others.

December 26, 2002 Another day at sea. We had gone to Kiribati, as the cruise line was required to dock at one foreign country before continuing the circuit of the Hawaiian Islands. The seas were still rough, so no one was allowed outdoors yet. We managed to get into the "exclusive" restaurant and found the food was no better than anywhere else onboard. This restaurant required dress-up clothes. The best part of the meal was the dessert called tiramisu. The food throughout the ship was good. They used lots of dishes and silverware on the tables, the service was excellent, and the presentation was superb.

December 27, 2002 The cruise ship arrived at the big island of Hawaii, and Marlow and I took the *Circle of Fire* helicopter tour. We had enjoyed it when we flew over Kilauea in a helicopter in 1988. This time it was raining, so we didn't expect the good views we had seen fifteen years earlier. The tour left from Hilo and flew around the crater, making sure it was a good distance from the edge.

He respected the possibility of a gas bubble blowing debris at his vehicle. In 2001 and 2002, creeping lava had swallowed up nine miles of surface. Molten lava flowed out to sea to enlarge the island.

We were seated according to weight so the heaviest people (two men) were stuck in the middle of the backseat with their spouses on the outside. Two skinny girls got the front seat. I shouldn't complain. I almost always got the front seat of sight-seeing flights. I was the only one trying to videotape the trip, so I was disappointed that I was crammed into a corner of the backseat with just a view from one side window. I was glad to learn the company sold videos of our ride. We bought one.

December 28, 2002 We took a helicopter ride to view Maui from above and flew over the extinct volcanic crater of Haleakala, then went from the dry side of the island to the wet side and back again.

The tour was scheduled with the same company that flew over the big island, so once more Marlow was in the center of the backseat, and I was squashed against the little back window. Half of the trip was a blur to me because of the glare on the windows. Never satisfied, am I? First rain, now glare. I was unable to take videos, so once more we bought the company-made tape of our trip. They had a camera inside the helicopter cabin taking pictures of the passengers from time to time as the pilot spoke their name. He must have had control of the camera as well as the vehicle. That way you knew you were buying a tape of your own ride. I wasn't too concerned with seeing Maui, as I planned on spending two weeks there in January with the Sierra Club. I knew I would get in some good hiking and see the land in detail.

December 29, 2002 Marlow and I took an eight-and-a-half-hour, four-wheel-drive trip around the isle of Kauai. That was so much more fun than the helicopter rides. You got it; I was back in my normal spot, riding shotgun. I had my camcorder taking pictures of the garden isle out the front windscreen.

The knowledgeable driver gave us a bit of a history lesson on the people of Hawaii. I heard a lot of information I had not known before. Didn't know the Portuguese and Puerto Ricans were slaves and kept in camps at the sugarcane and pineapple plantations. I was interested in hearing about their lives, intermarriage, and cultures. Over a couple hundred years, the people have mingled and mixed to make the Polynesian/Chinese/Portuguese/Japanese/Puerto Rican/Korean/Melanesian people that we refer to as Hawaiians. When the people say they are trying to restore their native culture, they are talking about the group that first arrived from the Marquesas. They are trying to restore Marquesan culture.

We visited tropical Waimea Canyon, where the *Jurassic Park* series of movies were made. The canyon was lushly covered with green trees, grass, moss, and ferns.

We went through abandoned sugarcane fields that were being taken over by cattle ranchers now that the market was not willing to pay the price for American labor to produce sugar. The United States no longer had slavery, so farmers felt it was not feasible to grow sugar or pineapple. America imported those products from third-world countries where people were willing to work for low wages.

December 30, 2002 We had a surprisingly easy disembarkation. We were not checked at all leaving the cruise ship area with our luggage. We were just told to help ourselves to luggage and leave through one of the multiple gates that led onto public sidewalks.

Unfortunately, in the excitement of seeing my niece, Trish, and her little son, Michael, waiting for us, we forgot one bag with Marlow's leather jacket and suit in it. We later went back to the dock to get it. There were about fifty bags left behind. The security guard told me to pick out whatever bags I cared to remove. As tempting as the white elephant offer was, I just removed our own bag.

After we settled into the military housing where Trish Kosey and her husband, Rick, lived, we went to the beach on Hickham Air Force Base. That was what people did in Hawaii; they went to the beach. The beach was nestled into a cove next to Honolulu International Airport. We sat in the sun on the sand and watched planes take off. We also saw military ships heading in and out of Pearl Harbor. Two-year-old Michael enjoyed seeing the various vehicles. He was such a cutie. It was going to be fun spending time with him.

December 31, 2002 Trish and Rick drove us to a secluded beach used by the Marriott Hotel. Trish knew all beaches in Hawaii had been made public. Hotels were no longer allowed to claim exclusivity to a beach. All we had to do at the hotel gate was ask to use the beach. There was no hassle; we were ushered right through. Everyone except Marlow went for a swim in the warm surf. Then we returned to the Koseys' home for a barbecue pork dinner and an evening of entertainment consisting of Michael doing shenanigans.

January 1, 2003 Marlow and I borrowed the Kosey car to go to the National Cemetery of the Pacific, a place where military men and their spouses were interred. The men fought in battles that took place somewhere in the Pacific Ocean or on its shores. The museum showing pictures and heroic stories of the men honored with congressional medals impressed us, but we were grateful neither Marlow nor any of our sons had seen combat duty. The cemetery was well organized, well kept, and a lovely setting.

We were told when we parked to take our valuables with us, as theft was a problem anywhere tourists went on the island. Theft in paradise! The security guard explained theft was prevalent because there was a bad drug problem. Drugs in paradise! Why would people need to escape reality if they lived in paradise?

January 2, 2003 We went to the *Arizona* Memorial and took the tour; there was only an hour wait to catch the boat out to the memorial. The navy ran the park. The memorial was respectful and well managed. I don't know what I was expecting, but it was not as impressive as I was led to believe. I thought we would be able to see the whole ship beneath the water—like seeing through a glass-bottom boat. We saw one turret and a small section of the ship. We saw the list of names of men who had lost their lives and were interred where they lie. The list made me sad. I thought of the number of heartbroken people left to live without these heroes. Surely someone will come up with a better solution to international problems than having a war.

January 3, 2003 Rick and Trish took us on a tour around Oahu.

Rick went for his first glider ride when we stopped at an airport. He enjoyed himself, much to Marlow's delight. Marlow was a glider pilot in his younger days. Trish was happy to keep her feet on the ground. Michael loved watching the big plane pull the little plane into the air with a long string. I felt better when the little plane was detached from the big plane, and Trish was more comfortable when the little plane landed safely.

Rick drove us to Waimea Beach, where good surfers go to catch the big waves. The surf was up and rough, and few people were braving the pounding breakers. The waves were twelve to fifteen feet high, and strong winds whipped them into froth. Surfing would have been unpredictable. We weren't tempted to get within reach of the water.

We ate an enormous shrimp and rice dinner off a "roach coach," the lunch truck parked in the shade near the beach. It had two picnic tables under the trees and the owners were doing a great business. Trish had scouted out good, cheap places to eat on the island since her arrival three years ago. Rick, a submariner, ate most of his meals on a navy ship.

January 4, 2003 The waves at Waimea Beach were up to thirty-five feet overnight. That was the highest they had been since 1985. It caused flooding in the areas we visited yesterday.

Rick went to work, so Trish chauffeured us to some touristy sights around Honolulu. She took us to Diamond Head, the extinct volcanic crater. It required a GPS to follow the twists and turns of residential streets.

At nine thirty that night, Trish drove Marlow to the Honolulu International Airport terminal that was less than two miles from their house. He left for Sacramento, California, and work at Aerojet.

January 5, 2003 I went for my usual morning walk. Each day since I'd arrived in Honolulu, I walked the neighborhood for an hour or more. The city wasn't hilly, so it didn't get the heart pounding, but hopefully it got the adrenaline cranked up a bit. Since it was Sunday in football season, I spent the next six hours watching games on television. Trish had her usual parade of friends stopping by for a visit, and Rick was at work.

January 6, 2003 Rick was off to work before I awoke. Trish, Michael, and I joined Trish's friend, Michelle, at the beach. The day was wonderful. I loved watching little people play. Michael had great fun with Michelle's two daughters.

I got the worst sunburn I've had since I was a kid. I thought we were only going to be there an hour like we had in the past, so I didn't take a long-sleeved shirt and long pants. We stayed almost four hours.

Fortunately, Rick gave me some aloe vera gel, which helped tremendously, and I got a good night's sleep.

January 9, 2003 My first day traveling on my own. I used Rick and Trish's car to go to Ho'omaluia Botanical Gardens and took every trail offered. I saw lots of tropical greenery, mostly untitled. The names I did read were words made up of vowels, and when I tried to say the Hawaiian words, they sounded like baby talk. I saw a mongoose and got a bit of a video of him. The park had a pleasant lake created by the Army Corps of Civil Engineers that was stocked with fish, mallards, and domestic geese.

I drove to Kailua Coast and sat in the shade on the beach. My burn was still raw, so I didn't want to agitate it. I watched the funny, snow-white tourists cavorting in the sunshine.

Then I went to Bishop Museum in Honolulu. I was too tired to cover it properly, though it did look interesting, so I planned to return when I could spend a whole day.

January 10, 2003 I spent the entire day at the Bishop Museum. The staff put on musical shows and told me (and others) stories. They showed us native artifacts and let us explore the night sky using charts. We charted our way from the Marquesas to Hawaii, the route of the original Hawaiian immigrants. I did a cursory tour of the Polynesian/Micronesian/Melanesian building and would like to have had a copy of the map showing where those three groups originated. The museum had a wonderful large map painted on the wall.

I didn't have energy for the garden tour. Sure missed the stamina I had ten years ago. Had no idea where I lost it; I wonder if I left it in the luggage room when I got off the ship.

In the evening Trish took me to see fireworks put on by the Hilton Hotel in Waikiki. She, Michael, and I joined Michelle and her daughters, Michaela and Becky, for a gala night of swimming, eating, drinking, and dancing (with the little people), topped off by fireworks. We were at the Hale Koa, a luxurious hotel bought by the military to house incoming families before base housing became available for them. All military personnel were allowed to use the facilities. The evening was lovely. I felt like I was living in an advertisement for visiting Hawaii.

January 11, 2003 I was the only passenger on the plane from Honolulu to Maui, where I joined the Sierra Club group leader and four other members for a treacherous cross-island trip to Hana. The leader's name was Linda. The others were Richard, Terry, Carolyn, and Peggy. We were part of a group of eleven Sierra Club members and three staff that settled into a luxurious condo on the Hana Coast. My roommate was Mary, a retired psychologist about fifty-five years old. She was a pretty lady, quiet-spoken, refined, and friendly. So far, so good.

Wine and *pupus* (hors d'oeuvres) were served before dinner. Dinner was smoked salmon, Oriental salad, daikon, Okinawan sweet potatoes, dried peas, and sesame crackers. Cookies and coffee were served during orientation later that evening. This could be a fattening experience.

The Sierra Club members consisted of five men and six women with a wide variety of personalities. There were three staffers, our leader, Linda, and two cooks, Carol and Lynn. Half the people were from California; the remaining people were from various other states. Linda gave us a rundown of what to expect over the next few days. She said the previous two years, two people had broken bones on the trip. She hoped we would all be extra careful. My stomach sank. *Please don't let it be me. Don't let that be the premonition I had before I left home that something bad was going to happen.* I vowed to be extra careful. Thank goodness I had reached that stage of life where I no longer cared if people called me a sissy.

January 12, 2003 We took a tortuous three-hour hike over large, round, movable lava bombs and along sharp, jagged cliffs to start the day. The day was beautiful, the weather was perfect, and the walk was exhilarating. I loved every minute of it, except for needing help climbing some of the rock faces with my backpack on.

Linda ended up carrying the backpack so I could expend my energy moving my body. Linda, like most of the group, ascended and descended the rocky outcroppings like they were polished wooden steps. I tested each step to make sure it was firmly in place and wasn't going to roll and throw me over a precipice into the foaming brine. The ocean battering the black cliffs a hundred feet below was a sight to behold, but I didn't care to get a closer look.

I commented that the rocks at the waterline were so rounded compared to the jagged ones we were climbing. With the next resurgence of water, I saw why. The waves washed the bowling-ball-sized rocks up to the face of the cliff, and then the receding water carried the rocks back to their place of origin or beyond. The sound of the rocks rolling into one another was quite audible. The ocean was a built-in rock polisher.

We ate our packed lunch at Wainapanapa State Park. I offered to watch the backpacks while the others trudged a half mile further to look at a cave (lava tube). As soon as the party left, a little mongoose came out of the rock wall where some of the folks had been sitting. He heard me turn on the video camera and scurried into hiding. I got a quick glimpse of a head and a tail. The mongoose looked rather like an oversized squirrel minus the bushy tail.

The afternoon was spent at Hamoa Beach. Sun, surf, sea, and hiking totally exhausted me by the time we returned to the condo. I slept well.

January 13, 2003 Today was a workday. We drove to Haleakala National Park, where the ranger offered us a variety of jobs. Five people were to hike up the trail and chop weeds with machetes. The ranger said it was an hour's hike, so I figured it would take me one and a half hours. I didn't think I would be useful with a machete anyway. Some folks were to clean out weeds and bamboo from along the roadside. Some were to cut down trees. Now, wasn't that ironic? Tree huggers cutting down trees! We were to clear hiking paths. Some were to houseclean bunkhouses for volunteer summer help. I chose the housework. So did Mary.

Mary and I washed windows that probably had not been touched for a couple of years. They were covered in salty scum. I scrubbed out the shower area and took inventory of the eating utensils for the ranger's information. We only worked a couple of hours.

Sierra Clubbers were called together for lunch and told that we wouldn't be needed in the afternoon. Not much of a work detail. I had expected to work every day during the time spent with the Sierra Club.

Three of us went to Hamoa Beach for the afternoon. The rest of the group went on another three- to four-hour hike.

January 14, 2003 The hike this morning was much more tolerable for my old joints. We walked on earth and gravel to get to Red Sand Beach. The "sand" part was a misnomer. It was red cinders that were murder on soft soles. Some people wore shower clogs. I wore hiking boots, so I was fine on the trail. The water was a wonderful temperature, and we saw a few fish while snorkeling. Snorkeling was the purpose of the destination.

The beach was for sun worshipers. A couple of old men with long, gray hair displayed their emaciated bodies. As the day got hotter, more people arrived, and it was good to see that not all nudists were so far over the hill, they couldn't see the crest behind themselves. All the nudists were men. There were women on the beach, but they wore swimsuits. The Sierra Clubbers wore swimsuits, snorkel fins, and masks. As we were walking out, we passed a group of twenty college kids going in. There was some hope the original men on the beach might get a good skin show. Collegian's hard, young bodies would certainly be more scenic than the middle-aged and infirm members of our group sporting their old fashioned 1960s-style swimsuits.

We ate lunch at the condo, and most of the group went on an afternoon hike to see waterfalls. I packed for tomorrow's transfer to another location, read, wrote, and snoozed.

January 15, 2003 We traversed the scenic, curvy, narrow Hana Highway. Some places the road was one car wide, and people played chicken if there was approaching traffic. Fortunately, I had a woman driver who didn't feel it was necessary to impress anyone with her daring. We lost every game of chicken.

In the evening we met our humpback whale expert—Dr. Marsha McGowan, a whale biologist, and her two assistants, Mike and Ryan. Dr. McGowan gave an interesting introductory talk about our first whale observation duties.

Some of the things I learned about the cetaceans were:

- Calves are born with no blubber. It has to be built up with rich mother's milk.
- Calves stay with their mother one year.
- Mothers give birth once every four or five years.
- Whale songs are more complex than birdsongs. A whale will sing the same song over and over. They sing only in the breeding area. They stop singing when they head north to Alaskan waters. The following year they return to the same place with the same song as the year before. Only the males sing. One singer will accompany a mother with her baby. The male singer does not attempt to mate with the nursing mother.
- When traveling in pods, the female and her mate will lead unattached females and males. When going home from the breeding ground, the mother will travel with her mate and her calf. Other males will fight to get her attention. She will not mate for four or five years and shows no interest in the males.
- In Alaskan waters the groups are separated according to gender. They participate in cooperative feeding, helping one another catch food.
- In the past twenty-four years, eighteen whale calves have been injured or orphaned off the coast of Maui by human behavior.
- In two months last year, the navy tested low-frequency sonar in the area; ten calves were injured or orphaned.
- Females chose the strongest males as mates (survival of the fittest?).
- Humpbacks and blues are baleen whales. Whales are divided into two groups, baleen and toothed.

- Life-span is thirty to fifty years.
- They weigh up to forty tons (*tons*!).
- They travel at a rate of up to eighteen miles per hour.
- The sound of their songs travels four and a half times further in the water than in the air.
- Humpback whales' voices will carry a hundred miles, though they have no vocal chords.
- Calves weigh up to two tons when born.

January 16, 2003 We finally got to do some "scientific" whale monitoring. My understanding was that was the purpose of the trip. I didn't know we were to do so much playing. We climbed to a lookout spot about half a mile from the shore. Teams of four were set up—two people with binoculars, one with a theodolite—a surveyor's instrument—and one with a pencil and pad to write down the results. I was the recorder for our team and hoped to learn the theodolite later in the week. The theodolite was set up for people six feet tall or taller. I said I would bring a stepstool with me from now on. The leader got the message and said one theodolite would be set up for short folks and one for taller people. A person with binocs would call out a position (there were crosshairs and a circle with degrees marked inside the eyepiece) and behavior of a sighted whale. The person with the theodolite would find the whale and verify the number of animals and position. The recorder wrote the info on the sheet. It got exciting after we started spotting whales.

After an hour Mary traded me binocs for record keeping. I couldn't believe how many whales could be seen with the excellent binoculars. It was my job to track one particular whale. It travelled parallel to the shore. It was a matter of watching in front of where I had last seen the whale and calling out his position and action (fluke flip, dorsal fin, arched back). A fluke flip was when they brought their tail out of the water, and it meant they were diving deeper and would be down longer. They may not be seen again for ten minutes. Otherwise they would come up every four or five minutes. When they propel their whole body out of the water, they disappear for a long time. What a sight to see! I loved experiencing this wondrous event.

On the way back to the condo complex, we stopped to see some petroglyphs. It was a six-mile hike from the parked vans. I could see the trail up was really rough, so I dillydallied at the car until the others had left. Then I carefully picked my way over strewn boulders and around tangled roots. I got halfway up the incline and saw that the trip would require a long distance of butt scooting along a precipice. It looked dangerous, so I decided to go back to the car and wait for the others to return. I had seen petroglyphs many times.

On the descent I tested every rock before putting my weight on it. Sure didn't want to take a tumble and miss out on the whale watching. I was about ten yards from the van on a roadside bank. Going downhill on loose gravel, I went sideways, with the theory that if my leading foot slid, I would only skin up my hip.

My left foot felt secure, so I lifted my right foot to take the next step. The left foot started sliding, with the arch of the foot on the ground. It hit something and flipped over so the arch was facing upward, and I went flying a hundred eighty degrees up and over the errant foot. I landed in the grass on the side of the path. I was so mad I had taken a fall that I pounded the ground and swore, knowing no one was within hearing distance. I knew from the pain that the ankle was sprained. That would mean pain for the balance of the trip, and the leader might not let me go on the whale-watching excursions. I was more angry than hurt. I thought that perhaps I could hobble back to the van and pretend like nothing happened. I would put ice on it when I got back to the condo and get an Ace bandage wrapped tightly on it. If I wore jeans, no one would be the wiser.

Just then, John, a highly emotional man, came upon me and started yelling, "Marilyn has fallen. Help! Someone! Man down! Quick, we need a medic! Get a doctor, get a helicopter, where are the nurses!" I could have throttled him. I told him it was okay; I was just crying because I was angry for being such a klutz.

I started to roll onto my stomach to get up. John knocked me down and held me there for the few minutes it took for me to be surrounded by concerned people. There were three nurses in the group, and under no condition would they let me move. The nurses discussed what to do. An Ace bandage was produced, and two people held my leg gingerly, but painfully, in the air while the third one wrapped it from toe to knee, including the shoe.

The two most athletic people carried me to the van and crammed me into the front seat. A long conference was held outside my hearing range. I tried to prop the aching leg up on the dashboard but couldn't move it without excruciating pain, so I sat still.

A decision was made. First I was to be moved to the middle seat where I could prop my feet up. Bob was to sit in the third seat and hover over me regardless of what I said. He was to hang on to my bare thigh and my upper arm and not to let me move until we reached medical assistance. Bob did his job.

The second van took the rest of the party to the condos while my van took the two athletes, the leader, and me to a medical clinic. One athlete, Laura, was a nurse and the director of this operation.

We arrived at the clinic at one o'clock. The nurses said the doctor was out, and they didn't want to take care of anyone until after they finished their lunch. Linda asked if there was another doctor on the island. The answer was no, but the one doctor shared by all residents would be at the Hyatt at two o'clock.

Linda didn't like the attitude of the nurses in Lahaina and decided to take me to the Hyatt. I was admitted to the doctor's examining room immediately, where a technician took x-rays. When he returned from developing the film, I asked him to explain to my companions that the leg was just sprained, and I really didn't need to wait for the doctor.

"I'm not allowed to tell you whether your leg is broken or not," he said. "That's the doctor's job, but I most certainly will not tell your companions that it is just sprained." He grinned a boyish smile. Oh no, a broken leg! How could that happen? Not again! I broke my foot on vacation in Australia in 1990 and didn't remove my hiking boot for a week until I got home. I couldn't walk on the broken foot, and people had to help me hop around. I was much younger then and could hop better.

Dr. Adams arrived thirty minutes later and read the x-ray. He told me I was mistaken about spraining my leg. I had broken the fibula and tibia. He congratulated my helpers on not letting me move and said it was a straight break, and they had saved me from requiring surgery to insert a pin. He warned me not to put any pressure on the leg whatsoever. He told the grinning tech to put a temporary splint on the leg. The temporary was all that was available at the Hyatt hotel. At the doctor's instructions, Linda took me to a clinic where a different, sturdier splint was applied. I was told that only an orthopedic specialist could apply a cast, and I would have to go to Honolulu to find such a person.

Bob, a Dallas Cowboy football player, and Laura carried me to the condo in a lawn chair, and Linda, the leader, put me in her luxury bedroom. She got the prescription for pain pills filled and bought a bedpan. Under no condition was I to try to hop to the bathroom during the night. I was to yell for her. She would sleep on the couch. Oh, what a nuisance. I humbly thanked all concerned.

January 17, 2003 The other Sierra Clubbers went to the cliffside to monitor whales in the morning. In the afternoon they went on a whale-watching tour boat. Linda stayed home and babysat me. I was so distraught over ruining her time as well as my own that I had a crying jag.

Well, how could I expect Linda to tolerate that kind of behavior? She didn't want to deal with me anymore. She called Trish and told her I needed to leave Maui. She asked Trish if I should be shipped to her house in Honolulu or to a hospital. Fortunately, Trish accepted me in her home. Linda made airline reservations, packed my bags, and drove me to the airport.

We met the others returning from the tour boat. They claimed they only saw whales at a great distance, and the boat was too unstable to take pictures. They assured me it was a flop as an adventure, and I hadn't missed a thing. People came by to wish me farewell. I just cried in return for their kindness. I was so disappointed to miss the whale counting. Or maybe it was the pain pills making me cry. I hadn't been that emotional for years.

Trish, Rick, and Michael met me at the airport. They transported me via a rented wheel-chair and their car to their home, where I fell into the guest bed and spent a restless night never far from dispiriting pain.

January 18, 2003 Trish took me to the The Queen's Medical Center Emergency Room in Honolulu. The personnel were kind, considerate, thoughtful, and unable to help me in any way (they sent $1,000.00 worth of bills after I got home, though they gave me no treatment). They said only an orthopedic doctor could attach a cast. The doctor could only do that after the swelling had receded and additional x-rays had been taken to see if the bones were still lined up. If they were not, surgery would be required. They had no orthopedic doctor in the hospital.

Trish and Rick spent the balance of their day getting me "comfortable." What a waste of a nice Saturday in paradise. I took pain pills and slept fitfully from nightmares.

January 19, 2003 A good old-fashioned Sunday with American football. Trish's team and my team both won their games. That meant they would play each other in the Super Bowl! It was Oakland Raiders against the Tampa Bay Bucs. A sure win for the Raiders was eminent.

Trish went to an all-girls' party. Rick, Michael, and I watched football on television.

January 21, 2003 I finally got in to see an orthopedic doctor. He did not order a new x-ray. He walked into the examination room and said, "Wow, I can hardly wait to operate on that good-looking leg." I said to just hang on, not to start sharpening his knives just yet. I was told the breaks were clean, and surgery was not necessary.

He reluctantly put a cast on after removing the splint. Dr. Murphy (phony name) put a quarter inch of padding on the leg under a half cast, which was attached with the toes pointing down like a ballet dancer. He said I was to come back in two days to get a full cast. A half cast goes from the knee to the toes. A full cast goes from the crotch to the toes (that meant I couldn't bend my knee while wearing it). My skin felt sore from the splints. I mentioned that to Dr. Murphy. The doctor told me to take as many pills as necessary to deaden the pain and not to bother with the dosage on the side of the bottle. He felt I would only be on pills for a few days, so I might as well be comfortable.

January 23, 2003 The full cast seemed to be one of Dr. Murphy's little jokes. I had worried about it for two solid days. He didn't bring it up, so I didn't either. He had half a dozen x-rays taken and said the breaks were still lined up, so he guessed he didn't get to operate unless I wanted him to.

He offered to give me one of those external scaffolding braces with pins running through my legs, saying I would get lots of sympathy from people. I rejected his offer and told him the cast was bad enough. I told him it felt like someone was pouring hot bacon grease over my leg. He said to elevate it above my heart and take pain pills more often. I told him I had been taking twelve pills a day to keep from screaming.

He said, "Okay," and gave me another prescription and told me to come back in a week.

January 30, 2003 Yea! Dr. Murphy heard me when I said I couldn't stand the burning pain any longer. He was surprised that it still hurt, saying he thought I would be off the pain pills by now. I told him I was worried about becoming a junkie at the rate I took them. They just barely made the pain tolerable, and I was still taking at least twelve a day. The bottle said not to take more than six a day.

Dr. Murphy had more x-rays taken and removed the cast. What a relief! My leg from the knee down was purplish-brown. It looked gruesome. He doused it in a solution that felt like a topical anesthetic. The burning stopped, and the skin felt numb. He put a new cast on. As he put each layer of plaster gauze on, he pressed it to my leg as hard as he could. It was so painful having the cast put on, I cried throughout the procedure. I hadn't cried for years. What the heck was wrong with my emotion control button?

February 3, 2003 The pain subsided to tolerable for twenty-four hours after the new cast was put on. Then it returned. I decided I had to cut back on the pain pills, so I limited myself to nine a day. I really suffered, waiting the last hour before taking another one. It took thirty minutes for the pain pill to offer any relief, and then it only lasted for an hour. I was miserable. I could find no comfortable position. I propped it at different levels while in bed; I let it lie flat on the bed; I dangled it while in the wheelchair. Each change of position alleviated the pain for up to ten minutes, then it returned. It felt like a tourniquet was on too tight and was shutting off circulation.

Little Michael brought toys to the guest bed and crawled up to play cars, trains, or soldiers with me. That distracted me, and I was determined not to let him know I was in pain.

Trish got me out of bed several times a day to avoid bedsores. She helped me shower, sat me in the shade in the yard to enjoy the birds, propped me in front of the television, sat me in the corner of the kitchen while she chattered away fixing meals. What an awesome home-care worker she would make. I would have lost my mind if I had been on my own at home.

February 4, 2003 I couldn't stand the pain anymore and phoned different doctors recommended by The Queen's Medical Center. It took a bit of calling to find a doctor who would treat one of Dr. Murphy's patients. Dr. Terrance (phony name) agreed to see me immediately. He looked at my toes and knee and said there was no reason for me to have been suffering as I had. He got out his saw and cut a one-inch-wide gap down the front of the cast. He said the cast had been put on so tight, it was cutting off circulation. If it had continued another day, I would have lost my leg. Yikes! What a thought! I am so glad I decided to change doctors before it was too late. After he made the cut, the pain started subsiding.

He said my leg looked like it had been tied with a tourniquet for six days. He said he had never seen a cast put on with no padding underneath. The leg looked like a wild brand of sausage. There were indentations in the swollen skin, and the anklebones were rubbed raw.

Dr. Terrance told me to take two Motrin four times a day, whether I felt I needed them or not; then if I absolutely needed a pain pill, to take it in between the Motrin doses. He said I would probably need the codeine for another day or two, and then I should start tapering off. He expected me to be using nothing but Motrin by the time of my next appointment in one week. What a relief!

February 5, 2003 I took eight Motrin and four codeine pills. A good start, down from twelve pain pills a day. I still had a "rain stick" affect. When my leg hung down while I sat up, it felt like little hot beads rolling from my knee to my foot. When I lay down and stuck my leg up in the air, the hot beads rolled back toward my knee. Guess the circulation was not 100 percent yet.

February 13, 2003 Dr. Terrance was pleased with the progress. He said to get a walker and start putting pressure on the broken leg. He said that would help it heal faster. Well, I'm for that! He said to just practice on the walker for a few minutes each day.

Dr. Terrance gave me the bad news that he was going out of town and wouldn't be back until mid-March. He did say I should be able to travel by late February and could go ahead and make reservations to go home at that time. Or I could go back to Dr. Murphy. Guess what my decision was.

February 20, 2003 With my new relatively pain-free life, Trish took me on occasional outings. We went to the beach one day with Michelle and her little ones. We went to a shopping mall on base a couple of times and went to restaurants a couple of times. I thought I might live through this after all. I was down to taking one codeine pill at bedtime.

February 25, 2003 My trip home: Rick came home from work at four fifteen in the morning, so all three could see me off. Rick drove to the airline departure door. He couldn't park there to take me inside, so I kissed the boys good-bye, and they drove around the block a few times while Trish made sure my luggage was checked and my ticket processed. We tearfully bid each other good-bye.

A young Mexican/Hawaiian man took my wheelchair and pushed me through security, past all the people waiting in line (at least one hundred) to a little gate on the side. They searched every inch of my camera case twice—two different people. Felt me up and down for weapons (in a little private partitioned-off place away from prying eyes). The boy, Phillipe, then pushed me through the terminal, chattering away all the time. He asked me where I was from, and I told him.

"I went to Northern California once, I have relatives there," he said. I asked where he went, and he said, "Ventura," which is suburban Los Angeles. I said I lived a bit farther north. He pushed at a speed and in a direction that was completely sane, and safe. He deposited me at the exit gate and made sure I was comfortable. I had an hour to wait for departure, so I propped up my foot and read the newspaper.

A lady came over and asked if I had seen her husband. She had gone to the restroom and told her husband to watch the luggage. It could now be confiscated and destroyed if left unattended in the terminal after security changes that took place September 11, 2001.

"Yes, he followed you down the hallway when you left," I said. She moved her luggage next to me, so security would think it was mine, and went in search of him and brought him back. The man limped back and sat down in his wheelchair again. They were in their eighties, and she was dressed up proper with hat and gloves like in the old days. He had on a suit and tie. I had on jeans and a T-shirt, with a sweatshirt tied around my waist in preparation for landing in cold Medford, Oregon. Phillipe brought up another person in a wheelchair and checked on me again to see if he could get me coffee or anything. (I tipped him $5.00) What a sweetie.

The three wheelchair users were first on the plane. They took me first because I couldn't walk at all. The other two could walk when they got to the plane. At the plane door, the airline staff changed wheelchairs and strapped me into one that was twelve inches wide. They pushed me through first class, and the steward helped me from the wheelchair to the window seat in the first row. I had no idea how to work the seat, as I had never been in first class before. So I just sat down, put on my seat belt, and propped my foot up on the wall in front of me at the corner where the vertical walls met. A second steward immediately asked if I would like coffee or juice while I waited for the plane to fill. I said no and asked if the little wheelchair was staying on the plane with me. He said, "Yes, but why do you ask?" I told him that as soon as I ate or drank anything, I would have to use the restroom. He said to just signal him, and he would take care of it.

Once all first-class passengers were boarded, we were given hot washcloths for our faces and hands. Then we were offered drinks. I skipped that again. As soon as the plane leveled off after takeoff, a steward came around taking orders for breakfast. He took orders from one row of seats at a time, two people. Then he went to the galley, and someone filled the orders. I ate the wonderful freshly made coconut pancakes, spicy sausage, and tropical fruit.

When I signaled the steward, he asked the gentleman sitting next to me to please get up so he could help me. He offered me his arm; I pulled myself up and hopped to the aisle. I waited for the wheelchair to show up. The steward said the restroom was only about ten feet away, so I should just hop. I said I needed more support than his arm, which fell to his side with each hop. He took my arm and put it around his neck, grabbed me around the waist and half carried me while I hopped to the bathroom. Bet that was entertaining for the passengers to watch. I returned to my seat in the same manner. I'll never see those passengers again. What do I care what they think of my lack of grace?

The Hawaiian sitting next to me started a conversation. He was an accountant traveling to San Francisco on business. It took about thirty seconds to discover we had nothing in common. We exchanged pleasantries from time to time but mostly just read during the trip. The movie was *Stuart Little II*. I tried for five minutes to get interested but couldn't. The ride was smooth, and the sky was clear. I could see some tiny white spots in the water from time to time that I imagined were whales but were probably just whitecaps.

At San Francisco I was strapped back into the little wheelchair to disembark as far as the ramp. There they put me in a regular wheelchair, and a man took me to my next gate. That was a scary ride, as he deliberately headed toward unsuspecting passengers. He would pull up to within a couple of feet and jerk the wheelchair to one side just in time to avoid a collision. He left me in front of the empty service counter and walked off. (I tipped him $0.) I wheeled myself to a restroom to relieve myself and wash up, and then back to an out-of-the-way spot by a window near the departure gate. There was one lady in the area. She was also in a wheelchair. The sign over the service desk said the next plane was going to Boise. I asked the lady if she was waiting to go to Medford, Oregon, or Boise, Idaho. She said Medford. We chatted for a few minutes. She was 90 percent blind. That was why they put her in a wheelchair. She was going to visit her son and grandchildren, whom she had not seen in ten years. She was ill, so this was to be her last trip. She was living with her daughter in New York.

The terminal filled with Medford passengers, about twenty of us. They started the boarding process by asking the blind lady and me if we could walk up the flight of stairs onto the airplane. The other lady said someone would have to help her get to the stairs and to her seat once she was on the plane. I said I could not hop that high. They took both of us in our wheelchairs back through the terminal to an elevator. We went down through an area with multiple signs saying, “Crew Only” and “Absolutely No One But Crew Members.” We were wheeled outside and deposited into a van. We rode a hundred yards back around the terminal to our plane, where they had installed a very narrow ramp. The blind lady was led up the ramp. I was transferred to a narrow wheelchair and pulled up the ramp backward while a second man pushed on my knees.

The wheelchair wouldn’t fit down the aisle where I was to go to the second seat. The travel insurance company had bought me two seats on this little plane so I could prop my foot up, bless them. I said I could hop that far.

A gallant Frenchman sitting in the first seat said in his wonderful Charles Boyer accent, “Nonsense, my daughter and I will move there. You will sit here in the front seat where you will have more room.” He immediately jumped up and moved, and his ten-year-old daughter followed. The only problem with the front seat was the armrest between the seats was not movable. I sat next to the window and propped my leg up on the armrest in a most unladylike manner.

The scenery was gorgeous from San Francisco to Medford—my beautiful, wonderful mountainous California. Mount Shasta was majestic. I could see the Marble Mountains and Scott Valley as well as Shasta Valley on our descent. I was ready to be back where I belonged.

My camera bag had been taken from me in the wheelchair transfer at San Francisco. I was glad to see it waiting for me along with the walker I bought and carried from plane to plane. The airlines wouldn't let me use the walker on the planes or in the terminals for insurance reasons. The pilot pushed me in my wheelchair to the terminal where Marlow was waiting.

Marlow took me to the baggage conveyor belt and then took my carry-on luggage to the car. He returned at the same moment the checked-on luggage arrived. We gathered my two bags and rolled to the front of the terminal, about fifty yards from baggage claim. He loaded me into his comfy seat-bed in the van—the middle seats were removable, and the rear seat lowered into a queen-size bed. Marlow loaded the luggage, and we were off down the road toward home.

February 28, 2003 I went to an orthopedic doctor in Yreka. The three doctors I had gone to for the broken leg all had different ideas. In Yreka technicians took x-rays from four different angles and showed me eight breaks. Imagine that! Unfortunately, the orthopedic doctor did point out one shard of bone that was in the cartilage of the ankle. He said I had a fifty/fifty chance of that restricting movement of the ankle later.

The first question the staff asked was why the slit was cut down the cast. I told them it had been so tight, it was cutting off circulation and felt like someone was pouring hot grease on my leg. They repeated the same thing the second doctor did. If I had obeyed the first doctor and continued to tolerate the pain by overdosing on pain pills instead of addressing the problem, I would have lost my leg. Ghastly thought! I really did love to hike and was looking forward to exploring the Marble Mountains in my backyard.

My new doctor put a cast on up to my knee, with lots and lots of padding and no slit. He said I absolutely was not to put any weight on the leg for the next month. I thought I would be graduating to a walking cast that day and be hobbling around with my walker. He said to stick to the wheelchair for at least another month. My next appointment was April 16, and he would decide then if the leg was healed enough to consider putting weight on it.

Dr. Terrance in Hawaii said I should put weight on the leg, as that would encourage healing. This doctor said not to do that. I was going to take the most cautious route in hopes of full recovery. Unfortunately, I had already been doing some standing on it.

Note: I was in a wheelchair for a total of nine months before graduating to the walker. I wore a permanent cast for eight months before graduating to a plastic blow-up walking cast. I used the walker for a month before returning to nonsupport. The leg healed with no further complications.

Fourteen

South America

2007

Marlow and I frequently celebrated our wedding anniversaries by doing something we wouldn't ordinarily do—something we couldn't really afford. For our fiftieth anniversary, we planned on taking a space shuttle ride. We thought the price would be about $10,000.00. It turned out to cost more than $1 million each, there was a waiting list, and travelers had to be in excellent health. We gave it a miss.

Ever since my awesome trip around the perimeter of Australia in 1999–2000, I had been talking of taking a year to drive from California to the tip of South America and back. Marlow said I could go if I could find a sharpshooter who could fix car problems as a travel companion. I couldn't find anyone willing to drive through Central America, let alone all the way to Tierra del Fuego. After Columbia hit the news headlines with their drug war, Marlow said I could go if I took a troop of US Marines with me. That sounded like fun to me, but the Pentagon wouldn't agree. Marlow knew I was getting close to taking off on my own, so he agreed to see South America with me on the condition that we fly from safe spot to safe spot, and only took a month for the trip.

What a bummer. After much consideration I figured it would be my only opportunity to see the southern scenery and meet our neighbors. I accepted his offer. Out of the thirty days, we spent eight in airports. On the way home to California from Portland, Oregon, Marlow came up with a good idea.

"You know what?" he said. "We could drive from California to Patagonia and back." What a concept, two seventy-year-old people in a psychedelic painted Volkswagen van tooling down the southern continent! I hope he hangs on to that idea, but I won't hold my breath.

March 7, 2007 Scott Valley residents received eighteen inches of snow last week. Marlow and I couldn't get out of the driveway, let alone get to Medford, Oregon's, airport sixty miles away.

What a difference a week made! There was a heat wave. The snow melted fast, the driveway and the highway cleared. All was "go" for us to start our trip to South America.

I phoned to confirm our airline reservations from Miami to Lima, Peru. Lan Peru had no reservation confirmations available.

"If you have a ticket, you have a reservation." So okay, the planes were still leaving at the time quoted, the gates quoted, and we still had the seats we requested, right? I guessed we would find out when we arrived at the plane.

Marlow drove my truck to Windmill Inn in Medford, where we planned to spend the night. My plain white seven-year-old Tacoma was less tempting to thieves than Marlow's shiny blue 2005 Tundra. We had a lovely room at the Windmill. It was quiet except for Marlow's continual coughing. At three a.m., I gave up on sleep and went to the hotel lobby to read. That was more relaxing than lying awake in bed with my head sandwiched between pillows.

Poor Marlow came down with a head cold the day before the trip. The cold spread to his chest overnight.

March 8, 2007 The hotel offered to keep my truck in their parking lot for the duration of our trip—free of charge! Incredible. That was an omen; this was going to be a good trip.

The motel shuttle delivered us to the airport at five thirty a.m. Check-in was easy at the little airport for a city of 76,000 population. The nice security lady even let me lock my bags.

The flight in the turbojet was flawless. We landed in Los Angeles on time, and a shuttle took us to the departure gate in the correct terminal to catch our plane to Miami. We didn't have to go through security at LAX. Yea! I love it when things go smoothly and people are thoughtful.

On the flight from Los Angeles to Miami, Florida, I sat next to a nice lady who conversed on subjects that were interesting. The five-hour flight went quickly. Marlow sat across the aisle and dozed. He was full of cold medicine, which kept him groggy.

The hotel in Miami was fine. I took a sleeping pill and slept soundly in spite of Marlow's coughing. We were hoping he had one of those twenty-four-hour bugs, but that didn't seem to be the case. Maybe the cold would go away when we arrived in the tropics.

March 9, 2007 Our flight from Miami to Lima, Peru, left exactly on time at five twenty p.m.

I finished reading my first book—*Wave Me Goodbye,* a fiction based on fact by Jura Sherwood, a fellow member of the Siskiyou Writers Club. Jura was born in England and was one of the children sent to South Africa at the start of World War II. Her novel was about two young lovers as they maneuvered a boatload of children to safety during the beginning of the war. Not all the children made it. The tragic endeavor was discontinued after Jura's childhood trip.

Marlow and I stayed at Hotel Antigua Miraflores in Lima, a city of almost nine million people and one of the poorest cities in the world. The hotel was picturesque and comfortable. It was located near the ocean in a safe area of town. There were other areas that the cab driver told us not to frequent.

March 10, 2007 Antigua Miraflores was a great hotel. The furniture was heavy Castilian carved wood. There was no air conditioning, so it was quiet even with the unscreened windows open. Our windows faced a courtyard with a fountain and flowers. We were on the fourth floor and there was no elevator so we got our exercise walking up and down steps.

A lovely breakfast was served—fruit, fruit juice, homemade rolls, and a variety of egg dishes. I ate a roll and had a glass of juice. Marlow had *jamon y huevos*, ham and eggs. We wanted to use our Spanish words as often as possible.

Rosa, the tour guide who met us at the airport the evening before, had studied English since grade school and spoke fluently. I liked her right off because she was a hugger. I love hugs. Rosa and a non-English-speaking driver met us at Miraflores at one p.m. and returned us to the airport. Customs was a breeze, as was getting to the departure gate with Rosa's help.

The plane ride from Lima to Iquitos, Peru, was another smooth one, which was surprising, since cumulous clouds were piling up in preparation for an afternoon thundershower. We arrived a little after five p.m.

Iquitos was a typical third-world city, with no yards and chipped and cracked adobe houses stuck together with their faces on chipped and cracked sidewalks. There was lots of wrought iron over windows and doors, and the roofs were made of corrugated iron or Plexiglass.

The town vibrated with hundreds of rickshaws powered with motorcycle motors. The drivers raced from one traffic light to another throughout the downtown area. It did look like a cheap way to get around.

The people were open and friendly. We felt no fear as we strolled along a promenade overlooking the Amazon River. In an open-air bar, we saw young people dancing. The band consisted of three drums and a flute. We thought they were practicing for a show. One young man directed the maneuvers and coordination of the others. We drank a beer and enjoyed their performance. The beer cost $1.00, cheap-enough entertainment for a Saturday night.

We walked along further and found other performers. There was a puppet show and a comedian whom we watched for a short time, hoping to hear the Spanish words we knew. The comedian picked us out of the crowd and asked where we were from. I told him and responded to a couple more questions. Judging from the laughter, we were the butt of his next few jokes. Oh well, it was all in fun. The lady standing next to me gave me a light punch on the shoulder while displaying a bright smile, indicating that we were welcome as long as we maintained a sense of humor.

I had *sopa criolla*, a delicious Creole soup, for dinner. There were Creoles in Peru as well as Louisiana. Marlow had fettuccini Alfredo. The menu was European/American foods. I was expecting spicier Hispanic dishes. I expected South America to serve Mexican food, which was a foolish notion.

We took the glassed-in elevator to our third-floor room and listened to the noise of the air conditioner and watched an American movie. I spent half an hour in the shower, as I suspected it might be the last hot one I'd have for a while.

March 11, 2007 We awoke to rain. Our palatial resort gave us breakfast under the thatched roof of a patio next to the swimming pool. Lovely setting. I watched the rain drip off the leafy overhang and fall onto the marble patio floor before flowing into a swimming pool that started outside but had a canal that wound into the lobby.

Marlow took a nap after breakfast—he was still taking cold medicine—and I chatted with rickshaw drivers who waited for passengers from the hotel. The driver named Alfred told me the population of Iquitos was 600,000, and there were 20,000 rickshaw taxis. I had no idea Iquitos was so large! I expected to learn it had about 20,000 inhabitants.

The taxis buzzed around the park in front of our hotel. Each started out a bit early when the traffic light was about to change from red to green. They all pushed the limit when the light was about to change from green to red—20,000 drivers playing chicken.

When Marlow awoke, Alfred took us to the boat dock in his rickshaw. Rain still fell, and he had a blue tarp up to his eye level so we couldn't see what was going on in front of us. It may have been better that way. We arrived safely, even though we could see rickshaw drivers on either side of us come within two inches of our vehicle as we raced down the road.

At the dock we met the American owner of the cruise ship—*Rio Amazonas.* There were enough cabins to accommodate eighty passengers on the hundred-ten-year-old boat. There were only five paying passengers for this trip! There were twelve crew members. Counting Pilar, the naturalist's fiancée, a total of nineteen people were on a forty-four-meter boat. That kind of crowd I could tolerate.

Our trip would be like having a private yacht. Maybe not exactly a yacht; we had no hot water, and the light in my bathroom didn't work, so I propped the door open, looking for slithery critters while using the facility. Marlow and I were assigned adjoining rooms. He had twin beds and a bathroom, and so did I. We each had a closet. That was the extent of our furnishings.

The chef was introduced as being the bartender and the person who would clean our cabins daily. His name was German—the word, not the language. German appeared shy and spoke as rarely as possible.

The three passengers accompanying Marlow and me were Angie and David, who were celebrating their thirty-fifth anniversary, and Richard, who was married but traveling without his wife, as she hadn't retired yet. Angie was the youngest tourist, and she was nearing sixty.

We left Iquitos at twelve thirty and were immediately served a buffet-style lunch—roast chicken, steamed rice, fried bananas, a salad, and papaya for dessert. Yea! Normal food in normal quantities, unlike other cruise lines. Aaaaaaand there was no waiting in line to be seated. We all sat at the same table, including our naturalist guide, Neil, and his fiancée, Pilar.

We were told our itinerary was altered, as President Bush visited Colombia yesterday. He was hated by many people in the world and had stirred up anti-American sentiments. We wouldn't go to Columbia or Brazil for safety's sake.

I started with sniffles and sneezes this morning, so I took antihistamine in hopes of keeping the germs to myself.

I sat on the deck and viewed the jungle scenery and the thatched hut villages along the shore.

We stopped at Neil's birthplace. He introduced us to his father, who had a distillery and manufactured rum and molasses. We had a rum-tasting party on the open deck of Mr. Guerra's home. Angie and I each bought a bottle of the potent liquor. The tiny sips we had at the tasting party made me sweat. Didn't think I'd be drinking much in the tropical heat. It was interesting seeing the distillery. Mr. Guerra used mule power to crush sugarcane into pulp because there was no electricity on his farm.

Mr. Guerra had a few head of water buffalo, which natives raised for beef. Chickens, ducks, and geese wandered the grounds freely. There was a large vegetable garden and fruit trees. Obviously, the plantation had been in business for some time.

Our after dinner entertainment consisted of getting acquainted with one another. There didn't seem to be any grossly obnoxious people, which was great. Richard was from the San Francisco Bay area, and Angie and David were from Toronto.

At bedtime I started reading a book called *Inés of My Soul* by Isabel Allende. The novel was a historical fiction that took place in Chile in the 1700s.

March 12, 2007 The boat docked at Pevas about three o'clock in the morning. Incredibly, the boat was navigated down the river at night without lights. It would be so easy to run over a fishing boat or any of the logs floating by. The captain told Marlow he could see in the dark.

I heard banging during the night and thought it was men running on deck. Later I learned the noise was logs hitting the boat and bouncing down the sides. We were in cabins *uno y dos*, one and two, which meant we were at the front of the boat, and the logs first hit the boat near our window. We were directly under the wheelhouse, so there were men walking above us. The steps to the wheelhouse were next to my bed's headboard. It sounded like the men were tap dancing, but I'm sure that was my imagination.

We took a rowboat (with a motor) to a Bora Indian village. We were greeted by a film crew! Jacques Cousteau's grandson and granddaughter were filming a documentary on the natives interacting with tourists. The film crew followed the five of us everywhere.

We were told about the natives' diet and lifestyle, and then they entertained us with music and dancing. Marlow had a young woman with big, bare breasts sit beside him on a log. The scene was humorous, watching him look everywhere except at the girl. He tried to look serious and interested in the educational parts of the interchange as she explained the meaning of the dance. He wouldn't dance and wouldn't drink the traditional yuca juice out of the community cup offered everyone (because of his cold). Angie and I got out there and bounced our boobies along with the bare-chested natives. I kept my shirt on so they wouldn't get jealous. I had fun. Of course, I didn't drink out of the communal gourd either, in case I had a cold developing.

When the show was over, I whipped out my Polaroid camera and took pictures to give the children. Everyone wanted to have a picture taken. Marlow said the film crew was following me closely during that activity. A couple of adolescents elected themselves as my bodyguards and protected me from being mauled by people wanting their picture taken. Good fun. I went through a hundred pictures—ten packs of film.

We returned to the *Rio Amazonas* for lunch, and then everyone except Marlow (nap time) went to Francisco Grippa's home in Pevas. I remembered studying Mr. Grippa's work in art history class in San Jose, California, back in the late 1960s. He was an up-and-coming artist at the time.

Mr. Grippa was famous in art circles, and his home was a mansion, Amazon-style. Each room was large, with open windows and no screens. It had no ceilings, except at the roof line. There was plenty of room for the air to circulate.

The house was several structures connected with covered verandahs. All were built on stilts. I thought I would die trying to climb the steep hill and then the two hundred steps to his second-story living-room door. I was beet red and breathing hard when I arrived. Francisco immediately escorted me to a bar stool and offered me a beer. Alcohol was the last thing I needed. I asked for bottled water. I recovered in a few minutes and was able to keep up with the conversation.

Mr. Grippa told us a bit of his history. He'd been painting professionally for over fifty years and had gone through numerous styles. He had pen-and-ink portraits, realistic landscapes, and wildly modernistic paintings on his walls. All were for sale, of course. Many were larger than our walls at home. I wandered from painting to painting admiring his techniques—not that I could afford to buy anything more than his postcards.

He offered me beer again, and I told him I didn't drink alcohol in the heat of the day. He was on his third or fourth beer by that time. He immediately said something to a young man, and a few minutes later, I looked out the window to see the boy chopping a coconut from a tree with a machete. I was soon served a fresh coconut with a straw sticking in a hole. Now, that's service!

I thanked Francisco and said I wasn't used to such attention. He said that if I were his wife, he'd treat me like a queen every day. Hmm. We had met his wife when we entered; she was twenty-four years old and a typical Amazonian beauty, with golden skin and jet-black waist-length hair. Angie asked Mr. Grippa how many times he'd been married. The young woman was his sixth wife.

"Maybe Marilyn could be your next wife," Angie said. I told him to keep me in mind when he got to number twenty. He laughed and said he considered that an acceptance to his proposal. (There was a proposal?) I wondered if there were many men trading in their twenty-year-old wives for seventy-year-old women.

We spent an hour with him and thoroughly enjoyed his stories. He had lived in Paris, New York, London, and Arizona and was now winding up his days in Pevas. I said he had made a good choice; I wouldn't mind staying there for a while. He immediately invited me to bring my family back sometime and stay as long as I wanted, living in his house. Did he do that with all his guests? There were several people lounging around the multistory complex.

When Angie and her husband, David, started talking about buying paintings and shipping them to their home in Canada, I excused myself and went down near the river to take Polaroids of natives.

That activity was always fun, but the pressure of so many people wanting pictures got a bit stressful. I wanted to be fair and give one picture to each person, but that was hard to communicate to children, let alone little ones who didn't speak the same language as me. I went through forty pictures and ran out of film. They were happy to pose for pictures with my digital camera after I explained I'd be taking those pictures home.

I took half a dozen pictures with my digital camera, then sat down to rest. The kids wanted to practice their English, and I wanted to practice my Spanish, so they taught me how to count (something I already knew). I did all right with that, so they started introducing themselves to me. That got them giggling. My funny pronunciations probably sounded like gibberish.

Our guide and fellow passengers appeared, and I rose to leave. A woman who had been on the perimeter of the activity came over, shook my hand, and said in very clear English, "Thank you very much." When she let go of my hand, I realized she had given me two little bracelets made from seeds. They will be treasured. I hoped the children grew up remembering that some Americans were friendly.

I took a shower. Who needed hot water in that heat? I felt so much better after getting my head cooled off and drinking a cool Coke (*no hielo, por favor*). I was careful to order all drinks without ice.

After sunset we went for a rowboat ride with Neil, the naturalist, and Fernando, the boat driver. Neil caught an eighteen-inch-long caiman (alligator), a snake, and several tiny frogs for us to hold, admire, and/or photograph.

March 13, 2007 I expected there to be leeches on the planned jungle hike, so I had on the knee-high socks that had been worn under my plastic walking cast when I broke my leg in January 2003. Then I wore heavy hiking boots that snakes couldn't bite through, jeans, a long-sleeved shirt, a hat, Deet for mosquitoes, and sun block. It was almost as troublesome getting ready to play in the jungle as it was to play in the snow.

The eight a.m. walk was postponed until two p.m. It would be mighty hot by then. I'd need some ice to pack in the crown of my hat. What a sissy I'd gotten to be.

The steamy jungle walk was hot, long, and fascinating. Richard, the man traveling single, collapsed on the way back. He'd made several stops to rest, but there weren't safe places to sit down or lie down in a jungle. He had football-damaged knees that gave out on him when walking on uneven ground. He also had asthma. When he collapsed, David, the prosecuting attorney from Toronto, sprinted back to the boat to get Richard's nebulizer. All ended well, with Richard making it to the boat in one piece.

Marlow and I hit the hot tub, which was filled with "purified" river water. The crew filled the tub soon after we boarded, let the mud settle out for a few days, and vacuumed that up from the bottom. The water was warmed by the sun but was cooler than the air. It felt mighty good, and we soaked for half an hour enjoying the serenity, greenery, and birds on shore.

It was siesta time; the Pevas natives on shore who hung out at the boat hoping to sell their crafts had disappeared. Our crew wasn't visible. Marlow went to his room to lie down. I read my novel. I was the only passenger awake, so I arranged deck chairs and tables to my liking and switched from one seat to another, according to where the sun hit the deck. Such a life!

My cold was better, so I quit taking antihistamine. I thought that might have contributed to my spaciness climbing to Francisco's house yesterday. (Note: We were on first-name basis, since we were engaged to marry.)

We passengers spent a pleasant twilight watching the children from Pevas play with a baby peccary. It followed its owner everywhere. Sometimes the boy ran faster than the pig, and it would squeal loudly until the owner returned. Boys were doing aerial somersaults into the river from the bank. Fishermen were arriving with their catch to be prepared for dinner. The people were so agile and healthy looking. We hadn't seen fat people, though a couple of the Bora women were slightly overweight. Perhaps they had access to store-bought food.

March 14, 2007 *Rio Amazonas* guests took turns having health problems—Marlow and I with our colds, Richard with his asthma attack and bad knees, and now David was confined to his room with diarrhea and vomiting. I was the most fortunate of the sick, as my cold was mild.

After breakfast everyone except David hopped aboard our rowboat taxi and took off for a remote Bora commune. We rode a bit over an hour in the lightly falling rain. We went up an Amazonian tributary called Ampiyacu River. We saw a three-toed sloth, plus the following birds-a greater toucan, purple martins (swallows), a greater ani, a falcon, a white-necked heron, and others including many parrots along the way. I loved watching the terns skip along just above the water and dip down for a quick bite when a tasty niblet swam under them.

We arrived at a mud-bank about twenty or thirty feet high. Neil chopped out something resembling steps for us old folks to climb. Two ladies inhabiting the village pulled us up over the crest. We were loaded down with cameras, wearing rain ponchos, and, well, old. Everyone made it without sliding into the river.

Sixteen people lived in the round communal house. The men were not home; they were working in the forest. Three women and half a dozen kids showed us their home and lifestyle. The large thatched hut had a loft with cubicles of mosquito netting for sleeping. The walls were sticks about two inches in diameter stuck vertically into the earth. They were tied together with strings made from plants, possibly pandanus spines. They would not keep out snakes and rats, but would keep monkeys and peccaries at bay.

Downstairs was an entertainment area with hammocks for men to lie on after using cocaine and a drum (a hollow log) for calling the neighbors to a party. The women dried cocoa leaves and pounded them into a fine, fine powder. At party time the men took large spoonfuls into their mouths and moistened the powder, then placed it behind their lower lip like baseball players do tobacco. All drugs were legal in Peru. The women did not partake.

In a kitchen area, a fire burned lowly under a single metal plate used for baking bread made of yuca flour. The yuca plant was also made into a drink. The ladies shared some of each with us. Marlow and I ate the flavorless bread, but rejected the drink, as once more there was only one gourd to be passed around to all drinkers. We needed to carry our own cups on future excursions to visit natives. I would hate to leave these generous people with a cold.

The natives had pineapples and bananas growing near the lodge. When the men were lucky with hunting, there was meat such as monkey, bird, or lizard, and there was always fish available. The woman also used roots and berries that were edible. That was the sum of their groceries.

The center of the lodge was the children's play area, but there was not a single toy to be seen. I asked Neil about toys, and he said playing consisted of practicing to be an adult. The boys practiced hunting, fishing, agriculture, and wood carving. The girls practiced gathering and making food and clothes and weaving hammocks. The women sat on the ground to do most of their chores.

They didn't appear to be aware they were poor, and they were happy as can be. The children were shy but polite. Infants were on mats inside a mosquito-net enclosure. The women were a bit shy, but cheerfully answered our questions and offered to share anything they had.

Possessions were scarce; these people existed on basic necessities. Kitchen utensils were almost nonexistent, and men's tools were few. There were no cupboards. They had no decorations except a couple of pictures of the Sacred Heart of Jesus. I assumed they were Catholic. There were not enough clothes visible to fill one closet, and there were sixteen people living there. I asked about the dozen shirts and shorts hanging on a clothesline, and it was explained that whoever needed a clean shirt or shorts took what he needed from the line. Clothes belonged to the community, not to an individual. I thought about stripping and leaving my clothing with them. I could make it back to the boat wearing only a poncho. Well, a poncho and my hiking boots. I don't do barefoot. By the time I had worked up the nerve to leave my shorts and T-shirt, Neil was herding us back down the embankment.

The fact that not many tourists came to visit was obvious; there weren't crafts to be sold. I wished I had my Polaroid camera, but had left it behind because I didn't want to wrestle with three cameras.

Fortunately, I had enough foresight to stick some notebooks, pencils, and erasers in my camera bag. I left them with the children.

Neil took us on a walk into the jungle for an hour. Richard stayed behind. He wasn't game to try another walk on unpaved trails. Just as well, as Neil used his machete to carve out a virgin trail. I would have gotten lost within minutes, but was confident that the native boy knew what he was doing. Sometimes we ended up in water six to eighteen inches deep, and everyone kept their eyes peeled for snakes. I'm sure they were nearby, but we saw nary a one.

Sure enough, after showing us many wonders of the flora and fauna, Neil returned us to the communal lodge. He had no worry of getting lost. It rained all through the trip, so I made no attempt to write down the names of the plants. Therefore I can't tell you what we saw except for beautiful red mahogany and orchids. Neil gave the names in Spanish as well as the local dialect and occasionally in English. I think it was English. Is *ficus* an English word? It's probably spelled *phycus*, if it is.

Richard said the women had taken food to the workers in the forest. Richard was six foot eight, so he wasn't game to try his luck in the people's hammocks. He sat on the floor to wait for us. The average height of Bora men was about five feet; the women were shorter. He said they wore no protection from the rain, which was coming down pretty hard. They just wrapped some of the yuca bread, cold fish, and something that looked like potatoes into a cloth, and off they went. I bet they thought we were silly wearing ponchos, hats, and boots. What an experience! It certainly gave us perspective on the necessities of life.

We had a hardy lunch waiting when we returned. I couldn't resist the salad made of heart of palm, red bell peppers, and tomatoes. David, the ailing passenger, said he watched the cook prepare last night's dessert. The cook peeled the bananas and then washed them in water before slicing them into the molasses from Neil's father. We took that to mean the cooks had been instructed to wash everything before giving it to us to eat.

At four thirty Neil gave us a demonstration for making and using a blowgun. A typical gun was four feet long with an oversized thimble, about the size of a shot glass, on one end. The thimble was called a "handhold." Straight limbs from the "pornographic" tree were chosen, the limb cut in half, and a tiny one-eighth-inch groove carved out and sanded smooth. The two sides were glued back together and reamed with a straight steel-hard piece of iron-bark tree. The tube was tied and wrapped tightly in palm leaves. The process took about two months to accomplish.

The pornographic tree was so-called because a new limb looked like a phallus.

The arrows were about eight inches long. They were sharpened on piranha teeth and dipped in a broth made from boiled poison-dart frogs. A tiny bit of kapok was twirled around the arrow about an inch from the unsharpened end. The kapok gave the arrow a surface on which to blow. Blowing on a one-sixteenth-inch-diameter stick in a one-eighth-inch-diameter hole would not create enough force to inject the arrow into its victim. The kapok gave the surface for the hunter to accurately blow the arrow forty or fifty feet. Amazing!

The guns were mainly used to kill monkeys or birds for food, but had been used in warfare. Only the tips were poisoned, so when the monkey tried to remove it, he'd brush his palm across the arrow, breaking it off with the poison still in his system. As soon as the monkey died, his throat was cut, and he was hung upside down to drain out poisoned blood. The monkey was then safe for human consumption. I don't know if the FDA would have approved that process, but it had worked for the natives for hundreds of years.

Our dinner was not monkey. I don't think so anyhow. Our chef had some strange combinations, but we were eating hardy and healthy at every meal. Tonight was no exception. We had pasta with garlic and olive oil, steamed rice, heart of palm mixed with green beans and pickles, and thin strips of beef fried with potatoes. Imagine having pasta, rice, and potatoes at the same meal at home. Mandarins left unpeeled in a bowl on the table were our dessert. Steamed rice had been served at every meal since we boarded the boat. Someone must have told the chef it was good for tourists, as we didn't see natives eating or growing rice. The people with intestinal problems were glad to see it served.

Marlow compounded his cold by getting diarrhea. That was something novel in our travels. I'm usually the one with digestive tract problems. Richard also had the bug, so all three men skipped the next scheduled side trip.

Our evening's entertainment was a rowboat ride looking for critters. The night was beautiful, clear, balmy, and pleasant when we got far enough upstream that Fernando, the driver, could turn off the noisy motor. We floated with the current back to the *Rio Amazonas.*

My only complaint about the *Rio Amazonas* was the continual noise. There was a huge diesel engine going all the time. Even when we stopped, the engine had to be run so there would be air conditioning in the cabins. The air conditioning made the rooms five or six degrees cooler than the outside temperature and may have removed some of the humidity. I would have preferred quiet rooms to slightly cooler rooms, but I'm sure I would have been outvoted if put to the test. Most civilized people have adapted to noise.

March 15, 2007 Marlow, David, and Richard were out of commission. Angie and I were the only customers for the six thirty a.m. bird-watching excursion. The creeks off the Amazon's tributaries were narrow in places, and we drifted through an archway of greenery. There were tropical flowers and vines—like morning glories draped over the multitude of ficus, mahogany, and unfamiliar trees. Neil gave their names in Spanish and Latin as well as the native dialect. It was all Greek to me.

We did indeed see lots and lots of birds. There were even a small number that sat still long enough for me to film them. The rarest bird we saw was the hoatzin, a bird that dates to the dinosaur days. It was amazing that they survived, as they were weak flyers and fed mostly on leaves of various plants. The young ones had claws on their wings, which enabled them to climb trees. If a predator got to the nest, they could drop into the water and then climb back up the trunk of the tree when it was safe.

We also saw oropendulum—a yellow-and-black bird of the magpie family that built tubular sausage-shaped nests about two feet long.

The black-collared hawk was found on several branches, as was the caracara, a bird of the falcon family. We managed to spot one greater ani. Angie and I saw a beautiful pair of blue-banded toucanets that have similar features to toucans but are smaller. There were jacanas on water lilies. The white-winged swallows and purple martins did aerobatic tricks in front of our boat for our enjoyment. Neil said they were clearing the mosquitoes from our path. Good for them.

We were honored to view a couple of blue-morph butterflies among the throngs of yellow, white, and multicolored beauties flitting from tree to bush to vine.

Several times Fernando turned off the motor, and we floated with the current, enjoying birdsong as well as the sight of them. We climaxed the trip by entering a good-sized black-water lagoon. The surface was glass smooth, with reflections of cumulous clouds. The edges of the lake were covered in a seaweed that gave the appearance of green beaches leading to the surrounding jungle. Neil explained that black water was the favorite haunt of piranhas, so we didn't dangle our fingers or toes overboard.

At nine o'clock Neil announced that we should return to the *Rio Amazonas* for breakfast and to check on our ailing mates. Angie and I could have gone on floating in paradise for two or three more hours before thinking about food.

Angie was a retired high school principal who was about fifty-five to sixty years old. She was enthusiastic about any activity and all of nature. She was a hiker, a real hiker who did hikes that lasted two to three weeks, walking twelve hours a day and often climbing five hundred to two thousand feet in elevation. She was also a writer and a genealogist, the same as me. We got along just fine. I just wouldn't volunteer to go for a walk with her.

After breakfast David came out of their cabin long enough to join us for some piranha fishing. I caught the first fish, and then that was all I caught. From then on I merely fed the piranhas fresh bait. Angie and Neil caught three apiece, and Fernando, the boat driver, caught the most, with about six. He was taking the fish off the hooks for us and had more than one person who needed help, so he quickly released one piranha and left it on the seat beside him while taking the fish off the second person's line. Yep, sure enough, the piranha bit him on the butt. I knew it must have been painful because Fernando jumped, but he didn't let out a sound. David pouted all the way home because he didn't catch any fish. Pilar, Neil's fiancée, giggled and cheered for each of us.

Pilar, a Peruvian beauty, was in law school. It seemed like she and David could converse since he was an attorney, but alas, they spoke different languages.

David returned to his cabin as soon as we docked, and we saw no more of him that day. Marlow was cooped up in our cabin all day. I think he slept most of the time, since he had no television to stare at and brought no books. The sleep probably did him good, since he'd been sick the whole trip.

After lunch Angie, Richard, and I went to a village of natives with Neil. The residents were called Riverinas because they lived on the Amazon shoreline. Neil said their settlement was temporary, and when the soil refused to nurture their crops, they would move on.

They were an exceptionally handsome people. They were short compared to Americans. I was five foot two tall by the time I was thirteen and in eighth grade. I talked to a twelve-year-old whom I had mistakenly thought was a first or second grader. The adult males were about five foot two to five foot four, and the women were under five feet.

That was the most prosperous village we had visited. Politicians promised people improvements if the people voted for them. The government gave the Riverinas a diesel generator and wired the town for streetlights. There were no streets, no vehicles to put on streets, so the government put in paved sidewalks. The government built a school but couldn't find teachers to occupy it. The individual houses had no running water or electricity, but they did have sidewalks and streetlights when they could afford to buy diesel fuel.

The homes were six to eight feet off the ground (flood proofing) and made of local woods with thatched roofs. There were chickens and ducks galore. The owners cut the wing feathers or marked ownership of their birds one way or another. Then they were all turned loose to run wherever as a group. The people must have been honest when choosing an animal for dinner or dividing eggs. We saw no pigs or peccaries, but there were a couple of water buffalo at the river's edge. They were community property; they didn't belong to an individual.

As soon as we arrived at the Riverina village, it began to rain. The man in the cabin closest to our docking spot invited us into his house for shelter. His name was Guerro. I thought he was a personal friend of Neil's, but learned later they had never met. Neil told us that if someone offers you shelter, and you refuse, you will never be allowed to enter that person's house again. Well, chances are small that we'll visit Guerro's neighborhood again, but still, I'm glad we left on friendly terms.

His living quarters were dirty. The floor was littered with fish heads and turtle shells—you know, typical stuff you find lying on a living-room floor. It turned out Guerro was smoking fish to preserve for later use. He had been cleaning the fish when we arrived. Oh okay, that's a pretty good excuse.

He had a fire going in a "stove" made of cement blocks with a rack about a foot above the smoldering embers. The rack was covered with fish and something indistinguishable. I didn't ask, but it might have been turtle parts.

His house consisted of one closed-in room surrounded by a ten-foot-wide covered verandah. The room was mainly used for storage; the verandah was where life was lived. The only furniture was a single hammock. Guerro was also brooding chickens in the "kitchen." It was the logical place to keep them safe from snakes and other predators.

Guerro's wife worked in the orchard. She chopped banana leaves with a machete the whole time we were there. The rain didn't slow her down.

A young boy peeked from the storage room a couple of times. I suspected he was a grandson, as Guerro and his wife looked to be close to my age. It was hard for me to judge the ages of people. I thought one young mother was thirty-something, and she turned out to be sixteen. Guerro and his wife may have been in their thirties, for all I know.

I was a Pied Piper with my cameras. Children crowded around so thickly, I could hardly walk. I missed most of Neil's educational lecture, not that I minded.

March 16, 2007 After breakfast we went on one more fishing trip. We had a full contingency today—all three men felt well enough to join Angie and me. A dozen small fish were caught, some piranhas, and some catfish. Only the tiniest were returned to the water. The rest were taken back to the *Rio Amazonas* and cooked for our next meal. I was glad Marlow caught a couple of piranhas. Then he followed my lead in feeding bait to the quick little buggers. They were only the size of sunfish.

We visited a modern town of 2,000 inhabitants. Around the large square were shops (not tourist places) with dirt floors and a few shelves of wares; there was a Catholic Church built of cement blocks. It was unlocked, and we went inside to admire the simple spiritual decorations. There was also a convent, an uninhabited school, a police station, and of course, a bar. There were sidewalks and streetlights, though no vehicles. People spent the afternoons lounging on their verandahs. There were several men swinging in hammocks or sitting on porch steps. The day was Friday; it was a little before noon, and children were everywhere, so I assumed there were no teachers for their schools.

Quite a bit of laughter came from the bar, but we didn't enter. Once more the people were friendly and happy. A group of children escorted us on our walk around town and were delighted to see their image on the back of my digital camera.

The houses were well constructed of wood as though they were done by professionals, and I wondered if the government had built them. No one appeared to be working except the occasional shop clerk; perhaps they lived on government subsidy. Neil said some people raised crops and sold them in Iquitos.

Thinking about it on the boat later, I realized Neil took us from the poorest of living conditions at the commune to the most modern, where people could buy their food instead of hunting or growing all of it. Some of the homes in this town had electricity. The one thing they all had in common was that people seemed content with their lot in life.

We didn't see a single doctor, hospital, or pharmacy. We saw no open schools. We saw no factories or places of employment except the few little shops in the last village. People fished, hunted, grew crops or water buffalo, and bartered for an existence. Neil said if they got sick and traditional herbal medicines didn't cure what ailed them, they died.

In the late afternoon, Fernando motored across the two-mile-wide Amazon and up a tributary to Monkey Island. What fun it was playing with baby spider monkeys and baby howler monkeys. The woolly monkeys ran, climbed, and swung from limbs all around us. They chattered, giggled, and argued. They were definitely showing off for the visitors.

One young woolly monkey, who was equivalent in age and attitude to a teenager, took a disliking to Neil. He bit him every chance he got. The monkey was chased off by handlers, and it ran like the wind in a big circle so it could come right back and attack Neil again. It bit his shoes when he tried to walk. Neil grabbed the monkey and tossed it into the air, where it reached out and caught a limb and made a circle around tree branches to end up jumping on Neil's back. I wish I could have followed him with my camcorder. The scene was quite amusing to watch, though I'm sure the monkey bites were painful when he hit skin instead of shoe leather.

We took refuge in a screened-in porch of the owner's large house, a real house built of wood on cement posts. It probably had half a dozen rooms enclosed, in addition to the verandah. There were outbuildings where the animals were sheltered while recovering from an injury or illness. The owner collected orphaned animals and brought them to his island to raise and release back into the wild, if possible. Sometimes the critters got too attached to humans and vice versa and had to live out their days on the island. The owner said his whole island was usually flooded once or twice a year. That was why no one outside of his family wanted to share the place with him. After each flood he had an influx of snakes to deal with. Gosh, just when I thought I'd found the perfect location to retire.

March 17, 2007 We had a morning landing at Iquitos. Was the trip already over? Aw shucks. I could have stayed for a month and not been bored a minute.

Neil organized a couple of petting zoo tours for us. They were great. The first had a tapir, anteater, jaguar (no, we didn't pet him, he was full-grown), and lots of funny monkeys.

The tapir was an animal the size of a large sow that was brought in as an infant and was affectionately attached to its handler. The handler went into the fenced-off paddock and called the tapir with a funny noise. The tapir lumbered up and lay at the handler's feet. Then he rolled on his back like dogs do for the handler to scratch his stomach. It stood, rubbed its snout against the handler's legs a couple of times, and then sauntered off into the brush from whence it came.

The anteater was the strangest creature, with his long snout and extra-long tongue. His fur was wiry six- to eight-inch-long hair. He had claws six to eight inches long also and was not good-natured. I kept my distance. Marlow got close for a photo, but was warned away with a story about an anteater tearing open his handler from throat to groin with one swipe of his claws.

The ornery woolly monkeys ran up and down the tourists like we were trees. They tried to take hair clips, caps, scarves, or any article of loose clothing. They also knew how to unzip purses and camera bags. I had one bamboozled, as I held my hand firmly over the zipper tab on my carry-all bag. He worked and worked with the zipper until it finally dawned on him that he needed to move my hand. By that time he was distracted by a handler bringing a bowl of food to the anteater, and the monkey ran off to harass the prehistoric-looking creature. He pulled the anteater's snout out of the bowl and held it while he got a few mouthfuls of chow.

There were good-sized caiman, six to ten feet long, in a jungle pond. We didn't try to handle them like we did the eighteen-inch one that Neil caught in the river on our first night excursion. We stayed well behind the flimsy-looking chicken-wire fence.

We went to a butterfly house where the larvae-to-butterfly transition was taught. The teacher was very good, I'm sure, but I was more interested in trying to take the perfect iridescent blue-morph butterfly's picture. I didn't succeed. I felt so fortunate to have experienced this outstanding creature both on the Amazon and at Eungella National Park in Australia.

Everywhere we went, I was impressed with the appearance of the people. They were clean, neat, handsome, and friendly. I've gotten used to little kids taking hold of my hand. I know they wanted me to take their picture on the digital camera, so they could see themselves on the screen. Come to think of it, I don't remember seeing mirrors anywhere except on the *Rio Amazonas*, which was outfitted for tourists.

At the second "petting" zoo we went to, there were anacondas. Thank goodness! I was afraid I wasn't going to get to see one up close and personal. The idea that I could touch one was exciting. I let Marlow hold it, as it looked heavy, and my back had been giving me warning twitches not to do anything strenuous, or it would send me to bed for a day or two. That's one of the little nuisances of getting old we learn to live with. The huge snake felt soft and smooth like others I've had the pleasure of holding. This anaconda was not a pretty color; it was a mottled cream or beige color and had no patterns.

I did hold the parrots—macaws, they were called. Some were called blue and gold, others red and green, or scarlet macaws. When I held out my arm for the transfer from Marlow, a bird bit me just barely enough to break the skin. I knew the bird could break a finger with his strong beak, so I stood still until the handler flicked it on the head like I've seen some parents do to kids to get their attention. After that the birds behaved well and let us hold and pet them.

A little girl came up and took my hand, and I walked to the salesroom with her. I bought her a piece of candy and myself a Coke. She kept hanging on to me even after I had taken her picture and shown it to her. She was a little cutie. First thing I knew, she was sitting on my lap to eat her candy.

When we got ready to move on, a woman walked up and pointed to the child and said, "Ten dollars." I thought she wanted a donation for the attention the child had given and waved her away, saying no.

"Five dollars?" the woman asked.

Like a naïve fool, I said, "La niña es bonita, porque no. No pesos o dollars."

I read that South America was trying to keep the Amazonians from becoming beggars, so the countries' governments asked tourists not to give people money for no reason.

Another woman approached and handed me a boy about three and said, "Five dollars."

It dawned on me that these women might be offering their children for sexual exploitation! I was horrified. I put the boy on the ground, glared at the women, and said firmly, "No!"

I spoke loudly enough that it attracted Neil's attention, and he walked back to see if I needed help. I told him I didn't want to give the women any money. He said something in Spanish, and the women with children went away. Later in Iquitos I saw a billboard decrying tourist pedophilia. It made me nauseated to think someone would think I was such a person. What on earth could a mother possibly need money for that she was willing to rent her small child's body to attain? The only thing I could think of was drugs.

March 18, 2007 Most of the day was spent lounging around the El Dorado Plaza Hotel in Iquitos. We watched the Sunday-morning parade of schools, businesses, and military branches. The parade was completely comprised of people on foot; there were no fire engine sirens wailing, police cars squealing, or horses prancing.

Checkout was at eleven thirty, after which we sat in the lobby waiting for a Brendan tour guide. We received a phone call from the travel agent telling us not to check out until three p.m., as they had cleared it with the hotel for us to stay in our room until we were ready to leave for the airport. Too late. Our room had been cleaned, and we really didn't feel like dragging our suitcases back upstairs. We left our bags behind the check-in desk and went for a walk.

I liked the waterfront with its parks, paths, and tourist shops. I bought a mahogany canoe about a foot long to recall memorable moments spent on the Amazon and its tributaries. There were always families or young lovers occupying shoreline parks. Well-behaved teenagers were found in groups practicing music or playing some sport. We stopped for a bowl of ice cream and watched the locals.

Iquitos's airport only operated from five p.m. to eight a.m. as vultures were so thick during the day, it was dangerous to fly jet airplanes in or out. The buzzards left a little before five to look for a safe place to roost for the night.

Our guide arrived in a van at three and escorted us to the airport, where we were booked on a flight to Lima.

March 19, 2007 We spent four or five hours at the zoo in Lima. Marlow spent 90 percent of the rest of the day in bed watching American television. He was so happy to be back to civilization, where he could see whether the men and women of *Law and Order* would really convict the bad guys or not.

I walked Lima sidewalks. I did an unscientific survey. I saw two women wearing dresses; the rest wore jeans, shorts, or slacks. Many people wore uniforms of one sort or another. It was a workday, and evidently employers supplied clothes.

Children wore school uniforms. At least they had teachers in Lima, if not on the Amazon. I spoke to a teacher while we waited for a traffic light to turn green and learned that all schoolchildren in Peru were taught English as a second language from grade school through high school—those that had teachers anyhow.

I saw no one smoking. A few people used cell phones but not many. Many people wore smiles and greeted me as we passed. I stood out as a tourist because of my pale skin and the cameras dangling from my neck.

The driving was crazy, with few rules being followed as far as I could determine, but I saw no accidents. There was a lot of horn honking, though.

And lastly, the general appearance of the people was handsome, fit, and content. Less than 10 percent were overweight or dangerously skinny. That was certainly different from any US city.

I rejoined Marlow, and we walked to a restaurant and had a wonderful meal in pleasant surroundings for a reasonable price. Restaurants were one place we got to practice our Spanish.

Then we returned to the Miraflores hotel for a sound night's sleep.

March 20, 2007 Marlow and I were up at four thirty, dressed, and on the way to the airport via taxi. Our tour guide did not show up to take us to the hotel from the airport on the nineteenth, nor did one show up this morning. I hoped they weren't in accidents. They should have phoned and left us a message explaining the negligence.

Check-in at Lima's airport went smoothly. It was such a blessing to have reasonable security people to deal with. We didn't have to remove our shoes or wait while they fiddled with our belongings. My bags were locked, and that didn't seem to concern anyone. They hand checked our film by request.

Once again I was assigned an inside seat and Marlow an aisle seat. We had requested window seats for Marlow and aisle seats for me throughout the trip. That very rarely happened. As soon as we were at altitude and allowed to unbuckle our seat belts, I skittered out of my claustrophobic middle seat to an empty aisle seat.

The movie was *Queen*, which I wanted to see, but I preferred to watch it in English. There weren't English subtitles, so I turned off the movie and listened to music. I enjoyed music in any language.

A Brendan tour guide met us at the airport and gave us a history lesson on the way to the hotel. Mercedes spoke with a decided English accent. She said her father was Argentinean, her mother was French, and she went to school in London before the war. Did she mean World War II? If she went to school twelve years before England got into the war in 1940, she was eighty-five years old! I should be so active at eighty-five. She got around like a healthy sixty-year-old.

Buenos Aires was extremely different from Lima, Peru. This place throbbed with money. There were eight-lane highways, hundreds of skyscrapers, and thousands of people milling on the sidewalks. Many folks carried shopping bags. It was popular to live in an apartment downtown. Therefore, there were grocery stores downtown. One could purchase an apartment for a mere $70,000.00 or upward to over $1 million. We were in a cleaner version of New York.

One noticeable difference between Buenos Aires and New York was the large amount of French provincial architecture, left over from two centuries ago when France occupied the territory. The old buildings were slowly being replaced by steel and glass buildings. There was also English Tudor and Italian Rococo architecture. Buenos Aires had a strong connection to Europe. The Old World apartment buildings had patios and window boxes sprouting flowers. Buenos Aires politicians decided many years ago it would keep the air cleaner if they put a park on every fourth block. That was good thinking. The people looked different than the ones in Peru. Ninety percent had European or North American ancestry. Very few Hispanics were seen, though everyone spoke Spanish.

The service in our dinner restaurant was extremely slow; it was early. People in Peru and Argentina ate dinner between nine and eleven p.m. We were at the restaurant at six. There were only a couple of other customers. The disappointing food finally arrived, and we ate as much as we wanted. Then the check came, and we were cheated. Welcome back to civilization.

I told Marlow to say something to the hard-to-find waiter. He wouldn't, didn't want to make a scene, as he didn't think he could communicate the difference between what we ordered and what we were paying for. I hate being cheated, so I pouted on the walk back to the hotel. I'm childish that way.

March 21, 2007 We took a tour bus to an *estancia* (ranch) to watch *gauchos* (cowboys) in action. There were nine other buses unloading tourists when we arrived. Pretty señoritas offered locally made wine or juice and empanadas—small meat pies—as we debarked.

The first activity we were offered was a horseback ride or a wagon ride to see the property. That sounded like fun. We were thinking thousands of acres and had our camera gear, so we chose the wagon ride. The wagon was only a hundred yards from the gate when we spotted burrowing owls standing guard at the entrance to their hole-in-the-ground homes. We went about a thousand yards out and back. Okay, that was a bit hokey.

We were promised a barbecue, and I wanted to see how they barbecued meat for nine busloads of people. The pits were about fifty feet long and twelve feet wide. They used wood to cook the meat, and it had been on the fire for a while. There were steaks, burgers, whole chickens, and sausages. The meat looked done, but it was supposed to be another hour before lunch. The meat was being turned with long-handled shovels like pizza paddles.

We wandered to the museum. It took Marlow about five minutes to cover the whole building. It took me a bit longer. As I exited, we heard the lunch bell tolling.

The all-you-can-eat meat was dry but tasty. I enjoyed the regular sausage more than the steak. Neither Marlow nor I tried the blood sausage offered. There was potato salad, coleslaw, bread, and apple strudel. It was one of the few meals I've eaten where people were expected to fill up on meat instead of starchy foods. Wine bottles were left on the tables for people to consume freely. Some folks chose beer or bottled water. I took advantage of the bottled water, carrying two extras with me as I left the table.

After the meal we were treated to tango and flamenco demonstrations that were greatly entertaining. Then a German-style band played dance music, and many guests danced polkas, waltzes, and fox-trots.

When that ended, the gaucho games began. We walked to covered seats along the playing fields. The mosquitoes were bad, but fortunately I had put on Deet before leaving the hotel. I had expected there to be cattle and cattle dung to draw flies on the estancia. The gauchos displayed their prowess with horse handling and then did a thing where they rode pell-mell at an arch that had a couple of rings hanging from strings at its apex. If the gauchos stabbed the ring with the little stick in their hand, they brought the ring to a lady in the audience and offered it in exchange for a kiss on the cheek. I was flabbergasted that a young gaucho chose me for his kiss. There were attractive young women standing beside me. I guessed his wife was in the audience, and he wanted to pick someone safe. I brought the ring home, of course. It was not something I needed to take to the jewelers to have appraised. It was a key-chain ring.

March 22, 2007 The flight to Iguazu (e-GWA-sue) Falls went well, except for the usual seat misassignments (that's a made-up word).

We were met by a sweet young thing named Carolina from Brendan and escorted to the super-plush resort called Cataradas Hotel. Cataradas meant waterfalls in Spanish. The girl was Brazilian and worked the falls from both sides of the border—three days in Argentina, speaking Spanish and English, and three days in Brazil, speaking Portuguese and English.

We settled into our large luxurious room and then went swimming in the pool. It had waterfalls, slides, a built-in bar, a volleyball net, and plenty of chaise lounges for sun bathing. There was a fitness center and a youth center in buildings beside the S-shaped pool. The grounds were beautifully manicured and decorated with pretty people going from one entertainment venue to another. We swam in the cool water for half an hour, then warmed up in the eight- shaped hot tub before returning to our room for a shower. We were squeaky clean when we went to dinner.

March 23, 2007 Cataradas offered a decadent spread for breakfast. There were probably twenty different breads and at least that many fruits, in addition to a dozen cooked dishes and cold cuts.

Our Brendan guide, Carolina, who preferred to be called Carol, met us in the lobby at a quarter till nine. We were off to see world-famous Iguazu Falls. Think of every adjective you can that means "awesome," write the words down with commas in between, and you will come close to describing Iguazu Falls. It was like seeing twenty Niagara Falls in a lush jungle setting. We walked miles on rainforest trails and expanded-metal catwalks to reach various outlooks.

When I didn't think I could walk another mile, we went down into the canyon and caught a Zodiac boat ride into the spray of a few falls. There were two hundred seventy waterfalls in twenty two miles of river. The boat ride was exhilarating. We were thoroughly drenched, which felt good after getting overheated hiking.

Marlow and I climbed a million steps at the end of the boat ride to get to a flatbed truck with benches that took us through the rainforest to meet Carol again. I thought the park staff might have to bring a wheelbarrow down the trail to haul me the last half mile.

March 24, 2007 Carol escorted us to the airport. On the ride Carol got credit for the best quote we had heard so far. We were talking about the care of national narks and she said, "Some tourists are not very polite toward nature." I suspected some local citizens were not very polite toward South America's nature either, a problem also prevalent in the US.

We were met in Buenos Aires by Barbara holding a sign saying, "Kill Patrick." Barbara was a pretty woman dressed to tango. She immediately hugged both Marlow and me. I love the warm, welcoming feeling of a hug, don't you?

As soon as we were settled into the car, Barbara began a sales speech. Did local merchants pay her for sending them clients? At any rate I wasn't interested in taking home any Argentinean leather or silver jewelry. I would have liked some of their national stone, rhodochrosite, but they were asking four times more for samples than what I would pay at a gem show in California. We were taken to our hotel, where a second lady awaited us.

Mercedes, the eighty-five-year-old wonder woman, took us on a tour of Buenos Aires. Neither Marlow nor I were city people, but we wanted to learn more about the area and the people. Mercedes was knowledgeable and talked nonstop about Buenos Aires and Argentinean history, politics, and culture.

We learned early that if we wanted to ask a question or insert a comment, we had to shout to get her attention. We did appreciate her stories and introduction to Jose San Martin, who was the father of Argentinean independence and responsible for the European settlement of Uruguay, Paraguay, and Peru, as well as Argentina. Why were school kids in the

United States only taught about Bolivar? I didn't recall ever hearing about the South American hero named Jose San Martin.

We rode past government buildings, embassies, and plush mansions built right out to the sidewalk and walled in with massive concrete fences. Maybe they had atriums or were built around a courtyard. Everything grew in this climate. Why didn't they have wonderful gardens and lawns? I guess it's the lack of room; ten million people were packed into twenty-two square miles.

The Boca area was colorful, clever, and entertaining. The homes were painted bright colors, rarely less than four colors per house. The original houses in the nineteenth century were covered with paint left on the docks by merchant ships. The homes were made of corrugated iron and must have been very uncomfortable inside—cold in winter and hot in summer. Boca was an artist's colony, and craftsmen were setting up stalls as we strolled the sidewalks.

We went to the famous La Recoleta Cemetery, with massive mausoleums kept in the family for generations. Eva Peron had a very nice one all to herself. To buy one cost as much as buying a modern house.

March 26, 2007 I went for a sunrise walk on Sunday morning and saw another side of Buenos Aires. The garbage trucks emptied Dumpsters and corner trash barrels every day of the week except Sunday. If you walked around Buenos Aires early on Sunday, you learned they were as dirty as New Yorkers, just better at hiring people to clean up their messes. They had homeless people living in parks, abandoned buildings, and even doorways of little-used buildings. You could see folks huddled in cardboard insulation if you walked early enough in the morning. They disappeared by ten o'clock. Buenos Aires was like a multitude of other big cities.

There was another misunderstanding! When Mercedes dropped us off at our hotel yesterday, she said she would be at the hotel at eight thirty to take us to the airport.

We packed our gear and dragged it to the front desk eleven floors down. Thank goodness the hotel had an elevator. We went to breakfast and then checked out of the room at eight fifteen. The desk clerk said we had reserved the room for another night and wanted to know why we were leaving early! We assumed Mercedes would arrive in fifteen minutes and straighten out the confusion. We waited forty-five minutes before phoning her.

"Ah well, no bother. I'll meet you tomorrow at eight thirty a.m.; your flights are confirmed, so you just go out on the town and enjoy yourself today."

Grrrrr. No bother for whom? We reregistered, and the bellboy helped us take the six suitcases (including two camera cases) back to our same room. We looked through the advertisements for local amusements, and I chose the Eva Peron museum. It was closed on Monday. Marlow picked the zoo. The advertisement said it was open from ten to eight, seven days a week. We hailed a taxi in front of the hotel. The taxi driver sat waiting for us as we walked to the zoo ticket window. It was closed. He thought he would be taking us back to the hotel or to another venue. Instead we decided to walk in that part of town. We were about five miles from the hotel, so we thought we could just walk until we saw something interesting to do, or until we got tired. We walked about two miles before it started raining. Marlow hailed a cab.

We returned to the dreary hotel room and watched old American movies on television while it rained until evening. We went to a local pizza parlor for dinner at about six.

March 27, 2007 Mercedes showed up promptly at eight thirty and called "her man" to spirit us away to the airport two hours before departure. Since she spoke the language fluently, I asked her to inquire if our travel agent in Yreka had informed them that I wanted an aisle seat. If not, could they please assign me one?

Mercedes smiled brightly. "All done! There you go. Up those escalators. Ta-ta."

Marlow was kind enough to trade my middle seat for his aisle seat once more. Then when he began to fade, I went to one of the many vacant aisle seats further back in the plane so he could stretch out a bit.

I should have dragged the dear, sweet man with me. The bulkhead seats were empty! Marlow could have had his cherished window seat, and still had room to stretch his legs straight. He was already dozing when I returned with that news, so I let him sleep and stretched out in the empty pair of seats myself. There was a shelf below the window at the perfect height for elevating one's heels. I placed the two available pillows between my head and the aisle armrest and began to read. Most unusual, I fell asleep!

I slept over an hour before waking to find we were over beautiful Patagonia. I wanted to dash up the aisle and get my camera out of the overhead bin but feared the scenery would be gone by the time I returned to the window.

The mountains were the most jagged, raw earth I had ever seen. Glaciers sparkled in the sun. Bare, new granite that had been magma only a short time ago, geologically speaking, jutted from the earth's surface, barely old enough to have dirt and trees on the lower slopes. It was autumn, and the leaves were orange, brown, and reddish brown. There were enough evergreens to offset the deciduous trees in their splendor. Fresh snow at higher elevations gave the Andes brilliant white caps to wear. Glacial kettles, round ponds left by retreating ice, were plentiful. What a country!

We flew over a thin layer of clouds, and a circular rainbow appeared out the window. In the center was the shadow of our plane. The shadow grew larger and larger as we descended. Beautiful, just beautiful.

As we glided down toward the island runway, I came back to reality. We left Buenos Aires three hours late. Did our Brendan guide in Ushuaia (oo SHWY a) wait for us? Did they know we were coming in late? Did the hotel hold our room? My questions would soon be answered.

Among the handful of people standing outside baggage claim area, I saw two men with Brendan signs and waved to them as I waited to have my carry-on camera bag inspected. The apple I had put in there an hour earlier was tossed in the trash, and I was told to proceed. No airline food allowed, we hadn't left Argentina, so it wasn't like we were bringing in foreign food.

Marlow was still waiting at the slowly moving conveyor belt. Finally half a dozen suitcases arrived. He waited. No more appeared. He waited. The conveyor stopped. Say what? There were two-dozen people waiting for luggage. The airline representative had each of us fill out a form saying where we would be staying and promised our luggage would be outside our rooms when we awoke the next day. Baggage was coming on a later plane.

The guides took us to the Tolkeyen Hotel, which was nouveau rustic. The building was only five years old and had a huge spa tub, a bidet, two queen-size beds, cedar-smelling natural-wood walls, and a corner heater. It would have been so cozy to use that tub and then crawl into clean flannel pajamas I had been saving for this part of the trip.

Instead, we went to the glassed-in bar/restaurant and took the corner table in an otherwise empty room. We turned our chairs away from the dining table and toward the floor-to-ceiling windows. We had drinks and tried to absorb the fact that we were actually in Tierra del Fuego. We had made it to the southern tip of South America. We were sitting there watching the wind whip up the waters of Beagle Strait. Charles Darwin may have stood admiring this same view. We had actually cruised the Amazon. We really did see the magnificent Iguazu Falls. This was not a dream. Luggage did not get left behind in a dream. We did not check out of the same hotel room twice on two consecutive days in a dream. By the end of the second highball, we had a long list of blessings to count. Lost luggage was a minor event.

Well, it was until someone pounded on the door about one a.m. and proudly announced he had our suitcase. Fortunately, I opened the door. The other three suitcases were on his cart but were marked in white chalk with the wrong destination. When I convinced the man that the tags matched my hotel registration slip, he gave me the suitcases.

All was well with the world. I went back to bed and slept soundly in the same clothes I had donned nearly twenty-four hours earlier.

March 28, 2007 The hotel served a lovely buffet breakfast attended by lots of folks who arrived on the later plane. They weren't in the hotel when we went to bed. They must have been from Buenos Aires, as they looked German and spoke Spanish.

Our guide met us promptly at eight and took us on a three-hour tour of Tierra del Fuego National Park. The soil was similar to tundra, and I was told it was peat.

"Isn't peat the stuff villains sank into and disappeared forever in nineteenth-century Scottish novels? Scotland was a long way from Tierra del Fuego."

Yes, they were one and the same. That was why it was important to stay on the wooden paths built for us. The ground looked solid; I rather doubted the guide, but he then went on to explain that not all peat was boggy. Where we were currently walking, peat had mixed with decomposed granite and was more solid. He took us to a very boggy bog, and we were careful to stay on the trail. That wasn't as easy as it sounded as strong winds buffeted us from side to side.

I was glad when we got into higher ground and walked among the wind-shaped juniper-looking trees. We were told they were beech trees. They are not relatives to North America's beech trees, but rather belonged to the same family that grows in Australia and New Zealand and dated back to the era when South America, Australia, and New Zealand were connected as Gondwana Supercontinent. There were two types of this same species, deciduous trees and low shrubs. I'm stalling here, hoping the name will come to me. Lenga! That was the name of the beech tree. They are the southernmost tree in the world.

As we left Tierra del Fuego National Park about noon, several buses arrived. I was glad we experienced the primitive land when few people were there. The Brendan van driver dropped us off at the travel office of *Mare Australis*, our cruise ship accommodation for the next few days. We checked in and stored our luggage.

While waiting for the ship departure, Marlow and I spent the next three hours at the naval museum. That might sound boring, but it wasn't. Each cell—oh yeah, I forgot to tell you, the museum was in a former prison—had the story of one voyage, one early explorer, or one prisoner. The prison was built so that it could be proven that Argentineans occupied the island. That way they could claim the land for Argentina. Chile and Argentina split ownership of Patagonia. Tierra del Fuego was the largest of several hundred islands. Indeed, Tierra del Fuego was one of the largest islands in the world.

I thought Tierra del Fuego, "land of fire," got its name from volcanoes. Nope. Sir Francis Drake saw the native's campfires burning along the shores and named the island. There were no volcanoes in the area. I learn something new every day.

The most southerly passage around Cape Horn was rejected for travel by early explorers after the straits of Magellan and Beagle were discovered to go from the Atlantic Ocean to the Pacific. The straits had much more calm waters and some protection from the wind.

We boarded the *Mare Australis* (*Southern Sea*) at six p.m., and I was pleasantly surprised to see our cabin had been upgraded. I didn't have to climb into an upper bunk as expected. We had twin beds, a dresser, a bedside stand, a large closet, and a functioning bathroom with hot water. We also had a nice large window and plenty of lighting fixtures. There was even a light I could use to read in bed without irritating my somnolent partner.

We toured the public areas of the boat, which took about ten minutes or so. We signed up for dinner reservations and proceeded to the captain's welcome aboard party. Waiters circulated with hot cups of liquid. I took one after learning all drinks onboard were included in the price of my passage. I have no idea what I was drinking. It tasted like apple cider but not as sweet. It made my cheeks warm, so it had alcohol in it. (We Irish descendants are good at detecting alcohol by feeling our cheeks or noses.) We each had a couple of drinks and a few of the fancy little canapés.

Dancers appeared and were introduced. Yea! We got to see another tango show. I wondered how many people were critically injured from that dance. It looked as though they were trying to trip each other. Sometimes the swift kick or jerked-up knee of the girl came between the man's legs, and I felt the male audience cringe. All seemed to work out well, and the couple went away as friends.

Later we met our dinner table mates—Monica and Marco from Barcelona, who had been married four days; Gema and David from London; Sonia and Richard from Zurich; and Linda from Calgary, Canada. All spoke fluent English (whew, my Spanish was getting me by, but I was not good enough to carry on a conversation). Linda was traveling alone, as her husband was tired of being away from home. They had just returned from another extensive trip.

Marlow and I took a liking to the newlyweds right away. The couple from Zurich was shy and preferred to converse between themselves. David from London knew the answers to all the world's problems (how nice for him). His wife, Gema, was proper English and decked out in lovely clothes for dinner. Tomorrow I'll change out of my jeans for dinner. In the meantime I'd watch which forks she used for which dishes and refrain from eating my peas with my knife. Linda was outgoing and conversational with everyone. She was a travel agent and loved to explore new places.

March 29, 2007 Decked out in warm winter clothes, rain ponchos, and floatation vests, we waited our turn to descend onto the inflatable raft to go ashore at Cape Horn. The captain sent a crew ahead to test conditions. The water was moderately rough with five- to six-foot swells. The wind blew thirty-five to fifty knots. The landing site was being battered with waves.

Marlow decided he didn't care to take the tumultuous boat ride to the gloomy island, which held nothing but a lighthouse and a memorial to dead people from the eight hundred or so ships that had sunk in the area. Were Zodiac rafts from cruise ships considered in that count?

The captain cancelled the excursion to the island. It was unsafe. We were glad he could see that. It gave us confidence in his piloting. We circled the island and rocked violently on the windward side of Drake's passage. On the windward side of Cape Horn Island, the squall increased to over a hundred knots per hour, and the swells grew to twenty to thirty feet in height. Sailors traverse that treacherous stretch of water with trepidation. The archipelago was the southernmost point of South America.

The *Mare Australis* headed up Beagle and Murray Channels looking for calmer seas. The captain found smoother waters at the Wulaia indigenous ecological site and let people go ashore. There were no people living there, just artifacts, so I chose to stay in our nice warm cabin and read or play solitaire. Marlow also chose to rest onboard. When the passengers returned, they said the only thing we had missed was being tossed about by frigid gusts of wind.

March 30, 2007 There were swells twenty to twenty-five feet in height as we passed from the Magellan Strait into the Pacific Ocean. Walls of water came toward the boat; when we were in a trough, all we saw was water through the ship windows. Marlow and I watched the spectacle from the third-floor meeting room, where we were attending a class on Magellanic Penguins. The speaker called a recess to the class for the twenty to thirty minutes it took to get from one body of water to the other. We were able to "wheeeee" with the others in the room without feeling like naughty children. Many wooden ships of explorers were only a third the length of our modern steel liner. Imagine being in such swells in small, wooden boats! Once we turned north on the Pacific Ocean, the water became smoother, and we resumed classes. We watched a video on the penguins and heard the history of the Magellan Strait.

We migrated up the west coast of Chile along the islands in Brecknock Channel, Cockburn Channel, Chico Sound, and Magdalena Channel. We admired the blue Plűschow Glacier, which was disappearing but didn't calf while we were watching. Groups of seals swam toward the ship. We suspected they were fed by the crew for the passengers' entertainment.

There was another treacherous transfer of passengers to Zodiacs to go up a fiord and see an ice field. Marlow and I had seen many ice fields in our day and chose not to join the group. An icy rain pelted them every minute they were gone. They did not go ashore; it was just a boat ride. We elected to watch Al Gore's Academy Award-winning documentary on global warming and sip hot tea in the comfort of the multipurpose room. All drinks, alcoholic or otherwise, were free on this cruise. We rarely felt like having alcohol. I occasionally had wine with dinner, and Marlow had a beer a couple of times.

There was a farewell champagne party with the captain starting at ten p.m. which we skipped so we'd be alert for the six a.m. trip to Magdalena Island. After a few cruises, we were finally learning that it's okay to say no to some of the activities.

March 31, 2007 Our wake-up call was at five a.m. Fortunately, the weather favored us with sunshine. Although there was a breeze, it was not gusting up to one hundred twenty miles per hour like it did yesterday. We wrapped up like Eskimos, putting on our flotation devices last. We packed twenty pounds of camera equipment and lumbered from the first floor to the fourth-floor bar, so we could go outside and walk down five flights of steps to the Zodiac raft. Who thought up that procedure? I guess they wanted us to meet in the bar/multipurpose room rather than out on the deck of the floor that held our cabin because of variable weather conditions.

We made a quick and pleasant raft trip to Magdalena Island, disembarked at a sturdy dock, and were greeted by almost 90,000 penguins. At least that's how many the naturalist said were living on the island at the moment. I thought it looked more like 5,000 myself but didn't count them. The experience of getting close to so many of the chattering little critters was wonderful. We spent over an hour there. I took lots of pictures with my heavy long-lens 35mm camera. When I looked at the counter and saw I was up to picture number forty on a roll of twenty-four shots, I knew something was wrong. I changed cameras and took a few digital shots and moving footage with the camcorder. Between Marlow and his big, heavy camera and my attempts, I hoped we got enough to recall the wonderful experience.

Marlow and I returned to *Mare Australis* for our last meal, breakfast. We stuffed our faces like we weren't expecting to eat again for a week. Actually, we didn't know what was going to happen when we reached shore. Brendan had not given us vouchers for the rest of the trip. We made several calls before leaving on the cruise, telling them we had not received anything for March 31 through April 4.

We disembarked, and I looked for someone holding a sign saying "Kill Patrick" or "Kilpatrick" or "Brendan." A young lady handed me a fistful of vouchers and helped load our luggage into a van. She took Marlow to a bank to exchange his Argentinean money for Chilean money, and then transported us to the bus station.

On the comfortable bus ride from Punta Arenas to Puerto Natales we saw rhea, a smaller version of emus and ostriches. We also saw guanacos, which are little llamas.

The two of us were greeted at the Puerto Natales's bus station by a Brendan representative, who transported us to a downtown hotel. The other passengers in our bus offered us sympathy when they saw we were being discharged at a purple-and-green building, the hotel of my choice. Never mind; it cost half as much as their socially correct brown building. Inside Hotel Saltos del Paine, we were greeted by two men like long-lost cousins. They wanted to do anything possible to make our stay comfortable.

The hotel had no other customers; it was so quiet. Our large room was comfortable, warm, and immaculate. We had a table with four chairs for playing cards or board games, a large dresser, a desk, television, phone, closet, nice bathroom, and two queen-sized beds. We didn't have the fitness center or swimming pool that expensive hotels had, but we never used those amenities anyhow.

Marlow and I walked the length of downtown Puerto Natales and chose a pizza parlor for dinner. I was still full from breakfast, so I passed on food and just had a *cerveza* (beer).

I want to tell you about some funny things we have seen on menus. Meals were literally translated into English. We had seen "cooked cow," "bread with grease," "pig and vegetables," and other assorted delicacies.

April 1, 2007 This was the grand climax of the trip. Today we got to see the real Patagonia, the Patagonia shown on public television, the Patagonia I saw from the airplane window as we approached Ushuaia.

The hotel clerk fixed us a splendid breakfast buffet. I hoped he had at least ten people in the hotel to help eat all that food. Homemade pastries, a variety of breads, fruits, juices, hot tea, fresh coffee, a choice of half a dozen types of cereal, creamy yogurt, cold cuts, and breakfast meats were laid out for us.

At seven thirty the guide, Christoforo, introduced us to our driver, Marco, as he piled overnight bags into the rear of a large van. The wonderful people at our hotel said we could leave any luggage we wanted in the room, and it would be there when we returned from our two days in Torres del Paine.

Yes, we were really off to Torres del Paine National Park! But wait, what was this? Marco was stopping for other passengers. Marlow and I had been spoiled by having guides all to ourselves. We each took window seats and spread our camera gear on adjoining seats.

Ah, those people looked familiar. They were on the cruise; they were the people who offered sympathy that we had to stay in a purple hotel (little did they know what they missed by not joining us at Hotel Saltos del Paine, Bulnes 156, Puerto Natales, Chile—just in case you're down that way looking for lodging). We went to another hotel and then another. There was one empty seat in the van by the time we left town. Everyone had been on the cruise. They were from Brazil, Spain, Germany, and Argentina. No one spoke enough English for conversation. We smiled, nodded, and added our few words of Spanish to communicate. Christoforo began his spiel on the history of Puerto Natales; I was amazed to find he repeated everything he said in three languages. I felt stupid when I met people like him.

Three hours later we arrived at the national park. Mountains appeared on the horizon. We rounded a curve, and Marlow spotted a guanaco! He yelled to Chris about his incredible find, but Chris ignored him and kept on with his canned speech. Marlow couldn't believe Marco didn't slow down one iota. Surely everyone on the van wanted to see the pretty three-foot-tall camelid.

We soon learned why Chris showed such indifference. We saw several dozen guanacos in herds ranging from four to twenty-four before the day was over. Finally, a young woman who had been flirting with Chris said she wanted a picture of one, and we slid to a stop. The squealing tires startled the animals, and they immediately headed for high ground. Only the first two people out of the van got any pictures, and those would have been of the animal's rear ends.

The scenery was magnificent beyond adjectives. The Torres were towers sculpted by talented ice, water, and wind. The jagged mountains were only thirteen million years old, mere toddlers. They were expected to surpass the Himalayas in height in eons to come. The tectonic plates were still vying for position, with one pushing the other into the magma, while the slab on top was thrust upward through the earth's crust. The glaciers had patiently carved and sculpted the scenery into what must have been some of the most spectacular on earth. Marlow and I compared them to the jaw-dropping beauty of Jasper-Banff, Canada, and came to the conclusion that the Canadian Rockies just might come in second.

The tour was a nice balance of riding in the van, walking on trails, learning new information, experiencing photo ops, and relaxing. Christoforo said we had chosen the right day. The temperature was in the sixties, there was a light breeze, and the sun was shining. He said he noticed that happened occasionally in autumn the day after the full moon. Perhaps a bit of malarkey was part of his repertoire, but at any rate, we were happy campers.

We spotted a couple of Andean condors gliding smoothly on waves of air off the ridges of the mountains. We watched several guanaco herds grazing in valleys or leaping up embankments at thirty-five miles per hour to escape our noisy vehicle. We even saw a few rheas running like children playing on stilts. Mostly the park was about startling geology.

About five o'clock we started toward the entrance to the park. I was so glad Marlow and I didn't have to leave. We were transferred to another van, which took us to Hosteria Las Torres de la Patagonia. Marlow got a bit nervous when we passed the tent campground, as he knew I made our lodging choice. It looked peaceful and inviting to me. Just kidding. I knew the temperature would drop to zero during the night.

We rounded a bend, and the ranch-style hotel came into view. Marlow exhaled when we pulled up in front of the luxurious accommodation.

We were treated royally and escorted to a lovely room with no television. We had passed through a rock, wood, and glass lobby that looked like a movie setting depicting where the rich and famous hung out. Down the hall we passed through a large lounge with a stone fireplace, several couches, easy chairs, and tables with straight-back chairs. Two-story-high windows displayed the surrounding mountains.

The first thing I noticed about our room was the stifling heat. Both heaters were turned to the off position. I turned them on and then off again to make sure they were turned as far as they would go. I called the front desk, and within a minute, there was a serviceman at our door. He fiddled and apologized in Spanish. He left and returned with a new thermostat, which he installed in minutes. Marlow complimented the man on the good service.

"Well, at $539.00 a night, it better be good," I said. I wondered if Marlow was rethinking the campground.

We went to a demonstration of what the resort had to offer in the way of activities. Every venue was far too ambitious for Marlow or me. They offered twelve-hour horseback rides into the mountains, rock-climbing, and strenuous ten-mile hikes gaining a thousand foot in elevation. Their guided hikes were at least six hours long. This was where the athletic hung out.

The wind howled all night, gusting at times enough to rattle windows and make the timbers groan. I was glad I wasn't in a tent.

April 2, 2007 We discussed plans for the day. We—well, probably only half of we—wanted to hike. Not the six- to twelve-hour type hike, but something more like one or two hours over gently rolling terrain. Marlow, ever the good sport, agreed. But he wanted to eat breakfast first.

The breakfast was gourmet food arranged by artists. I bet there wasn't a single person in the hotel that had cheesecake or German chocolate cake with whipped cream for breakfast at home, but those were only part of the decadent array of foods offered. Marlow got his usual assortment of eggs, cheeses, and meats. I had the yummy creamy yogurt over fruit with granola. Oh okay, I'll admit it. I also had a slice of the chocolate-peanut-butter cake with butter-cream icing. What the heck. I might get blown off the mountain in an hour and never get another chance. Chile's rich coffee went down real easy after the gooey sweet treat.

I checked with the front office to see if we could stay in our room until the three p.m. pickup by Brendan. No problem. I sure didn't want to pay for an extra night for not checking out of the room by noon.

Marlow and I gathered the minimum amount of camera gear possible, a bottle of water, and headed for the hills. He was whistling as we strolled across the resort lawns toward the towering monoliths. What a guy! I had known for fifty years that he didn't like to hike. He had known for fifty years that I loved to walk.

The wind was blowing hard enough that we had to face each other to be heard. We walked about a quarter mile when Marlow spotted a bird he wanted to identify. I couldn't hold my camcorder still enough to see what it was through the telephoto lens. Marlow walked all the way back to our bedroom to get binoculars. He rejoined me thirty minutes later, and we went a bit further. We made it across a wooden bridge over a ravine, which was very scary in the gale-force winds I thought for sure the wind was going to knock me over the side. Marlow wasn't whistling anymore. We braced against the oncoming wind for another thousand feet. The problem was that when we put all our weight into pushing against the wind, it changed directions and attacked us from the sides. We hadn't gone far when we gave up and returned to the lodge. If it isn't fun, I don't want to do it.

We enjoyed the bright sunny day from the large, comfortable lounge with a roaring fire in a marvelous stone fireplace. When I tired of staring at the glorious mountains or dancing flames, I read. When I tired of reading, I walked the length of the hotel, looking at all their pictures.

How did they take those great photos in the wind? The photographer must have arrived on the day after the full moon in autumn—that one day of the year when the weather was perfect.

We sauntered around the grounds of the resort and found a kiosk that serviced the campground, where we were able to get bottled drinks. I had taken one teensy bottle of alcohol from the fridge in our room the night before, and it cost $8.00. We were afraid to ask how much a twelve-ounce Coke would cost. It sure seemed as though the drinks in the fridge should have been included in the price of the room.

Our driver arrived to escort us to Puerto Natales at three o'clock as promised. He didn't speak English, so I couldn't ask him to explain Chilean driving habits. The whole way through the park the day before, Marco had driven on the wrong side of the road. He didn't even attempt to move over on sharp curves. The ride was nerve-racking. Today our driver also drove on the wrong side while on the dirt roads of the national park. What's up with that? I can see doing so on a straightaway where one side is smoother than the other, but that was not the situation here. Both sides were equal, so why endanger yourself and your passengers' lives? Someday a Chilean driver will meet up with a tourist on a curve. We concentrated on looking out our side windows. We watched for animals or scenic geology. There was plenty to take our minds off the fact that we might die in a head-on collision at any moment.

We arrived safely at our purple hotel at seven, just as the sun was setting. The hotel clerks were glad to see us. Maybe they knew how the Brendan drivers drove. Sure enough, our room was just as we had left it. Our suitcases had not been touched.

Marlow and I walked to a nearby restaurant and had *hamburguesas y papas fritas*. No, they didn't taste like American hamburgers and fries, but they were close enough for the two dollars they cost.

Marlow watched Tom Cruise overcome the evil Gene Hackman in the movie *The Firm* on television. I loved to read the Spanish subtitles at the bottom while listening to American words. Some are literal translations, some not so much. Every time an American used that favorite four-letter word for intercourse, the subtitle said, "*mal diction*," which translated to "bad word." At any rate Marlow was glad to be back in the world of television.

I showered and repacked for the long trip home. I wanted to leave behind all the winter clothes I had brought and as much other stuff as possible. We were short one suitcase that broke a zipper, and I wanted to be sure we didn't over pack the three remaining ones. Plus, I always leave clothes behind in poorer countries. I'm sure someone in Patagonia would relish the hot-water bottle, flannel pajamas, hand-knit sweater and thermal underwear.

April 3, 2007 We were offered the usual big breakfast at six thirty before our seven o'clock pickup. I really liked their creamy yogurt. It must be the high-fat kind or something. It tasted so much better than my nonfat type at home.

We were shuttled to the Puerto Natales bus station for the three-hour ride to Punta Arenas. The bus company gave assigned seats and supplied careful, safe drivers. Marlow and I were one row back from the driver. The well-padded seats were comfortable, and we relaxed to enjoy our last views of wonderful Patagonia.

At the airport we tried to check our luggage all the way to Miami so we wouldn't have to struggle with it in Santiago. No such luck. I handed the clerk all of our remaining ticket information. She said we didn't have tickets for the American Airlines flight from Santiago to Miami. I told her they were electronic tickets. She couldn't check luggage without a physical ticket. She did some button pushing on her computer and printed a ticket so she could complete check-in. At least she did give me an aisle seat, bless her heart.

Our departure time was two hours away, so we entertained ourselves watching the airport luggage handlers chase things in the wind outside the terminal windows. They chased hats, tarps, papers, boxes, and suitcases. One man parked his luggage cart without setting the hand brake, and it kept rolling down the runway after he walked away from it. What a horrible job to have in this land of perpetual wind.

The kiosks opened half an hour before takeoff, so I was able to buy a book written in English called *Across Patagonia*. The story was nonfiction written by Lady Florence Dixie from London. That would entertain me for the long ride home. I also bought a bottle of water, as I get dehydrated on planes. Marlow was afraid to buy water because of the American rules about taking three ounces of liquids onboard. It was much simpler to board a plane in Chile than it was in the United States.

The Lan Peru flight left Punta Arenas promptly on time at noon. The flight was amazingly smooth. The wind had no effect on the plane. I was a bit leery of wind shear and other stuff I learned about in 1990 when I took flying lessons. Sometimes a little knowledge gives you an upset stomach.

The trip to Santiago, Chile, was considerably shorter than we'd expected. It only took three hours. We had a five-hour layover in Santiago. Neat! We could check our luggage for the next flight and then take a city tour. Wrong. American Airlines wouldn't let us check our luggage until two hours before the flight was due to leave. Welcome back to American rules.

We dragged our belongings to seats and sat for two hours, then waited in line with fifty or sixty other people for another hour. When we got to the front of the line, I laid the printed information on the counter and gave the lady my passport. She stumbled around a couple of minutes and finally admitted she didn't have a reservation for us. She looked and looked at our electronic ticket and finally found a little "LP" in one corner, so she called Lan Peru on her phone. Sure enough, we were booked on Lan Peru. Maybe the Lan Peru clerk in Punta Arenas could have checked our luggage through to Miami if she had seen the little "LP."

I took one look at the long line of passengers in the Lan Peru queue and knew there was no way I could stand there for another hour. The American Airlines clerk read my mind, stepped through the scales where our luggage had been sitting, took us to the front of the Lan Peru line, and explained to a clerk what had happened. The clerk took care of us immediately.

Free of luggage, but with only two hours until boarding time, we couldn't leave the airport. I decided to see if I could find a restaurant where they served the national drink—*maté*—that I had read about in the books by Isabel Allende and Lady Dixie. Sure enough, there was such a place. The clerk spoke no English, but I could tell she was giving me a choice of three flavors. I communicated that I wanted her to give us the flavor she liked best. We got two delicious cups of strawberry punch. Very nice. I found it hard to believe that was the drink that grown men longed for after a hard day of riding the range, but I may never know what the original drink tasted like. When the Spanish arrived in the 1600s and 1700s, they soon traded their habitual cups of coffee or tea for the wonderful indigenous people's drink—maté. I'd look it up on the Internet someday but only expected to learn that it was the preferred drink of Chile and Argentina, and that I already knew.

Lapis lazuli was the national stone of Chile. I wanted to see if I could get a mineral sample reasonably priced in the duty-free shop. They had globes exactly like the one on our coffee table at home where the oceans were lapis. I knew how much I paid for that globe two years ago, so I could ask how much the one in the duty-free shop was to compare prices. They wanted $1,000.00, four times more than I paid in California! I came away without any lapis.

We boarded the plane a little after nine, an hour late. The loaded plane sat in the terminal for another hour. The pilot finally announced they had to take some luggage off, as someone had checked luggage and then had not boarded the plane. That left the huge 757 plane with one empty seat. Thank goodness the Lan Peru clerk had given me an aisle seat for the nine-hour flight to Miami.

They fed us dinner at ten p.m. and breakfast at four a.m. Neither meal was appealing at the hour offered. Marlow catnapped off and on in the stuffy, noisy plane, but I couldn't find a comfortable position. I read most of my new book and watched the movie *Happy Feet.*

We were dragging when we got off the plane in Miami. Then we had to face customs, get our luggage, and get to the hotel. We booked a room for April 3 and 4, as we knew we had an early-morning arrival and would want a shower and sleep before proceeding to the West Coast.

Days Inn cancelled our April 3 reservation because our travel agent had not told them we would be arriving in the early hours of April 4. They assured us we could check in after two p.m. as we still had an April 4 reservation. I cancelled the reservation and called a couple of other hotels offering shuttles from the airport. No rooms. I was in no mood to talk nicely to people, so I turned the chore over to Marlow. He found a room on his second try and didn't ask the price. Whatever, we would pay it.

We checked in to the luxurious Wyndham Inn looking like homeless people off the street. We took showers, brushed our teeth, and slept for about two hours. Sleep, blissful sleep.

We watched television, walked around the lovely hotel grounds, watched the golfers from our bedroom window, read, and dozed. At eight o'clock I took a sleeping pill and slept for twelve hours. I knew it was going to be a long time before I got restful sleep again.

April 5, 2007 Muffins and coffee in the room. I like to think of it as breakfast in bed. Marlow thought of it as a crummy snack.

I took one more long, hot shower and dressed for the day. We got caught up on the horror stories called news on television. Not much had changed in a month. I envied the tribes on the Amazon with their lack of electricity to run televisions.

We checked out of the room a few minutes before the ten o'clock deadline and played on computers in the lobby until one, when Marlow decided we needed to get to the airport. This was the United States, so check-in and security would take a while. We shuttled to American Airlines' front door. It was three hours until boarding time. We window-shopped at crowded duty-free stores then settled into seats at our departure gate. There were duty-free stores for liquor, perfume, cosmetics, clothing, and groceries. One of the first announcements we heard at the gate was that the three ounces of liquids applied to duty-free items also, and no one would be allowed onboard with more than three ounces of any liquid. I saw a security employee throw away all kinds of cosmetics a woman had just paid good money to buy. They ought to shut down duty-free stores until the United States got back to normal.

Marlow made friends with a reggae band traveling from the Virgin Islands to Hawaii for a gig. They were pleasant young men, and we enjoyed hearing their stories. A lady sitting on the other side of the musicians told them that Hulk Hogan, the wrestler/movie star, was sitting a few feet away. They went to check it out. Marlow went to check it out. Everyone within hearing range of the woman went to check it out. Sure enough, the man with gigantic muscles was posing for pictures with passengers and signing autographs. I wanted to take a picture of Marlow comparing biceps with Hulk, but Marlow wasn't game.

Our flight was delayed an hour. Five hours after arriving at the airport, we boarded the plane. I read more of my book about crossing Patagonia in the 1800s on horseback. What an incredible true story. One of the most surprising things to me was how seldom the author, Lady Dixie, mentioned the wind as a factor in their travels.

I may have even dozed off a time or two. I wondered if Hulk Hogan was sleeping soundly up there in his wide, plush, leather, reclining seat in first class. Probably not. There was noise in the front of the plane also.

We arrived in Los Angeles with fifteen minutes to catch our connecting flight to Medford. We dashed from one terminal to another, which took ten minutes. Thank goodness we didn't have to drag our luggage with us; it was booked through to Medford. I excused myself and ran in front of other people waiting in line at the Horizon Air check-in counter. I told the first available clerk that we needed to get checked in for the flight to Medford.

"Oh honey, that flight was cancelled. You'll have to rebook on another flight. See the lady in customer services."

We dragged our tired asses to customer service and waited in line an hour and a half before approaching the counter and having the young woman tell us there was no problem; we could catch a flight to Portland at six a.m. and then transfer to a plane going to Medford. The cancellation was their fault, so they would put us up in a hotel, but we would have to be back at the airport in six hours to check in. Marlow knew from past experience that it would take us two hours to get settled in at a hotel, so he rejected that offer. He asked the girl to see if they could book us on a different airline. Ten minutes later, after a lot of typing on her computer, she found a flight leaving for Redmond, Oregon, in thirty minutes with a connecting flight to Portland, Oregon, where we could catch a commuter flight to Medford.

"We'll take it," Marlow said.

The clerk sent him downstairs to get our luggage from the load waiting to be put on the plane leaving at six. Marlow found the clerk in baggage claim to be one of those sloth-like people that moved at one speed—extremely slow. When the employee located our luggage, she assured him she would retag it for our route. He had little hope of seeing the luggage again for a week.

The Horizon Air clerk serving me was surprised at Marlow's news, but accepted the baggage claim clerk's word and gave us our boarding passes. We ran to security, tolerated their histrionics, and boarded the plane just in the nick of time.

The small turbojet flight to Redmond was fine. We arrived at midnight. We had no luggage to claim, so we sat down and checked our tickets for the details of the connecting flight to Portland. *Six a.m.*! Good grief, another six-hour layover.

Passengers from our arriving plane cleared the terminal, and Marlow and I were the only customers in the building. There were two security men on duty sitting in little offices at either end of the terminal.

Marlow found padded benches with no armrests where we could lie down. We actually fell asleep. I woke up shivering an hour later. I quietly left Marlow snoring away and went to the far side of the terminal and jogged in place. The security guard saw me and asked if I was okay. I told him I was cold and asked if he had any of those little airplane blankets. "No." I remembered that I put a sweatshirt in my camera bag because it wouldn't fit in a suitcase. I put it on and lay back down. Sleep eluded me.

At four a.m. terminal staff arrived. A woman opened the snack bar and started coffee. Good, something warm would really hit the spot. Marlow awoke and joined me for coffee.

At five o'clock an announcement came over the loudspeaker that anyone traveling to Portland needed to be processed through security immediately. We were so spacey, we actually put our camera bags on the x-ray conveyor belt and walked through the metal detector like people do in South America. *Beep, beep.* We went back through and took off our shoes, emptied our pockets, took off belts and watches. Marlow made it through. The man made me turn around and go back and put the wallet I had in my hand in my hip pocket and walk through again. Jerk. What possible difference could it make whether the wallet was in my pocket or in my hand? Do they have a lot of terrorists trying to blow up twenty-passenger planes between Redmond and Portland? Once we were declared nonterrorists by Mr. God, we had to wait half an hour for the plane crew to arrive. Five minutes before six, we boarded the plane.

The plane left on time. We listened to the usual warnings about airline crashes from the stewardess, but fortunately she didn't take herself too seriously. She told us that our seat cushions were flotation devices in case we had to ditch over water. We would be flying over the Rogue River. Then she reminded us that those cushions were the property of the airline and we would be expected to return them after use.

There was a three-hour layover in Portland before boarding one more plane for the final leg of our flight to Medford, Oregon, the city nearest Fort Jones that had a commercial airport. We knew we didn't have a ghost of a chance of seeing our luggage upon arrival in Medford, so we started for the door to go to the Windmill Inn to pick up my truck. Then and only then did it dawn on me that the truck key was packed in my checked-on luggage. Oh no… What a sinking feeling.

We sank into nearby chairs. We'd have to wait for that six a.m. Horizon flight from Los Angeles to Portland and then whatever flight was leaving Portland to bring our luggage and truck key to Medford. I looked up just in time to see one of our suitcases about to make the full circuit on the conveyor belt and disappear behind rubber curtains. Our luggage was in Medford! Oh happy day! The luggage clerk in Los Angeles did reroute it. We loved her.

We picked up my truck at the motel and started for good old Fort Jones. I was sound asleep in the truck as soon as we were on the freeway. I was awakened every once in a while as we crossed the Siskiyou Mountains by Marlow jerking the steering wheel. I asked him if he wanted to pull over and sleep for a while, but he said he was okay. I was totally zonked out and went right back to sleep. After we were safely in our driveway, he admitted he was too spacey to drive and kept finding himself staring at the vehicle in front of us in a trance.

It took over twenty-four hours to get from Puerto Natales, Patagonia, Chile, to Miami, Florida. It took over twenty-four hours to get from Miami to Fort Jones.

On the way from Portland to Medford, Marlow leaned toward me and said, "You know what? We could drive from Fort Jones to Ushuaia."

Fifteen

Australia and Vanuatu

2008

My grandson, Joshua, announced his engagement, saying he and Michelle would be married at Easter timc. I wanted to be in Rockhampton, Queensland, Australia, for the hoopla building up to their wedding. I wanted to meet the bride's family and get to know the chosen lady. Therefore, I chose to go to Australia two weeks before the ceremony. Marlow preferred to continue working at Aerojet until the big day. He stayed in Cameron Park, California, while I jetted off to the South Pacific.

March 12, 2008 I finished last-minute packing, took a shower, and ate breakfast before the airport shuttle arrived at our Cameron Park, California, home. The driver had expected to transport a few people to the terminal, but due to a spate of cancellations, I was his only customer. I had nothing to say to this stranger, so we rode for an hour and a bit without talking.

At the Sacramento terminal, I slipped the strap for the backpack camera case over my head while the driver removed the suitcases from the rear of his van. I offered him a tip. Before I let go of the twenty dollar bill, I asked for change. He had none. I told him I'd get change inside the terminal and leave him five dollars at the shuttle counter. He groaned and crawled into his driver's seat.

Incredibly, I was the only person in the check-in line, so I was quickly separated from the suitcases that were marked through to Brisbane, Queensland, Australia. The clerk commented on the large, clear identification tags and said there would be a lot less lost luggage if everyone used such tags. I smiled in gratitude for her acknowledgment of me doing something right.

Free of luggage, I had two and a half hours to wait for my flight. I settled in with a book given me by a friend. *The Potato Factory* was such a depressing story about Australia's early European occupants that I left the book behind when I boarded the plane.

The first leg of my flight was to Portland, where my vibrant young cousin, Susan, met me at the terminal. Susan had spent 2007 traveling and shared a multitude of pictures and stories. The two-hour's layover flew by with Susan's fascinating company.

I boarded another plane and was whisked off to Los Angeles, a two-hour flight from Portland. Thank goodness I had no luggage except the camera bag as I dashed from LAX domestic terminal to the international terminal. I was the final passenger to board the Qantas flight to Australia. I was panting from my dash and gladly accepted the friendly stewardess's offer to carry my camera bag as she escorted me to my seat.

What a pleasant surprise it was to find I had a perfect spot. The huge transport vehicle had two aisles and a center section with five seats across. I feared I'd be stuck in the center of those five seats. Instead, I was located where the plane's tail started to narrow, and there were only two seats on the wall side of the plane. No one occupied the seat beside me. There was a space of about twelve or fourteen inches between the window seat and wall. The indented window had a foot-thick sill sloping toward the arm of the chair.

I could see out the window just fine and had room to sit with my legs propped up on the empty seat while watching movies. A screen was imbedded in the seat back in front of me. Best of all, I had room to prop my feet on the windowsill and lie across two seats when I was ready for sleep. I have a rule for traveling—I'm never going to see those travel companions again. I don't care whether they think I'm dignified or not. Comfort is my number one priority.

Although I slept off and on during the flight, it wasn't restful, and I arrived in Brisbane fourteen hours later, dazed and gasping for breath in the high humidity. While waiting in line to turn in my agriculture form promising I had brought no bugs into Australia, I noticed I got dizzy when I moved my head. I was unsure of my balance. I had checked all the boxes on the form with the pencil given me by the stewardess on the plane. The agriculture clerk made me fill out a new form in ink. The line behind me grew as two additional planes landed.

Next I went to claim my luggage at turntable three, where Qantas told passengers they would find their property. Over two-hundred-forty eager passengers pushed their way against rails of the empty turntable. I stood back, leaning against a cement post supporting the ceiling. Thirty minutes later an announcement came over the loudspeaker saying the turntable was broken and the luggage was being transferred to turntable one.

Turntable one was already jammed with boxes, suitcases, strollers, surfboards, golf clubs, and myriad paraphernalia from a plane that had arrived from Japan. A few brave souls from my flight fought their way through the crowd, wrestling items free from the moving conveyor belt.

I stood well back from the melee, feeling more and more ill. I was fighting for oxygen, feeling light-headed, and my knees seemed to be losing the ability to hold my weight erect. I looked at each piece of luggage as it appeared through the exterior door and fell onto the turntable. My suitcases did not appear.

After thirty or forty minutes, I asked a uniformed lady where to file a lost luggage report. She pointed to a queue of about fifty people. While in line I watched the turntable. There were about eighty suitcases going around and around not being claimed by anyone. There were probably people in Timbuktu looking for those suitcases. So much for my large bright yellow name tags. They didn't help the bags make it to the correct location.

I made my lengthy report and was sent to customs with my camera bag. I joined a thousand chattering incoming visitors, some with luggage and some without. We snaked our way past a series of officials. The first person was to check our passports and visas. I told her I had pneumonia and was about to pass out from the claustrophobic conditions. She saw I had only one bag and picked it up with the command to follow her. She promptly escorted me to the front of the line. I'm sure that saved me well over an hour of misery.

Once through customs I collapsed in the nearest chair and fought for air. My vision was playing tricks on me. People looked like they were passing my chair in slow motion.

I planned on going to a motel to shower and rest for twenty-four hours before descending on my friends, the Nugents. Once more I forgot to account for the lost day crossing the International Date Line. One would think, with the number of times I've traveled to and from Australia, I'd remember that little item. I wrote the Nugents telling them I'd be at their house on March 14. Lo and behold—today was March 14 in Australia. I left Los Angeles at eleven p.m. on March 12 and arrived in Brisbane at six thirty a.m. on March 14 after a fourteen-hour flight.

I knew I was in no condition to hire a rental car and drive, so I hailed a taxi. I relaxed in the rear seat and watched the cityscape roll past the window.

Pat and Christine Nugent greeted me with enthusiasm. After hearing my woeful story of lost luggage, Christine drove to a shopping mall to buy me pajamas, toothbrush, and two new outfits. I gratefully soaked my body under their rainwater-soft shower while she was away.

Pat was busy packing items into the trunk of his car. They had scheduled a trip to New South Wales. As soon as Christine returned, we were off on a five-hour trip to Iluka. We arrived at the lovely home recently purchased by the Nugents' dear friends, Michael and Rhoda. I was spacey and incoherent, so I soon excused myself and dropped into the bed allotted me. I slept soundly for about twelve hours.

March 15–16, 2008 Michael and Rhoda welcomed me to their retirement home on the Clarence River outside Iluka, New South Wales. The cheerful couple had not yet moved into the house, so furniture was scarce. They had been wise enough to supply the place with beds and outdoor furniture. We sat on the expansive lawn soaking in the warm sunshine, listening to birds, and watching the river float serenely by their four acres of tropical vegetation.

Michael and Rhoda had had a hardscrabble life, working long hours to make ends meet. Now, in their later years, the real estate market had skyrocketed, and their poor, small home was on prime property. They were able to sell for a substantial amount, retire in style, and live happily ever after.

The weekend of rest was just what I needed. My health improved before Sunday evening found us on the road back to Brisbane. Once we arrived at the Nugents' home, their daughter, Kim, said Qantas's deliverymen told her my suitcases had gone to two different locations in New Zealand before finding their way to the Brisbane terminal Sunday afternoon.

March 17–18, 2008 I got acquainted with the Nugent grandchildren as they came and went from their grandparents' home. Daughter Kim, her husband, Allen, and their children lived about a hundred yards from Pat and Christine on acreage property that had been in the Nugent family for generations. Son Anthony, his wife, Nikki, and their children lived about two hundred yards further down the same driveway.

All the children were precious and had distinct personalities, but it was two-year-old William who stole my heart within a few minutes of our meeting. He was a macho miniature man. His elbows stuck out to his sides as he walked with a swagger. He lowered his voice when talking, trying to sound as much like Dad and Grandpa as possible. He would have no trouble holding his own against his three older sisters.

I cherished every minute spent with the Nugent family. Pat, Christine, Marlow, and I had been dear friends since 1973. I was sorry I hadn't allowed more time with them, but alas, I was also eager to see my own son, Scott, and his family.

March 19, 2008 Scott, his wife, Meleese, my grandson, Joshua, and his fiancée, Michelle, met me at the airport in Rockhampton, Queensland, when I arrived. I looked forward to an evening of visiting, then retiring to the solitude of the old farmhouse to relax in the sounds of nature.

Scott and Meleese had twelve hundred acres. The main house was a modern brick place near the highway. The original farmhouse was about a mile further from the highway on a dirt driveway. Two of Scott's building contracting customers wanted him to tear down their old houses and build new homes. Instead, he bought and hauled their old houses to his property and set them up for relatives to use. One was attached to the original farmhouse, and one was a quarter mile farther into the bush. Rod and Merle, Meleese's parents, lived in the latter place.

Scott and Meleese had six children, Joshua, Rhys, Caleb, Mikaela, Shinnay, and Elijah. They ranged in age from eight to eighteen. Josh lived in the original farmhouse; the rest of the family lived in the main house. The afternoon and evening were filled with the hubbub of getting reacquainted. I thoroughly loved that. I was also glad when Scott announced he was taking me to the farmhouse for the night. I stayed in the house adjoined to the original farmhouse and was asleep by eight thirty.

March 20–23, 2008 Easter was a few days away, and no wedding plans were underway. When asked, I was told the wedding had been postponed; I phoned Marlow and told him not to catch a plane to Australia. I'd let him know as soon as I was given a new wedding date.

Countrywide preparation for Easter had begun. I spent Thursday riding with Scott on his "run," checking last-minute emergencies and a multitude of queries before the long weekend. Scott was Queensland's largest building contractor and had a number of houses under construction. As the day wore on, it became progressively harder to reach merchants and workmen. Everyone who could took off early.

Good Friday was spent at Scott's residence. He mowed the large paddock down the hill from his six-bedroom brick home. There was to be an Easter egg hunt in the field. Scott had multiple problems with his old tractor and finally announced the egg hunt would take place on the lawn surrounding the house.

Meleese, Michelle, Mikaela, Shinnay, and I did housecleaning and laundry. One of my favorite tasks was hanging clothes outdoors, so I opted for laundry. With such a large family, there were eleven loads to be washed, dried, folded, and stored. It seemed like 90 percent of the play clothes were the same size. I'm sure the children had to search through their siblings' drawers to find a full outfit to wear after I stored things.

Saturday was food prep day for Meleese. Her family—parents, five siblings, their spouses, and assorted nieces and nephews, would spend Easter at the house. I laundered the family's wearing apparel from the previous day and made another sweep through the busy house picking up toys and discarded food wrappers. In the evening all the children joined me in egg dyeing—not an Australian tradition. We loved seeing what combinations each artist produced.

Sunday morning Merle and Rod, Meleese's parents, arrived first, followed closely by Meleese's sister, Coreena, her husband, Gabriel, and eight of their nine children. Meleese and Coreena's brothers and their families appeared, and a general melee took place while women displayed a wide variety of holiday dishes on the large breakfast bar. Meleese produced turkey, ham, and chicken, two kinds of potato salad, coleslaw, tossed green salad, three-bean salad, and pavlova. Her mother, sister, and sisters-in-law filled any empty space with bowls of scrumptious-looking delicacies. The dining-room table accommodated ten people. Picnic tables in the yard were arranged for children, and the food was relished amid laughter and stories.

Scott gathered everyone under ten years old into a room, and with his commanding manner, kept them enthralled with the story of the true meaning of Easter. Meanwhile the older children ran about outside, hiding dozens of colored eggs, chocolate eggs, and jelly beans.

I brought a couple dozen paper Easter baskets from America, which were distributed to the little folks, and they scurried about looking for treats. Excitement ran at maximum pitch until every inch of the yard was scoured. That was the first Easter egg hunt for the cousins, and a vow was made to make it a family tradition henceforth.

Grandpa topped off the celebration by bringing a tractor and wagon of hay to the house. He managed to pack all the children and several adults on to the hay and took them for a ride around the dirt roads of the farm.

As the sun dipped low, fond farewells were exchanged, and the house nearly emptied as all nonresidents left.

March 27, 2008-April 3, 2008 Even though March 27 was Shinnay's tenth birthday, she didn't get to celebrate until late evening. Elijah was in a school performance that evening. All of us went to see the third grader's singing, dancing, and poetry recitation. Afterward, Scott treated his family, plus Michelle and me, to dinner at Sizzlers. We sang "Happy Birthday" to Shinnay when dessert was eaten. Then at ten p.m., Shinnay was allowed to open her presents. She was very tired, but was gracious in her appreciation of each item received.

The next morning Michelle's sister, Danielle, who was in town for spring break from university, drove Mikaela, her cousin Heidi, and me to Byfield National Park as well as the beach near Yeppoon. Mikaela and Heidi were also on spring break.

While at the beach, I found a dying sea snake on the sand. I didn't know how long it had been out of the water but did know that no one should touch it. Their bite was deadly. I tried to find a large rock or something heavy to dispatch it to snake heaven, but had no luck. I went to a sailing club, where I found a woman working in an otherwise deserted building. She said she would send a man with a shovel to dispose of the snake.

No one showed up during the next hour. Danielle, Heidi, Mikaela, and I stayed with the snake. It died, probably of dehydration, but I still didn't want a curious little boy to pick it up. The snake was shimmery silver and looked like something one of my boys would have brought home for show-and-tell. Heidi wanted to test and see if it was completely dead. She brought a can of water from the sea and poured it over the snake. The skin immediately turned coppery brown. The snake remained dead.

I picked it up with a stick and carried it to a trash bin. That incident gave the girls an exciting tale to tell at the dinner table.

April 4, 2008 The family was up at the crack of dawn and off to Vanuatu via Brisbane. The flight to Brisbane went smoothly, and a rented van awaited us at the terminal. Half the group wanted to go to a shopping mall, so Scott drove them to the front entrance, and they went off in search of the perfect buy.

The second half, Scott, Rhys, Caleb, Elijah, and me, went to Sea World on the Gold Coast.

The zoo/amusement park was delightfully entertaining. The cutest things were tiny penguins that stood about twelve or thirteen inches tall. They were called fairy penguins and came from Australia's southern shores. The dolphins, sharks, rays, starfish, and other critters were also nice to see. We had a wonderful time.

Scott and Meleese owned two condos in Rydges's resort in Brisbane, and that is where the family stayed while in town. We met up with the shoppers at Rydges, and there was a flurry of showers and dressing for an evening meal. We ate at Ahmet's Turkish Restaurant and were served a wide array of tasty Turkish treats. This was my first time eating Turkish food. I hoped it wouldn't be the last time.

Scott, Meleese, and I strolled along the riverfront shopping area. There was a gem and mineral store that caught my eye. We spent about an hour drooling over all the wonderful fossil artifacts and jewelry on display. Meleese showed me an exquisite bracelet she had her eye on. I hoped she would own it someday.

April 5, 2008 The eleven people in the Kilpatrick entourage caught our plane to Vanuatu without a hitch. Upon arrival at Port Vila, Efate Island, Vanuatu, we hopped aboard a shuttle and were taken to a ferry that deposited us on the island resort of Iririki.

As we were waiting to be escorted to our assigned quarters, Scott handed me a velvet pouch, saying, "Here, I picked this up for you." My mouth dropped open when I saw it was the bracelet Meleese had pointed out in the Brisbane jewelry store window. I was flabbergasted and mumbled words of gratitude before slipping the bracelet into my pocket. I didn't want Meleese to see it. Oh my goodness, how could my son have given me the very bracelet his wife wanted? She would be so hurt. I couldn't accept it.

Scott, Meleese, Josh, and Michelle went to a restaurant nightclub while the balance of the family stayed with me. I had a wonderful evening playing rummy 500 with the youngsters.

As soon as I was alone in my room, I started worrying again about the bracelet. Scott would expect me to wear it when we dressed up for dinner. I slept fitfully. I came to the conclusion I'd give the bracelet to Meleese for her birthday in May, and then I was concerned that would hurt Scott's feelings. How could he have bought his mother something his wife hoped to own? I felt like I was living a soap opera.

April 6, 2008 The day was spent partaking of water sports offered by the resort. We went snorkeling, then off to the rental shack, where the kids were taught to drive Jet Skis, sail catamarans, and ride in the three-man inner tubes pulled behind a Jet Ski. I went on a tamer glass-bottom boat to admire the coral and fish.

April 7, 2008 Another active day. We caught a morning flight to the island of Tanna and took the short ride to White Grass Resort. The taxi was interesting for the kids, as it was a pickup truck with two benches sitting back to back in the rear. The young people hopped up there for the bumpy ride while adults jockeyed for position inside the four-door cab.

We had little cabins, with an average of three people to a building. I shared my cabin with Shinnay and her twelve-year-old cousin, Heidi. The buildings were woven bamboo on wooden frames. They had proper roofs covered with palm fronds to make them look quaint. Each cabin had a front porch with comfortable chairs. My cabin overlooked a sloping lawn dotted with bougainvillea, palms, and tropical flowers. The lawn led to the coral/lava beach of the ocean. What a perfect place to let all tensions drain away.

I started on a solitude walk through a rainforest and found myself at a bay occupied by several Kilpatricks snorkeling. The name of the beach was Blue Hole One. Elijah told me that if I kept on the path, I'd come to Blue Hole Two. I went on until the track ended but found no snorkeling site. On my return I met Scott and Shinnay looking for the same destination. Scott was wise enough to ask the locals if we were on the right track. We weren't. But we did have a nice walk along coral-strewn beaches. Finally, I had the opportunity to talk to Scott about the bracelet. I told him I couldn't accept it, that he needed to give it to Meleese.

Scott laughed out loud. "Meleese would never wear something like that! She picked it out as a gift for you. She said six months ago when we first saw it that it looked like something you would like. She showed it to you in the window to test her theory. When she told me your reaction to seeing it, I bought it for you. Meleese knows you have it."

I doubted his words, saying he misunderstood Meleese. She really wanted it for herself. He said he'd ask her when we returned to the villa.

Scott, Shinnay, and I followed directions to the main road, which had foot-high grass growing in the middle. We found a sign announcing we had arrived at Blue Hole Two. The hole was a cove off the main part of the bay.

As soon as we returned to the group, Scott asked Meleese if she would like for him to hire the jeweler to make her a duplicate of my bracelet. She laughed.

"My goodness, no. I'd never wear anything like that. I like tiny jewelry with just a single stone." My bracelet had three rows of brilliant-colored gemstones set in sterling silver.

Scott explained my trepidation, and she confirmed that what he had told me was true. She had picked it out for me. Yippee! I have a fantastically beautiful bracelet to wear in case a member of royalty invites me to visit.

April 8, 2008 Holy Toledo! What a day!

The Kilpatrick group took the morning tour of a native village. The Melanesian people were like the ones I'd seen on television specials on New Guinea. They shared the same ancestry. I had wanted to go to New Guinea for thirty years to meet these fascinating people before they became modernized. I wanted to know all about their culture.

I took my Polaroid camera along and left the people laughing at themselves. That was a good icebreaker. Even the most masculine of men giggled like teenagers when they were handed pictures of themselves.

We met family groups, and they showed us games and dance steps. The community dressed in costumes of grass skirts and nambas and performed ceremonial dances for our delight. My younger grandchildren joined them in the dances. Nambas are U-shaped gourds covering the penis but not the testicles, tied in place with a leather thong attached to the narrow, pointed end of the *U* and reaching around their waist. The length of the namba decided which tribe they belonged to. Some islanders were known as the Big Nambas, and others were called the Little Nambas.

The ladies showed us how they made the thatched huts, which were much larger than I expected. Some were approximately twenty by forty feet. It wasn't until much later in the tour that I learned a hut that size housed ten people. There was a single, central hut for all the women in the village to use for food prep.

I wanted to move in with the people for a year or so to learn everything they knew, but alas, time came for the group to head back to the resort to partake of a Western meal.

After lunch we were loaded into two pickup trucks to be driven to the active volcano, Mount Yasur. The ride took two and a half hours. The four-wheel-drive roads were the worst I've ever seen. Mud in places was a foot deep, and other places had volcanic rocks threatening oil pans. People stood along the road near their villages and shouted, "Hello" or cheered as we passed. My older grandchildren were riding in the rear of the truck in front of me. I watched them hang far off the bed of the truck to slap palms with other children and young men along the road. We were only traveling about five miles per hour at that point.

When the drivers got to a dry, flat bit of roadway, they raced ahead regardless of people or animals in the road. The road rule was every man or animal for himself. On mounds of volcanic ash, we rode at angles dangerously close to tipping the vehicle on its side. Now I knew where people got the idea to build roller coasters.

We crossed a wide river with the driver's head out of his side window, looking for solid footing in the sand/ash river bottom. When we reached the far side, we made a U-turn and discovered we were on the edge of a waterfall. We mothers were surprised to see how close the family had been to going over the precipice along with the rushing water.

We arrived at Mount Yasur at sunset and made our way up the incline to the exploding crater. The air we were breathing smelled strongly of sulfur and was filled with breath-choking ash. We wore heavy yellow raincoats to protect ourselves from falling ash.

The climb was well worth the effort. We were on the rim of the crater looking into the angry boiling soup. *Boom*! The magma gas exploded, and bombs were thrown high in the air. They landed back inside the crater and hissed. Popping sounds were prevalent the whole time we were on the rim. Dark smoke billowed for a few seconds before each explosion. Bright-orange bombs of various sizes and shapes were thrown into the night sky and fell helter-skelter, still glowing, onto the crater walls a few feet in front of us.

White steam hissed and bubbles roiled and popped, followed by foul-smelling sulfuric gas filling the air. A third explosion filled the night air, and bright plumes of fire lit up the night sky. As the sky darkened, the explosions appeared more often, with bombs blasting higher and higher. New fissures appeared along the crater wall and competed for attention. It appeared more violent because it was more visible against the night sky. We spent quite some time staring in awe. We knew that nowhere in America or Australia would civilians be allowed anywhere near such a violent act of nature. This was a once-in-a-lifetime experience.

Scott and Meleese finally felt it was time to herd the group down the ash mound. The trail was not marked, and in the light of our crank flashlights, it would have very easy to take a misstep and roll to the bottom. Fourteen-year-old Caleb came to my aid and had me walk with one hand on his shoulder. He chatted gaily the whole way down the path to distract me from imminent danger. I developed a fear of falling after breaking my leg in 2003.

A head count was made, and we were relieved to find everyone made it back to the vehicles. Our ash-covered raincoats were returned, and we climbed aboard our chariots for the ride to the resort.

Louie, the driver of the truck I was riding in, plummeted down the winding, narrow, rock-strewn crater path at excessive speeds. I was riding in the front passenger seat and braced myself by hanging on to the dashboard with both hands. I asked him to slow down, and he ignored me. What a harrowing ride!

After several minutes Louie explained that he had a bad front tire and wanted to get in front of the other vehicle in case he had a blow-out. Great plan!

Louie tried to get Yalu's attention with a flashlight when we reached a straightaway. That was to no avail. Yalu, the second driver, was about half a mile in front of us. Louie told me to hold the flashlight out the window and keep turning it off and on. The light was so dim that it barely showed on the front fender of the passenger side of our vehicle.

Louie took a corner on two wheels, and suddenly the other vehicle was right in front of us. Louie asked me for the torch (flashlight), and he aimed it at Yalu's rearview mirror. We were no more than twenty yards from the rear of Yalu's truck. He saw the light and slowed to a stop. Louie went to Yalu's window and explained the situation.

Scott suggested we change the tire immediately. The two drivers spoke with animation in their native tongue for a few minutes. There were lots of hand gestures and arm movements, and we could tell the drivers were accusing each other of something bad. Louie returned to our truck, seated himself, and slammed the door, indicating the discussion was closed. He pulled around Yalu's truck and took the lead. We tourists sat glumly silent. The two vehicles proceeded at a reasonable speed. My family members shrugged their shoulders and said nothing.

Oh no, we'd forgotten about the river crossing! I expected the drivers to walk across the river to find the best path since it was pitch black and they couldn't possibly see solid ground by looking out their side windows. Louie plowed into the water without slowing. He promptly became mired in muck. He revved the engine and spun the wheels, digging us in deeper.

For the next hour, people from both vehicles pushed and pulled the vehicle. Some dug volcanic muck from around the tires, which was immediately replaced while the laborer worked on a second tire.

It dawned on one of the men to jack up the wheels and put rocks under the tires. Louie didn't know how to use a jack. Kilpatricks came to his rescue and pumped up the front right bumper, only to discover the tire was completely flat. Boys and men scoured the sandy, ashy soil for rocks but found none of reasonable size.

A third truck came along. We were rescued! It turned out to be more natives on their way to the crater. They drove a few miles to the start of the crater and returned with a truckload of rocks.

Scott thought to ask the third driver for a second jack (Yalu had none), as the workers couldn't get both the front and rear of the vehicle out of the muck at the same time. The river was flowing so fast that ash buried the front tires mounted on rocks by the time the rear tires were on rocks.

The newcomers also had a rope, which was tied to the rear of our vehicle. Yalu turned his truck around and tied the rope to its rear end. Meleese and the younger children were still sitting in the rear of Yalu's truck.

Suddenly, without warning, Louie was reversing toward Yalu's stationary truck at full speed. The rocks under all four wheels spewed out in front of our vehicle, where several people stood in the water. Scott, Meleese, and their children were screaming, "Stop!" Louie ignored them—he later claimed he didn't hear them. Louie crashed into Yalu's truck with a loud crash. I had the awful feeling that one or more of the workers had been standing between the two trucks. I was suddenly vomiting out the side window. Thank goodness, my women's intuition had been wrong. No one was between the vehicles. Everyone was traumatized but no one was physically injured.

Louie turned to me and said, "Why did Yalu stop?"

I told him Yalu wasn't in his truck, he was standing in front of us in the river with the older Kilpatrick boys, who had been working on the elevation of the wheels.

Caleb walked up to my window to see if I was okay. I assured him I was and asked if anyone in the other truck was hurt. His answer, "Nah, just Mum and the little kids were in there." I guess he thought they were indestructible.

I opened the door and turned to get out. Louie grabbed me from behind and told me to stay put. He'd check on the others. He disappeared into the darkness, and I got out and verified no one was injured.

Yalu and Louie yelled at each other until they got their anger out of their system. The tourists began the chore of changing the flat tire. Neither driver had ever changed a tire before and knew nothing about the mechanics of doing so.

We made it across the river and bounced along the muddy road to the resort. Louie's two-way radio had a flat battery, and Yalu had no two-way, so no one at the resort knew why we didn't return. We arrived two hours later than expected. That type of thing must have happened often. No one at the resort was alarmed at our tardiness.

April 9, 2008 A snorkeling trip was planned to Blue Cave. The ocean was choppy after recent storms. With trepidation I agreed to go along. We would swim through a tunnel to get to the cavity. There were lights inside, and it would be a marvelous snorkeling adventure.

We were loaded into two fourteen-foot "tinnies" (metal rowboats) and rocked and rolled over the ocean's surface for more than two hours to arrive at a lava mountain with waves violently slamming the shore. I immediately knew I couldn't get in that water. Even if I survived the swim to shore, I'd never be able to get myself back to the boat after the cave experience. I suggested that the three youngest children stay in the boat with me. Scott and Meleese assured me the children were good swimmers and would have no trouble.

Overboard they all went. Within two minutes I heard shouts of, "Lige! Lige! Somebody save Elijah! Shinnay's in trouble. Somebody get Shinnay. Shinnay! Shinnay!" The oldest boys were able to rescue the two smaller children from the crashing waves and drag them to the tunnel entrance.

The family plus Michelle and Heidi successfully dived under water and went through a short tunnel, emerging inside a cave of murky, fast-moving seawater. Evidently seawater was entering from more than the tunnel. Thirty minutes later they climbed back into the transport boats with tales of horror, rough water, claustrophobic tunnel swims, and impossible snorkeling.

The return trip was shortened by thirty minutes because of currents and prevailing winds. Once we were close to the resort, the boat driver realized he had no path to cross over the reef, as the tide had gone out. We waited in the ocean until the second boat arrived and showed our driver a path. Our boat had a steeper keel and was caught on the coral several times. Four men, including Rhys, climbed into the water, picked the boat up, and heaved it forward a few inches with each wave.

Finally, we were in calm water and floating to shore. The family decided to snorkel in our docking spot, as the water was calm on the landside of the reef. I joined them. We saw the most beautiful, colorful coral I'd ever seen. The coral was lavender, pink, green, and all shades of the rainbow. The fish were brilliant fluorescent in their bright-colored costumes. We enjoyed a wonderful show floating serenely in the cove.

The late afternoon was spent resting or exploring our surroundings individually or in pairs. We needed a little downtime. I reclined on a lawn chair beside the pool and read a history of Vanuatu written by a native who had learned English from missionaries. Some of the stories were so primitive, it was hard to believe they were talking about people living in the twentieth century.

We had an early night. Shinnay, Heidi, and I were sleeping soundly when a 7.3 earthquake awakened us at eleven thirty p.m. The girls became hysterical. I watched the bamboo walls wave the opposite direction from the way my bed was going but was much too tired to care. I told the girls to quiet down, assuring them the earthquake would pass in a few seconds. They cried, they howled, they clung together. Heidi encouraged her younger cousin with tales of horror, claiming she saw flames, and that the cabin was being carried into the ocean. Shinnay was sure the volcano, which was several miles away, was spewing lava down on top of us. They carried on for an hour before exhausting themselves. Both girls slept through the aftershocks. I opened one eye to make sure nothing was going to fall on top of us, turned onto my stomach, covered my head with a pillow, and went back to sleep.

April 10, 2008 In the light of day, after eight hours sleep, I was ashamed of the way I reacted to the earthquake. I should have taken the girls outside and comforted them, and assured them we were not going to die. I apologized, but neither girl was ready to forgive my misjudgment.

Our flight was scheduled to leave at eleven thirty a.m. We were to be at the terminal for check-in at ten thirty a.m. The taxi was to pick us up at the resort at nine thirty a.m. We would leave Tanna Island and arrive at Iririki Resort at one p.m. It was a nice, well-organized plan. I liked organization.

Our taxi driver nonchalantly rolled to a stop in front of us at ten a.m. He visited with friends and/or relatives for ten minutes while we loaded luggage in the rear of the pickup truck and scuttled aboard ourselves. I thought we'd never get through check-in on time. Of course, I had completely forgotten that the airport terminal was only five minutes away.

Meleese kept all the tickets to facilitate travel expediency. She marched to the counter and handed the lady all eleven tickets while we dragged our suitcases behind her. She had one ticket missing—mine. Not to worry; the clerk gave me a boarding pass anyhow. This definitely was not America.

The clerk weighed each suitcase. Twenty kilos was the maximum limit. Mine weighed nineteen and a half kilos. The clerk gave me a toothy grin and put her thumb and forefinger together in what was evidently an international symbol of "okay."

The lady processed all the luggage and stamped tickets and boarding passes and handed everything back to Meleese. Meleese counted tickets—there were only seven, and there were eleven people. There were ten boarding passes. How could they disappear right there at the counter? The clerk looked around a bit, then gave Meleese another, "Not to worry, just show ticket taker your receipt. Him know you paid eleven people."

We would only be in the crowded terminal a few minutes. It was time to board. I walked toward the door leading to the runway. There was no plane on the tarmac.

A small plane that would hold about fourteen people landed at noon. About thirty people jumped up and got into line. That did not look good. Meleese showed the ticket taker her receipt. He looked at it for two minutes before telling her this was not her plane. Whew. We were glad to step back and let other people fight for seats.

The taxi driver strolled up to Scott and said, "Me take you to resort. Nice and cool. Me come get you when plane comes." Scott had traveled in Vanuatu enough to know it was best to go with the flow. At the resort we learned from the English manager that our plane had motor problems and was expected to arrive at two o'clock.

We ate lunch and lulled about in comfortable open-air lounges. We wished we had swimsuits and snorkel gear, but that was hopefully locked in safekeeping at the airport.

At one thirty our taxi arrived, and we went back to the airport. At two o'clock the same fourteen-passenger plane landed again. It was obvious the plane was only going to hold half the people in line. The line moved forward at a snail's pace. When Meleese worked her way to the front of the line, she was told the plane was full, and we would have to wait for another. When will it arrive?

"At two thirty."

Scott called it to the man's attention that it was currently two forty-five.

"Ah, maybe plane be here at three thirty." Meleese went to the ticket counter and asked what was happening. The clerk explained that the plane that was just loaded would take those passengers to Port Vila and return for us. She warned Meleese to be first in line when the plane returned. What a way to run an airline!

We knew it was slightly over an hour flight, so the plane would not return until at least five o'clock. Scott called the resort, and they sent the taxi to come get us. The taxi driver stayed at the resort visiting with employees. When we saw the plane fly over the resort at four forty-five, we dashed to the taxi and got to the terminal in time to be first in line before the ticket taker took his position at the door.

We got on the small plane and took the smoothest ride ever over the azure water and green islands of Vanuatu. We arrived at Port Vila to find a taxi driver who had been waiting for us since noon. He drove us through the bustling capital city to the ferry.

The ferry was so small, it took people on the first trip and returned for our luggage. It was seven o'clock when we arrived at the resort. The clerk smiled and said she had expected us at one o'clock. Would we please have seats; our rooms should be ready in an hour. Say what?

We were handed keys an hour later and made our way along the torchlit sidewalk to two villas. Scott's was still under construction. There was no furniture, as the interiors had not been completed. He returned to reception to tell the surprised clerk. She eventually found space to ensconce the whole tribe of Kilpatricks.

I was unpacked, showered, and in bed when room service showed up with dinner for the four boys sharing my villa. Sleep sounded much nicer to me than food.

April 11, 2008 It was a beautiful, calm morning. The water looked perfect for snorkeling. I got up at six thirty and was tempted to go snorkeling alone. I knew that was never a good idea. The buddy system was always better in waters filled with critters that bite or sting. Instead, I strolled the circumference of the island, reveling in the perfect weather and beauty that surrounded me. I loved the tropics. I wondered how long it would take me to become laid-back like the natives who never worried about time, appointments, schedules, phones, televisions, or the other paraphernalia we Westerners thought was necessary for survival.

A couple of hours later, family members appeared here and there on my path and told me they were going to the restaurant for breakfast. Eating in the tropics was fun. There was such a bounty of fruit that it was hard to choose one, two, or three. I usually ended up leaving the cafeteria-style counter with a little bit of everything, which created a heaping platter. Then I needed a second platter for the variety of breads offered. I would definitely have to wait an hour after breakfast before going in the water.

When I did get to the cove and was putting on snorkel gear, a gentleman sat on the opposite bench at my picnic table. He commented on water conditions. I responded, and he immediately said, "You're a long way from home!"

That started a conversation. He said he had gone to the University of Michigan in the late 1950s. I said I shouldn't talk to him. I went to Ohio State in the late 1950s. He laughed, and we bantered back and forth about the traditional football rivalry. He said he was married in 1957. So was I. He had a son about a year later. So did I. He said that was where the similarity probably ended. My son's first words were probably not the same as his sons. I disagreed, saying my son's first words were "mama and dada." He said his son's first words were, "Oh, oh, oh, how I hate Ohio State."

We donned masks and flippers and waddled to the water's edge, where we parted company. I tucked chunks of stale bread into my life vest and pulled out bits to coax fish within two feet of my mask. I held an underwater camera in the other hand, and snapped pictures of iridescent parrot fish, clown fish, and many whose names were unknown to me. I suspected when the film was developed, I'd have pictures of bubbly water and nothing else. Fish moved quickly. Actually capturing them on film was an art.

After snorkeling Meleese and I took the children to the water sports complex. They played on a tire swing dangling from a tree limb, buzzed back and forth on Jet Skis, and bounced on the water's surface on an inflatable toy pulled behind a Jet Ski. The three older boys went on a catamaran. It all looked like fun.

Another excellent day in paradise ended as I watched the sunset over the water while sitting in a hot tub on the verandah of our villa.

April 12, 2008 Everyone climbed onto the ferry by five thirty for our trip to Efate Island. The bus met us at the Port Vila dock for transport to the airport. Meleese was told to arrive at the airport at six o'clock. We did.

We arrived an hour before the terminal was open. We stood on the sidewalk outside the terminal watching city folks make their way through morning traffic using a variety of transport methods—bicycles, motor scooters, twenty-year-old vans, and thirty-year-old pickups that doubled as taxis.

Terminal staff arrived a few minutes before seven and opened the doors so we could check in for our flight to Pentecost Island. We each had to be weighed. The adults groaned as the whole world became aware we were overweight. Who was the only one who said, "Don't anybody look," when she stepped on the scales? Shinnay, who weighed in at twenty kilos.

Meleese was told one person would have to go on a smaller plane, as there wasn't enough room for everyone on the larger plane. I rode in the eight-seater, dual-prop plane with other tourists. It finally got off the ground at eight thirty.

We landed on a dirt track called an airstrip and unfolded our bodies so we could slide out the door. The terminal was such a delight, I forgot my grievances against the airline company. The terminal was a thatched hut with bamboo walls. The one room was about fifteen by thirty feet. A counter displayed a carefully hand-printed sign saying, "Check-in." There were two benches made of bamboo. Of course, there was also the ominous scale in the center of the room.

The single employee at the terminal told me no larger planes were scheduled. My plane would bring the rest of the family. As there were ten people left in my group, that would take two trips. The trip took one hour each way. We were in for another all-day terminal experience.

I was pleasantly surprised a few minutes later to see a sixteen-seater make a circuit over the dirt track and line up for a landing. The plane took a lot more space to come to a stop and had coasted half a mile past the terminal. All my family was soon bouncing toward me aboard a pickup truck.

I climbed aboard the pickup, and we were taken to the old terminal—a concrete-block building left over from World War II. A few natives shyly peeked at us from around corners. We were told we had to wait at the old terminal until the land divers were prepared. That took another hour. We were there to view the sacred ritual, when farmers tied vines around their ankles and dived off homemade towers in a quest to please the agricultural god, so they would have a good crop of yams. I would have given up farming and opened a mortuary if I had been born on that island.

There was no drinking water at either terminal and only the most primitive of toilets. We were told this would be our last chance for toilet facilities for four or five hours, so everyone dutifully used the smelly outhouse, carefully looking for snakes and spiders before entering.

About noon we were told the land divers were ready for us, and we trailed up the muddy, slippery, steep hillside to the tower perched above us on a cleared slope. The heat and humidity had everyone sweating profusely. It rained most evenings, so the ground was perpetually wet. We chose our viewing sites by their shade content. There were no seats, and there was no flat ground. There was only mud and chopped-down brush on the edge of a clearing.

The seminaked farmers sang and chanted as each man climbed the rickety-looking seven-story tower. The divers were intent and prayed fervently as they tied lianas to their ankles. They religiously pleaded with their god to hear their prayer.

The music—drumbeating and singing—became more intense, and the divers' chants became more demanding. Then suddenly all was quiet as the man fell forward. The first man arched his back far enough that when his face and shoulders hit the cultivated dirt, it did him no permanent damage. He stood up beaming broadly. I thought surely he wasn't supposed to actually hit the ground and later learned that the men made their own vine cables and were expected to know exactly how long to make them to stop their downward fall six inches above the dirt.

I'm sure the farmer and his family were relieved that he lived. The last diver of the previous week had died of a broken neck. The tower had collapsed. The natives believed that the custom had not been followed. It took three months to build the tower, and the construction crew was to stay at the site, pray, and meditate the whole time. In fact, two men who helped build the previous tower had committed a taboo of sleeping with their wives while the construction was underway. Blame it on the women. The sinners had to pay the widow five pigs each. Their wives were severely beaten.

We watched four more divers fall from successively higher points on the tower. The men were heroes and proudly stood beside white people to have their picture taken. They wore nothing but a namba.

I migrated to where Melanesian women and children were gathered in the shrubbery and whipped out my Polaroid camera. I asked if I could take pictures of the toddlers and was given permission. When the first picture dried, I handed it to the mother to keep. I took two or three pictures before people crowded around wanting group shots taken. I went through two rolls of film in a matter of minutes and was surrounded by laughter and big smiles.

When it was time to leave, two elderly ladies took my hands and led me down a grassy, gradually falling slope. The path was a hundred times easier to navigate than the trail we had climbed to get to the performance. The rest of the family arrived at the old terminal covered with mud from falling and sliding down the dangerous terrain of the original trail.

The ladies took me to what must have been their pride and joy—an outhouse with a ceramic toilet sitting over a hole in the ground. They proudly nodded and pointed, and I could tell they wanted me to use the facility. It had no door. No one else was around yet, so I perched over the bowl and managed a tinkle. The ladies clapped. There was no toilet tank or lavatory, but there was a bucket and a water tap. I poured a little water in the toilet bowl and washed my hands under the tap. I smiled at the women waiting outside and thanked them. They were pleased to see I appreciated their modern fixture. It was their show of gratitude for giving them pictures.

At the terminal the guide who had led us up the trail to the tower wanted us to follow him to the beach, where a picnic was waiting. The mud was knee-deep in places along our path. When we arrived at the beach, all waded in deep enough to wash. The water felt so good, I was tempted to submerge myself totally with my clothes on. As the local ladies wore Mother Hubbard dresses, I assumed a white woman coming out of the water in shorts and a wet T-shirt would not be proper. I didn't want to have to pay anyone pigs for committing a taboo, so I stayed knee deep in the water and splashed my face. In traveling from island to island, I was conscious of the variety of cultures and tried not to offend anyone.

Finally, a bottle of water was produced. I accepted two four-ounce glasses and quickly downed them. There only seemed to be one bottle of water and one bottle of sweet juice for twenty-four people. Sandwiches were produced. They had meat of some kind, and I knew they arrived on the plane from Port Vila with the family, so they had been sitting in the heat for four hours. I declined the sandwich. Miraculously a second bottle of water appeared. The water was a bit cloudy, and I suspected it was filled at the water tap I had used before coming to the beach. I really didn't want Montezuma's revenge to catch up with me in this remote place. I chose to go for a walk while the other tourists ate and drank the treats offered.

A native lady joined me, and we spent an interesting hour exchanging bits and pieces about our lives. Madeline was dressed in a worn but clean ankle-length muumuu, sandals, and hat and carried a parasol to ward off the noonday sun. She walked with a proud demeanor, so I knew she was an important person.

Madeline was the island physician. Her knowledge, medicines, and rituals had been handed down from her grandmother. She never prescribed modern medicine, but used herbs, roots, homemade potions, and spiritual rituals. She did as much as possible for her sister, but the curse put on the sister that gave her breast cancer was too strong. The sister went to a modern hospital on Espiritu Santo (of Black Sheep Squadron fame during World War II), but of course, those doctors knew of no way to remove the curse either. The sister died of her affliction.

Madeline mentioned there were three causes for death. I could think of many more and asked what three she knew about. Madeline said that people either had a curse put on them by a witch or other practitioner of witchcraft, they committed a taboo, or they died of old age. I asked about the children who succumbed to death. Madeline said they died because someone had put a curse on them or their parents. The curse was on the mother in cases of miscarriages or stillbirths.

I didn't mention that I had been an aerospace engineer to this woman who proudly proclaimed she had once seen a television show in Port Vila, Efate, during her one trip to the main island. I thought my career was a stretch too vast for her to comprehend and felt no need to pretend superiority for having been in the right place at the right time to have the opportunity to take part in the US space program.

Madeline spoke English very well, so I asked where she had learned it. Missionaries, mainly from Australia, had lived on the island in the past and built schools. She went to one of those schools for a couple of years. Also, there had been US soldiers on the islands before Madeline's birth, and they taught a few privileged chiefs to speak English. The chiefs in turn taught tribal leaders. Many people knew how to speak Pidgin English brought back to Vanuatu by freed slaves who had been taken to the sugarcane fields of Queensland, Australia, in the 1800s. That language became known throughout the archipelago as the common language. Madeline's mastery of the English language was superior to Pidgin. She also spoke French fluently and six native tongues. Each tribe had its own language. She said she was one of the wisest people on the island. I believed her.

Madeline said she had lived a fortunate life, as the most important man on the island, her uncle, had taken her as his concubine. I asked if his importance was because he was a chief. Heavens no, he was important because he was the only person on Pentecost Island who knew how to talk to pilots flying in airplanes. I visualized him meditating to make contact, but Madeline went on to say he used the machine in the bamboo terminal and pushed buttons and turned knobs at just the right time to talk to the pilots and could hear them when they spoke to him, even though they were far away.

I was rather sorry when our guide said it was time to board the taxi for the ride to the terminal. I wanted to spend at least a week with the ladies of Pentecost. Well, I wanted to fly back to Port Vila and get a couple of forty-four-gallon drums of clean water, then return to Pentecost and stay for a week.

Two planes arrived within minutes and ferried all the outsiders to Port Vila. The Kilpatricks boarded the private shuttle bus waiting to take us to the Iririki ferry dock.

Every available shower in the two Kilpatrick villas was occupied within fifteen minutes of our arrival. I beat the boys to the one on my floor—each villa had three stories and three bathrooms. I let water run into my mouth while I scrubbed caked-on mud out of my hair.

What a wonderful day.

April 13, 2008 We spent the day on Iririki. I snorkeled in the bay and then swam in the freshwater pool before collapsing into a chaise lounge and watching my grandchildren buzz up and down the waterway between islands on Jet Skis, catamarans, and various other water toys. The toy area was on the opposite side of the mile-wide island from the snorkeling site, thank goodness.

In the afternoon Scott arranged for us to tour a unique waterfall on Efate Island. Meleese knew what to expect, so she told her children to dress in their togs. "Togs" is Australian for swimsuits. The cascading waterfalls were like a giant water park. The water dropped about a hundred feet over an escarpment before spreading out into several ponds flowing over huge boulders—I mean, like rocks that are twenty feet in diameter—into other pools. Some pools were three feet deep, others were ten feet or deeper. The older boys slid over the boulders into the ponds. Elijah and the girls, Mikaela and Shinnay, tried everything their teenaged brothers did. Sometimes a big brother had to pull the little ones out of a dangerous spot. There was a trail going to the top pool, which everyone except me climbed. The trail was completely underwater but was marked by a rope handrail. I was determined to make it through this trip without breaking any bones or any cameras. That meant I had to forego youthful antics.

April 14, 2008 It only took a half hour to pack my luggage for the trip to Rockhampton, Queensland, so I spent the balance of the morning reading the fascinating history of Vanuatu.

The Kilpatricks spent the afternoon and evening in airports or on airplanes. We arrived at the farm at bedtime, and all slept soundly.

April 26, 2008 Twelve-year-old Mikaela spent the afternoon and night with me at the farmhouse. After a couple of games of double solitaire and a game of rummy 500, we wanted exercise. We started on one of my favorite trails on the farm headed for the old campground. Mikaela carried apples to feed her maternal grandparents' goats, and I carried cereal bars called Weet-bix, which were compressed Wheaties.

The goats were happy to see us and gleefully accepted our gifts. The male goat dropped his half an apple, and Mikaela reached into the tall grass to retrieve it for him. He promptly butted her. We decided we had worn out our welcome and left the goat pen.

We saw red-tailed black cockatoos and a pair of pale-headed rosellas, as well as dozens of rainbow lorikeets, melodic magpies, and butcher birds.

We followed the cattle trail, so it was inevitable we should find cows. We were on a ridge between heavy scrub and a *billabong* (pond) when we saw a calf blocking our path. I kept walking, thinking he would move when we got close. Mikaela grabbed my arm and said, "Wait a minute, that's the calf of the mean cow! She will chase us if we get too close to her baby."

I'm not very good at outrunning angry cows. Okay, I'm terrible at outrunning anything other than snails. I shouted, "Shoo!" and waved my arms. The calf looked at me like I was a silly old woman. Imagine that.

I picked up a grapefruit-sized rock and bowled it toward the calf's feet. The rock missed the calf and rolled down the hill into the sticker bushes. The bushes rustled, and the calf took off like a shot out of a gun. We expected to see an angry cow charge toward us from the brush. Instead, we saw a big group of wild boars take off at a run away from us.

"Holy moly, holy moly," Mikaela said as I counted the departing pigs. My count was up to twenty when Mikaela grabbed my arm and pointed to the brush twenty feet from us.

I looked in that direction and saw a sow with about eight piglets suckling.

"Run, Mikaela," I said quietly. I didn't want to break eye contact with the sow, but I backed away as quickly as I could. When I had gone twenty or thirty feet, I turned and followed Mikaela as fast as my little fat legs would carry me. We trotted along past the possum house, goat pen, horse trough, sour tangerine tree, and up to the farmhouse in a quarter of the time our outbound journey had taken.

"Okay, that's enough exercise for one day. How about another game of rummy five hundred?"

May 10, 2008 It was my day to spend alone with ten-year-old Shinnay. We went into Rockhampton and started our day at a pretty little side-walk café. Yuck! The food was terrible. I ordered the spinach and mushroom omelet. All I could eat were the six slices of mushroom and six pieces of spinach. They were inside sticky foam that had no egg flavor—had no flavor at all. The texture was disgusting; it was slimy and oozed between the tongs on the fork. Shinnay had a favorite Australian children's breakfast of baked beans on toast. She only ate about half her serving, so I don't think it was tasty either. The check came to $25.00. I hoped our day would improve.

We went to the theater and bought tickets for an afternoon dance competition called "Eisteddfod." Shinnay has taken dance lessons, and I thought she would enjoy seeing her fellow dancers perform. She knew some of the youngsters in the contest.

Attached to the theater was an art gallery. Shinnay and I enjoyed drawing, painting, and coloring together, so it seemed reasonable we would like professional's work. I paid for tickets and went through the double doors. Whoops! The art gallery was under renovation. There were two small rooms open to the public. That was a bummer.

The first room was filled with an amateur collection of dream interpretations. First through third graders had produced better art. The second room had a display of silver sculpture by jewelry makers. The second room was quite nice, and we oohed and aahed over the pretty semiprecious stones set in silver. That killed half an hour.

We had two hours before the dance recital started. We walked along the river, then decided to create some art of our own. I brought drawing material to a picnic table, and we spent a lovely hour and a half sketching our surroundings. Shinnay showed a definite spark of talent. I hoped it would be ignited.

We went to the theater and learned the producer had changed the starting time from two p.m. to one p.m. Our tickets said two o'clock, so I was disappointed we had missed half the show. We waited until the current performer finished before entering the theater and finding seats. I thought we'd be in the last or first row because of our late arrival. There were about twenty bored members of the performers' families in the theater. We chose middle-of-the-theater seats about ten rows back. I wish I had that luck at all live performances.

An Irish jig was announced. Yea! I loved Irish music. Five girls performed the exact same dance to the exact same music and were judged. Shinnay and I agreed on first-, second-, and third-place winners.

The same music was played for the next five girls; they were judged and awarded ribbons. This was repeated five more times before a new song was played and a new set of five girls performed. Shinnay and I politely applauded for each girl. We stayed an hour before quietly leaving and returning to the farmhouse.

I read her stories after dinner, and we retired early. I knew the day had been disappointing and hoped she would give me another chance for a fun day sometime in the near future. I would research places to go other than the shopping mall—which was her suggestion when we left the theater. Shopping was my least favorite social activity. I suggested a camping trip. She thought sleeping on the ground sounded terrible. Surely we could compromise and share a pleasant day together.

May 11, 2008 Shinnay and I agreed I fixed better breakfasts than the restaurant. We had muesli, yogurt, fresh fruit, and hot herbal tea.

We walked to Grandma Geiszler's to present her with a card and poem Shinnay had bought her the day before. Grandpa Geiszler joined us for a *"cuppa"* and a visit. I loved this couple dearly and thoroughly enjoyed any time spent with them.

Shinnay and I bid them farewell and went for a hike in the bush to pick wild flowers and count who could find the most birds. I offered Shinnay five cents for each bird she could correctly name. She thought they were all called "bird." She went home without any money. I drove her to her parents' brick home on a hill. She was glad to be there.

Meleese fixed a lamb extravaganza for Mother's Day lunch for her mother and me. That didn't seem fair, since Meleese mothered six children. The meal was delightful, and we ate until we couldn't hold another bite, then started clearing the table.

Josh, his younger brothers, Rhys and Elijah, his friend Carl, and Michelle's brother, Shawn, had gone crabbing the night before. They presented Meleese with a huge crab as her Mother's Day gift.

Meleese, Rhys, Elijah, and I went to the beach near Yeppoon, a thirty-minute drive from Meleese and Scott's home. It was blissful watching the waves caress the shore. We searched for sand dollars and found a few. Elijah got the trophy for finding the most unbroken ones.

Meleese spotted an echidna waddling among the rocks of the embankment holding the highway. Meleese and Rhys tried to catch it to take it to the safety of the farm. It would be better off away from the speeding traffic.

The frightened little fellow clung desperately to the cement at the top of the bank. Meleese was afraid prying his claws loose from the concrete might cause him pain or injury. The critter depended on his claws to dig for ants, termites, and other edible insects. We left him clinging to his security.

Scott gave me a beautiful red leather carry-on bag for my travels. It was filled with rose-fragranced bath products. I would feel so decadent lying in a tub of rose-smelling water.

When I returned to the farmhouse, I learned Josh had given me a large crab as a Mother's Day gift. I was surprised and pleased he thought of me! I graciously accepted the gift. After thinking it over during the night, I confessed to him the next morning that I was allergic to crab. I had developed the allergy sometime over the past five years and was afraid to take a chance on getting sick. He was more than happy to take the cooked treat and consume it for his breakfast. Nonetheless, the crab was one of the most unique gifts I'd ever received.

May 18, 2008 I had a surprise birthday potluck lunch at Kershaw Gardens for Meleese's birthday. About eighty to ninety people showed up and had a lovely time sitting in the shade of the trees in the botanical park, visiting with friends, relatives, and neighbors.

The weather was perfect, the food plentiful, the cake beautifully decorated. Meleese smiled throughout the day. I knew she was uncomfortable being the center of attention, so I was pleased that she laughed so much and really enjoyed herself.

In the evening she rode to the farmhouse on a quad to thank me for my thoughtfulness. I confessed that I couldn't have pulled it off without a lot of help from Scott. He knew what people to invite; I didn't.

She had asked him for a day of complete peace and quiet. I told her I had set it up with him to have her spend the following Saturday at the farmhouse completely on her own. She could color in my coloring books, draw, read, make jewelry with my tools, walk in the bush, eat the multiple snacks I would leave, and nap. I'd spend the day at her house, cooking, cleaning, doing laundry, and yelling at kids. She smiled politely and said that wouldn't be necessary.

June 28, 2008. The previous month had been a stressful marathon in preparation for the nuptials of eighteen-year-olds Joshua and Michelle. The wedding had originally been planned for Easter time. That was why I had arrived in Australia the middle of March. The wedding was postponed. Now, the day finally arrived.

Marlow flew to Australia two days before the wedding and planned on staying two weeks. He joined me at the farmhouse, which we would now be sharing with the newlyweds.

The wedding was a spectacular outdoor affair at Byfield National Park. The girls looked like they stepped off magazine covers in their lovely gowns. The handsome young men tolerated pastel-colored formal outfits the whole day. The reception dinner and dance went on late into the night, with everyone in attendance having a good time.

Fortunately, Scott and Meleese had made arrangements for several guests to stay in the cabins at Byfield. Marlow and I enjoyed the rustic room and the sounds of critters singing to one another during the night.

The day after the wedding, we joined Michelle's family in admiring the surroundings and wildlife. There were about two dozen kangaroos of various sizes grazing on the lawn where the wedding ceremony had taken place.

July 4, 2008 On July 2 Meleese and Scott had taken the honeymooners to the airport to catch a plane to Melbourne, Victoria, for a two-week honeymoon.

Scott talked his father into extending his stay until September. All the Kilpatricks except the honeymooners took a Southern Hemisphere midwinter break in the tropics. Meleese and Scott treated Marlow and me to an all-expenses-paid trip to Cairns, Queensland, and environs.

We flew from Rockhampton to Cairns. At the Cairns airport, Scott and Meleese rented two Mitsubishi sedans. I was consigned a rear seat in the car Scott drove for the duration of the trip. Not a bad spot. The car floated on air, and the seats were soft and comfortable.

We took our luggage to the luxurious Aquarius Hotel. Marlow and I were assigned an eleventh-floor suite with two bedrooms, two bathrooms, two balconies, a living room, a dining area, and a fully equipped kitchen and laundry. The accommodations were as large as the mobile home Marlow lived in when he worked at Aerojet in Sacramento, which we considered our second home.

We learned the second bedroom and bathroom were to be occupied by sixteen-year-old Rhys and fourteen-year-old Caleb. They were good company and would make fine roommates. The size of the accommodations made a bit more sense.

July 5, 2008 I started the day with a decadent shower. The shower stall was four feet square, and the nozzle head was a foot wide. Taking a shower was like standing in a warm summer rain. I would have been completely happy to spend the day at the hotel, lying on the chaise lounge, snacking from the stocked fridge, and reading. I probably would have taken a couple more showers just for the sheer joy of it.

Meleese phoned with instructions to meet her and Scott in the lobby. It was time to start our vacation. We looked over the small city, a major tourist location, and the boys were soon enticed to try the go-carts. Adults took younger children with them. Rhys and Caleb drove their own cars, and everyone raced around and around the rubber-tire-lined track.

Some people wanted to "shop," so we wandered around the mall for a couple of hours before returning to the hotel for an early evening. Marlow watched television. Rhys, Caleb, and I played cards.

July 6, 2008 The two cars wound up the curvy mountain roads onto the Atherton Tablelands. Meleese had packed sandwiches for a picnic at a picturesque lake. We had the park to ourselves. Shorebirds and ducks played at the water's edge, a breeze rustled tea trees, and bright sunshine warmed the grassy expanse dotted with picnic tables.

After lunch we went on a boardwalk trail to see the Curtain Tree, a fig tree that had been uprooted in a hurricane and fell into the saddle of another fig tree's major limbs. As the years passed, the two trees sprouted numerous roots from the first trunk and other major branches reaching to the ground, thereby forming a curtain several yards wide.

We spent the afternoon and evening at Grandview Bed and Breakfast, which was strategically located on the crest of a hill. There were views of rolling hills, farmlands, and forest. The kids found bicycles and a tennis court to expend excess energy.

King parrots and crested pigeons entertained Marlow and me. Meleese and Scott amused themselves with the hot tub, garden paths, and video library.

When the children were finally out of energy, we went to a pub for dinner. It had the usual assortment of country characters found in such places, along with a display of historical farm machinery. The boys got acquainted with a farmer who explained the machinery, which kept them entertained until the food arrived.

July 7, 2008 Our breakfast food was supplied, but we had to do the cooking. It was a bountiful feast, with enough meat and bread left for luncheon sandwiches.

We had just gotten underway to our first destination when we came across a place called Windy Hill. We stopped to check out the orchard of windmills generating electricity. The wind was blowing so hard, it was difficult to keep my balance while walking. I'd lean into the wind and then be hit by a gust from the side that threw me off course. It was like a pedestrian carnival attraction. Of course, the kids enjoyed accidentally, on purpose, bumping into one another. Thank goodness they didn't do that to grannies. I tended to break when I fell anymore.

We arrived at our place of lodging for the night to discover we were sleeping in 1914 train cars. Marlow and I shared our room with Mikaela and Shinnay. Meleese is so good at planning vacations. She incorporated so much variety.

Shinnay and I went for a four-kilometer walk to Atkinson's Point. The most interesting thing we saw was a tree growing from cracks in a boulder and a momma wallaby with her joey. I loved spending time with the children individually when we could talk without sibling rivalry interfering. Shinnay was delightful; she looked for beauty in everything she saw. She examined leaves, twigs, and bushes and found dozing birds in trees that I would have missed.

In the evening we went on a guided tour to the entrance of lava tubes at Undarra. The humorous guides kept us smiling as we walked to a hilltop for champagne and hors d'oeuvres. We watched the sunset along with a visiting mob of eastern gray kangaroos. A whistling kite swooped down to grab a morsel of cheese before gliding gracefully away.

We arrived at the lava caves in time to see hundreds of tiny bats exiting for a night hunt. At times snakes extended from the lip of the cave to catch bats for their own sustenance. In summer there was estimated to be a quarter of a million bats in the cave.

We walked into the enclosure, and everyone on the tour was asked to take flash pictures at the same time. The lights frightened the bats, and they made a U-turn back into the depths of the cave. After exploring and hearing the history of the cave, we climbed up out of the depth of the cavern, slowly feeling our way along the footpath back to the parked cars. The guides knew the way and made it to the cars first. They turned on headlights so the rest of us could find our way.

July 8, 2008 The Kilpatricks drove down the mountain range, arriving in time for our scheduled Skyrail cable-car trip back to the crest. The Skyrail stopped at Barron Gorge, and we took a rainy hike into the rainforest. The umbrella trees, a palm species, protected our heads from water most of the way along the trail. We were in the tropics, so it wasn't as though we were going to catch a cold from being in the warm rain.

We remounted the Skyrail cars and rode the rest of the way to Kuranda over top the rainforest. Once there, we went to a butterfly farm. The large glass house was home to an assortment of colorful butterflies and tropical flowers. Once more I felt like a character in a Walt Disney movie—I should skip along the trail with the butterflies landing on shoulders or outstretched arms. The aroma of the flowers was heady in the steamy heat.

Too soon it was time to hop aboard a train pulled by a steam engine and descend the mountain. We rattled over trestles and through lush forests, getting closeup views of a flowing river and waterfalls.

July 9, 2008 The family caught the morning catamaran ride to Green Island on the Barrier Reef. The weather was cool and windy, so the ride was choppy. I brought my snorkel equipment, but the conditions were not conducive for that sport.

Instead I went into the submerged observatory and on a glass-bottom boat to see the colorful fish and coral. As many times as I've been snorkeling, I should be able to name the fish. There were clown fish, and a…let me see, blue fish, yellow fish, and, oh yeah, some angelfish.

There were brain coral, cauliflower coral, crown of thorns starfish, and a bunch of other kinds. Sorry, that's about as technical as I can get. The one word that described the whole scene was magical.

The family went to a crocodile farm and listened to naturalists expound on the prehistoric monsters. A five-meter-long crocodile was enticed to extend himself from the murky water and take a dead chicken from a pole. The mechanics of such an animal jumping vertically would be interesting to learn. The size and power of those animals kept me out of murky saltwater rivers in northern Queensland. When there weren't chickens available, they were known to take a tourist or two.

We all walked the circumference of Green Island. It always amazed me that so much vegetation could grow on an island of sand and coral.

July 10, 2008 Scott and Meleese took the two cars filled with family to Port Douglas, which had become a wealthy people's enclave in recent years. The settlement was a fishing village the first time Marlow and I took our young sons there in the 1970s. Australians had become more prosperous since then, plus numerous international tourists had found our old stomping grounds. The beaches were the best in the world. The weather was rainy and cool, so the only water sport we partook in was the hot tub.

When the rain let up for a while, Marlow and I walked through the quiet rainforest that ran along the edge of the beach, enjoying some exercise. We liked the smell of tropical plants and the sight of Australia's beautiful birds. It was sunset by the time we returned to our accommodations, so we sat on the balcony and watched giant fruit bats gracefully wend their way to eucalyptus trees endowed with gum blossoms.

July 11, 2008 We had breakfast with the birds at a wildlife refuge. I had been to the place eight years earlier and spent four hours communing with the critters. I was so glad I was able to share it with my grandchildren. Fortunately, it had not changed, and the whole family had a great time. The animals were loose, and tourists walked among them.

Well, the birds weren't free to fly off; they were inside huge landscaped domes. The whole experience was good for one and all. We even got to see a black-necked stork family—mother, father, youngster, and an egg in the nest. We learned the bird's name was changed from jabiru after the government learned the name was Portuguese, not Aboriginal.

It was my seventy-first birthday. I couldn't think of anywhere I'd rather be or anyone I'd rather spend the day with than my sweet, super-tolerant husband, my handsome son, and his family.

In the evening we went on a guided tour through private property covered with rainforest flora to look for critters. We found wide-awake crocs in the rivers and sleeping birds in the trees. We were gone long after dark and were several hundred yards from any other tour groups, but the leader saw something called a path. I loved it, just loved it. What a perfect way to spend a birthday. We listened to insects and frogs and were enveloped (literally at times) by vines, roots, and branches of brush. Wahoo! Who has more fun than people?

July 12, 2008 I thought last night's trip was the highlight of the vacation. I couldn't imagine feeling happier than I did exploring the wilderness. I was wrong. Meleese had another surprise.

Meleese, Mikaela, Rhys, Caleb, Elijah, and I hiked up, up, up a very steep hill to a little building that turned out to be the start of a zip-lining experience. The building had a turntable with cables attached. The cables stretched across to a platform on a tree several yards away—maybe a hundred meters away. Cables were going from that platform to another tree fifty yards further, and then there was another platform and more cables. We each wore a harness that enclosed us from our shoulders to our crotches. We wore hard hats.

A worker attached my harness to a strap dangling from the cable and told me to step off the first platform. Step off into midair fifty meters above the ground. Holy cow! The worker turned to help a cute teenage girl get into her harness. I became invisible to him. I inched my way to the edge of the platform, saying, "I can do this. I can do this." I stepped off the platform. There was immediately a snapping sound and a loud crack as something broke on the harness.

"Excuse me. Excuse me. Something just broke." I felt like I was screaming, but the sound coming out of my mouth wasn't audible to the flirting couple. Finally, I took a deep breath and yelled, "Hey! Something just broke!"

The attendant turned quickly and grabbed the cable, pulling me back toward the platform. When he assured himself that whatever broke wasn't important, he gave me a gentle shove back out into mid-air. I asked him what would happen if I passed out.

"We'd drag you up onto this platform. Do you feel like you're going to pass out?"

I took two large gulps of air and announced I was fine. He set the cable in motion, and I floated above treetops, over a gorge, seventy-five meters over a river, and to the next platform.

It was easier to step off the second platform, and by the time I got to the third one, I was completely relaxed and thoroughly enjoying myself. I was to the point where I could even do flips midway between platforms. I was flying! For the last expanse, I flew upside down, laughing all the way. I wanted to beg Meleese, "Can I do it again, Mommy? Can I, huh? Huh? Can I?"

The flying experience kept our motors revved up all day. But that wasn't all Meleese had planned. In the afternoon we went on a Daintree River boat ride. The boat was several barges connected and painted to look like a train. The primary animals we saw were crocodiles sunning themselves on the banks. The boat driver said the animals needed the sun to digest their food. They couldn't digest it in the cold river. Soooo, even if a croc grabbed me while I swam in a murky river and swallowed me, he couldn't digest me until he was lying on a sunny bank. That was comforting to know.

In the evening we got dressed up and went to a very fancy dinner. We were taken by bus to Flames of the Forest, on an Aboriginal reserve. We were greeted with champagne or apple juice at an outdoor bar, and Aboriginal waiters in tuxedos and waitresses in black-and-white dresses carried trays of hors d'oeuvres from person to person. The location was lit with candles wired to bare trees, and torches lit the pathways. The setting was beautiful and romantic.

We were escorted to our table, which was set with white linen, crystal glasses, bone china dishes, and silver utensils. We had front-row seats for the performances of dancing, singing, and poetry recital. Part of the entertainment consisted of dreamtime storytelling. According to legend a rat mated with a duck. Their children were the first platypuses. Oh, so that explains that mystery.

The seven-course dinner consisted of crocodile, kangaroo, beef, chicken, and an assortment of exotic vegetables and fruits prepared in dishes I'd never eaten before. The service was excellent, the show entertaining, the ambience exquisite. The warm summer night air was filled with the aroma of eucalyptus mingled with the spices of food. Wine flowed freely. I was glad a bus was taking the guests to their lodging after the meal.

What a splendid evening to top off a fantastic day.

July 13, 2008. We drove from Port Douglas to Cairns and returned to our first hotel of the vacation—Hotel Aquarius.

Marlow and I toured a replica of a 1606 Dutch boat. We learned about early navigation by tiny boats on the seas, most of which was done by the sun and stars. The captain and first mate had private quarters where logs, maps, and precious cargo were stored. The balance of the crew slept in hammocks that were removed from their hooks during the day. There was very little storage space for crew members, about enough for the typical carry-on bag on an airplane. There was a galley where food was stored, but the cooking was done aboveboard on the foredeck in a brick enclosure about the size of a barbecue pit. That particular replica had sailed to Holland, Indonesia, and around Australia. It would be leaving on another voyage soon. It took eight crewmen and eight volunteers. Oh, to be fifty years younger. I couldn't volunteer because part of the job required climbing the rigging. That would have amused the crew, but wouldn't have done anything to further their travels.

July 14, 2008 The family flew to Rockhampton. Marlow and I were driven to the old farmhouse, where we continued our residence until the first week of September.

During our last six weeks of sojourn in Australia, Marlow and I took turns riding with Scott on his rounds to inspect house-building sites. It was nice to watch our son at work. We marveled at his ability to keep so many facts, figures, dates, and timelines in his head. He had several houses under construction, and each was at a different stage of development. Scott kept things flowing smoothly with the help of his conscientious staff. Meleese managed the office staff and kept things running smoothly there.

We attended sports outings where our grandchildren were playing basketball, tennis, or swimming. We watched in amazement as Meleese juggled a full-time job and most of the chauffeuring of children to myriad social engagements, schools, sports, and musical affairs. "No child left behind" took on a whole new meaning to me.

Sixteen

New York, London, and Paris

2010

In 2006, when my stock was still worth money, I promised my granddaughter, Bethany, a high school freshman, that I would take her to Europe to see real art as her high school graduation present. At the time she was painting watercolors and dating a boy whose father was a professional artist. Well, my stock tanked after making that promise, but a young man I mentored at Aerojet several years previously was now a supervisor and in position to give me a temporary job to refill my coffers. I was able to fulfill my promise.

I studied sites on the Internet and mapped out an itinerary starting after Bethany's mid-June commencement. I made reservations with Servas hosts for homestays, at hostels and at hotels and booked transportation and educational tours in New York, London, and Paris.

Bethany and I were going to bond before she became engrossed in adult life.

June 22, 2010 Marlow took our eighteen-year-old granddaughter, Bethany and me to the airport. We arrived two hours before our flight to New York. It took twenty minutes to check in and get through security. No hassles, no delays, the Sacramento airport staff made the start of our trip smooth.

Once in New York, we wended our way to baggage claim. Bethany gathered luggage while I negotiated a phone call to our hostess for the night. The first airport terminal phone I tried was out of order. I lost a dollar before realizing it was not working. A man was using the phone next to me. He hung up in anger and walked away. I tried his phone. After dialing the number, I got a recording saying, "Hang up the phone and dial 6-1-1." I did so after depositing a second fifty cents for that phone. The operator asked what number I wanted, and I gave it to her. A minute or so later, she came back on the line and said the call had been rejected by the recipient. I was flabbergasted, as my instructions were to phone the hostess when we landed in New York. The operator suggested I try a different phone.

That didn't make sense to me, but I did it anyway, and got the same recording saying to call 6-1-1. The 6-1-1 operator mentioned the recipient was not accepting collect calls. I explained I wasn't trying to phone collect! The operator suggested I try a different phone.

Fer gorsh sakes! What's with the phone company? Were all the phones in the terminal wired for collect calls only? Before leaving the third phone, I pressed the coin return and was rewarded with $3.00! That made up for all the coins I had deposited so far.

The fourth phone worked fine. The call was completed, I apologized to Inna for the collect calls at the late hour—it was near midnight—and explained the airport phone situation. The hostess said the key was in the mailbox. We were to stay in the first room on the left after we entered the front door. I told her we'd be very quiet so we wouldn't wake her. She laughed and hung up.

A man approached after we exited the terminal and asked if we wanted a taxi. I said yes and kept walking toward the queue waiting in line at a designated taxi stand. A New Yorker told me the man who approached me was a "hijacker." Startled, I asked what she meant. She said local people get tourists to go into their private cars thinking they are taxis. Then the driver charges whatever he wants instead of the going taxi rate. Whew. I was glad to hear we escaped a hijacking. That was a reminder to avoid looking like a naïve tourist.

We entered a Yellow Cab, and the polite driver took us through heavy downtown traffic (after midnight!) and through lower middle-class neighborhoods before descending into a deserted industrial area. When he started looking for the house number, we were in a sad, poverty-stricken area, and I told Bethany I didn't like the feel of the place.

The driver couldn't find the address and drove around the block. He was getting fidgety and at a traffic light asked for his cash. I told him I would pay him when he delivered us safely to the address. I didn't want him to dump us on the street in that neighborhood. He said he couldn't find the address and needed to get back to the airport.

The second time around the block, Bethany spotted the address and checked the mailbox before I alighted from the cab. She confirmed the key was there, and it unlocked the front door. Our taxi meter said $62.00. I handed the driver four twenty-dollar bills, expecting eighteen dollars in change. He gave me a handful of bills, and I peeled off five ones and gave them to him as a tip. I felt $67.00 was enough to pay for a single taxi ride. I stuck the rest of the money in my pocket; he got our luggage from the trunk and quickly departed.

Bethany and I went into the dimly lit hallway. The place reeked of insect repellent. The hallway walls were solid brick, and we saw only two doors and a stairway. This was clearly not a private home, as I was led to believe from the Internet advertisement. I got the address from a company called Home Stays and had communicated with Inna, a lovely sounding lady with a Russian accent, and the owner of the building. I thought we were staying in one of her bedrooms.

The key had a tag saying "F," and there was a door on our left saying "F," so we let ourselves into the nearly bare room. There was one full-size bed, one folded-up rollaway bed, a tiny table with wobbly aluminum legs, two fold-up chairs, and a fan. There were two doors inside the room. One led to a closet. I assumed the other led to the bathroom, but it was locked. We heard movement behind the second door, so we didn't try it again. I put one folding chair against that door, one against the front door, and pulled the heavy velvet drapes closed against the wrought-iron-clad window. The room was hot and humid, so we turned on the fan.

I put things from my pockets onto the table, including the change for the taxi. There were three ones! I realized the taxi driver had already given himself a ten-dollar tip before handing me change. The creep accepted $15.00 for a tip! Not unreasonable for the time of night, but it would have been nice for the driver to tell me he was charging that much.

The accommodation had no bedding, but we brought our own, so we fished it out of our suitcases. I wanted to use the bathroom before retiring, so I went into the hall. I wasn't about to try the other door at the end of the hall, as I heard people in there. I saw a young woman sitting on the staircase, talking on a phone, and asked her the bathroom location. She pointed down the hall on the second floor. I made my way to a clean, community bathroom, took care of necessities, and rushed back to our assigned bedroom. (Bethany did not use the facility during our whole stay. She was afraid to leave the bedroom. She must have a bladder the size of a cantaloupe! Mine is the size of a walnut.)

Once inside the bedroom, with the door locked and the folding chair against it, I headed for bed. The folding chair couldn't keep anyone out, but the scraping on the bare floor would alert us to the door being opened.

There was a knock on the door. I enquired who was there, and a male voice with a Russian accent said, "It's the manager. I need to tell you something about your room."

I told him to tell us in the morning. I wasn't about to open the door at one o'clock in the morning. We slept fitfully.

June 23, 2010 First thing we wanted to do was change accommodations. We were scheduled to stay in this scary place two nights. No way could we stand a second night.

I knocked on the other first-floor door expecting to find our hostess, Inna. A sleepy lady answered, and I asked if she was Inna. She said no. I asked if that was the manager's room. She said yes. She turned and called to someone in another room.

As we had no cell phone, the handsome, smiling, young Russian manager of the "rooming house" agreed to phone a taxi for us. He was polite and couldn't really understand why we would have any objections to our accommodations. He was sorry to see us leave. We weren't sorry to leave! I knew I'd be billed for a two-night stay, but money was the least of my problems at the moment.

I had no idea where to find lodging, so I asked the taxi driver to take us to the airport so I could look at their hotel references. I phoned JFK Hotel on a direct line (I didn't want to attempt the public phones again) and asked if we could come straight over. They said they would send a shuttle for us. What a relief.

By two o'clock we were ensconced in a real motel, took badly needed showers, and were ready to face a day of sight-seeing.

We got instructions for going to the Statue of Liberty from the hotel clerk. He sent us down the street two blocks and around the corner to a grocery store, where he said we could buy bus tickets. The grocer didn't know what the hotel clerk was talking about, but said we could get tickets across the street and down a block at a check-cashing place. The clerks at the check-cashing place didn't know what the grocer was talking about, but said a bus to the subway stopped a block down the street. The subway would take us to the statue. A customer standing behind me said they were wrong, we needed to cross the street and walk up two blocks.

We left that establishment and asked several people—all polite and thoughtful—how to get to the Statue of Liberty. We got on a bus headed the direction most people told us to go.

I asked the driver if he took dollar bills and if so, how much was the fare to the subway station. He said he only took "meetro and kines."

"You mean you don't take money?" I asked.

"Jes kines."

"Coins, Grandma," Bethany whispered.

The two of us dug for coins in our backpacks as the bus headed for the next stop. The fair was a dollar each. We came up with a total of seventy-five cents. The driver told us to keep the "kines" and sit down.

He was offering us a free ride just because we were silly tourists who didn't know how to negotiate the bus system. What a kind fellow! After sitting we came up with enough pennies and nickels in various pockets to pay for one fare, and Bethany bravely marched forward and deposited it.

When we debarked, I thanked the driver for his kindness. He smiled broadly and said, "Ave a gut die." (I don't know where the man was born, but I knew his mama reared him right.)

After asking the subway ticket salesperson directions, we managed to get on the subway headed the wrong way. After about an hour of riding underground, I noticed the next stop was Columbia University. We were headed north instead of south to the bay!

When we alighted from the subway, I spotted one of "New York's Finest" and asked where to catch the train going the correct way. He pointed across a trestle to a set of tracks. I asked how we could get over there.

He pointed. "You should go down those steps to the station and buy a new ticket, then climb the steps on the other side of the trestle. But follow me, and I'll take you in the back door so you don't have to pay an extra $3.00 each." He did, and we didn't. He wasn't going to qualify as a rude, arrogant New Yorker either. Where were those people we were told were the rudest in America? All we had met were people who wanted to help us. No one was rude. Well, we also met one devious taxi driver.

I told Bethany it would be near sunset by the time we got to the statue and suggested we get off somewhere else and enjoy a bit of daylight in New York. When we got to Central Park, she said, "Let's get off here and see some trees and grass."

That sounded heavenly to me. We bought freshly made chicken sandwiches from an Italian mom-and-pop deli and took them to a pond in the park for a picnic. We walked around the park and down Fifth Avenue before heading for the hotel and a sound night's sleep between clean, cool sheets, with the air conditioner humming gently in the background.

June 24, 2010 We were up at five thirty, ate the free breakfast offered at the hotel, and took the free shuttle to the airport. The hotel was run by people of Indian descent, and every one of them was sunny and polite. The shuttle driver inquired of our destination for the day and I told him London. He was as enthused as we were. He was sure we would have a wonderful time.

We finally met our first rude New Yorker. The American Airlines clerk asked me what I was doing as I stood at a computer in the lobby. I told her I was reentering my passport number as requested by the check-in computer after it said my passport was invalid. She grabbed my passport from my hand and gave it to Bethany and said, "Old people are too stupid to operate computers. Let her do it for you."

Bethany was startled and said, "What am I supposed to do, Grandma?"

I told her to swipe her passport on a different computer and see if it was accepted. She did, it was. Then she swiped mine, which was also accepted, and we answered the computer's questions and were issued boarding passes.

The balance of the staff greeted us like welcome friends, including the security staff, who ushered us into the first-class security line so we wouldn't have to mingle among the common folks. Okay, okay, maybe he didn't really think we were first-class material. Maybe he just wanted to give some work to the x-ray people who were standing idle.

The security people were friendly and helpful to everyone, being sure to give extra assistance to the elderly, or those with children or other handicaps.

The plane departed within a few minutes of the scheduled time, and we settled in for an eight hour ride to London. At Heathrow we circled for forty-five minutes before the plane was permitted to land. I told Bethany to consider it our first tour of London.

My seat partner slept from takeoff to touchdown, so I watched three movies. Bethany's seat partner was too shy to speak, so Bethany dozed and read magazines. Her movie screen wasn't working, but I didn't know that until after we landed. I would have had the stewardess look for a vacant seat with movie capability. It must have been a long ride for Bethany.

We caught a taxi outside baggage claim. The taxi meter said "fifty-two" when we arrived at our hostel. I offered the driver euros, and he acted like I was offering him something too hot to handle. He needed pounds. Fortunately, the hotel clerk could exchange my euros for pounds, so we didn't have to spend the night in *gaol* (jail in American).

We were staying at the least expensive hostel with rooms available I could find in London. I made reservations last January. The room cost $150.00 a night, so I was expecting nice accommodations. We were directed to a seven- by twelve-foot bedroom along a maze of corridors and narrow steps. The room had a window overlooking a ten-foot-square "courtyard." The four brick walls surrounding the courtyard were a minimum of two stories high. A ten-foot ladder leaned against one wall. When we walked out of our teensy room, we noticed the door that exited into the courtyard was marked "Fire Escape." Heaven help us if there was a fire!

Although there wasn't walking room between our beds, we did each have a beloved fleece blanket. We both loved fleece, winter or summer. We had a clean bathroom and a little table that held an electric kettle, cups, tea, coffee, dehydrated milk, and sugar. And we had an armoire to store our suitcases. We were set for another perfect night's sleep.

June 25, 2010 Bethany and I dressed and went for the free breakfast. The dining room had thirty people crammed into a space meant for fifteen. We couldn't pull a chair away from the table far enough to squeeze our bodies into a seat at the first table. The second table had a bit more space. We figured a way for four people to sit in chairs side-by-side with every other person facing a different table. There were two people facing each table. One end of each table was against a wall. If a person next to the wall wanted out, everyone between him and the narrow pathway had to get up and move his chair. We were warned that Europeans were used to smaller living quarters than Americans. We just hadn't imagined their areas would be made for Lilliputians.

We got directions from the desk clerk and entered the population milling about downtown London. The hostel was in an excellent neighborhood, next to a luxurious-looking Best Western hotel, clean, neat row houses and just a few blocks from Victoria train station.

The most impressive thing about London (so far) was the volume of noise. The cacophony was horrendous! The second most noticeable thing was the harried people scurrying from place to place. I was assaulted on all sides by roaring diesel buses, growling cars, streams of wailing emergency vehicles, and various loud mechanical devices used by construction workers and street cleaners. No wonder the unsmiling pedestrians had their teeth clenched.

We eventually found the location to exchange our e-mail confirmation for a valid ticket on the double-decker open-air tour bus. The buses looked so quaint in pictures. Of course pictures don't show you the noise level surrounding the buses or let you feel the heat from the summer sun. Of course we chose to sit on the open-air roof-top seats.

We spent several hours viewing all sides of every wonderfully constructed building in midtown London. The age varied from twenty-three-hundred years old to built yesterday. There was old, new, modern glass, ancient Roman stone, marble, brick, and cement construction. There were no wooden buildings. Didn't I learn about a tremendous fire in London in the 1800s in my history class? Oh yes, and didn't they survive multiple days of bombing during World War II? Of course there were no wooden buildings.

We craned our necks from side to side viewing historic monuments to man's ingenuity as we listened to a recording explaining what the edifices represented.

Our tour included a boat ride on the Thames (pronounced *tems*, which rhymes with gems). We were so eager to get on the quieter boat ride that we boarded next to the Tower of London without bothering to go see the crown jewels held there.

The weather was perfect. Tour directors were friendly, hospitable, humorous, and helpful. The first day in London was instructional, nerve-racking because of noise, but entertaining.

I ate a delightfully delicious sandwich in the respite of our tiny hostel quarters, and fell asleep by seven p.m. I slept sound until four thirty a.m. when sunlight told me to arise and greet another day.

June 26, 2010 The long summer days stretched from four in the morning to ten at night. We took a different bus tour of merry old London. This bus was enclosed, air conditioned, and quiet. We saw different buildings and memorials and a few duplicates of yesterday. Exclusive Embassy Row had no lawns. That surprised me. At least the buildings were separated by ten feet or so. Commercial buildings and homes were connected, just as they are in New York or any other major city.

In the afternoon we took a tour of splendid Windsor Castle. The palatial home of monarchs was posh, historic, and large. The interior was decorated with red and gold. Bethany was an outstanding partner to share the experience with me. She was interested in every detail and didn't mind my obsession for getting to places early and staying as long as it took to read placards or hear the audio tour.

After a long day of walking, sunshine, and learning, we were more than happy to veg out in front of the telly and watch a soccer game in the evening. The United States lost to Ghana two to one in the try for the World Cup.

June 27, 2010 The weather forecast was for the hottest day of the season. Sunday was beach day when the temperatures were high, so lots of folks joined us at the bus station. They were going to the beach; we were going to Paris.

The bus driver ushered us aboard. Bethany and I got front-row seats. It took an hour and a half to get out of London. Then we had a delightful ride through the countryside of Kent. We stopped at Gillingham and Canterbury to drop off or pick up new passengers, and arrived at quaint little Dover a few minutes before noon.

Once onboard the ferry, going across the channel, Bethany and I shared a scrumptious hot meal—lasagna, bread roll, cheese, and a fruit tart. Our first sit-down-in-a-restaurant meal since we left Sacramento tasted so good!

The water in the channel was smooth, the air temperature warm, and the humidity high. The ferry had only one small deck from which to enjoy the weather, so it was crowded. We stayed in the restaurant, where we had softly padded window seats.

The advertised "free" shuttle in Calais costs two euros each, but it took us directly to the train station with our heavy luggage without hassles. We waited there for the next train to Paris via Lille/Flanders.

The train went through flat farmland and the occasional village to Gare du Nord station in Paris. A slew of private taxis waited outside the train station for passengers. Our hotel was in Montmartre, a five-minute drive away.

The elevator at the hotel was too small to hold two people and two suitcases, but that wasn't a problem. We took turns. The luxury hotel ($240.00 a night) was small, but we did have room to walk between our beds and to open our suitcases beside our beds. We had a built-in closet and a modern bathroom. The building had no air conditioner, but since we were on the fifth floor, it was safe to open the windows. Our view was of other buildings—all well maintained and clean looking. The people in the courtyard appeared to be kitchen help and maids, and it was delightful to hear their chatter and laughter. Bethany and I fell in love with the city listening to them.

We were really in Paris! Paris, France! *Ooh la la*!

June 28, 2010 We slept in late and then had pastry from a boulangerie for breakfast. We took the subway to our prearranged all-day bus tour starting point. We admired two thousand years of French history in the form of architecture.

We walked the Louvre's Tuillerie Gardens, which were disappointing, as there were no flowers. There were trees and bushes, wide snowy white sand-covered paths, and a carnival. A few park benches were found, and one section had picnic tables. The place was set up to accommodate hundreds of thousands of tourists. Several were there fanning themselves in the shade on that sweltering day.

To take the subway, it was necessary to walk down two flights of stairs, buy our tickets, walk up two flights of stairs, over a bridge, and then back down two more flights of stairs to get to the correct track. My knees creaked by the time we stepped into the crowded train. There was a musician playing a violin on the platform between stairs, and his music drifted throughout the area. That made the steps much more tolerable.

We had difficulty speaking the language but managed to communicate our desires. Younger people spoke English and kindly pointed us in the right direction to attain our destination. The streets and sidewalks were crowded and noisy, but people didn't appear as stressed as Londoners.

I had on shorts and a blouse and was given the evil eye by older women wearing dresses. People were polite, but it was evident women over twenty-five were expected to wear skirts. There were a few women in their twenties wearing slacks, but only teenagers or younger wore jeans or shorts. I took the hint. That night I'd put my shorts away until I was back in California.

We ate at a sidewalk café across from our hotel and had our first glass of wine. After all, we were in Paris! Paris, France! The restaurant didn't have what I think of as French food—rich in cream and butter. We ate salads and bread rolls.

June 29, 2010 I awoke at seven thirty—maybe my sleep was regulated to local time. Yippee! I took a shower and packed to leave the hotel before awakening Bethany. Her showers take an hour—that's why she looks beautiful afterward, and I merely smell better.

We went to our Servas hostess's home to drop off our luggage. Madame Camille, Cheri, and Michel lived on the fifth floor (ground-floor level was considered zero, and up one flight of stairs takes you to the first floor). There was no elevator. I managed to drag my fifty-pound suitcase up one flight but was relieved when fourteen-year-old Cheri offered to take it the rest of the way. She huffed, puffed, panted, and stopped after two levels for a rest. I needed a rest by that time from just dragging my body up that many steps.

Cheri gave us a key to the flat and showed us how things worked and what wasn't working before shyly retiring to her bedroom. Bethany was glad to see they had a cat. She missed her pets.

Bethany and I went to the Eiffel Tower, built for the 1889 World Exhibition. The tower replaced the Washington Monument as the world's tallest structure. It remained the tallest structure until replaced by the Chrysler Building in 1930. I've lost track of how many structures have been built taller than the Chrysler Building.

We joined the visitors wending their way through the lines waiting to ascend the Eiffel Tower, many of whom were rude, loud, aggressive Americans.

We were able to go to the top as there was no wind. When the wind is above a certain velocity, the tower is closed. The temperature was great and the views divine. We could see for miles and miles in any direction. Mostly what we saw was city—a city with several interesting-looking monuments near the tower.

We dined in the lovely restaurant, where we had window seats. Bethany's Americanism crept out when she ordered a hamburger and fries. Everyone should have French fries on their first trip to France. Right? She did celebrate her Eiffel Tower experience with a glass of champagne. I stuck to a salad and water, didn't want alcohol to make me sleepy—there was too much to enjoy.

We took a delightful boat trip on the Seine and admired the historic buildings along the way. The Seine had several places where steps descended from street level to a platform where people could sunbathe, picnic, or set up stalls to sell crafts.

Teenagers, Cheri and Michel cooked roast chicken and vegetables. There was also a tossed salad. Cheese and fruit were served for dessert. I thought it was an exceptionally sophisticated meal. Camille, mother of Cheri and Michel, was a lawyer and worked long hours. She came home for dinner, which was served at eight thirty, and then returned to work. She had a golden retriever to protect her on the walk to and from her nearby office. Cheri and Michel cleaned the table and then returned to their bedrooms. That was disappointing. We were hoping to get acquainted. I did dishes, set up my air mattress, and admired the view of the twinkling Eiffel Tower through the French doors in the living room. The Martins had no television, no air conditioning, no working stovetop on which to cook (just an oven, an electric skillet, and an electric pot to heat water), and worst of all, no hot water or working shower. Strange that a lawyer didn't make enough to get those things fixed. Bethany washed her hair by kneeling in the tub and using the cold water from the tap.

By eleven o'clock it was finally dark, and the squealing trains at Gare Lazare, a major train station across from the apartment, became fewer and fewer. I slept well.

June 30, 2010 I awoke at six o'clock fully rested. I expected the trains to wake me up but didn't hear them during the night.

I ate breakfast and visited with our hostess. She left for work about eight, and I had one more cup of tea before heading out to a nearby art gallery—Gallerie Lafayette. When I arrived, I found the gallery to be a shopping mall. There was a dome of stained-glass windows and gold-leaf trim on plaster curlicues and sculptures over De Beers, Cartier, Tiffany, Louis Vuitton, and Dior establishments. The vendors didn't have individual stores; they had counters in the open floor space. It was like being in Macy's except each counter was a different store. I think the mall was originally a cathedral. I only stayed a few minutes after turning over the bargain basement shoes and seeing the price range was 150 to 300 euros. Imagine paying $450.00 for a pair of shoes.

Later I learned that those were the prices for a single show at the Lido or Moulin Rouge! Thousands of tourists felt compelled to pay those prices to watch half-dressed women dance for a couple of hours. I had been looking forward to seeing the cancan, but could never bring myself to put out that much money for a show. Bethany was disappointed about my decision, but accepted it without argument.

I viewed Trinity Church, built during the Renaissance, before going back to the apartment. When I arrived, the two girls were just waking up. Michel and Camille were at work. Camille told me earlier that Cheri was self-conscious about her lack of good English, so she didn't want to join us on a tour of the Arc de Triomphe.

Bethany and I went to the glorious arch. The horses Napoleon stole (confiscated during battle) from Vienna were no longer symbolized on top, but the twelve-story structure was still awesome. We later found the horses on the duplicate arch at the Louvre. The Arc de Triomphe was based on the Arch of Titus in Rome. The monument was located on Champs Elysees in the middle of Place Charles de Gaulle Park. Bethany and I walked to the top and took the elevator down after viewing the widespread city. Major roadways radiated out from the arch like spokes on a bicycle wheel. I wished I had a rental car so I could drive them all and admire the neighborhoods. At the same time, I was relieved I didn't have to drive in city traffic.

We went shopping (mostly window-shopping) along exclusive Champs-Élysée, and Bethany bought a pair of Ray-Ban sunglasses.

We tried to go to the Concorde to find the museum where Margo Scandella, Bethany's other grandmother, told us we would find some wonderful impressionist art. The bus driver misunderstood my question and said, "*Oui, oui,*" when I asked if his was the correct bus to the Concorde. He took us to modern downtown Paris with glass and steel structures and a modern arch. Parisians were proud of their new arch. We got off the bus at the end of the line, a place called Le Defense.

We found our way to a subway station and took the train back to the Servas hostess home. Camille worked late. I offered to take the family out to dinner. Only Cheri was home. After conversing with Camille on the phone, it was decided we would take Cheri to a restaurant, and Camille and Michel would take care of their own meal.

Cheri was charming. Bethany finally broke through the shyness, and the girls spent a pleasant evening exchanging words for animals, plants, and other objects while playing a French version of Clue. It was my favorite evening of the trip because Bethany and Cheri were laughing and having fun.

I spent the evening writing in my journal and glancing at the well-lit Eiffel Tower. It is covered with twinkling lights that come on hourly, and then it switches back to spotlights for luminescence.

July 1, 2010 Bethany and I made it to the Louvre, originally a palace. First thing I did was pinch myself to see if this was just another dream, or if I was really at the Louvre in Paris, France. I was delighted that the pinch hurt. It meant I was really, truly in Paris.

The Louvre was last used as a palace by Louis XVI before he moved the government to Versailles. The structure was started in the 1300s. Amazing! Many of the stone buildings built in the mid-1800s in California had fallen down. This palace was five hundred years older.

The best way to express the experience of the Louvre is to borrow the French expression, "*Ooh la la*!" We took a tour with an English-speaking French lady to make sure we hit the highlights. The *Mona Lisa* was encased in glass, so there was no way to take a good photo or video. The reflections of the multitudes admiring the painting were reflected in the glass. I was surprised to see oil paintings displayed this way, as an art teacher taught me that oil paintings should never be encased in glass. I hoped Mona wouldn't end up with a moldy smile.

We saw the armless *Venus de Milo* and winged *Goddess of Samorace*. The real ones, the originals! We saw *Liberty leading the People* in the French Revolution against the monarchy, the *Wedding at Cana*, and many masterpieces of Italian and French artists. We admired Greek sculpture, and Bethany viewed Egyptian art. My legs gave out before I got to Egypt.

We needed to go back another day to see the Richelieu wing. Perhaps I'd have enough energy to see the pharaoh's treasures at that time.

We were too tired for any additional touring, so we went to the apartment. Since they had no hot water, I decided to take a cold shower and shampoo. I forgot the shower didn't work. I knelt to rinse shampoo from my hair under the tub tap. Getting down and up from the tub was an adventure at my age.

July 2, 2010 Our Servas hostess left for a swim at six a.m. By the time she returned, I was dressed, fed, and packed. Bethany was ready soon after, and we shared air kisses all around (that's French-style kissing—kiss the air next to a person's ears), then departed.

We got a taxi and delivered our luggage to the next hostess's home. Suzanne was at work, but her boyfriend, Marceau, did his best to show us the functioning of their apartment. The unit consisted of a ten-foot-square bedroom, a three-foot-square bathroom off the bedroom, a three- by four-foot water closet (toilet room), a four- by six-foot kitchen, and a ten- by fourteen-foot lounge that was turned over to us as a guest room.

The first things we noticed were the lack of screeching trains and the access to a shower. We would be happy here. The previous hostess was generous to share her home with us, had wonderful children, a grand view, and taught me how women were supposed to act and dress (sexy but classy).

We visited with Marceau, who spoke halting English. We drank the pitcher of cool lemon water offered and admired his paintings.

It was only nine in the morning, so we bid Marceau farewell and wended our way to the subway heading for Notre Dame. We arrived before crowds of tourists and walked directly into the church. Bethany wanted to climb the tower, so she did that while I took a leisurely stroll around the interior and exterior of the cathedral. The church was started in 1163 and finished a couple hundred years later in 1345. What an incredible feat performed by the workmen (slaves?). The stained-glass windows were beautiful, the wood a pleasure to touch, the floors and internal grave markers impressive carved marble.

The Gallery of Kings over the external portals showed twenty-eight Judeans. The flying buttresses were massive, and gargoyles as ugly as expected. I marveled that such a tall building could have been built before the advent of mechanical lifting devices. They must have used scaffolding with ramps and let men carry the heavy stones upward toward the heavens.

Bethany was jazzed by her trek to the top of the cathedral tower. Of course, she made new friends on her way up. The people climbing all those steps were under thirty.

We later listened to jazz musicians in the park beside the cathedral. We loved all the live music in Paris. Jazz was an American form of music, so most of the songs were ones I'd heard at jazz festivals in California. The balmy summer air was filled with delightful sounds.

We dragged ourselves away from the concert and down the steps to a flea market along the river. Men of all ages flirted with Bethany until they realized she was with me. If she noticed, she didn't indicate any interest.

We stopped at a pharmacy to get rehydration powder before returning to our host's home. Bethany and I both felt drained after a minimum of activity in the summer heat and humidity. We needed to replenish our mineral salts.

July 3, 2010 The phone rang and woke us up, but not our host. It was our hostess, who had gone out earlier for a Saturday-morning singing/dancing session with friends. The session had been cancelled, her bike was stolen, and she was soaking wet from the rain.

Bethany and I didn't answer the phone, as we knew who ever was calling would speak French, and we also knew no one was phoning us. Suzanne went to a store and bought new, dry clothes before contacting a friend and spending the day with her. She told us about her phone call when she got home that evening. We felt properly guilty.

Bethany and I ate bananas and yogurt I bought from a local grocer and made our way to the subway (Metro). After two hours of walking, waiting, and riding, we arrived at Musée d'Orsay.

What a wonderful museum of impressionist art! Manet, Monet, Cezanne, Van Gogh, Gauguin, Millet, Whistler and many more were represented. We wandered from masterpiece to masterpiece with our audio guide attached to our ears.

I had no idea Auguste Rodin was a painter. I probably knew it forty years ago but had forgotten. Rodin's paintings of his wife were superb. The artist captured her personality and expressed it through oil paint. She exuded so much love from her joyful, creamy-rose face. I envied his talent. The depiction looked so real, I expected her to intone some endearment to her husband at any minute.

Suzanne, Marceau, Bethany, and I spent the evening eating cheese, bread, sausage, radishes, and tomatoes, and drinking red wine while sitting on the floor around the coffee table in the lounge. Bethany and I were entertained listening to Marceau and Suzanne tell stories. A most pleasant evening was had by all.

July 4, 2010 Marceau was off to sell trinkets at a flea-market booth. Suzanne was having lunch with a friend. I needed a day off sight-seeing, and our hosts left me to relax in their home. Bethany decided to go to the flea market with Marceau and came home with treasures—a sundress, a 35mm-film camera, and glowing stories.

I read, ate fruit and cheese, listened to music performed in the street by a local brass band, and took a long, luxurious shower. The water was room temperature, not cold, not warm. I shampooed, did my nails, lathered my starving pores with lotion, and relished the solitude.

July 5, 2010 We spent the day transferring from one Servas host to another. When we arrived at Gif sur Yvette, we were supposed to phone the host to pick us up at the train station. We could find no phones that took coins. I walked to the post office and bought a phone card to make a single call. The card cost 7.5 euros (US$10.00). On my way back to the train station, I got lost. Fortunately, there were enough friendly folks working in their yards to guide me to the destination, where Bethany waited with our luggage.

I asked young people where there was a phone so I could use the card. They didn't know—they had their own cell phones. We found a phone a hundred yards away and phoned our hosts, who picked us up and took us to their delightful home high up a hill.

When Michel showed us to our bedroom on the second story, he said, "Feel free to take a douche if you like." I politely declined. Then as soon as I was settled in, the first thing I asked was, "Could I please take a shower?" I later learned *douche* was the French word for shower. Oh, the embarrassment of not speaking the local language.

We joined Michel and his sister, Inez, at the dining-room table and made hesitant conversation until Francine got home to interpret for us. Inez was a delightful middle-aged woman who relished the opportunity to recall her high school English lessons. She explained that she was in town to find housing for her daughter, Michela, who would be attending college in the autumn.

Francine, our hostess, arrived at seven, and we ate dinner at nine. Inez fixed dinner, and everything we ate was different than anything

I'd had before. The main course was a mixture of grated zucchinis and eggs fried into a skillet-sized cake. It was delicious. We ended the evening meal with cheese, bread, and fruit—great choices of cheeses and fresh French bread. I'd gain a ton. Everyone drank wine with dinner.

July 6, 2010 Bethany and I walked and walked and walked around the charming, quaint town of Gif sur Yvette and in the nearby woods. The architecture of the homes was modern French, with brick, stone, and wrought iron. Every yard was *Better Homes and Gardens* perfect. The layout of the narrow streets reminded me of many World War II movies. It was sad to think of these beautiful buildings and lovely people in jeopardy of being bombed.

The first level of the Gif sur Yvette homes was garages and workshops. The second was living quarters, and the third was bedrooms.

Our current Servas host had a bathroom on the second and third floors. They had hot water. We took showers at least once a day. Bethany was so glad to finally get proper hair care. She didn't feel comfortable taking a shower in Suzanne's apartment, as the bathroom was part of the bedroom—when you stepped out of the shower, you were in the bedroom.

Inez, Michel's sister, went home. Michel took Inez and Michela to the train station. Bethany and I saw them on our walk to town and wished them "Bon voyage." I went to give Inez an air-kiss beside her ears, and we bent our heads in the same direction at the same time and bumped noses. Thank goodness she had a good sense of humor!

In the evening I treated the family to a meal at a restaurant. Everyone except me had Italian food. I had magret de canard (duck). It was wonderful, but there was too much food, so I offered some to Bethany. She couldn't eat all of her own food, let alone part of mine, so Emaline and Etienne, the teenagers, finished off the leftover food on our plates. That made me feel more at home with them.

We learned it was good manners in France to never take seconds until everyone was finished with their first serving, and it was bad manners to leave food on your plate. Take what you want to eat, no more, no less. I was the slowest eater and wondered why everyone watched me after their plates were empty when we ate at home. They wanted second helpings. Everyone ate robustly at all three Servas homes, but no one was overweight. I think the tricks were that they didn't eat between meals, and they walked or rode bicycles everywhere.

July 7, 2010 We spent the day doing laundry, reading, and resting. We took a lovely walk in the woods two blocks from the house. Bethany tried out her flea-market Nikon camera. She was so enthused about finding a film camera. I hoped it worked well for her.

July 8, 2010 We toured Musee Rodin and the Forum des Halles and Invalids, where Napoleon was buried. The military museum, the Forum, showed many pictures of Americans and other Allied military men fighting to free the French from the Nazis. They had not forgotten Normandy.

We went to Rodin's home that is now a gallery of sculptures. Rodin took up sculpture later in life, creating *The Thinker* for his *Gates of Hell*—doors made of copper. He made use of the pose in other sculptures. He also created the beautiful statue called *The Kiss*. There were so many exquisite statues to see in Rodin's lovely home and garden.

We were about to cross the street while on Embassy Row (plush mansions) when a cavalcade of motorcycle police stopped in front of us and motioned us back onto the sidewalk. Two long black cars stopped in front of us. Security guards emerged from both cars, looking in all directions. They scrutinized Bethany and me. One man made a motion with his head. A security guard opened the back door of the first limo, and out stepped Sarkozy. The French president! He was quickly surrounded by guards as he walked to meet a lady emerging from the second limo. I don't know who the lady was for sure, but thought it was Angela Merkel, Chancellor of Germany. The primary subjects shook hands and chatted for a few minutes while we gawked.

A security guard said we were free to proceed across the street if we wanted. We did. Bethany was on cloud nine after actually seeing the President of France. Who wouldn't be impressed?

"He looks just like the cartoons!" she said later.

That evening over dinner in the garden, Bethany related the story to our host and family. They were not stirred. Though pleasant to us, they seemed devoid of sentiment. The only time the children showed any emotion was when requested to do something. Then they whined noisily. Don't all kids?

July 9, 2010 We left the quiet village with its green hills, green lawns, green trees, and flower gardens. Michel offered to drive us to our next place of lodging in Versailles so we wouldn't have to wrestle our luggage down and up train station steps. What a blessing! Vive la France!

Eighteen-year-old Emaline was aroused from her bed at nine o'clock. She liked to stay there until noon while on school holidays. I thought she was being told to say good-bye to us. Actually, Michel had Emaline drive while he talked her through the motions of handling a car. She maneuvered around construction zones, down detours, and got us to our hotel safe and sound. She didn't even drive fast like so many learners. It was a pleasant country excursion.

We arrived at eleven. The hotel staff let us store our bags in a closet, as it was too early to register. They directed us to a tourist agency, where we bought tickets to tour Versailles Palace and Gardens.

We spent the balance of the day gaping at the wonders of the huge palace that started as a hunting lodge for Louis XIII, and ended up being a building covering several acres with gold, marble, exquisite oil paintings, crystal, and more gold. Even the front fence was clad in gold leaf and I was reprimanded when I rested my hand on the fence to take a picture through the bars.

Louis XVI was the last monarch to rule from there. He had over twenty-two thousand people living in the palace at one time, as Versailles was the seat of French government after he moved out of the Louvre.

Incidentally, there were several monarchs between Louis XIII and Louis XVI. Louis XIV was not the son of Louis XIII. It took over a hundred years to build the palace.

The hall of mirrors where dances were held was the most impressive room in the building. Several others were dark and dreary, with mahogany wood, deep-red velvet walls and drapes, and dark marble floors. One of the funny customs about monarchies was that a special room was set aside for people, dozens of people, to watch the king and queen undress for bed or get dressed in the morning. Every article of clothing had a ritual that had to be performed before being donned by the royal person. When the queen gave birth to her children, several people were required to be present to attest to the fact that the baby actually was delivered from that woman. Yuck!

Louis XVI and his wife, Marie Antoinette, were beheaded at the start of the French Revolution. After hearing their stories, I think they were ignorant of the extent of poverty in France. Had they been better educated, perhaps they would not have spent so lavishly while peasants starved.

We made no attempt to see the grounds that day. Bethany didn't appear to have much more energy than I did in the summer heat. I was near collapse by the time we fell into our beds. I slept eleven hours without so much as a single potty break. I'm not usually so easily tired out. It had nothing to do with my approaching birthday reminding me that I'm old.

July 10, 2010 We spent a delightful day of music, water fountains, water ballet, flowers, shady trees, and watching boaters on the man-made lake behind Versailles Palace. The classical baroque music floated from loudspeakers throughout the grounds. The gardens covered eight hectares (twenty-two acres) and were divided by twelve-foot hedges, so one felt he was by himself from time to time. People strolled among the gardens instead of rushing helter-skelter like they did in Paris, London, and New York (and all other major cities in the world).

Bethany and I spent a delightful four hours there before wandering off to a *creperie* for lunch. We went to the hotel, bathed, rested, watched CNN, and played cards until seven p.m. and then had a leisurely dinner at a sidewalk café and meandered to the palace to join the folks gathering for the fireworks. According to the restaurants we had visited, Italian was the favorite food of the French.

Versailles's gate opened at nine, though it was obvious sunset was a long way off. Classical music played. The fountains sprayed artistically, and thousands of people found spots to sit on steps, garden walls, or the lawns.

The fireworks started at eleven and lasted fifteen minutes. They were disappointing, but people who had never seen the spectacular show offered at the Sacramento fairgrounds on July 4 were impressed. I liked the *bon vivant* of the people around us, the music, and the pleasant evening temperature. Some people brought picnic baskets; many brought children.

A darling little girl sitting behind us explained everything she saw with excitement. I agreed with her and ooohed and aahed. She asked a question and didn't understand my response.

I explained to her mother, "*Je no parle Francais*." A few minutes later, the father carried the child away. When she returned, she acted afraid of me. I pointed out a fountain spray dancing to the tune of the music and she grabbed her mother's neck and hid her face. I got the message. Those who don't speak French are bad people.

We walked the mile (give or take a bit) back to our hotel without a fear of mugging or such activity usually associated with women alone on the sidewalks near midnight. The streets were filled with jovial tourists.

Our room was stifling, and the open window offered little relief. We slept fitfully. The only place we've found air conditioning was in a pharmacy.

July 11, 2010 I awoke at eight thirty, quickly dressed, and went down for the breakfast we had paid for the night before. I gathered a platter of pastry and a glass of orange juice to take to Bethany. The breakfast room closed at nine.

After Bethany ate, we made the tortuous trip from one lodging place to another. The clerk at the hotel laughed joyously when I asked for a taxi to take us to the railroad station four blocks away. No taxi would travel such a short distance! Well, at least I finally heard a French person laugh out loud. This same lady told me the credit card from Scott Valley Bank had expired in March. Good grief! Why hadn't the bank notified me? I had enough euros to pay the bill in cash.

We dragged our suitcases down the sidewalks to the station, up a flight of stairs, down a hallway a city block long, down two flights of stairs, and boarded the waiting train. My suitcase still weighed fifty pounds in spite of giving away six books, a pair of shoes, and two outfits of clothes along the way. I had bought no souvenirs except a deck of cards. I didn't understand the weight.

We transferred trains at Notre Dame Station in Paris and headed for Charles de Gaulle Airport. On the map it looked like the airport was one stop beyond our hostel. Not so, of course; it was several miles away and cost 60 euros (US$90.00) to get a taxi driven by a madman to take us from the airport to the hostel. He thought we wanted to experience the Grand Prix. I thought at times we would get whiplash from the ninety-degree turns he made while changing lanes on the highway. He was determined to be first in line and cursed anyone who got in his way.

Bethany and I arrived at St. Christopher's Hostel frazzled and in no mood to hassle. I had lost my Citibank MasterCard in Paris. Somehow it was dropped while in the pharmacy and not noticed. No one tried to use it in the intervening time before I got it cancelled. I had a backup American Express card and a Scott Valley ATM card, which was also a Visa credit card, but out of date, according to the last hotel clerk.

The hostel wouldn't accept my American Express card. We scrounged through our pockets and money belts and came up with enough cash to pay for the first night's lodging. That meant we immediately needed to find a bank and withdraw more euros.

We walked the few blocks to the bank machine, where we had no trouble using my expired Scott Valley ATM card. Then we went to lunch at a kosher pizza parlor. Don't know why I was expecting kosher pickles or borscht on crust, but we had a heavy cheese pizza. Kosher pizza was no different than Christian pizza! Who knew?

We retired to our immaculate sixth-floor room with a balcony overlooking the Baisson de Villette, a lake surrounded by cement walls, city streets, sidewalks, and the occasional tree. Bethany showered, then napped. I napped, then showered. Bethany played Sudoku, and I entered this page in my journal.

We went to the dining room/bar for dinner and a happy hour drink. We had pasta with vegetables and salad for 6 euros (US$9.00), our cheapest meal in Europe. Well, it would have been cheap if I hadn't added a $5.00 beer and Bethany an $8.00 mojito.

The room was crowded with football fans, and we were soon immersed in World Cup Soccer. What fun! The game was for the championship and went one-hundred-seventeen minutes before Spain made the solitary goal. They beat the Netherlands, which set off celebrations that lasted all night.

I love soccer or any other kind of football, so I was quite content to whoop and holler with the other patrons in the festive room before walking the short distance to the elevator and the solitude of our private room.

Bethany couldn't stay awake for the whole game, so she went to the room thirty minutes before me. She was asleep when I entered. I tiptoed to the balcony and relaxed on the mattress, only to realize the celebrations in the streets would keep me awake. I brought the mattress into the room and slept on the floor. There were only two other rooms on our penthouse floor, and only one of them was occupied, so we weren't kept awake with celebrants dancing in the halls.

We were awakened at four o'clock by a terrific electrical storm that washed humidity from the air and football celebrants from the sidewalks. I was glad I had moved indoors before the storm hit. When the rain stopped, I opened the sliding-glass door to let the refreshing air circulate.

July 12, 2010 Bethany wanted to see Salvador Dali's art museum, so we went there and also to Sacré Coeur Basilica. That meant walking miles and miles of crowded streets, all of which went *up*hill (or was it just my imagination?).

Dozens of young men were illegally selling souvenirs. As we climbed the steps of Sacré Coeur, I saw a vendor rubbing the upper arm and back of an elderly woman, trying to sell her cheap ribbons. She kept walking and ignored him. I should have done the same.

Instead my temper began to build before we reached the point where he would approach us. The man started to reach for me, and I slapped his hand as hard as I could with a folded map. I yelled loud enough that everyone nearby heard, "Don't you touch me!" He smiled and reached toward Bethany. I smacked him again and said, "Don't you *dare* touch her!" People around us stopped, waiting to see where the confrontation would lead.

I glared at the man, and after a couple of seconds, he put both his hands in the air to indicate surrender.

"Leave her be," his coworker said. "She's a racist." I immediately wanted to deny that but kept silent instead. We walked on unmolested. Whew. Afterward the thought dawned on me that if I'd done that in the United States, I might have been arrested for assault.

Each time a salesman—all very dark-skinned, approached us the rest of the morning, I shouted at them, "No, we do *not* want your wares!" They backed off, startled at my aggression. I'd guess we had at least twenty men approach us over an hour's period.

As we arrived at the Metro station by the Eiffel Tower, several souvenir salesmen were running this way and that. Some were being let into the station exit by coworkers as we tried to make our way out.

"It's a police sweep," Bethany said.

I, being older and wiser, said, "I don't think so. They're trying to sneak onto the train without paying."

Once we were on the sidewalk, we saw several men running, and Bethany pointed to the policemen chasing them across flowerbeds, shrubs, and busy city streets. One policeman collared a salesman in the middle of the two-way street and swung him around. The salesman dropped his cheap imitation Eiffel Towers, and they were broadcast over a wide area. Traffic came to a standstill. Pedestrians with digital cameras and cell phones took pictures of the action. There was a lot of commotion for a couple of minutes as police handcuffed culprits. We saw police vans and policemen in several locations doing their job of loading dozens of vendors onboard. Youth beats old age at observance once again. Bethany was right, I was wrong.

By the time we walked two blocks to the Eiffel Tower, salesmen were back in force. They worked the crowd as though they had every right to be there.

"They're like cockroaches!" Bethany exclaimed. I agreed with her but secretly felt sympathy for the poor men who had seen the horrors of war and escaped. They were now probably in France illegally and trying to make enough money to buy food and pay rent. Perhaps they were trying to make enough money to help another wretched soul escape their homeland.

Bethany said the police chase was the most exciting thing since seeing the president. I mentally calculated the amount of money spent on museums and tourist attractions. We could have stayed at our first place of lodging in Harlem in New York City, and she would have had plenty of excitement.

We walked around the base of the Eiffel Tower and through the gardens until we found the right spot to take a picture of Bethany holding up the Crooked Kilt T-shirt for a picture. The Crooked Kilt was the name of Brian and Heidi's (Bethany's brother andfuture sister-in-law) place of employment, and they sent their T-shirt on the trip since they couldn't go themselves.

Once more we were accosted by gypsies wanting handouts and salesmen wanting to sell us trinkets.

One young woman walked up to me and said, "Do you speak English?"

"A bit," I responded, thinking she was about to ask directions.

She held up a card that said, "I'm from California and am visiting France. I've been robbed and have no money to get home. Please help me." I turned the card right side up, so I could read it, then handed it back to her and said we really didn't want to help her get to California. I explained that the people in California read English right side up. She giggled, apologized in French, and looked for another sucker.

By the time we settled at a sidewalk café for lunch, I was in a grouchy mood. We ordered duplicate salads and tap water. The waiter spoke perfect English. He asked if we wanted a large or medium bottle of water. I said, "Une carafe d'eau, s'il vous plait." And for good measure repeated, "Tap water, *not* commercially bottled water."

The salads arrived, and the waiter put an Evian bottle in the center of the table. I mentioned that it was strange the restaurant put tap water in a commercial water bottle. Sure enough, when the bill arrived, there was a charge of six euros for water. I refused to pay it. The waiter said, "You didn't have to drink it." I threw up my hands and walked out of the restaurant. I really, really hate being cheated.

July 13, 2010 We left St. Christopher's Hostel in a taxi and arrived at Gare du Nord half an hour later. The train station had such a beautiful exterior. It fit right in with the historic buildings of Paris. The driver let us off at the door closest to the Eurostar departure gate. The Eurostar was the super-fast train that went under the English Channel and had passengers in downtown London in two and a half hours.

I bought tickets before we left home, so it was merely a matter of going through security and sitting in the waiting room for thirty minutes before the train left. I thought of buying a Parisian T-shirt but didn't want to add one more ounce to my suitcase.

I loved Paris, the architecture, the museums, the Seine, the Eiffel Tower, Notre Dame, the musicians, and the flirts. I loved Versailles, the sidewalk cafes, the glorious gardens, the serene residential streets, the pleasant people. But if I were to design my own Parisian souvenir T-shirt, it would say, "No, I don't want any cheap trinkets or overpriced water!"

Once on the air-conditioned train, our luggage stored in the incredibly small space provided, we took our cushy assigned seats, which faced each other across a table.

I watched the French countryside slide past for an hour before falling sound asleep. I missed the "Chunnel" experience. I woke up as we pulled into Victoria Station.

We went to Blair Victoria Hostel, where we were again given one of the smallest rooms in the Western world. We had to leave the bathroom door open to get in and out of the shower. That's okay; we hadn't planned on setting up housekeeping. The hostel was clean, safe, and it only cost $120.00 a night. That sounded like I had lost my mind – "only cost" and "$120.00 a night" in the same sentence.

Chris Tzinieris, our English cousin, met us at Blair Victoria, and the three of us walked to Victoria Station, where we caught a train to his hometown of Richmond. I grabbed the first seat available when I boarded the rush-hour train. Chris and Bethany spent the half hour carrying on such a vivacious conversation, I doubted either of them noticed the passage of time.

We debarked in the quaint town, and Chris phoned his wife to let her know we had arrived. There was a slight drizzle falling, which was quite pleasant and cooling. It gave me a chance to use the one item from my suitcase that had not yet been used—a sweatshirt. It really wasn't that cold, but I wanted an excuse to wear the shirt after toting it from California.

Chris explained that he lived two miles out of town and that his wife was on her way to meet us. What he neglected to mention was that Sarah was walking with her mother, Sue, and her two children, Dimitri and Isabella. Isabella was six months old and Dimitri four years old. Imagine people walking two miles in the rain just to meet Bethany and me! Incredible!

We went to a real English pub and had fish and chips and a delightful evening of conversation. The babies were cute and cuddly.

Sarah recently obtained her graduate degree in international relations and was looking for a job working with Israel and Palestine. What a courageous woman! Chris was a chemical engineer working with petroleum. If we had more time, I'm sure he could have told us some great stories about his job. Sue was a personable, lovely, smiling lady and devoted grandmother. I wanted to spend days getting to know this group. What a shame we only had a few hours.

July 14, 2010 From London to New York, the flight went smoothly. The service was good; the plane left on time and arrived on time. Customs was a breeze. We caught a shuttle to JFK Hotel and relished the large air-conditioned room with two queen-sized beds. The room cost $120.00 the same as the teensy place we had in London. We were so happy to be there, we didn't even want to leave for dinner. Bethany ordered Chinese delivered. We watched television shows where we understood what the people were saying and slept soundly throughout the night.

July 15, 2010 We made another attempt to reach the Statue of Liberty and Ellis Island. We made it? Yea! We caught the correct bus and deposited the correct "kines." We caught the correct train and went right to the park where the ferry left for Liberty Island. The only glitch we had was that the quota for going to the top of the statue was full. We didn't make that climb. Dang. Oh okay, I really only intended to buy one ticket, and it wasn't for me. Actually, Bethany didn't appear devastated about not climbing the spiral stairwell either. When I expressed my disappointment to her, she responded with, "I think I'll go buy an ice-cream cone."

We did the audio tour and thoroughly enjoyed the construction and renovation stories as we wandered around the base of Lady Liberty.

We boated to Ellis Island and were impressed with the beauty of the museum and the well-laid-out audio tour. We followed the steps of the immigrants and heard their stories. The experience was humbling, learning what people endured to become citizens of the United States.

Back on the mainland, we walked through Central Park and chatted with a group of Russian ladies trying to figure out the subway system. Yes, we too had to ask directions. A kind police lady gave us her map and perfect directions to get us on our way. We caught the correct bus and once more rode through the fascinating neighborhood called Jamaica Plains, where there was a storefront church on every block. I loved the names of the churches and wished I'd brought paper and pen to record them. The church names expressed a desire to survive everyday life with a little help from above.

The hotel let us use the microwave in the breakfast room to reheat leftover Chinese food, and we snuggled into clean, cool, large beds after refreshing showers.

July 16, 2010 Was it anticipation? I don't know. I just knew I was awake at four o'clock and couldn't get back to sleep. I sat in the lobby and was amused by the night creatures checking into the hotel. The woman was obviously a prostitute, and she had two grinning men with her.

The hotel clerk didn't want them in the establishment. After hassling for a while, the woman remembered that she was already registered and sharing a room with another woman. She gave the other woman's name, and the clerk phoned the room. The second woman soon appeared in the lobby and verified that she had been waiting for this group to join her. Hmm.

The rest of the day was spent in hell! Delta Airlines booked us from New York to Indianapolis to Minneapolis to Sacramento. The first flight was to leave New York at noon, so we arrived at the airport at ten. We stood in an extremely long line and waited for ten minutes while watching the clerk type on her computer to confirm we were on the flight. It took that long for each customer. What a system! When asked how many bags we were checking in, I responded two—one apiece. That would be $50.00 each. I reluctantly paid it, as I knew my heavy suitcase could never be hoisted over our seats on the plane. Other people who had traveled on Delta before knew to bring three carry-ons. The bins were filled by the first few people on the plane. The plane departed an hour late. The time was going to be close for catching our connection. When we arrived in Indianapolis, we dashed to the next departure gate, only to learn that plane had been delayed an hour and a half.

We boarded the second plane two hours later and made the hour-and-a-half flight to Minneapolis. Guess what? That plane was delayed also. Bethany phoned her mother to tell her we were expected to be three hours late arriving in Sacramento.

After we boarded the plane at Minneapolis, the pilot noticed he was low on fuel and had to order a truck to bring some. We sat on the plane for over an hour while it was refueled. The customers were cranky by the time we took off, but the staff didn't mind. They went about their chores in the usual manner, never offering an apology or an extra packet of pretzels.

July 18, 2010 A five-hour drive brought me to beautiful Scott Valley nestled in the bosom of the Siskiyou Mountains. Fort Jones, with only a handful of people cruising down Main Street, looked like the perfect place to return after spending time in three of the largest cities in the world. It was a good place to rest and plan my next travel adventure.

15064939R00343

Made in the USA
San Bernardino, CA
13 September 2014